THE MAMMOTH BOOK OF

NEW EROTIC PHOTOGRAPHY

EDITED BY
MAXIM JAKUBOWSKI

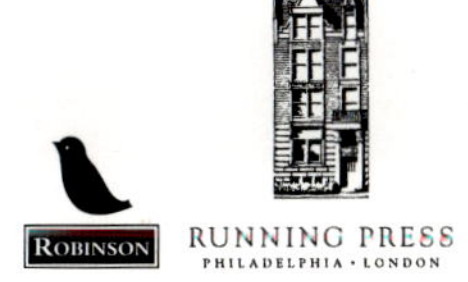

Constable & Robinson Ltd
3 The Lanchesters
162 Fulham Palace Road
London W6 9ER
www.constablerobinson.com

First published in the UK by Robinson,
an imprint of Constable & Robinson, 2010

A copy of the British Library Cataloguing in Publication
Data is available from the British Library

UK ISBN 978-1-84901-384-0

1 3 5 7 9 10 8 6 4 2

First published in the United States in 2010
by Running Press Book Publishers

9 8 7 6 5 4 3 2 1
Digit on the right indicates the number of this printing

US Library of Congress number: 2009943392
US ISBN 978-0-76243-999-7

Running Press Book Publishers
2300 Chestnut Street
Philadelphia, PA 19103-4371

Visit us on the web!
www.runningpress.com

Printed and bound in Italy

Design and layout by Susan St Louis

Photograph credits
Imprint page: Michael Combs, contents page: Gary Breckheimer,
page 6: Elisa Lazo de Valdez and page 8: Gary Mitchell

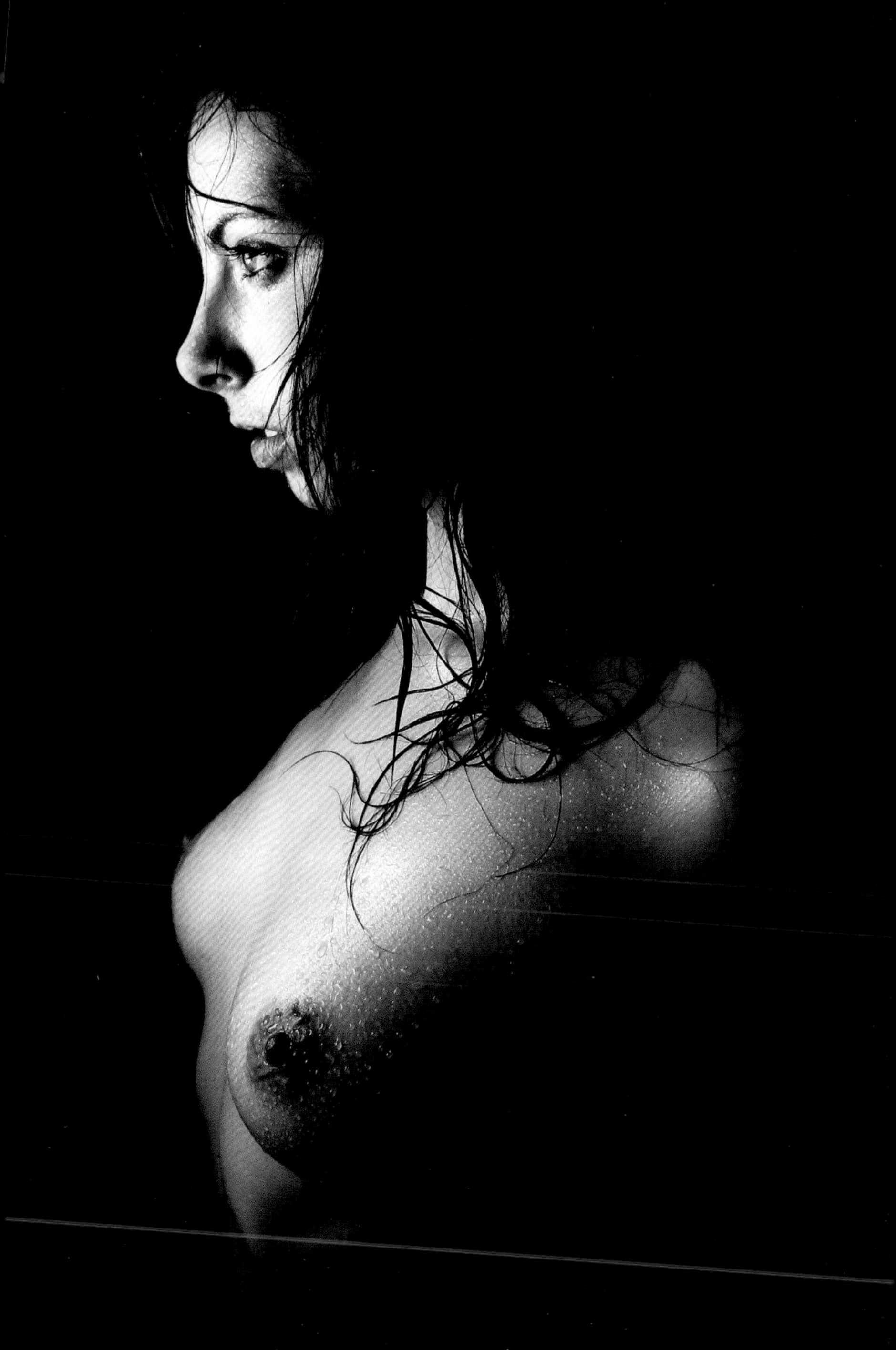

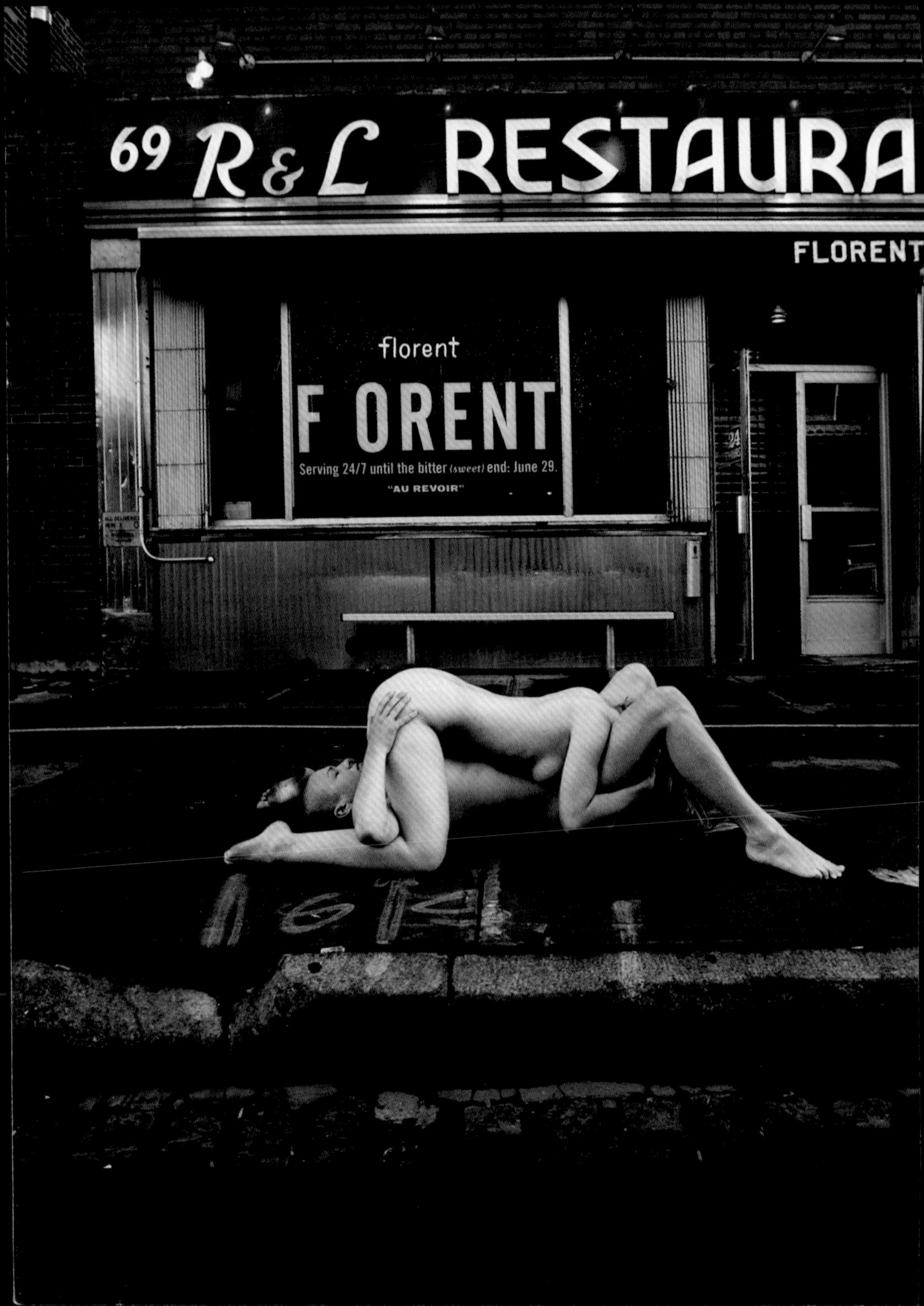

69 R&L RESTAURA
FLORENT
florent
F ORENT
Serving 24/7 until the bitter (sweet) end: June 29.
"AU REVOIR"

list of photographers

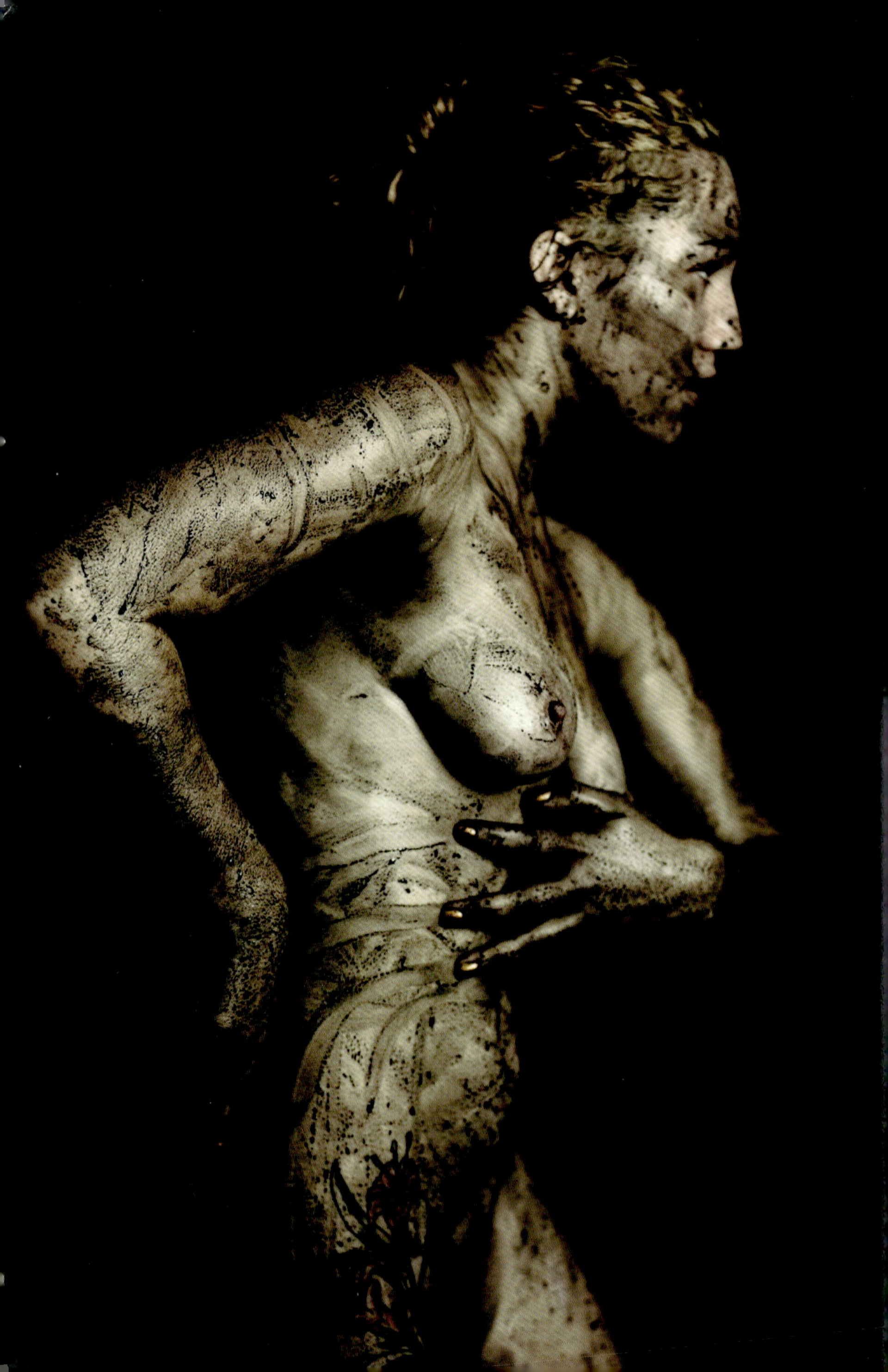

introduction

Poets, writers, singers and painters throughout the ages have worshipped women and sung their praises without ever exhausting their fount of inspiration. Beauty is, of course, highly subjective and it could be argued that it's only with the advent of photography that we have been able to judge at first hand how beauty is seen by others. The camera has been able to capture evanescent moments in time, the curve of a shoulder, the spark in an eye, the flow of hair against diverse backgrounds, the colour of skin, the delicate texture of flesh and life in its hypnotic lens like no other observer could before. But as well as providing us with unforgettable visions of female reality it has also simultaneously conjured up a fascinating other world of fantasy images where women become unreal, representations of lust and innocence that can appear miles away from the ordinariness of everyday life.

The initial volume in the *Mammoth Book of Erotic Photography* series appeared in 2001, followed by another in 2005, so a further five years have since passed during which mighty winds of change have blown across both the photographic and the publishing world. The majority of photographers now active in the field mostly work in digital format, although there remains a wonderful hardcore of traditionalists who intend to continue working with film. On a separate note, Polaroids have come to an end. The landscape has changed, to say the least. In addition, the Internet has also become an added and valued source for material and publication which was not as generally available a decade ago.

But one thing has not changed: the sheer beauty of the female form.

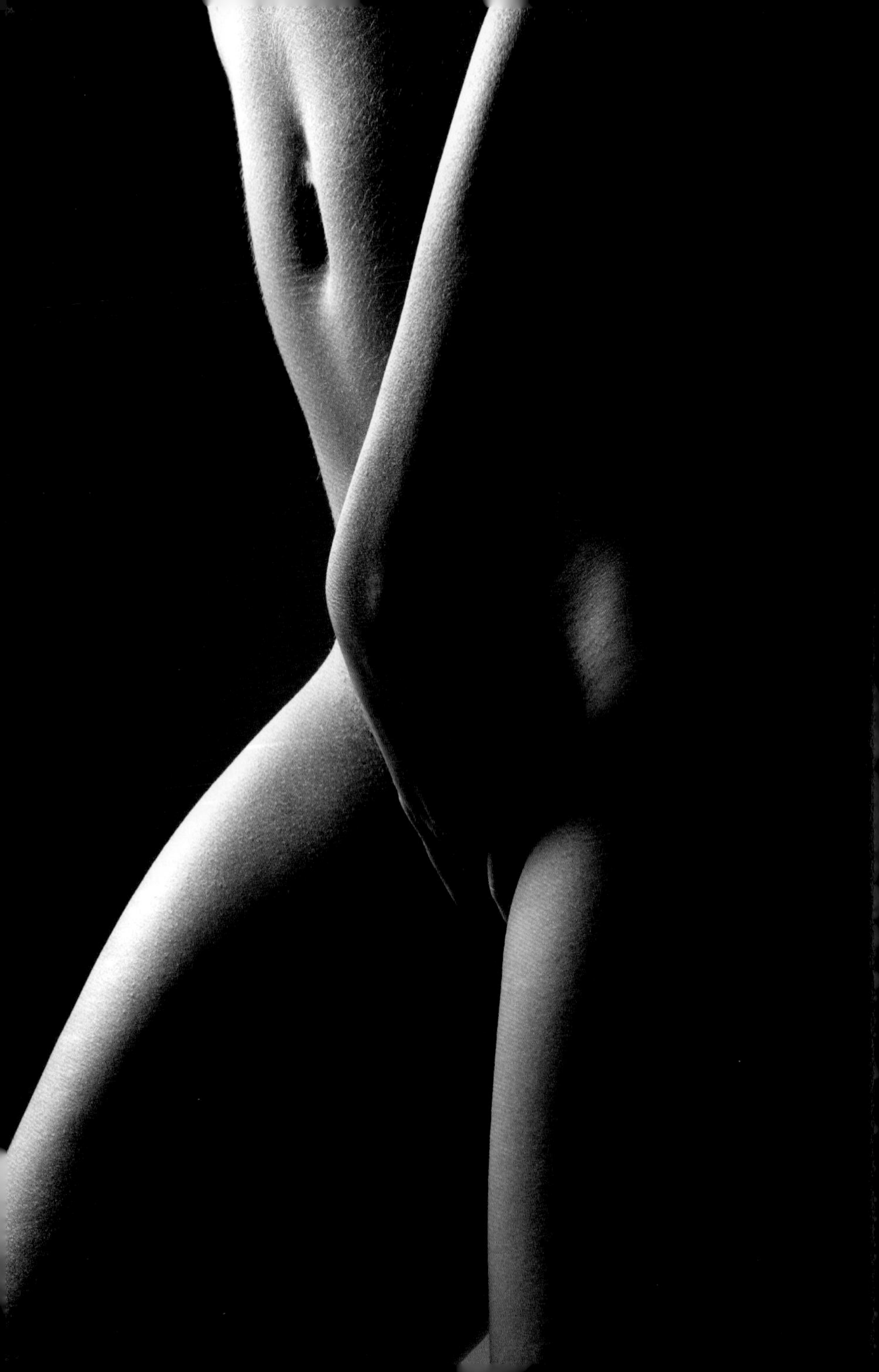

It was often thought by primitive tribes that photographs of people could steal their souls, while others believe that the act of presenting images of women only serves to objectify them, and skews our perception of their essence, and demeans them. I disagree strongly with both strands. There is an inherent lusciousness about the body of women and in these books we have tried to celebrate it, not exploit it. It's interesting to point out that over the course of the three volumes we have published, we have discovered an ever increasing number of female photographers as we widen our net for talented photographers and artists throughout the world, and that actually many of these women enjoy doing self-portraits in addition to taking images of other models, many of which are not even professional. So does the female eye differ from the male one? It's a question others would answer better than me, but all I know is that both visions are exquisite when talent lies behind them and the hundreds of photos I have selected for this volume prove to be a perfect demonstration.

I never cease to be amazed and pleasantly surprised at the sheer amount of variations the photographers we have selected this time around have been able to conjure up. It might be assumed that the number of poses, lighting combinations and angles at the disposal of the photographers is limited, but they always come up with something new, a novel way of catching the uncatchable in their visual net and delighting us, the viewer in the process. Indeed, occasional models can be found – I will leave the detective work to the reader – in different portfolios by individual photographers, and they look completely different (albeit still wondrously beautiful).

So leave your prejudices at the door and relish this celebration of beauty.

Maxim Jakubowski

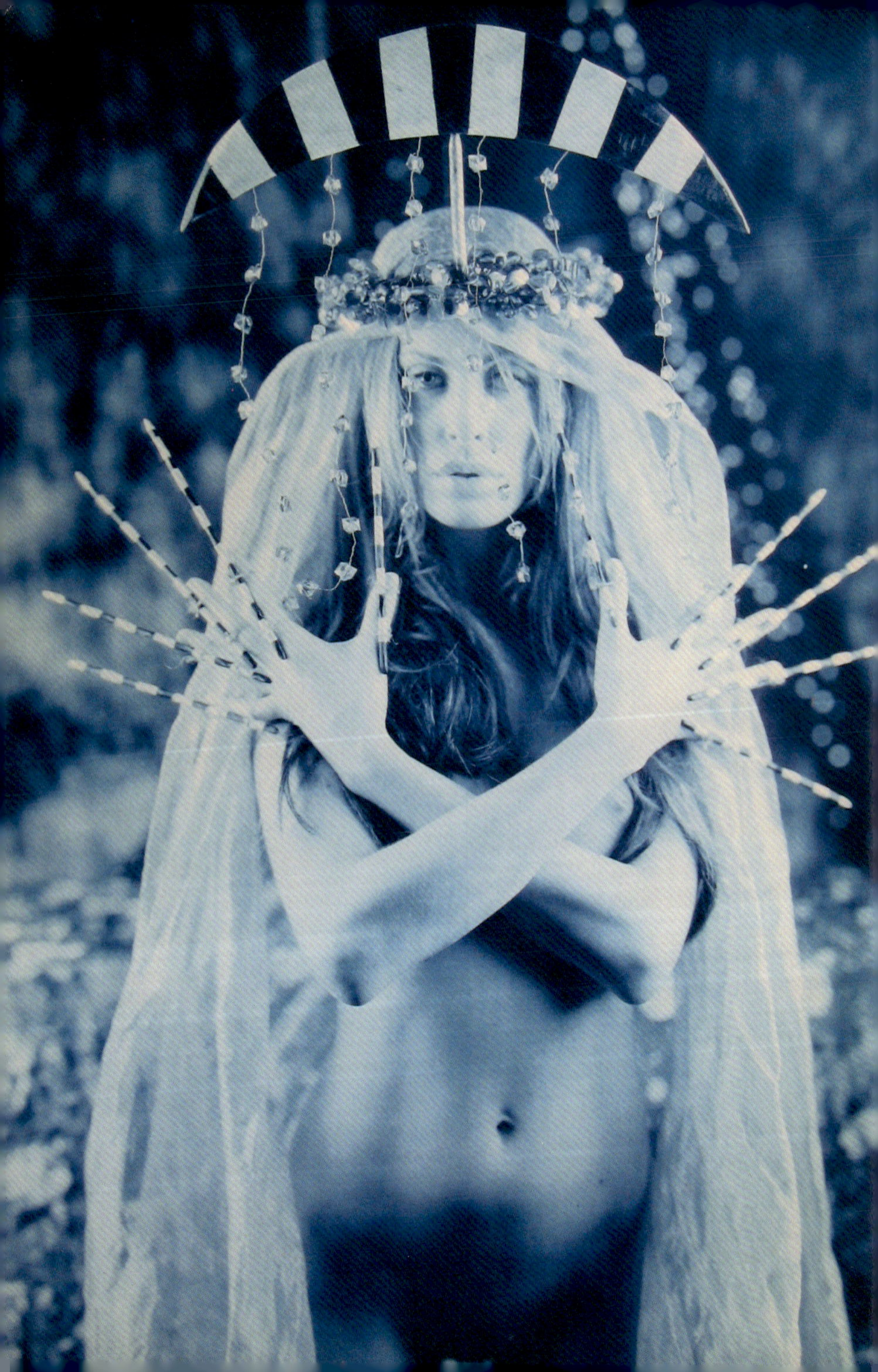

patrick alt

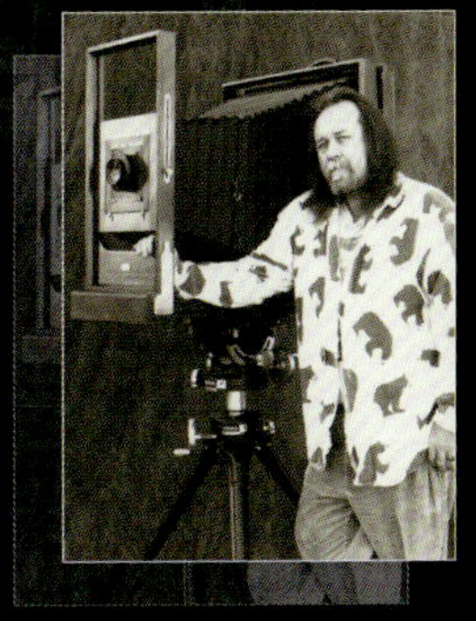

BORN IN 1950 IN WISCONSIN, Patrick moved to California in 1970. He has widely exhibited and his first book *Unknown Tuscany* was published in 2006. His photographic work continues the tradition of film-based large format black-and-white photography, concentrating mostly on the platinum/palladium and cyanotype printing processes, as well as silver gelatin prints. Nothing digital is used in the making of his work. He uses numerous large format cameras to create his images. His work reflects the Pictorialists' sensibility - their belief in beauty as the primary source and inspiration for image-making and the view that eroticism is the last frontier to be examined and explored.

www.patrickalt.com

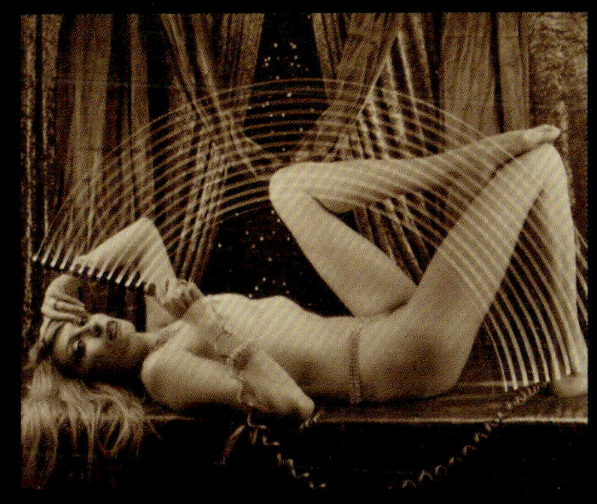

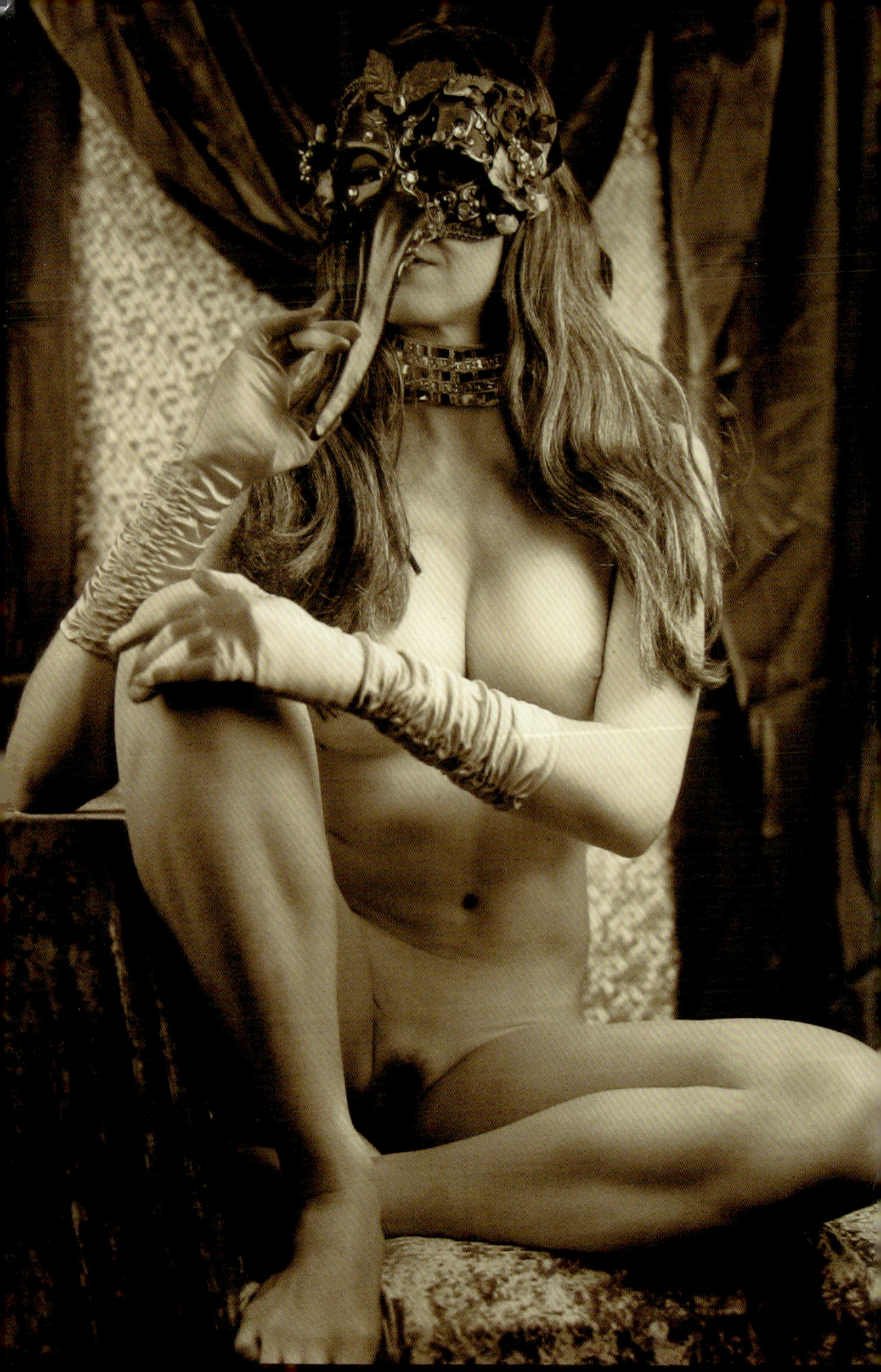

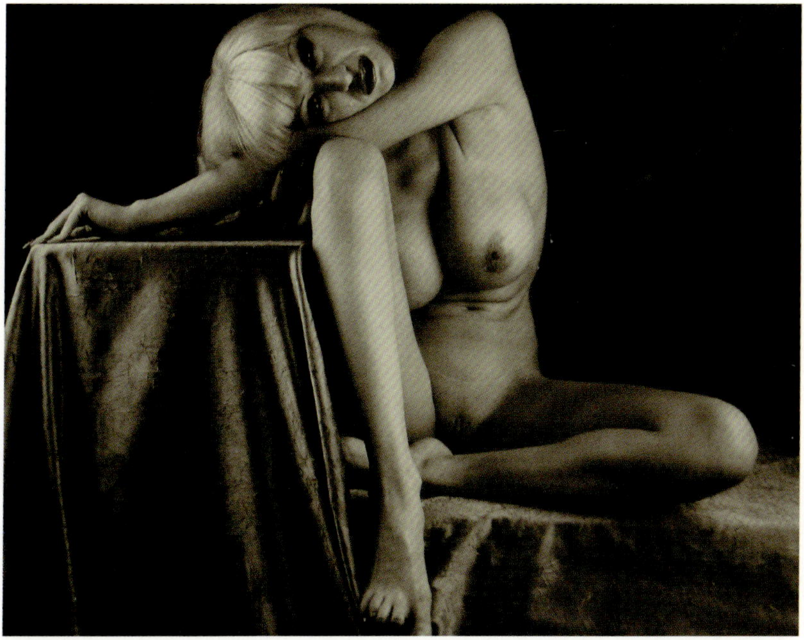

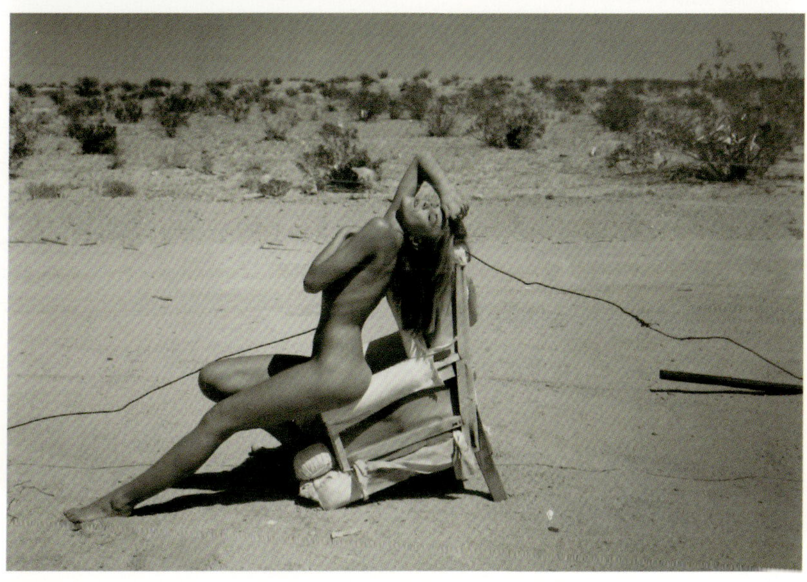

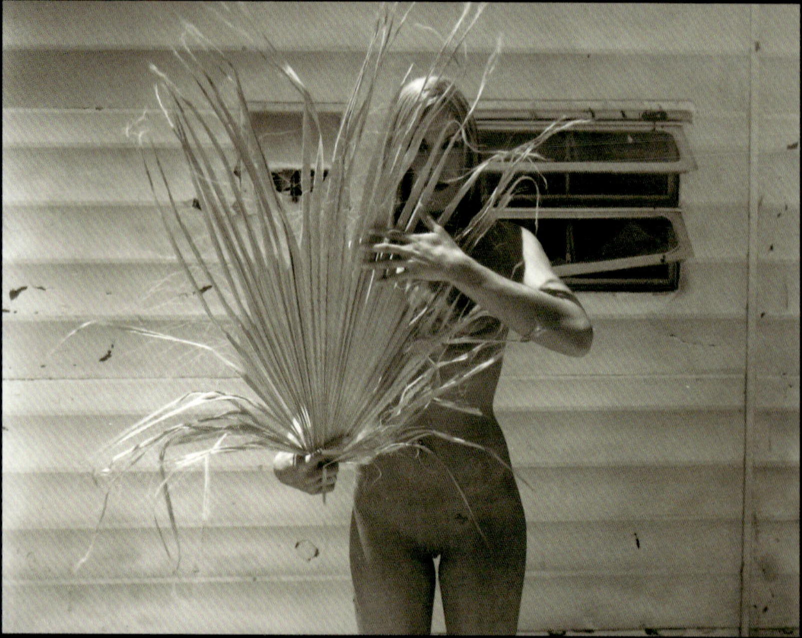

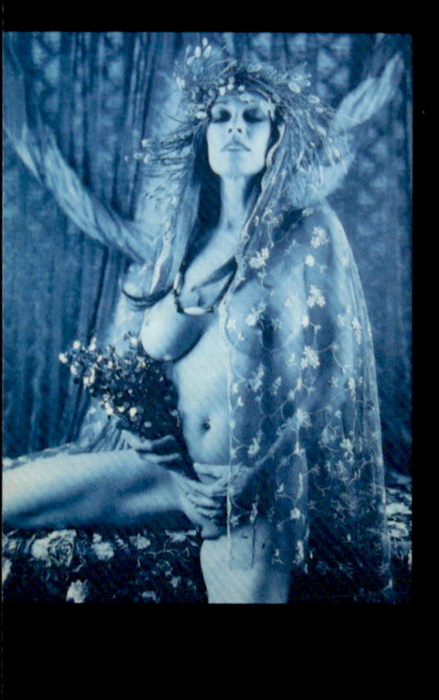

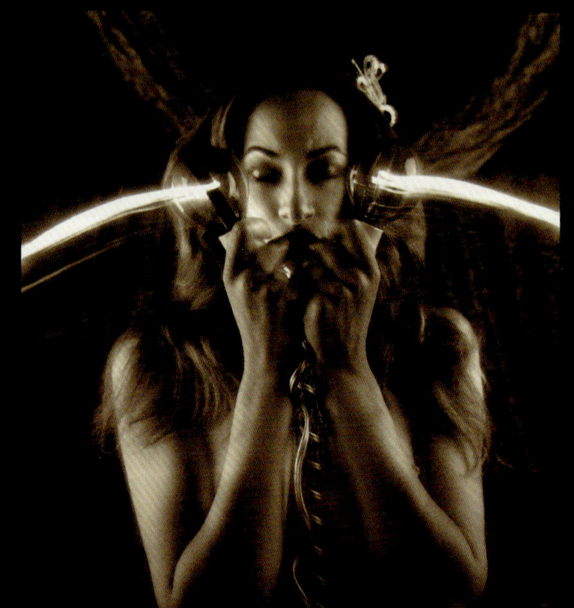

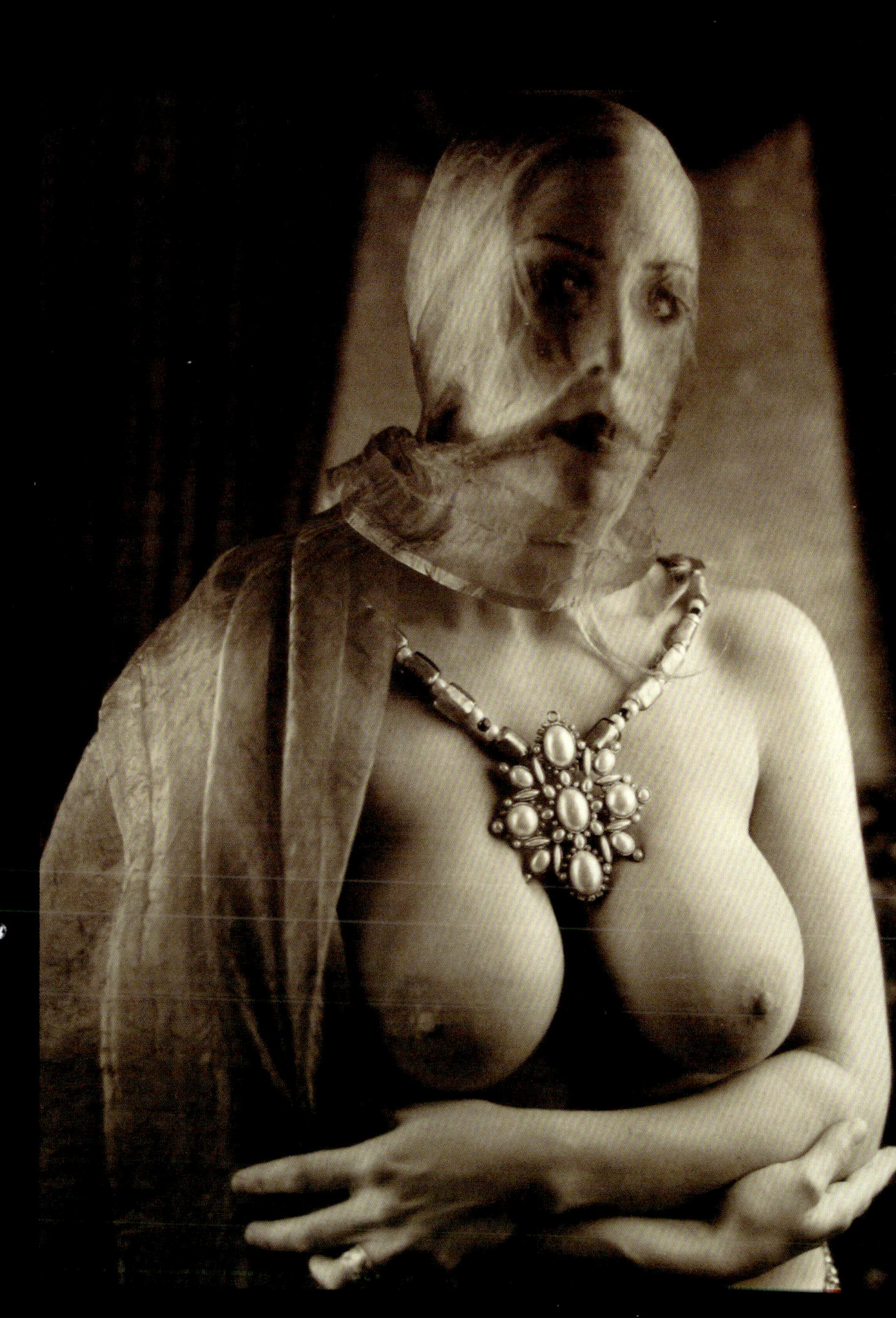

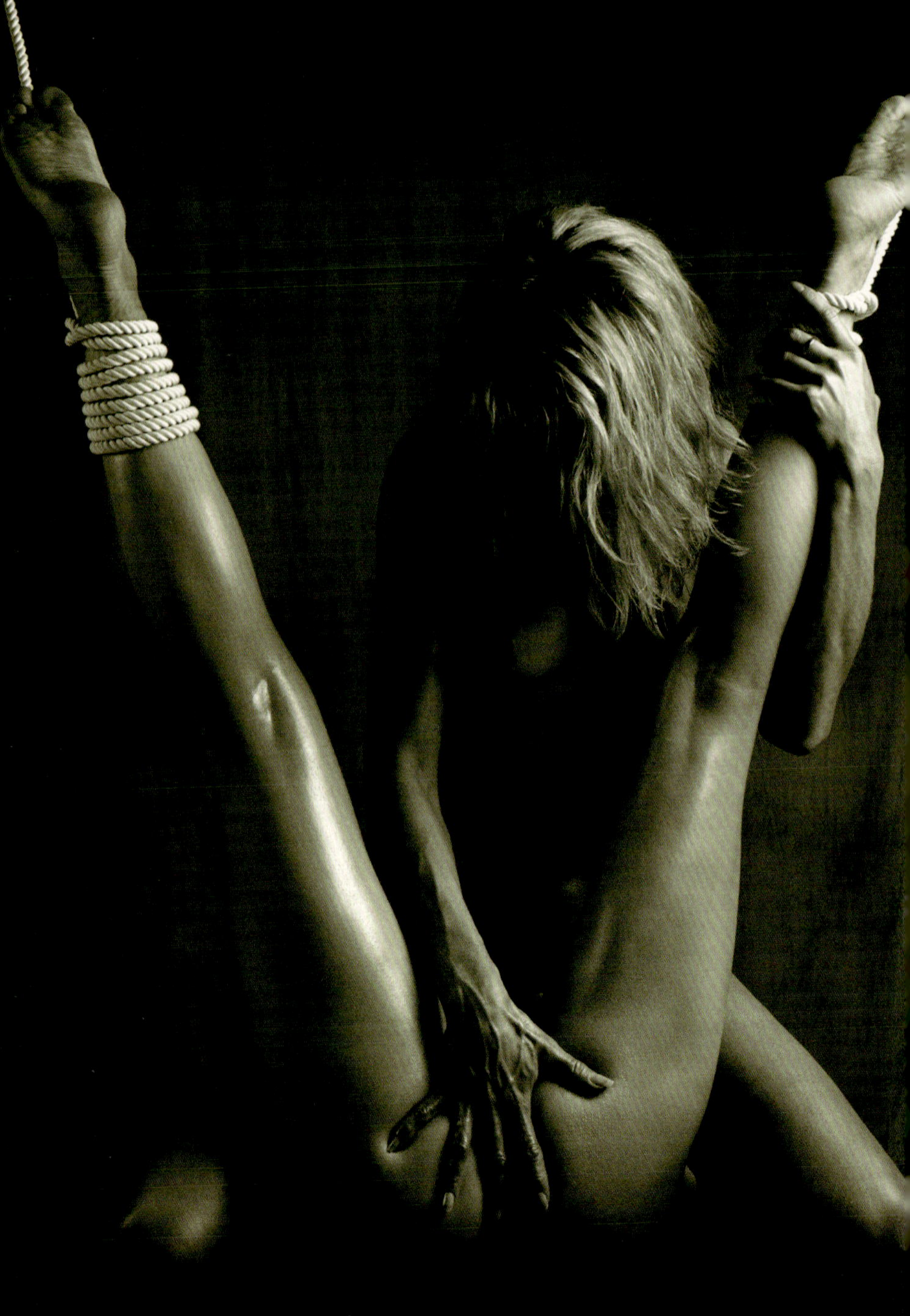

igor amelkovich

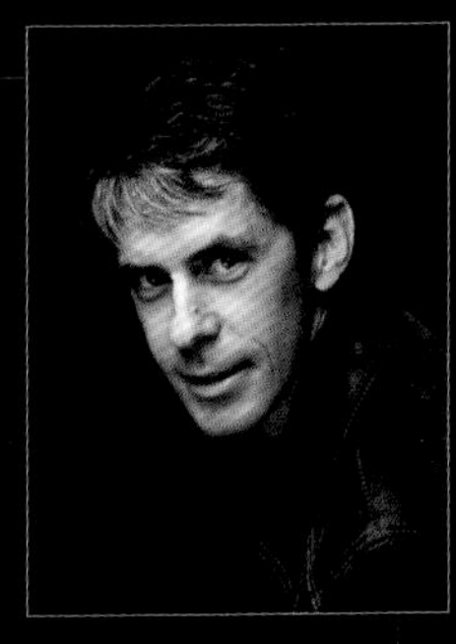

IGOR LIVES IN CHELYABINSK, in the southern Ural mountains of Russia. He studied radio engineering but photography has been his focus since 1999. He is self-taught and had not held a camera before. His work is film-based and he uses a Hasselblad 503CW. Artistically, he maintains two interests: landscape photography and the nude. For him, woman is nature's concentrated form of beauty. His work has won several regional and international awards.

www.amelkovich.com

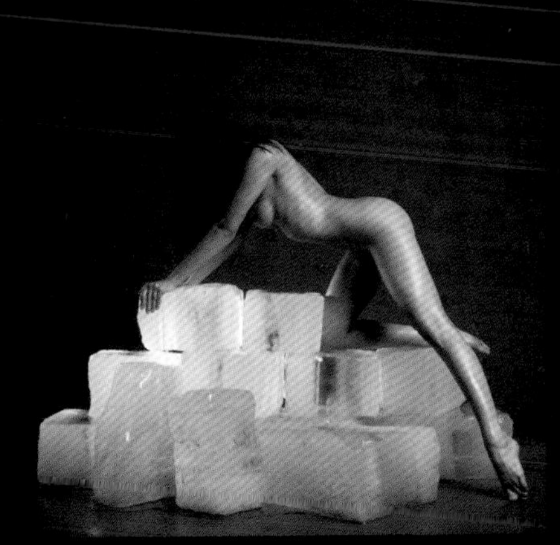

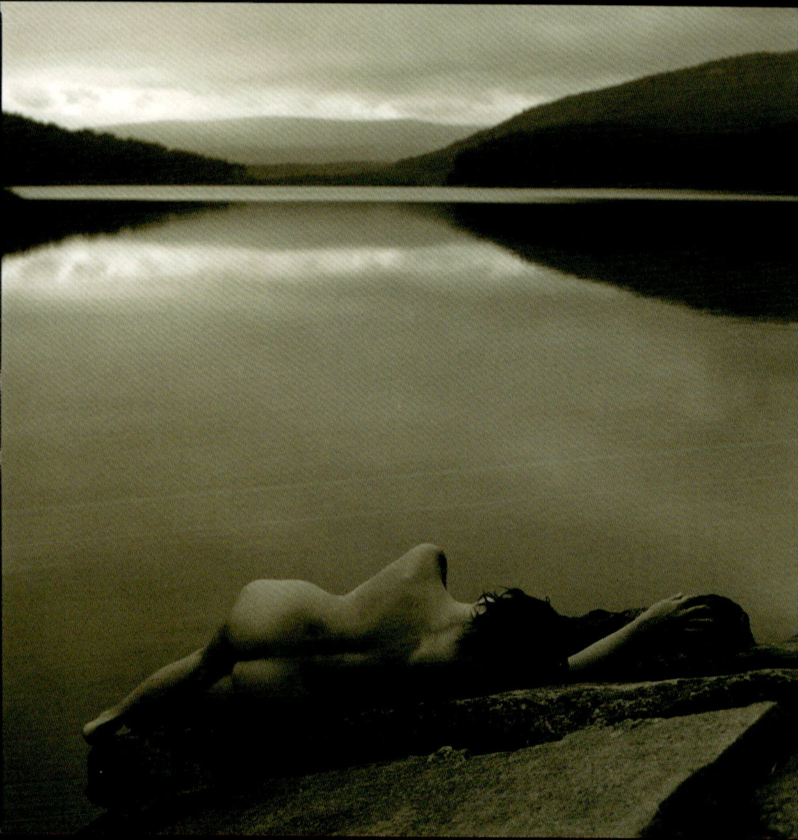

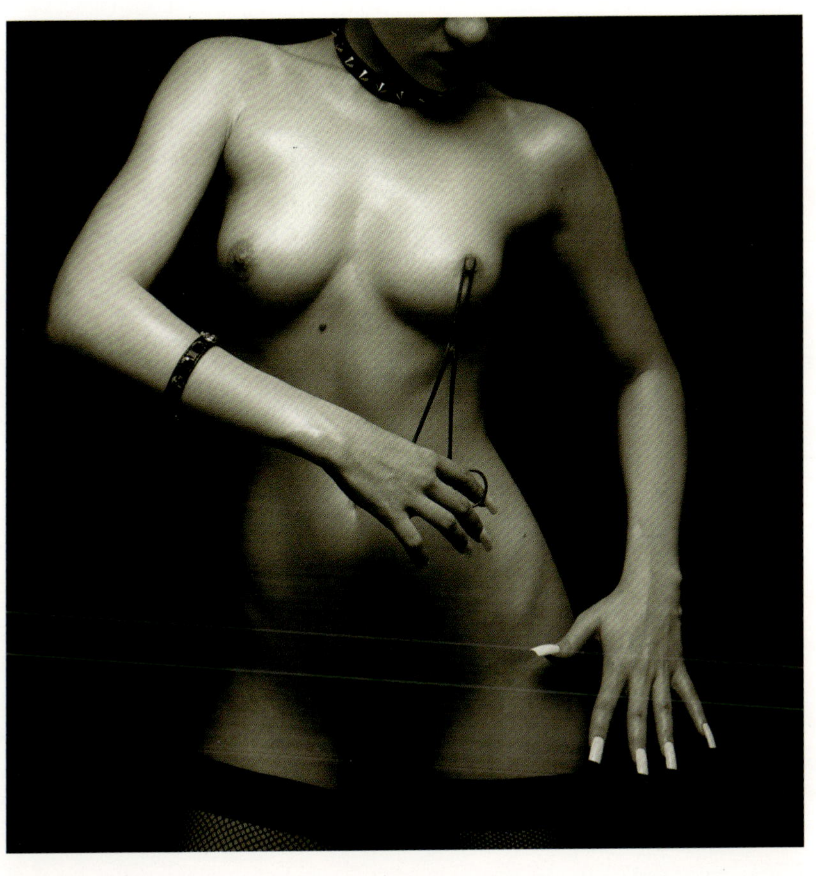

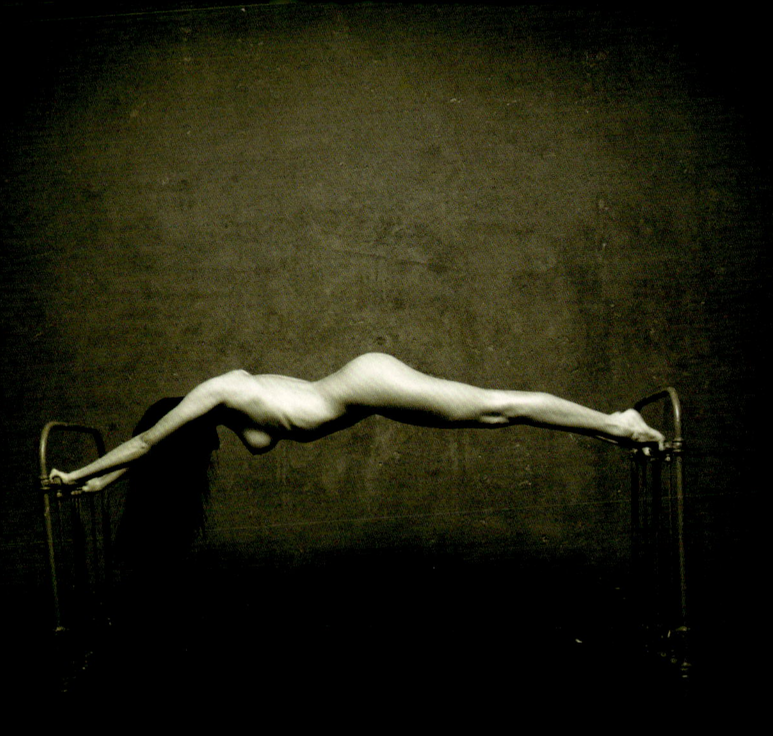

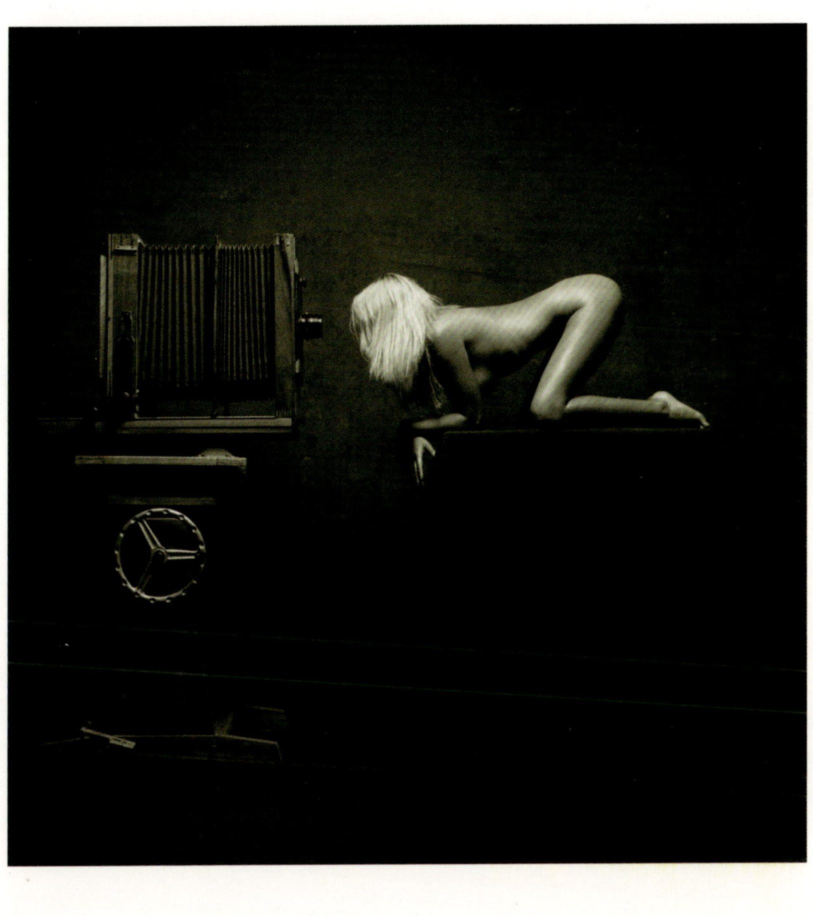

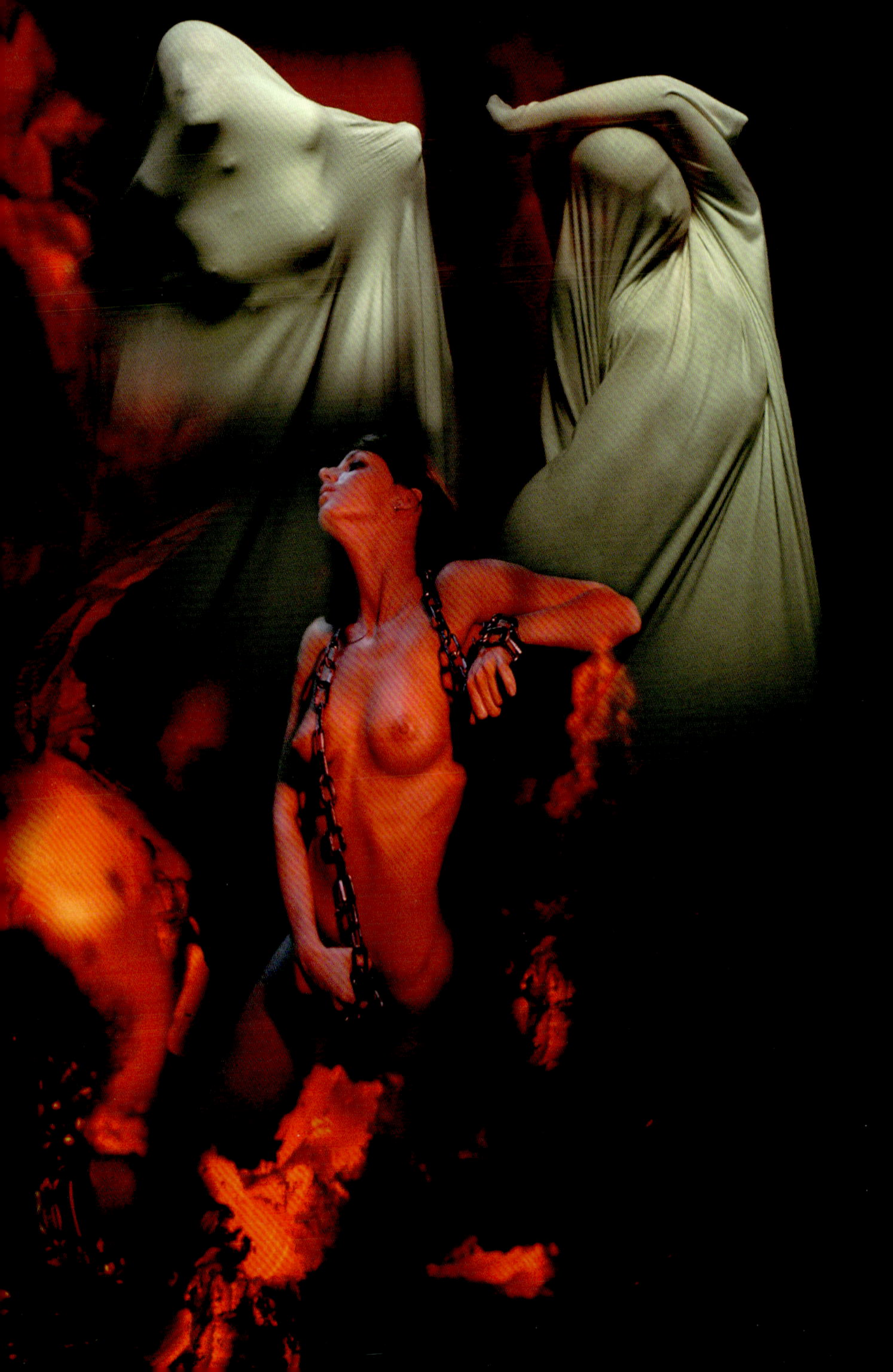

jean jacques andré

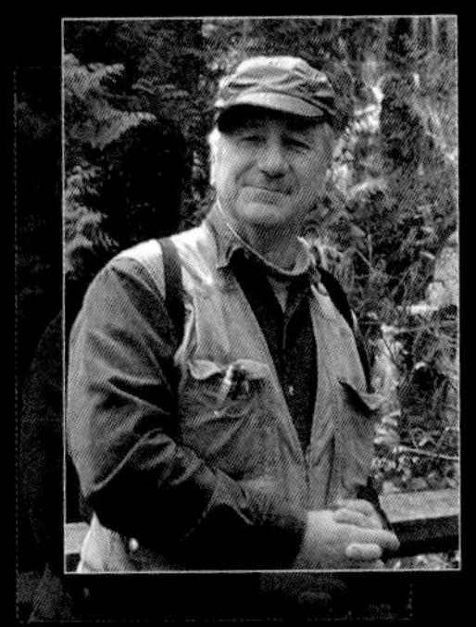

IN THE MID-FIFTIES, when he began figure photography, straight photographs of the nude alone were not fully satisfying to Jean Jacques André. In his mind, regardless of composition, form and lighting, they did not have great artistic value. They lacked meaning. Their use was that of a sketchbook – notes, poses and angles to be developed later into a body of work with more depth and creative merit. By 1956 he began to experiment with photomontages. Dark room 'magic' opened the doors to what was to become a lifelong dedication. It would enable him to express emotions and experiences stored away in the years from his youth to the present. Exhibitions, publications, workshops and of course the web have all been ways and means to communicate and share the joy of discovery.

http://jjandre-ca.com

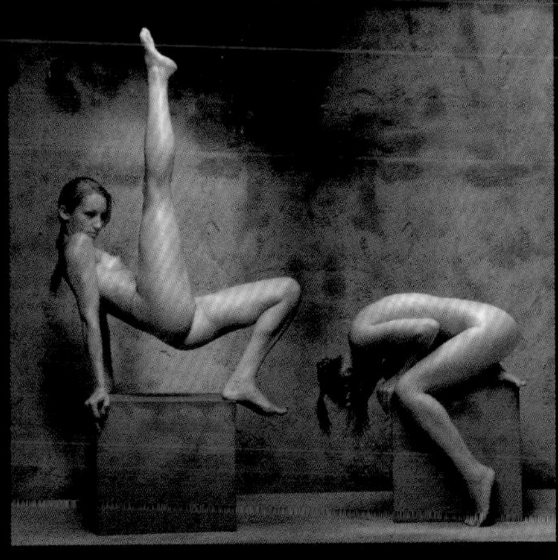

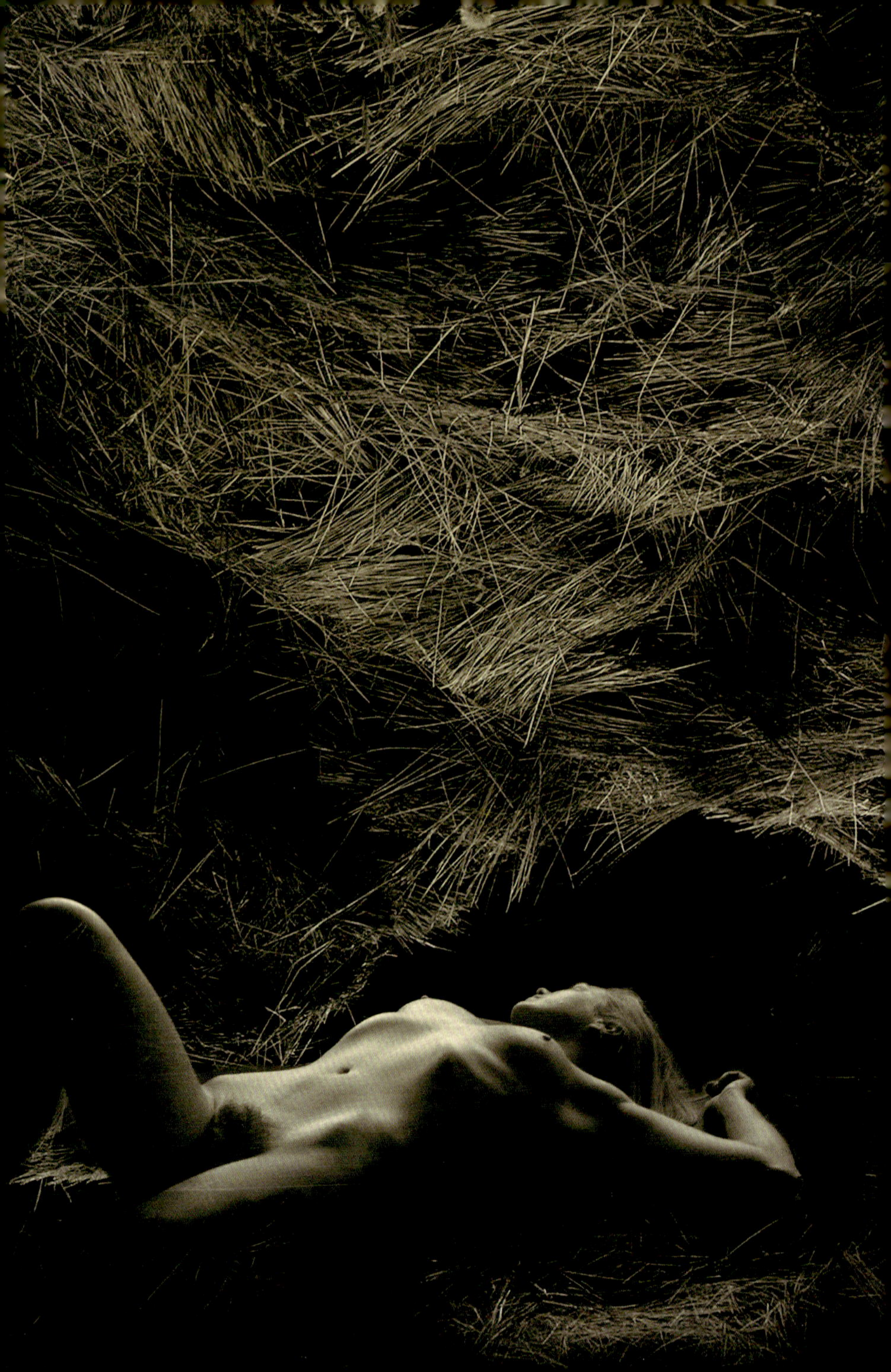

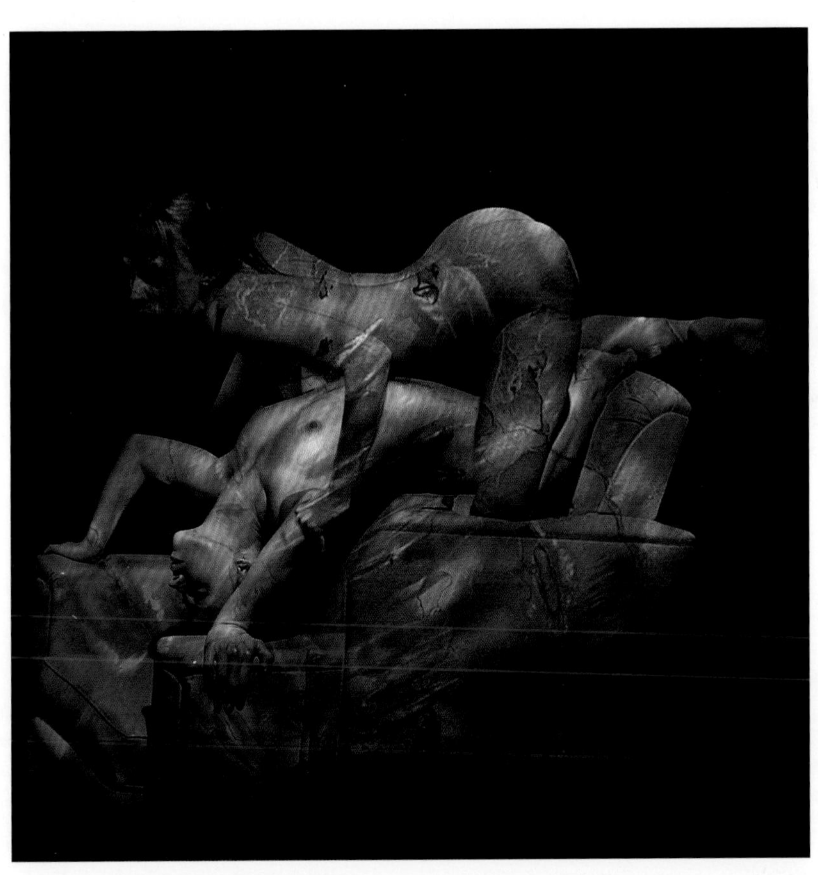

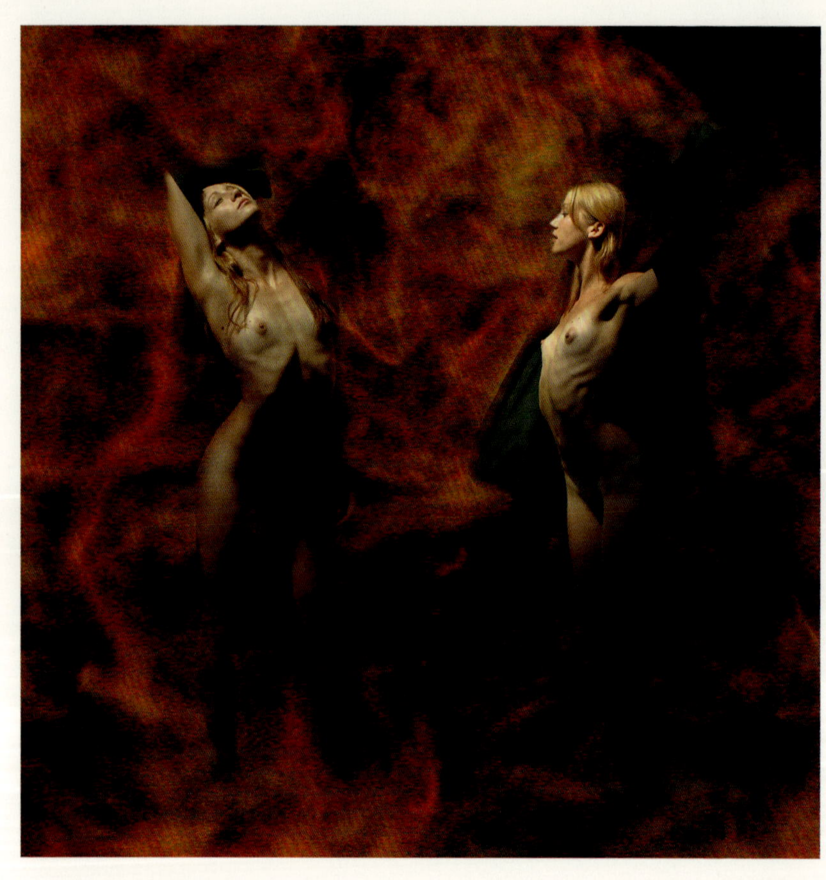

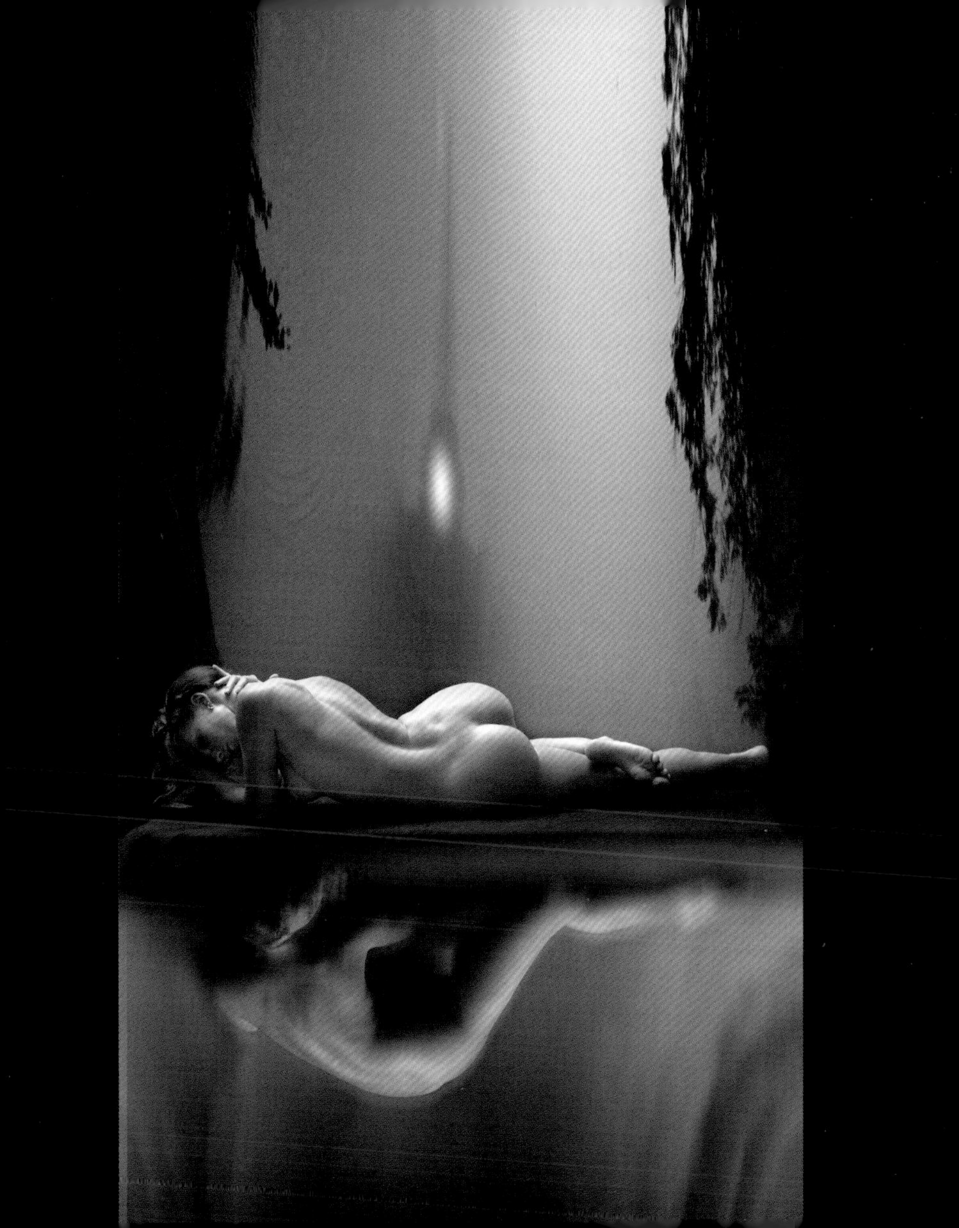

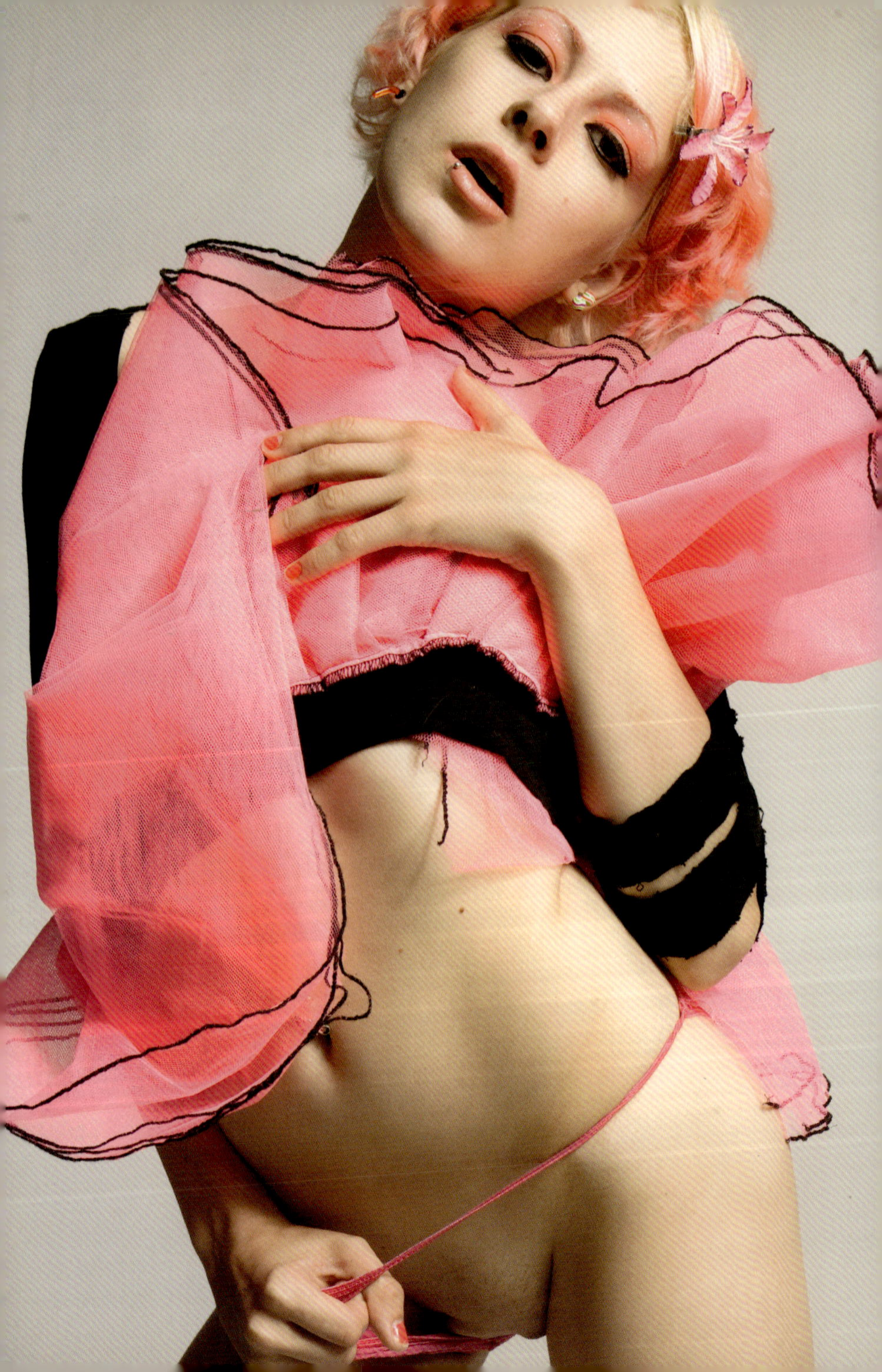

robert baham

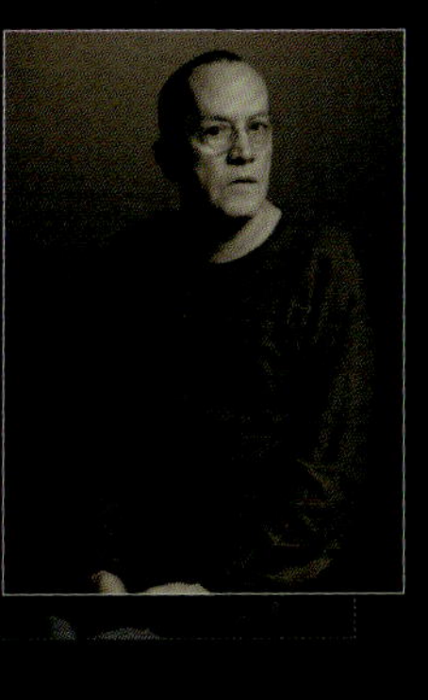

AS POETS AND PHILOSOPHERS have always known, there are only two things in life worthy of serious consideration: sex and death. American photographer Robert Baham's work is about the former. But it is not sex without love. He loves his models while they work together and remains fond of each of them forever. He does not work with professional models. In most cases, this is the first and last time his subjects will be photographed this way. Their generosity is an act of pure grace. The best of his work is unplanned and spontaneous. He just gets lucky sometimes.

www.chapapeela.com

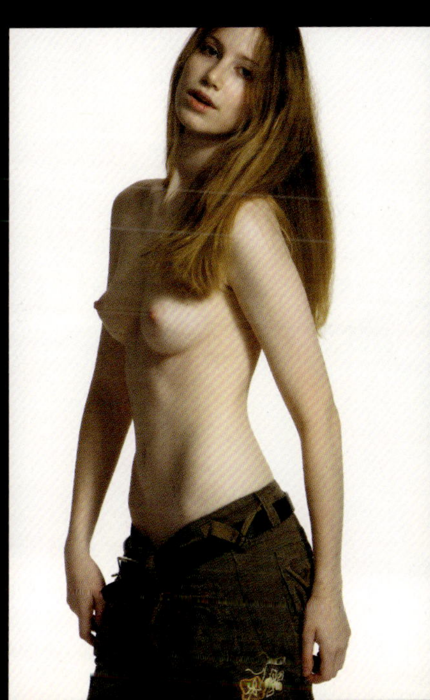

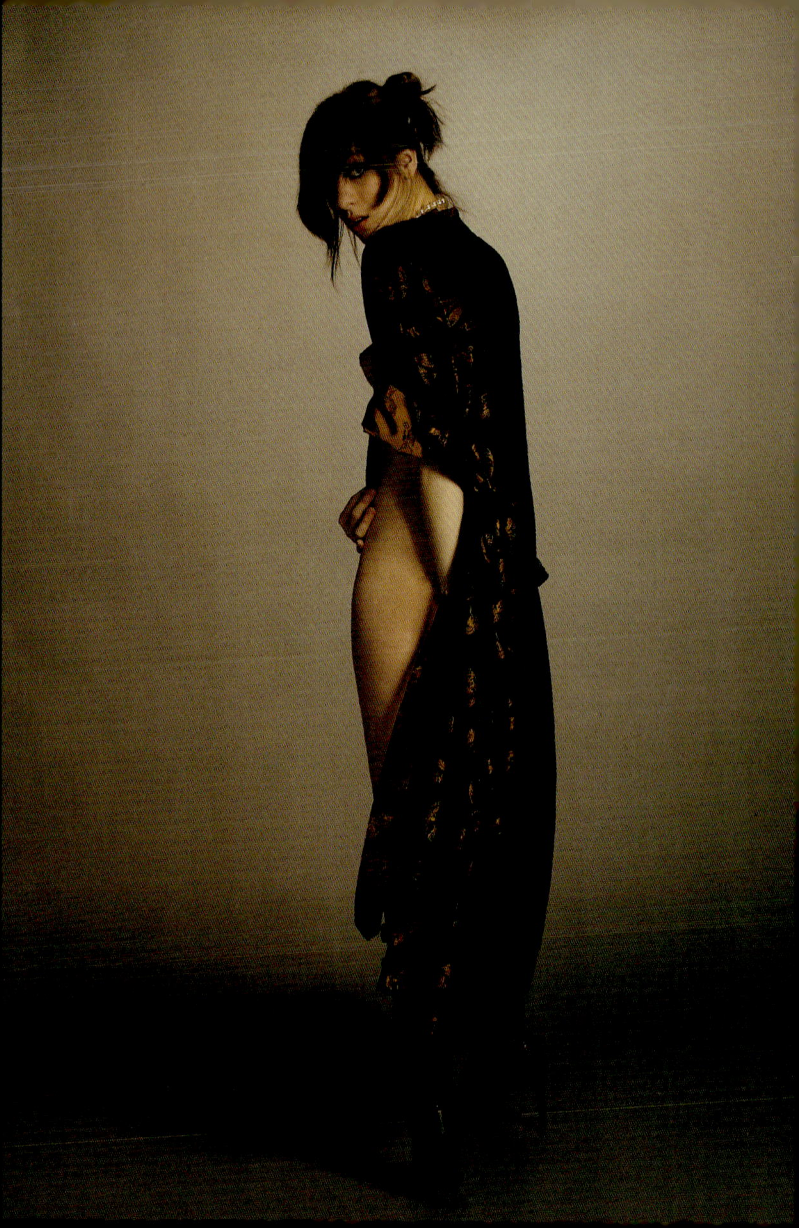

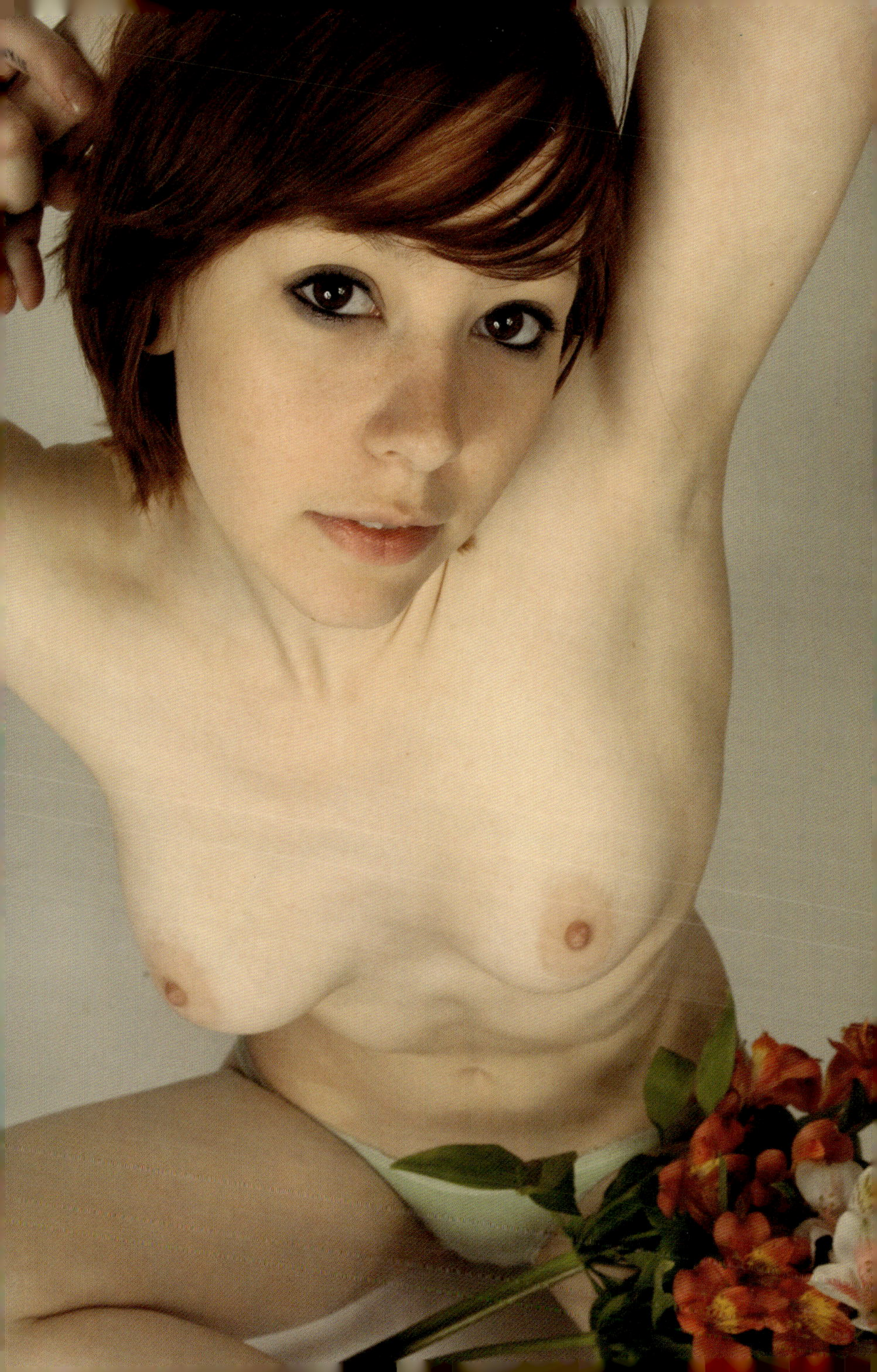

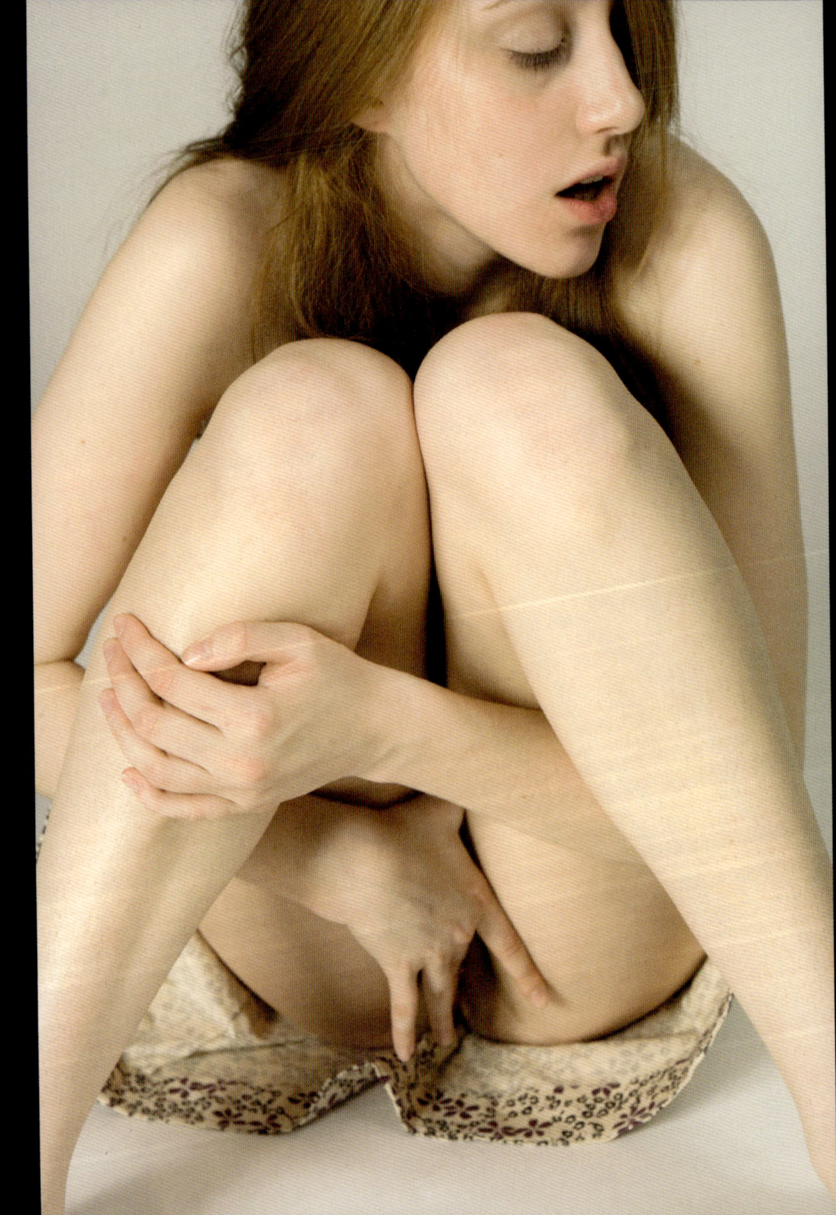

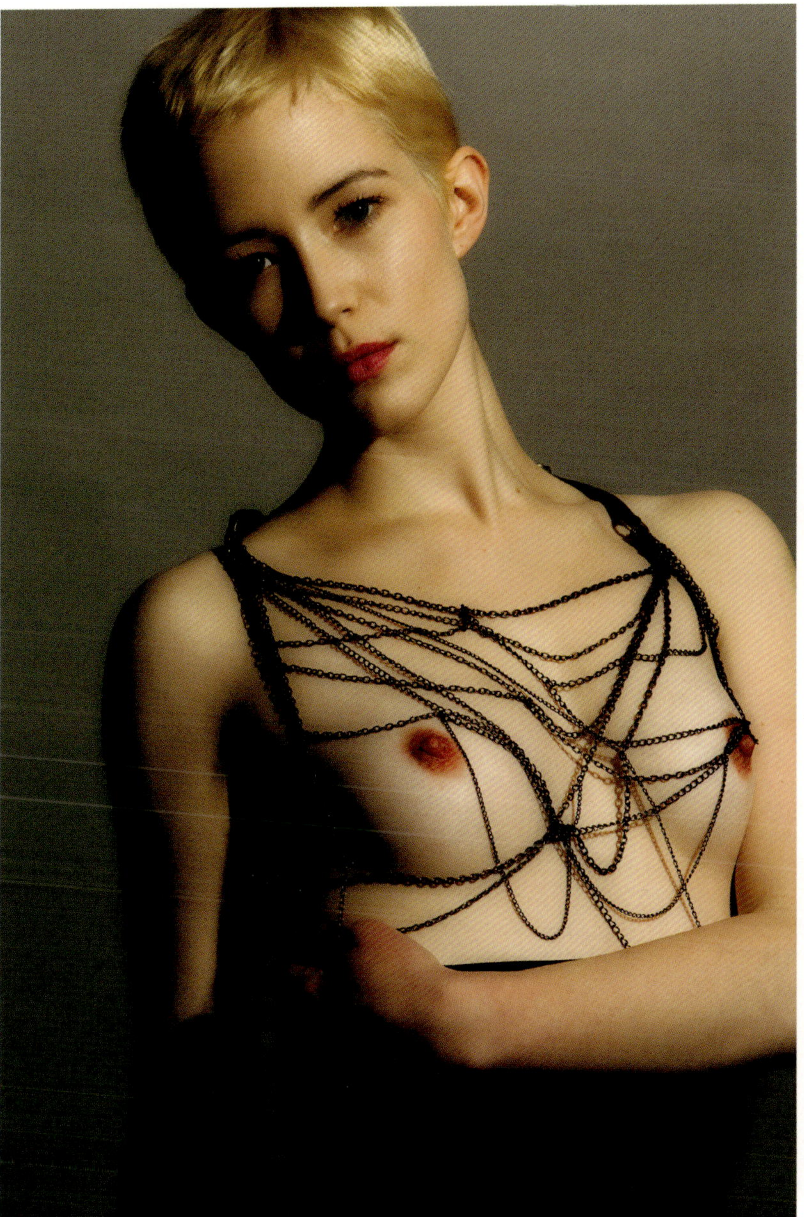

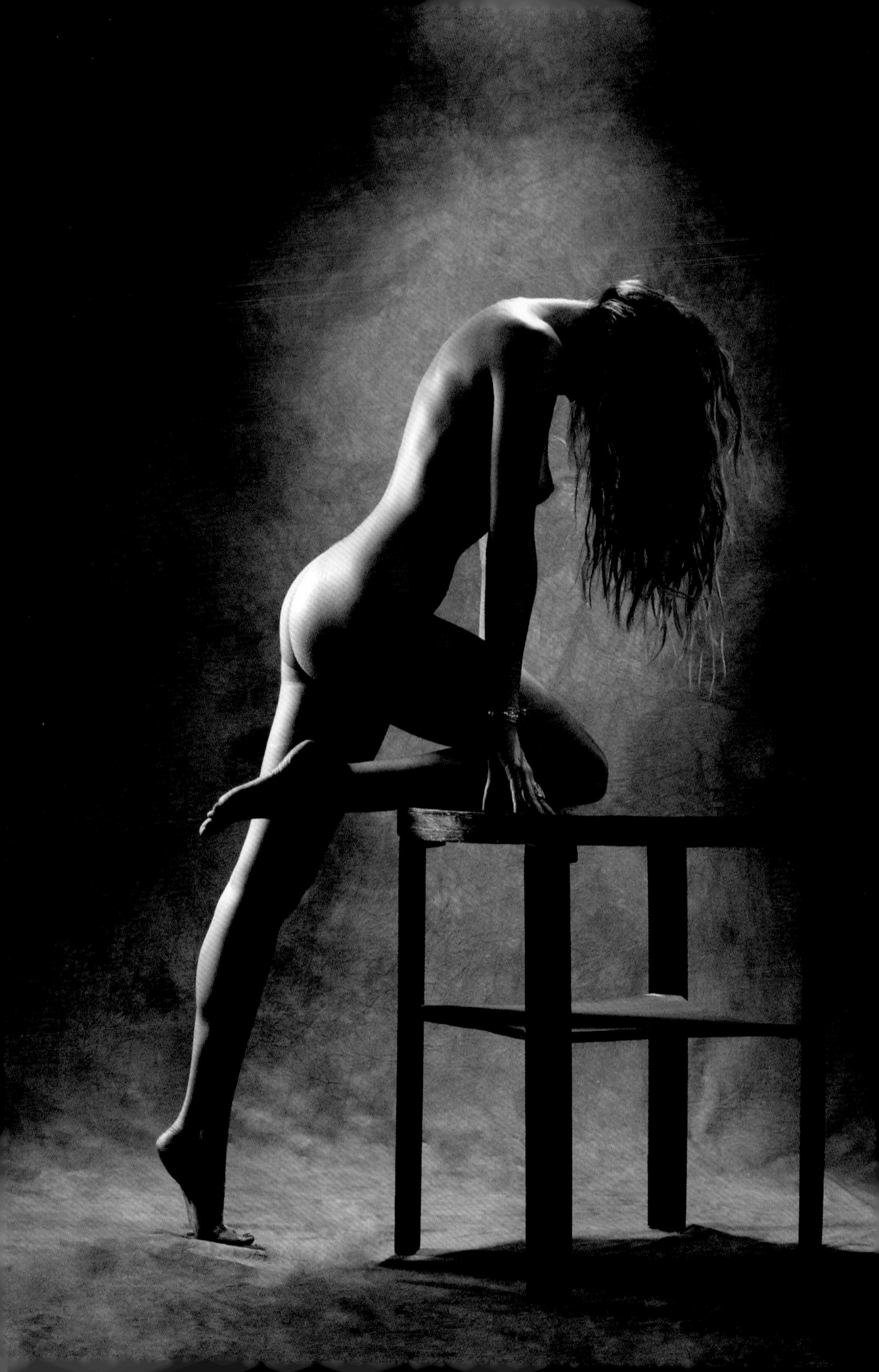

valery bareta

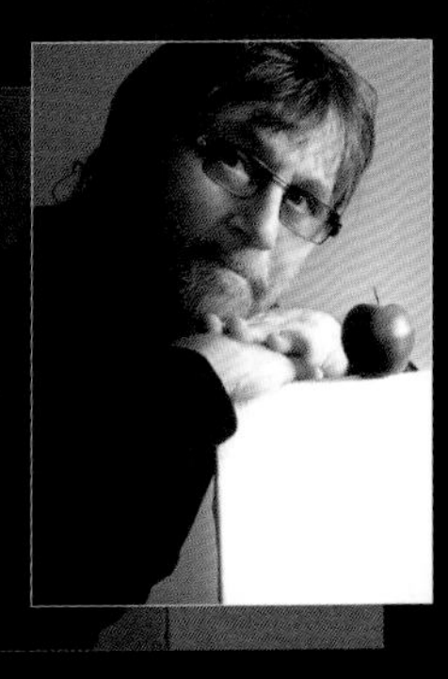

VALERY IS A RUSSIAN PHOTOGRAPHER, born in the Ukraine, who now lives in Tallinn in Estonia. Following technical studies and his degree, he joined the Soviet army and spent time in Kamchatka. He enjoys taking pictures of women, both classical and innovative, and likes metamorphoses as well as allegories.

www.valerybareta.com

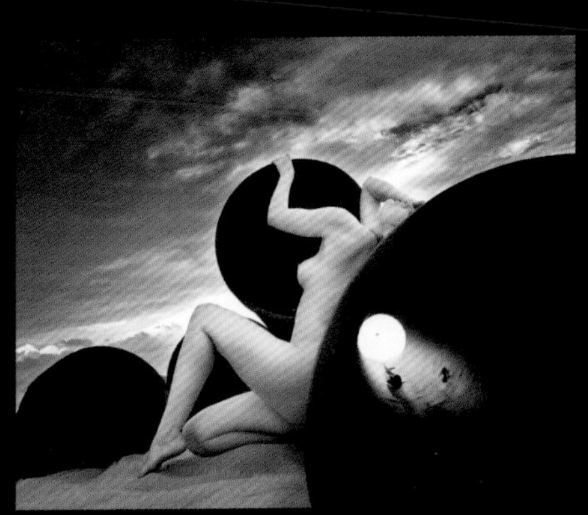

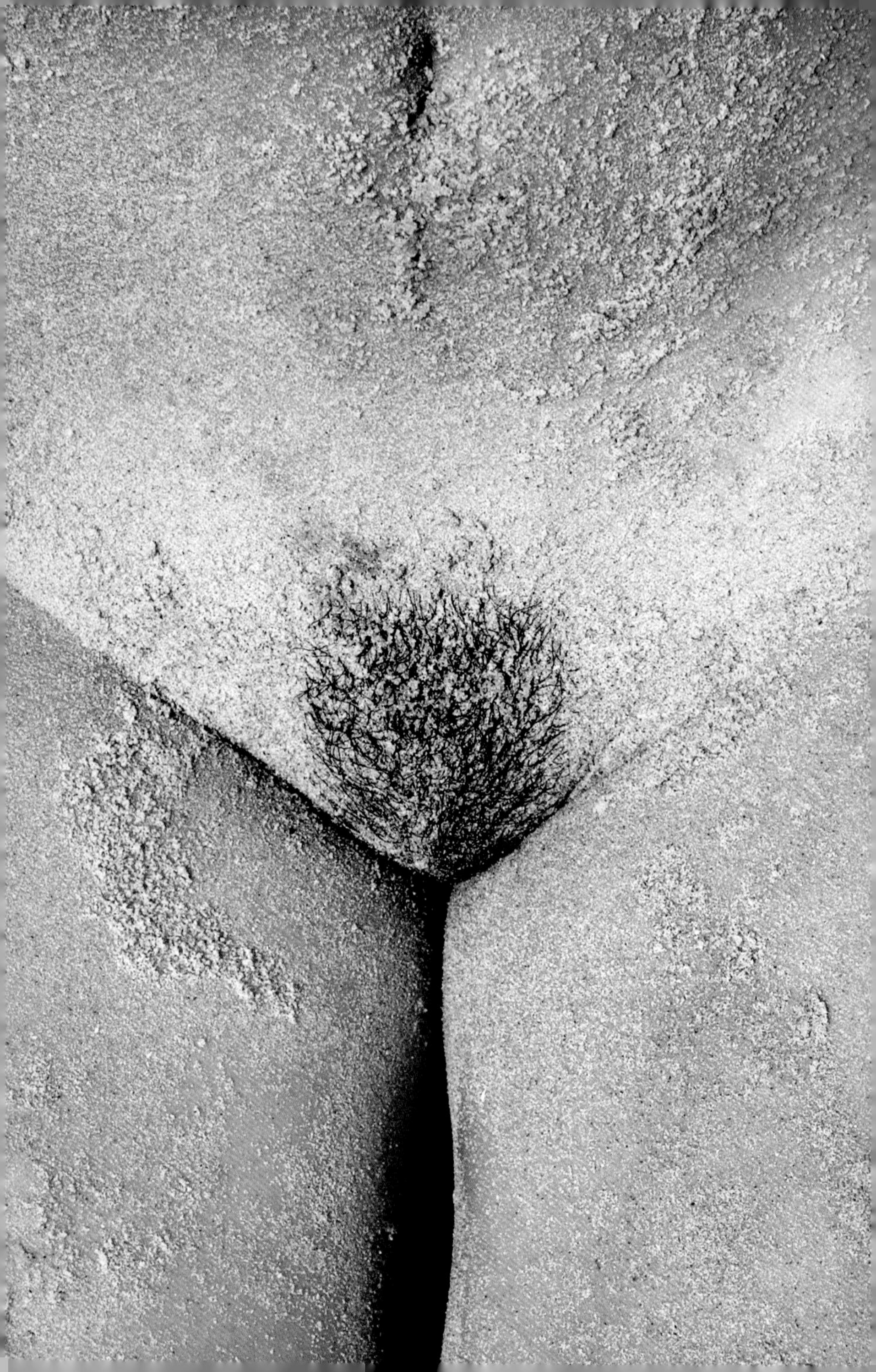

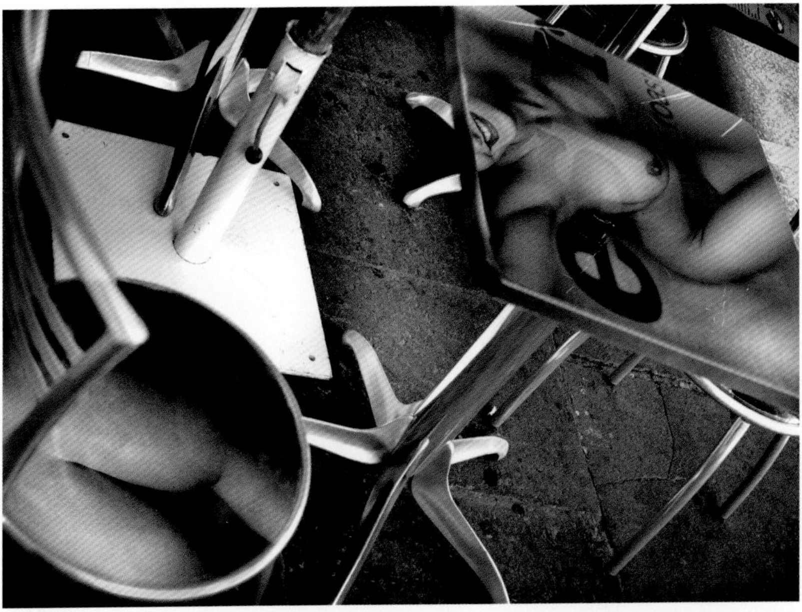

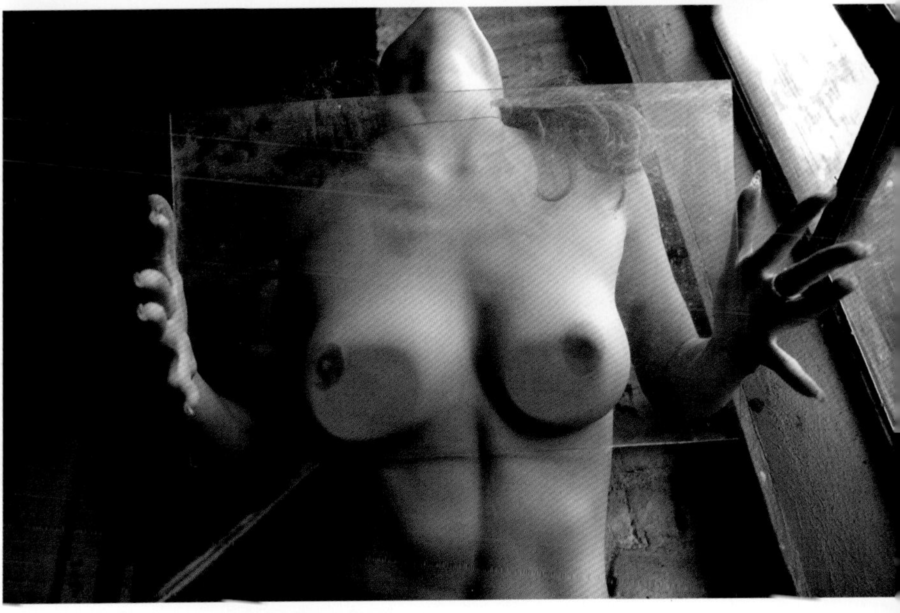

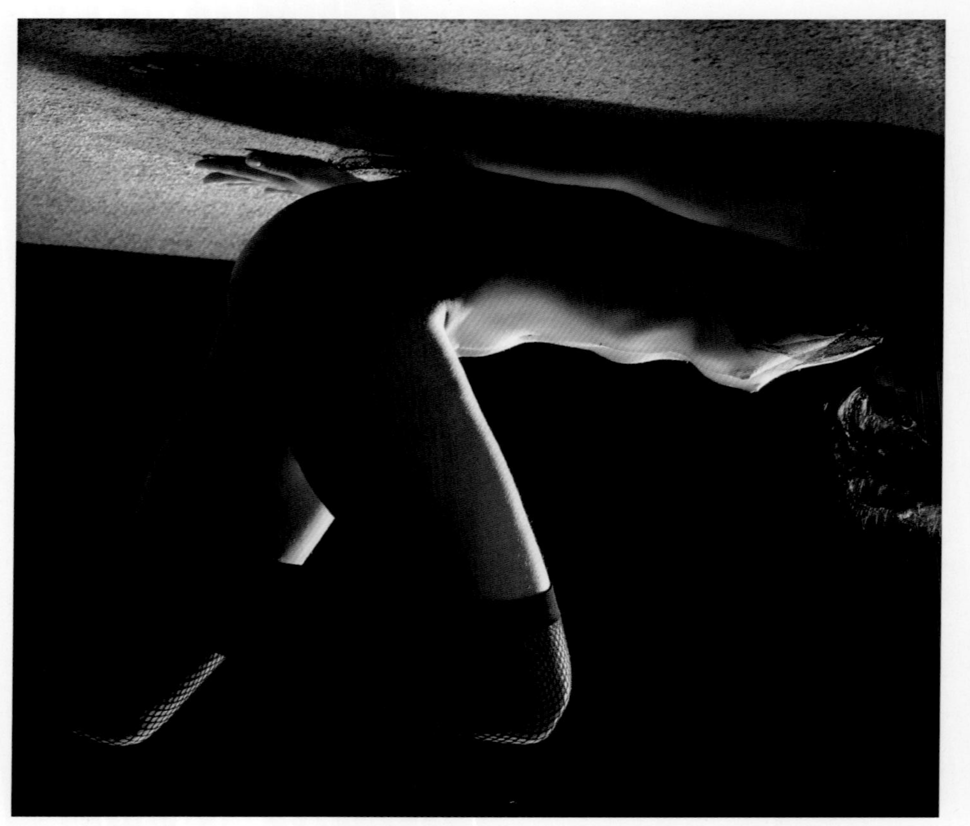

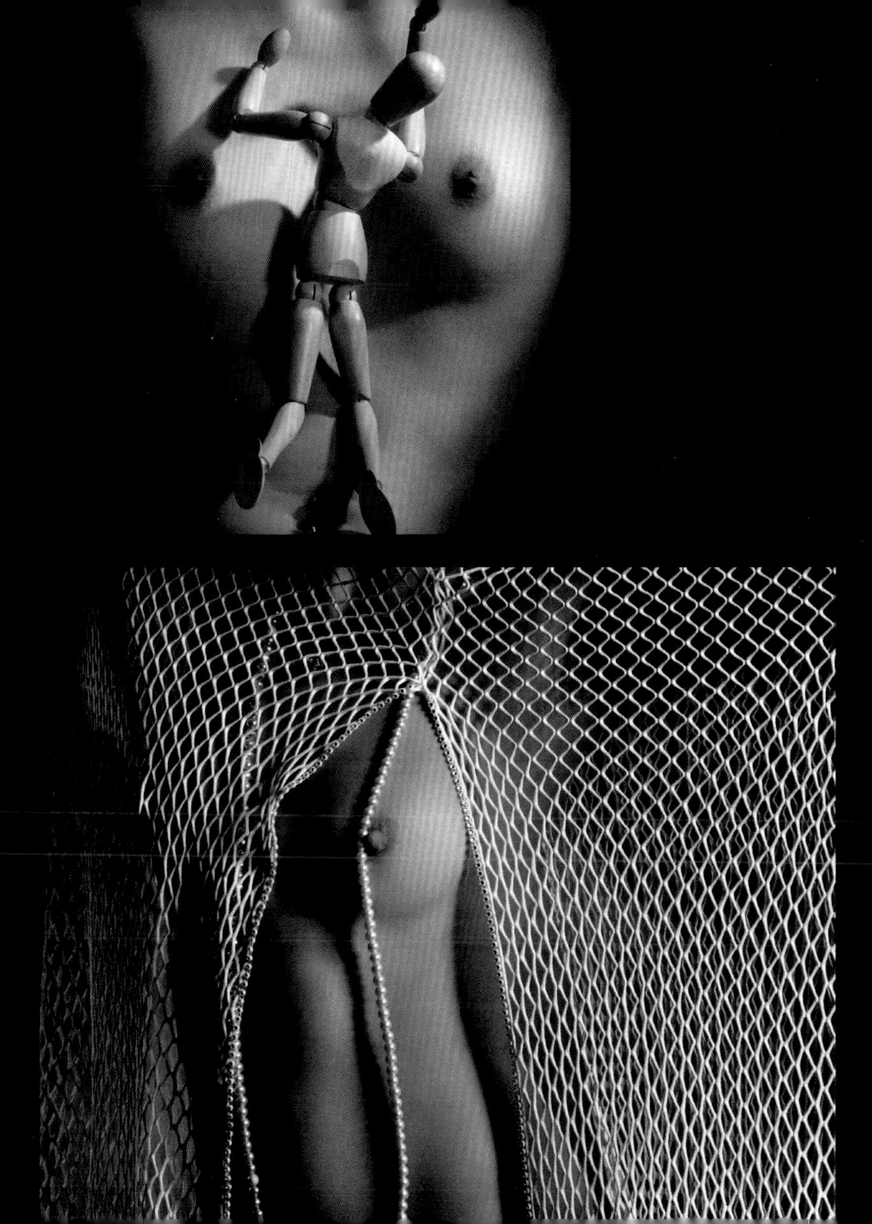

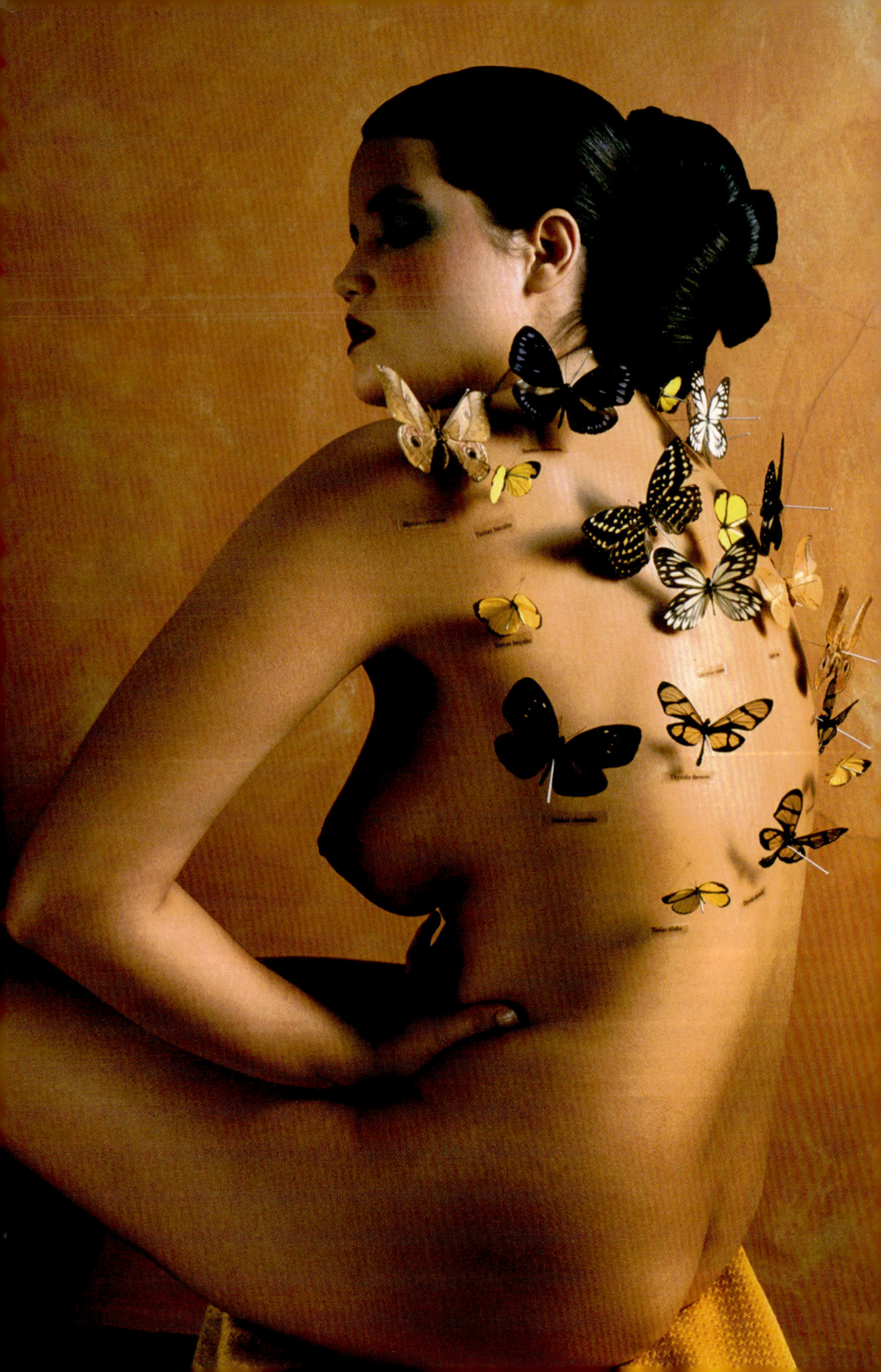

alva bernadine

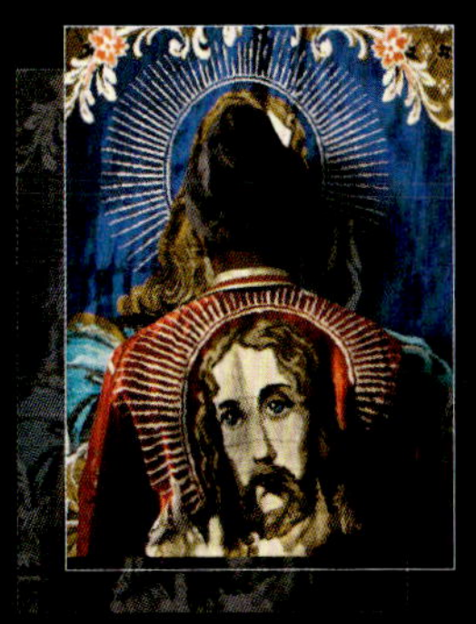

ALVA WAS BORN IN GRENEDA, West Indies and moved to London in the UK at the age of six. At age ten, he bought a toy camera that took blurred images, some of which his mother still has in the family album. He began seriously interested in photography at the age of twenty-one and his first pictures were of London tourist spots; a year later he began practising his present style. He is self-taught and has never been an assistant. He has worked for numerous magazines all over the world and, in 1987, was the winner of the Vogue/Sotheby's Cecil Beaton Award. He was voted Erotic Photographer of the Year in Great Britain in 2002 for his book *Bernadinism*.

www.bernadinism.com

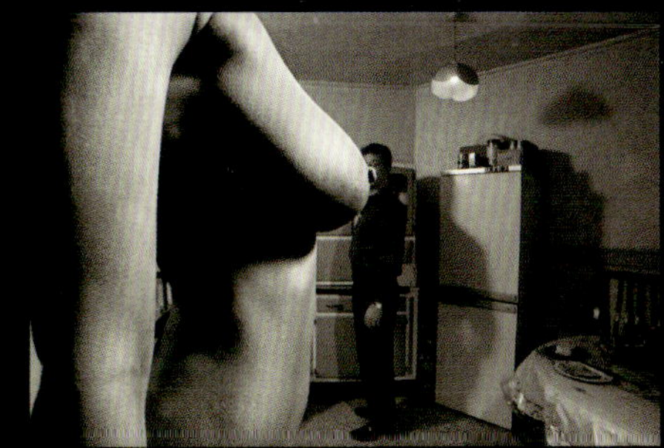

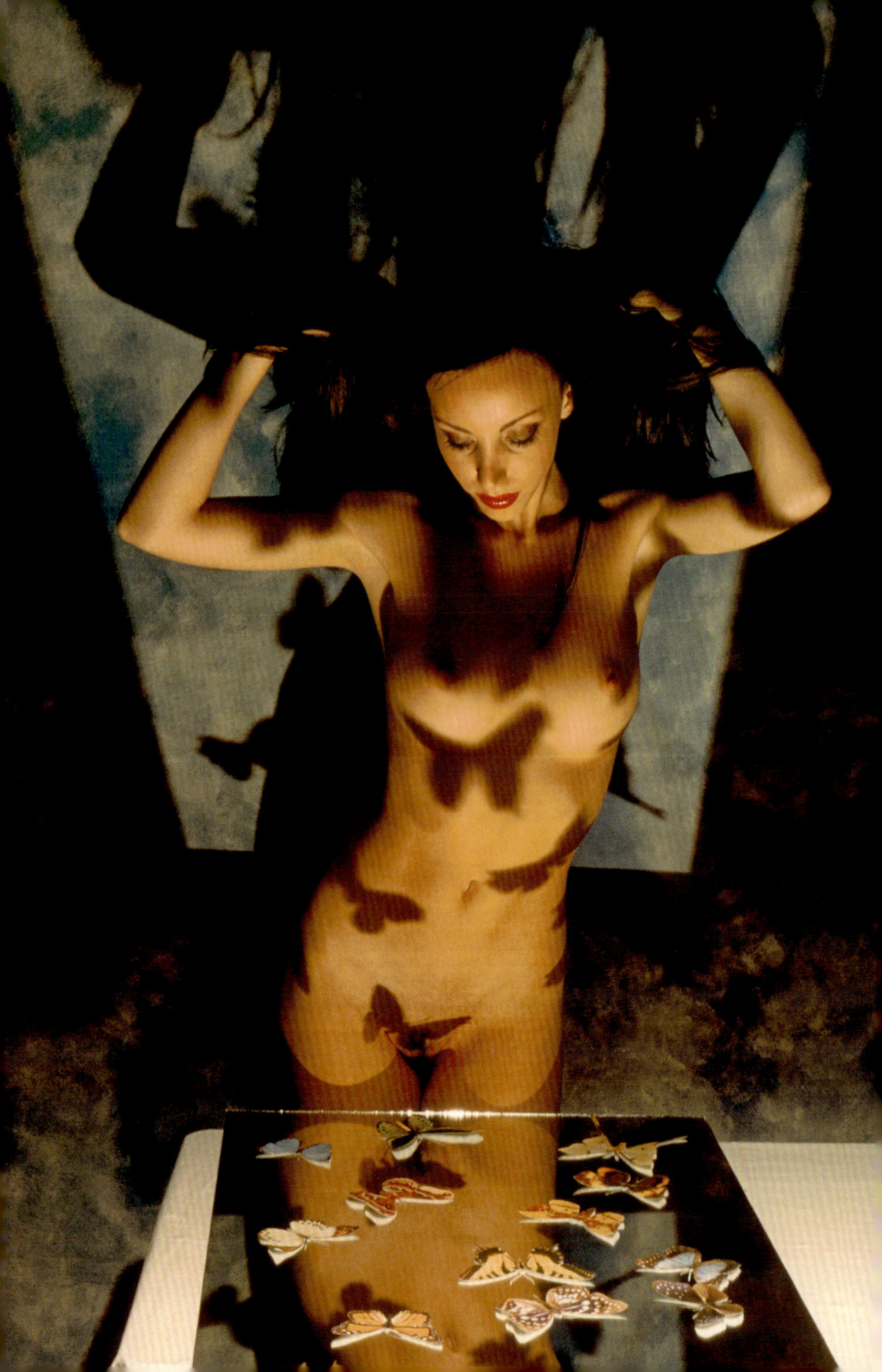

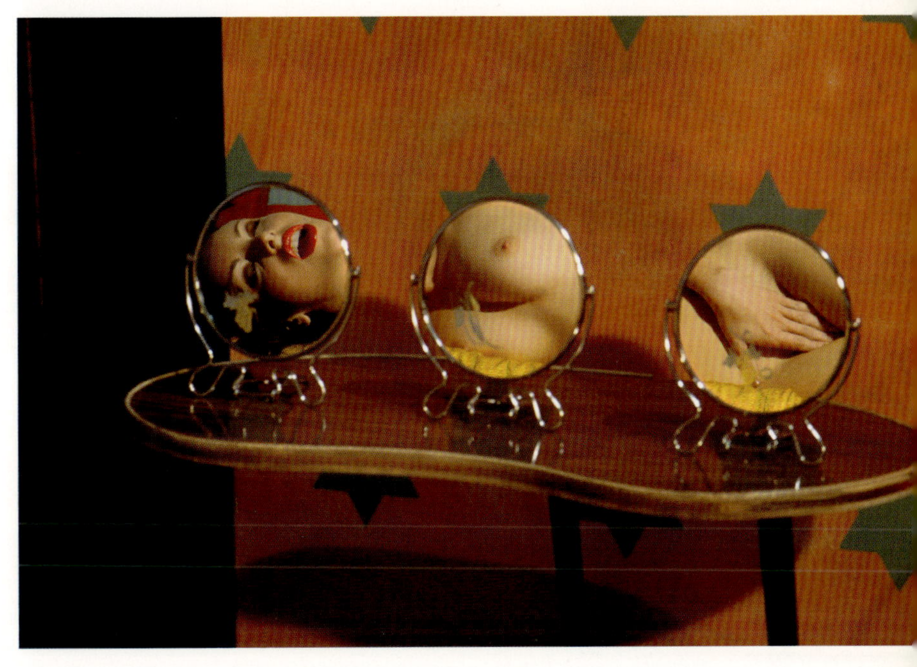

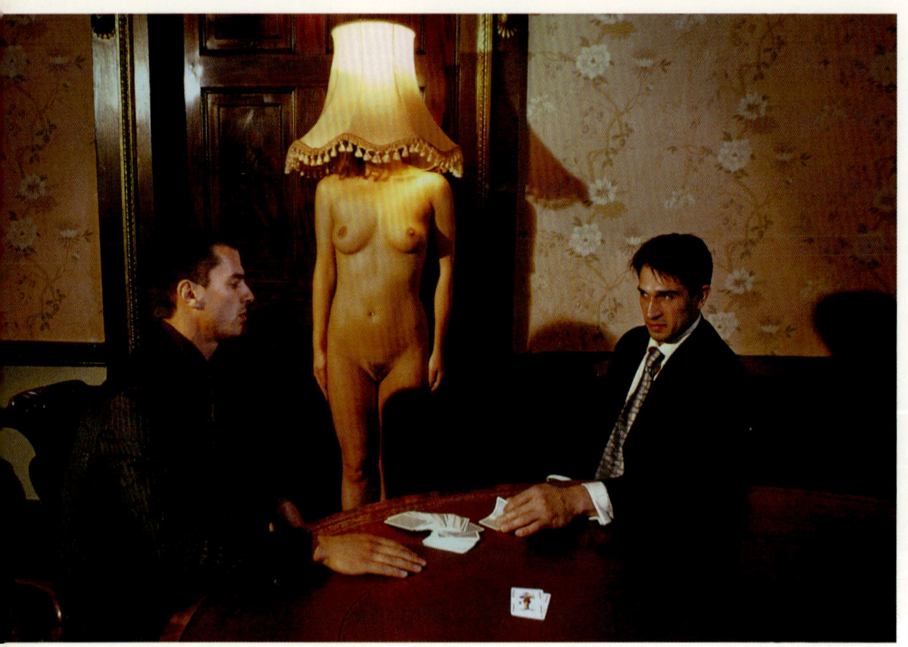

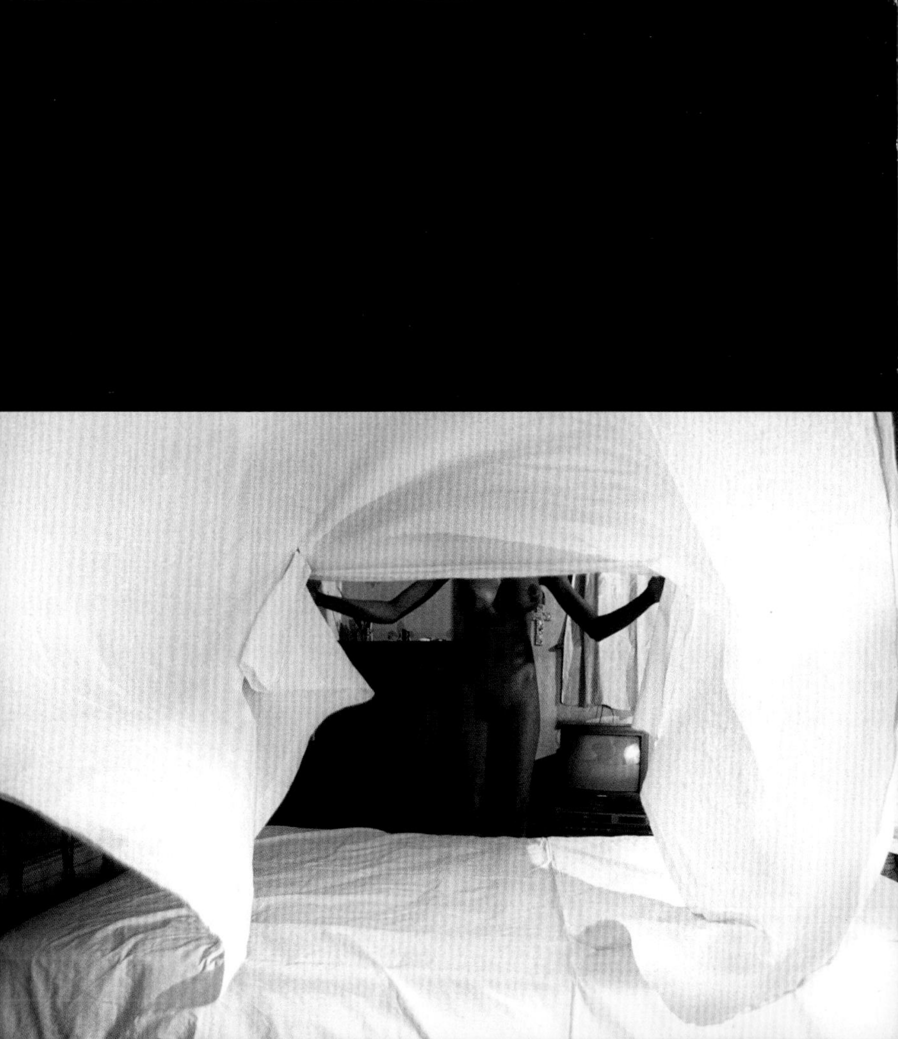

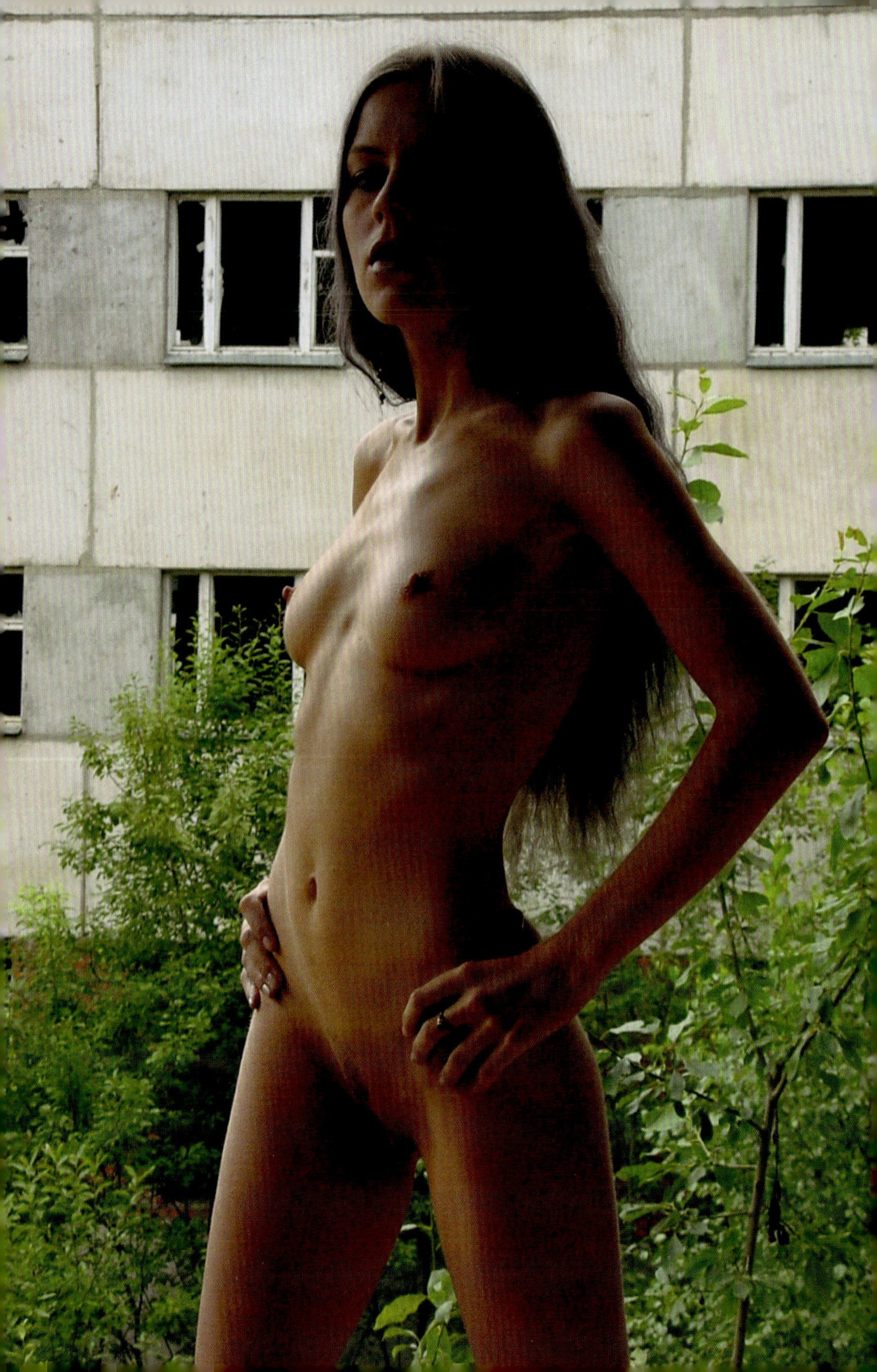

kirill borgia

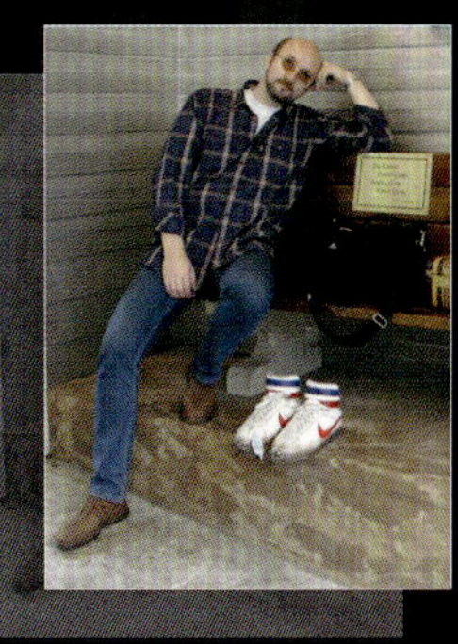

KIRILL BORGIA IS A PSEUDONYM for a well-known fine art photographer from Moscow. He emerged in the 1990s when Russian erotic photography first saw the light of day on the Internet. Since then he has become a brand name. All his models are non-professional girls next door. They are young, bravely nude and provocative, yet one never gets the feeling they are other-worldy untouchables. This appealing aura of naturalness and simplicity is what makes Borgia unique.

www.borgia.bos.ru
www.girls-of-russia.110mb.com

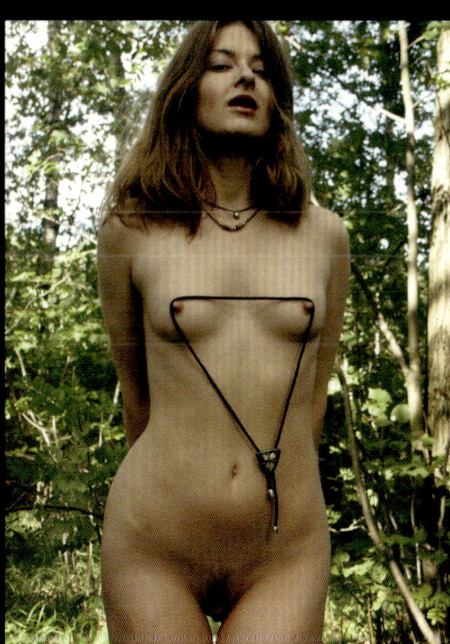

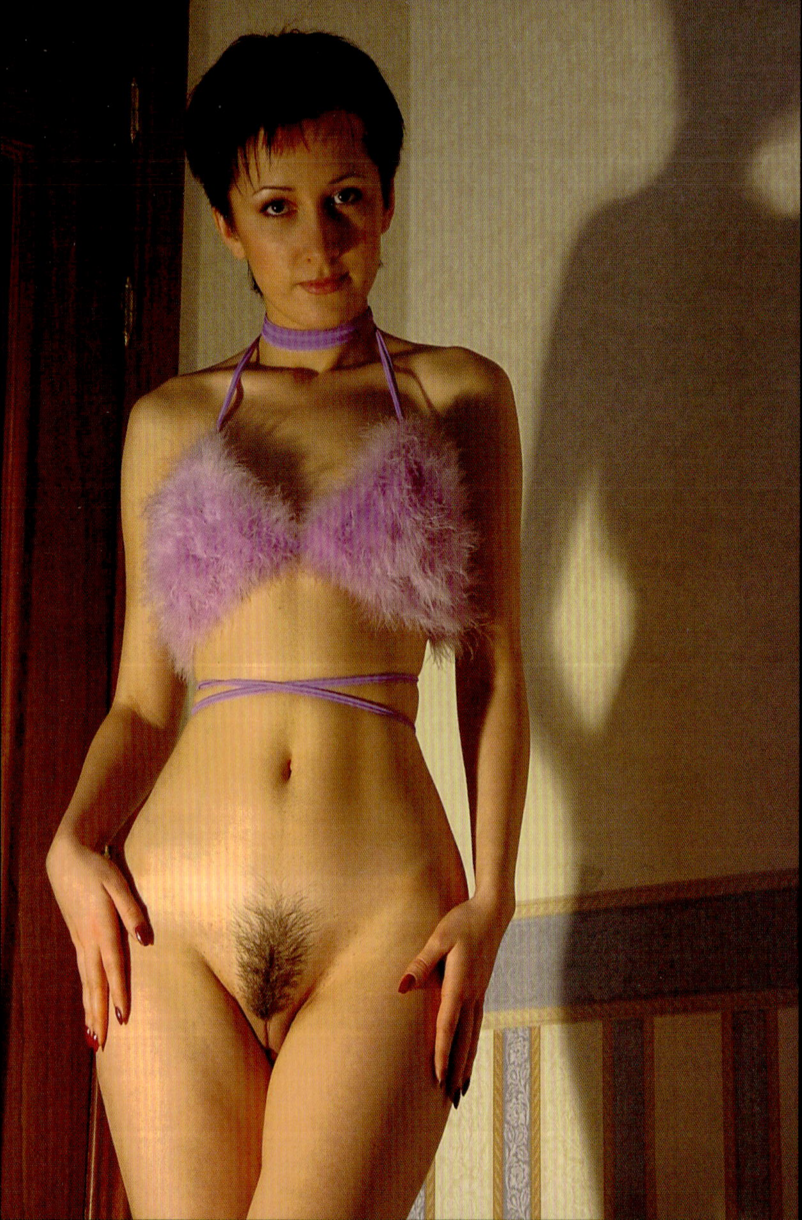

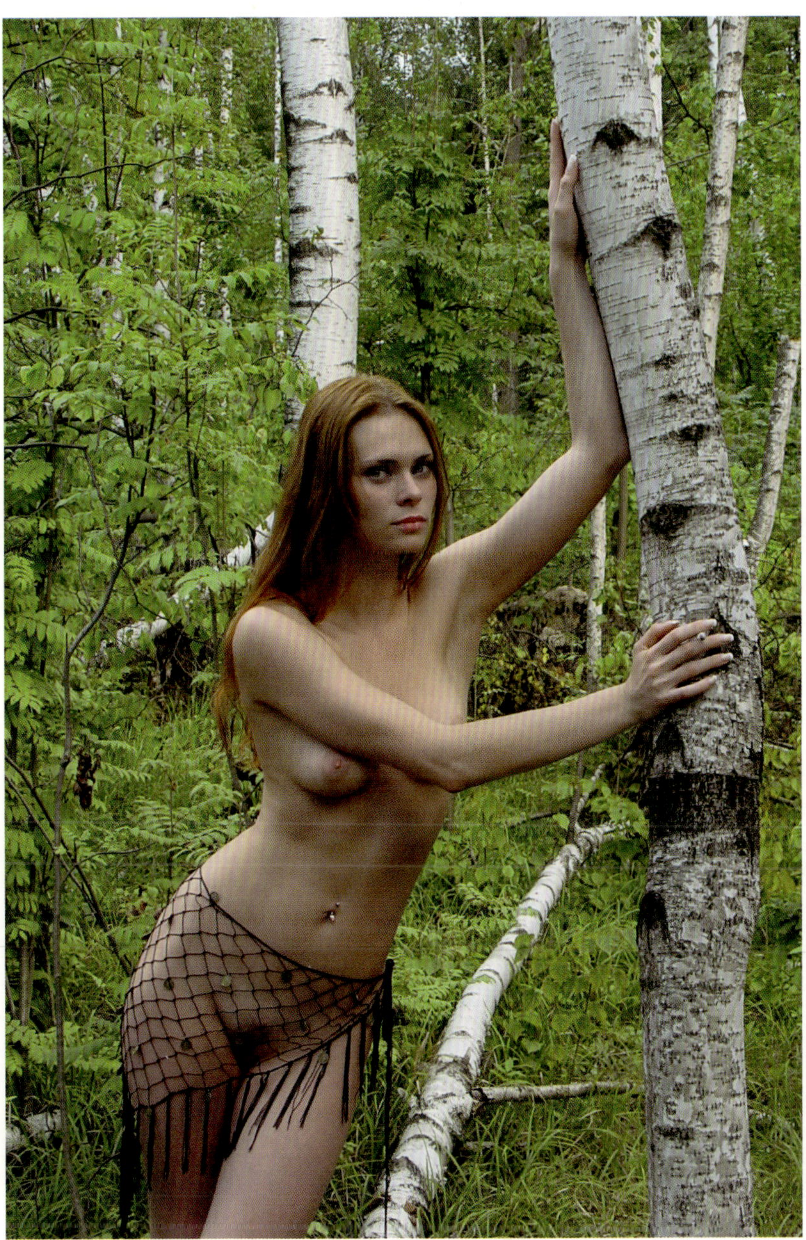

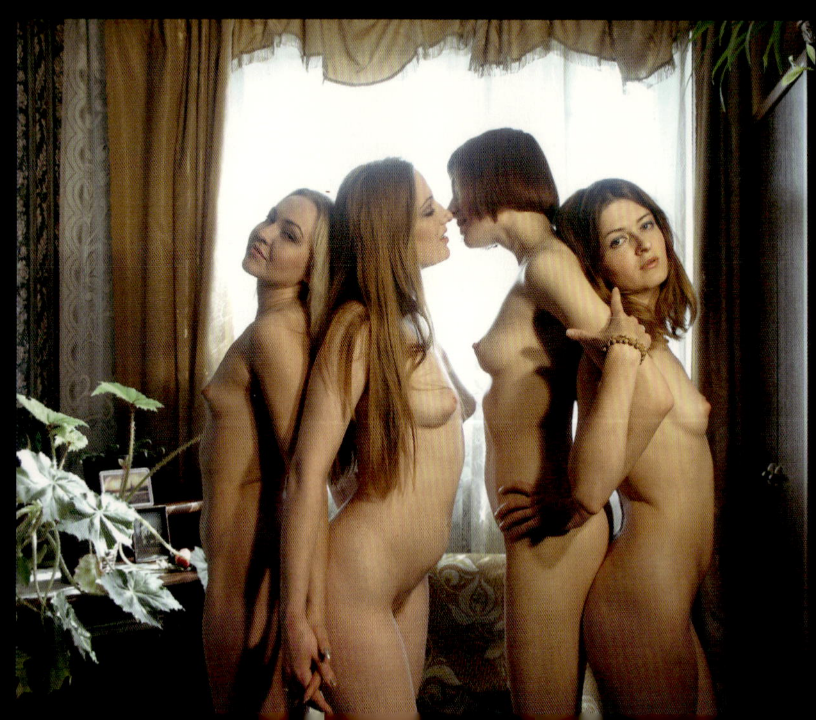

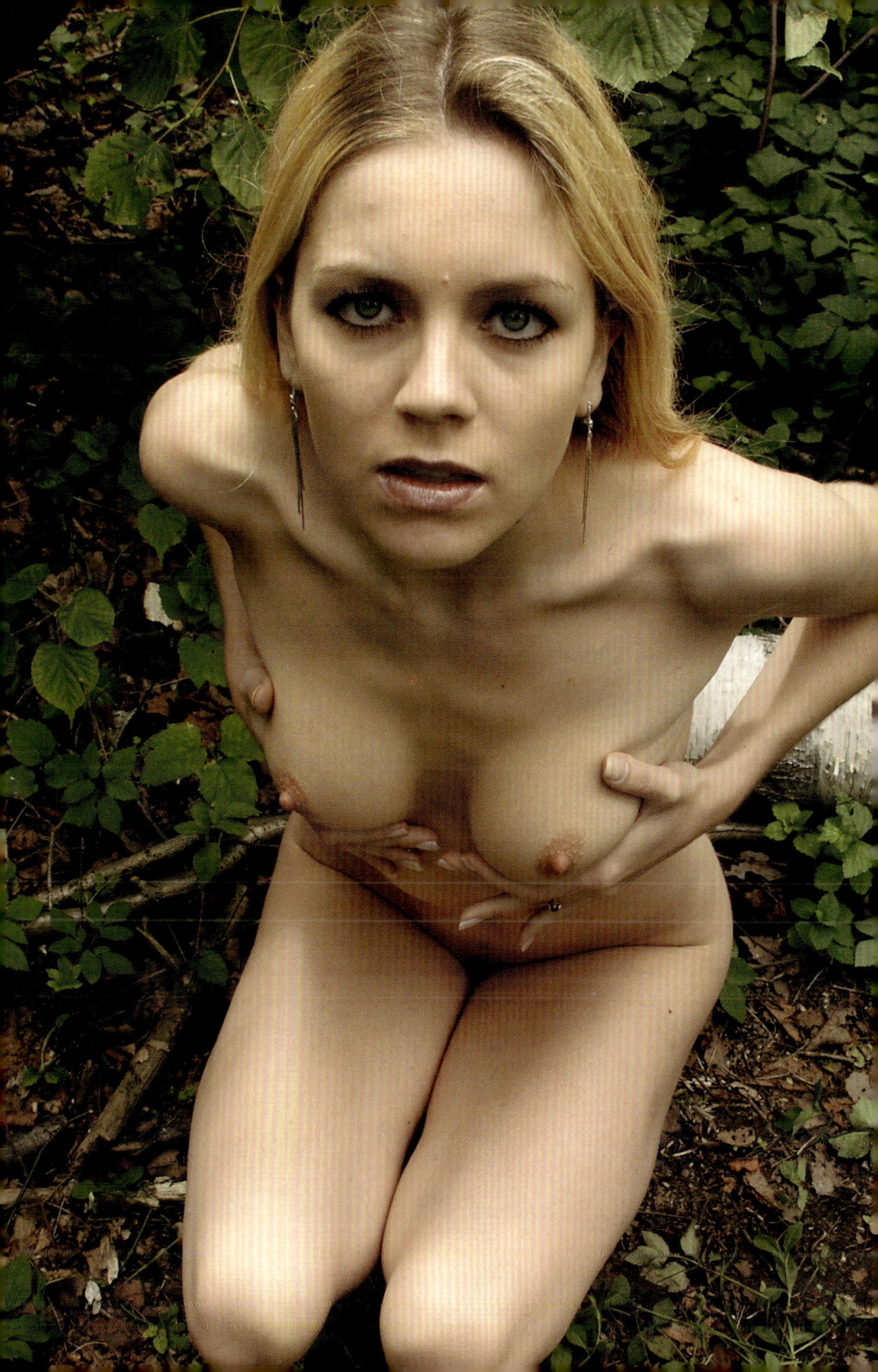

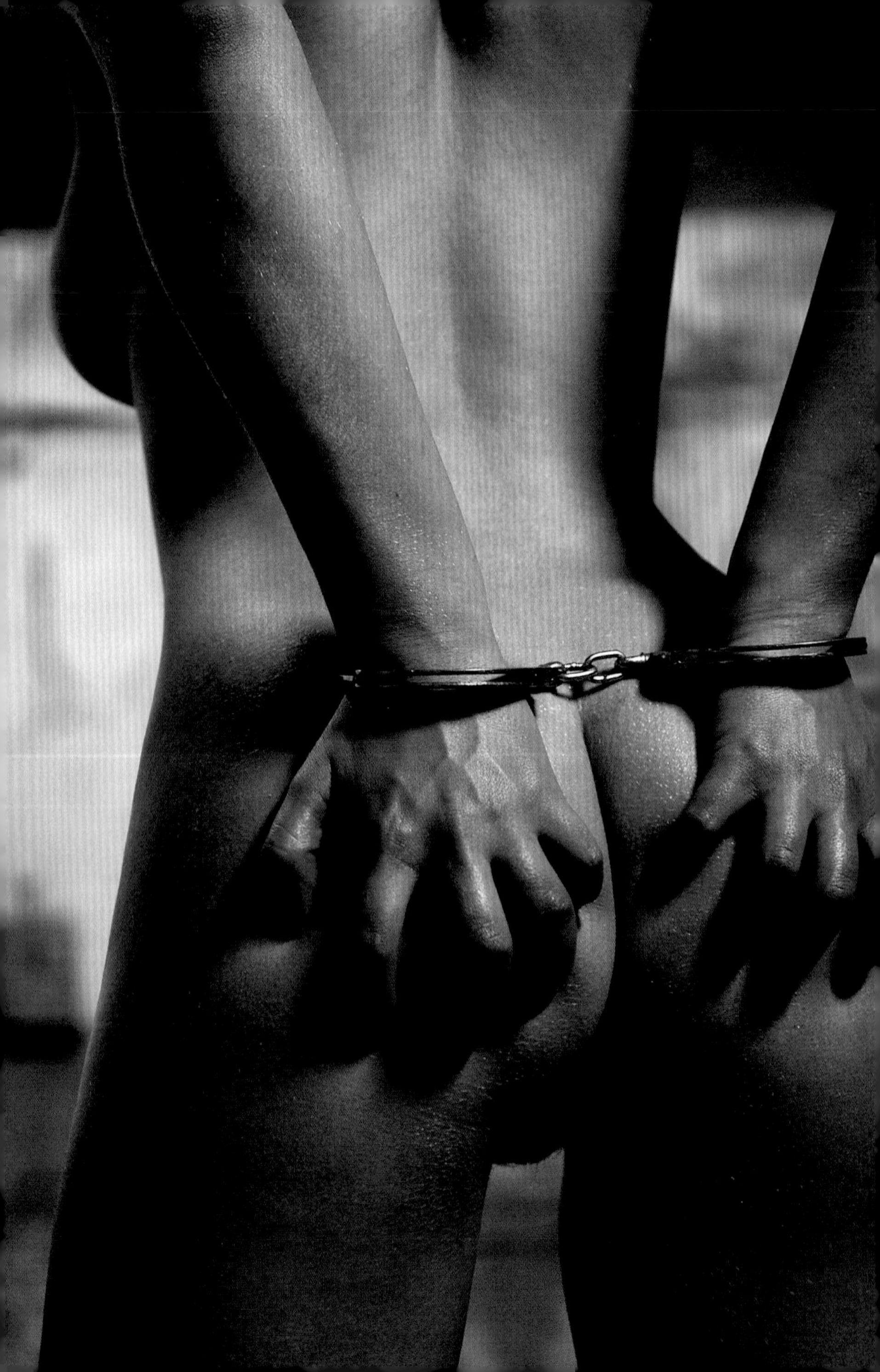

walter bosque

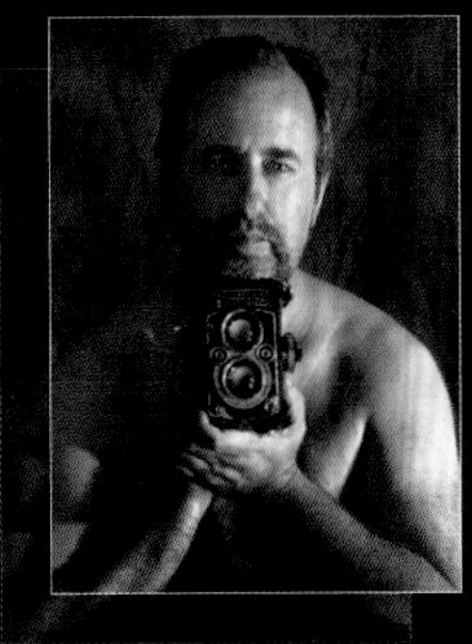

WALTER IS THE LEADING Argentinian photographer of the nude. For him, photography is a way of life. In relation to nudes, he works with amateur models. They pose for him because they love art and they do it with passion in each photography session, despite facing drawbacks, long delays, hours of travelling, extremes of temperature on occasion, and just long walks on others. They are the other part of his art, since they provide passion and effort with each photograph. To make photography a way of life was a hard decision driven by the heart. He refers to the ultimate truth on photography uttered by the master Henri Cartier-Bresson: 'Photography is to locate in the same line of sight the mind, the eye, and the heart.'

www.walterbosque-art.com

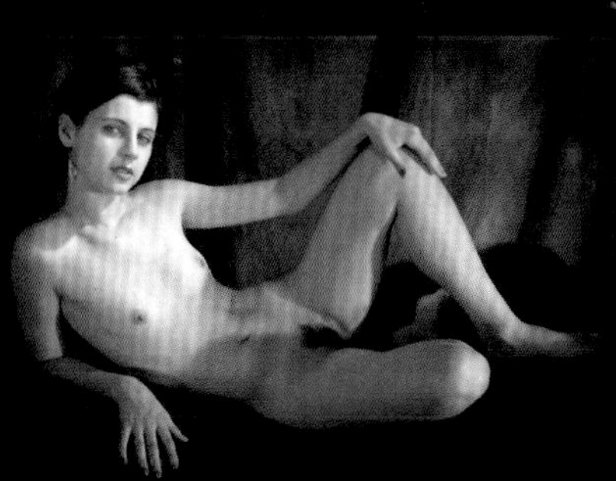

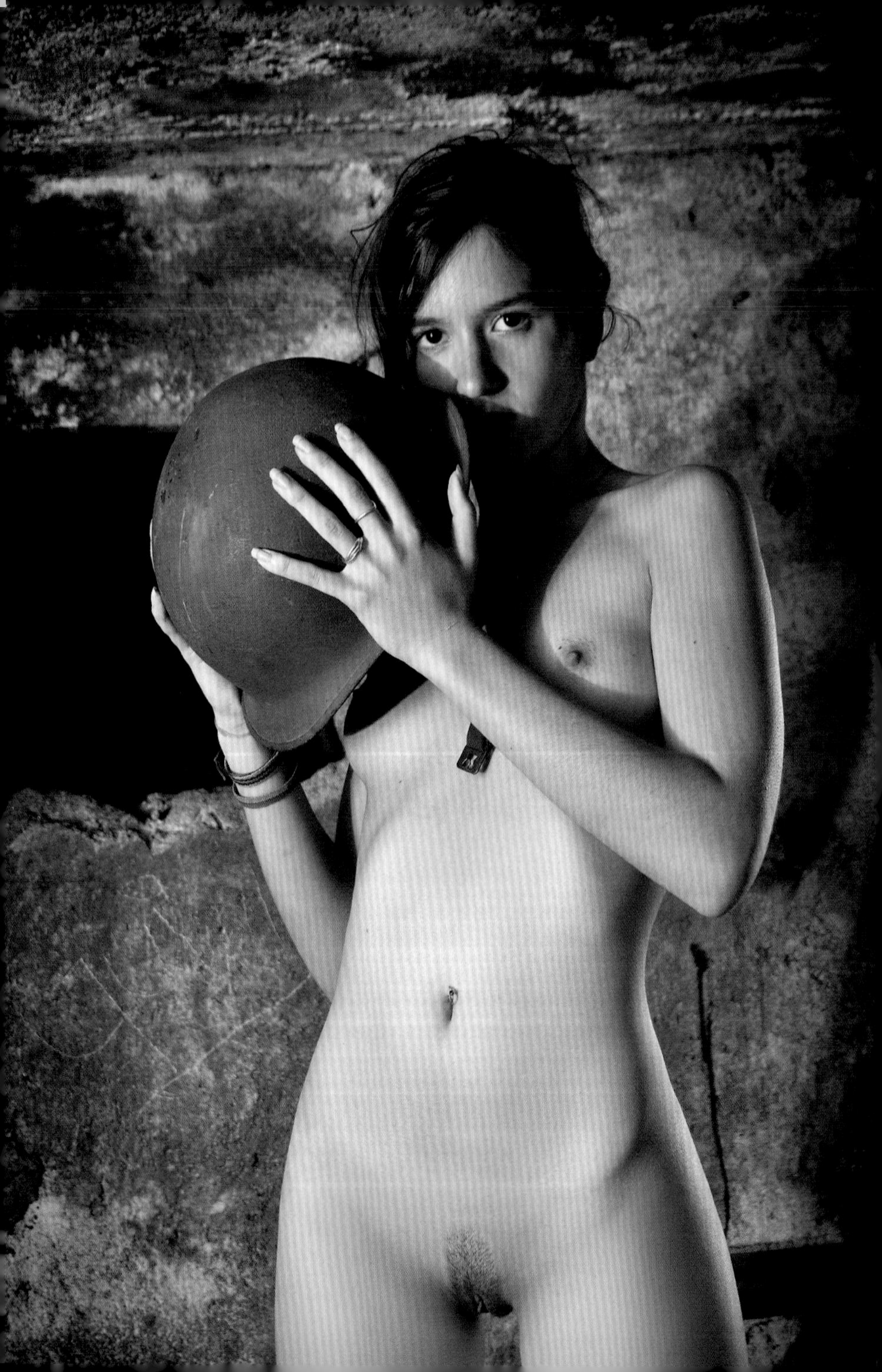

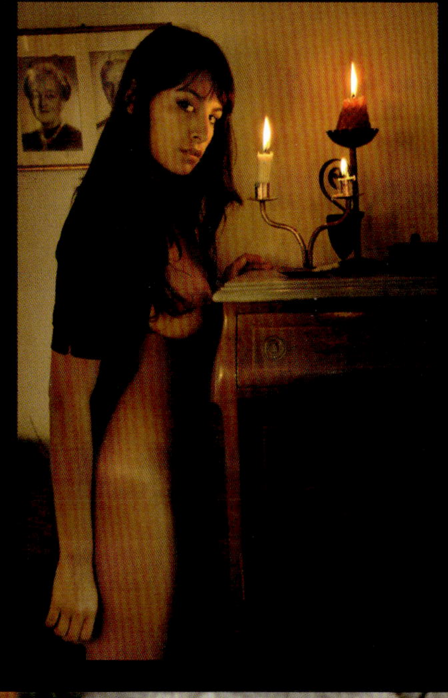

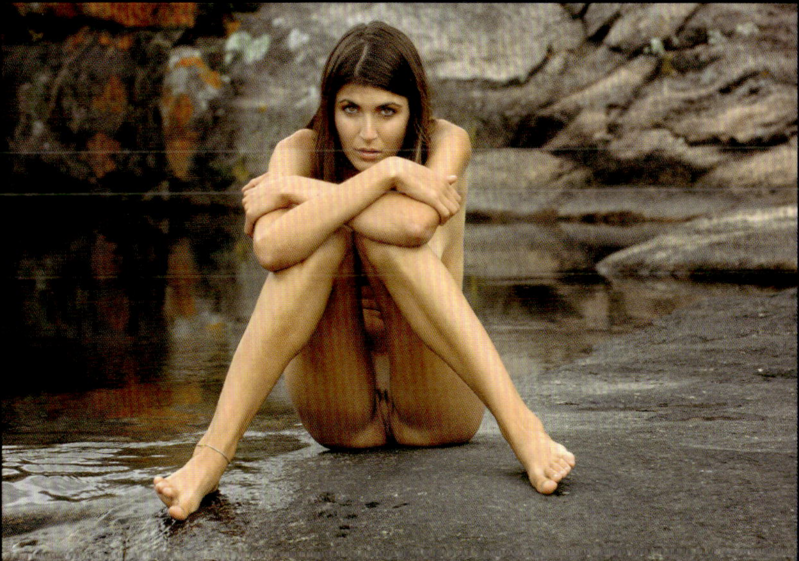

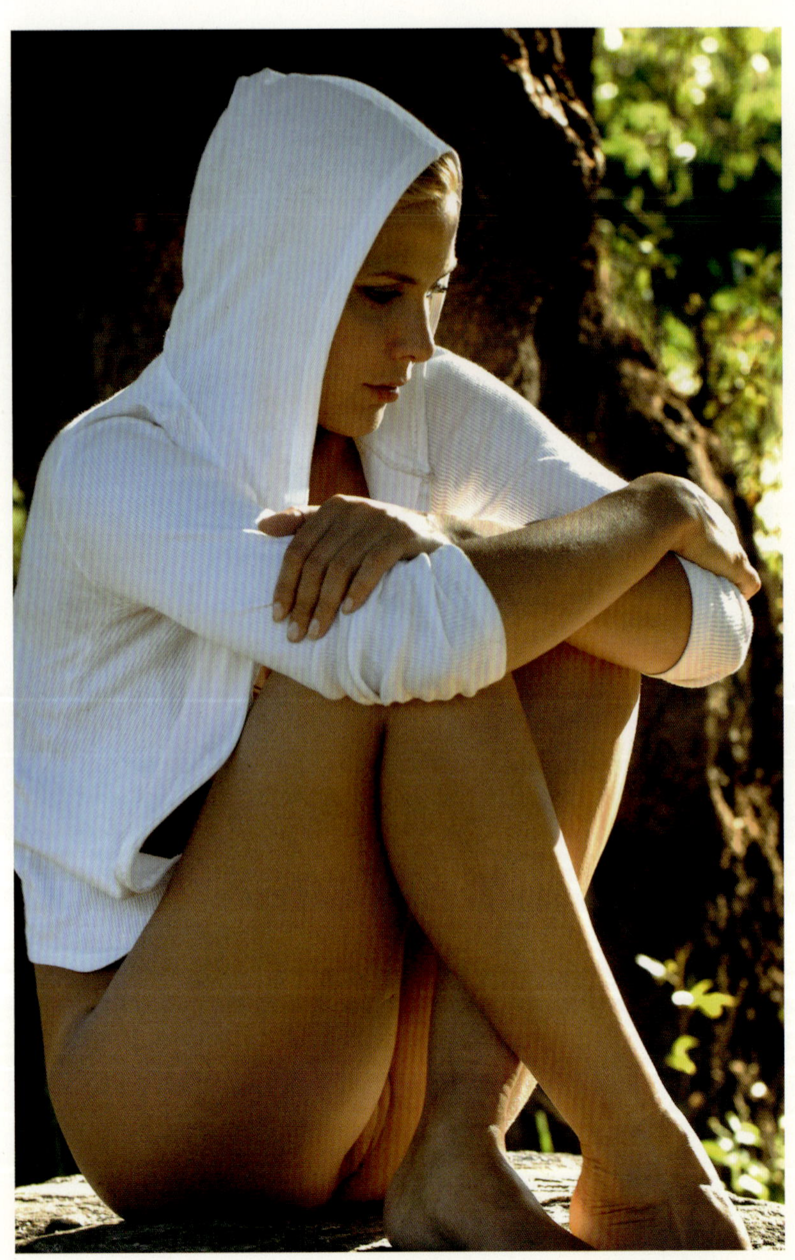

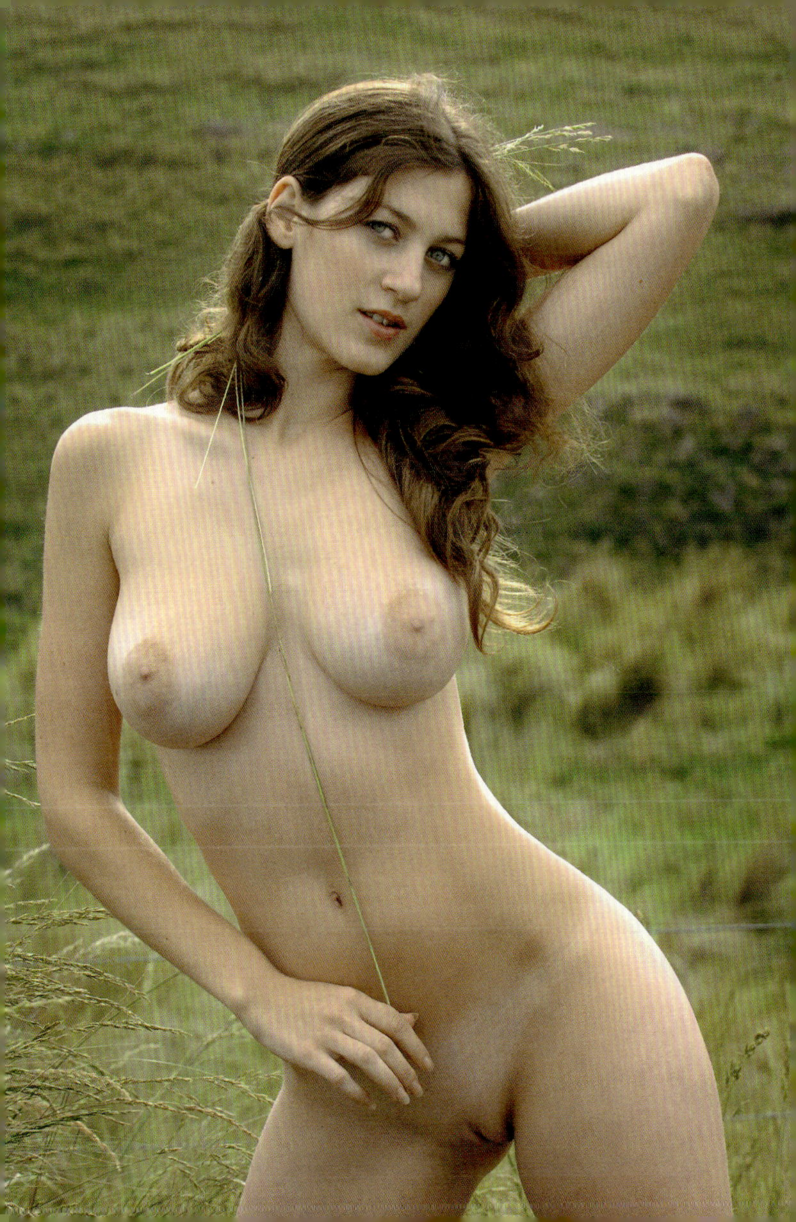

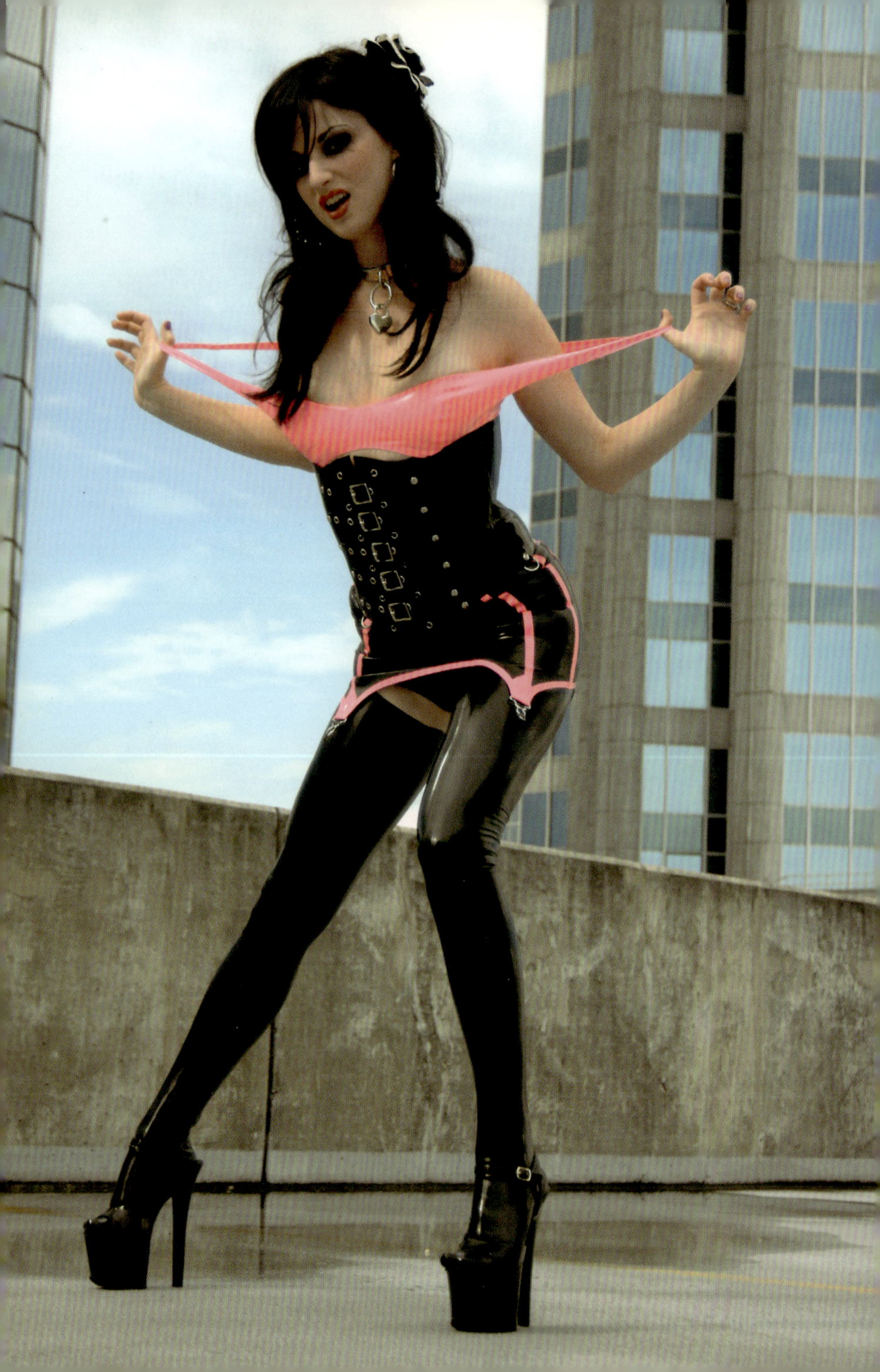

larry bradby

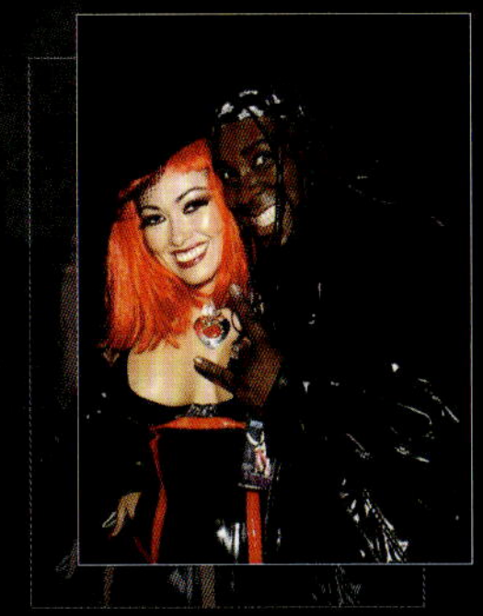
Larry Bradby on right

LARRY BRADBY IS A WELL-KNOWN photographer in the Washington, DC area. He has been shooting professionally since 1995. His work is very creative and set apart from many other photographers on the scene. He has shot for Versatile Fashion, NightDreams, Pink Label Corsets, SugarKitty Corsets, Exquisite Restraint and many other clothing lines and clubs.
He has been published in *Secret*, *Marquis*, *Elegy*, *Gothic Beauty* and *Stiff Magazine*.

www.larrybradbyphotography.com

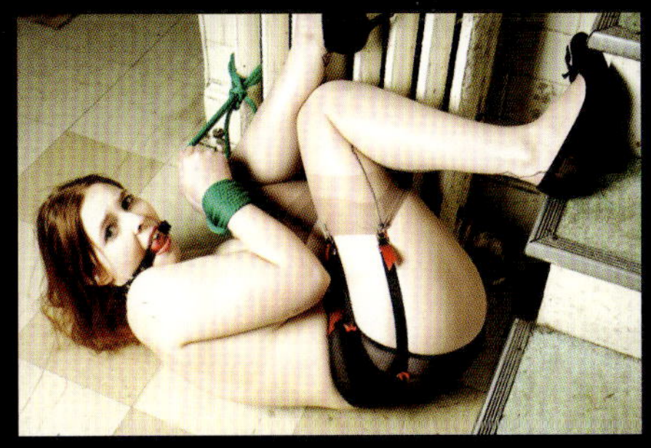

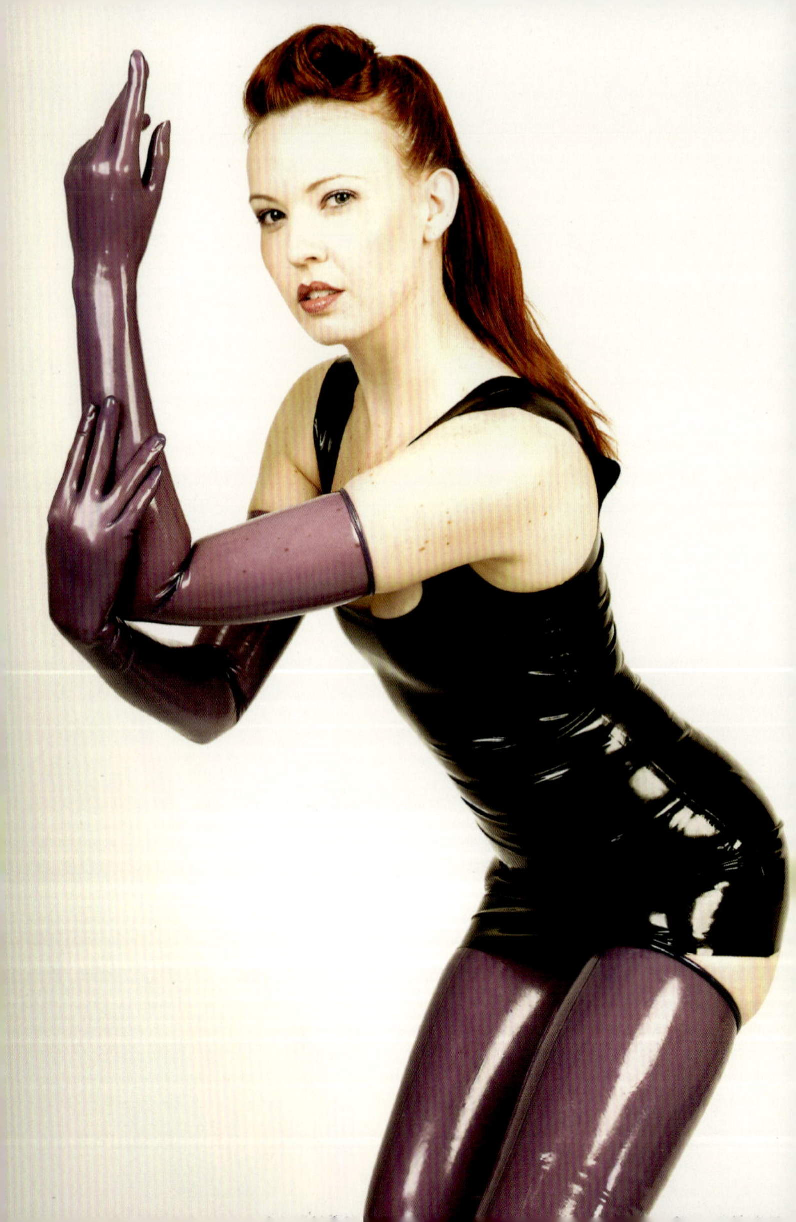

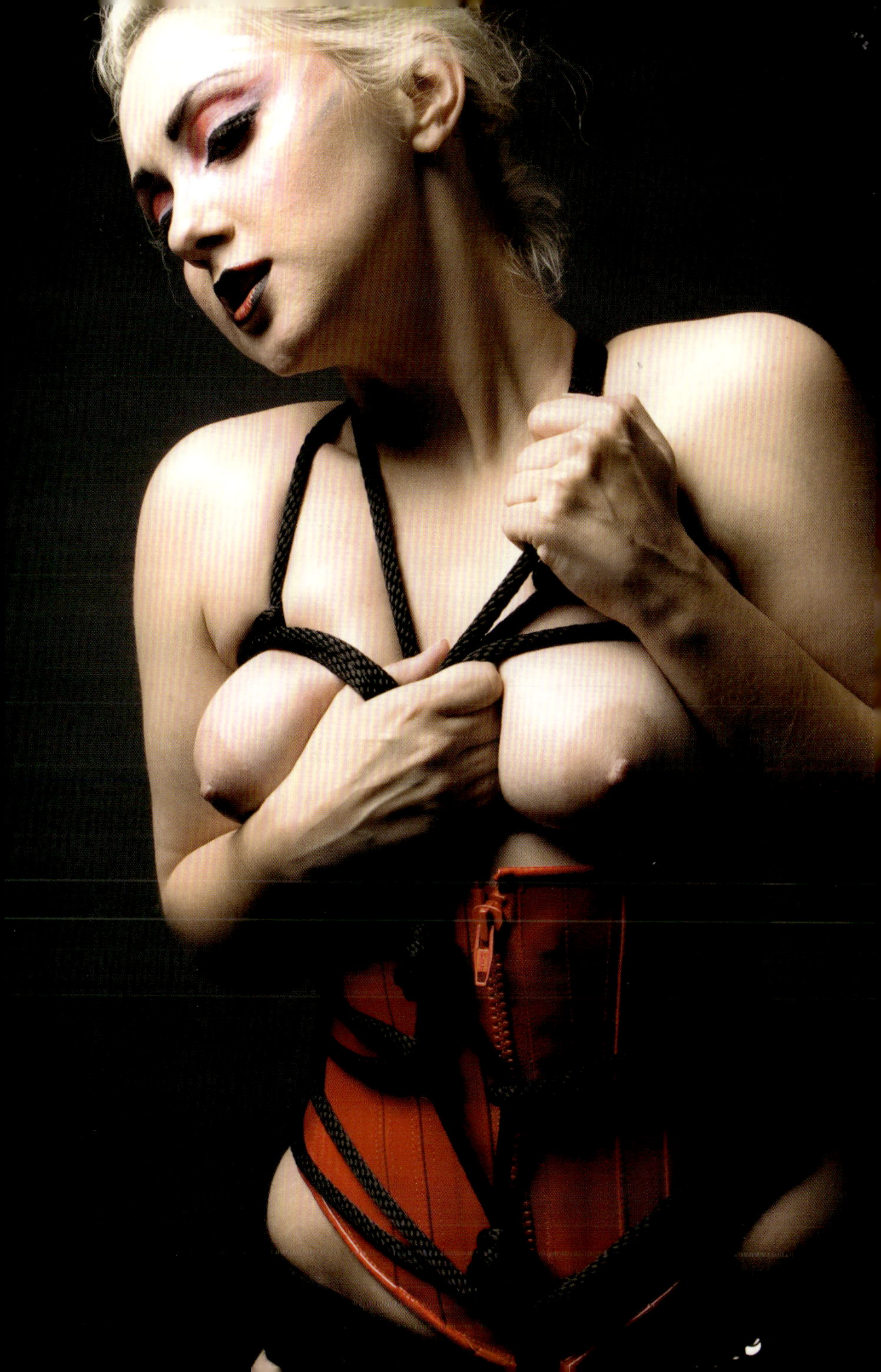

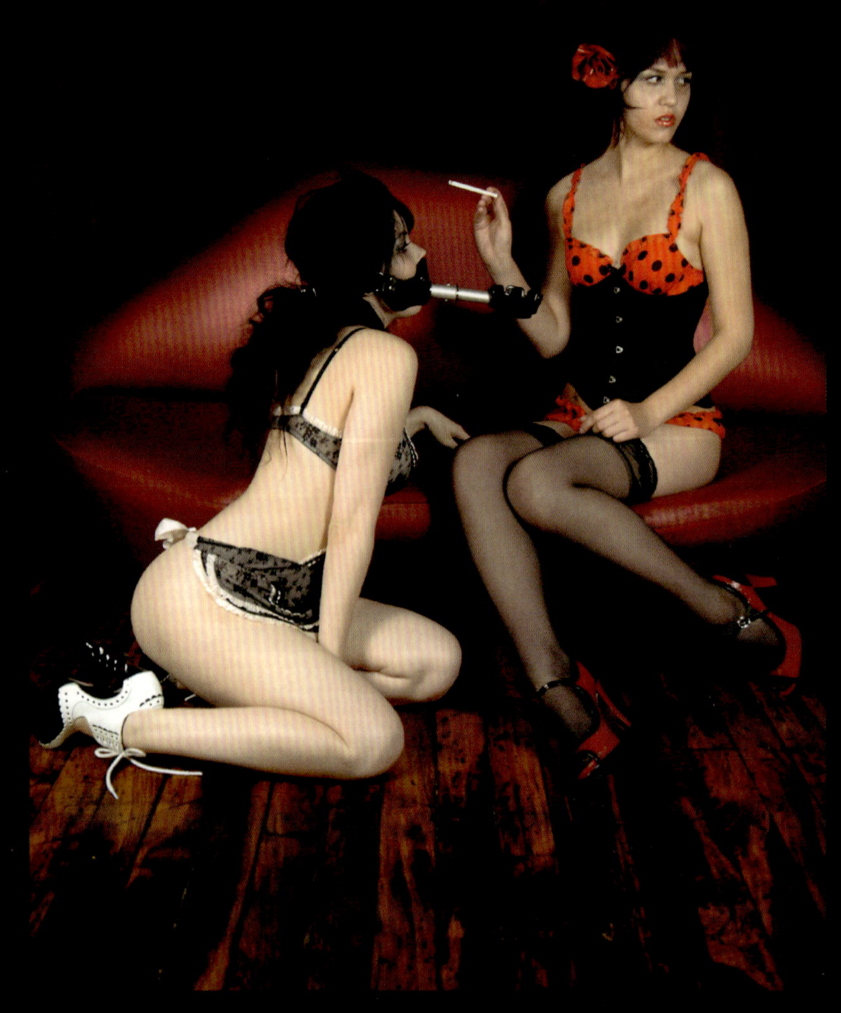

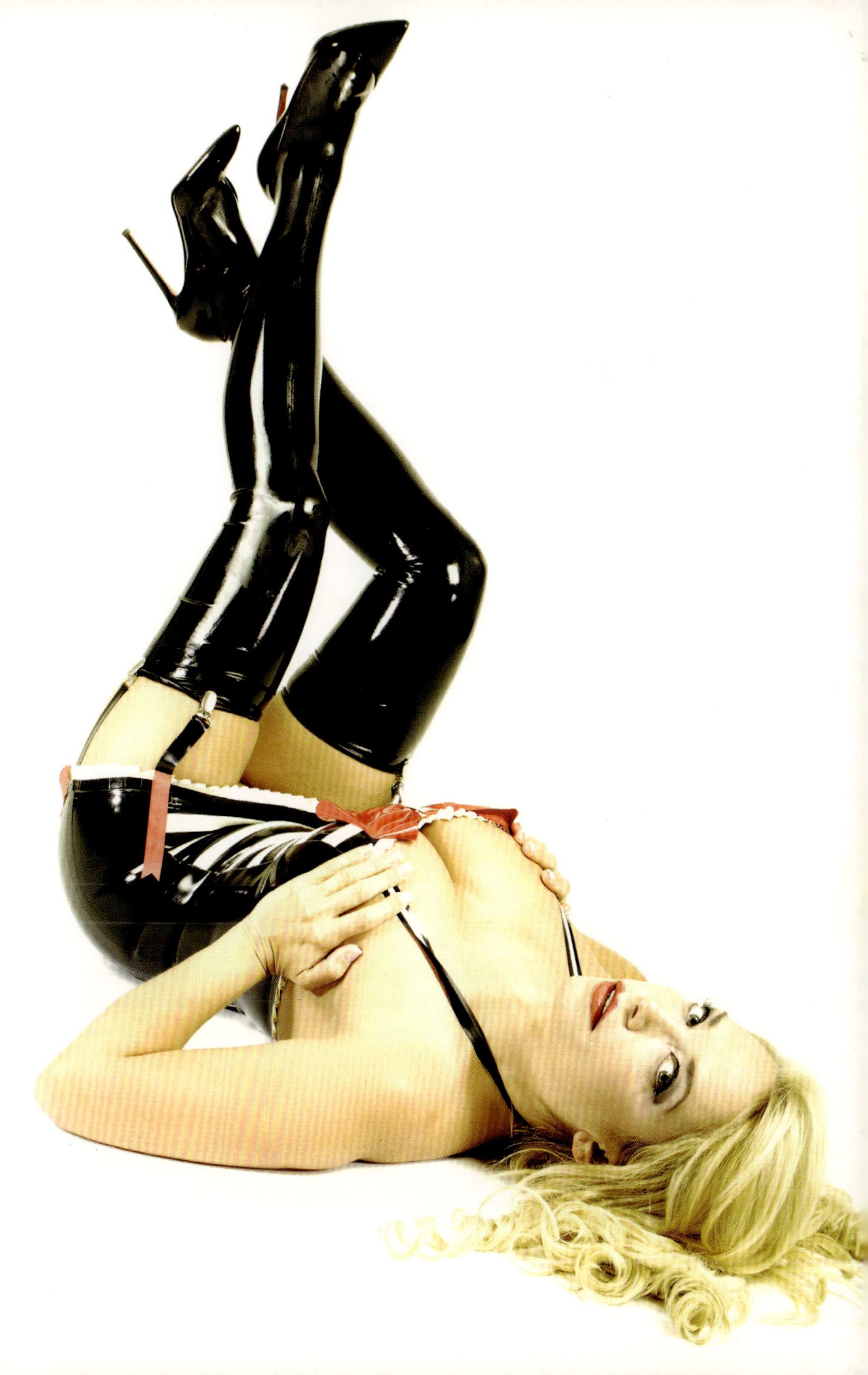

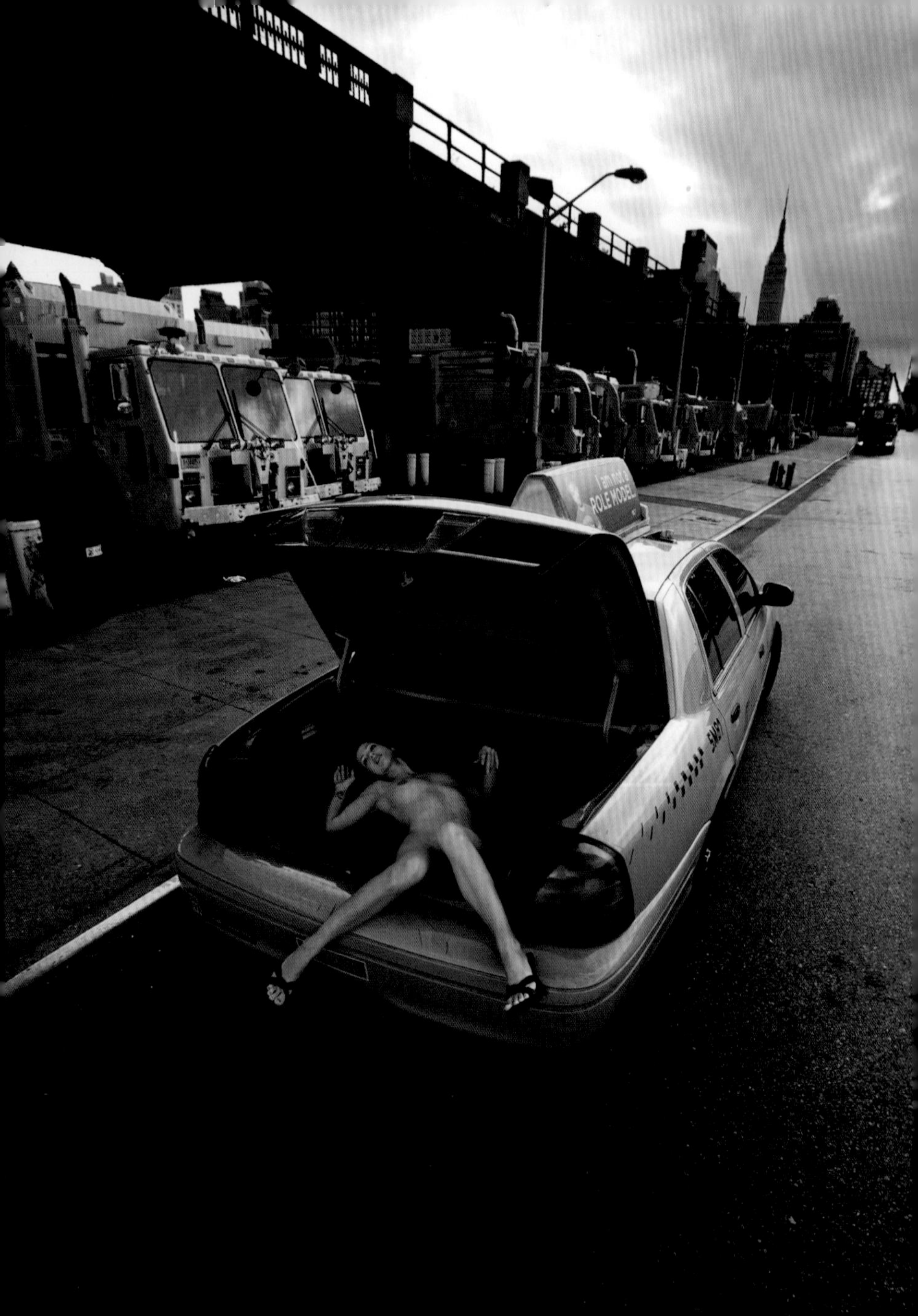
I am not a
ROLE MODEL.

gary breckheimer

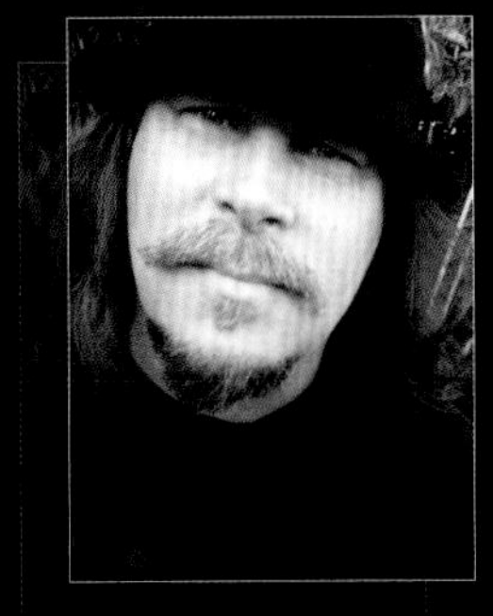

GARY IS A NEW YORK CITY-based photographer, who has been pursuing his craft for over two decades. His work can be seen internationally in galleries and magazines. He explains, 'By juxtaposing the beauty of the female form in the harshness of our urban surroundings, my intent is to allow viewers to contemplate the relationship of man with his environment. As an artist, my goal is to create pictures that tell a story. I consciously incorporate paradoxes for that element of the unexpected mixed with an overtone of solitude yet erotica in my photos.'

www.garybreckheimer.com

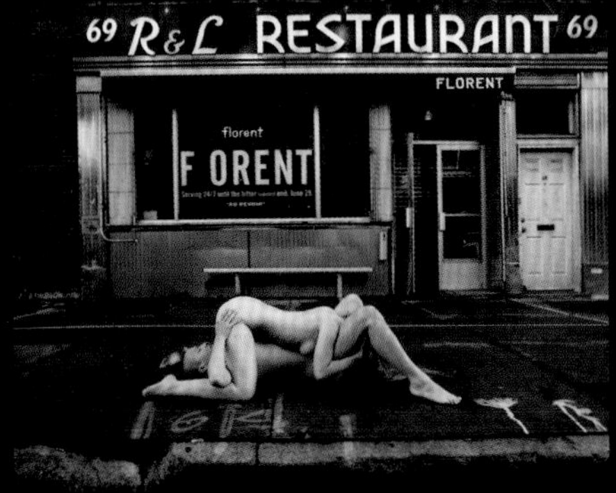

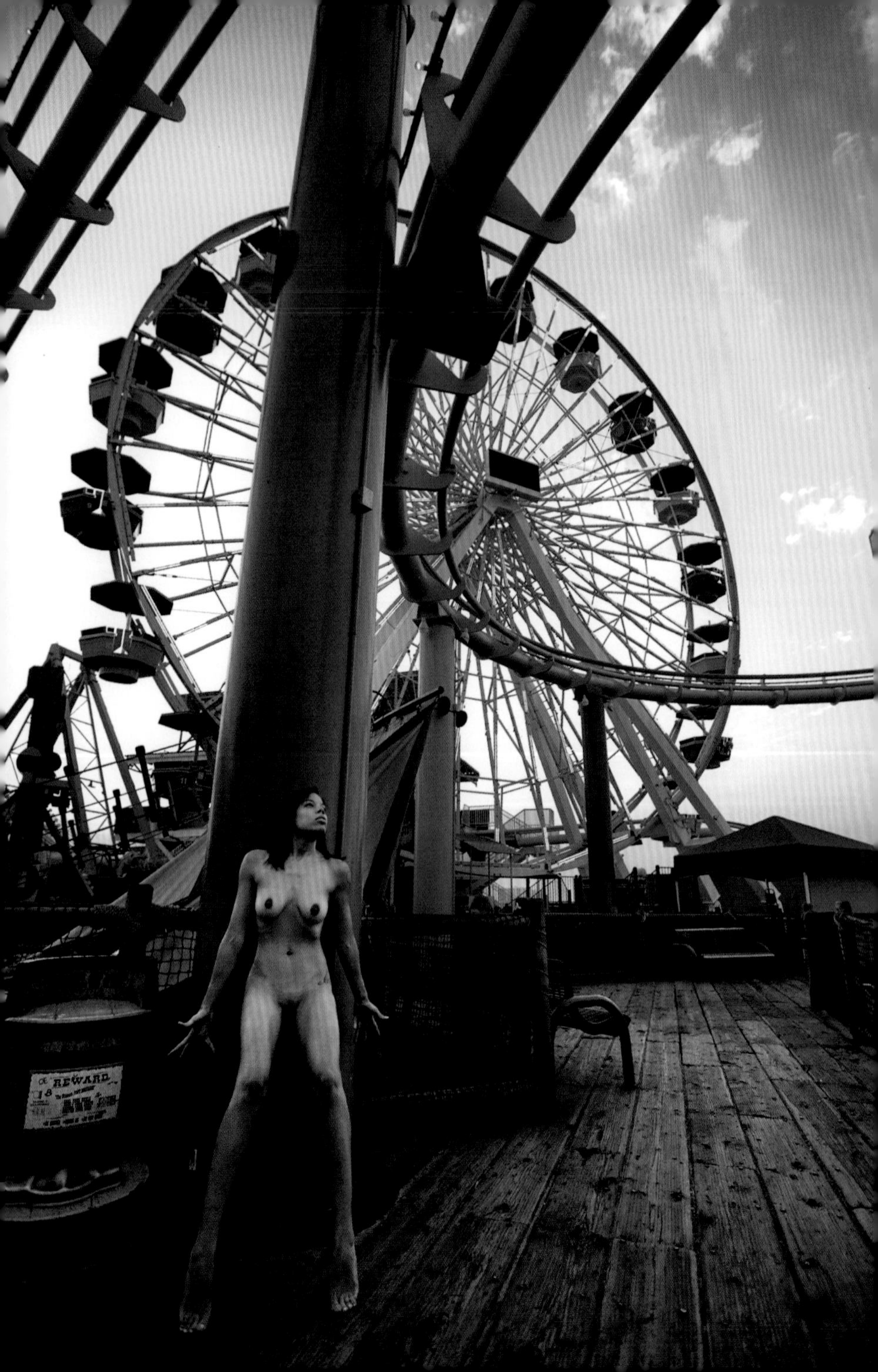
REWARD

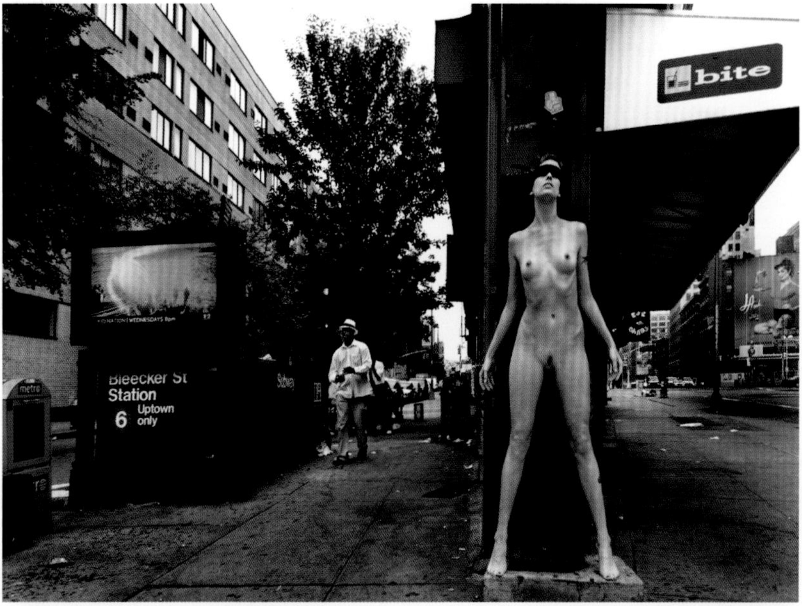

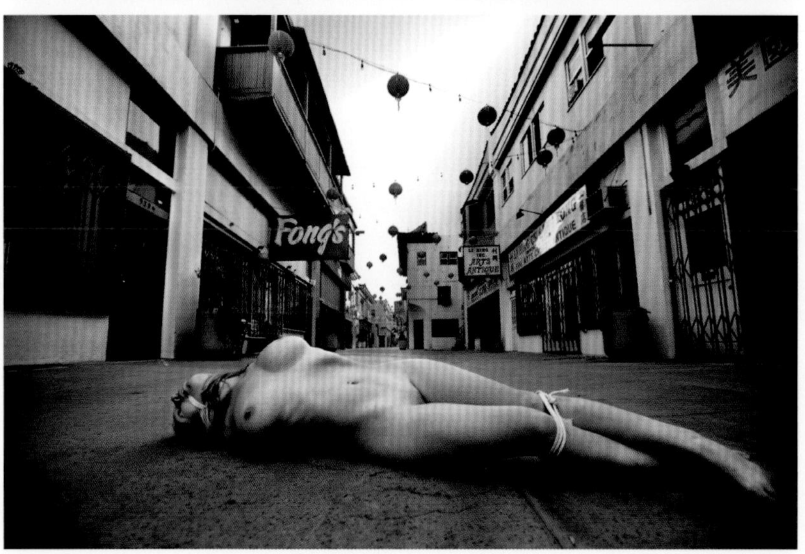
Fong's

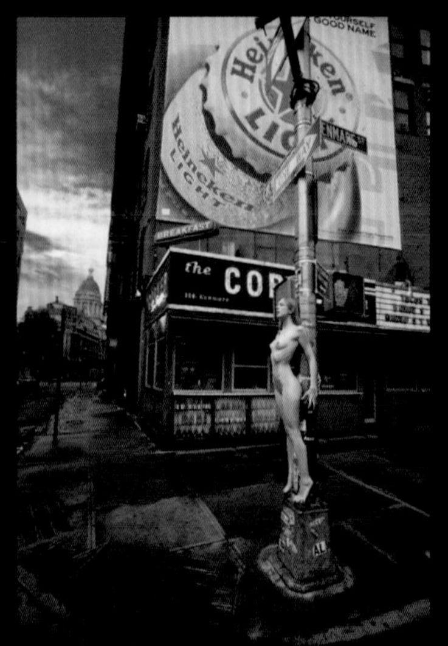
GOOD NAME
Heineken
the COR

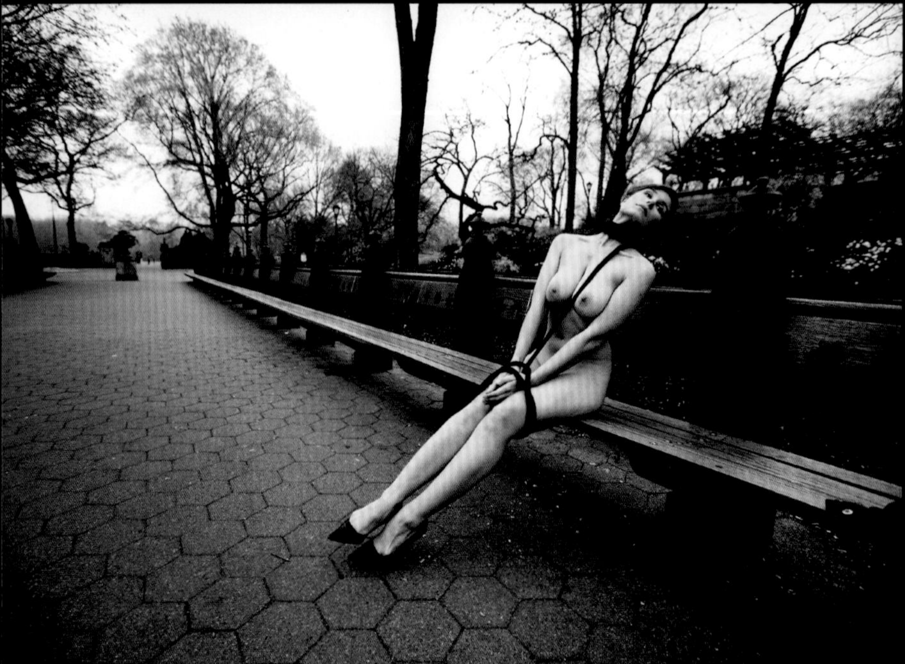

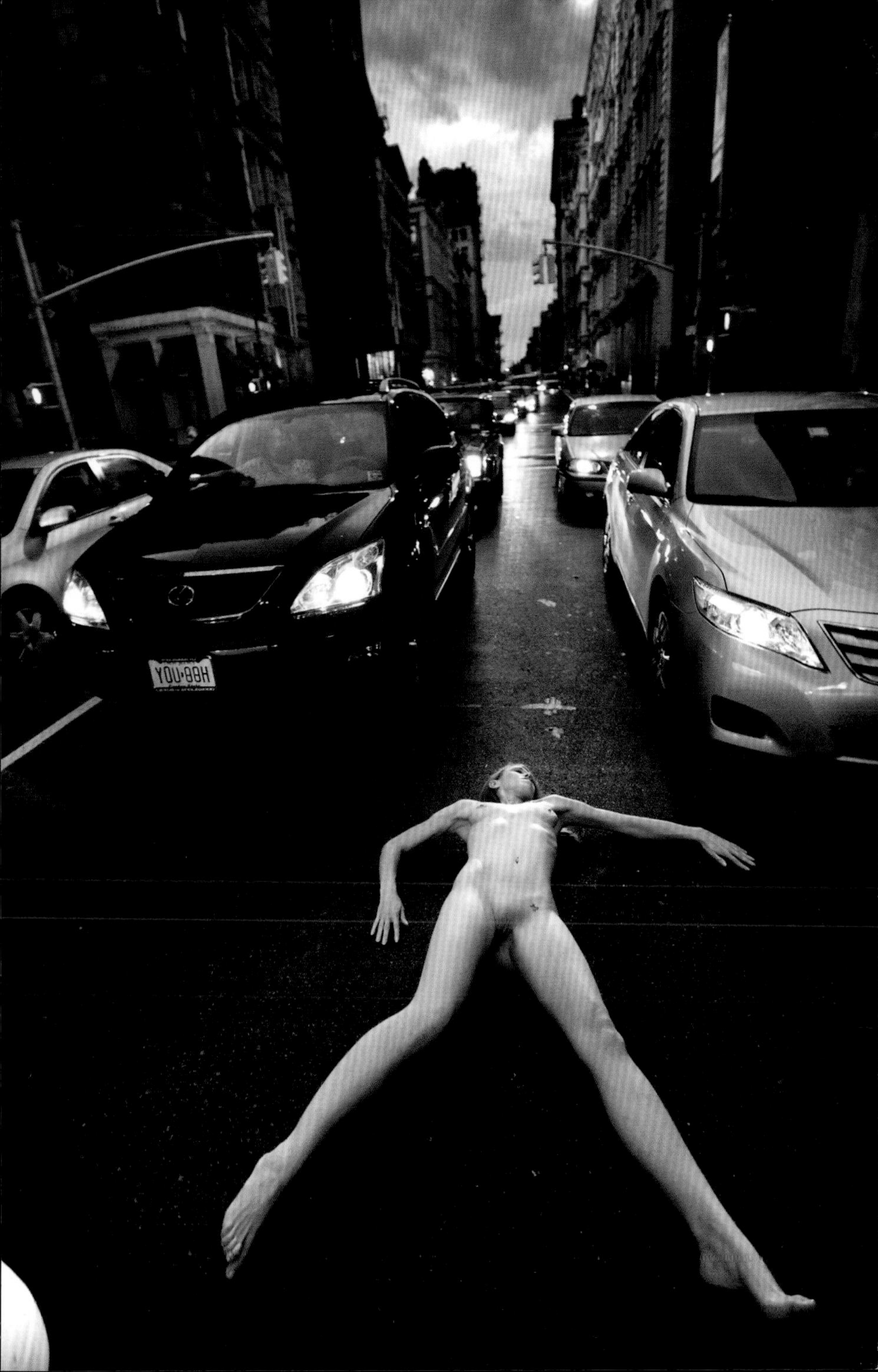
YOU·88H

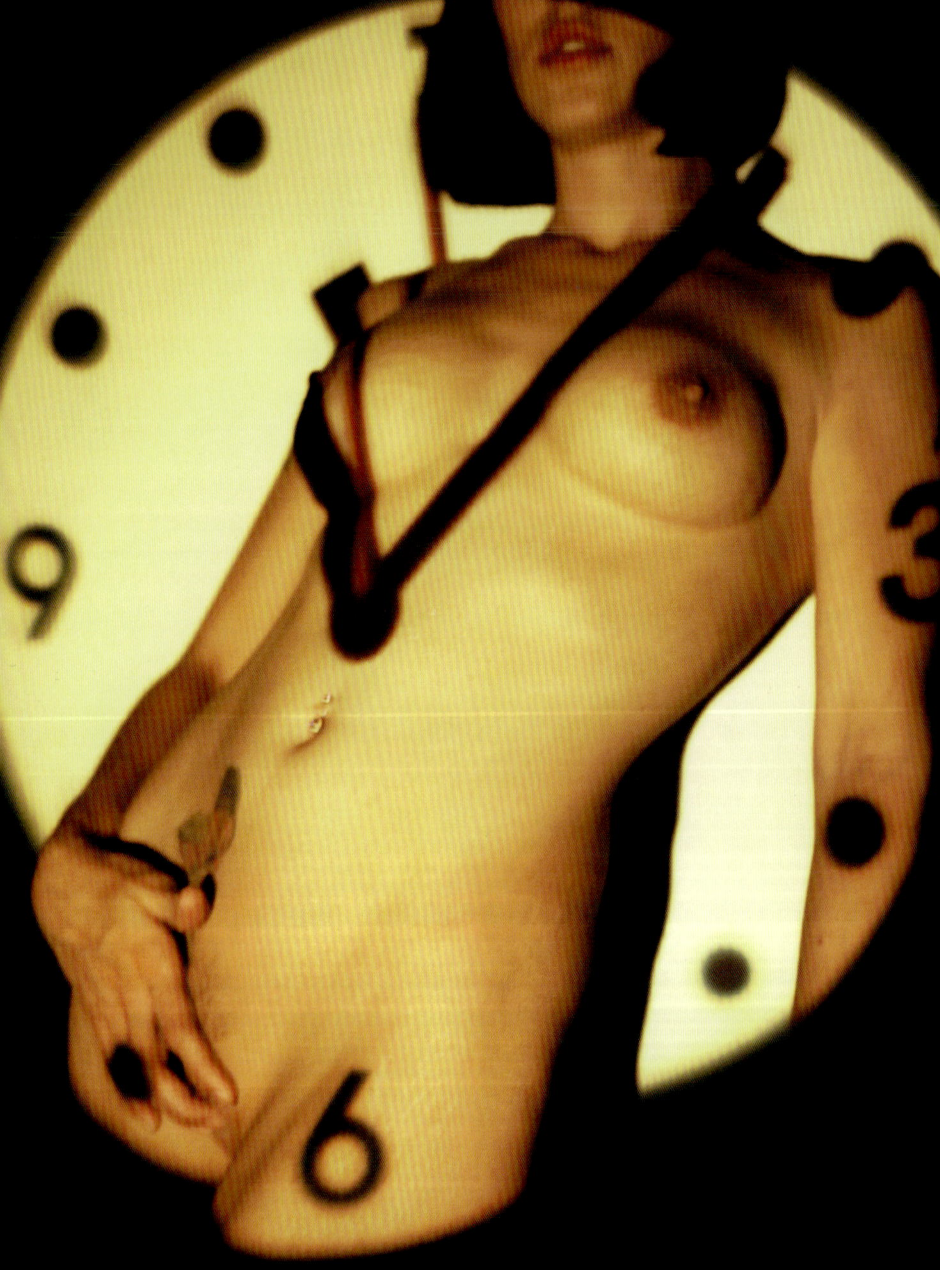

james christopher

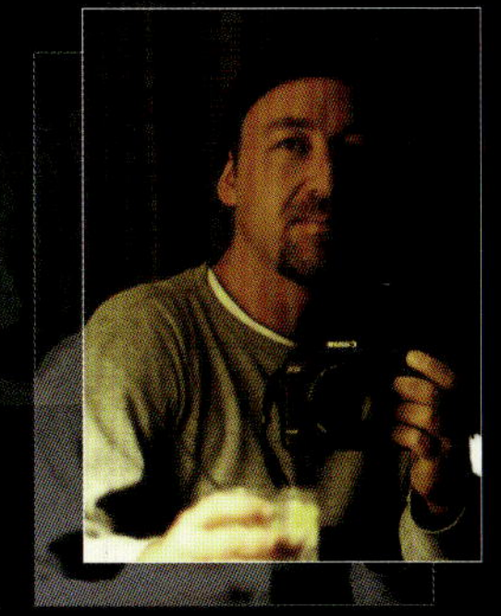

JAMES CHRISTOPHER BEGAN taking pictures the day his mother put a camera in his eight-year-old hands. His college years and early career saw a focus on film-making – which influenced the way he would capture images more than a decade later. James is a contemporary photographer inspired by his love of modern architecture, pop art and film-makers such as Stanley Kubrick. His works explore the relationship with space, light and the spontaneity of his human subjects; whether working with models or ambience, his shoots are rarely planned. Viewing James's simple portraits and sensual nudes, there is a sense that his subjects have been empowered rather than objectified. His photography is both surreal and mystifying, capturing the essence of the person and the feel of a moment. At times his photos are erotic, tranquil or emotional; the powerful range of emotions explored in his photos makes him a genre-defying artist capable of capturing timeless beauty.

www.moderncitizen.com

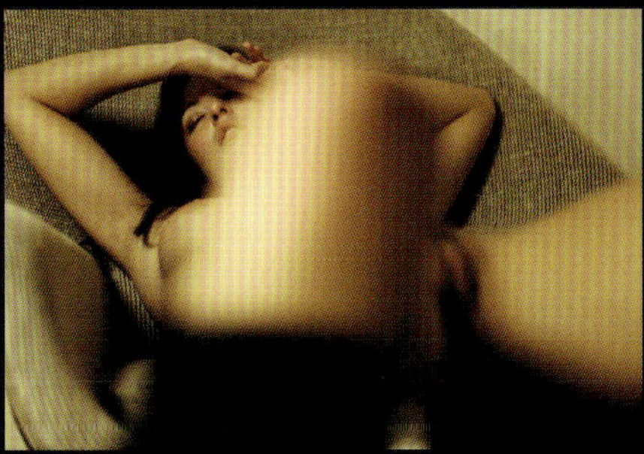

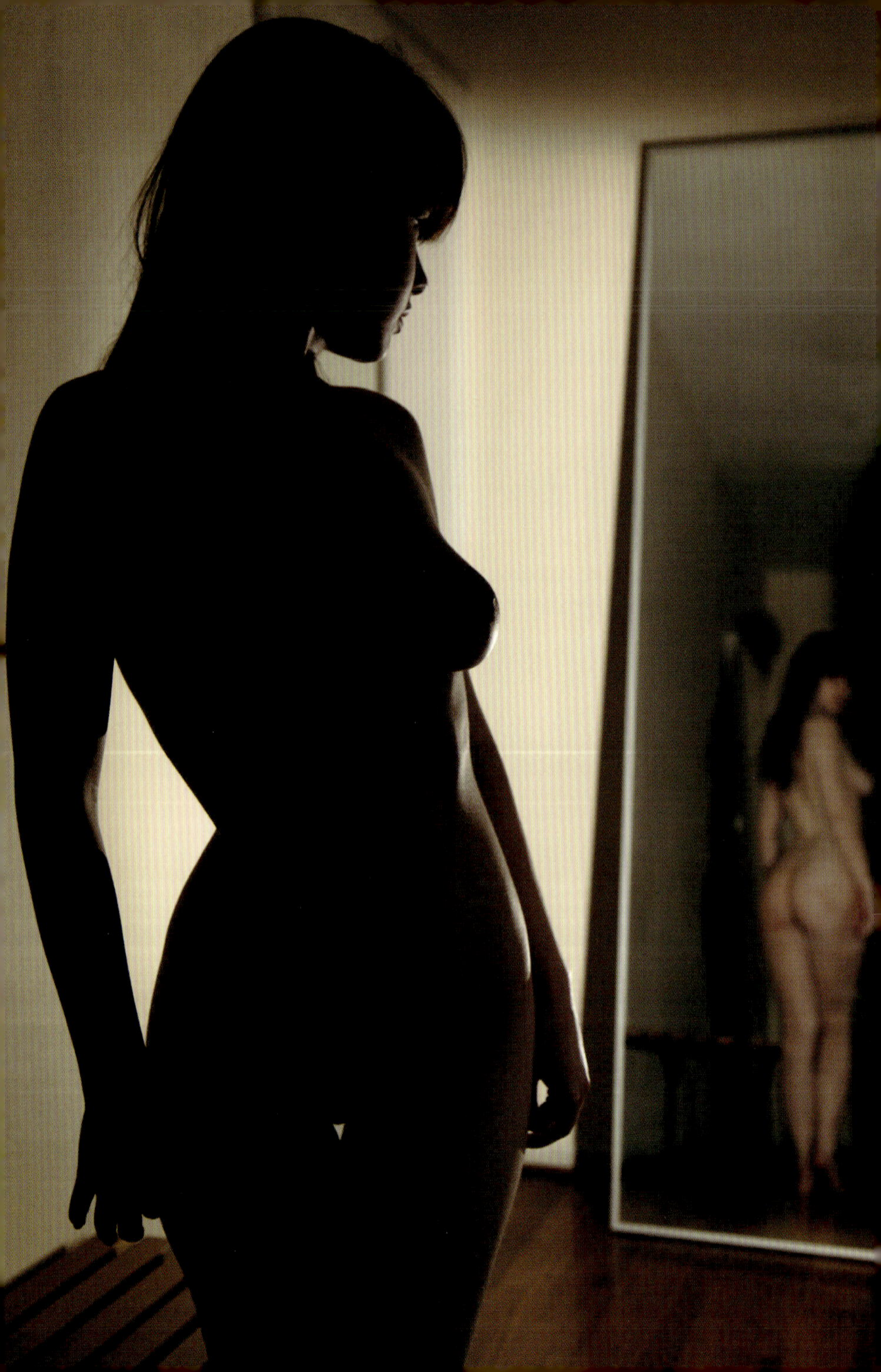

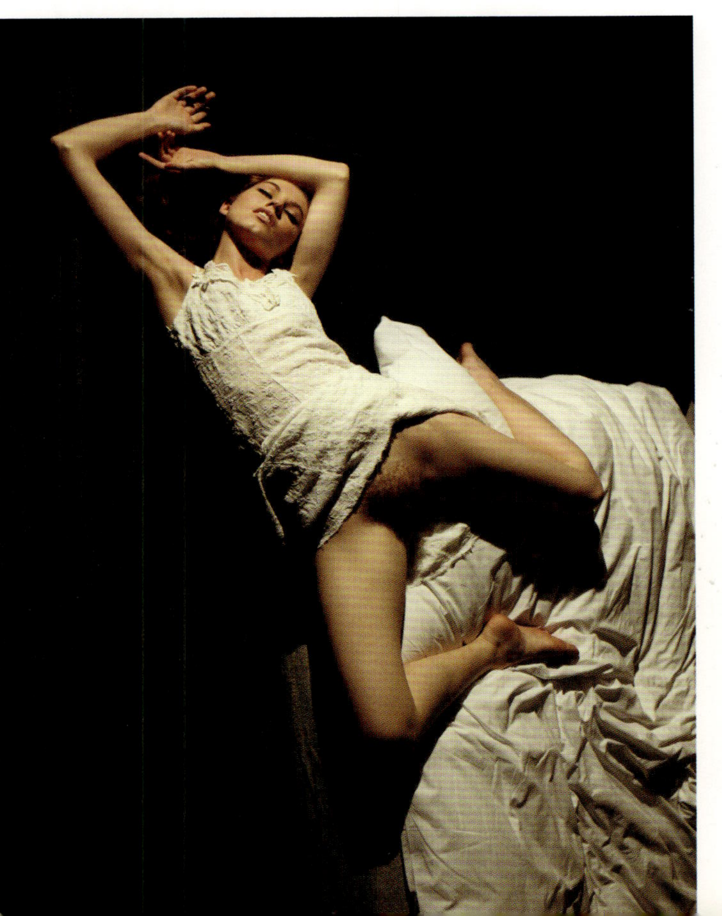

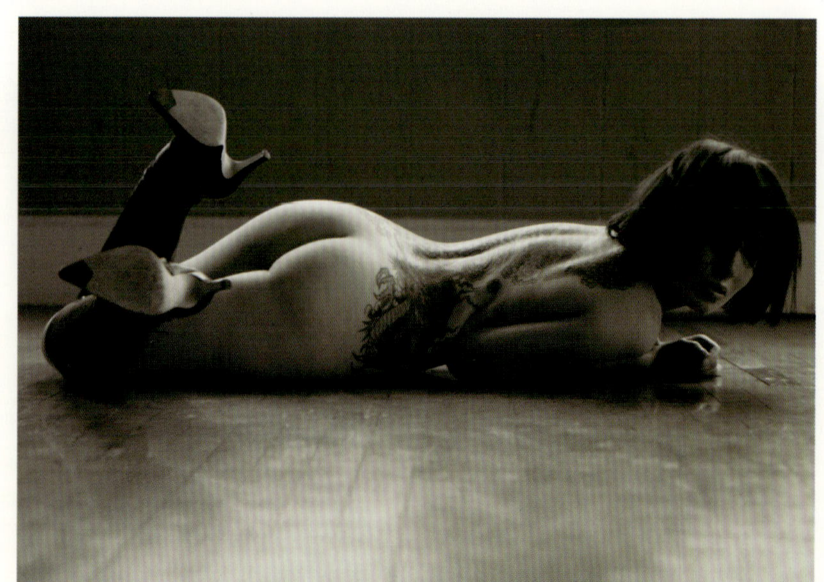

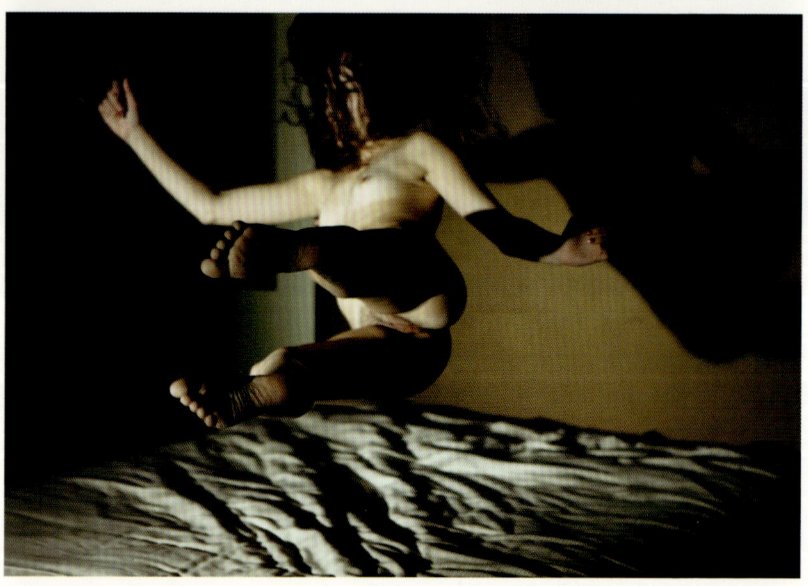

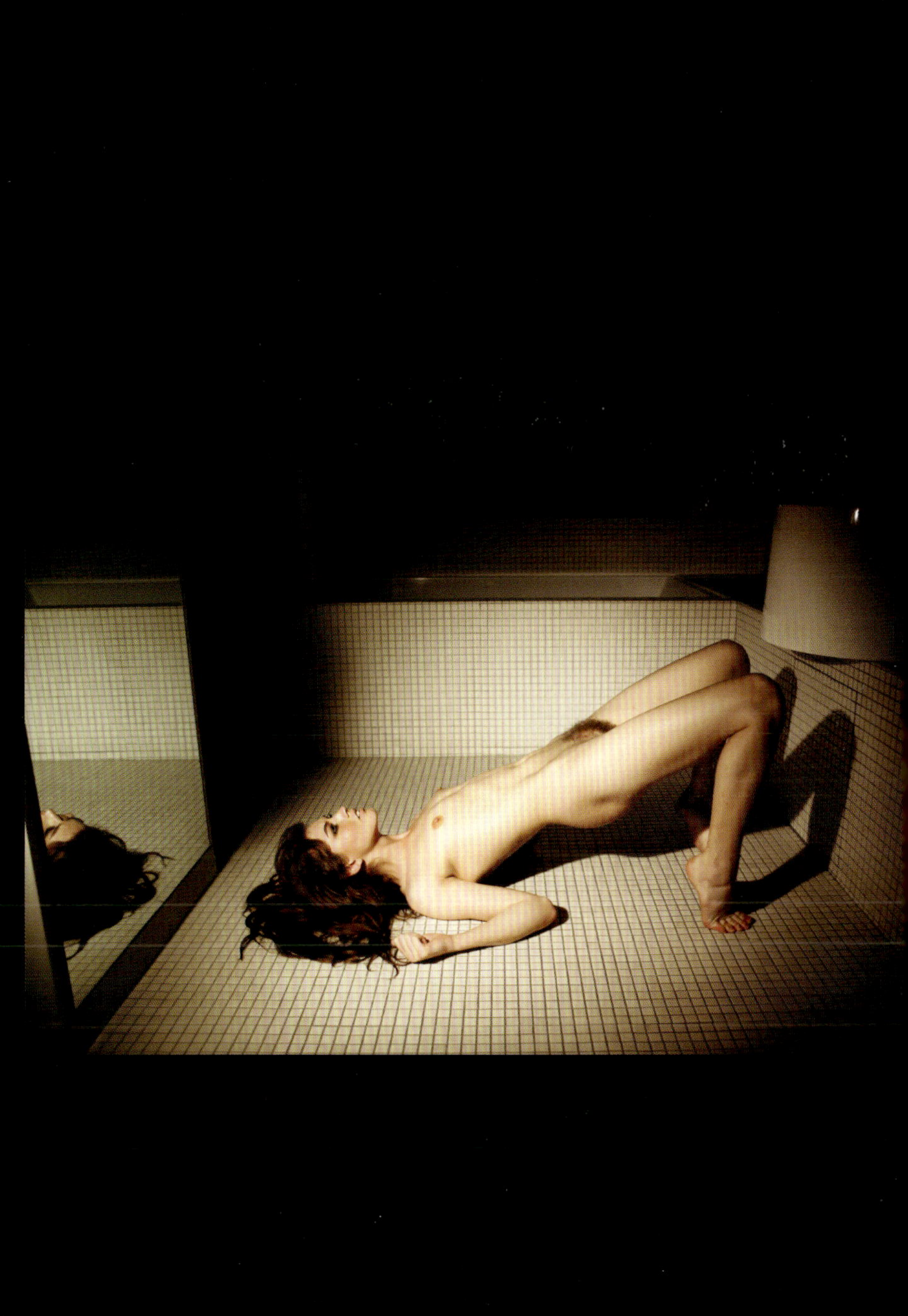

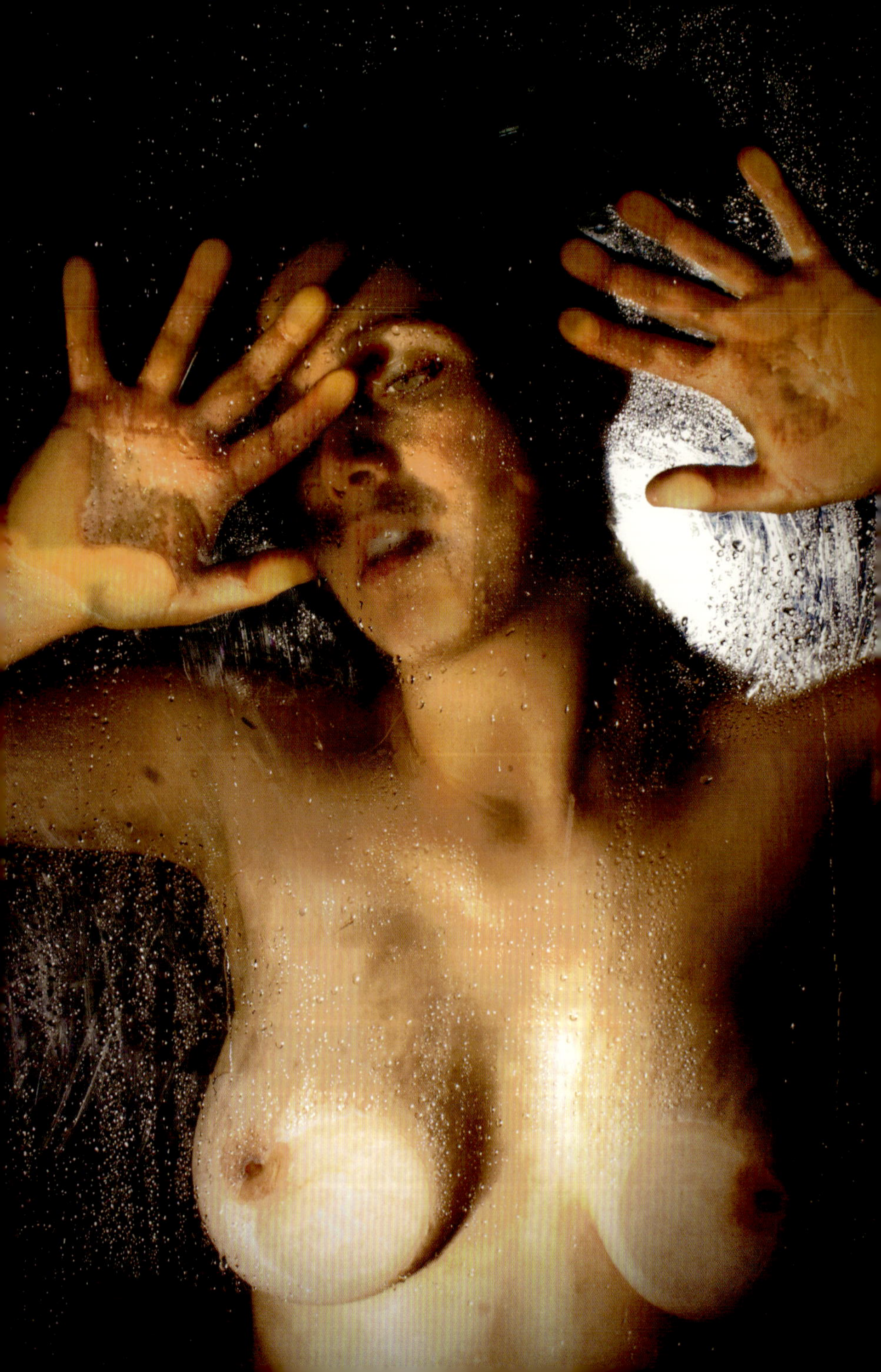

michael combs

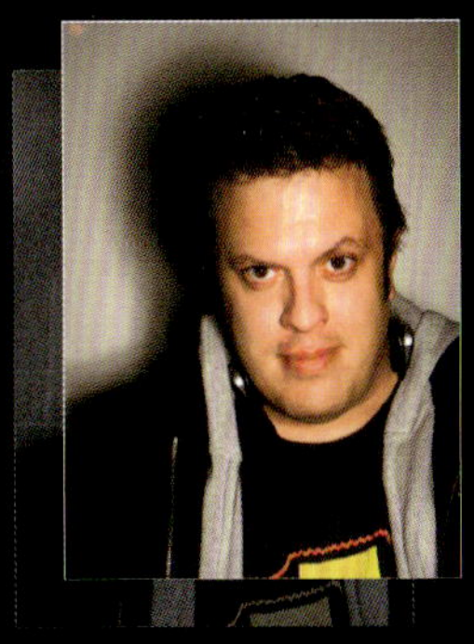

MICHAEL'S LIFE-LONG FASCINATION with the female form began during his mostly unwashed youth. Way at the back of the drawers of a huge steel desk, based in his grandfather's office, lived artefacts of the hidden world of adults. There were pens with pretty coeds on them, whose clothes disappeared when flipped upside down; calendars of comically surprised women in various states of undress; and key fobs that, when held up to the light, revealed what the butler saw! He got into nude photography because of his grandfather. Each image he creates is to honour him and that secret world of his, filled with the beauty, humour and grace of the female form.

www.fmlphoto.com

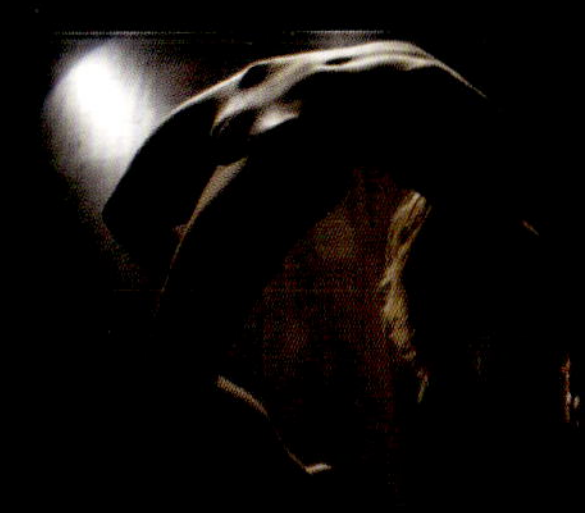

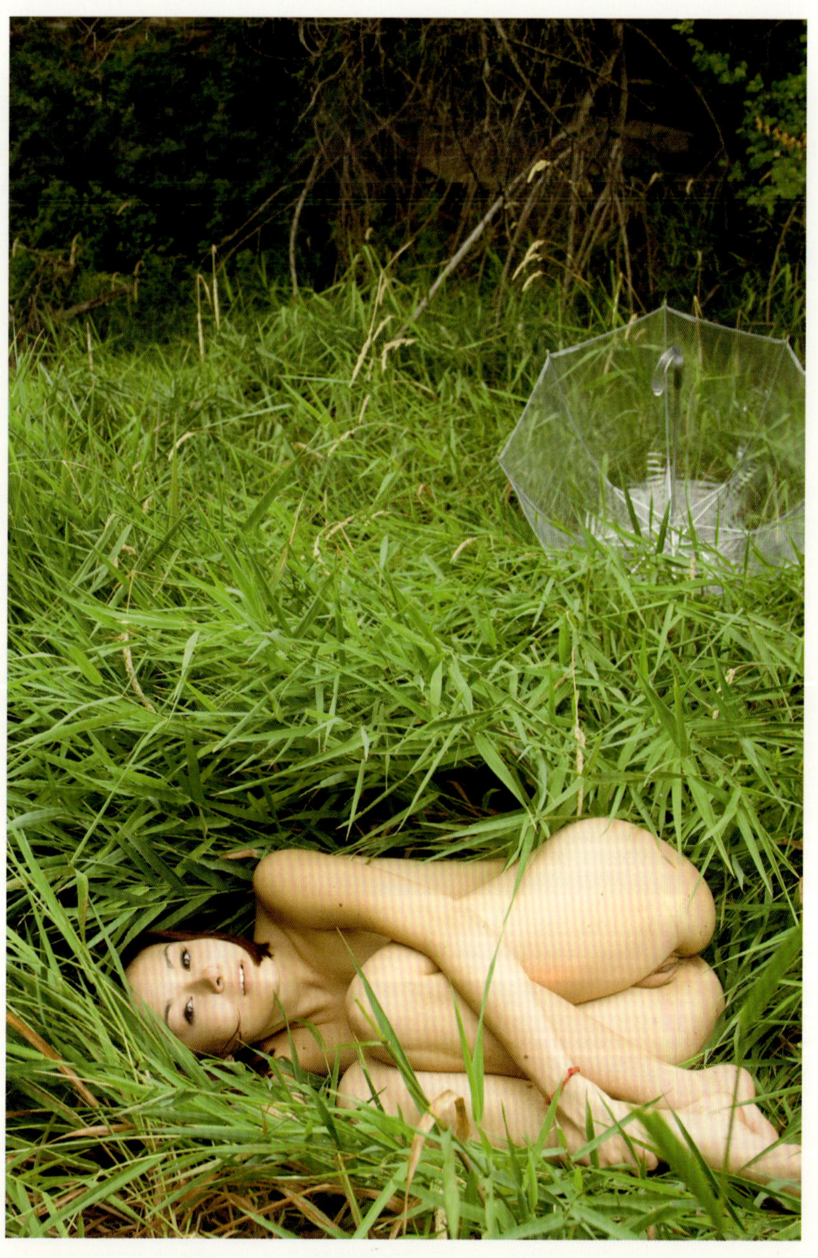

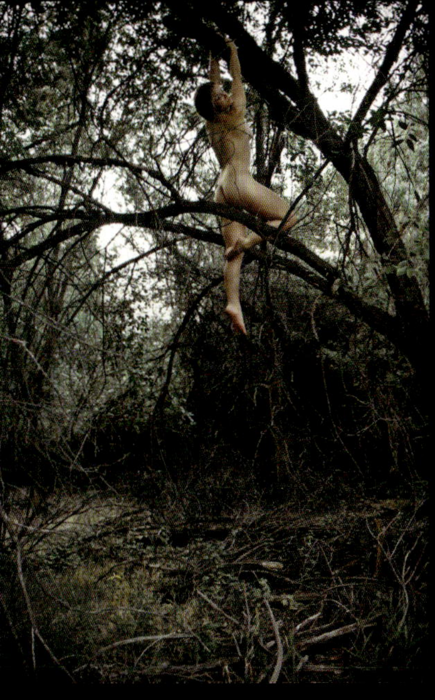

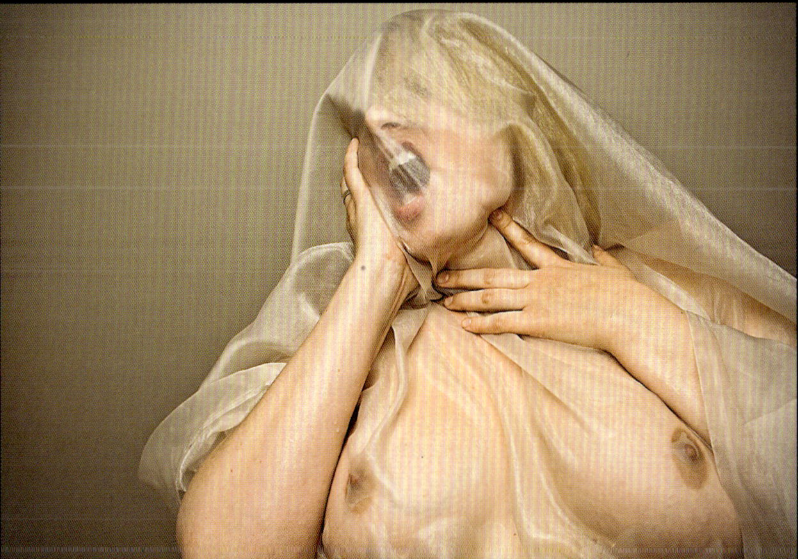

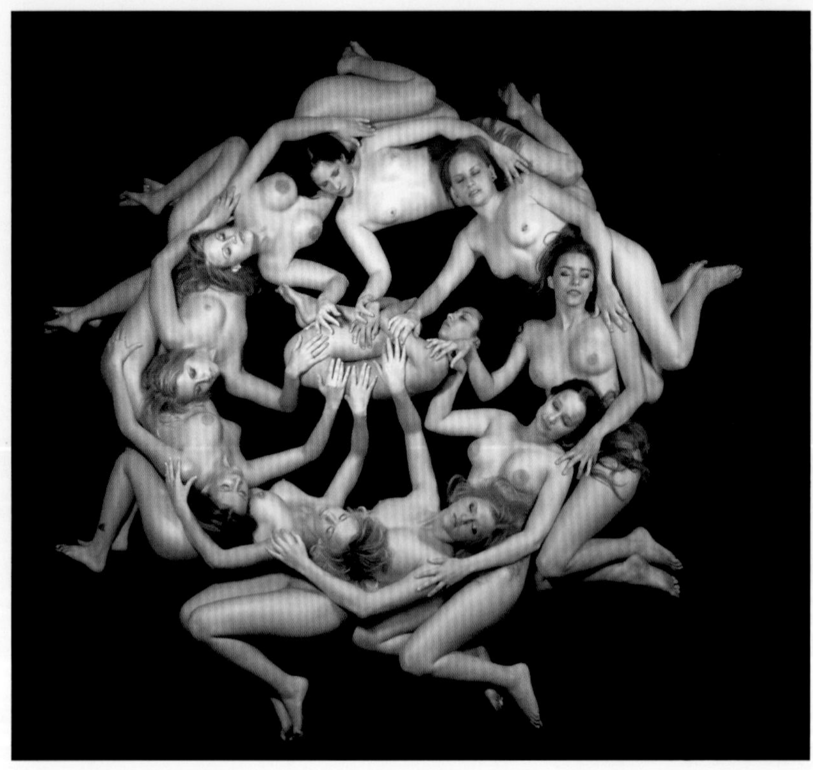

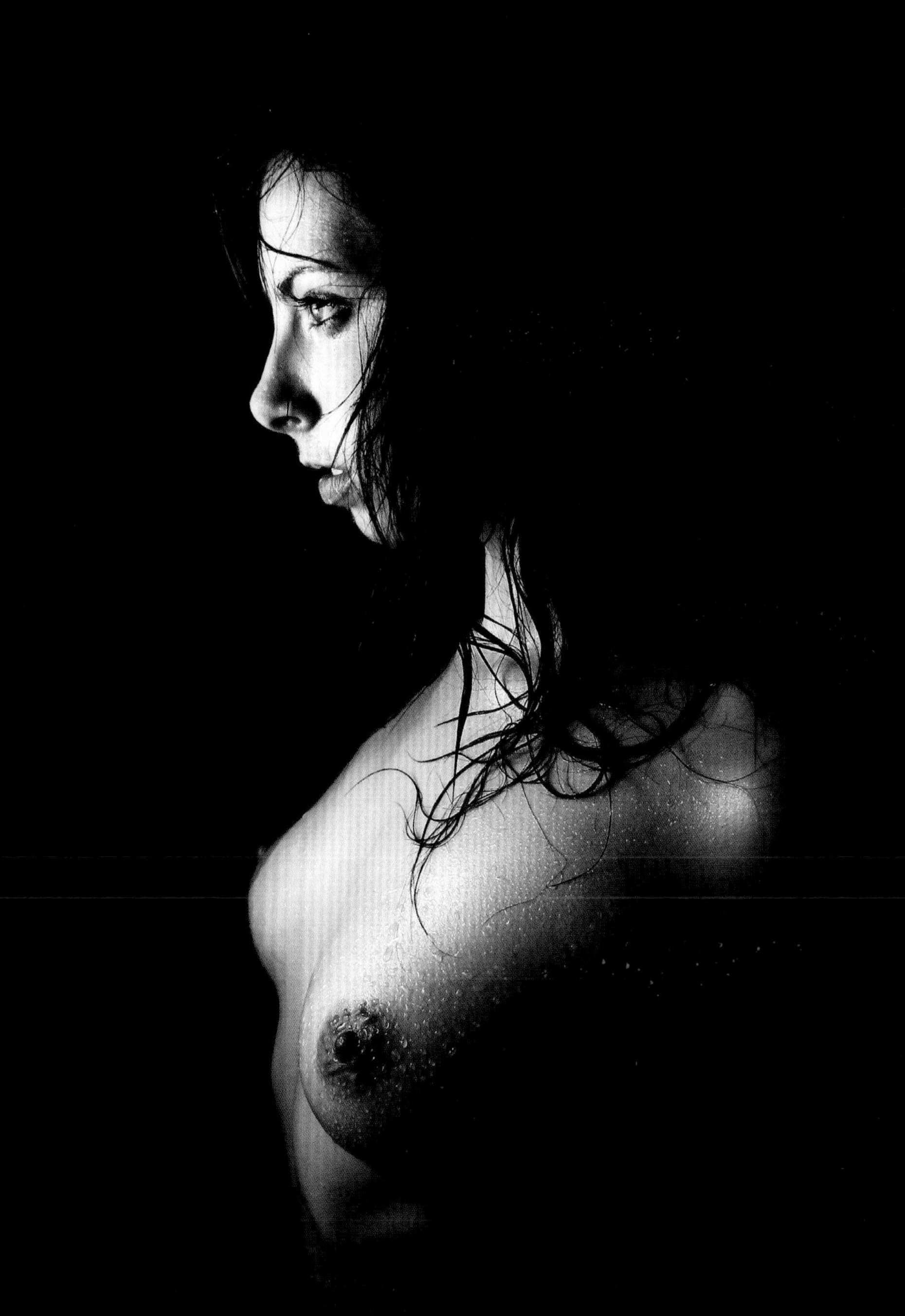

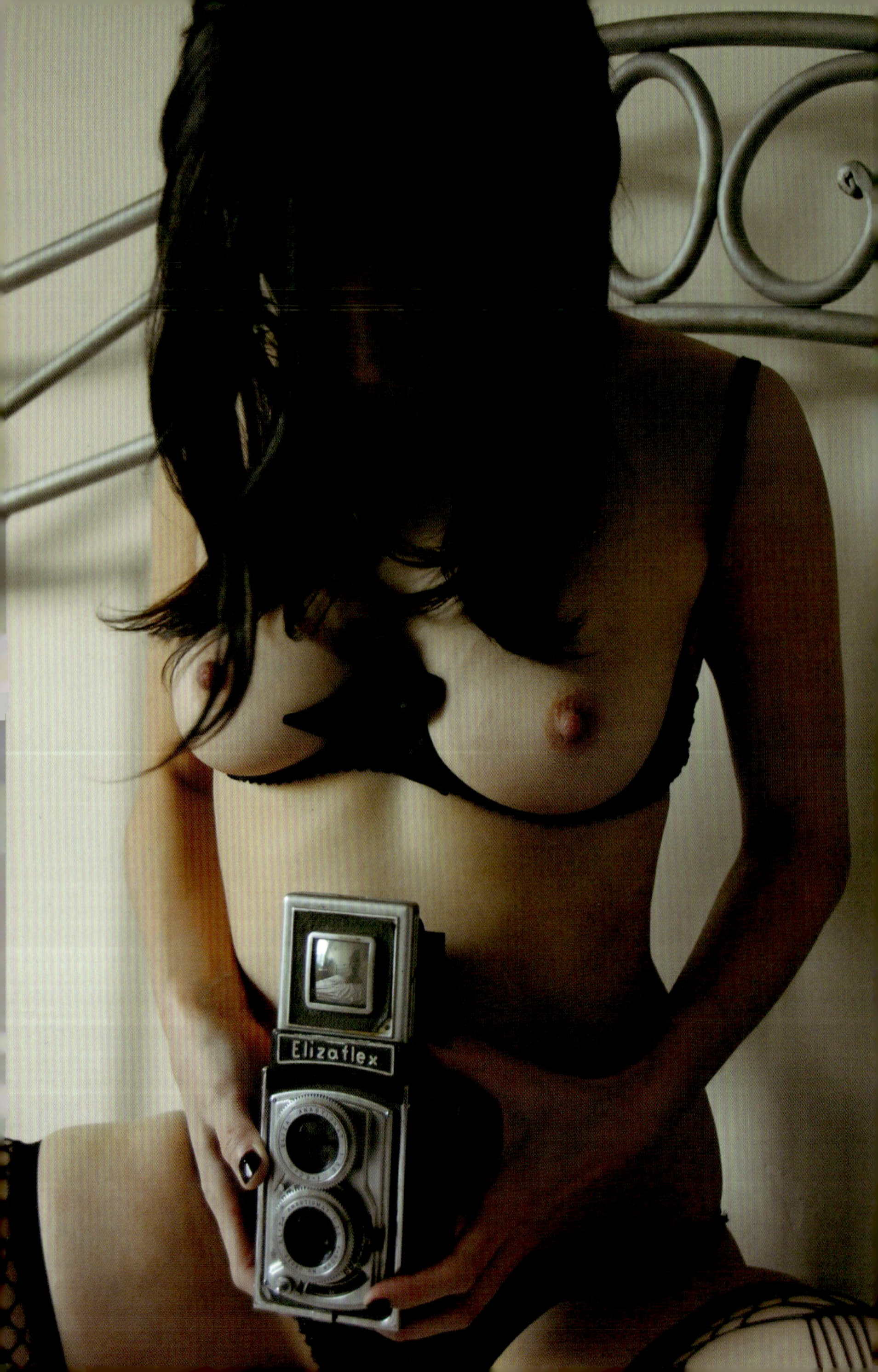
Elizaflex

tommy cuellar

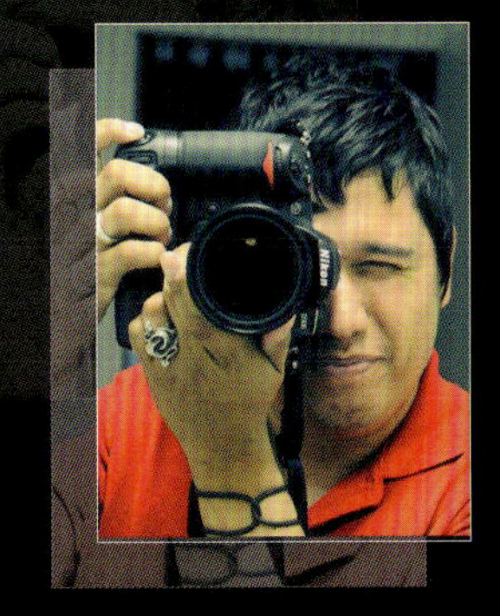

TOMMY IS BASED OUT of San Francisco. His interest in photography began at an early age, but seriously picked up while teaching in Japan in the mid 2000's. Here, he shot street fashion in Harajuku and Shibuya and documented the underground goth and fetish scene. His work has appeared in many books and magazines. The majority of his work revolves around shooting professional dominatrices in their dungeons, often during live BDSM sessions. His unobtrusive manner allows him to take photos from a variety of interesting angles while a session unfolds naturally and undisturbed.

www.glowstar.com

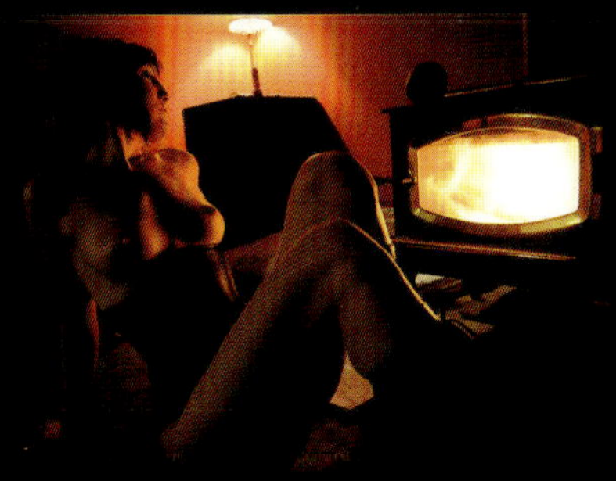

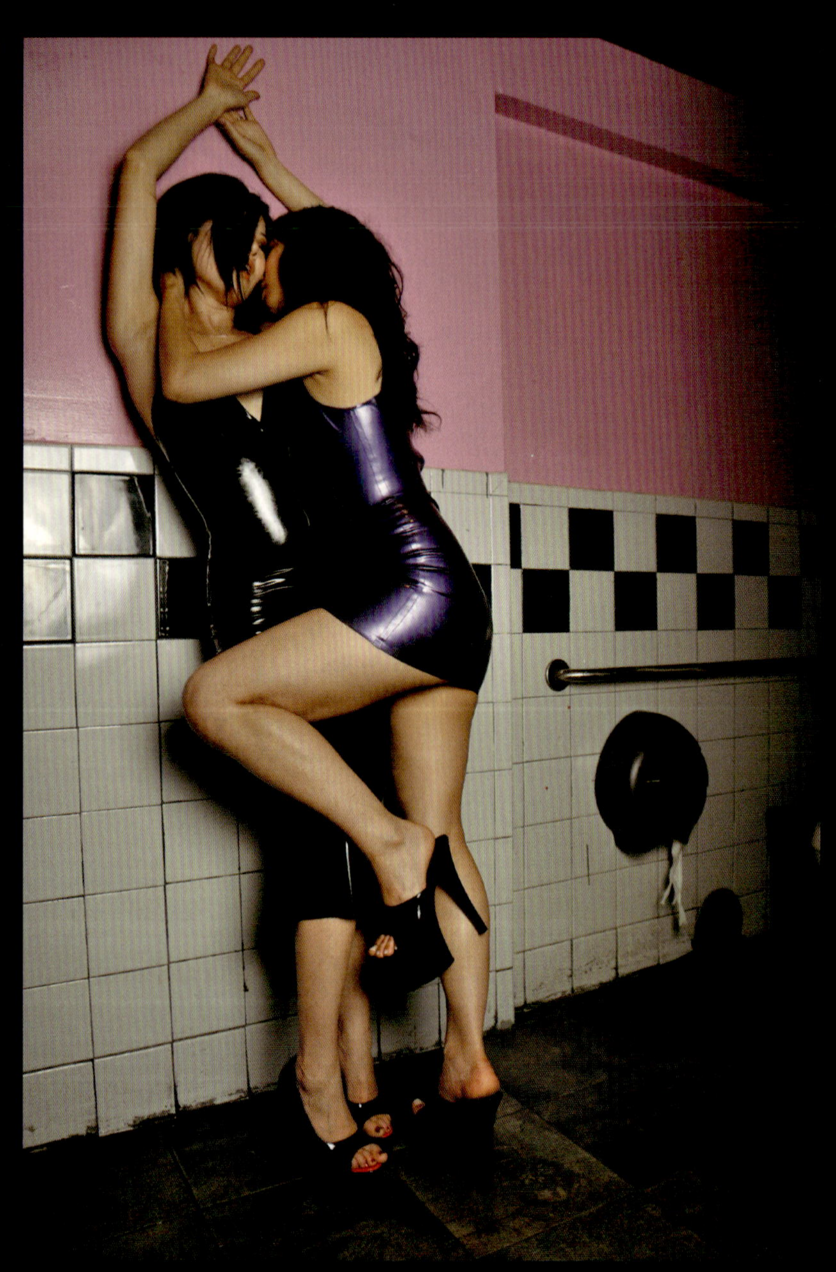

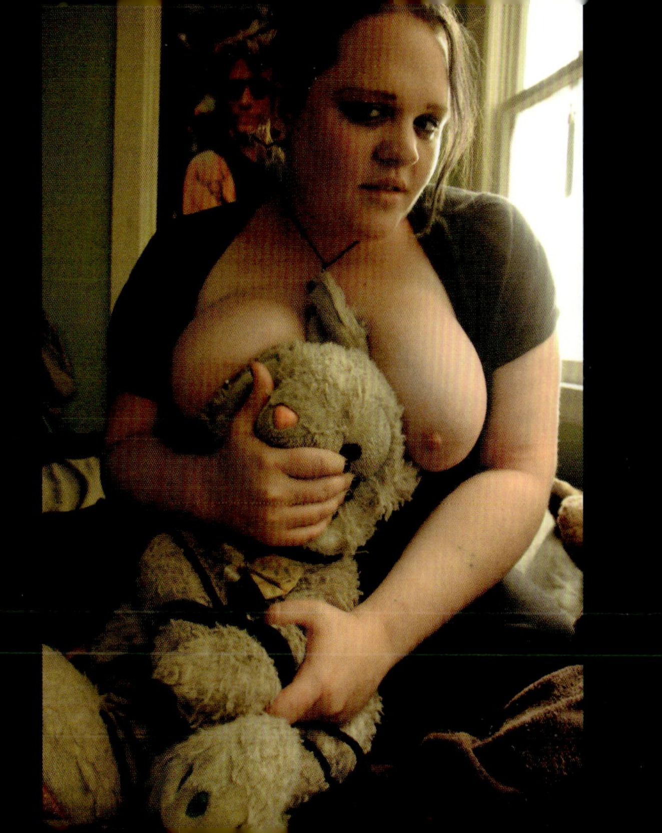

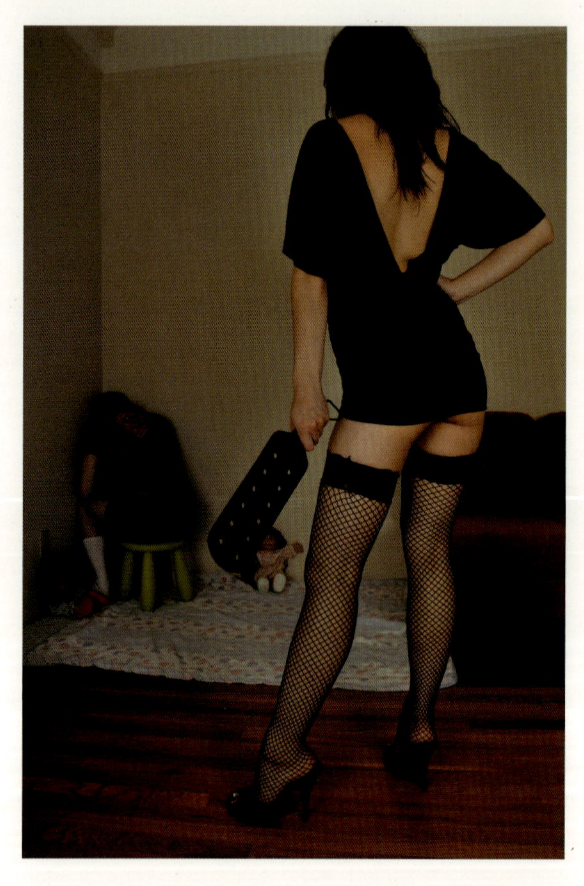

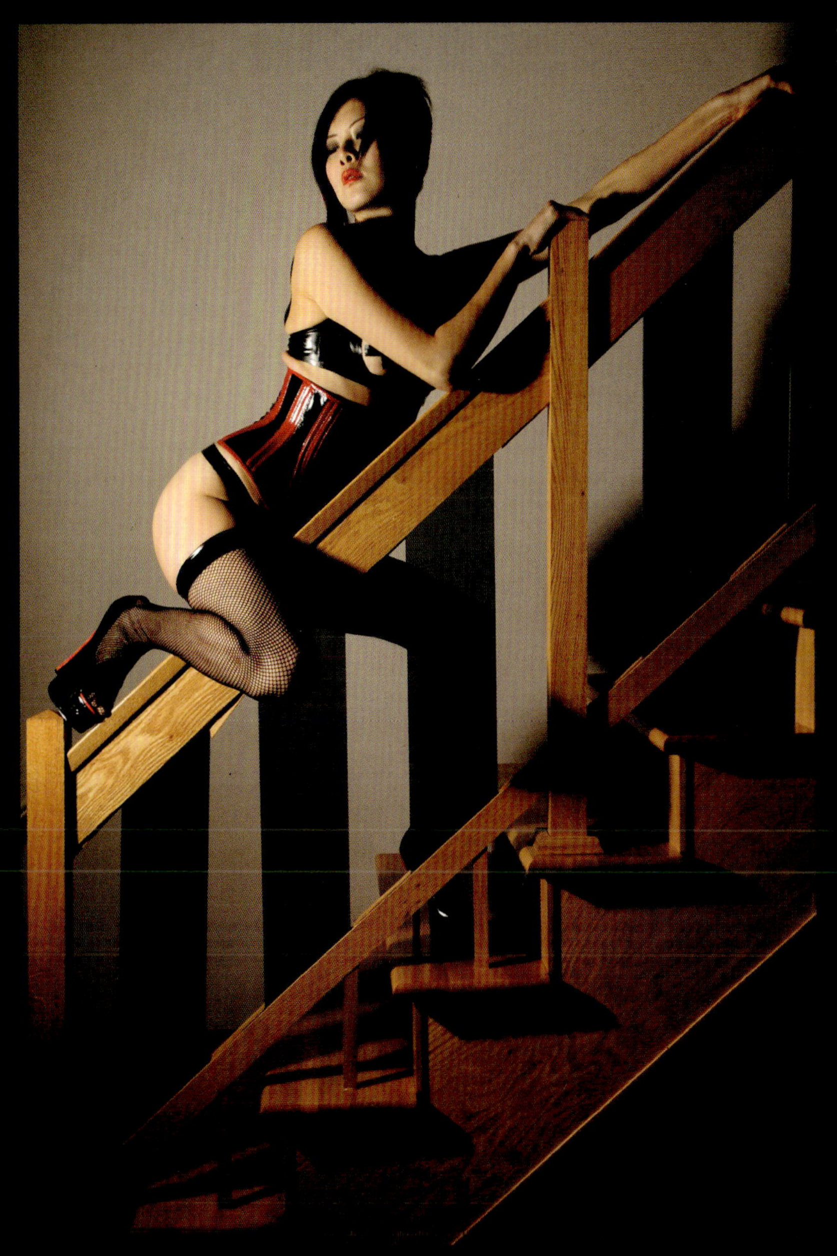

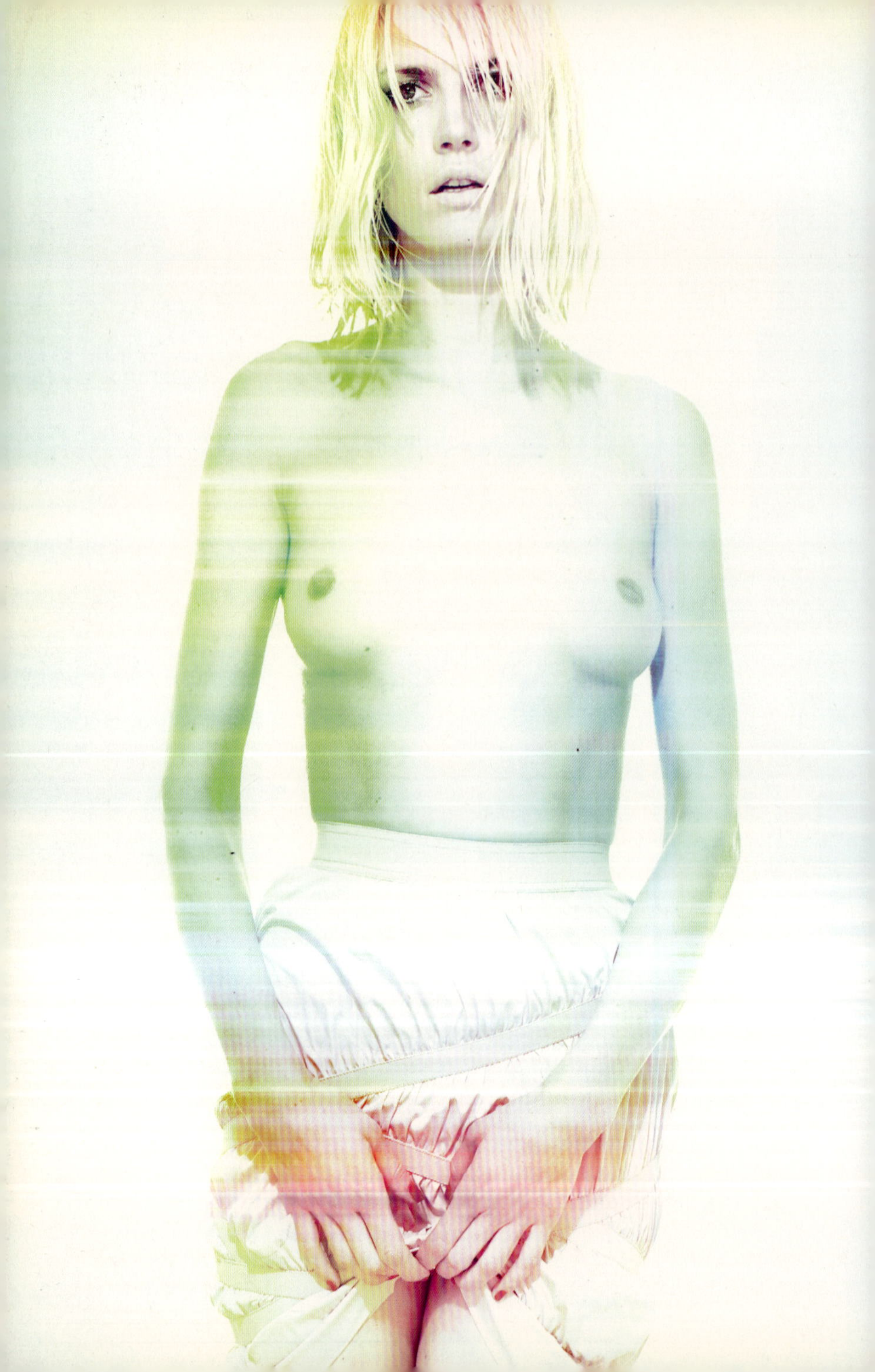

pierre dal corso

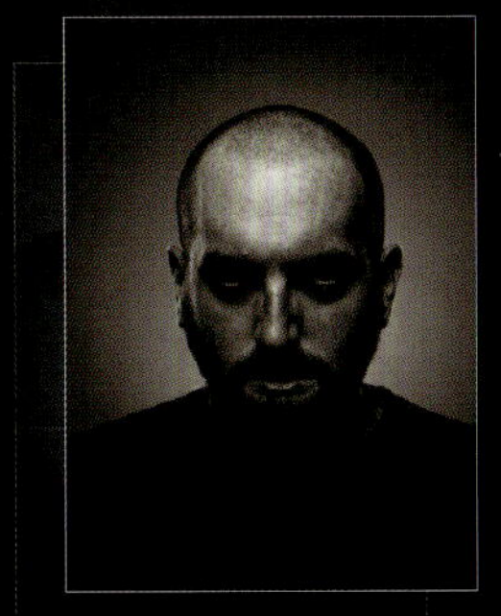

PIERRE WAS BORN IN 1977 in the south west of France. After studying Art History, he moved to Paris and then to New York, where he lived as a photo assistant for five years. He is now back in Paris, working for fashion magazines and on personal art projects.

www.pierredalcorso.com

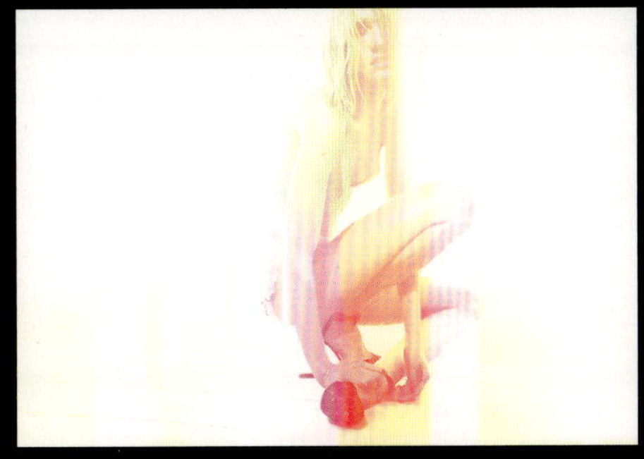

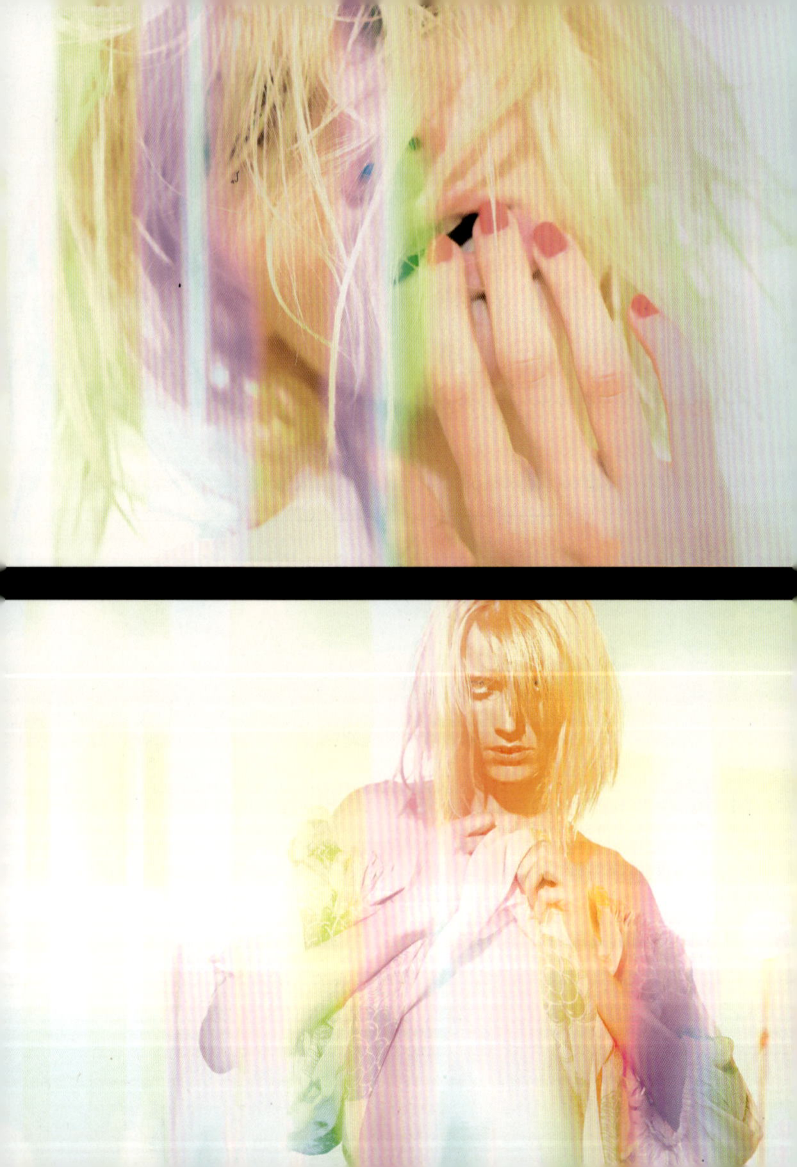

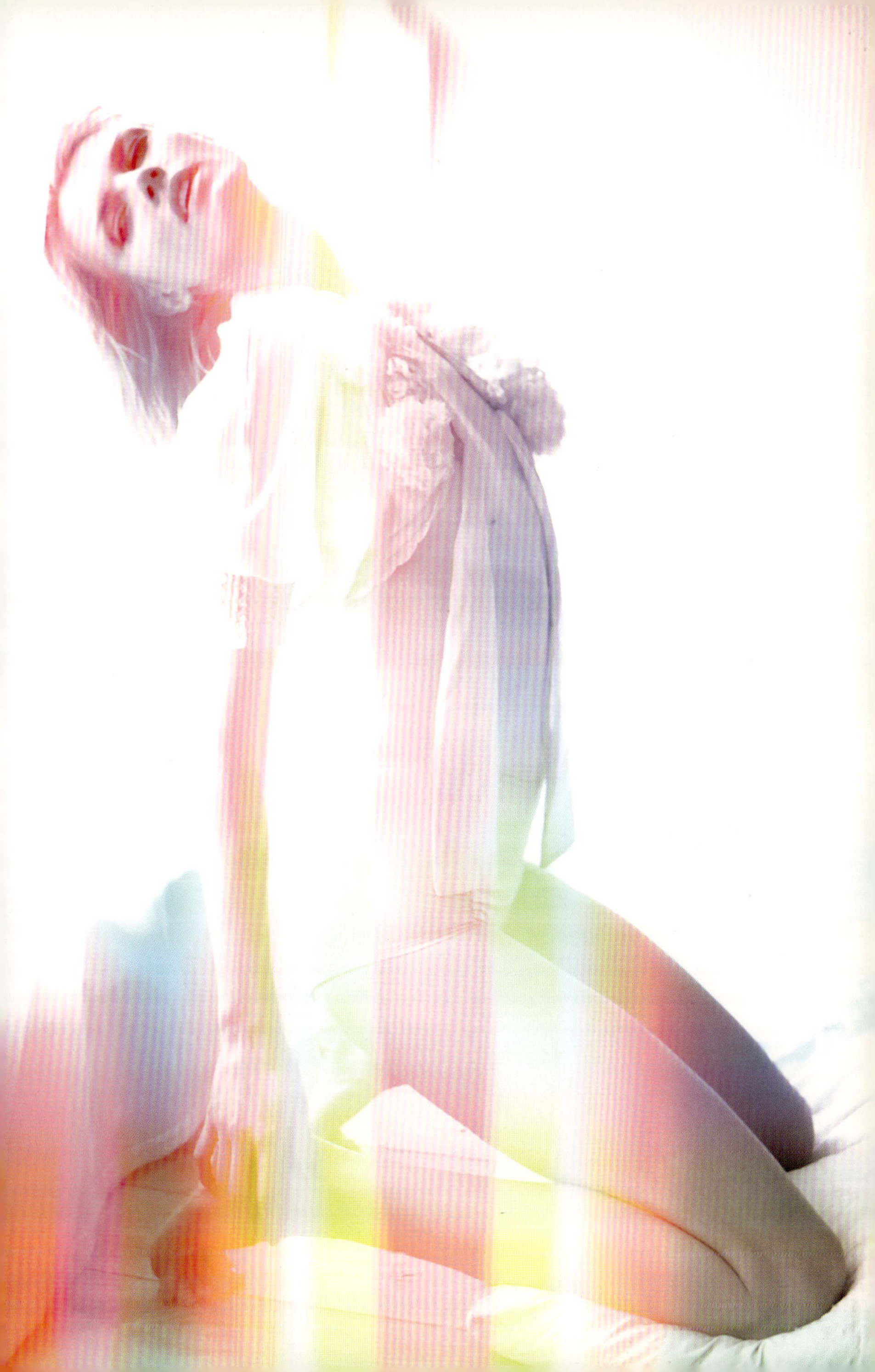

PIERRE DAL COR

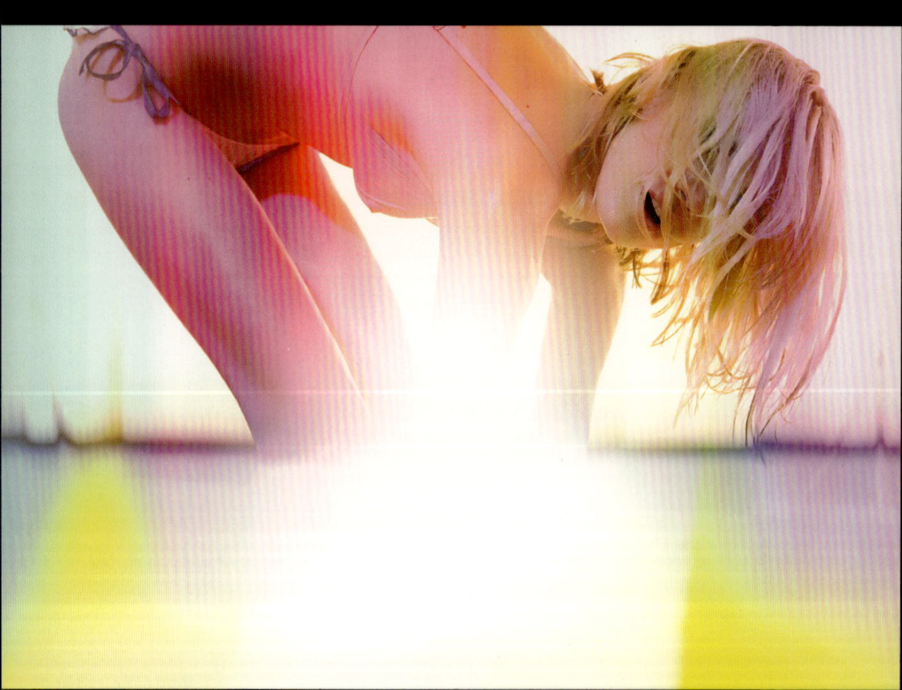

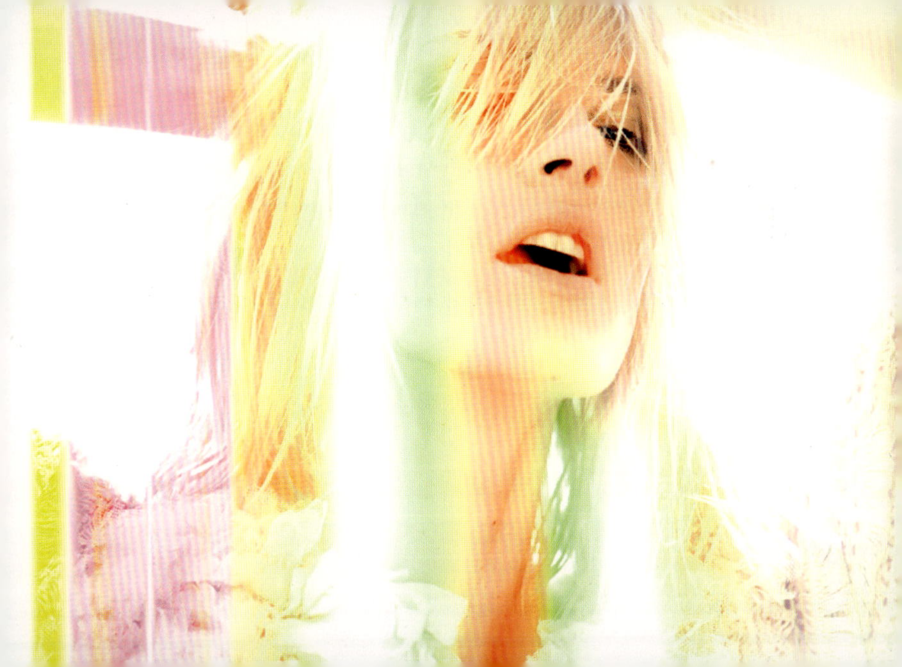

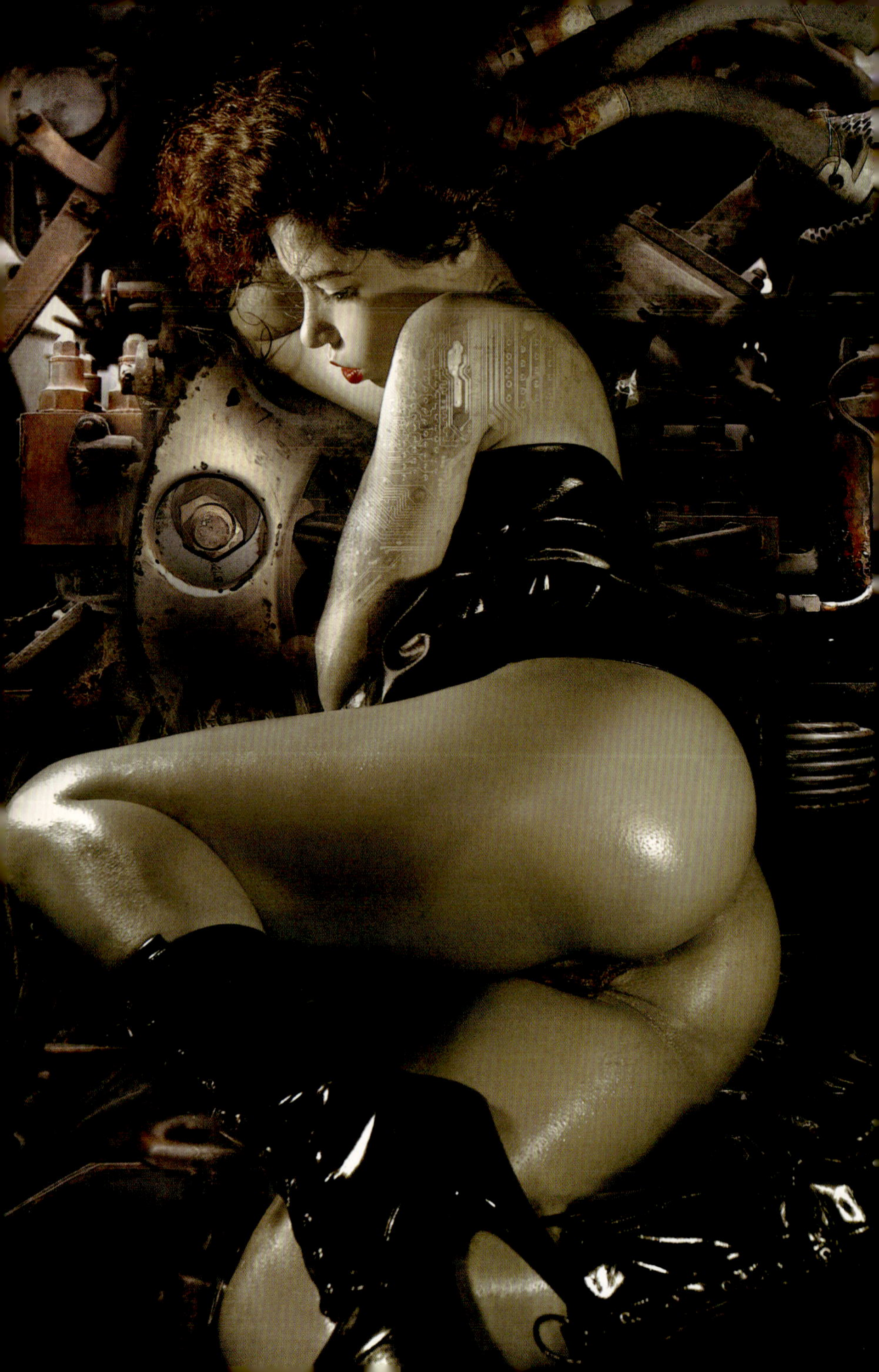

luis durante

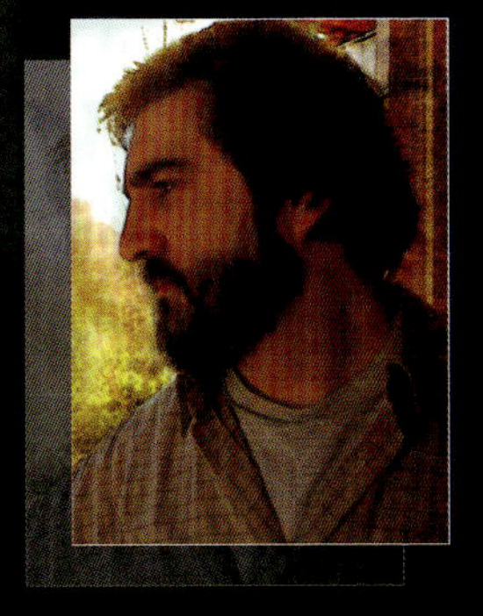

LUIS WAS BORN IN SORIA, the most romantic place in Spain, in 1955, and spent most of his childhood in Madrid, drawing and painting. When he was seventeen, he lived in a hippy community putting on theatre and street performances across Spain, England and other parts of Europe. At twenty-three, he left the community and went to Paris, where he studied photography. Four years later, he returned to Spain, worked in advertising, and published several books featuring his girlfriend and muse, Idoia.

www.duranteart.com

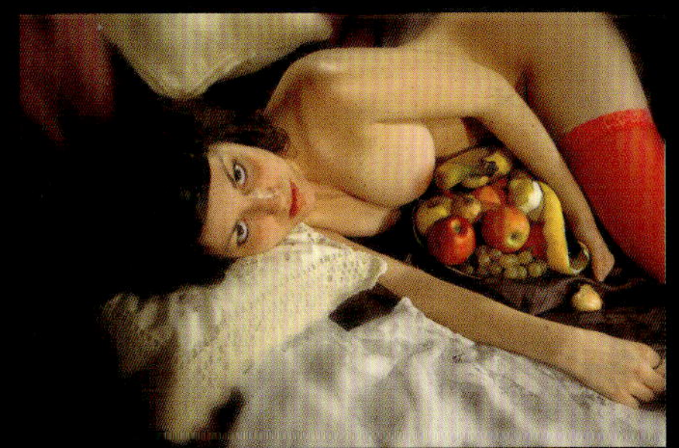

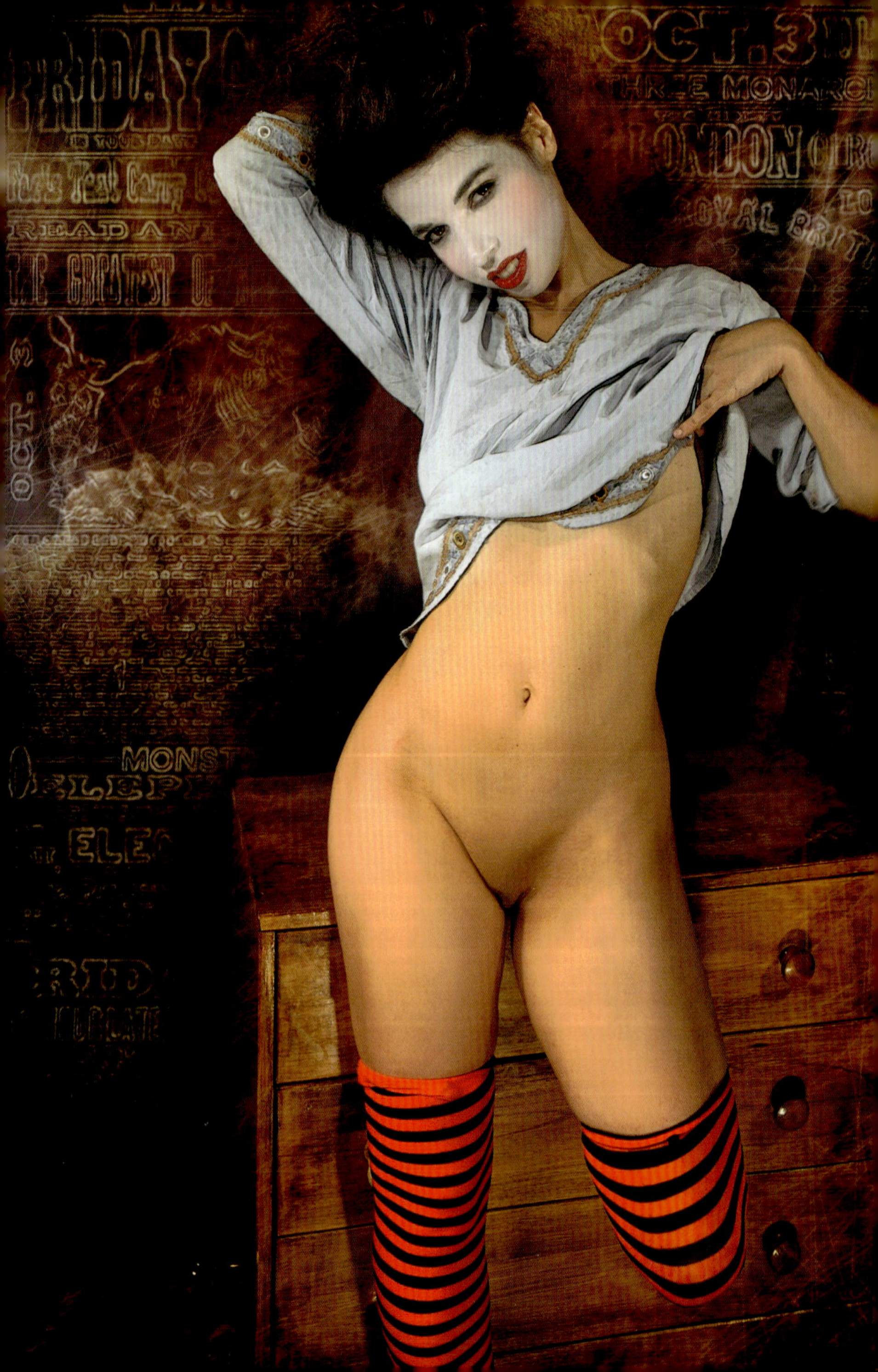
FRIDAY
OCT. 3
LONDON

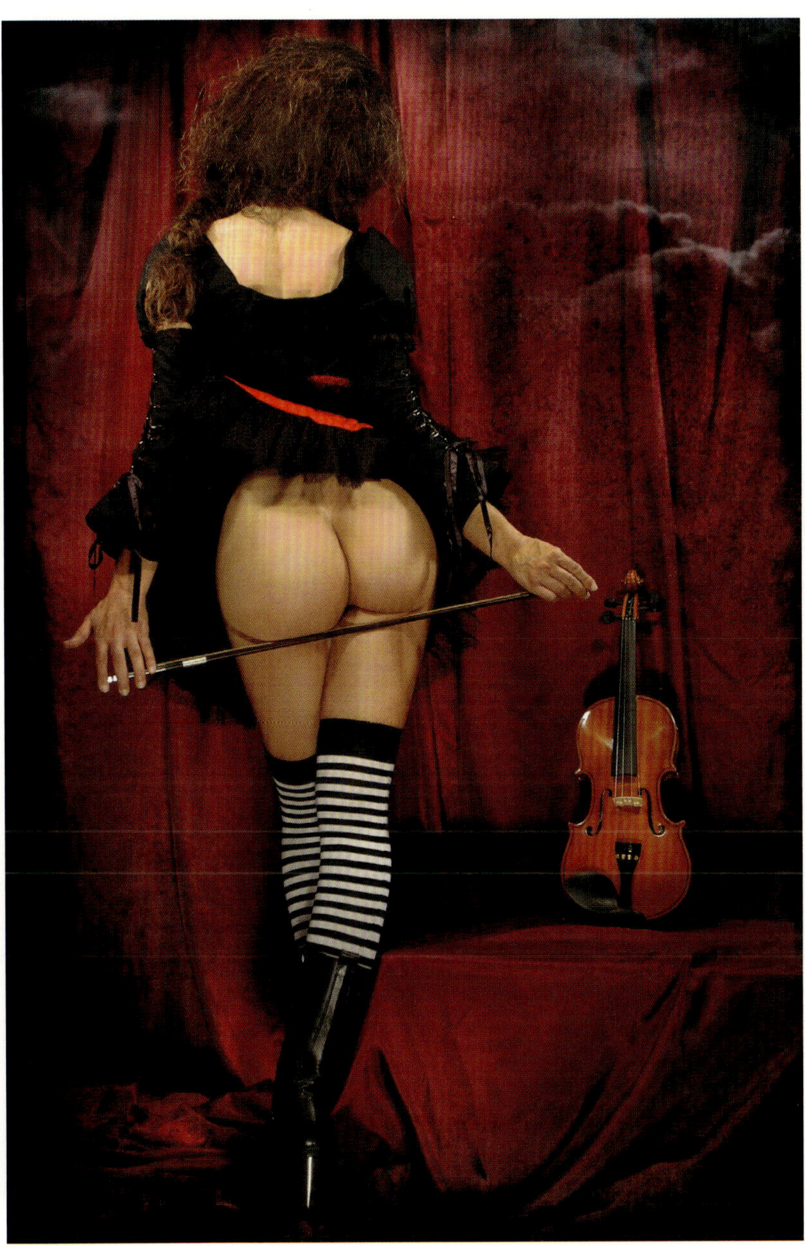

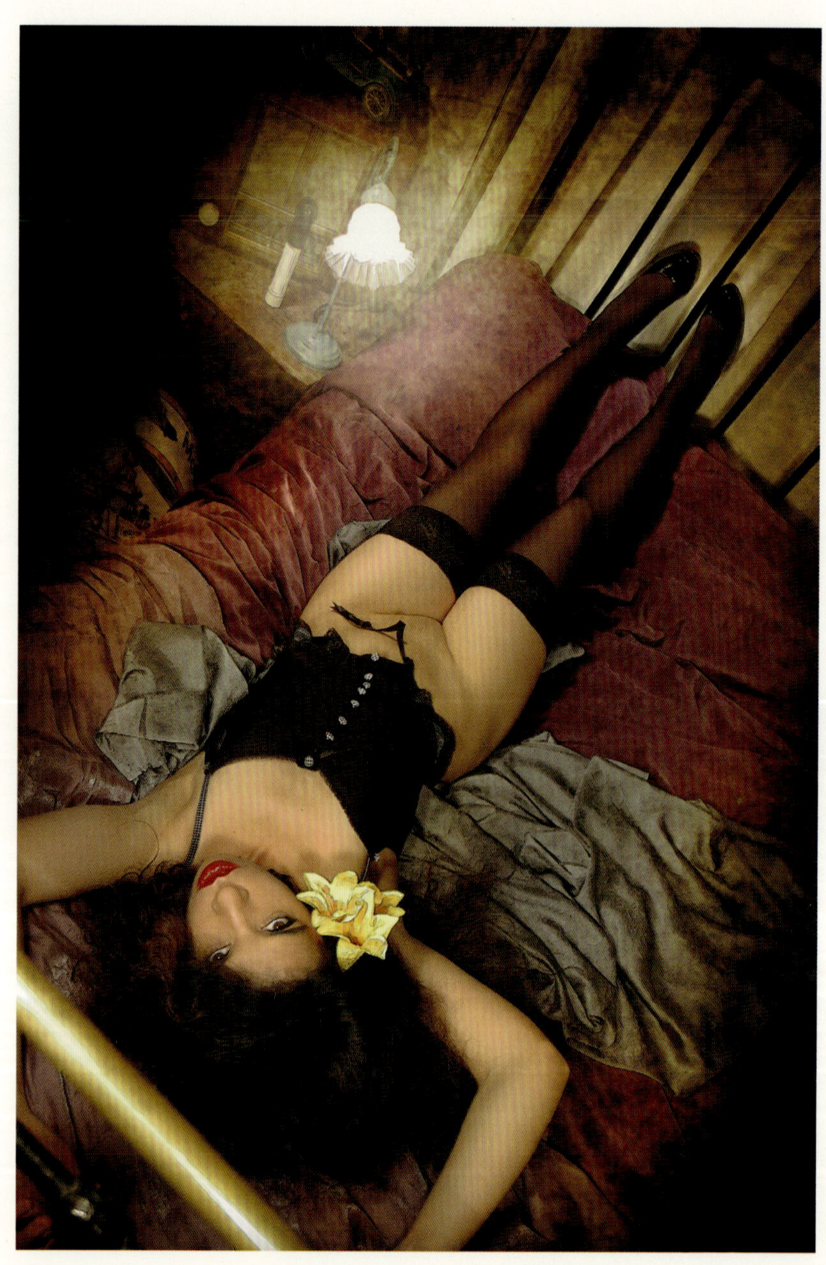

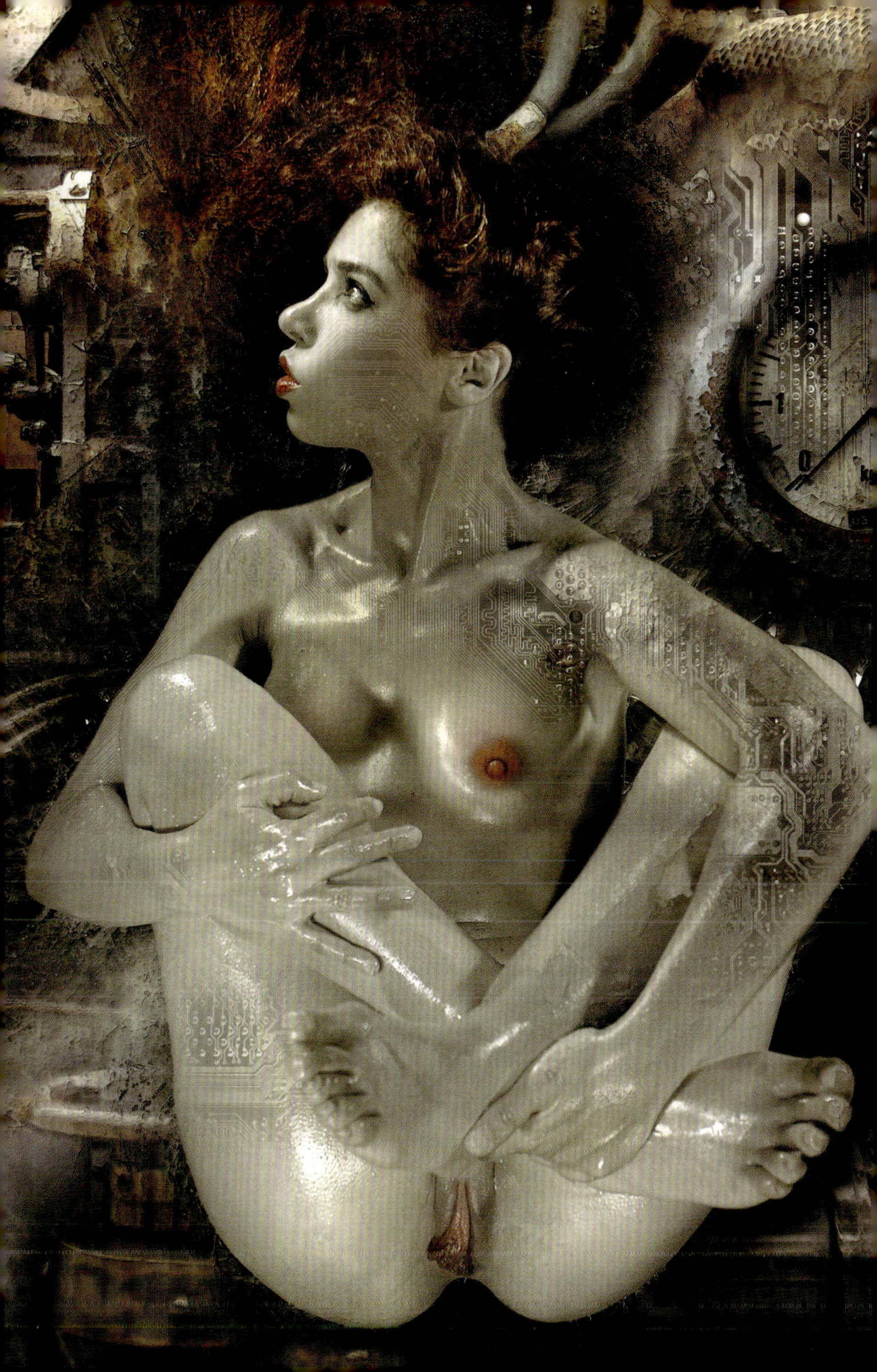

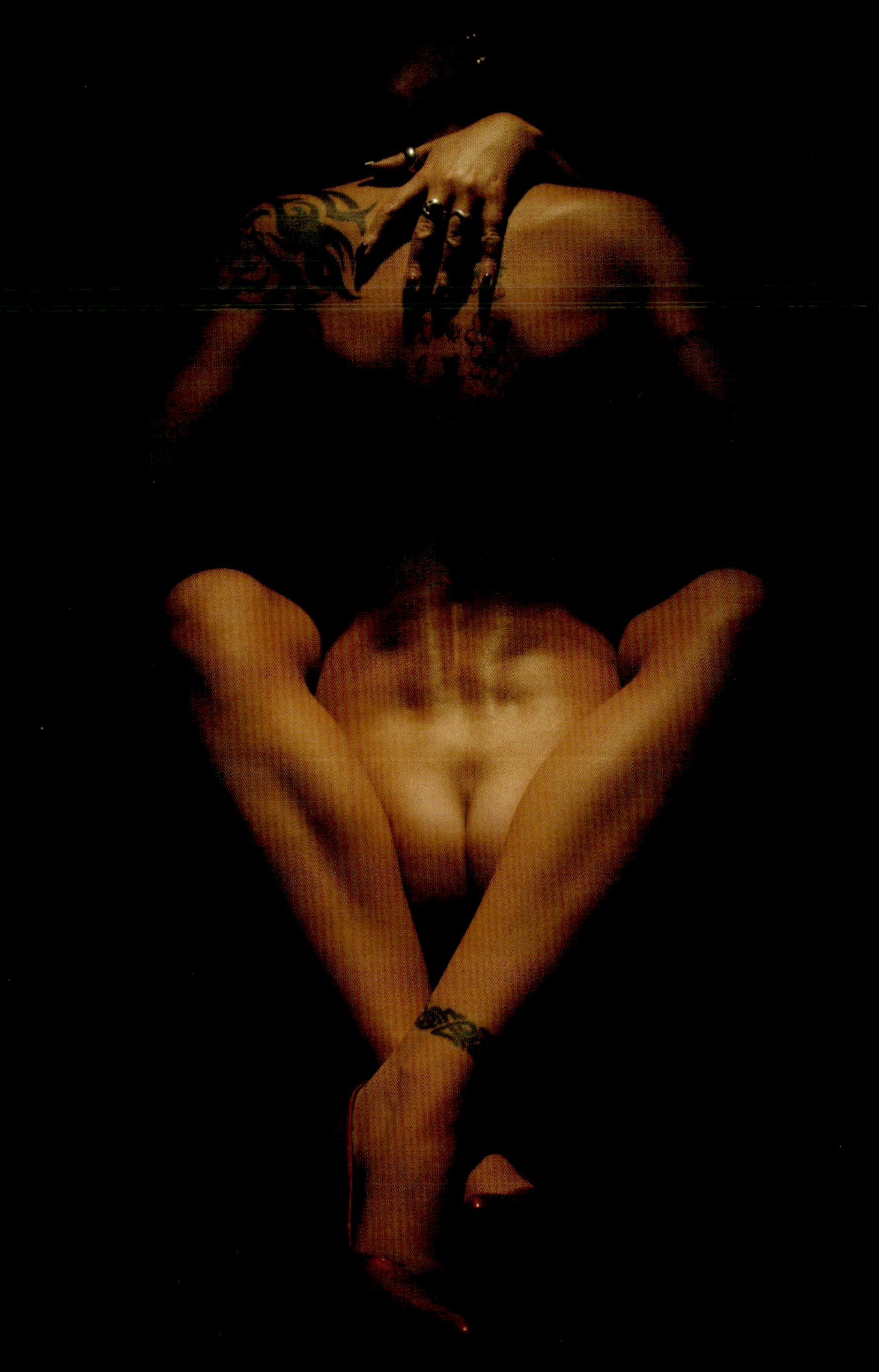

kai eckhardt

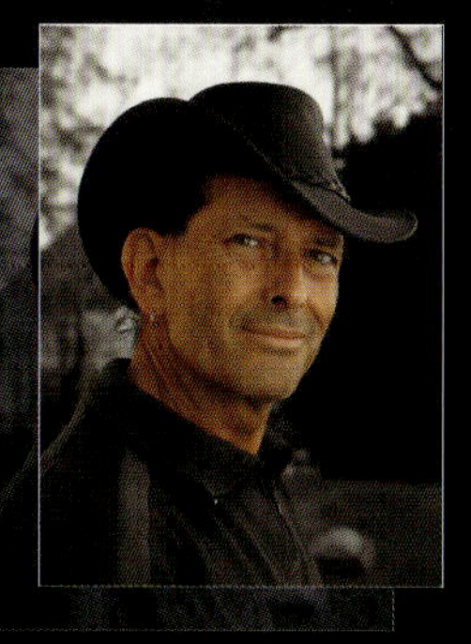

KAI WAS BORN IN 1960, and raised in Kiel, in the north of Germany. He is a self-taught freelance photographer and artist, and now runs his own studio and a small gallery. The focus of his work is both the erotic and fine art nude photography. His passion is to play with skin, light and shadow.

www.ke-erotic.com

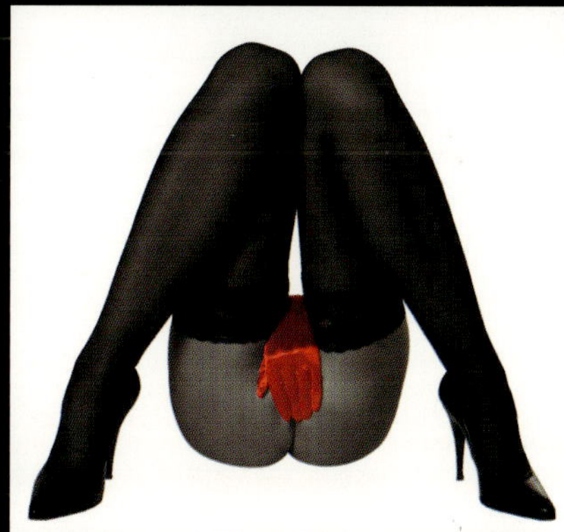

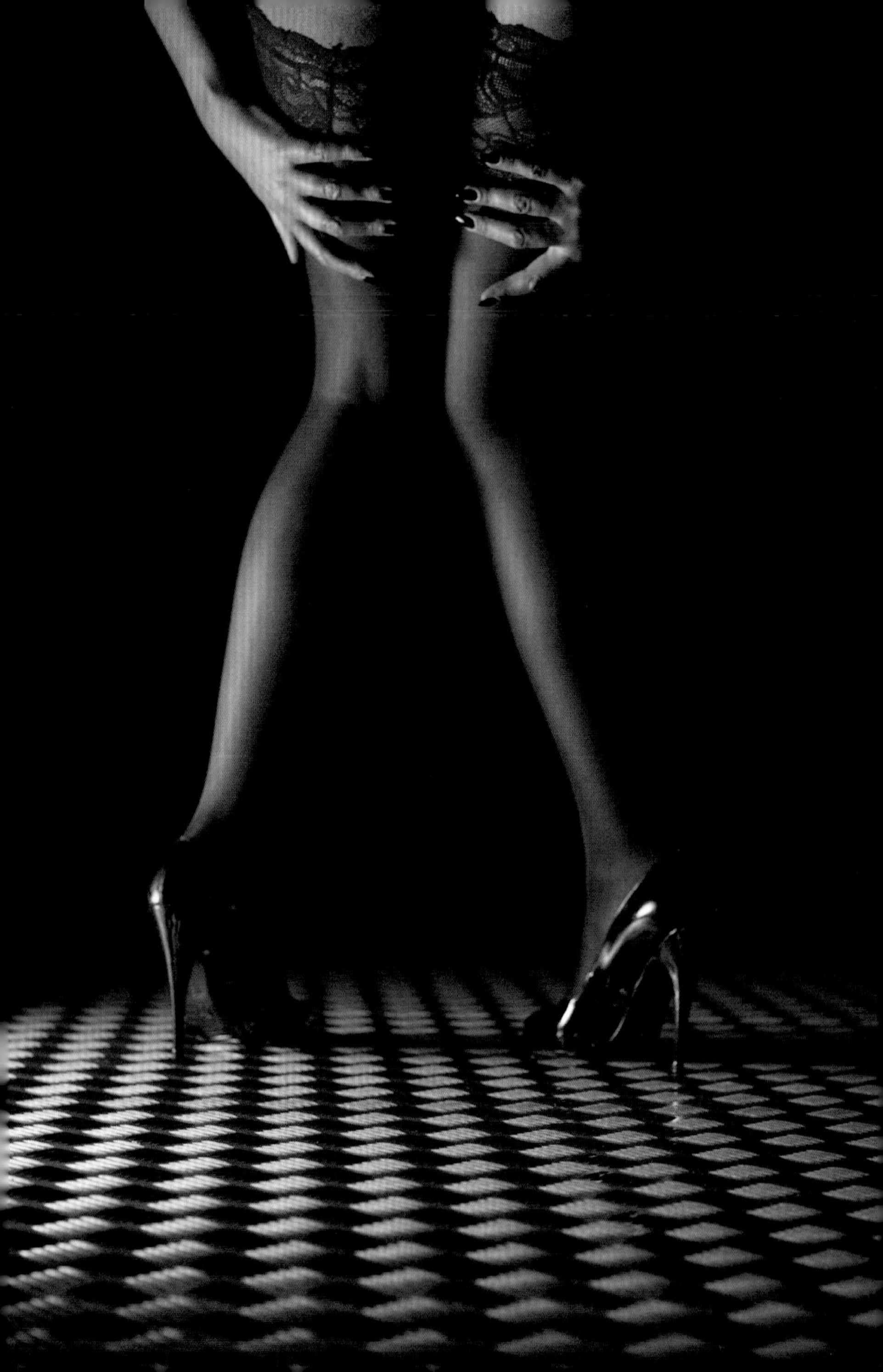

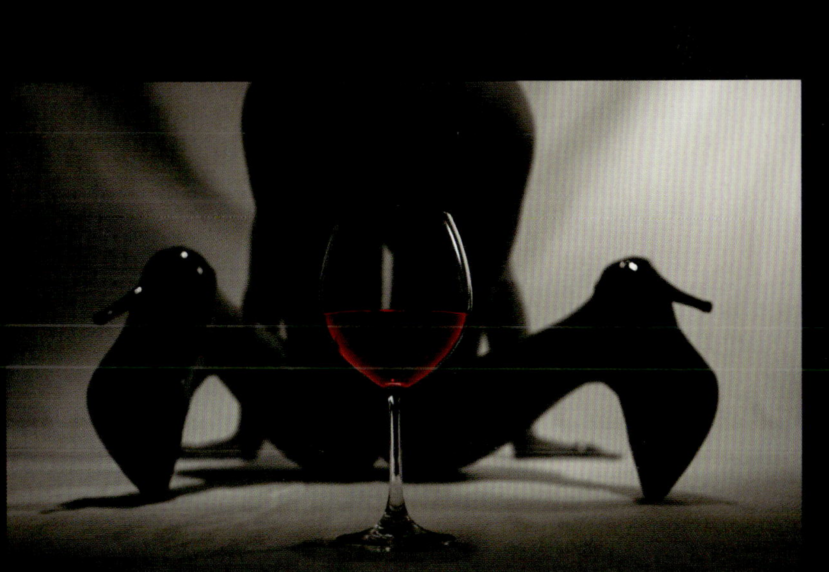

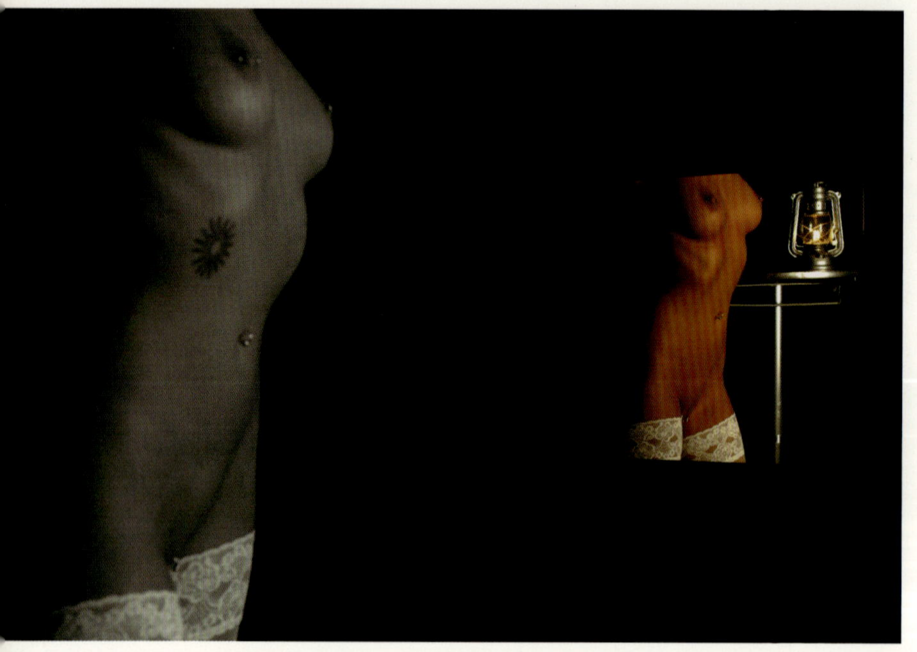

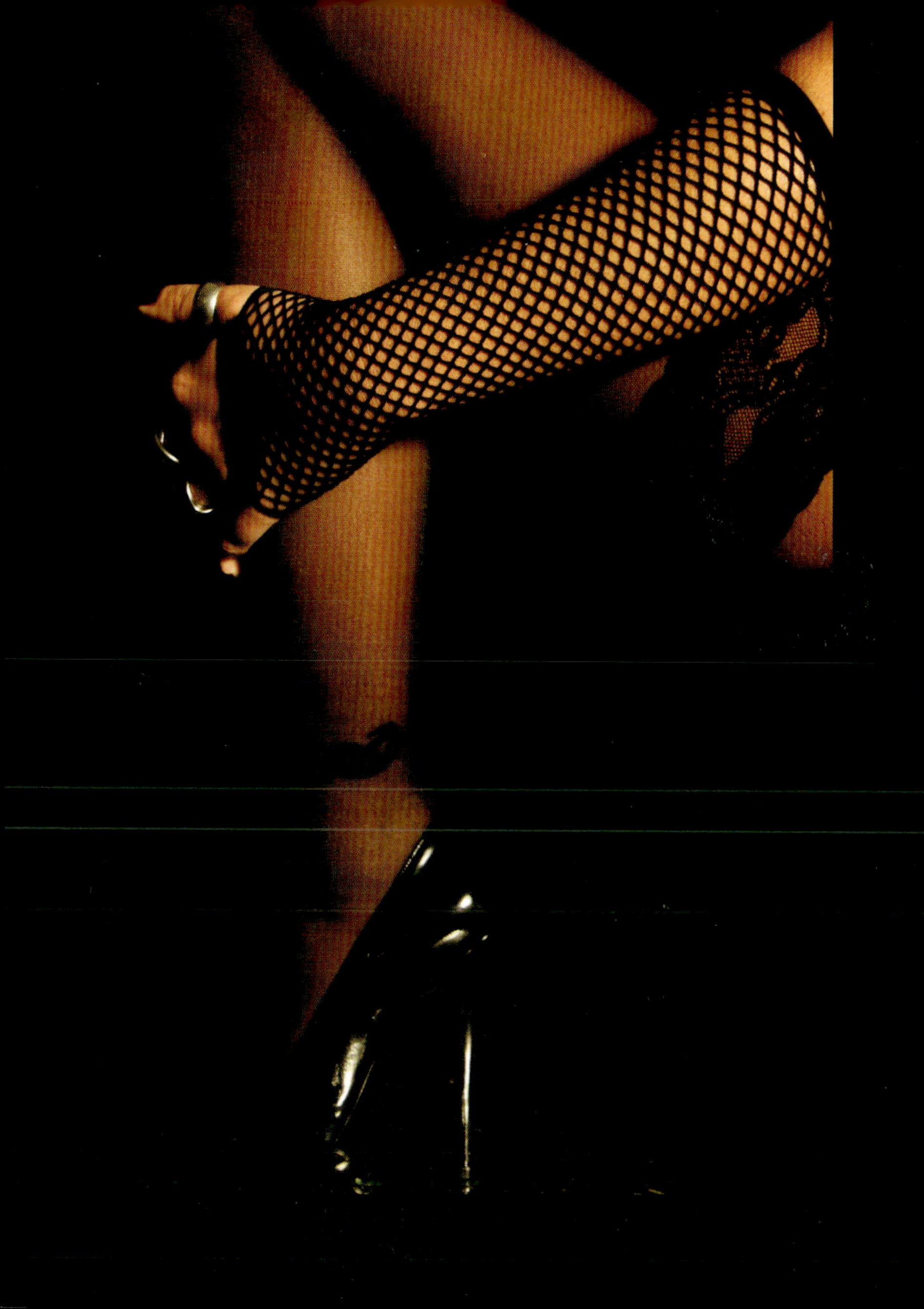

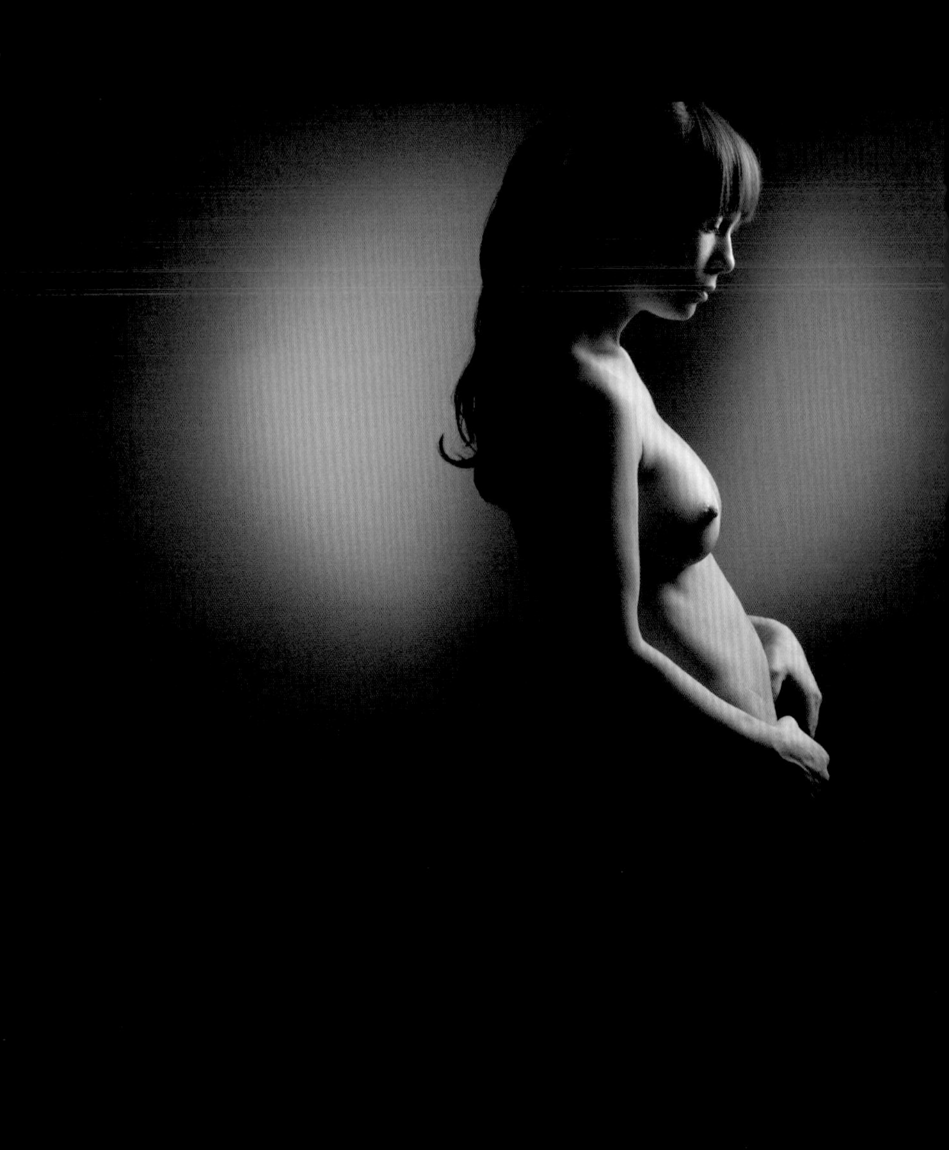

estergom

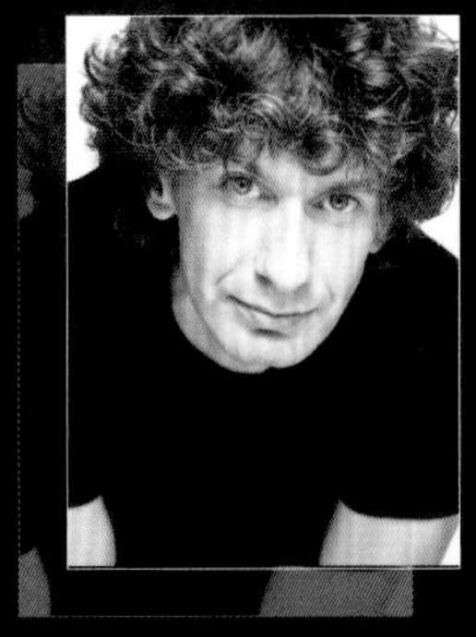

ESTERGOM IS THE NAME used by photographer Anastasiy Mikhaylov. Born in Poland, and educated in Russia and Hungary, he became a sought-after Director of Photography on films, TV programmes and documentaries. In recent years, he has devoted increasing time and effort to his photography, to the point where it is no longer a mere hobby, and has participated in several exhibitions in Moscow. His work is influenced by cinema (Antonioni, Bertolucci, Tarkovsky, Wong Kar-Wai) and master photographers like Helmut Newton, Irving Penn and Albert Watson. He has a strong preference for minimalist monochromic images with simple compositional structures and uses natural light or tungsten lighting.

www.estergom.com

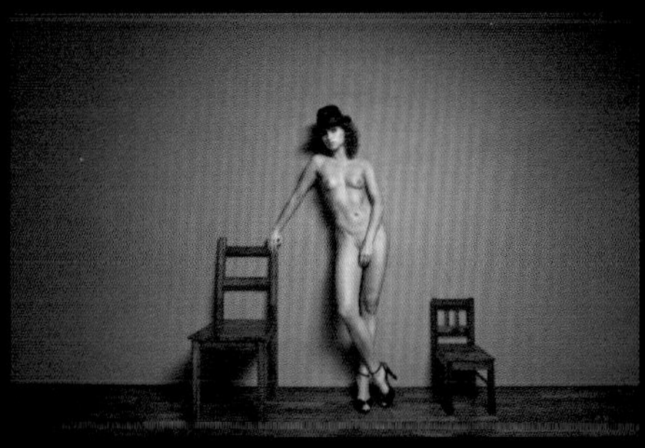

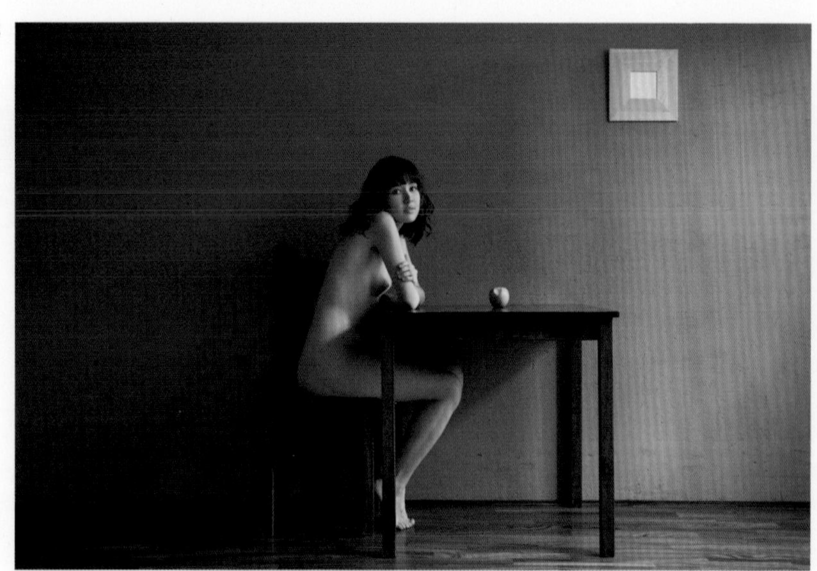

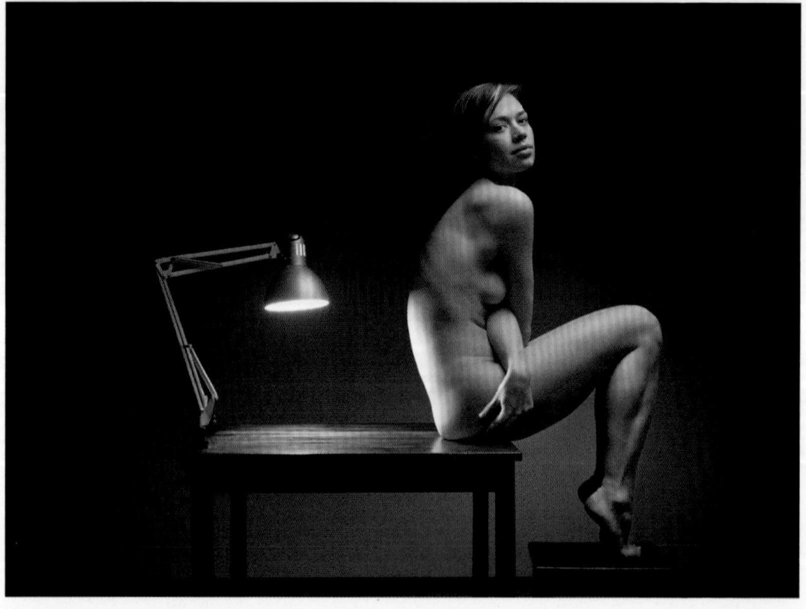

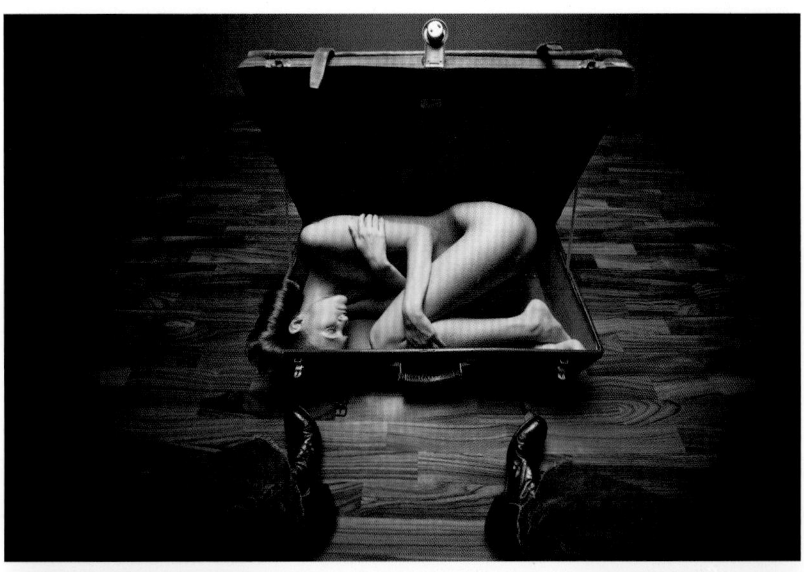

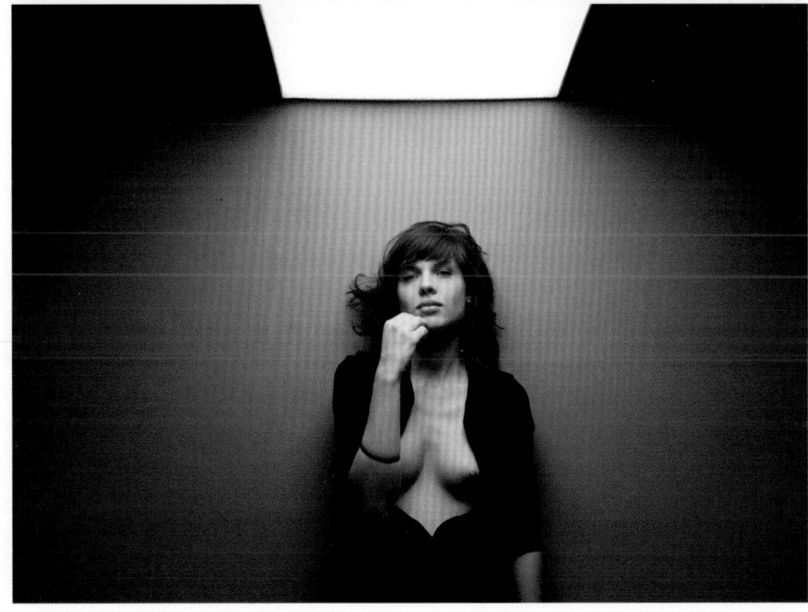

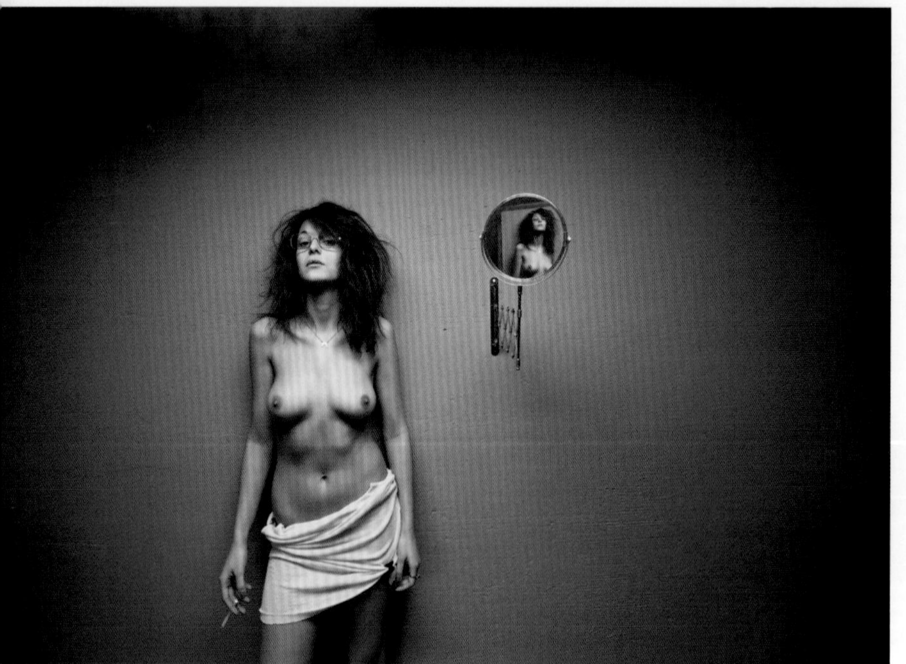

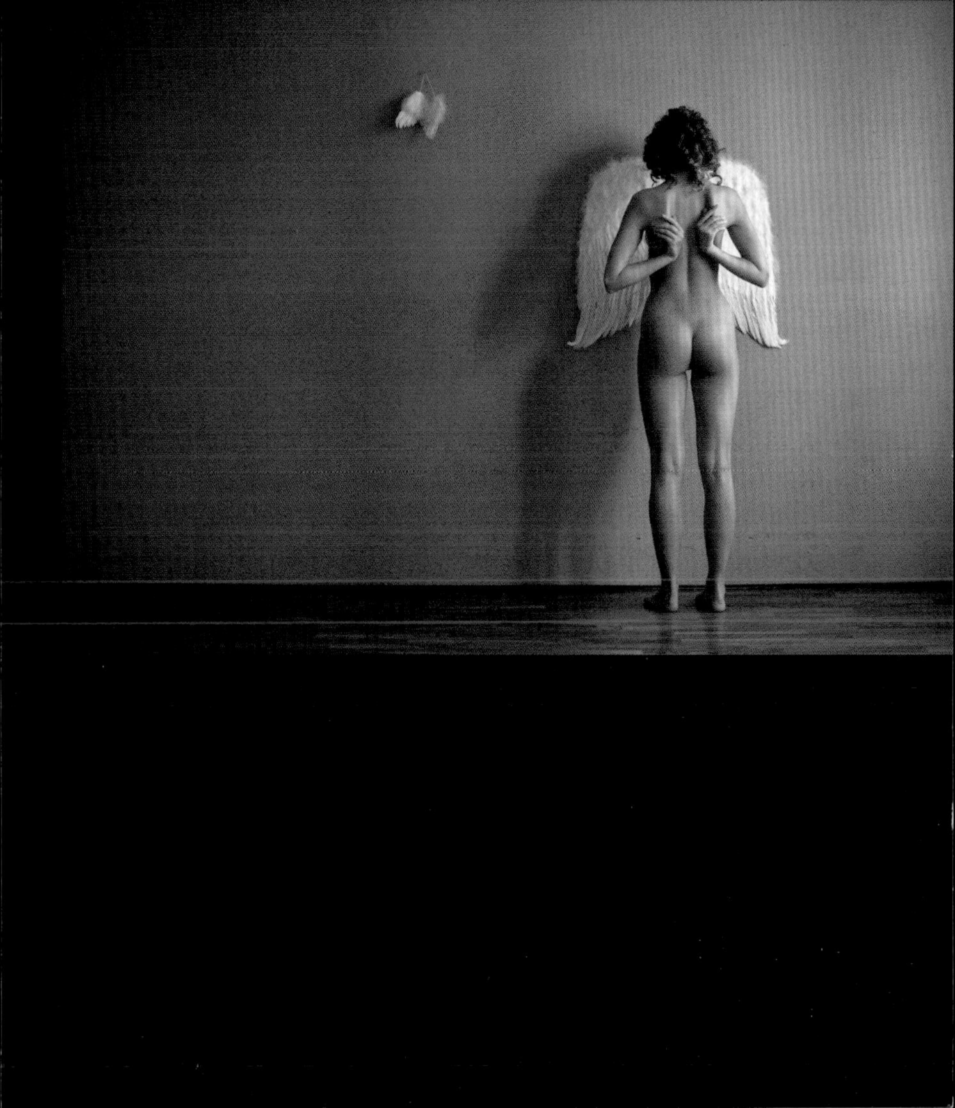

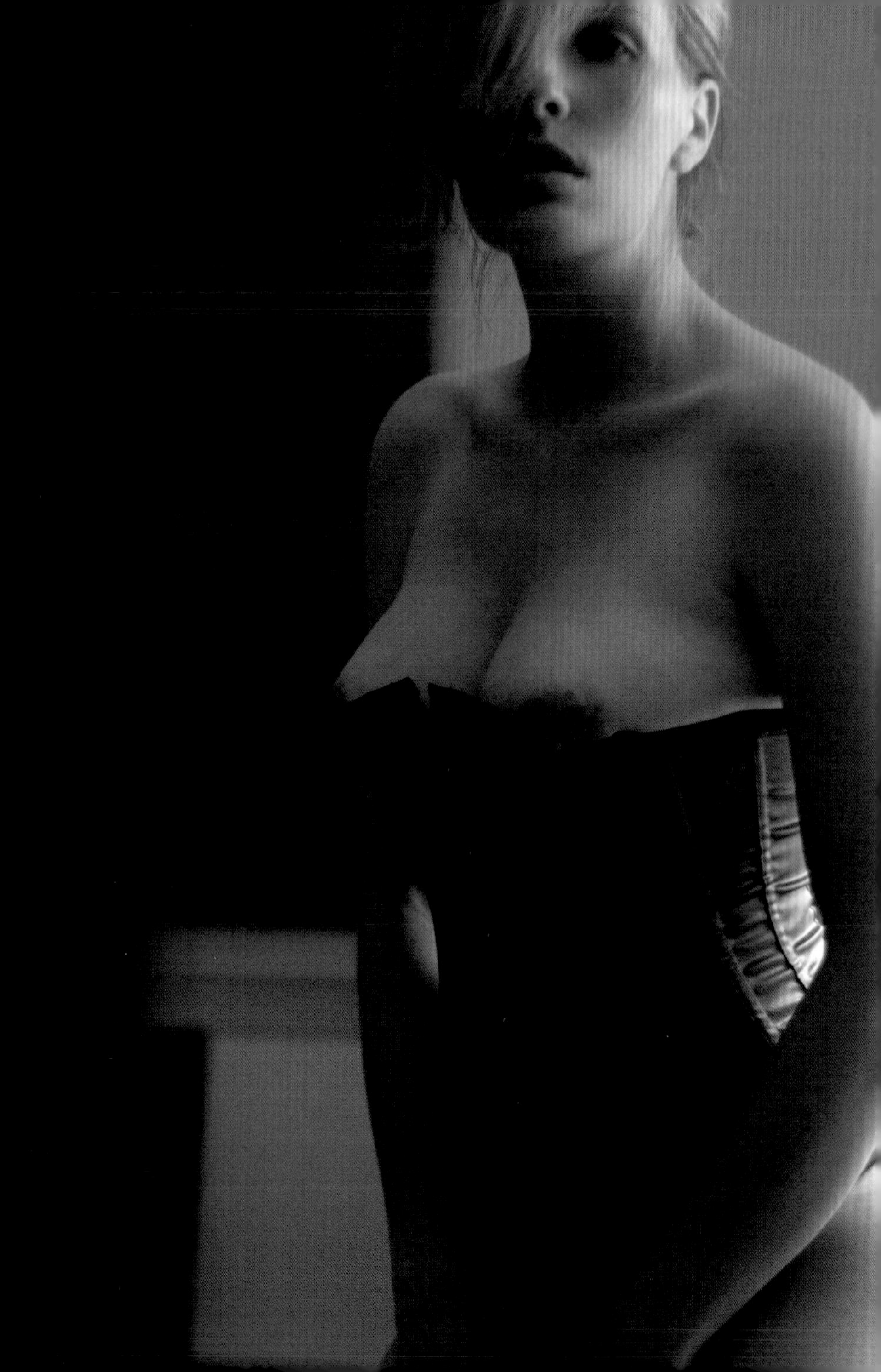

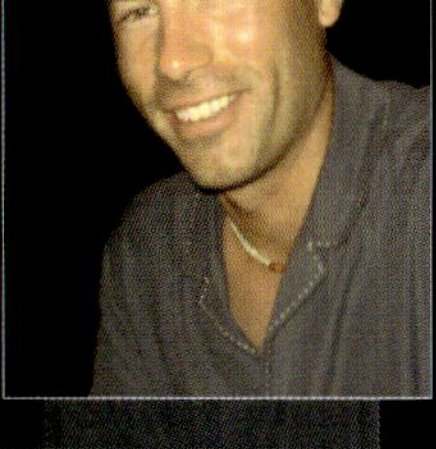

inspired this young American photographer. Ben Fernon has always loved to create. Photography had always intrigued him so he naturally took it up as a hobby: 'I used to draw and paint but now I just like the instant gratification of pushing a button.' He attempts to capture real candid moments of beautiful women in a natural setting.

www.flickr.com/photos/benfernon

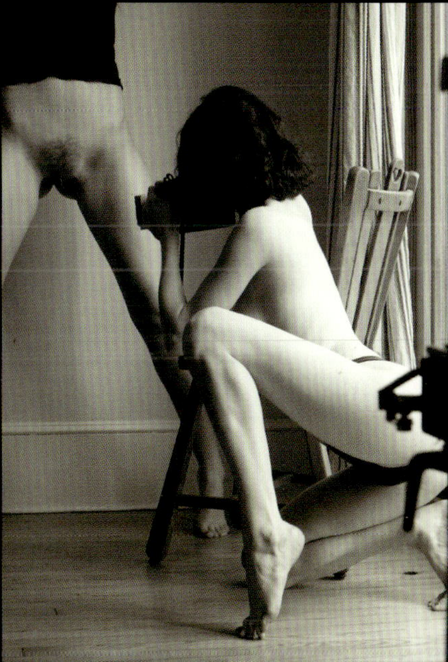

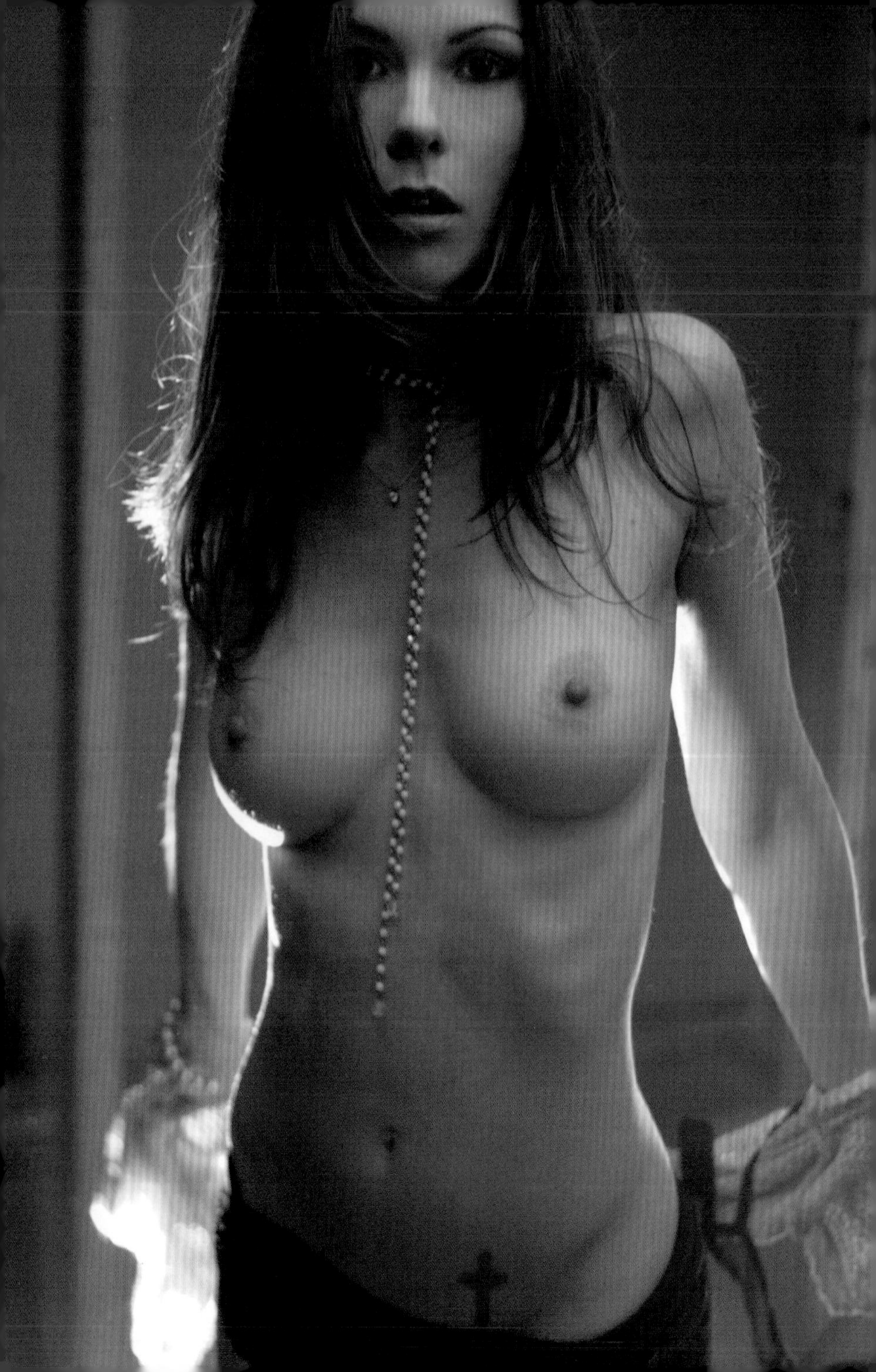

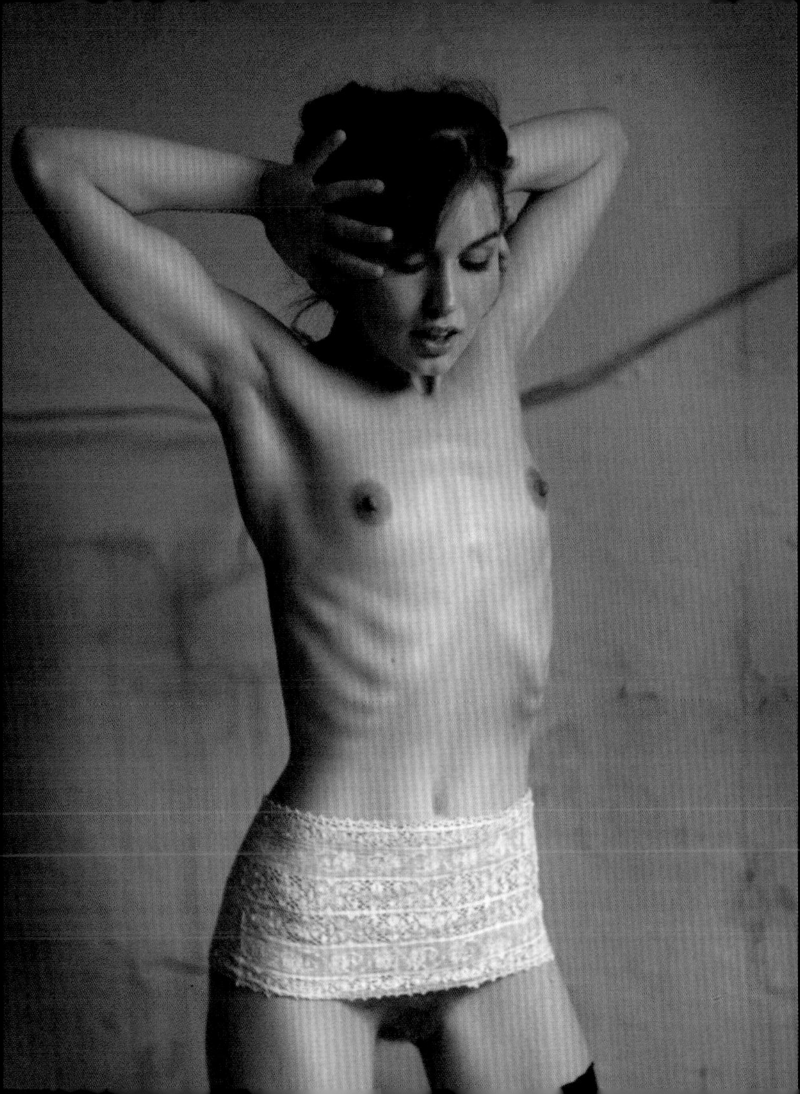

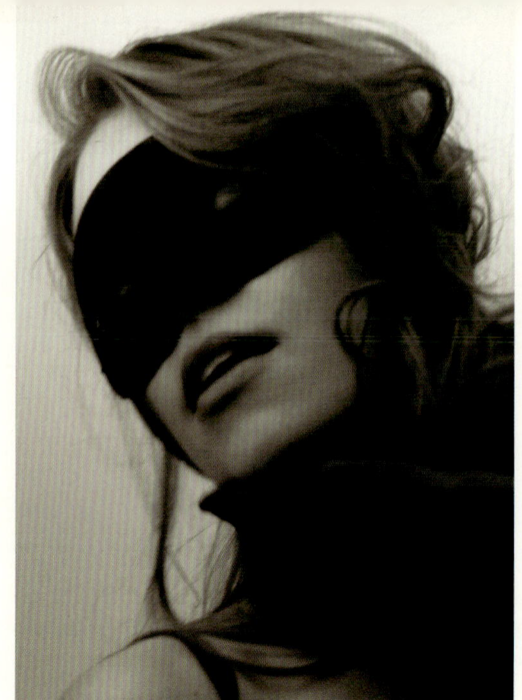

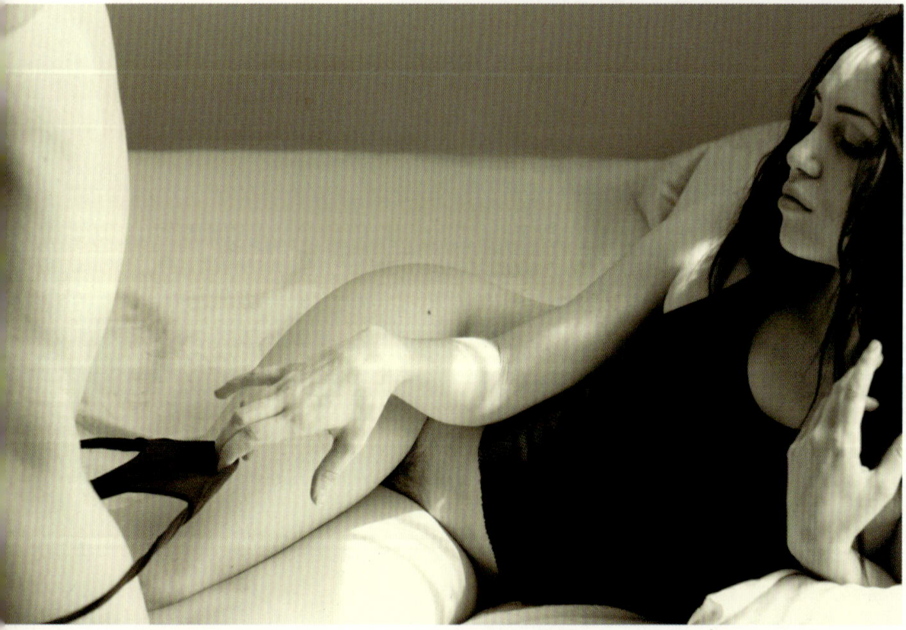

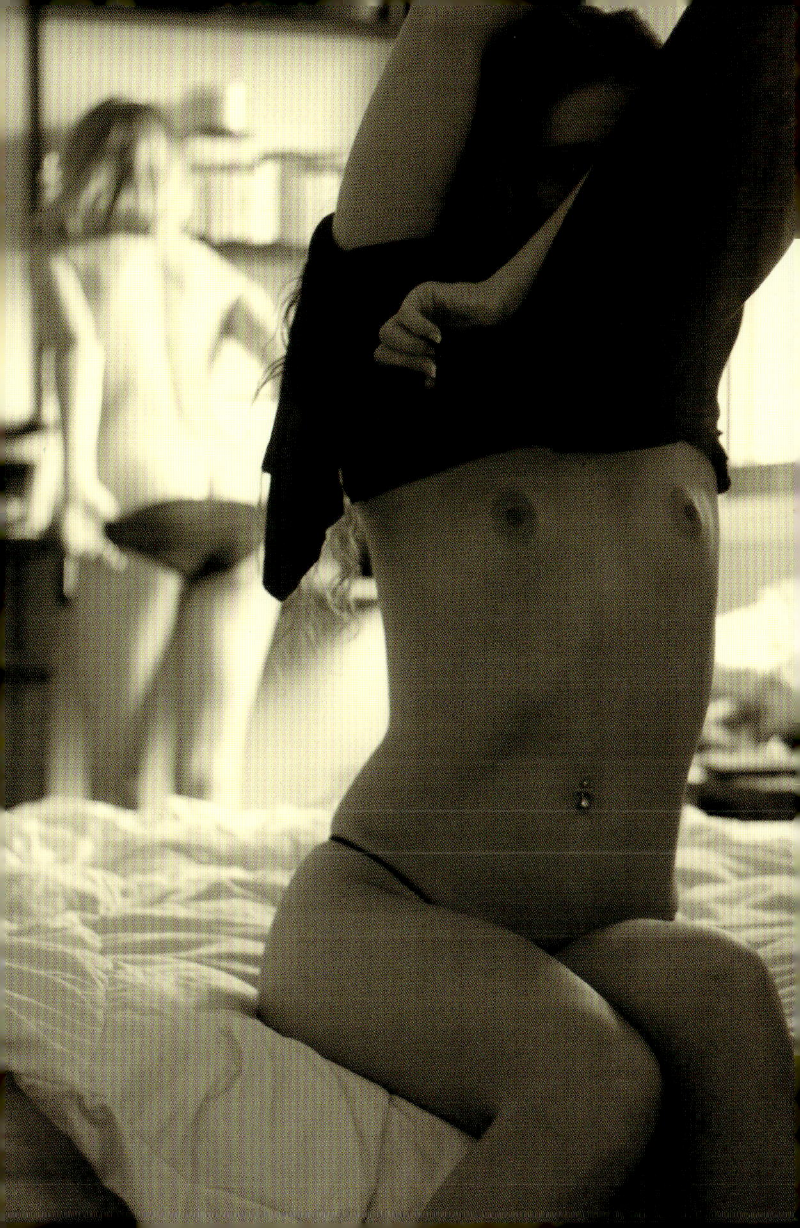

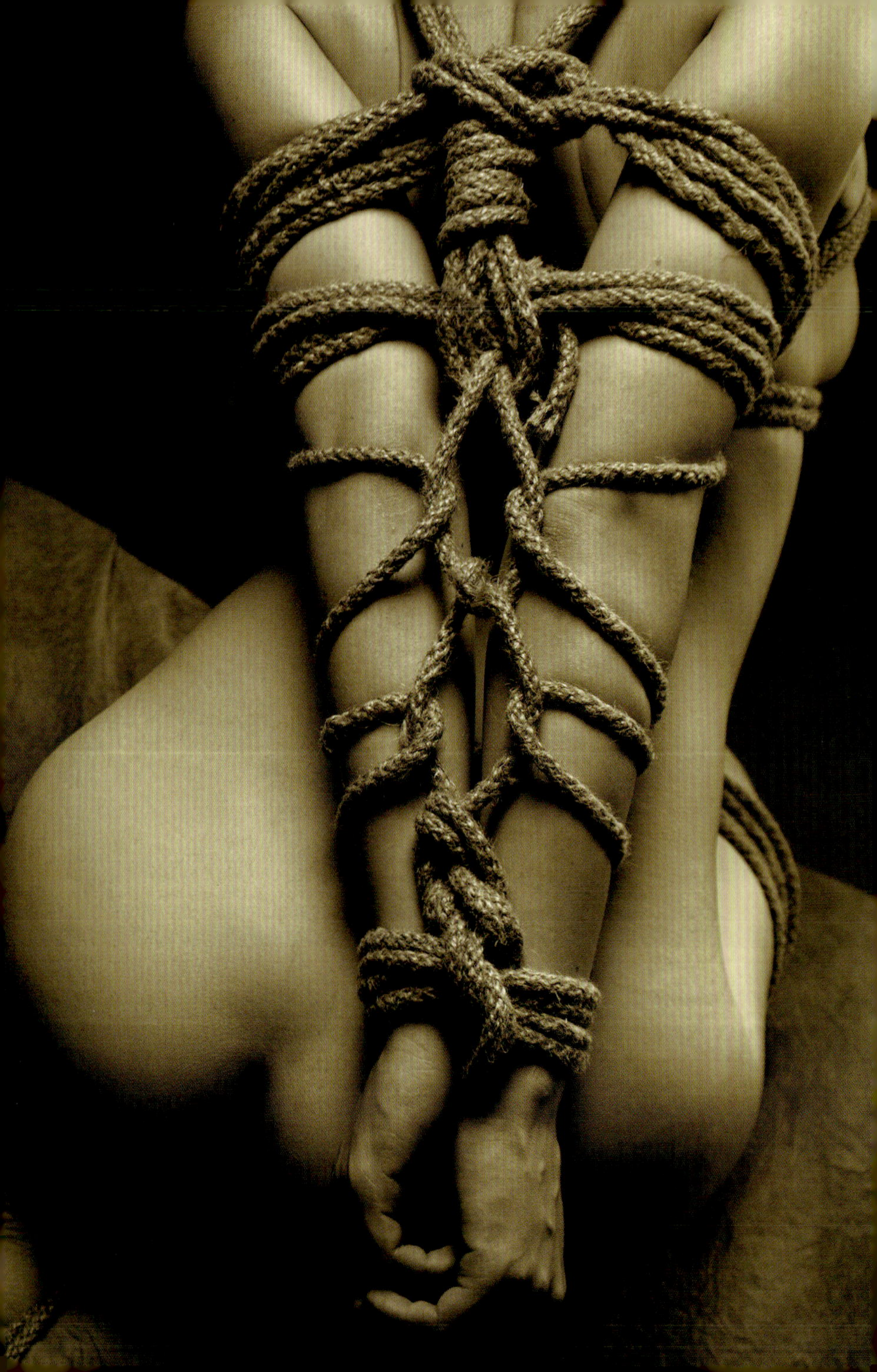

vlad gansovsky

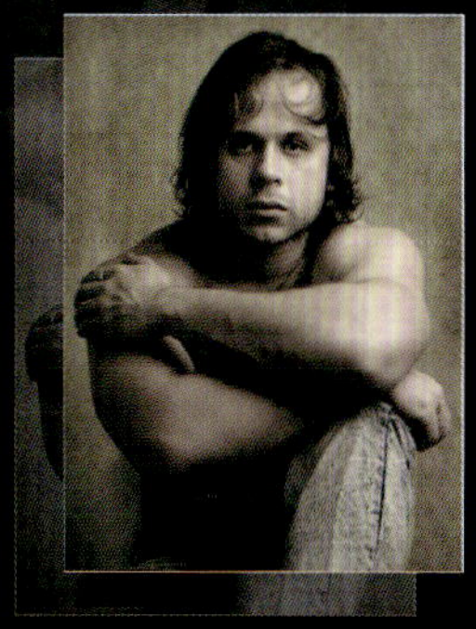

RUSSIAN PHOTOGRAPHER Vlad Gansovsky seeks maximum openness – not only spiritual but also physical. He aspires to reveal and demonstrate those things usually perceived as taboo. In photography, his interests lies mainly in people and the way they relate to one another, and in emotions and intimacy, which he likes to capture within his frame.

www.surart.ru
portait by Neoromantika

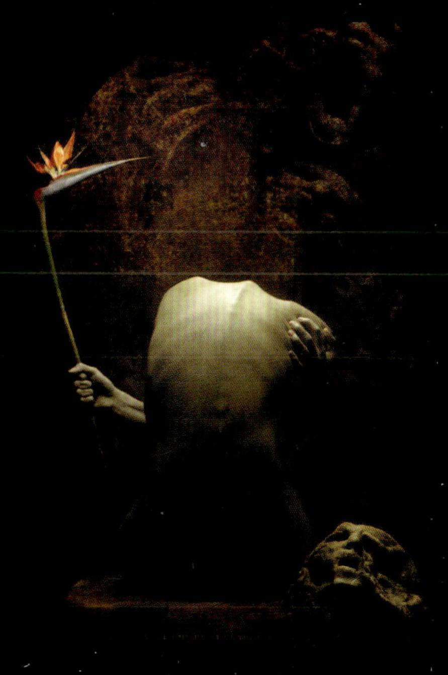

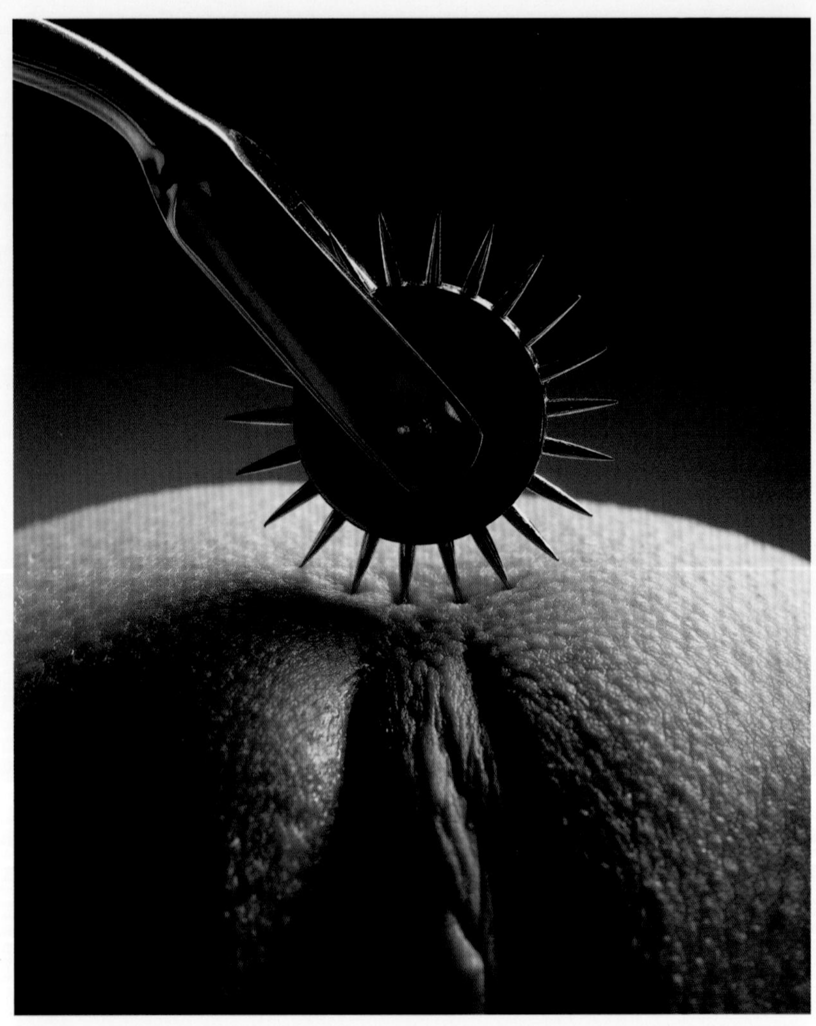

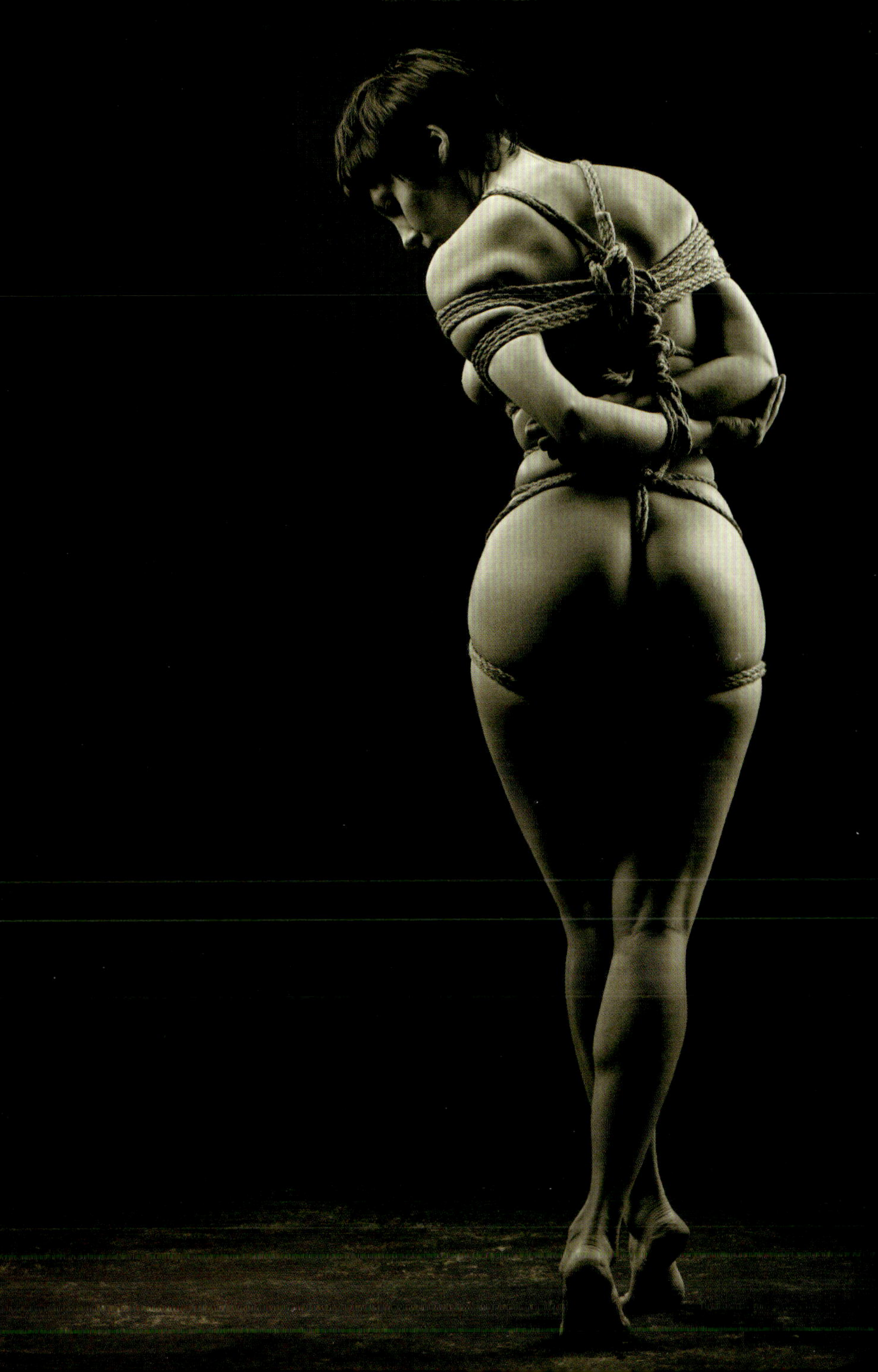

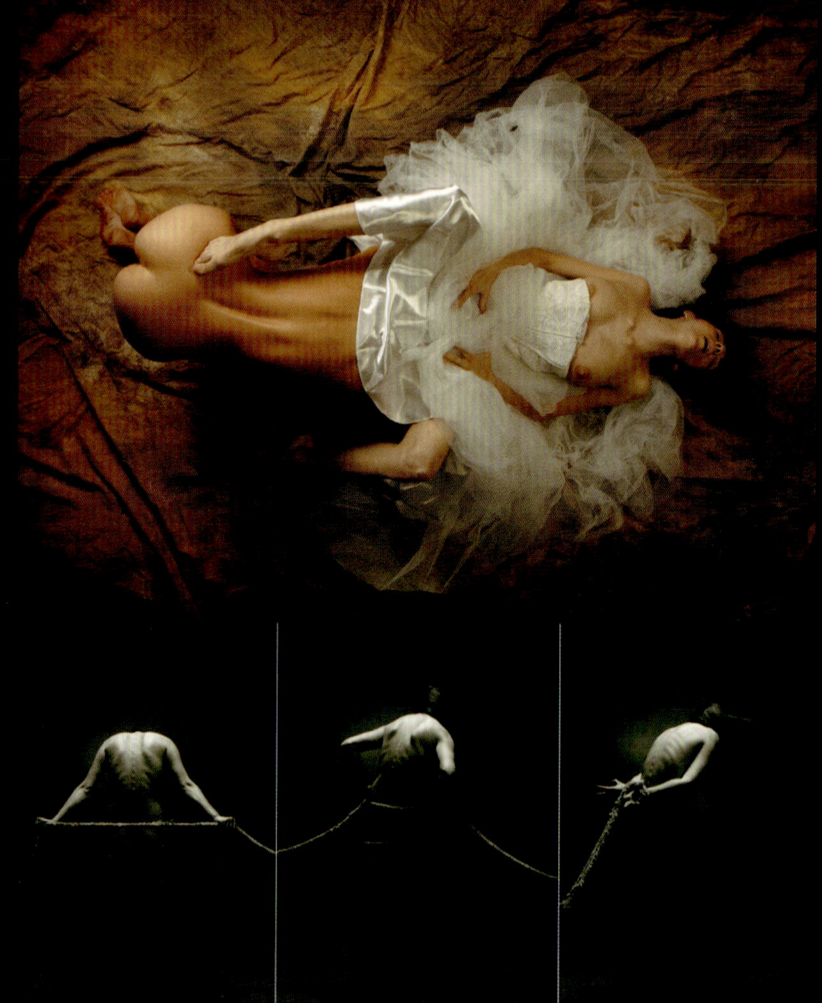

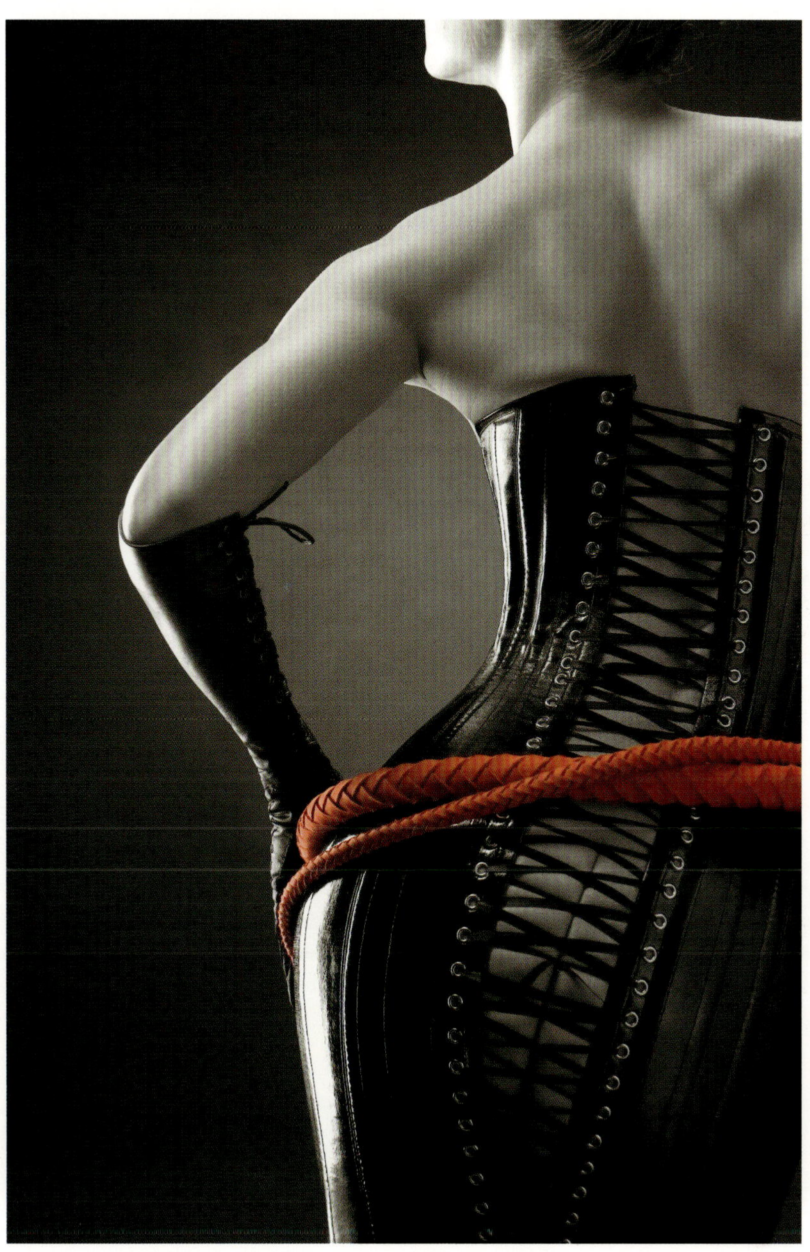

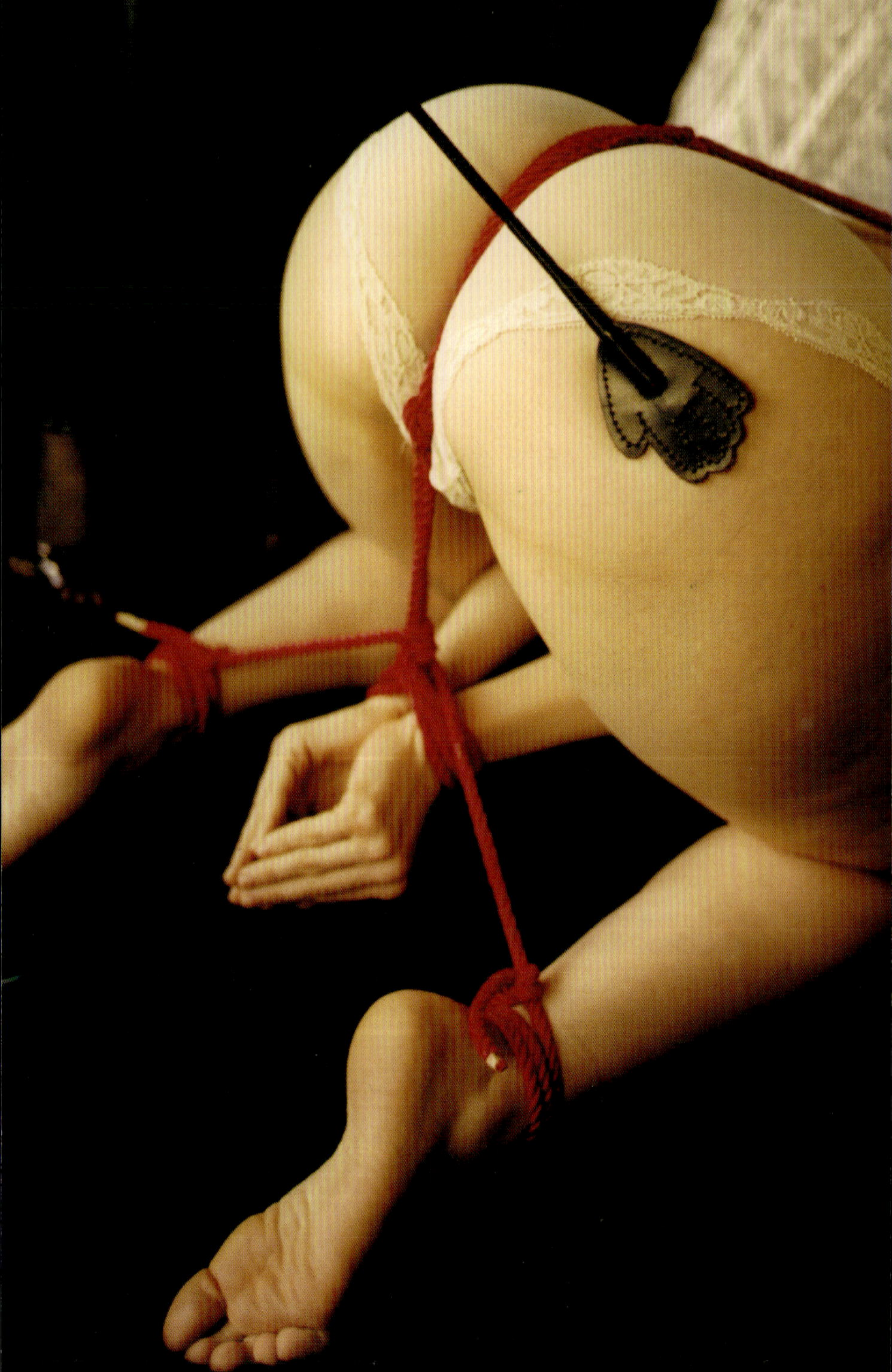

charles gatewood

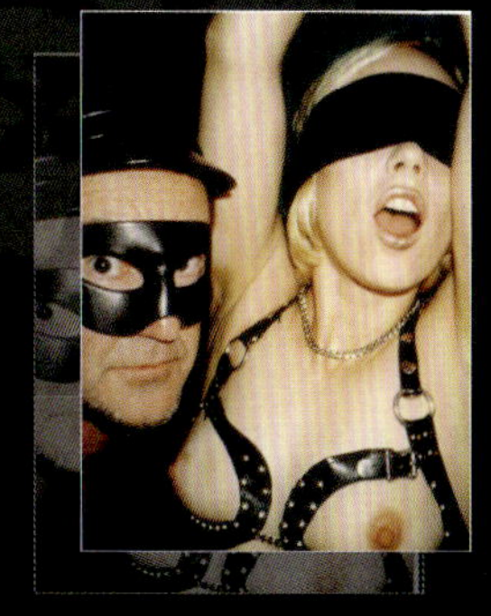

GATEWOOD HAS BEEN CALLED the 'family photographer of America's sexual underground' and has documented alternative culture for over forty-five years. His books include *Sidetripping* (with William S. Burroughs), *Pushing Ink* (with Spider Webb), *Hellfire*, *Primitives*, *The Body and Beyond*, *True Love*, *Badlands*, *Messy Girls* and *Photography for Perverts*. He has been given many awards and been the subject of two documentary films. He lives in San Francisco where his underground adventures continue.

www.charlesgatewood.com

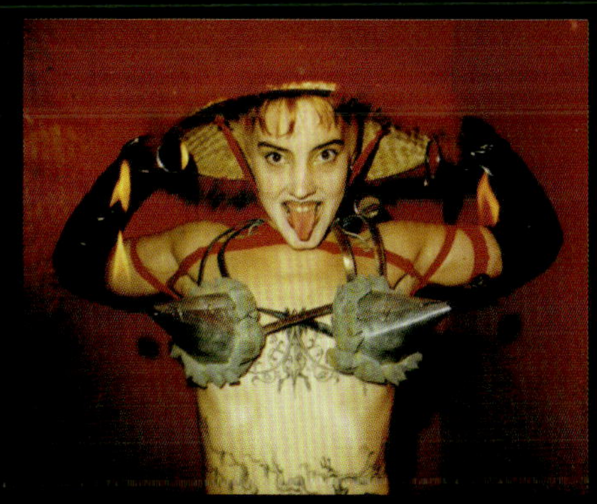

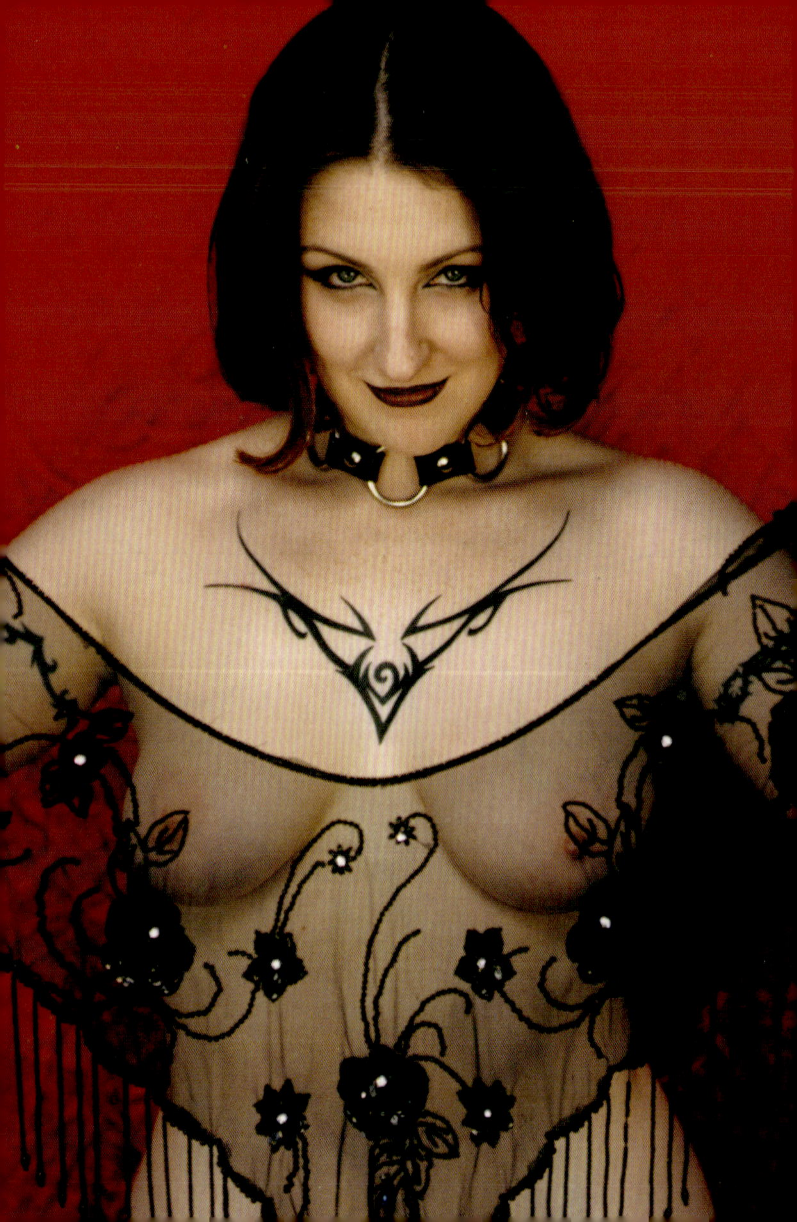

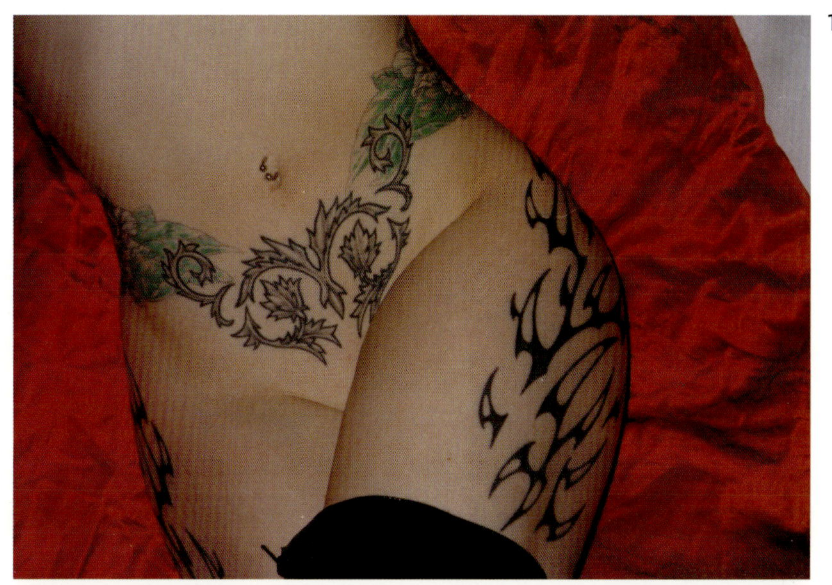

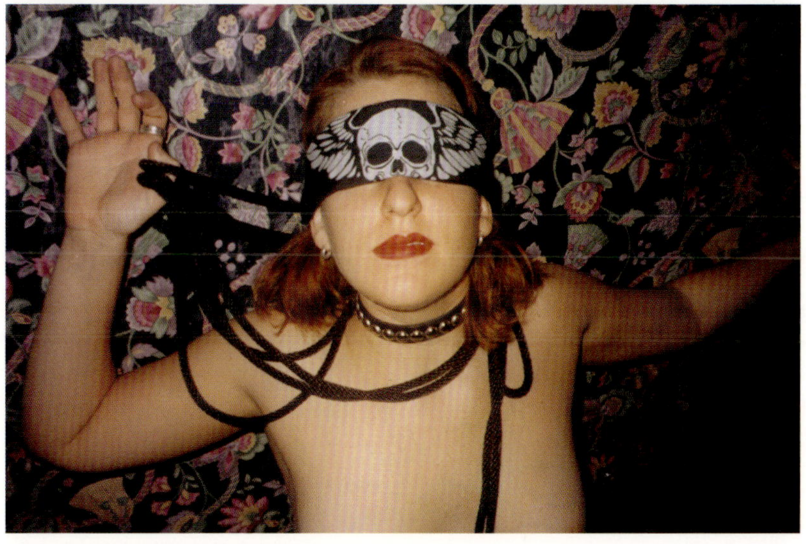

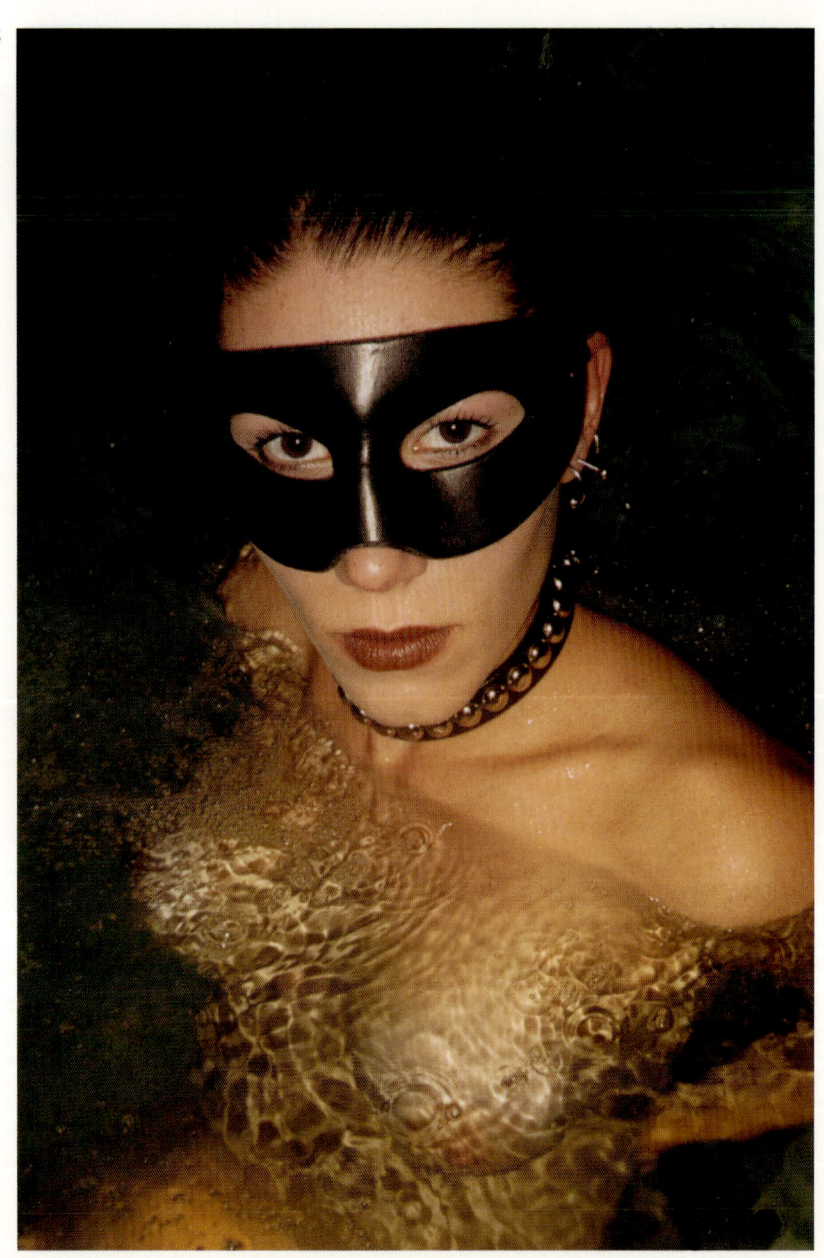

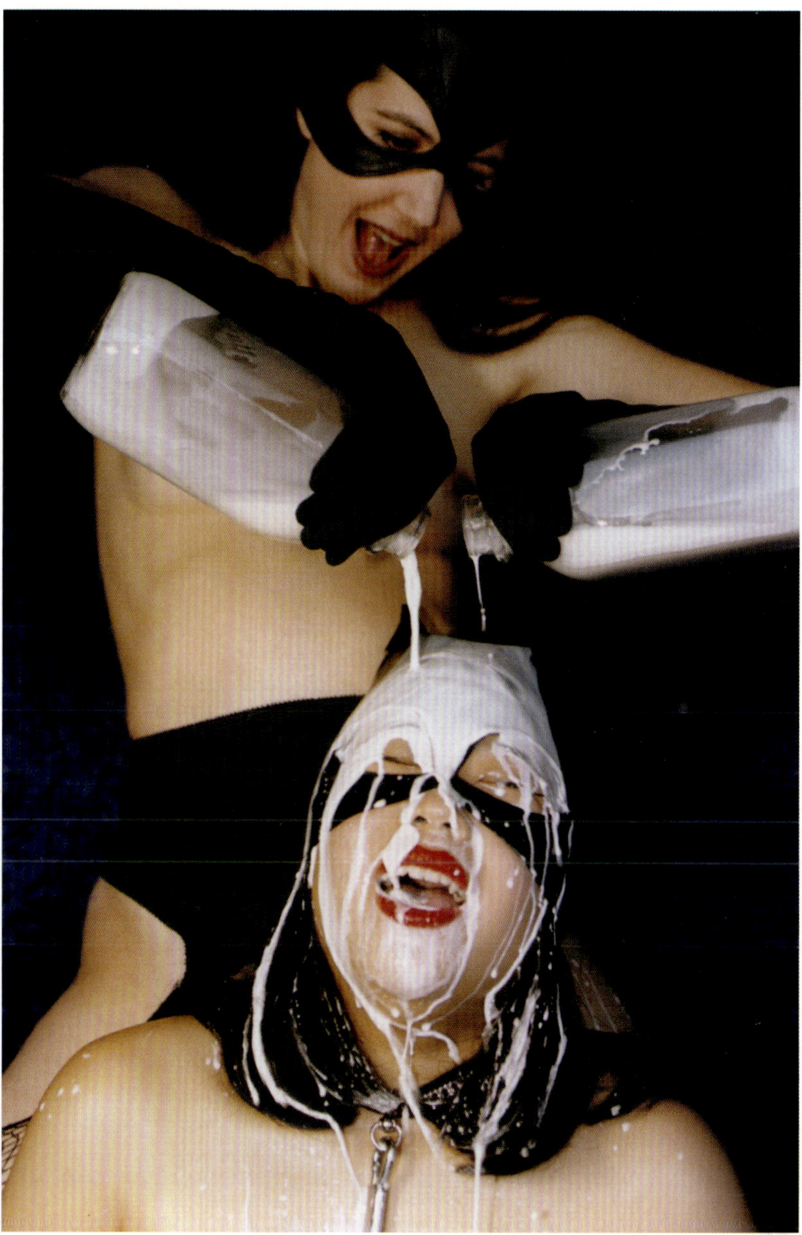

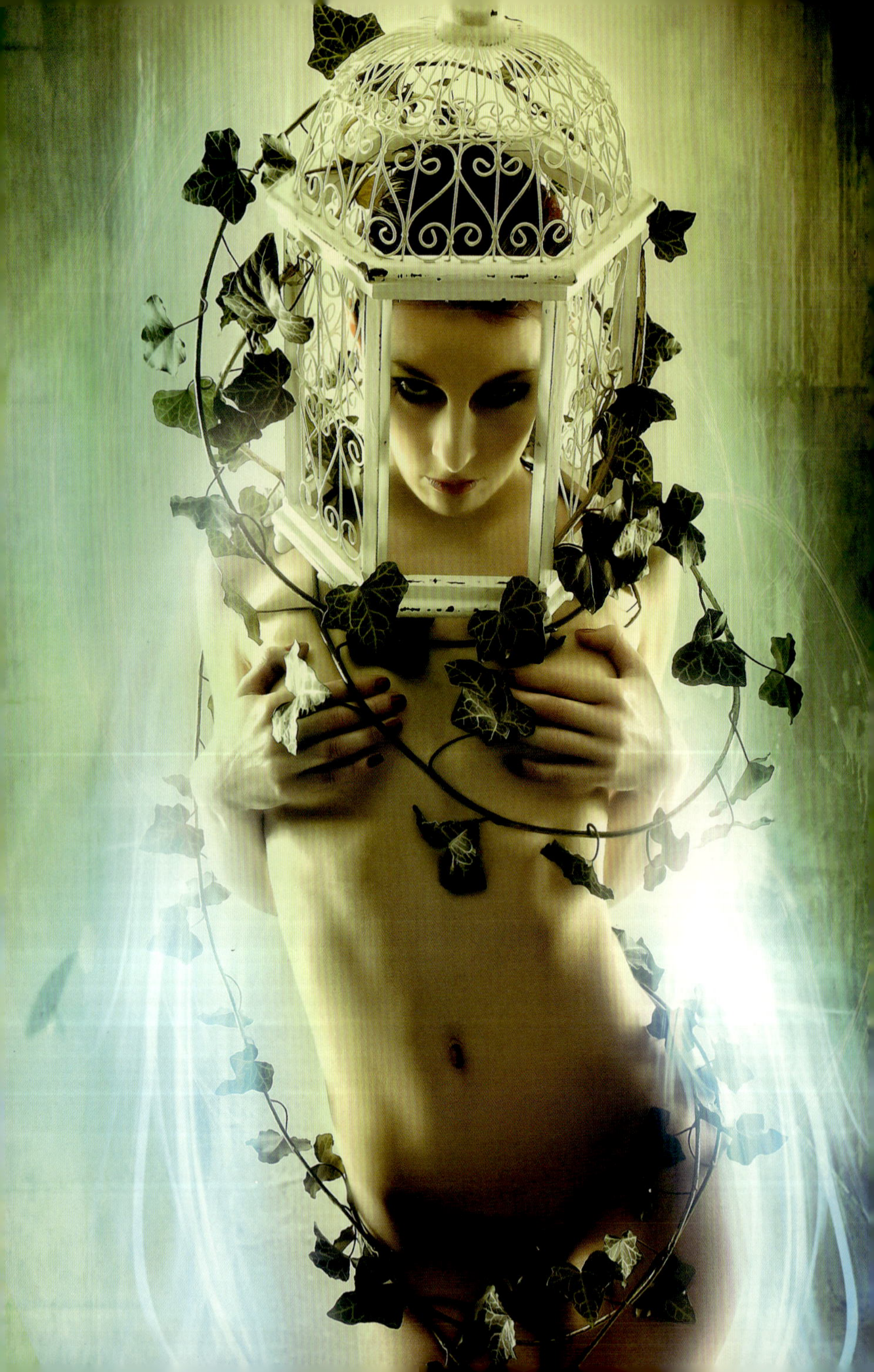

stefan gesell

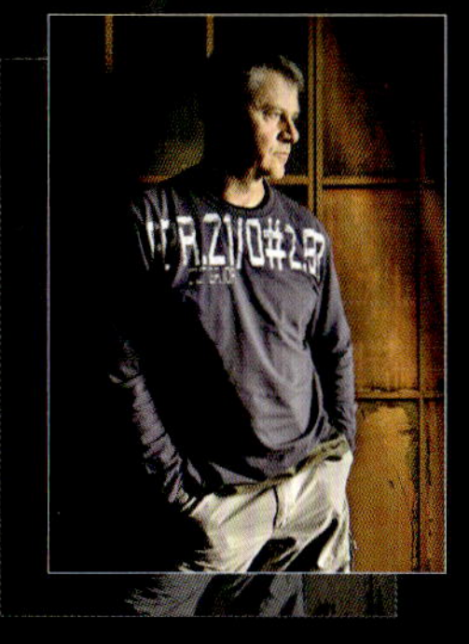

STEFAN WAS BORN IN northern Bavaria in 1959. His early creativity was restricted to house walls and car bonnets. But his drawing sketches could never be contained by the page, and a larger canvas was required. It was only with the arrival of digital photography and an Agfa camera borrowed from his father, together with the universe of options opened by computer processing, that he came into his own. His photos have been widely published and are soon to be the subject of his own book.

www.fotosym.de

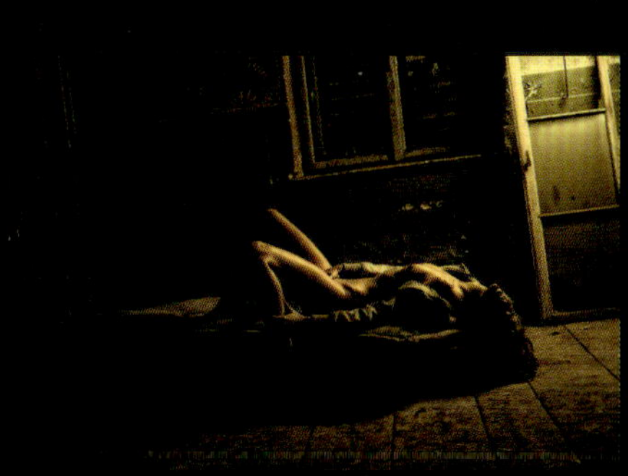

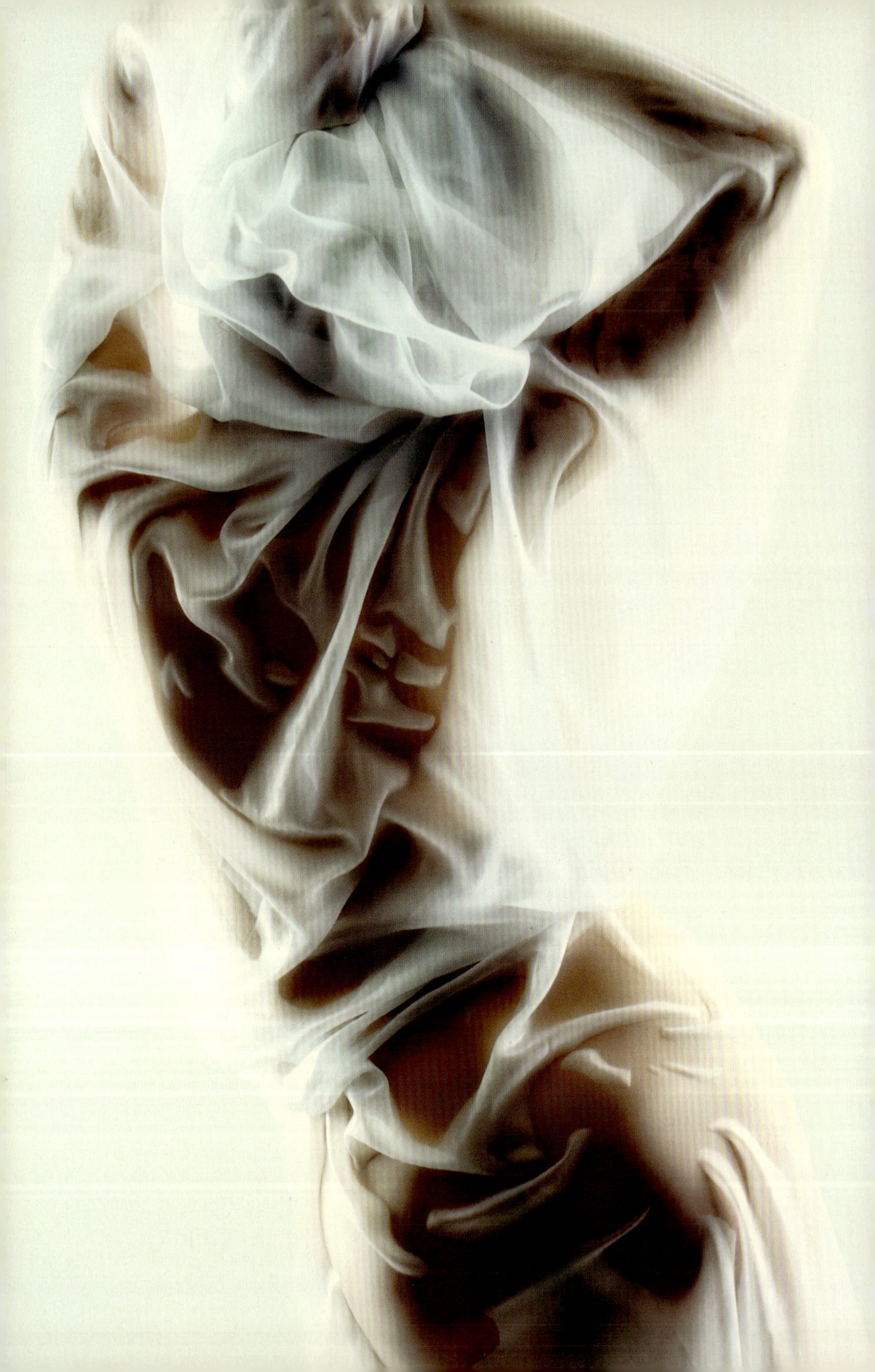

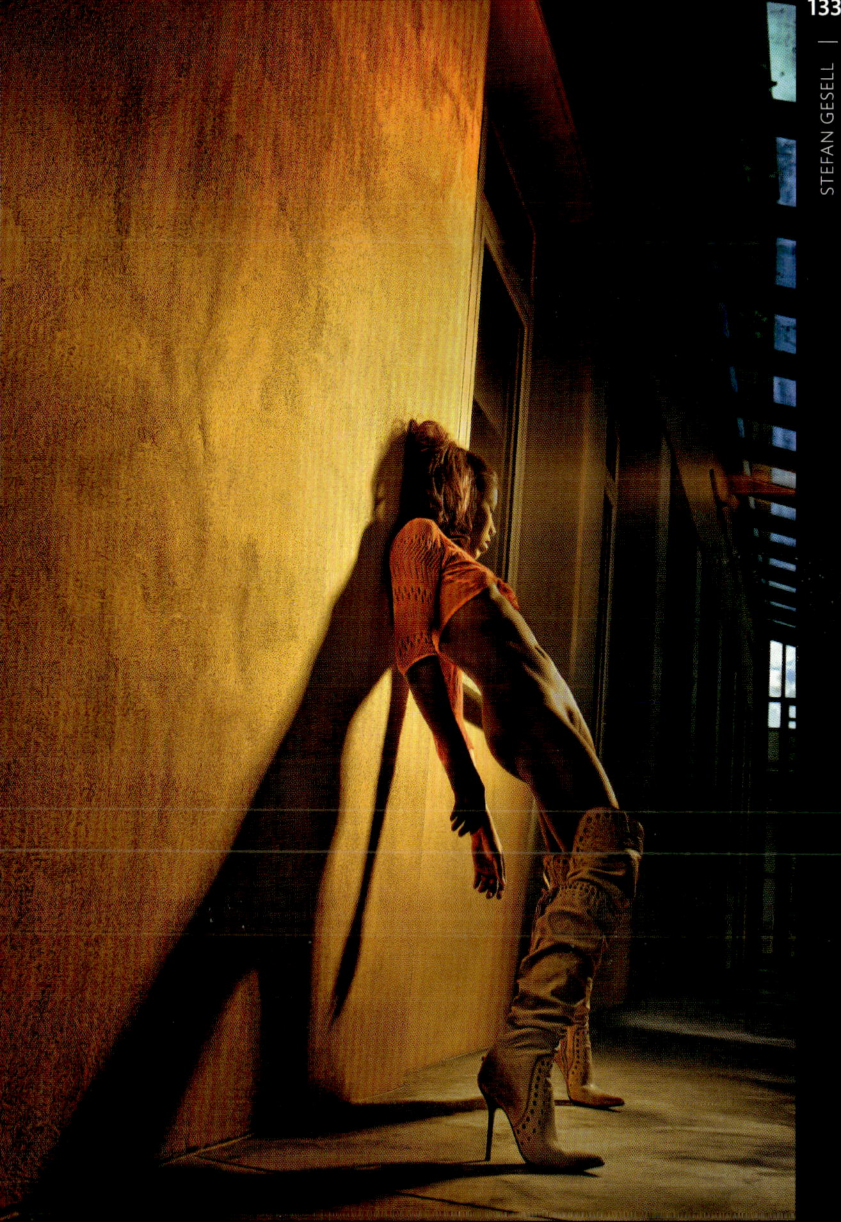

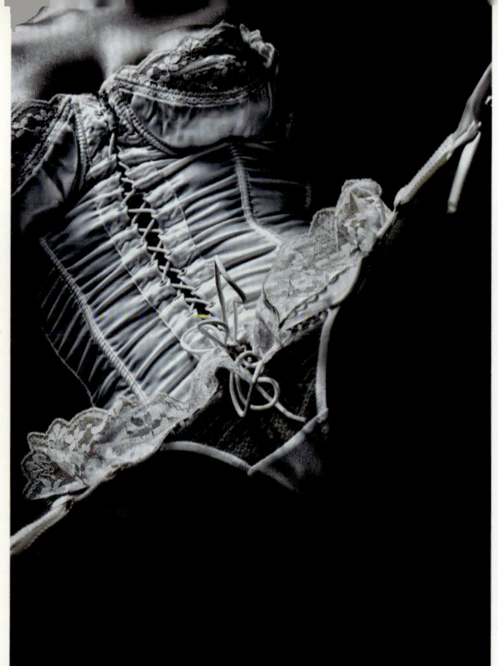

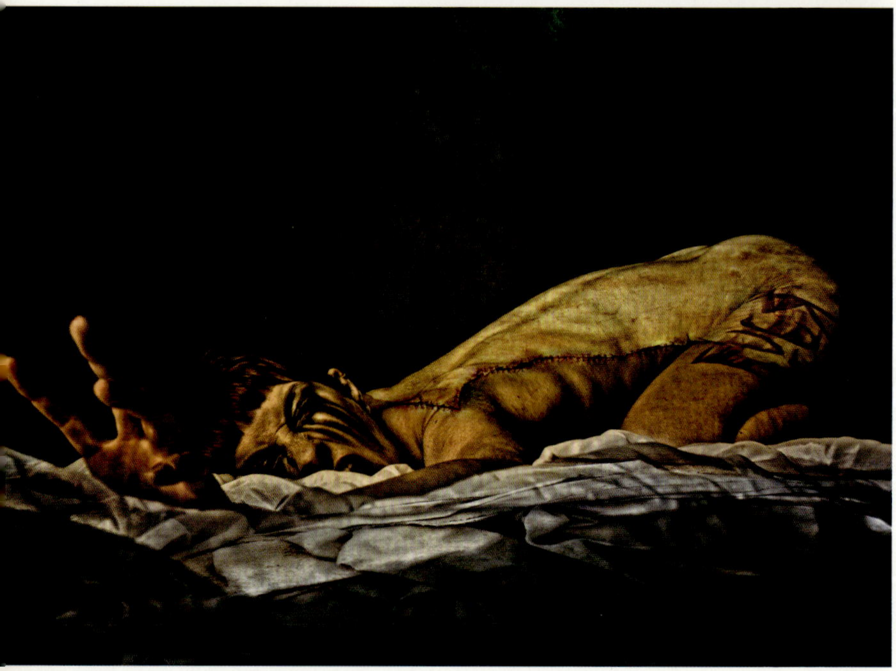

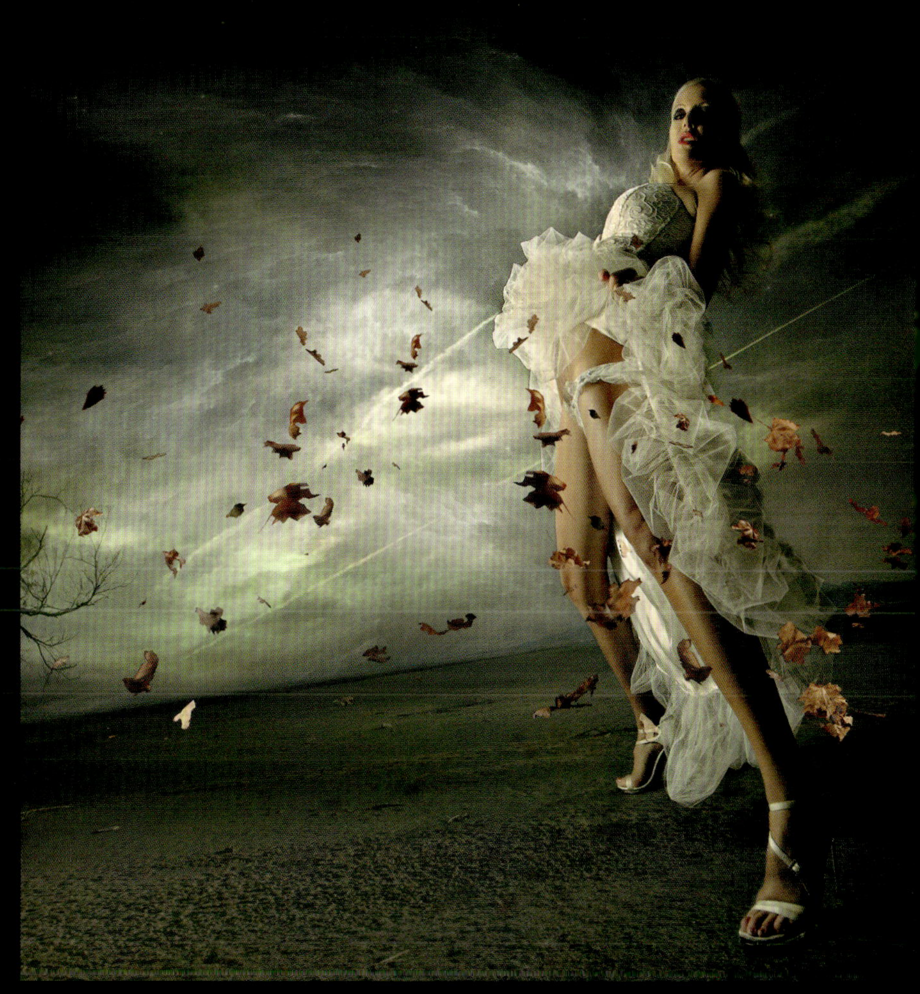

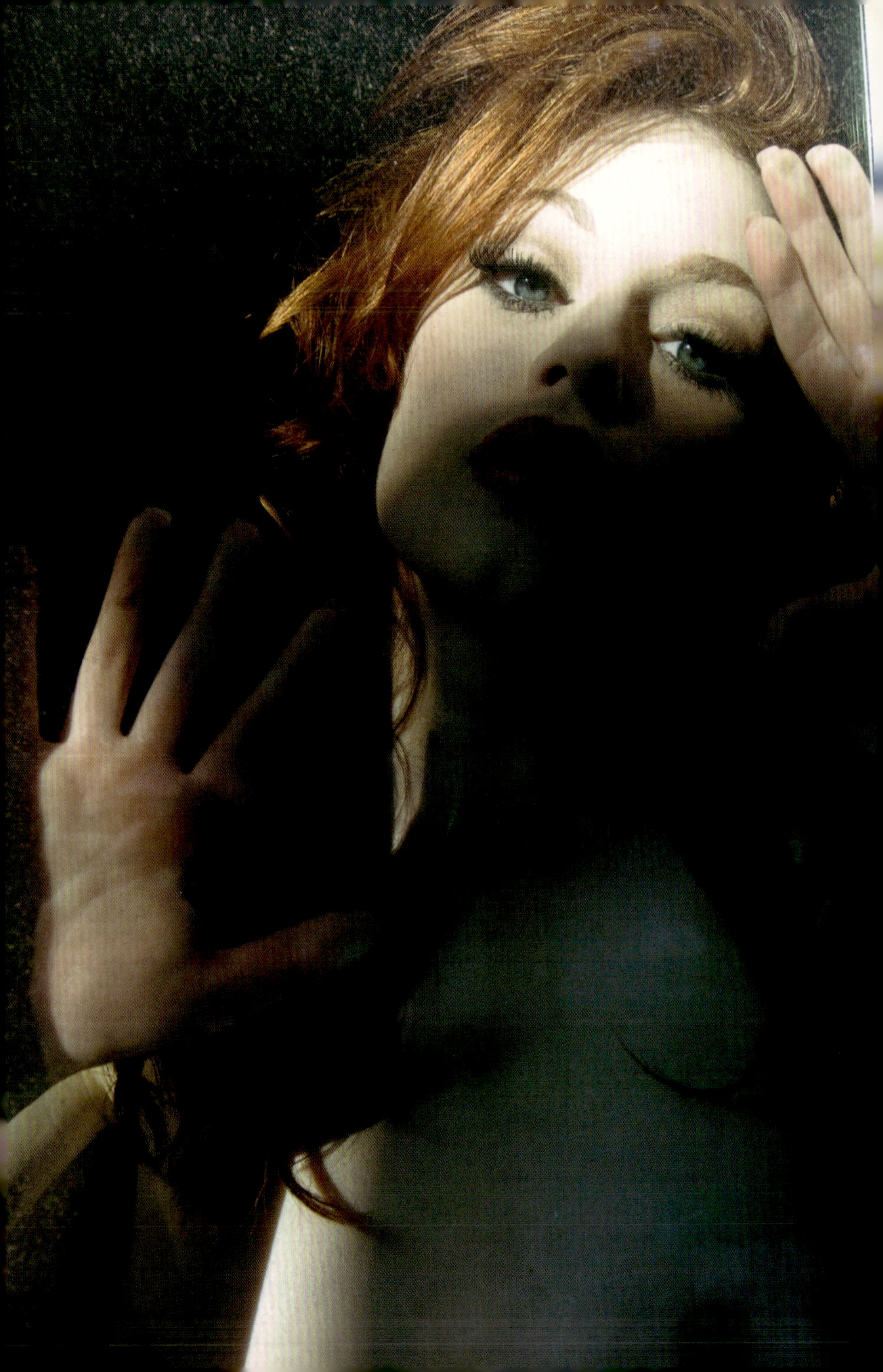

steve diet goedde

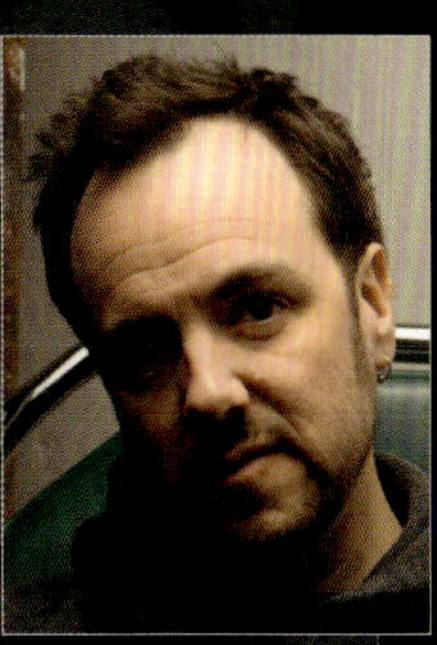

STEVE DIET GOEDDE (pronounced 'die-it geddy') has been a fine art erotic photographer for nearly twenty years. He is known for his subtle approach to photographing alternative fashion in a very ethereal, down-to-earth style. His attention to composition and to black-and-white tonal quality have given him the title of the Ansel Adams of erotic photography. He established his photographic style in the early 1990s in Chicago, where he photographed the contents of his first book, *The Beauty of Fetish* (Edition Stemmle), which was released in 1998. That same year, Steve relocated to Los Angeles where he continued to define his evolving style. This west coast work was later compiled in his second book, *The Beauty of Fetish: Volume II*, in 2001. In 2006, Slish Pix released a DVD compilation of his work entitled *Living Through Steve Diet Goedde*. In 2009, Steve collaborated with French composer Robert Waechter on a CD entitled *GoeddeConcerto* (ReadyMade Music) in which the Concert Master of the Nice Philharmonic Orchestra interprets twenty-one of Steve's photographs into twenty-one mini-concertos.

www.stevedietgoedde.com

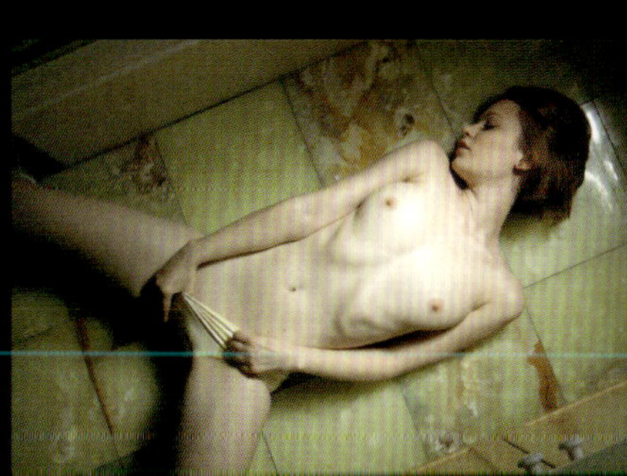

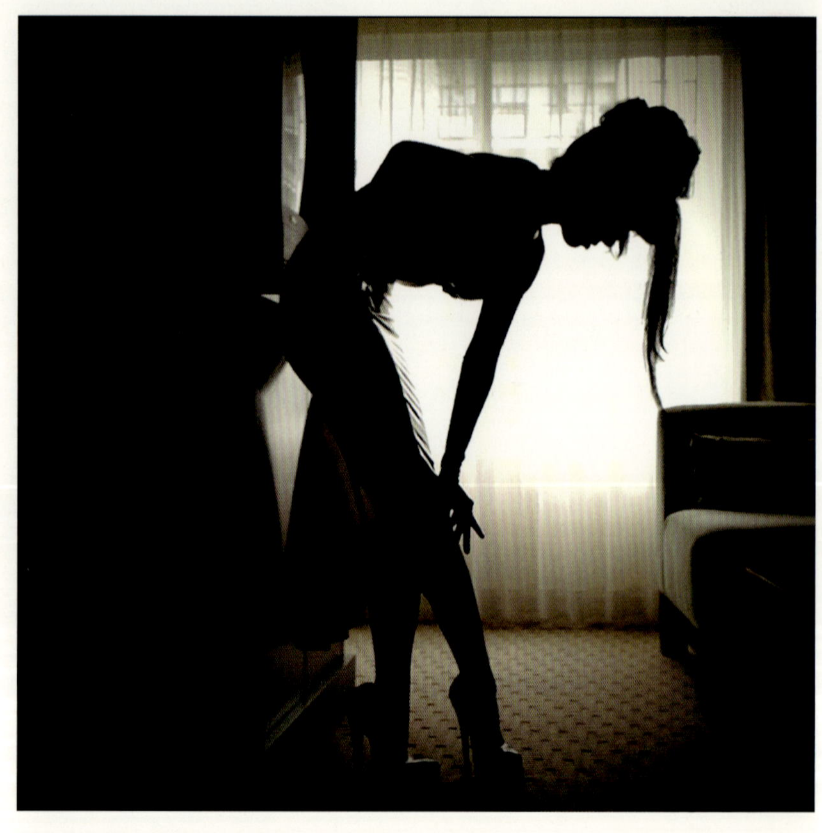

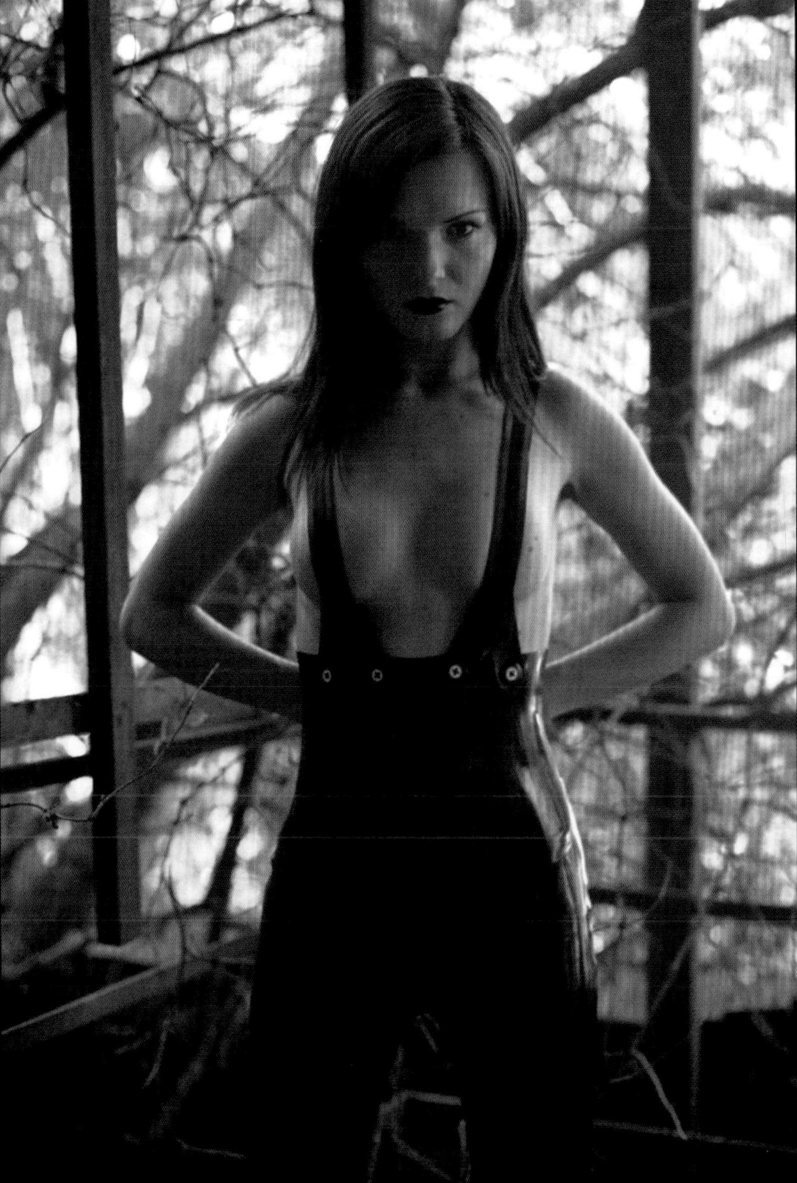

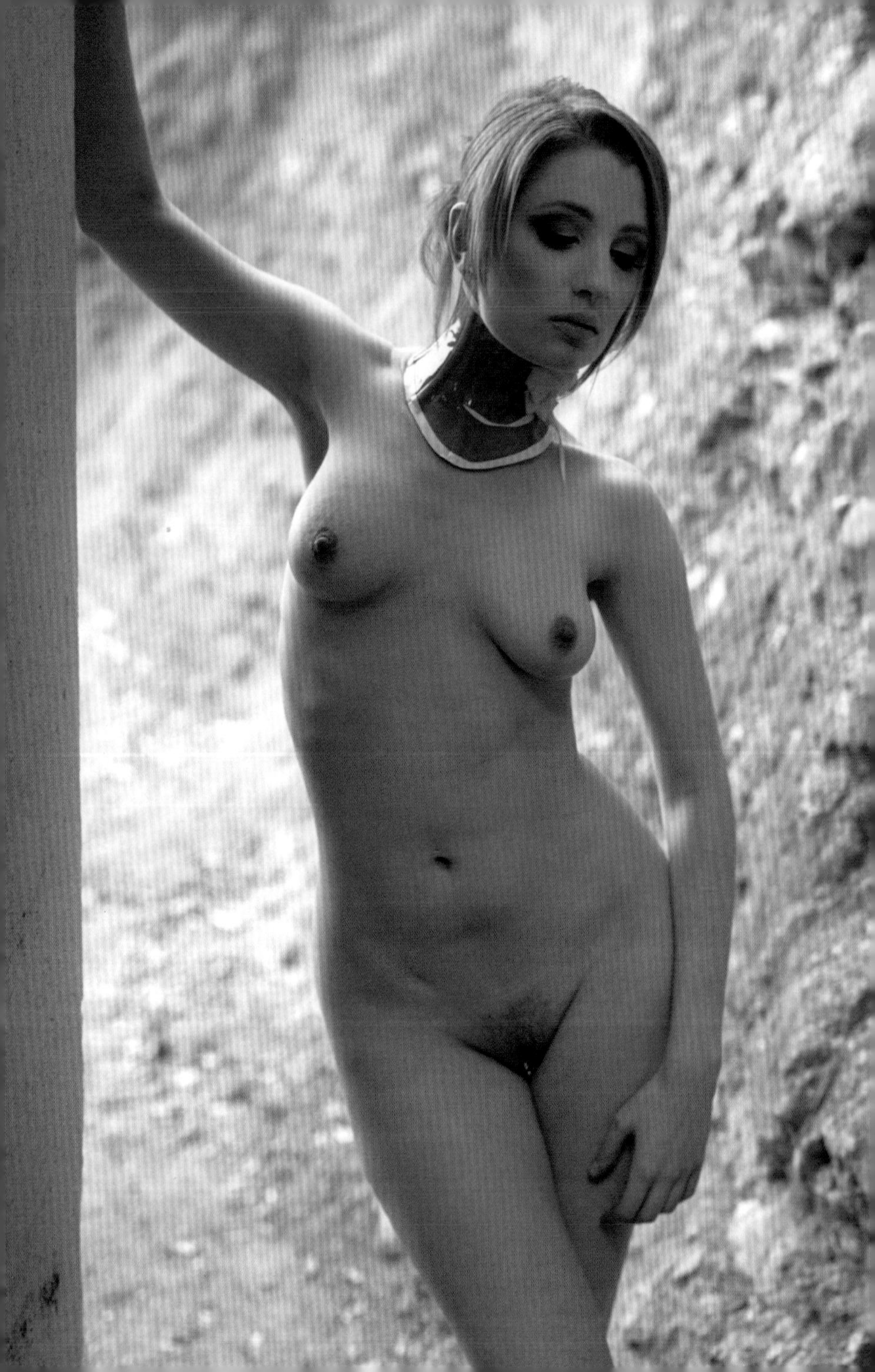

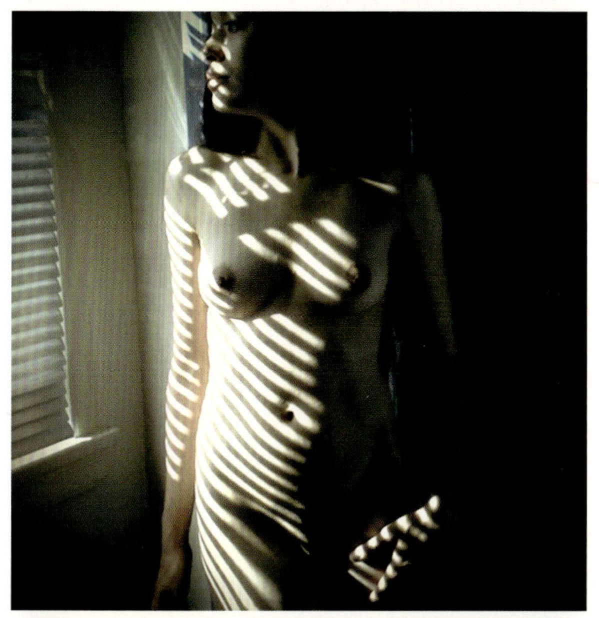

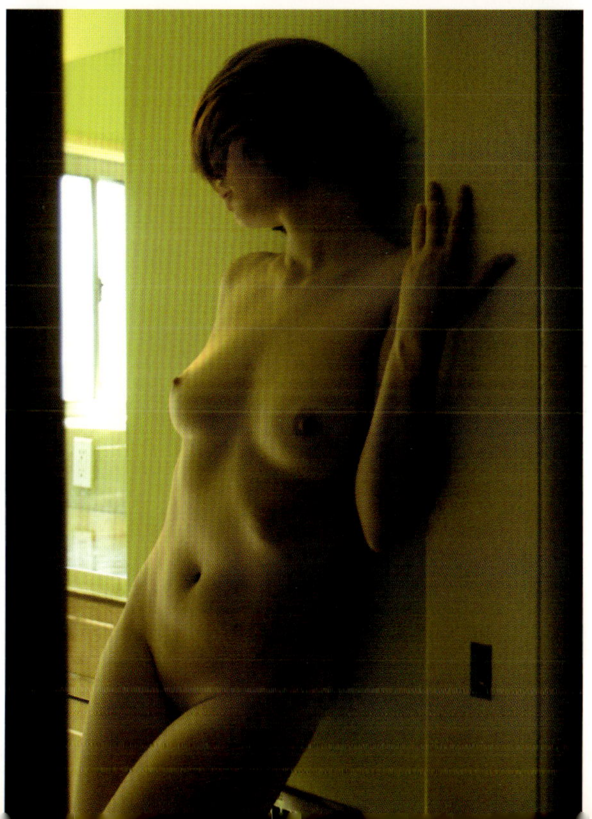

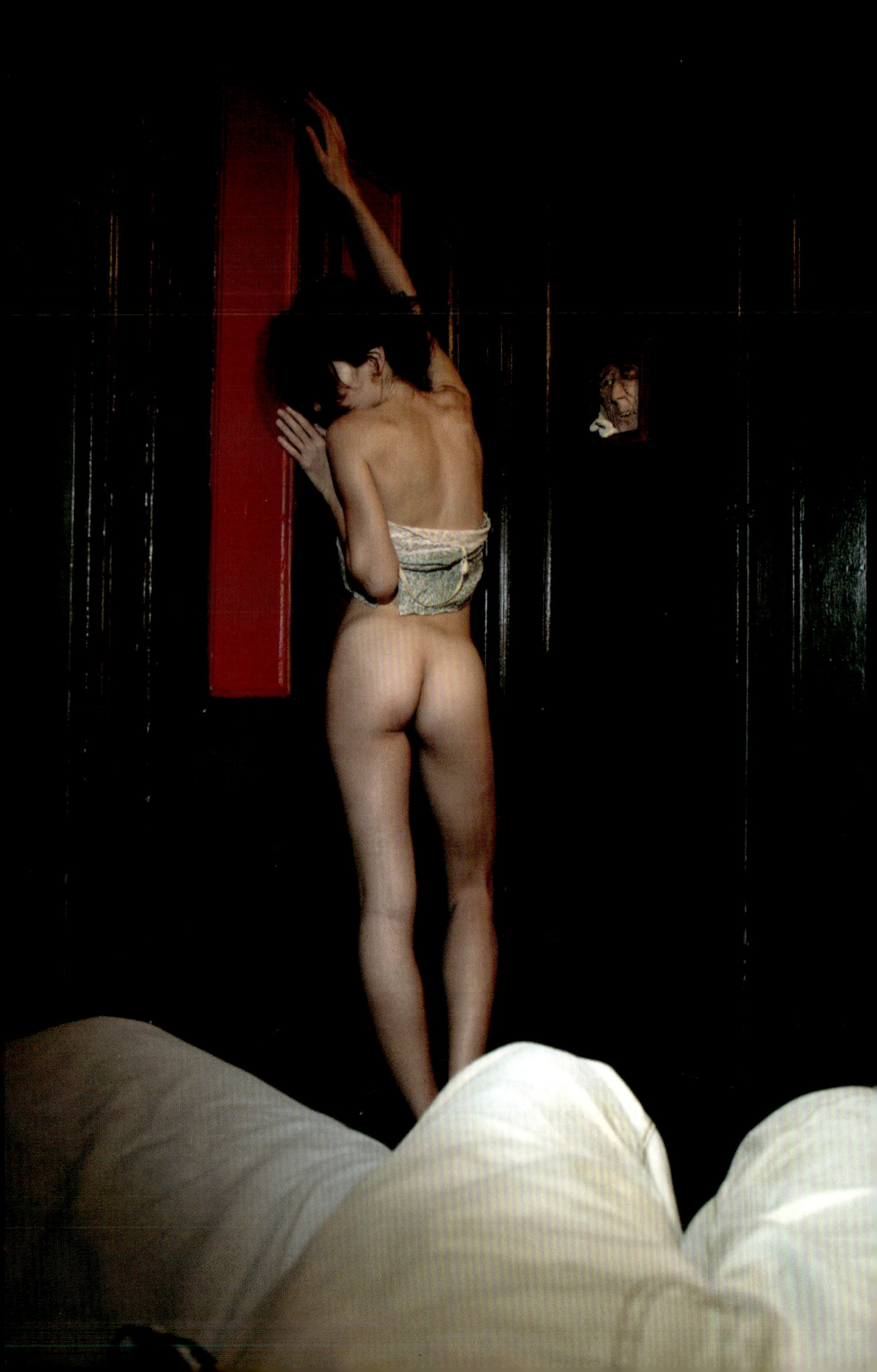

peter gorman

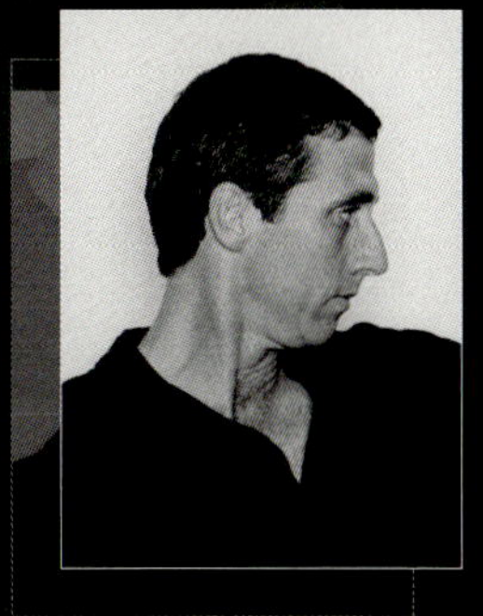

PETER WAS BORN IN 1961, in Binghamton, NY. He moved with his wife Rachel to New York City in 1994. His first book was published in 1991. His titles include *Touch*, *Stripped Naked*, *Naked Rooms* and *Naked in Apartment 7*. He has been featured in many other books of erotic photography and in all the major magazines in the field.

www.petergorman.com

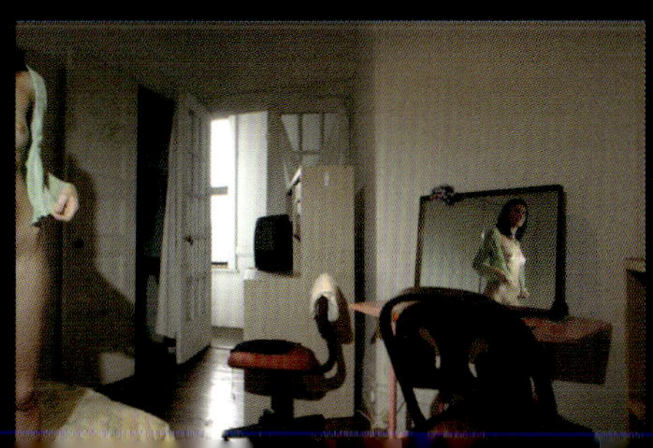

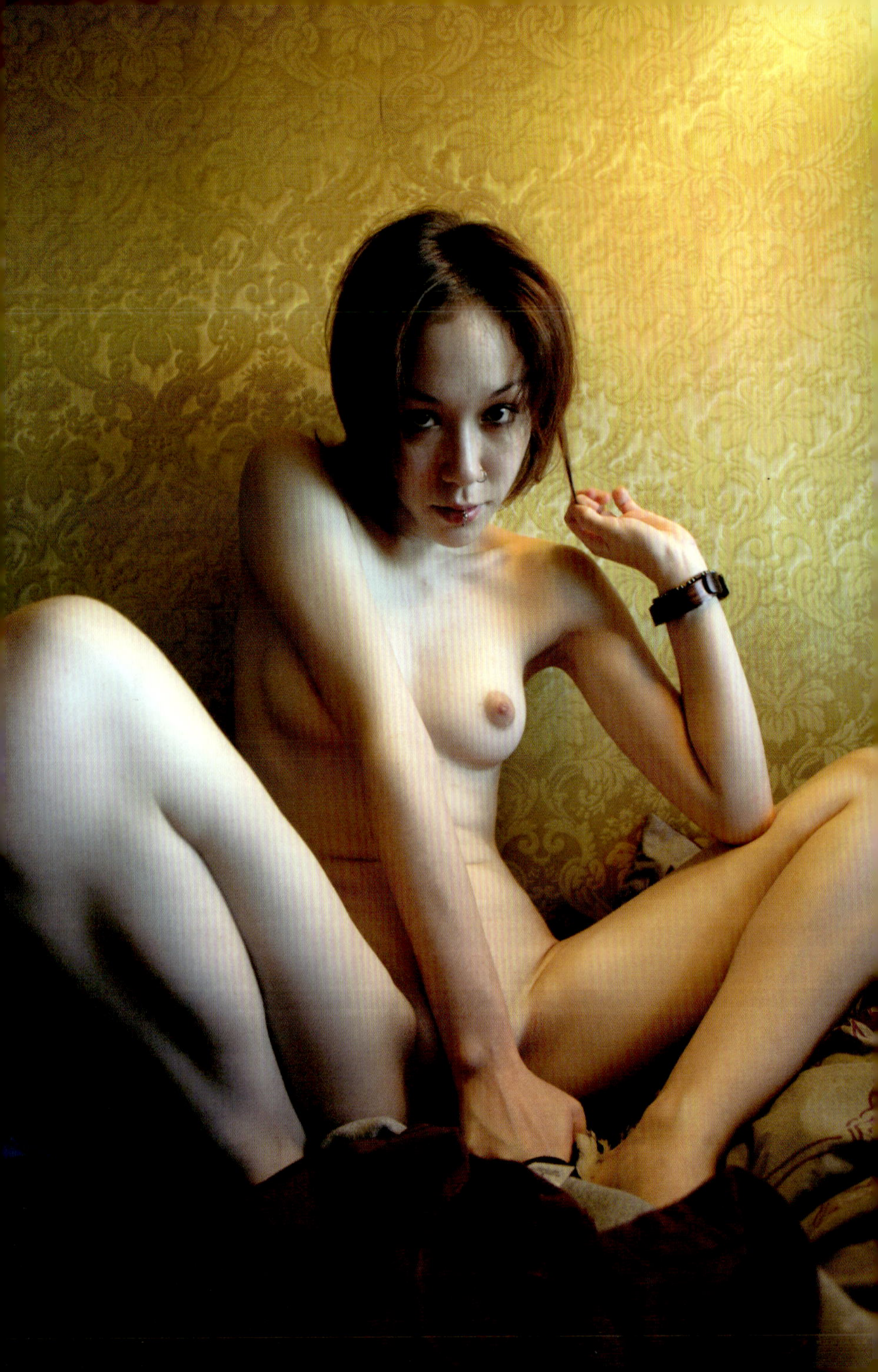

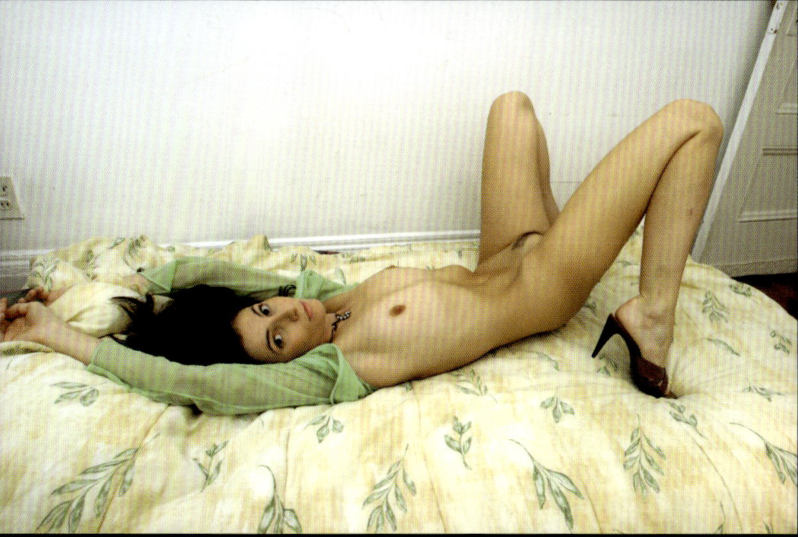

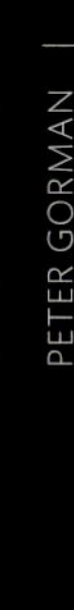
PETER GORMAN

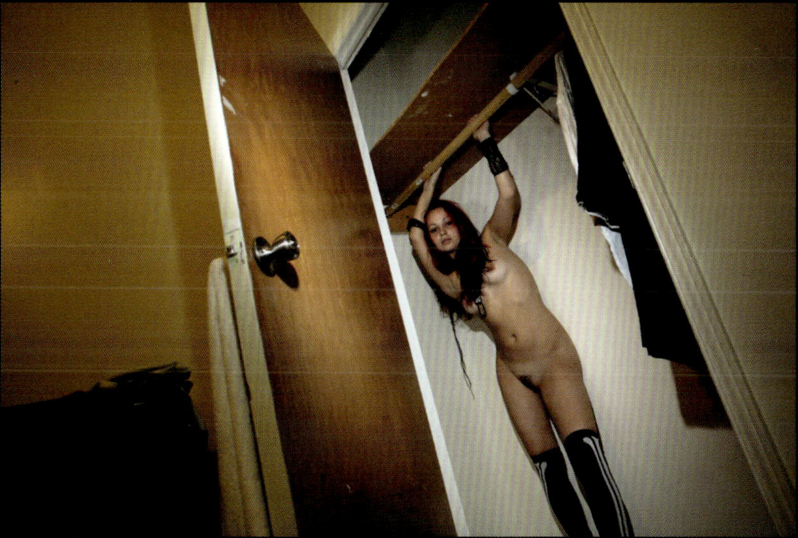

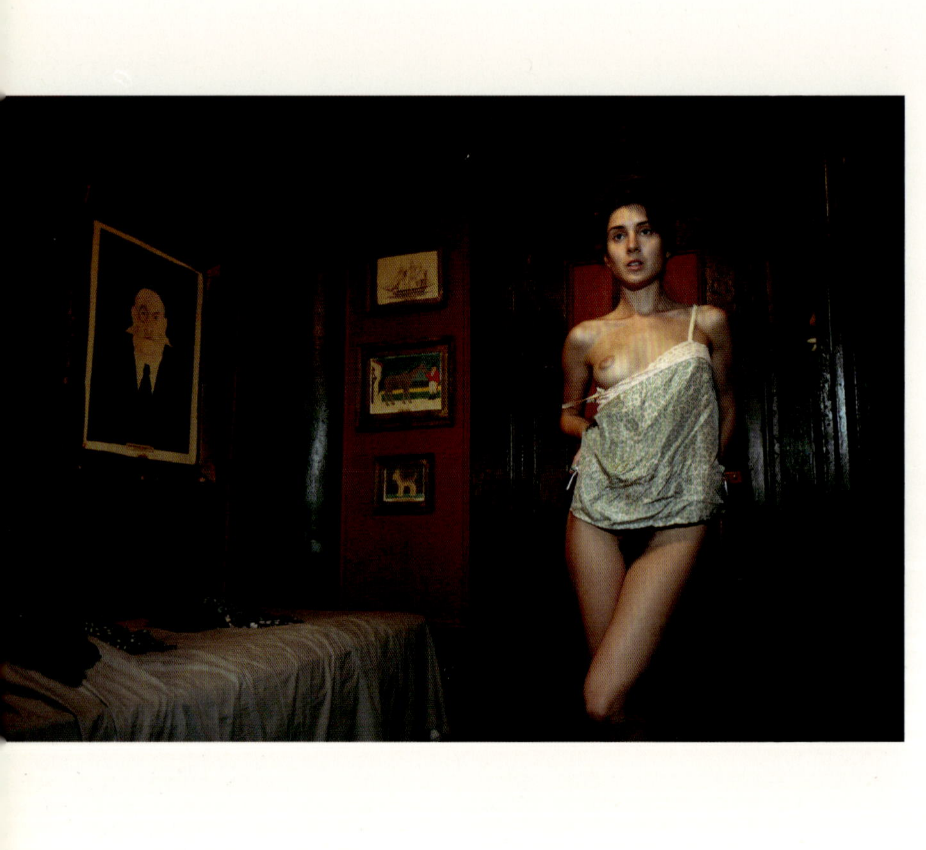

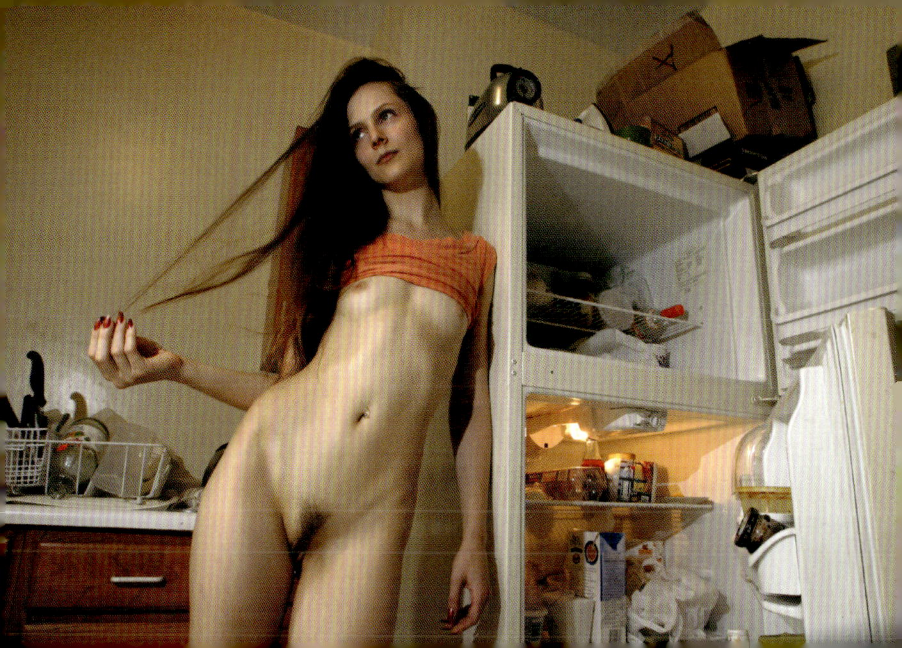

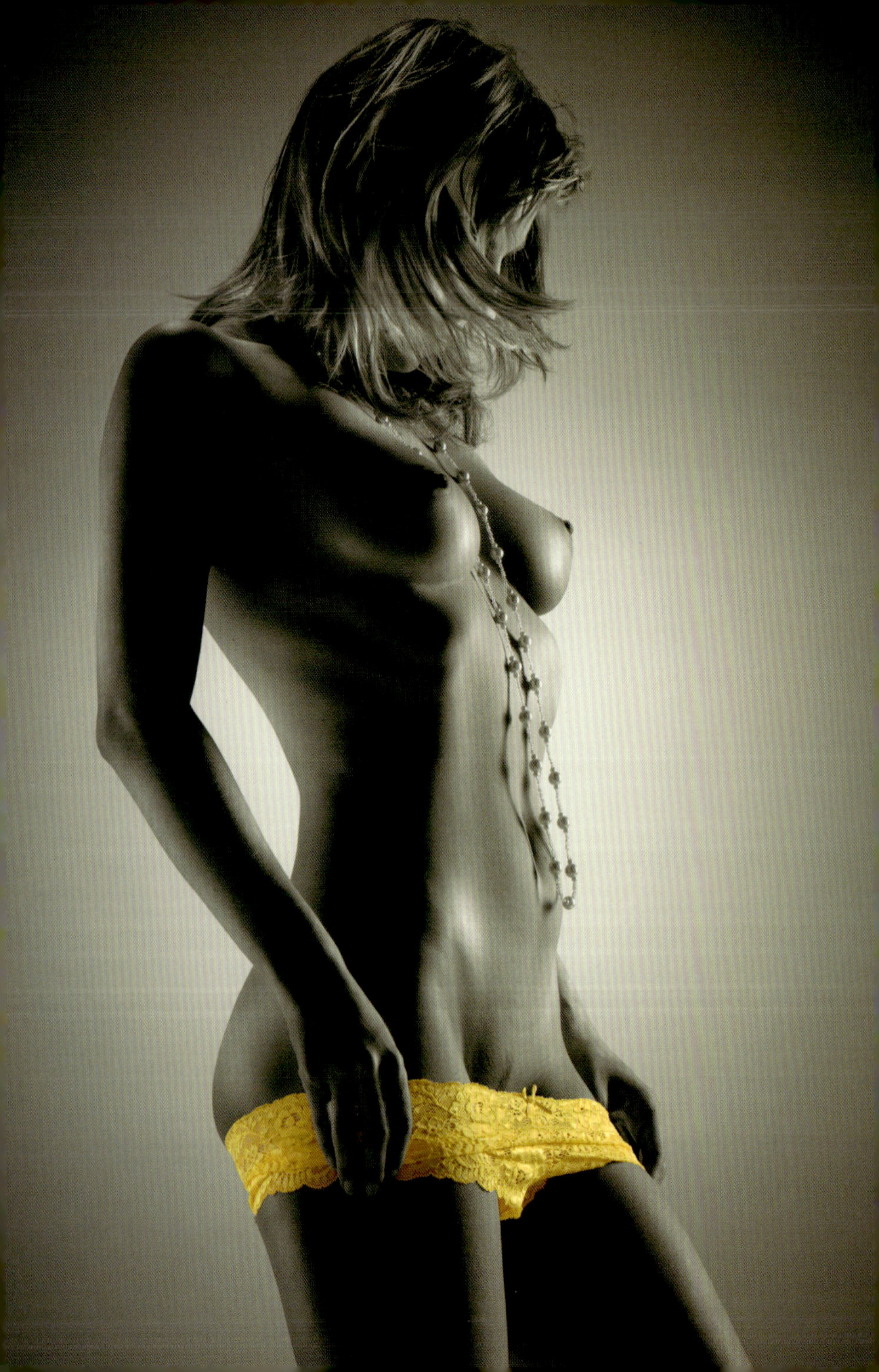

gero gröschel

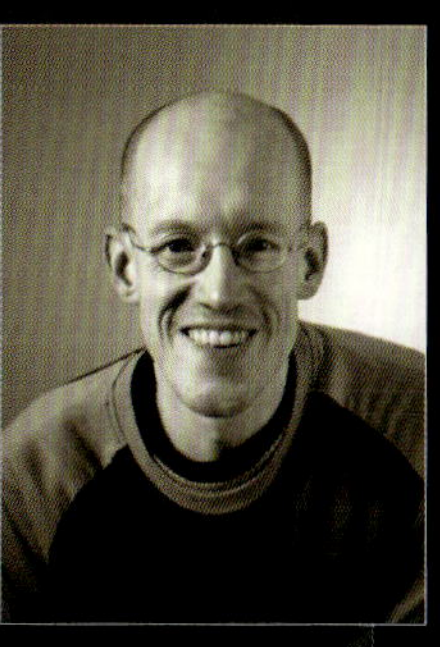

GERO GRÖSCHEL LIVES IN GERMANY. He works as a commercial photographer and photo artist. He stages and shoots photographs that are mostly sexy, but that alwyas have an aesthetic claim. His pictures are striking and the parallels to advertising photography are not accidental. Reduction to the essential is an attribute of his way of working, which often adds a graphical component to his work. Whether classic or vanguard, his pictures are straight to the point. All works shown here have been produced in his studio, which gives him ideal conditions to achieve the often perfect lighting.

www.geroart.com

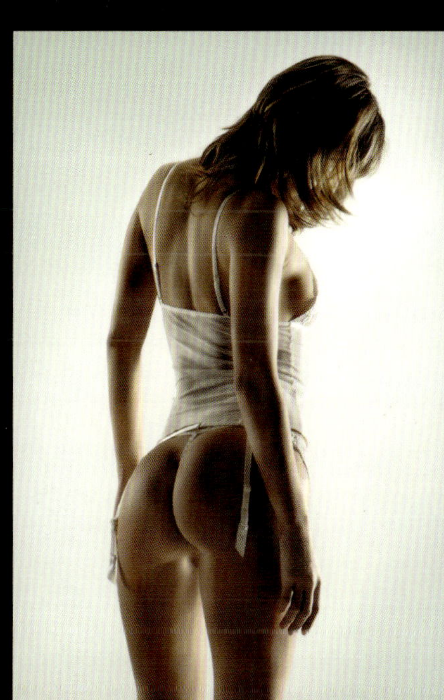

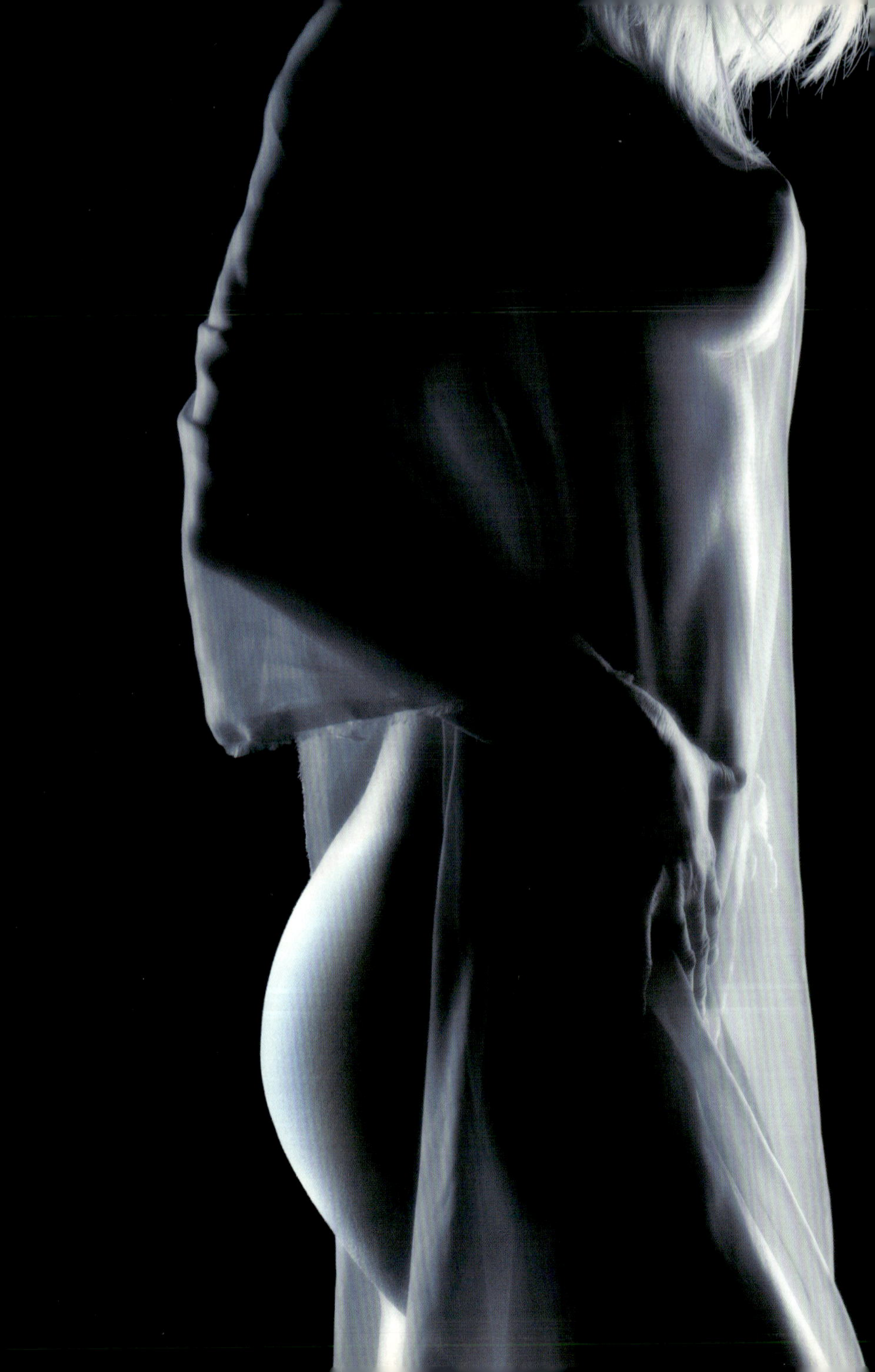

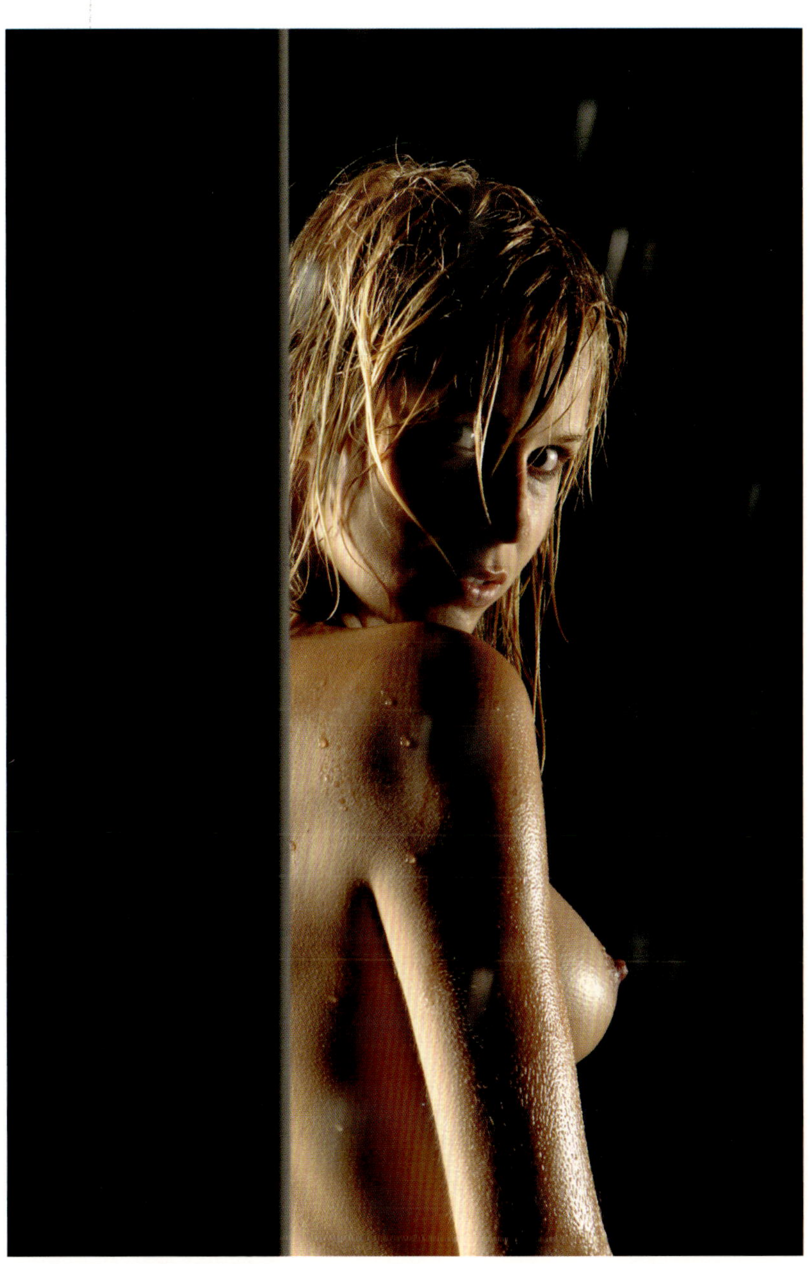

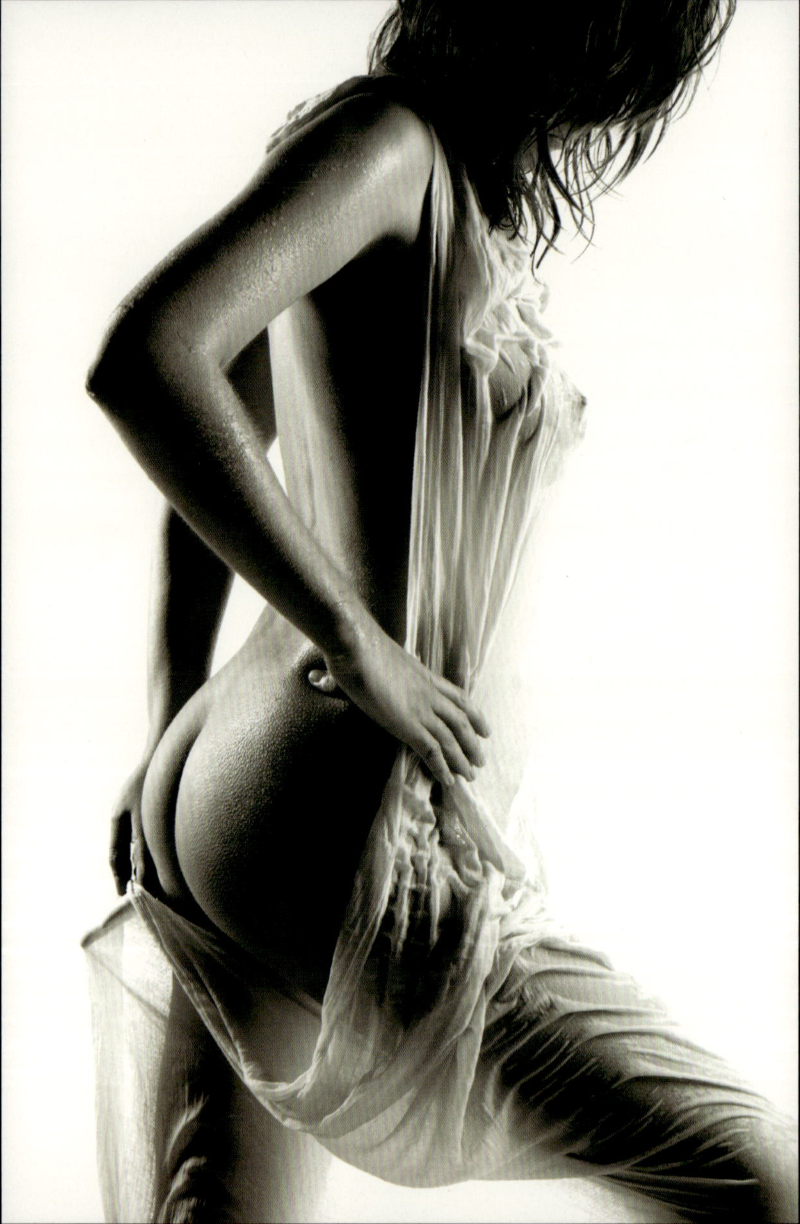

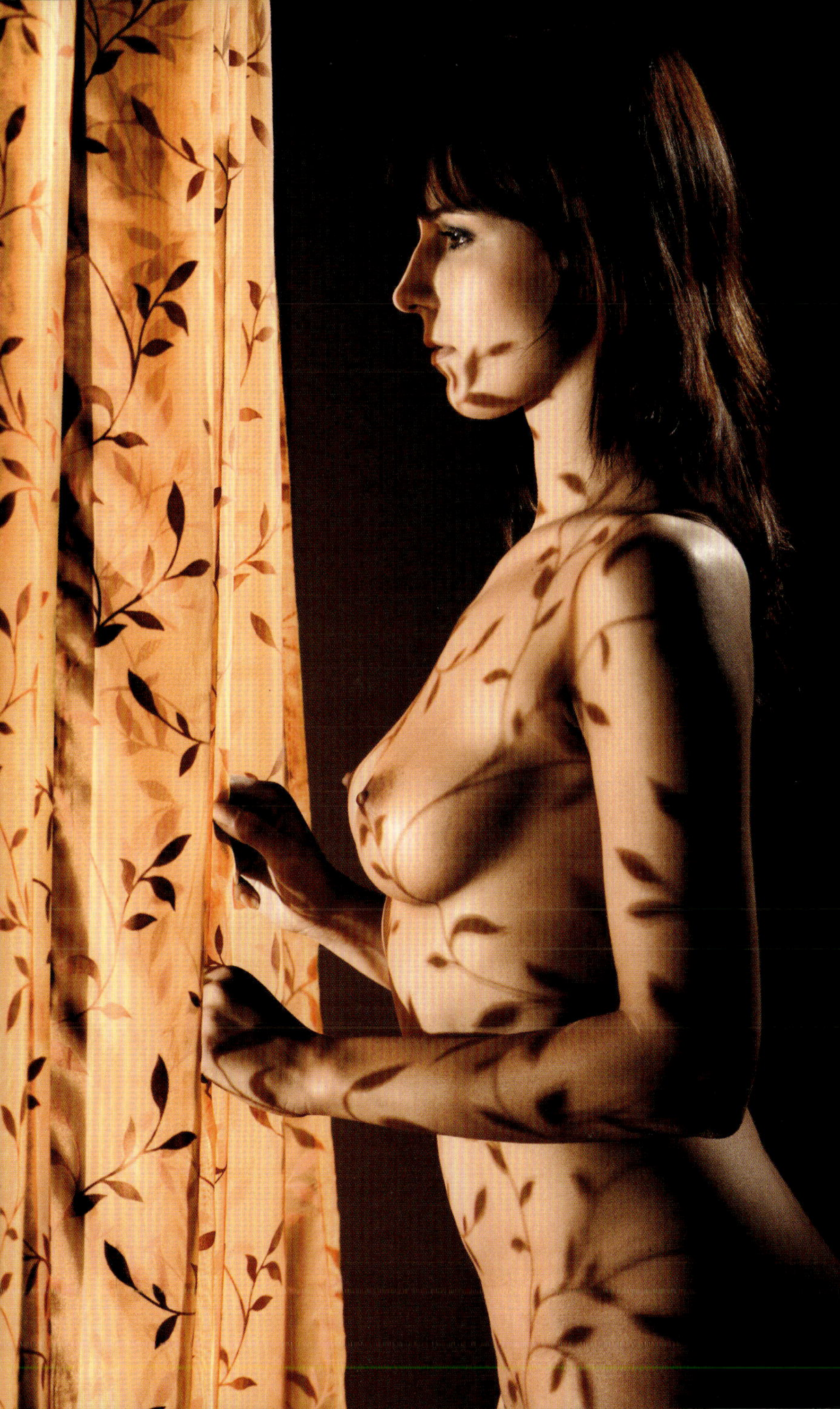

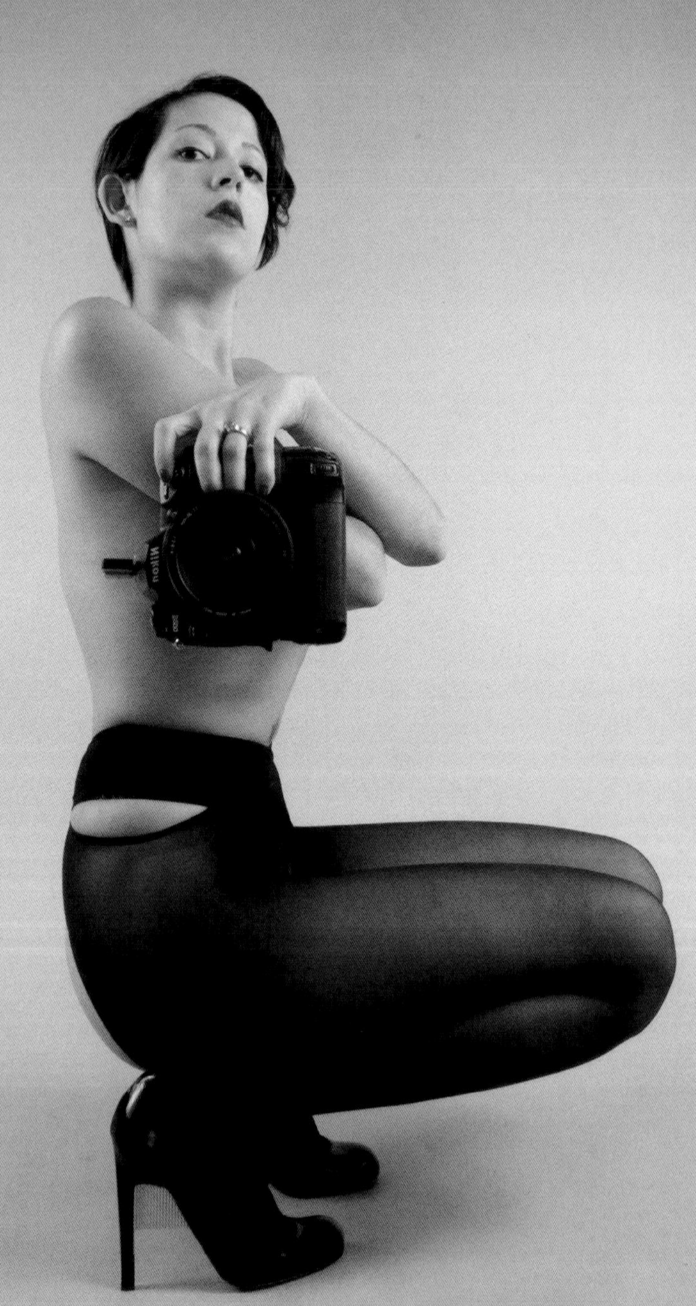
Nikon

alejandra guerrero

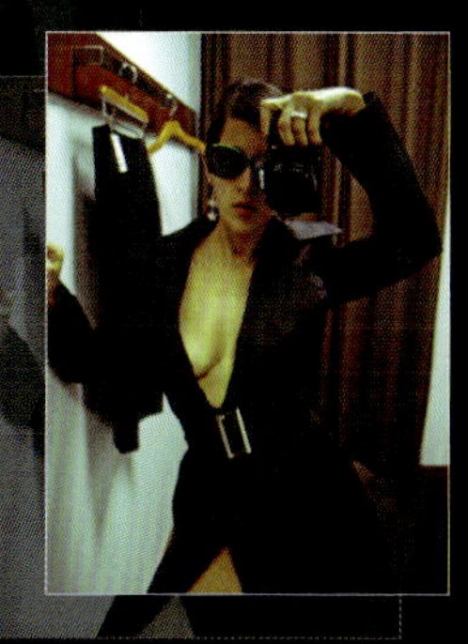

'IN A PROJECT FOR A NEW MEDIA class in Fine Arts School, we had to recreate ourselves in an alter ego. To me back then it was clear that I pictured myself as a sort of Vampire Femme Fatale. So I looked around my mom's old clothes to see if I could find something that I could use for the outfit. Found this alluring long black dress from the 1970s, got a wig, went to a cemetery and some other "dark" old spots in my city, set the camera on a timer and took some pictures of myself that depicted me as a gothic, dark Vampiric woman. Many years later it would transform somehow into my known alter ego, Corporate Vampire. Eight years later, I discovered that my mother wore that same dress to a Christmas party in 1978 where one of my dad's aunts said she looked too sexy, as if she was selling her appeal... nine months after that day, I was born.'

www.alt-er-ego.com

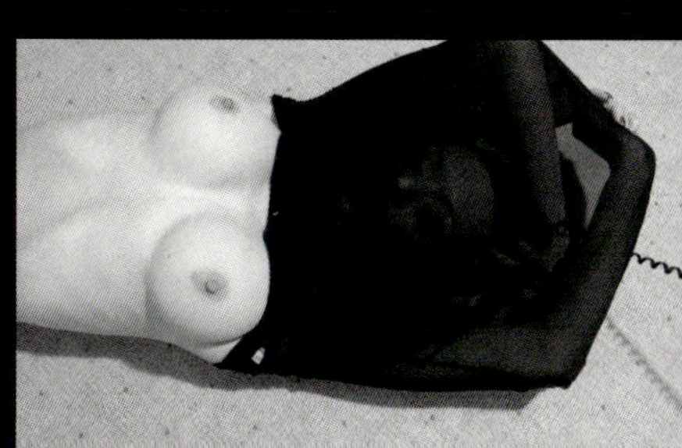

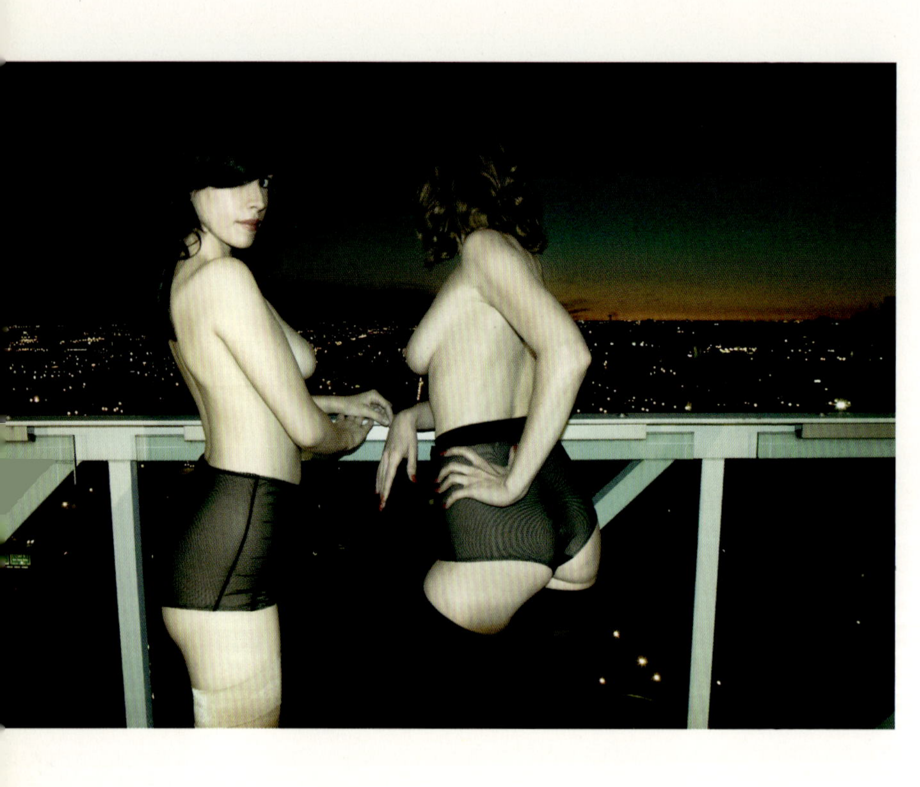

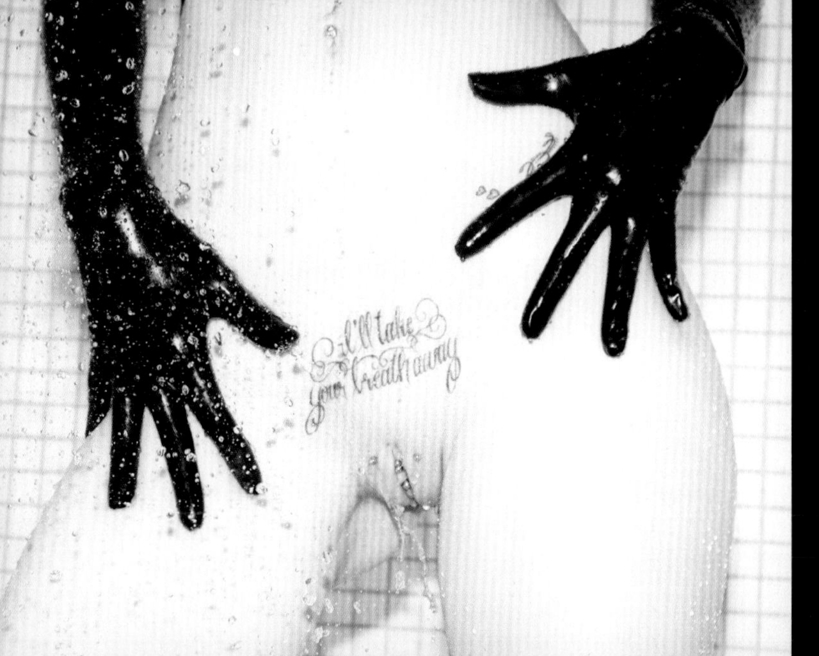
i'll take
your breath away

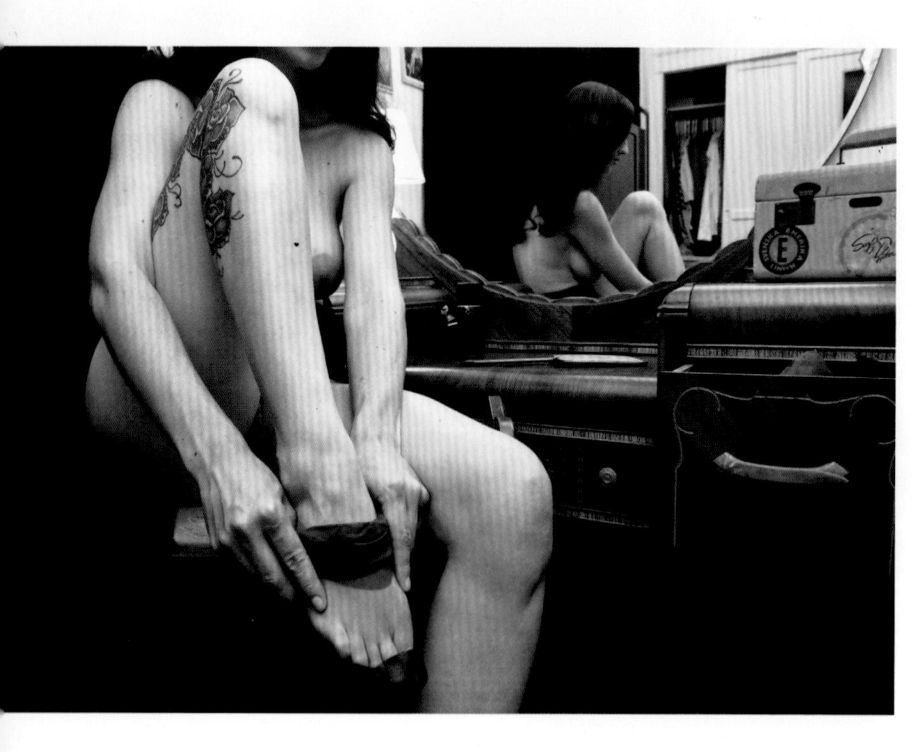
SVENSKA AMERIKA
E
LINIEN

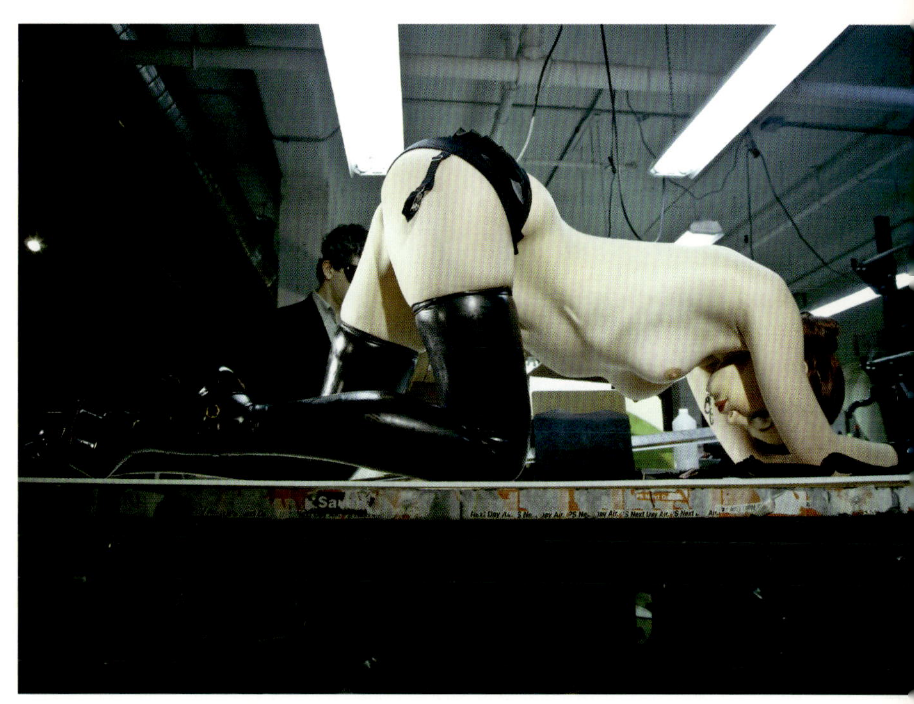

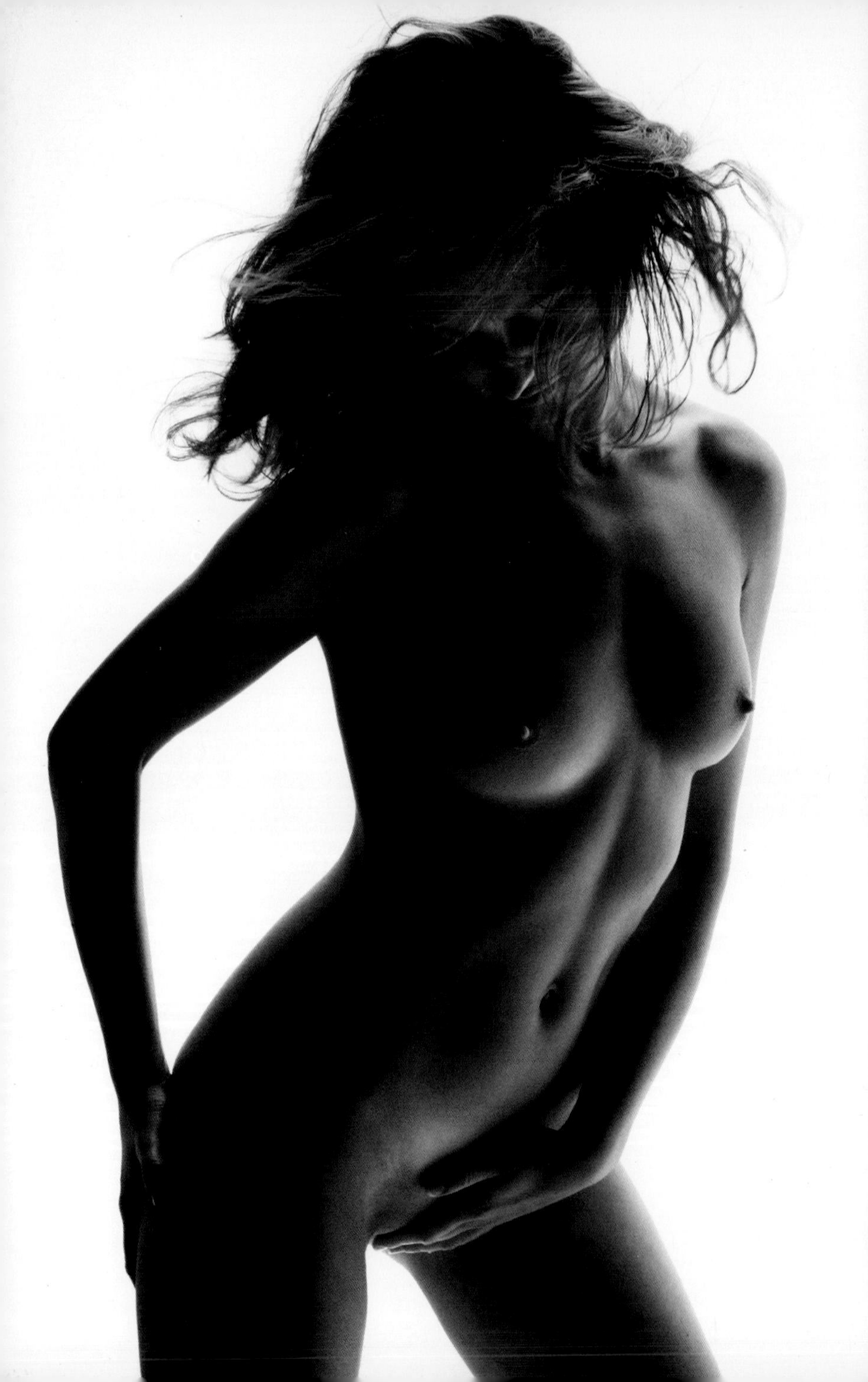

norbert guthier

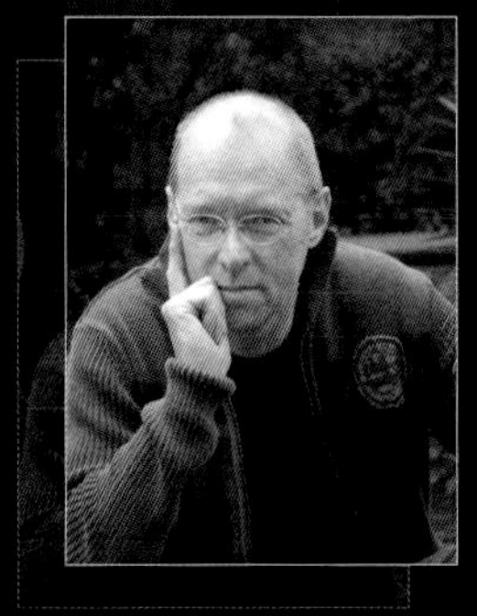

NORBERT WAS BORN IN 1954 in Heppenheim in Germany and has been self-employed as a photographer since 1982. He lives and works mostly in Germany and Spain. His books include *Frankfurt: Faces of a City, Bodytransfer* and *Guthier Nr 3.* His work in the field of the erotic has been widely acclaimed and his images of the female body '... seduce us ... grab our feelings, indulge the narcissistic exhibitionism that is prematurely taken as obscenity. They rebel against social mores, and this is what makes them so secretive, so sensual, so erotic ...' (Helmut Ortner).

www.photoicon.com/darkroom/43/
www.fotodesign-guthier.com

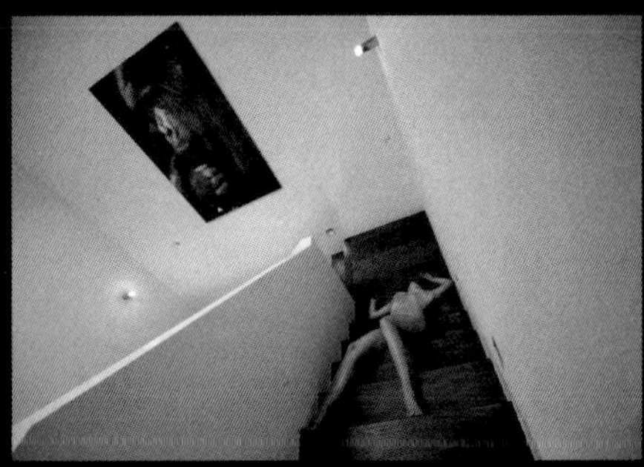

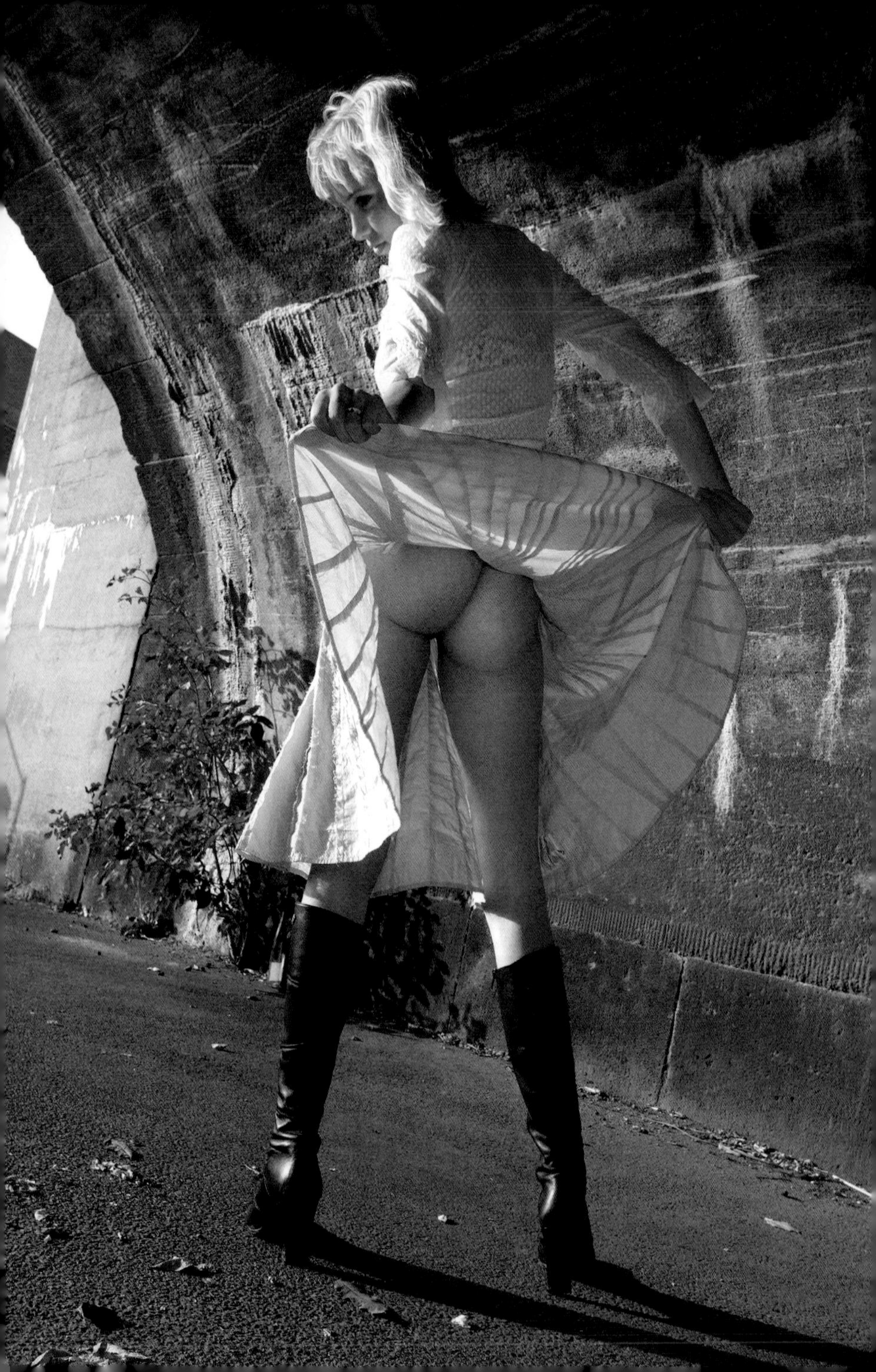

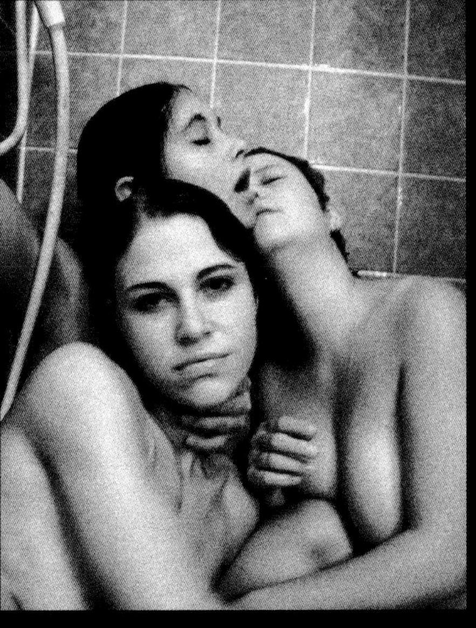

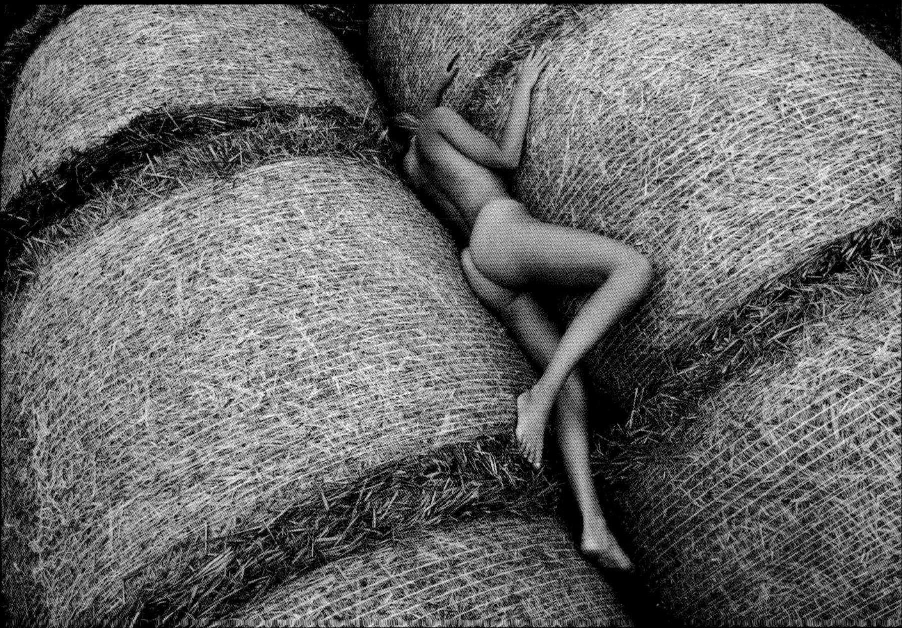

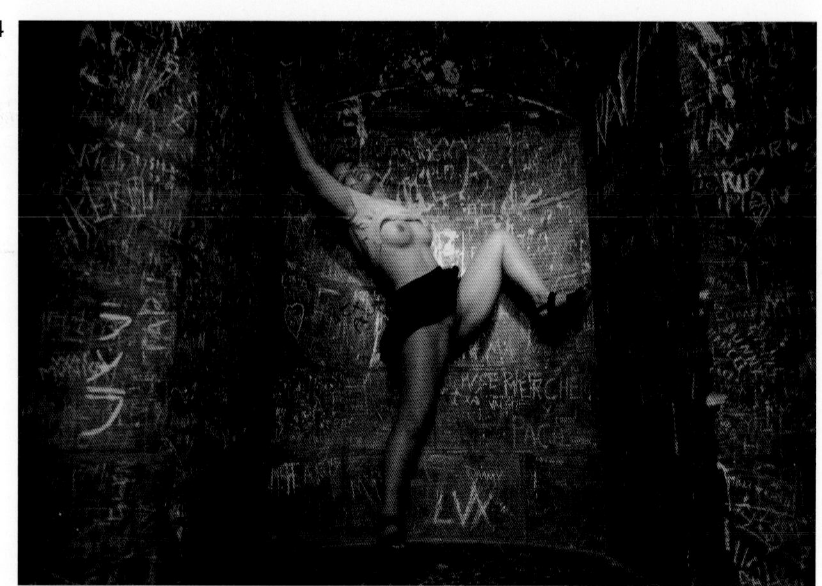
LVX

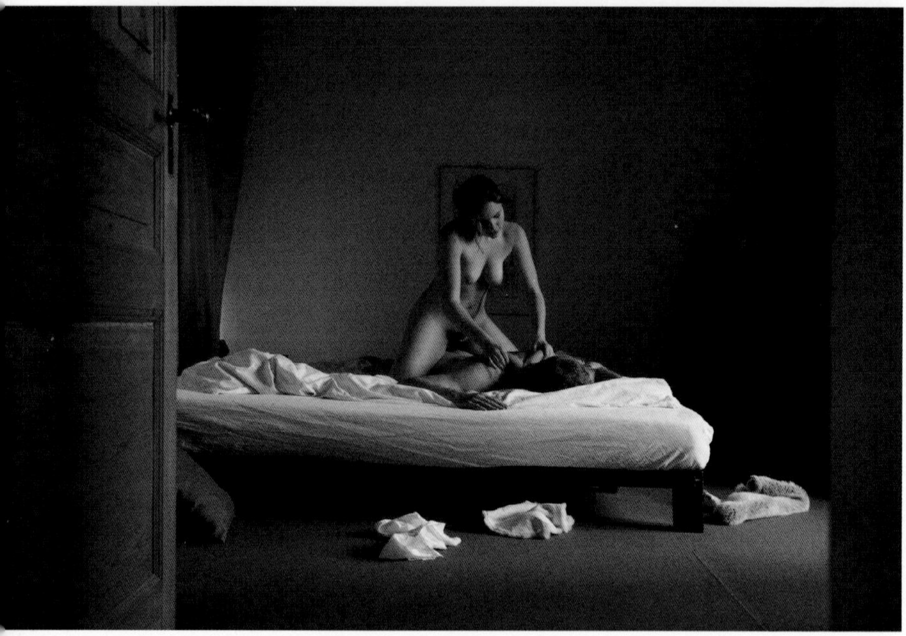

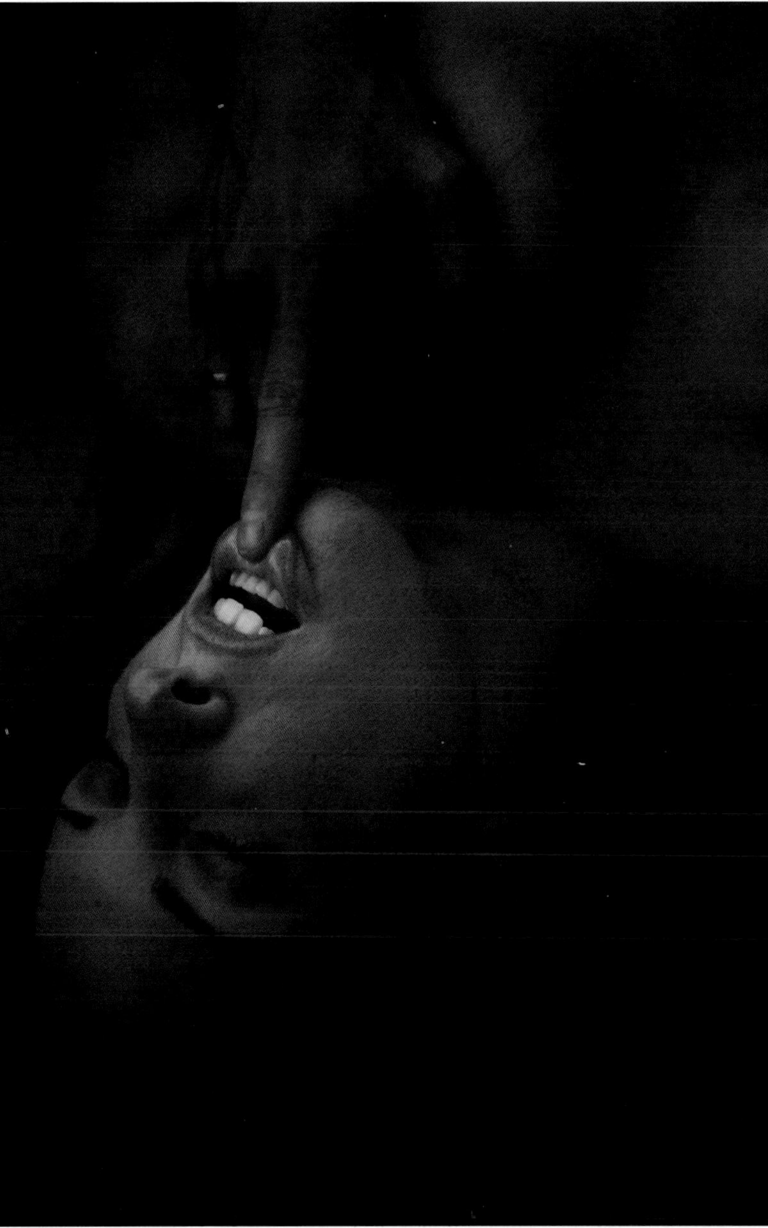

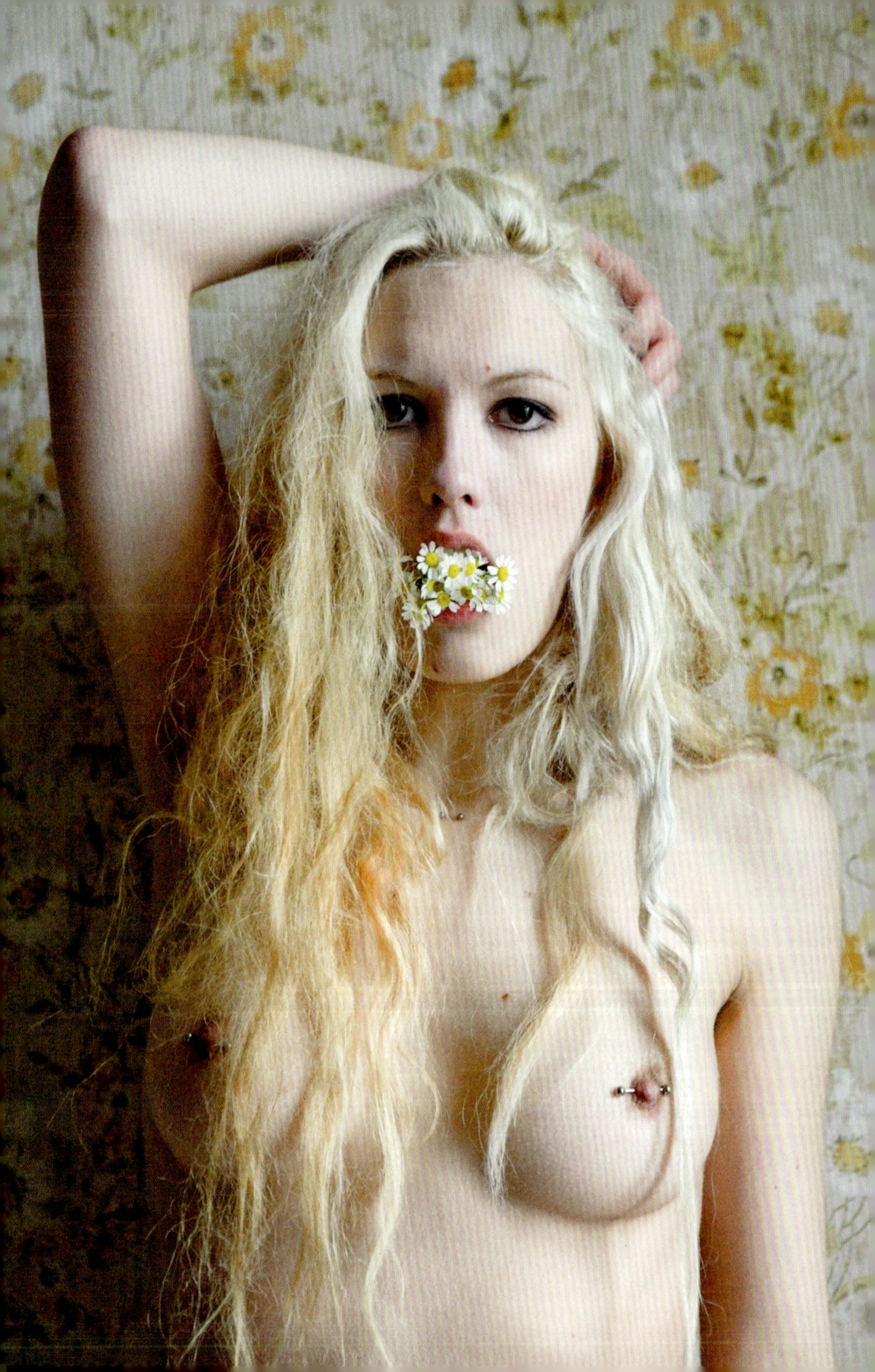

aaron hawks

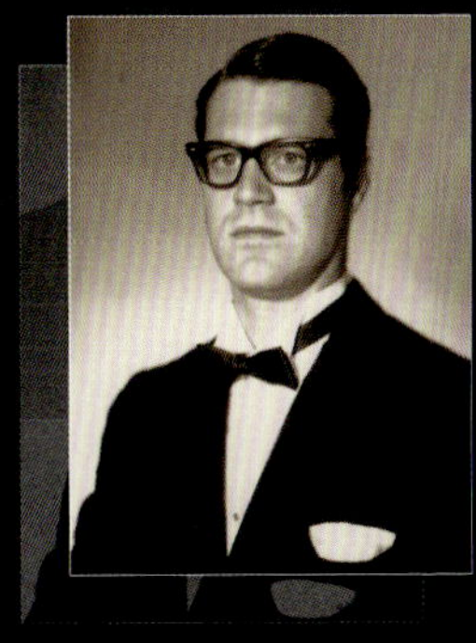

FROM SEATTLE, WASHINGTON originally, and now living in Emeryville, California, Aaron has been photographing for fifteen years, honing his skills as master of the melancholic still. The women in his sets are artists, real sex workers and fetishists whose beauty, grit, intensity, and self-awareness inspire his art, culminating in the untraditional documentation of timeless records of sexual noir. The secret to Aaron's art isn't just his technical capability or the subconscious interpretation of sexual messages that his portraits deliver, but the actual sets, which are hand-built and designed in his warehouse.

www.aaronhawks.net

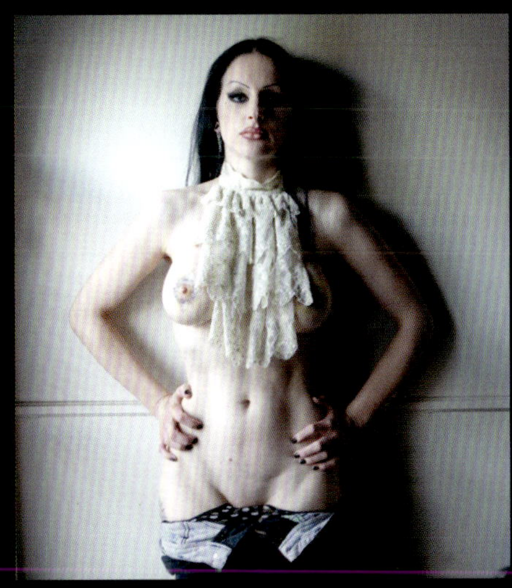

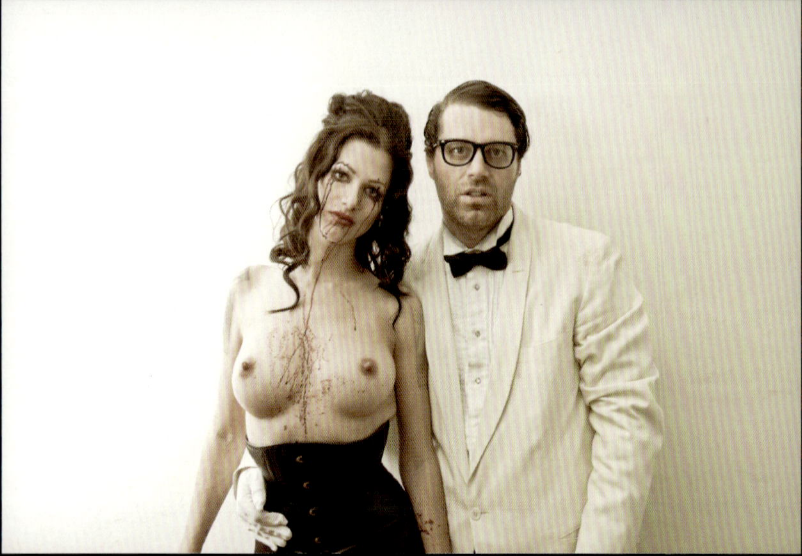

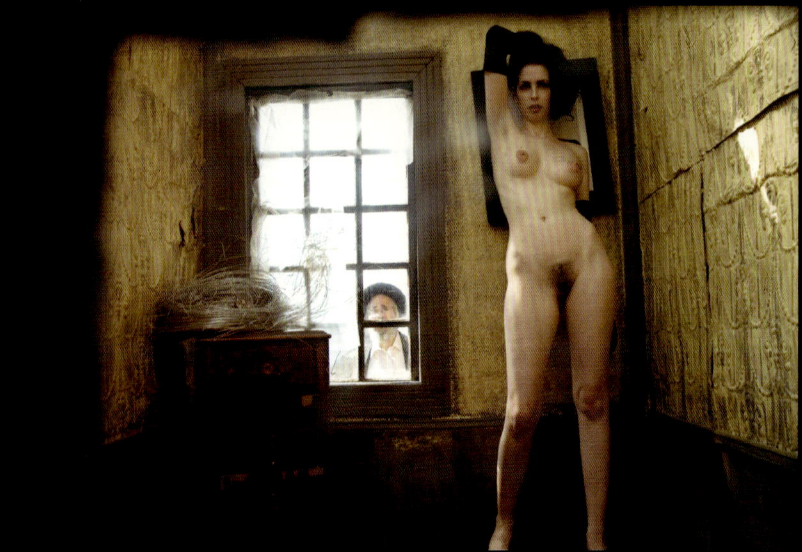

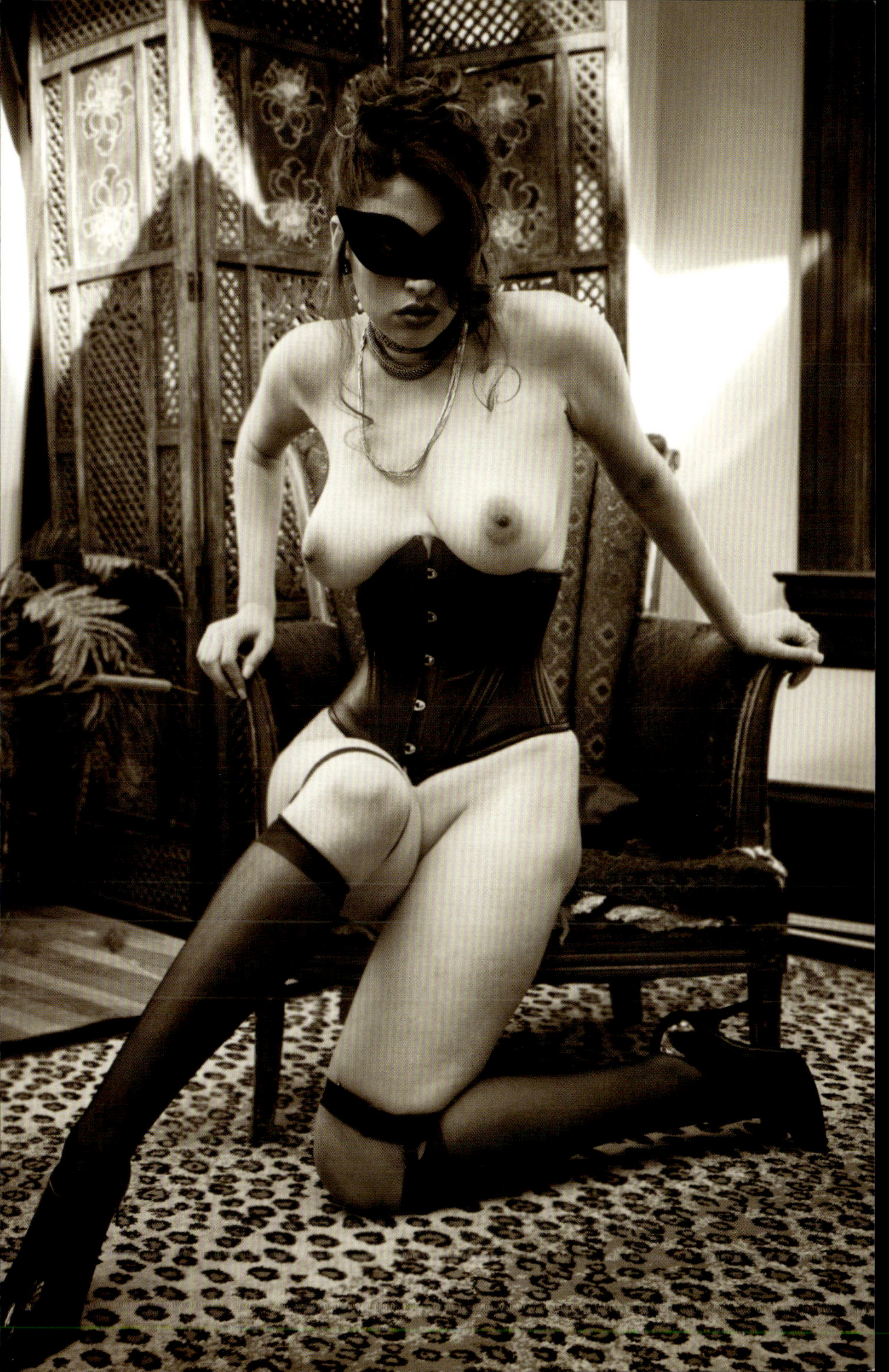

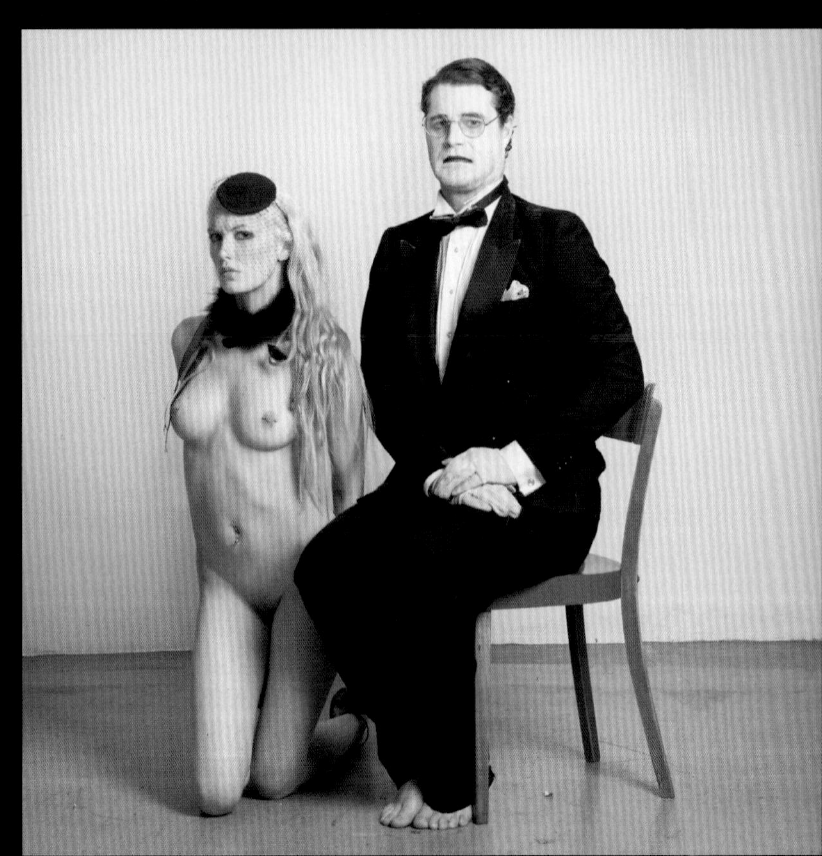

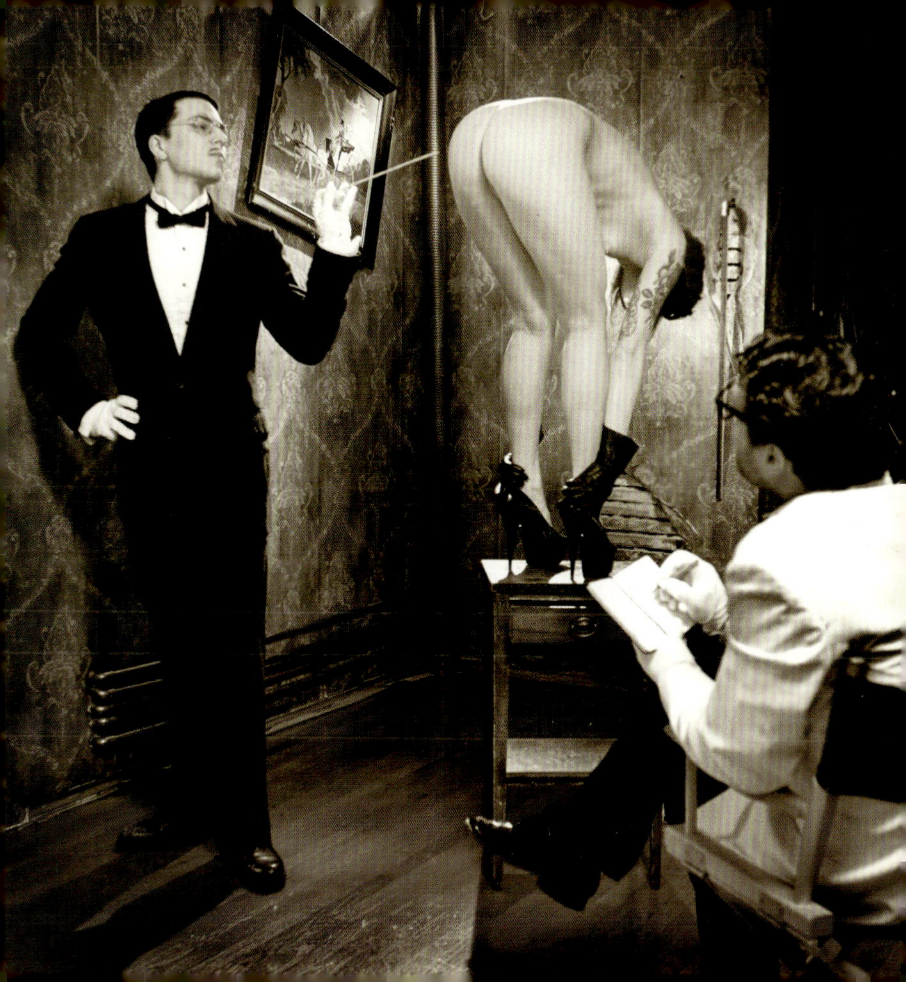

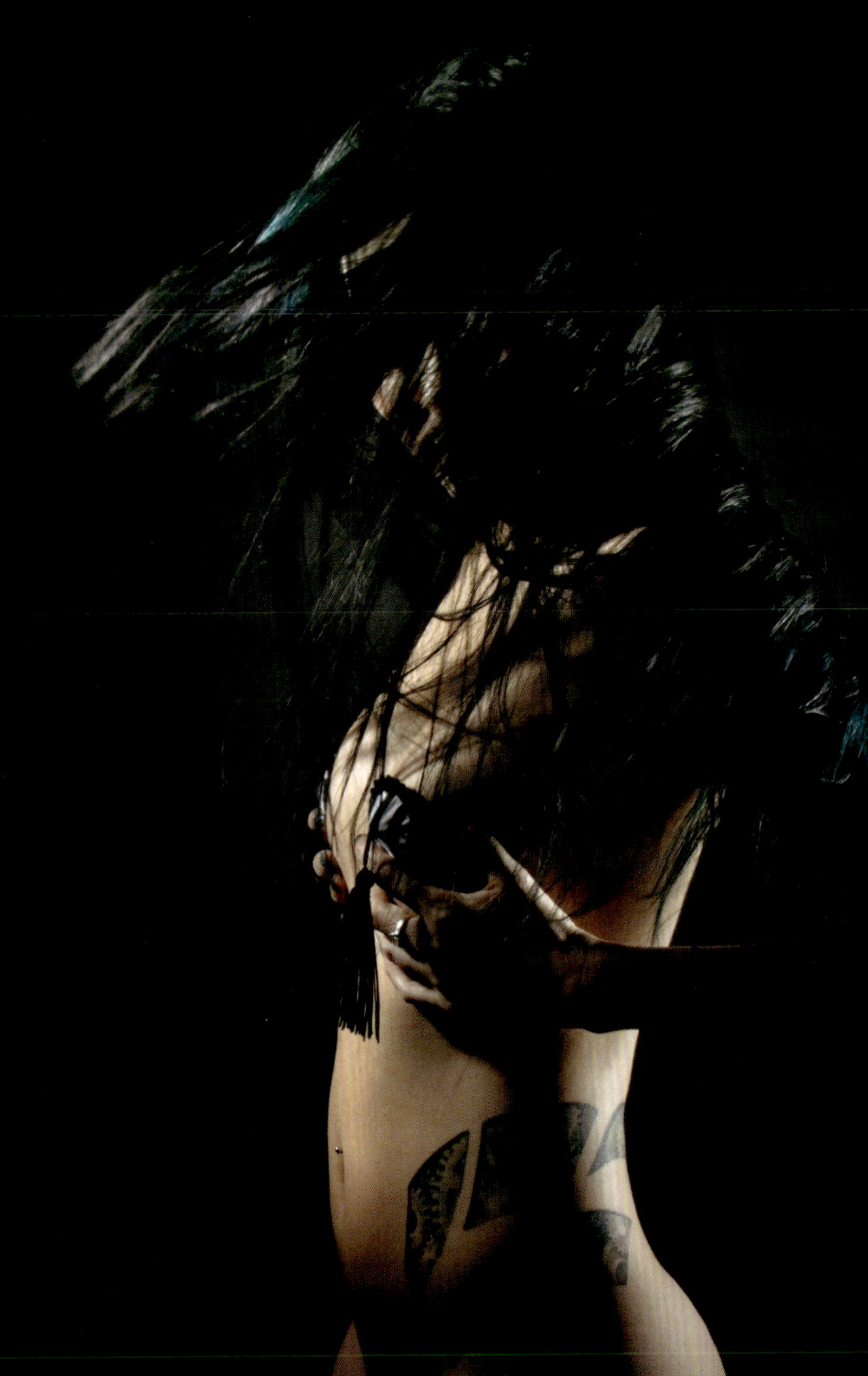

kevin hundsnurscher

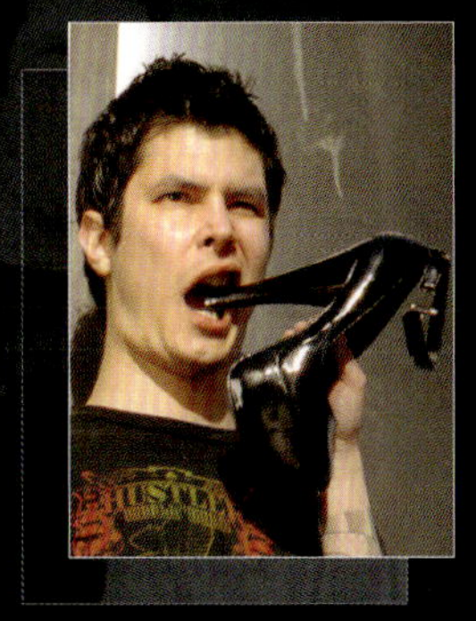

KEVIN IS FROM THE SEATTLE area, where he takes public and candid pictures of models, friends and bands, as well as doing more conceptualized shoots in semi-public locations. He is driven to create images that feature people completely transformed or incongruous situations. Since all his work is done outside the studio, every photo has its own story and he tries to communicate this story through the picture, hoping that the viewer's experience of his work is as rewarding as it was for him to capture: light and shadow, the cream and the dirt ...

www.photo.net/photodb/user?user_id=246170

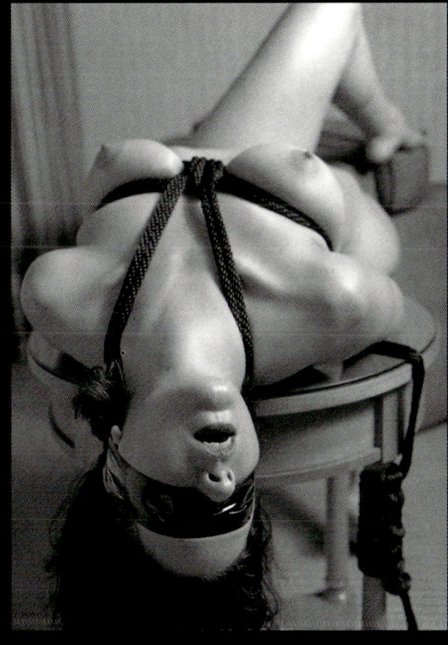

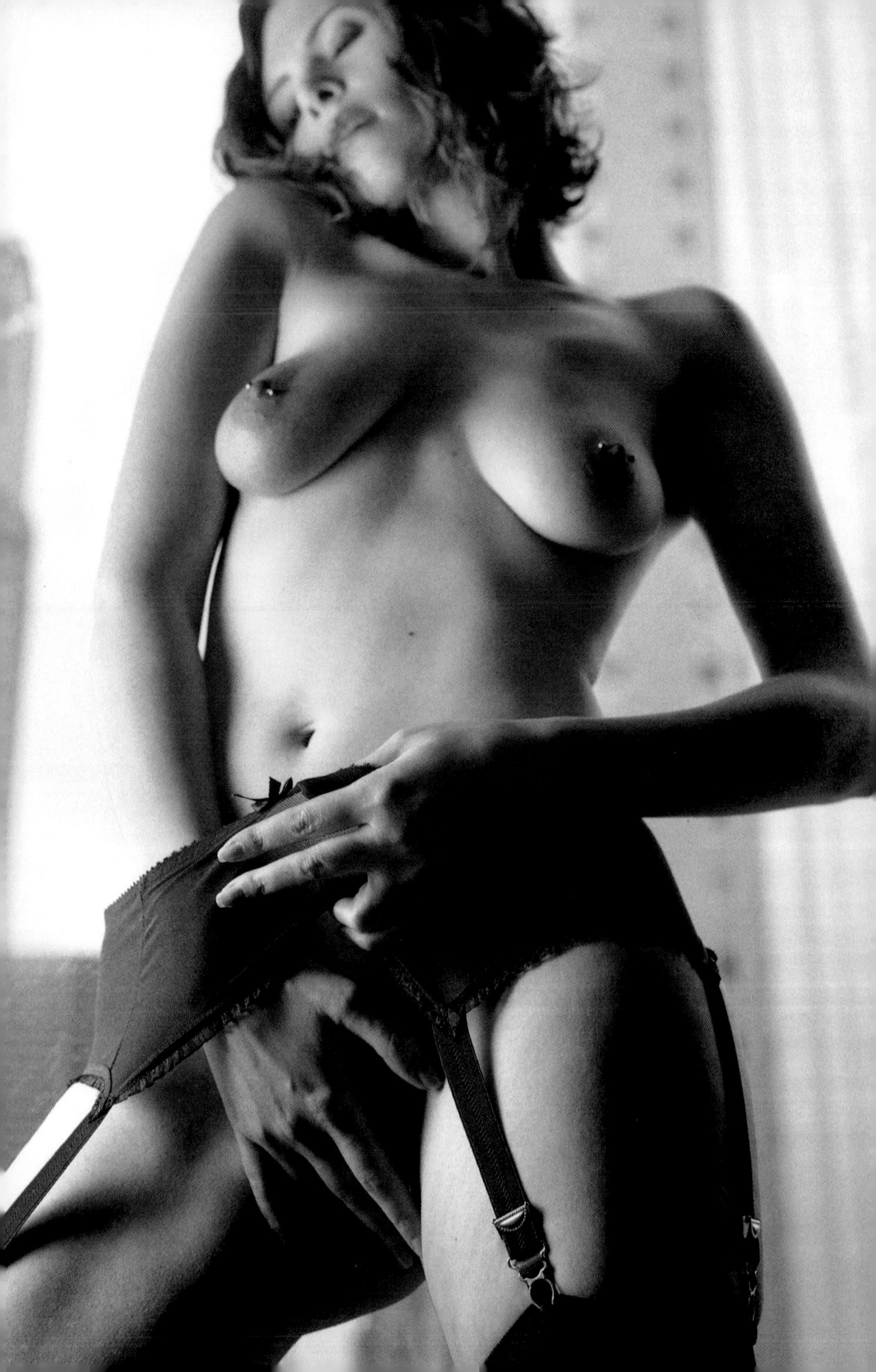

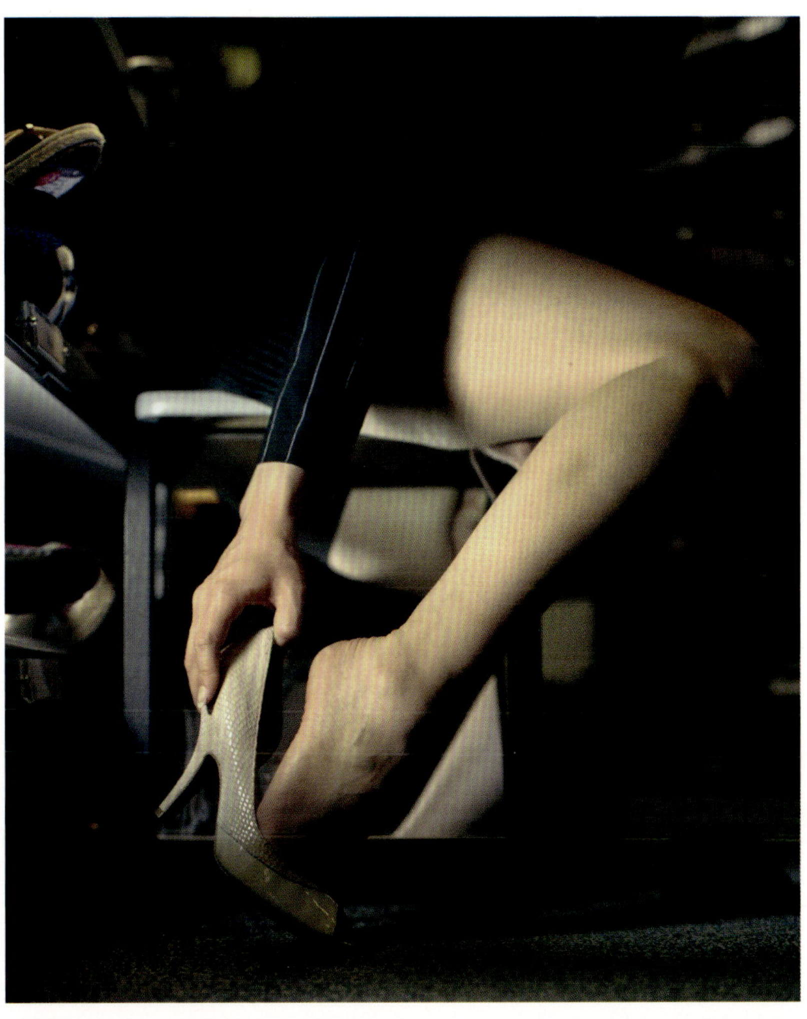

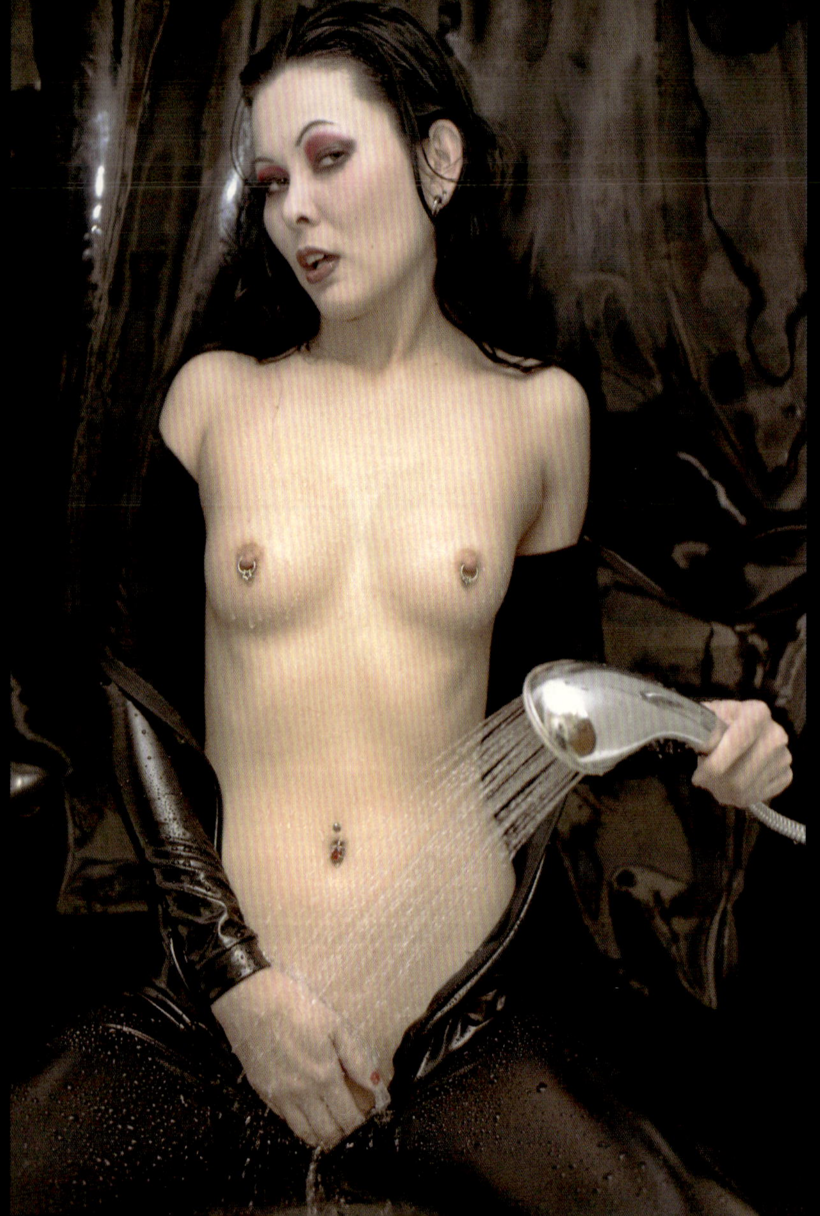

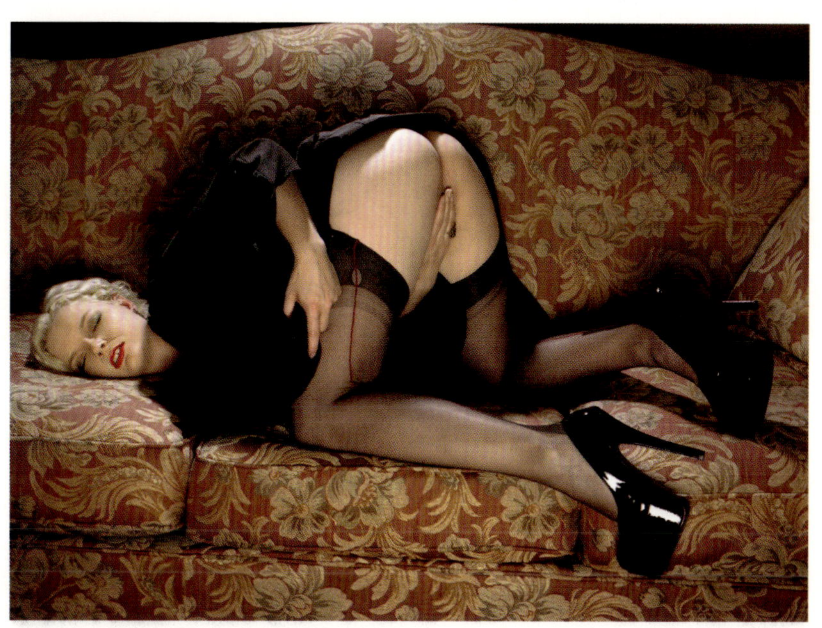

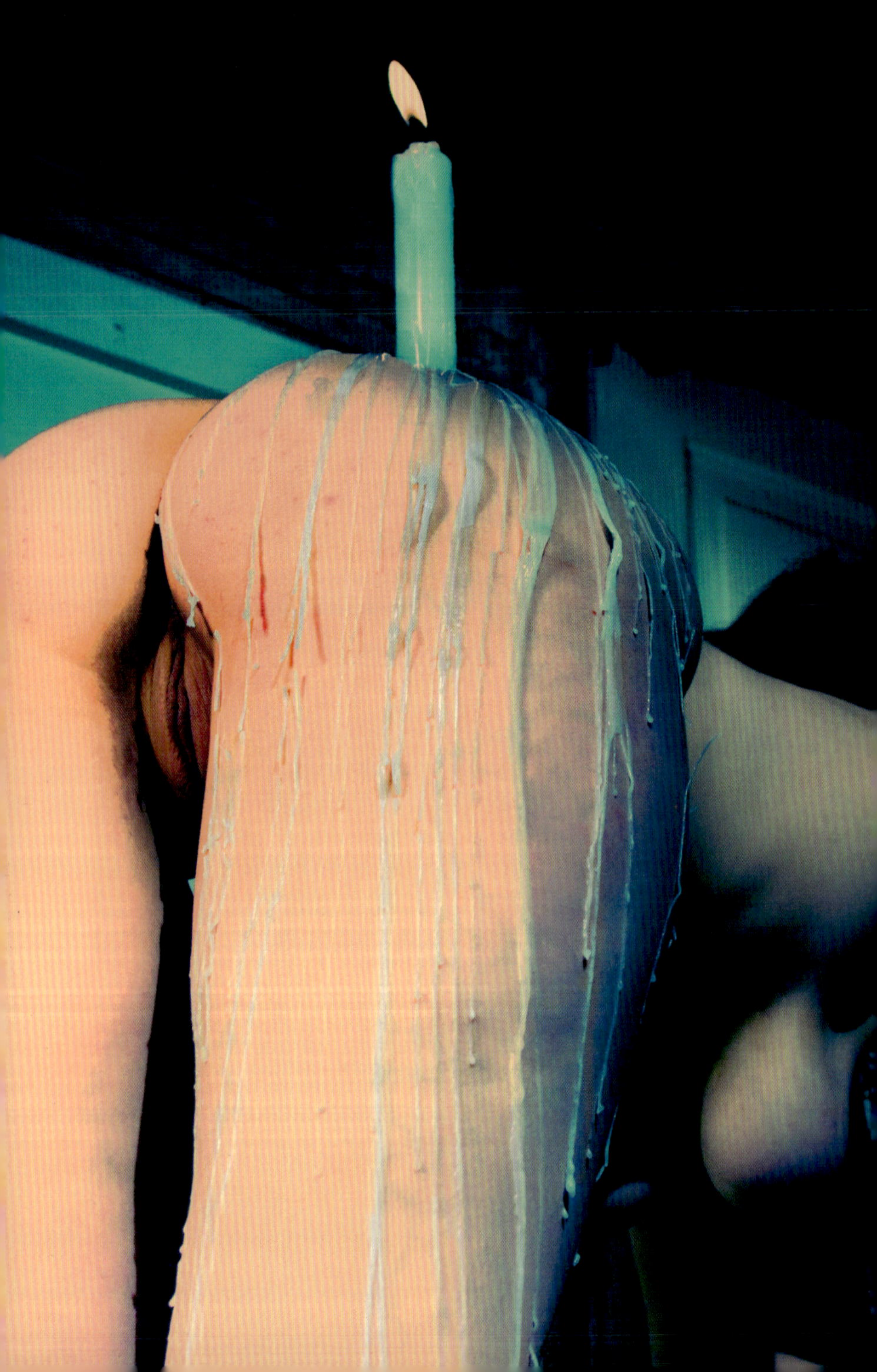

richard kadrey

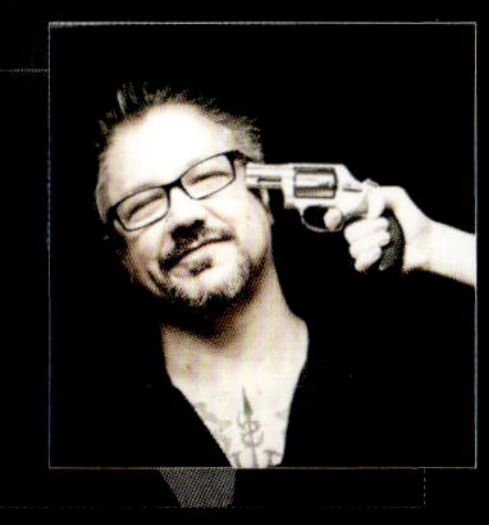

RICHARD KADREY IS A FETISH photographer and digital artist living in San Francisco. He shoots under the name Kaos Beauty Klinik, exploring his own and his models' fetishistic impulses. Very concerned with light, he's worked with everything from traditional studio strobes to long exposures illuminated with a $6 plastic flashlight. Kadrey is also a writer. His latest novel, *Kill The Dead,* is published by Eos.

www.richardkadrey.com
www.kaosbeautyklinik.com

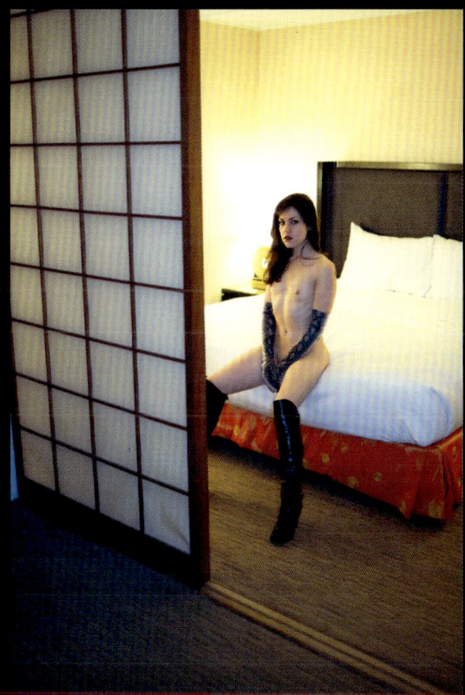

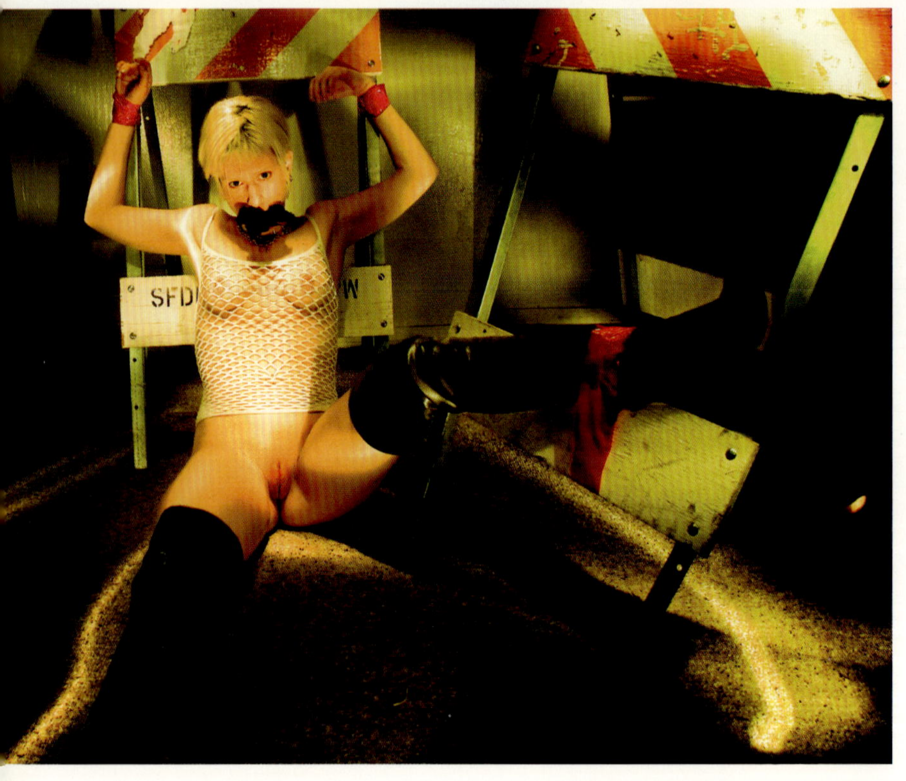
SFD

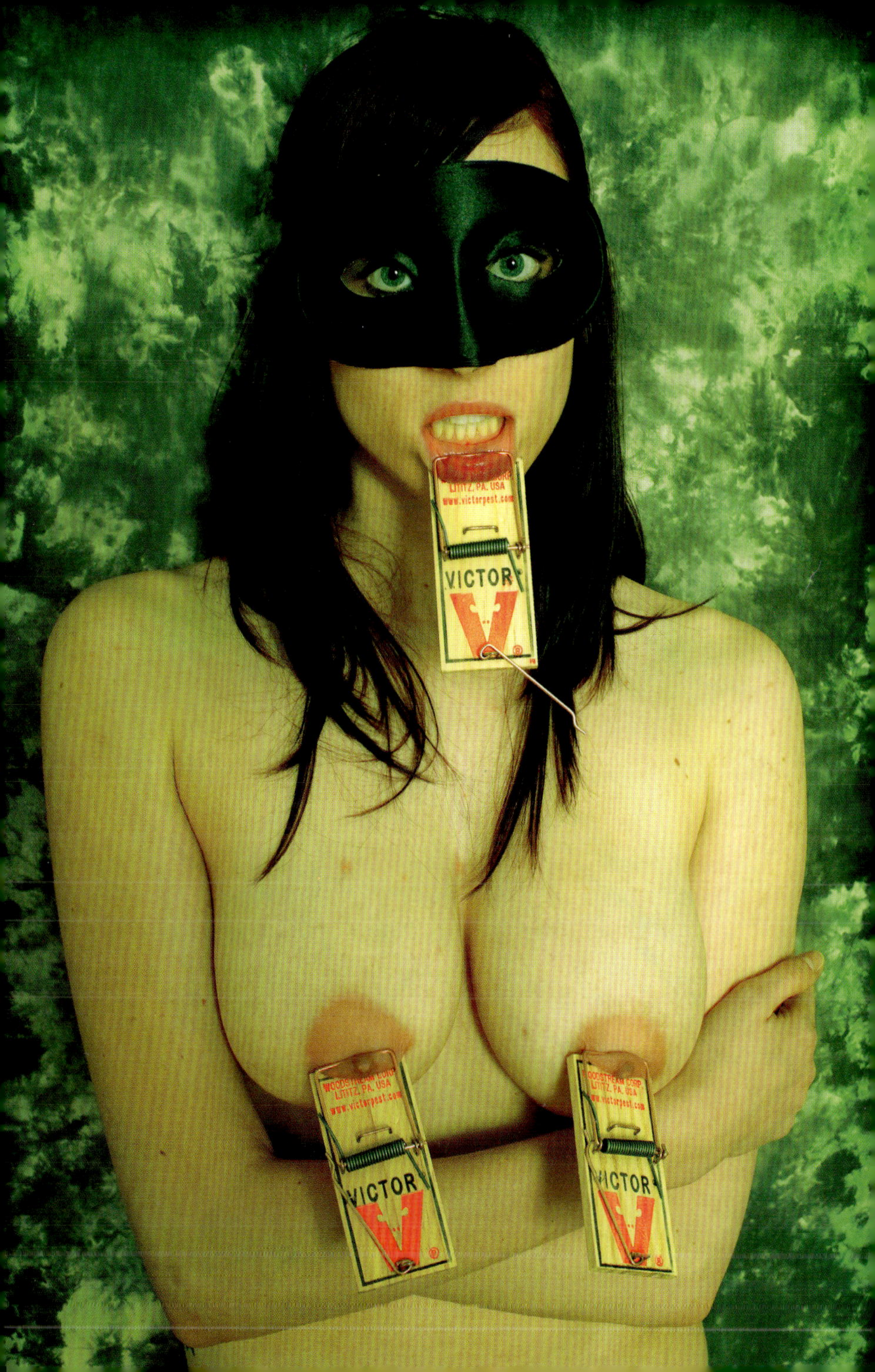
LITITZ, PA. USA
www.victorpest.com
VICTOR
WOODSTREAM CORP
LITITZ, PA. USA
www.victorpest.com
VICTOR
WOODSTREAM CORP
LITITZ, PA. USA
www.victorpest.com
VICTOR

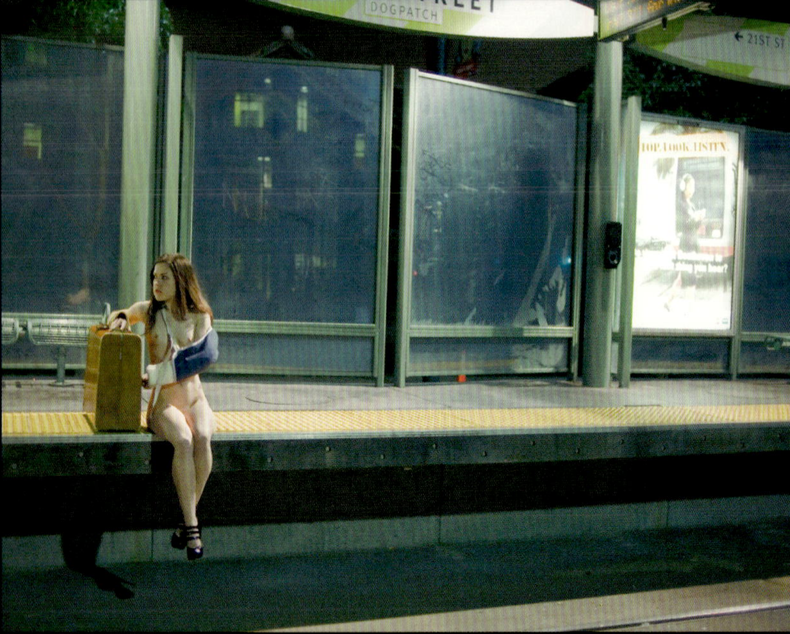

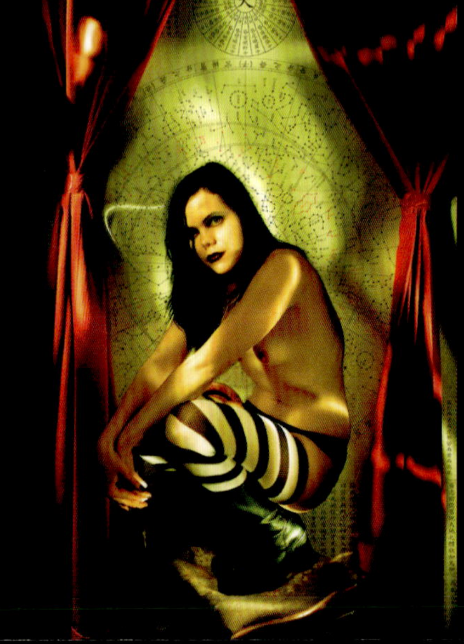
天

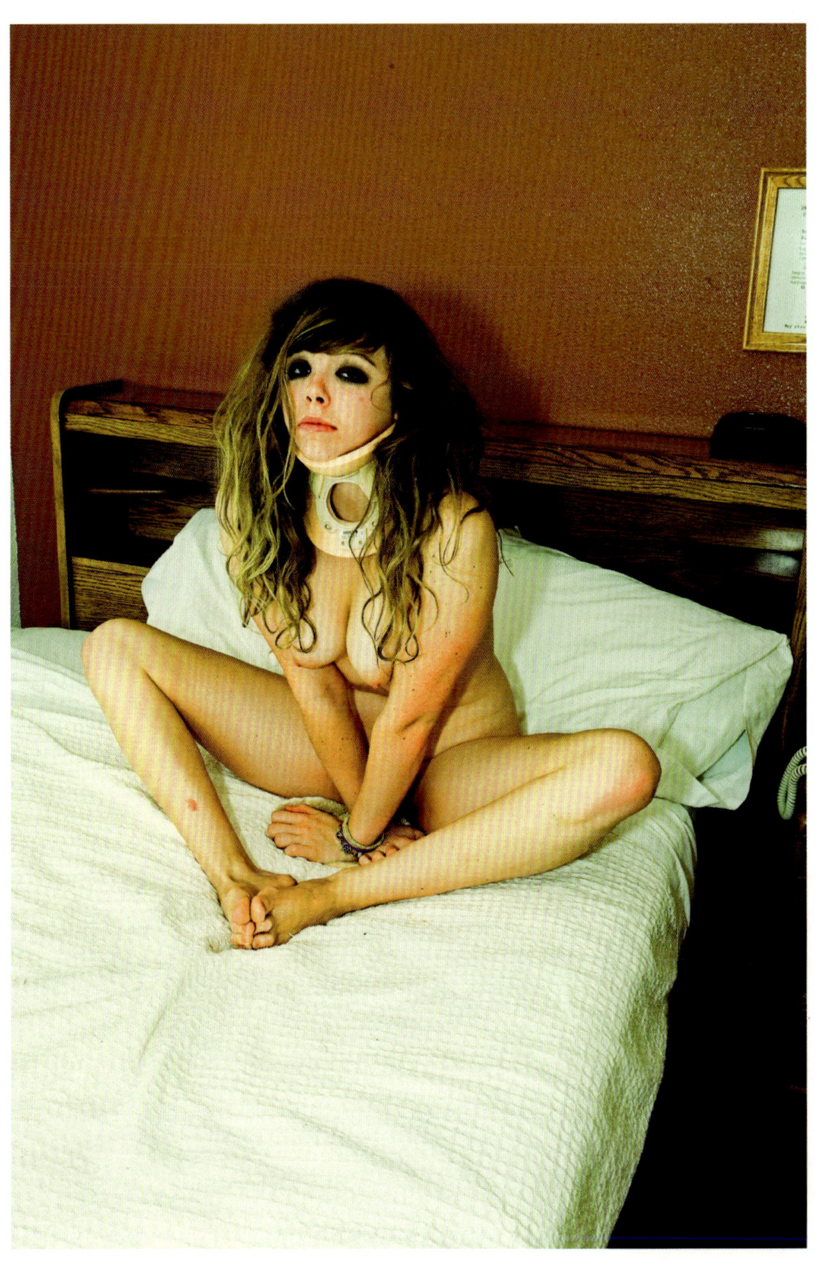

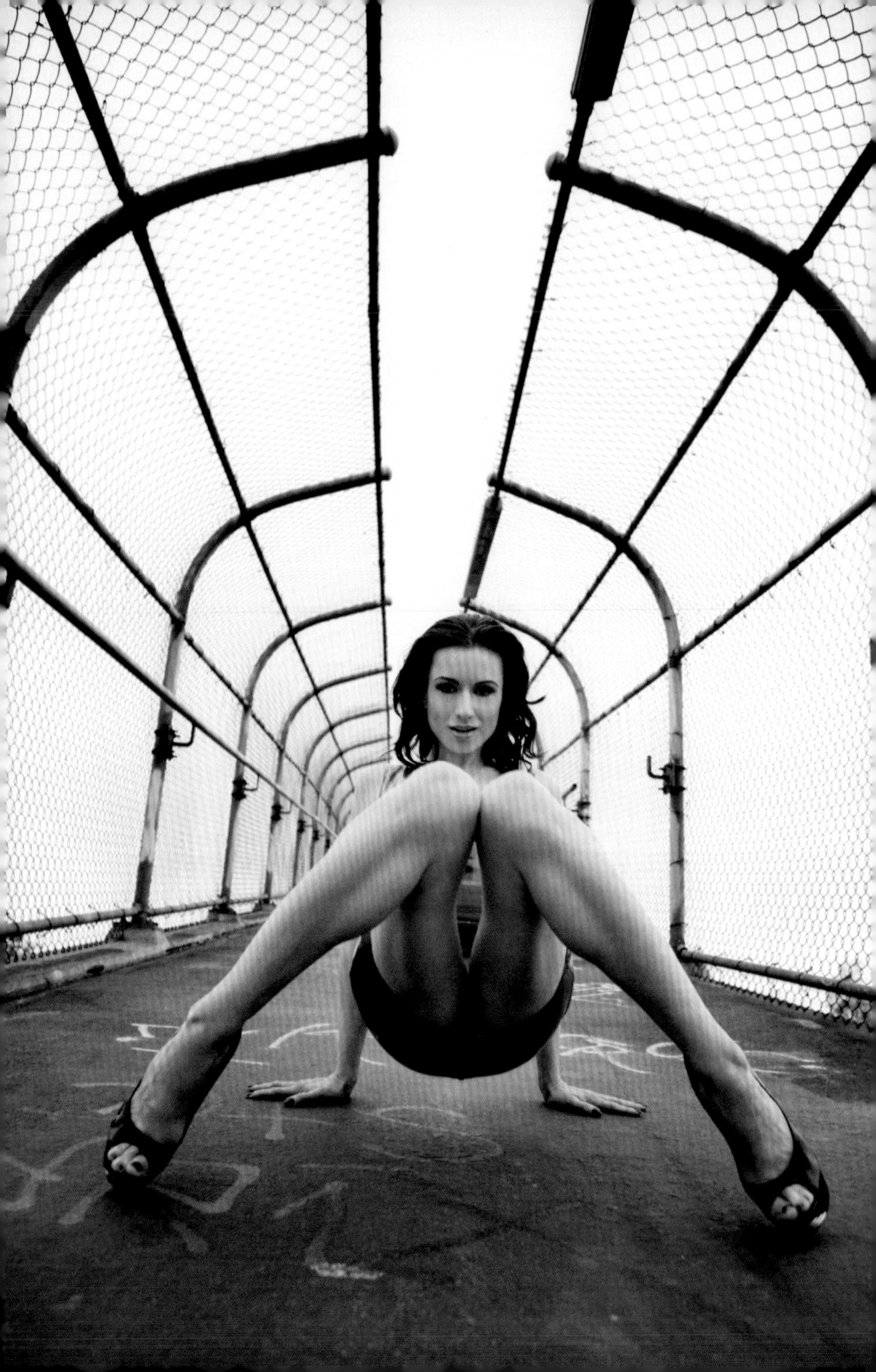

christine kessler

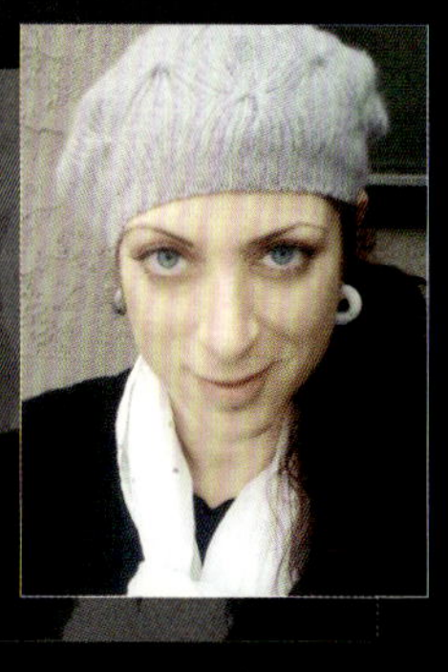

AMERICAN PHOTOGRAPHER Christine Kessler decided ages ago that ogling boobs and buying lube by the gallon beat working for a living. She keeps the dream alive at her pay website, www.myfetishdiary.com. She also pens *Bizarre*'s monthly Fetish Fanatic feature and her second book, *Nylon Girls*, hit the stores in 2009.

www.christinekessler.com

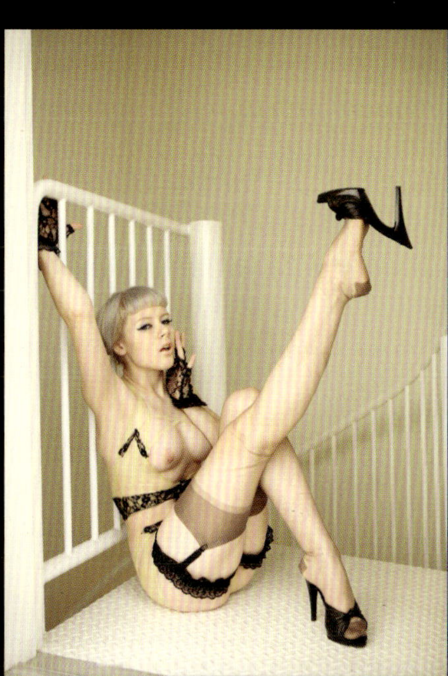

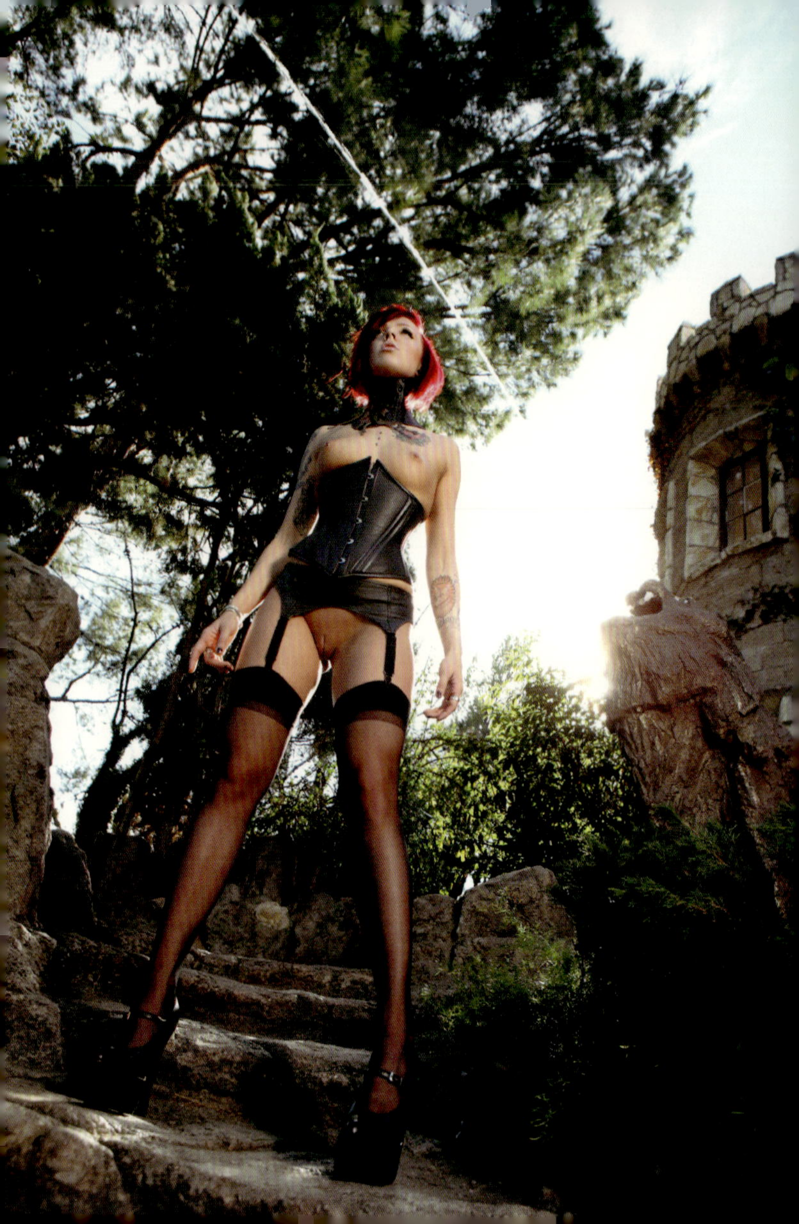

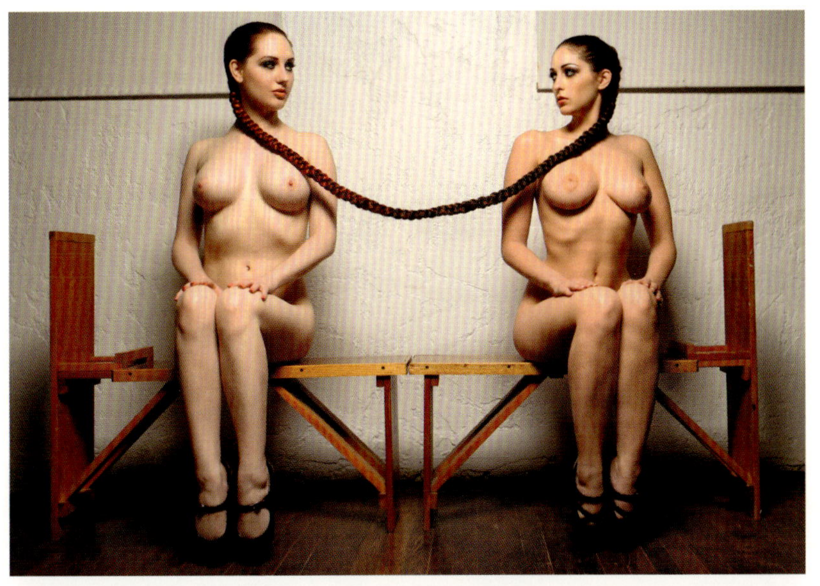

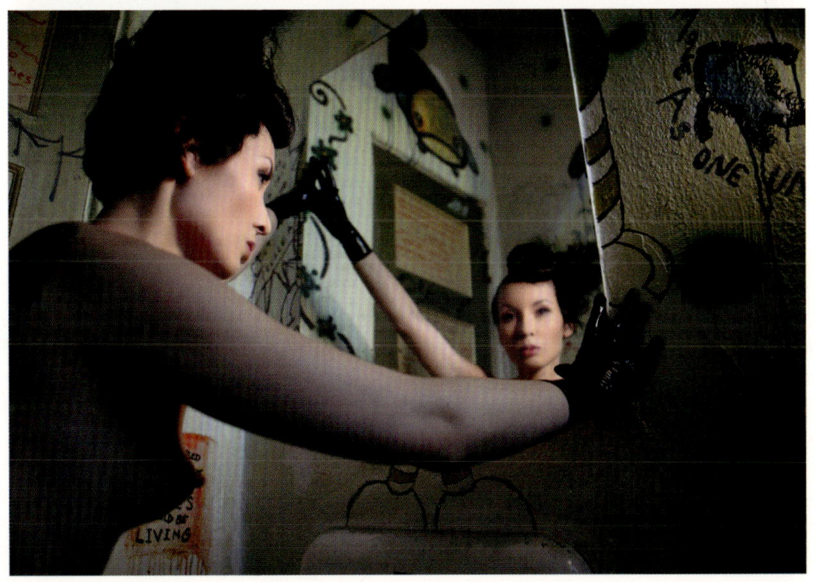
ONE
LIVING

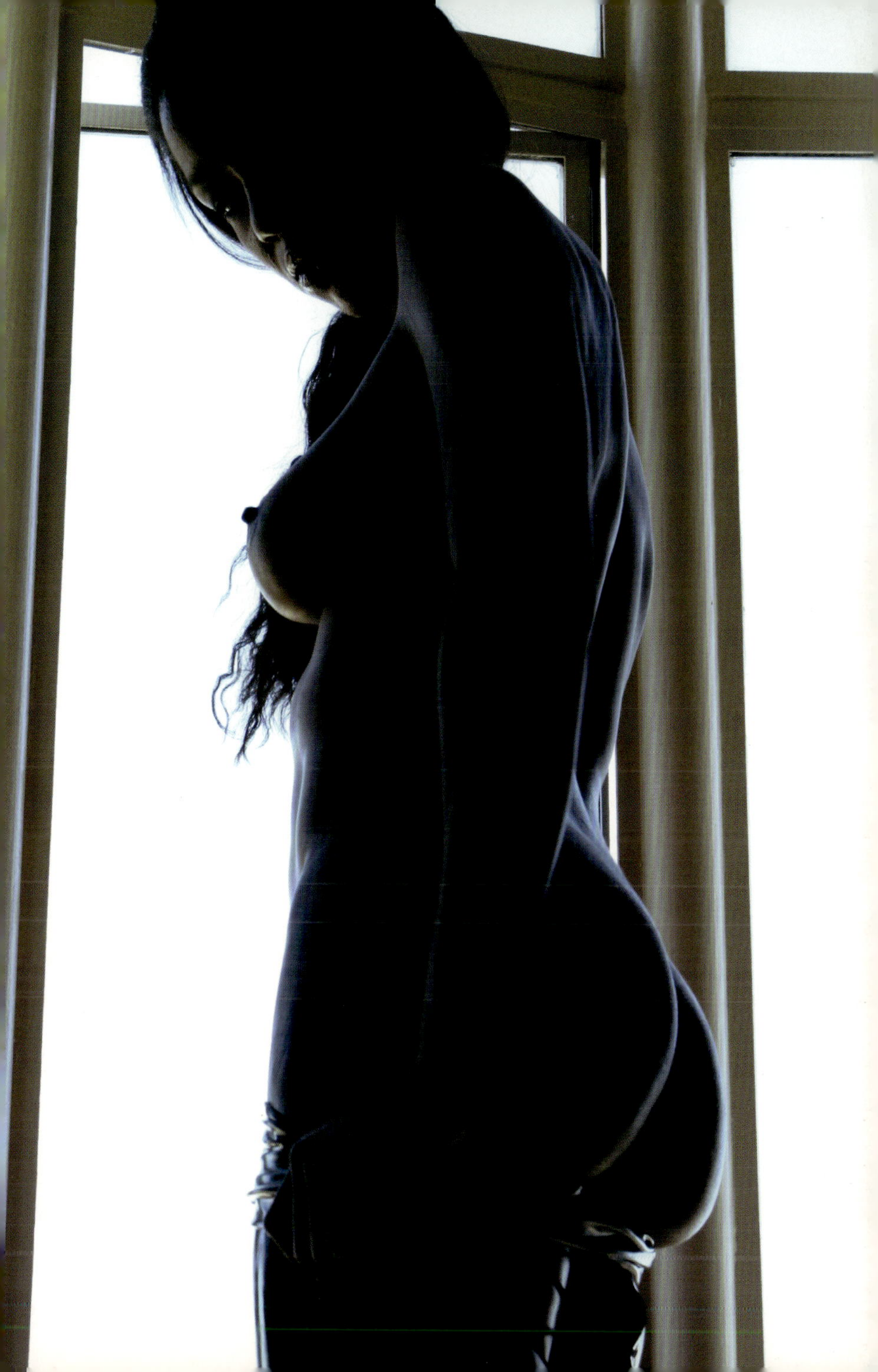

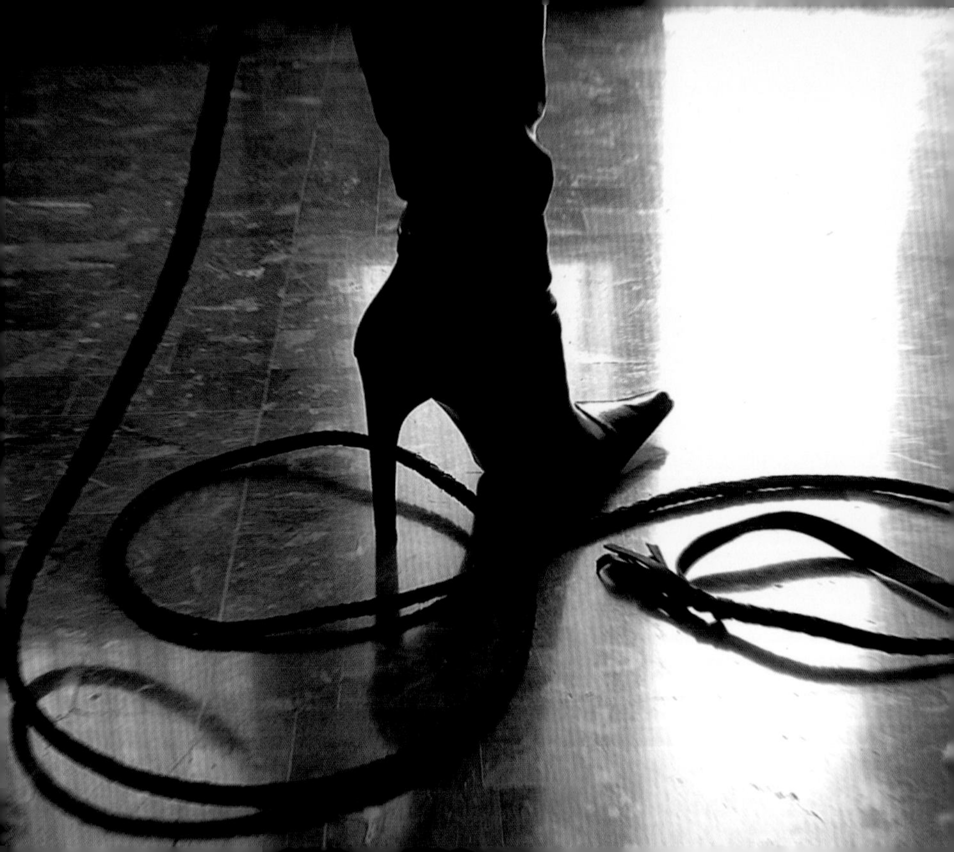

koshka

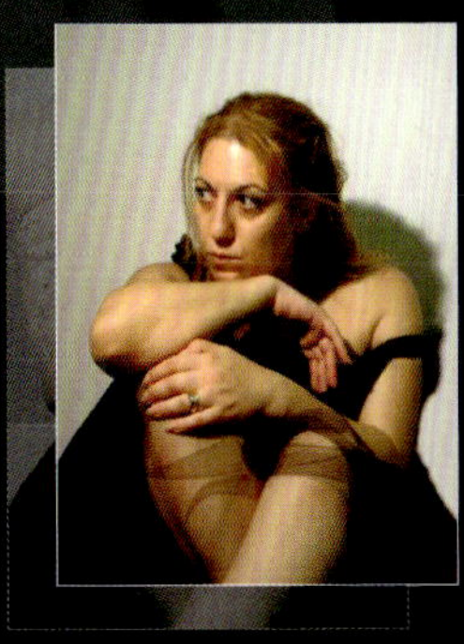

MOST OF HER WORKS are self-portraits but she feels they are something more than what might appear at first sight to be simply the expression of a narcissistic attitude. They are brief stories in which she plays a role. When she creates these images she behaves like an actress but is also the director and the author of an inner screenplay flowing in her mind and through her senses. Koshka is her pseudonym and it is related to her love for cats and Russia (she has a degree in Russian Language and Literature). In Russian 'koshka' means 'cat' and sometimes she feels free and lonely just like a cat. She lives in Italy and works as a writer, translator and editor.

www.koshka.it

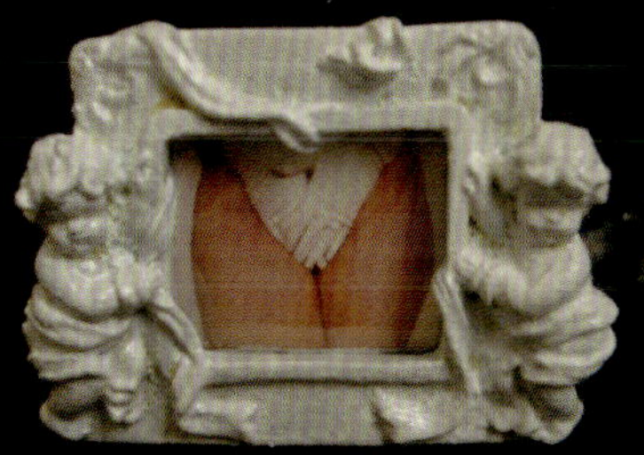

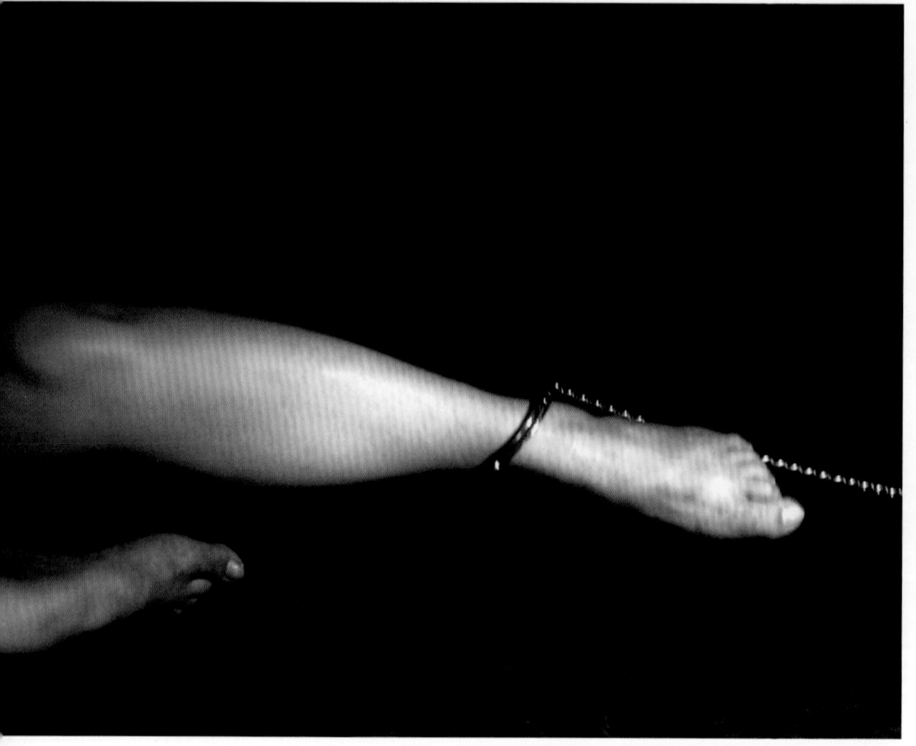

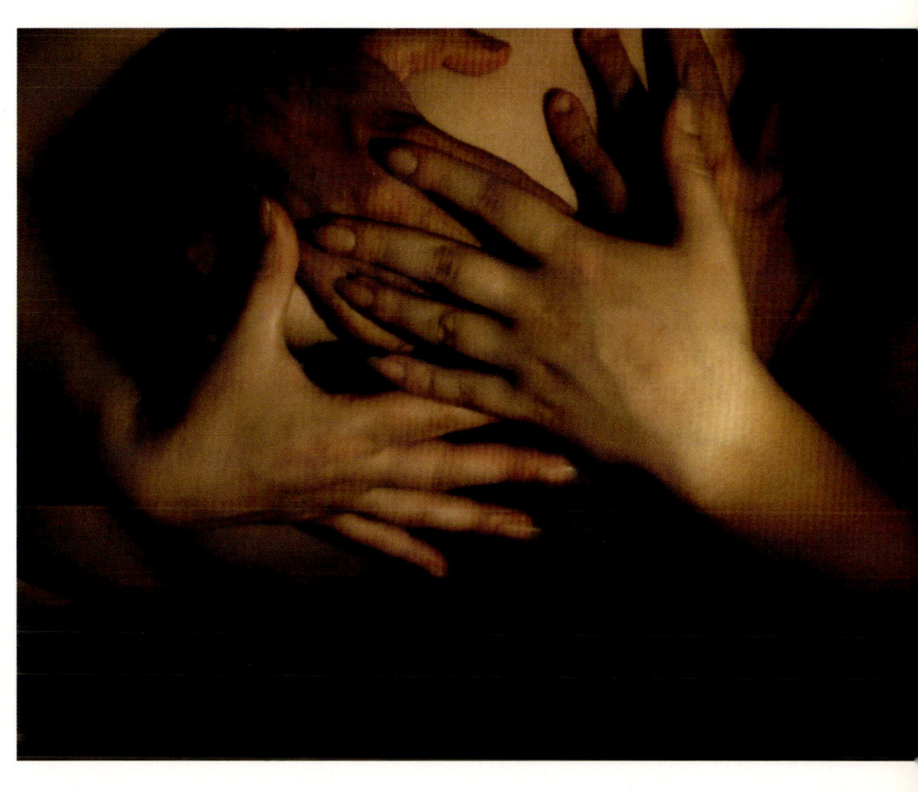

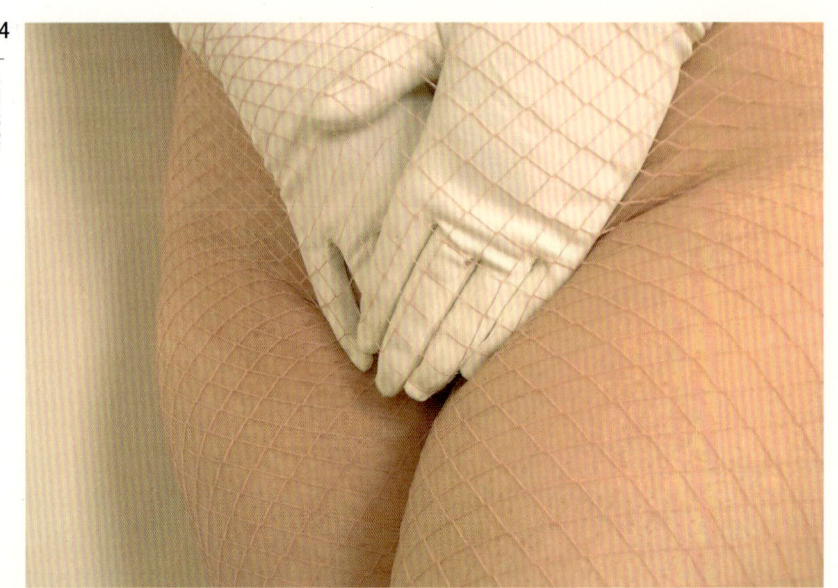

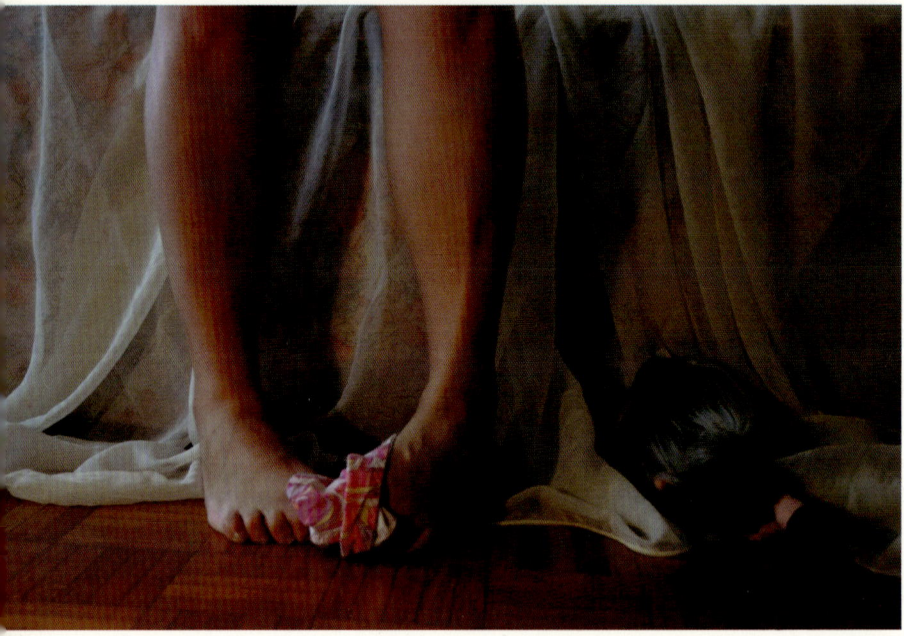

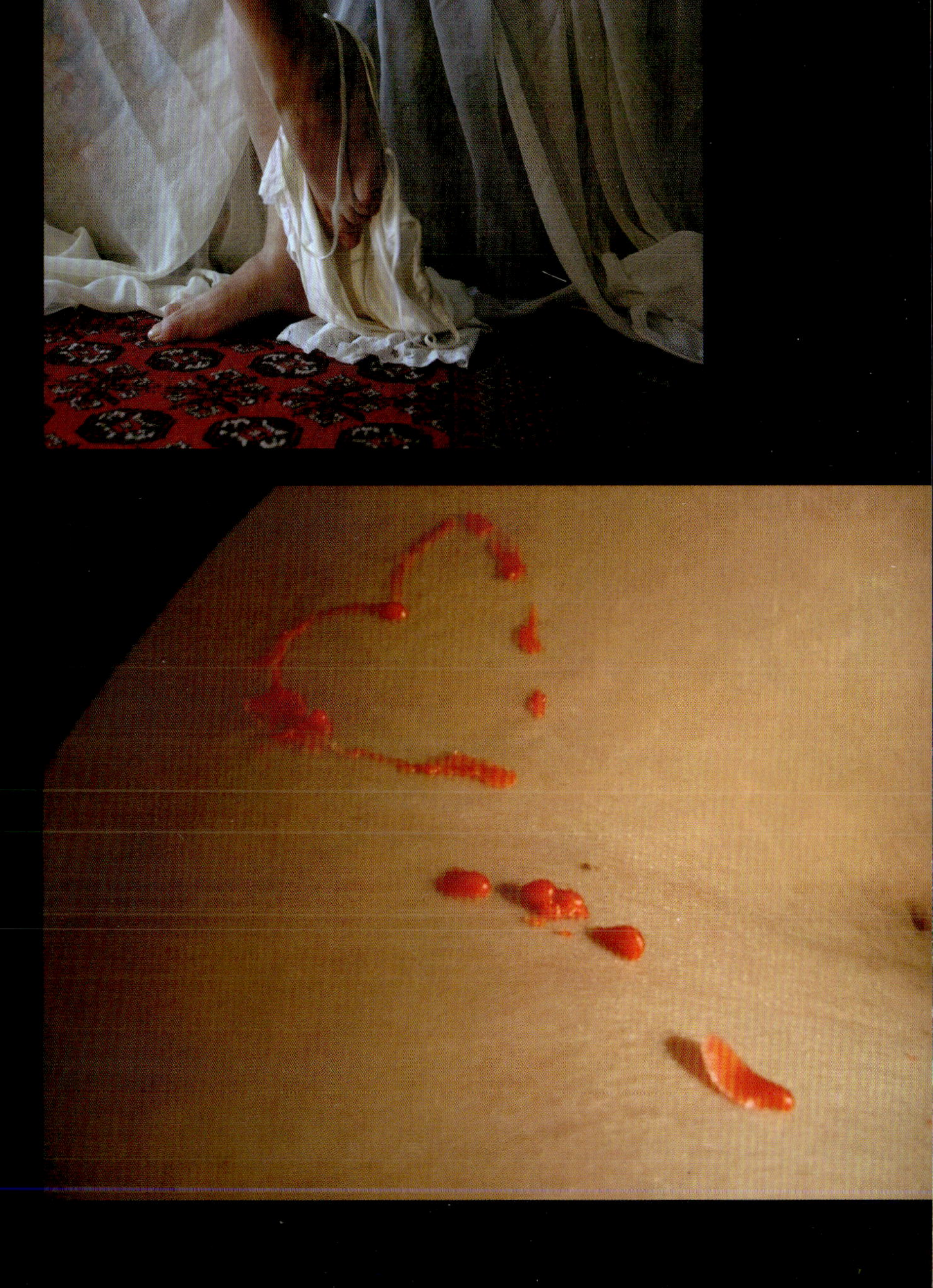

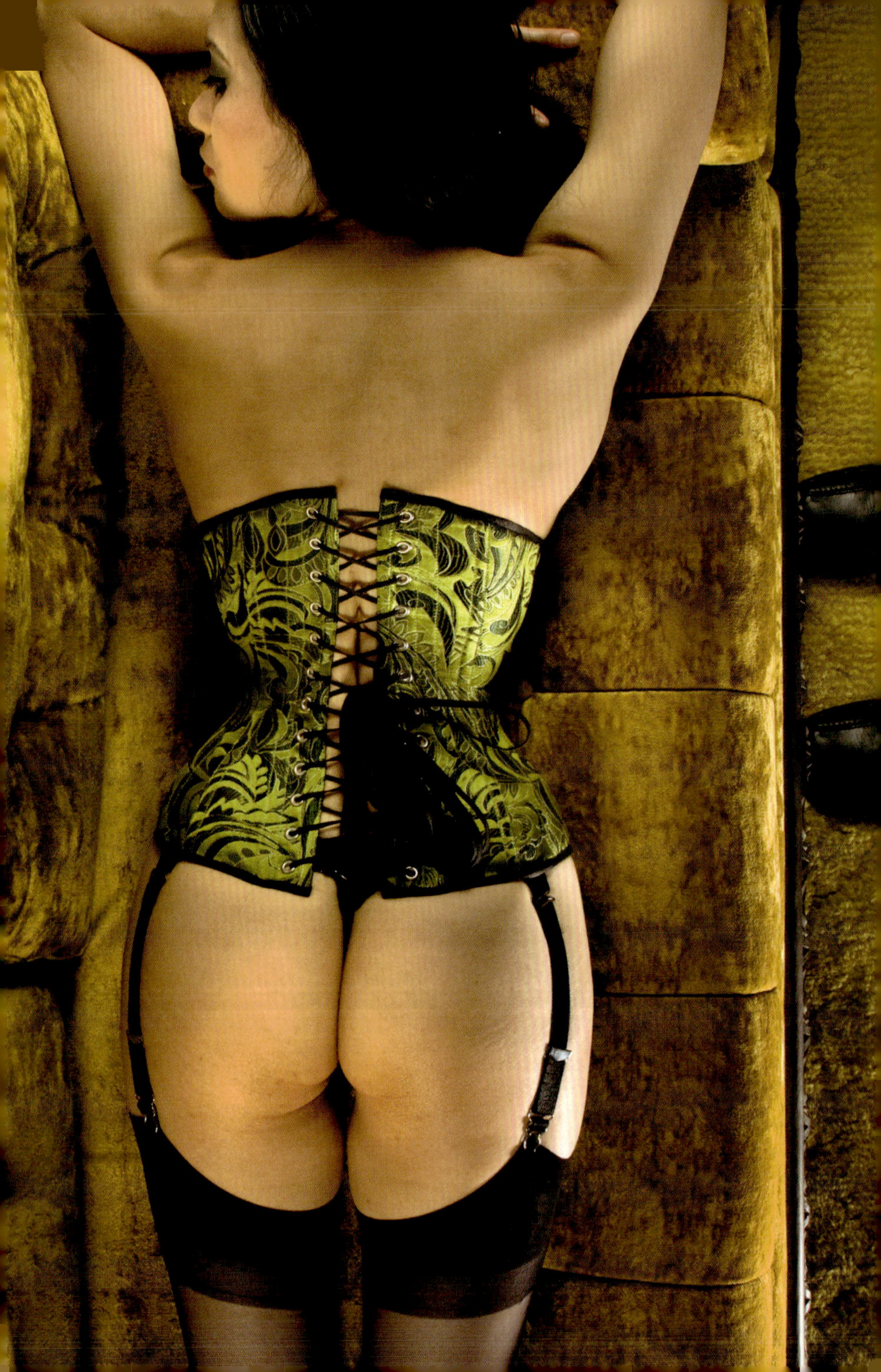

chas ray krider

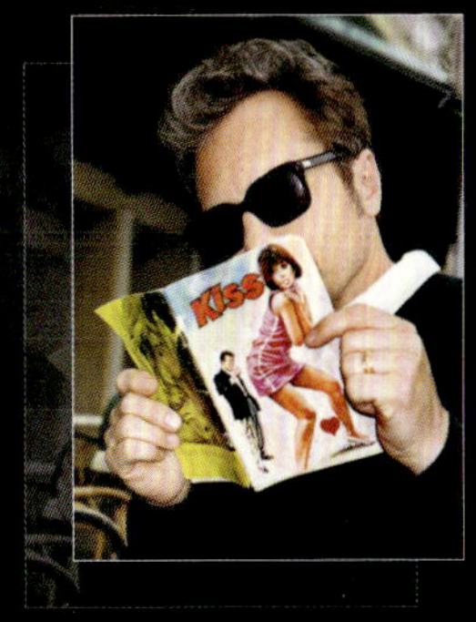

US PHOTOGRAPHER Chas Ray Krider's images are part of a tradition of erotic art that employs exaggeration, mystery and the guilty pleasures of voyeurism. The photographs are about the forms employed in narrative-based erotic art as contrasted with erotica crafted merely to display the explicit. The work concerns the art of presentation, the mystery of anticipation and the universal human curiosity about sexuality. There are 'fine art' references within these photos but there is no attempt to use the formal desensitizing techniques of 'high' art photography to distract the viewer from the sexually charged visual aspect of the narrative. Krider has published two books: *Motel Fetish* and *Do Not Disturb*.

www.motelfetish.com
www.chasraykrider.wordpress.com

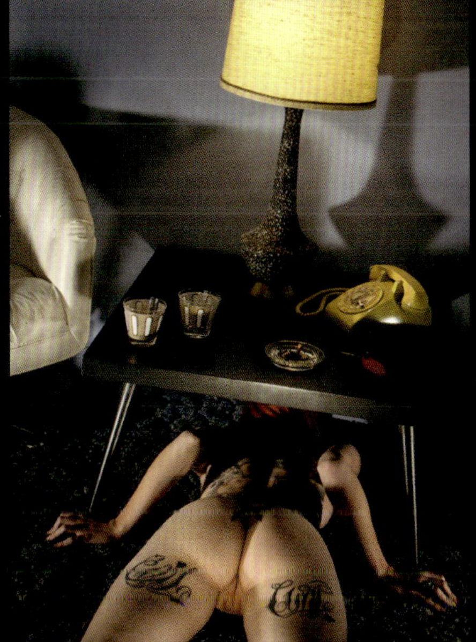

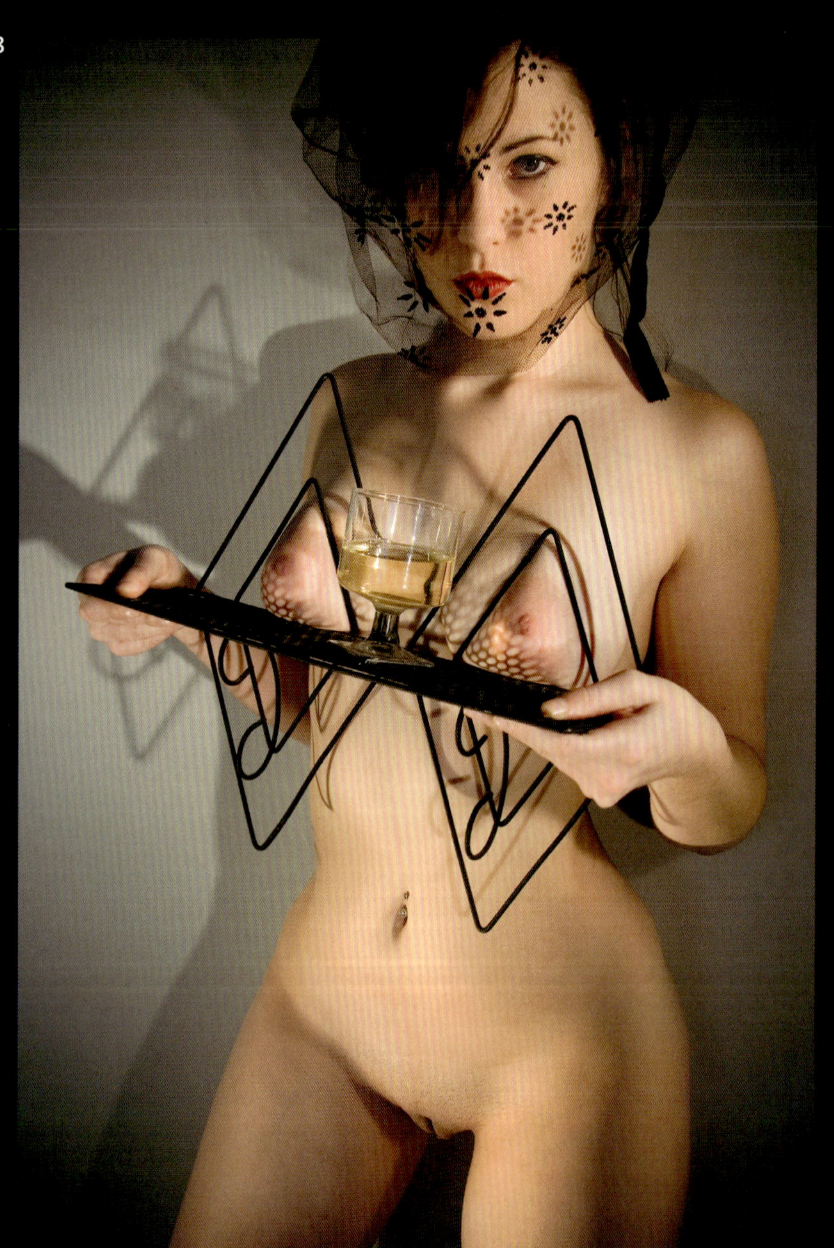

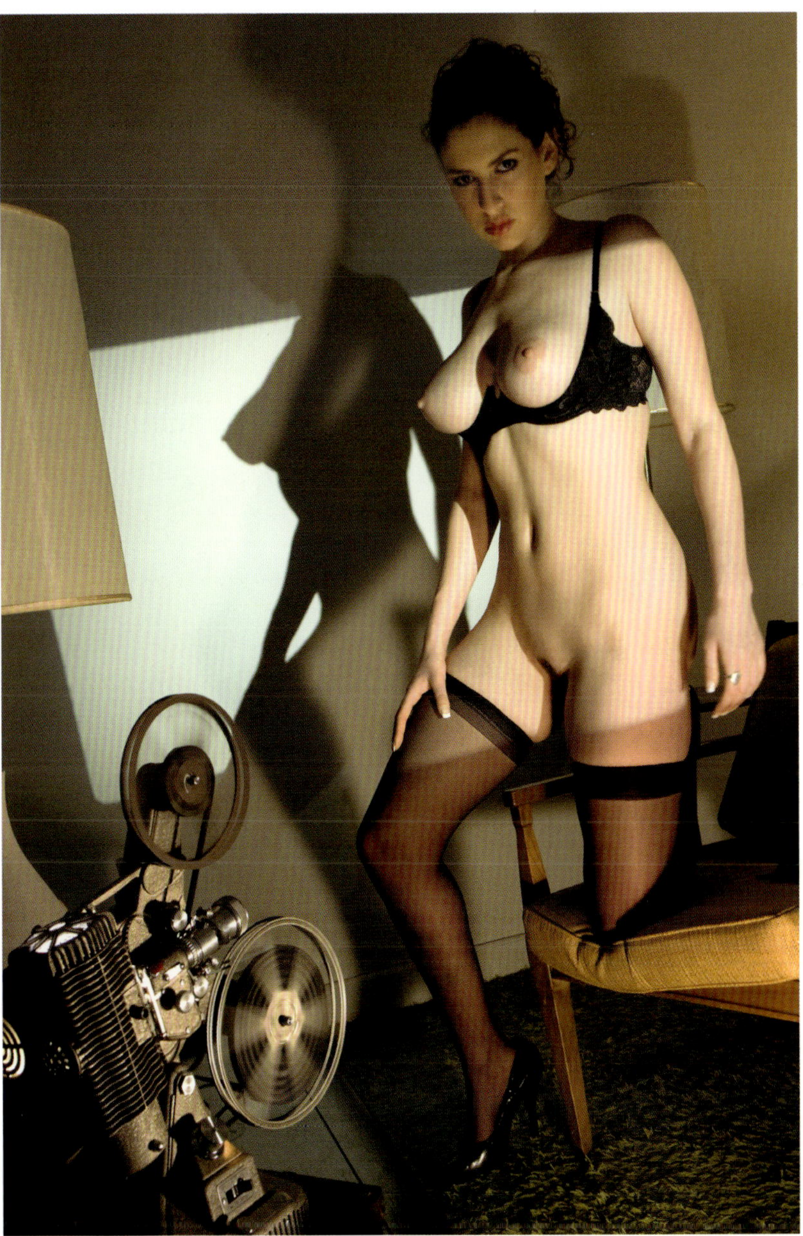

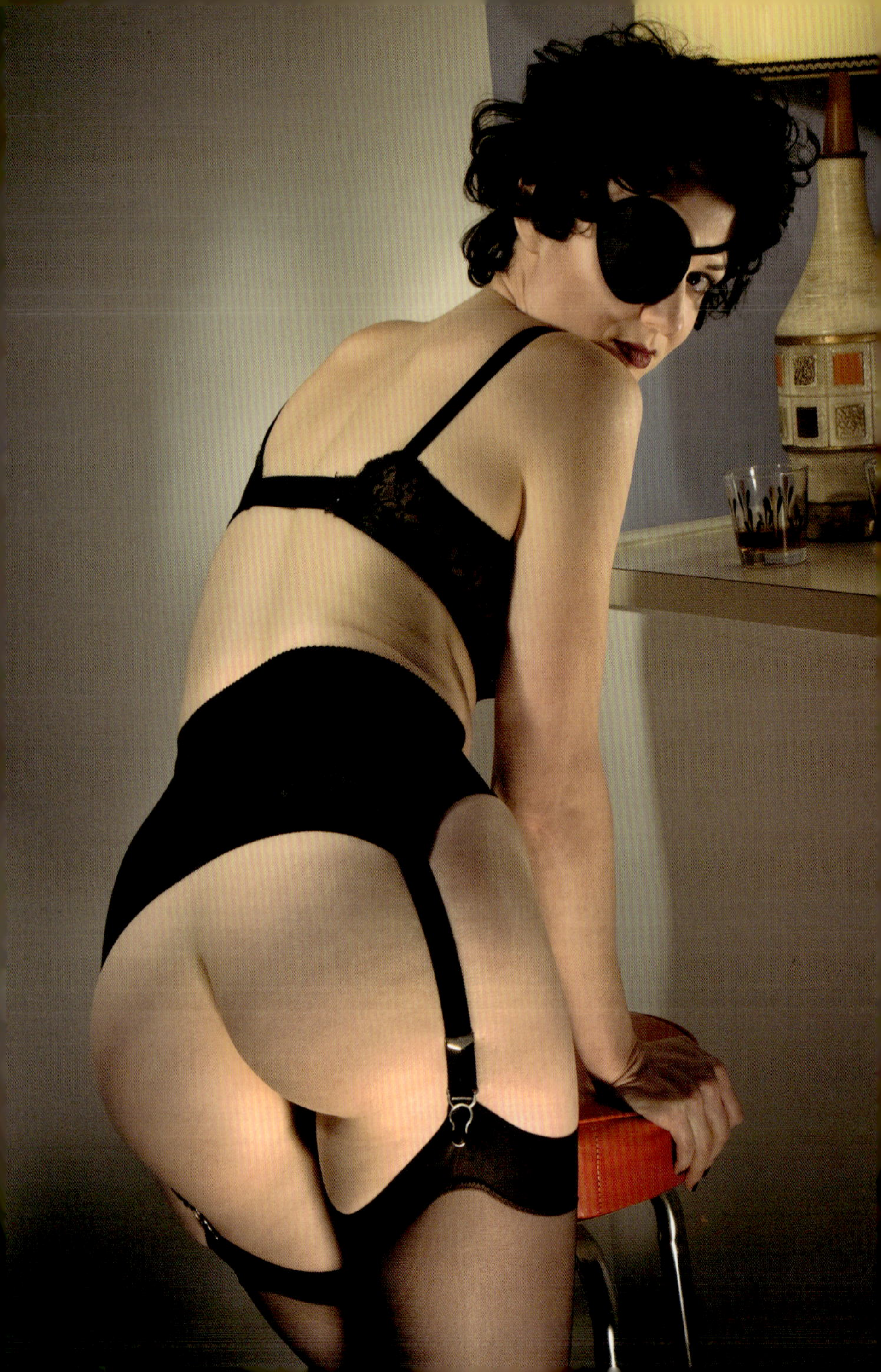

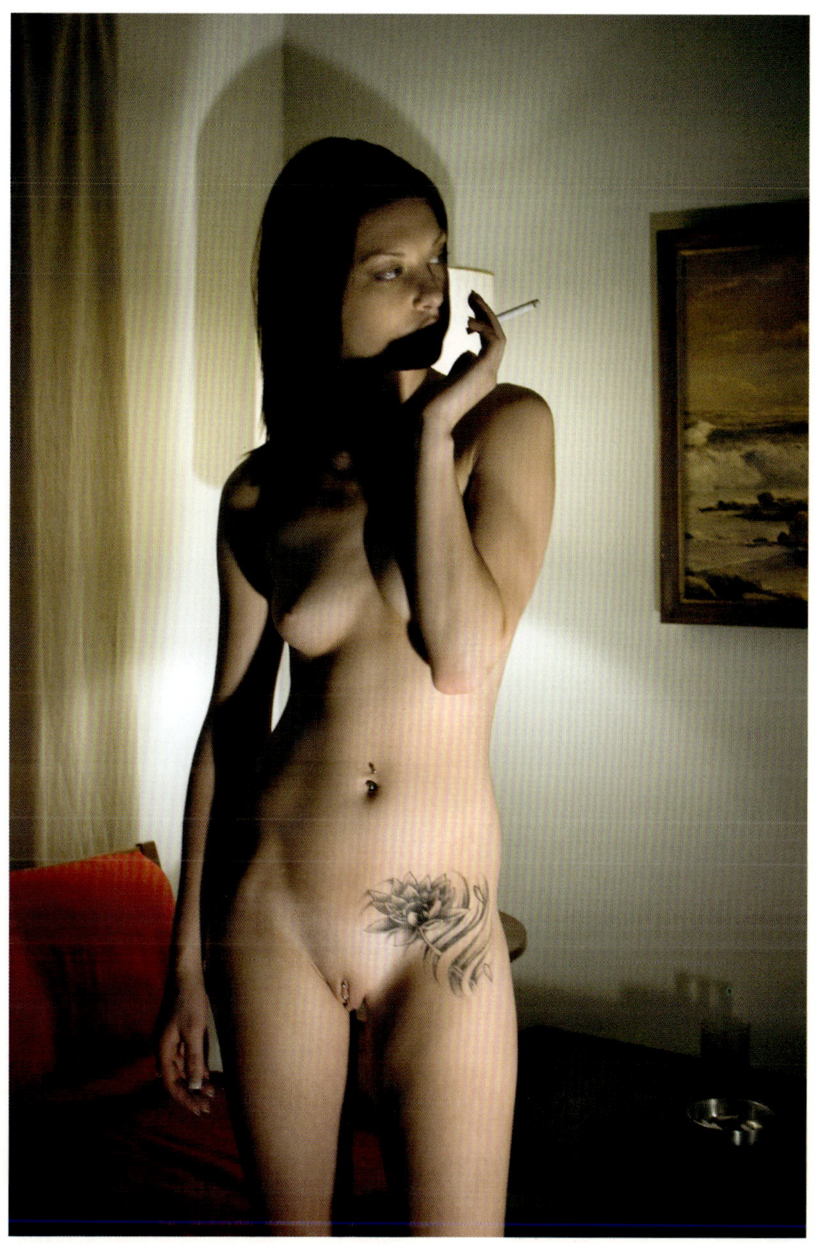

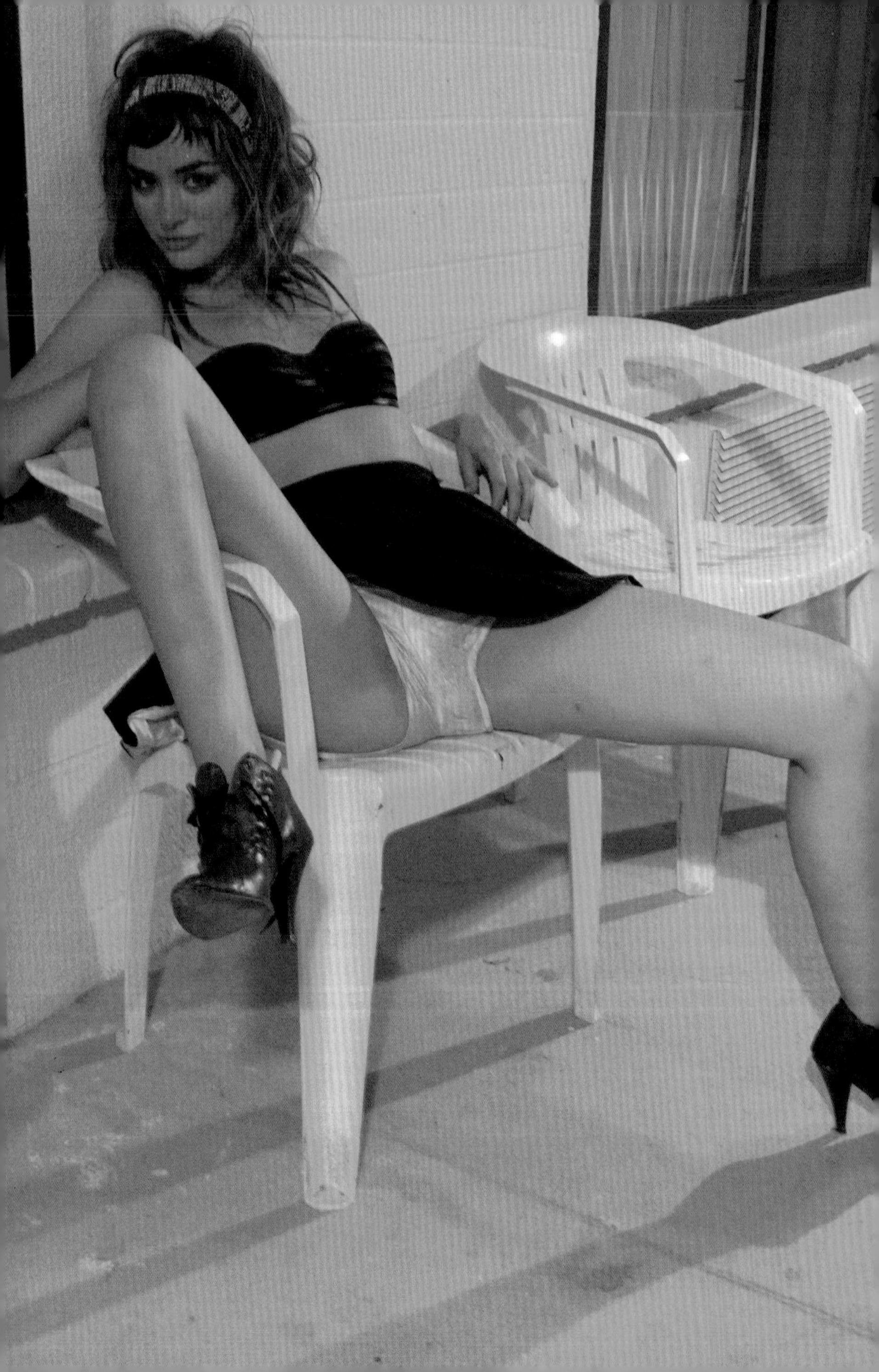

eric kroll

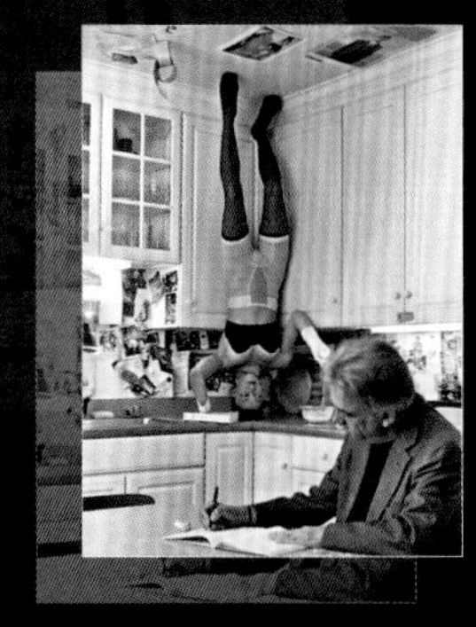

NOW IN HIS 60s, and resident in Tucson, Arizona, Eric Kroll is one of the all-time masters of erotic photography, with many books to his credit, including *Sex Objects*, *Fetish Girls*, *Beauty Parade* and the two volumes of *The Transformations of Gwen*. He also directed many films in the fetish area, and collaborated on Taschen's bestselling erotic books series. He has also contributed to the *New York Times*, *Vogue*, *Der Spiegel* and other leading publications and has been on-set photographer for major movies.

www.fetish-usa.com

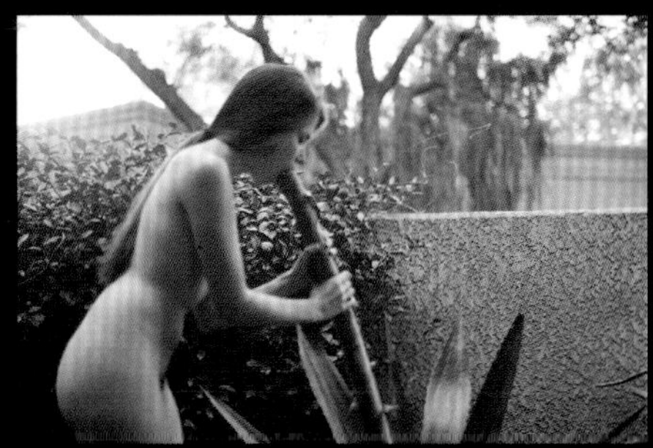

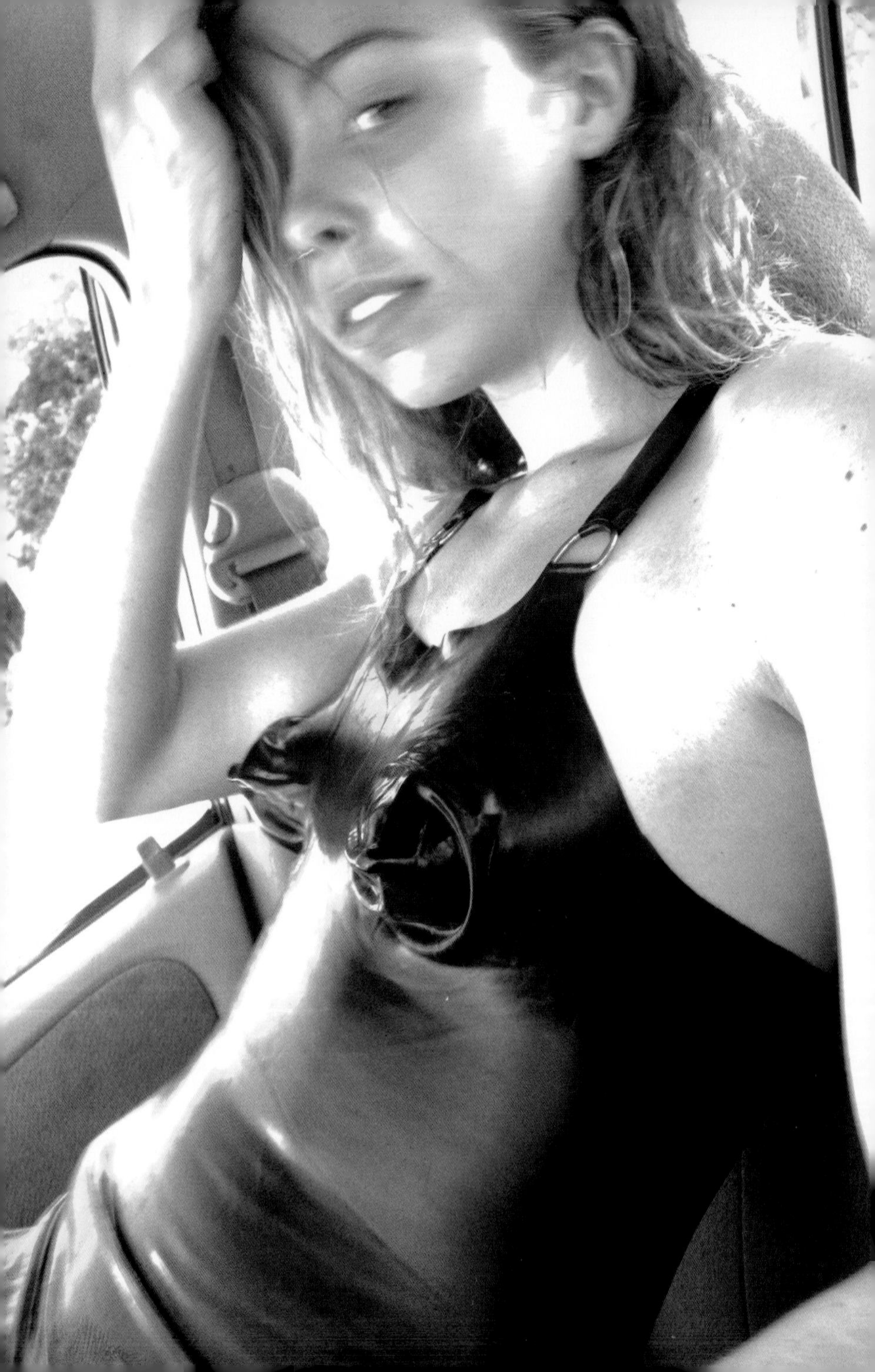

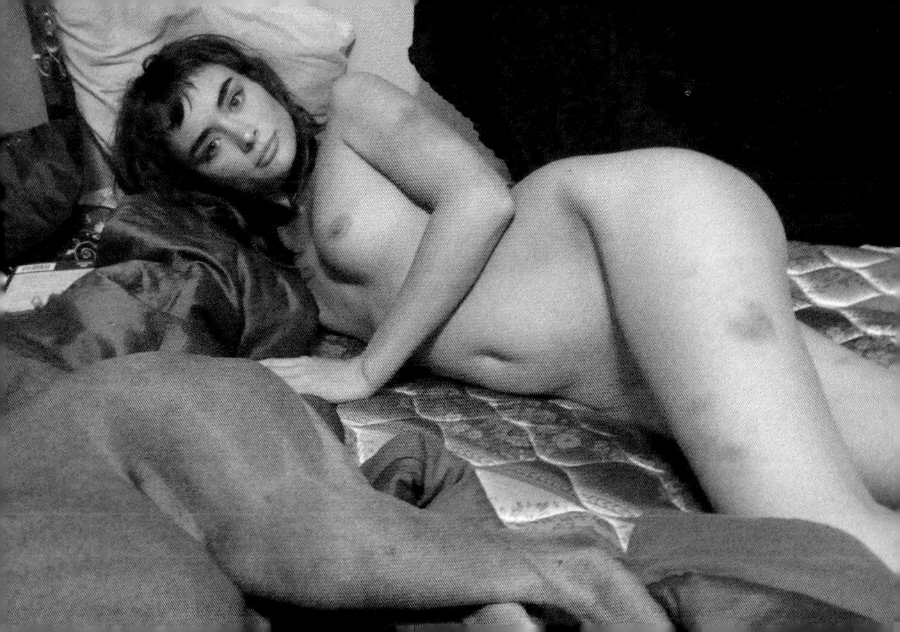

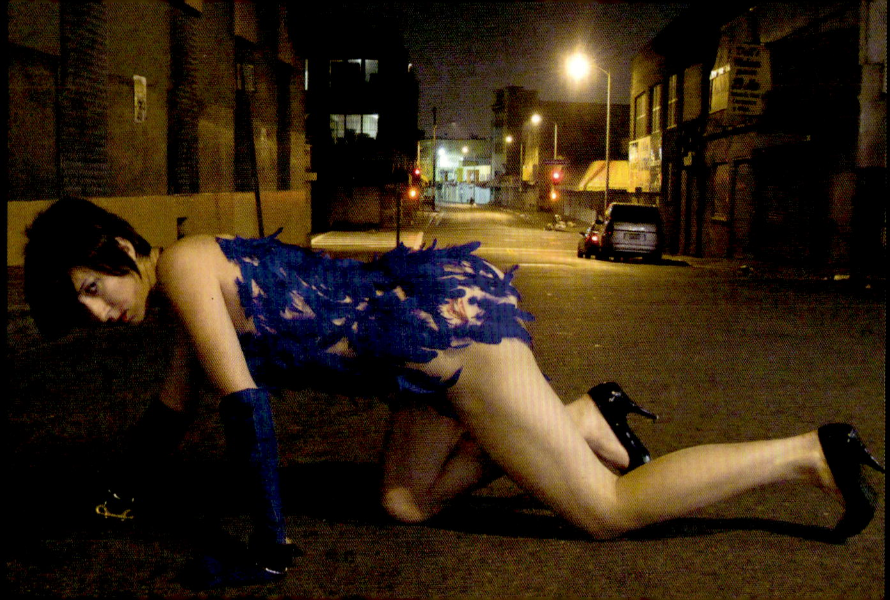

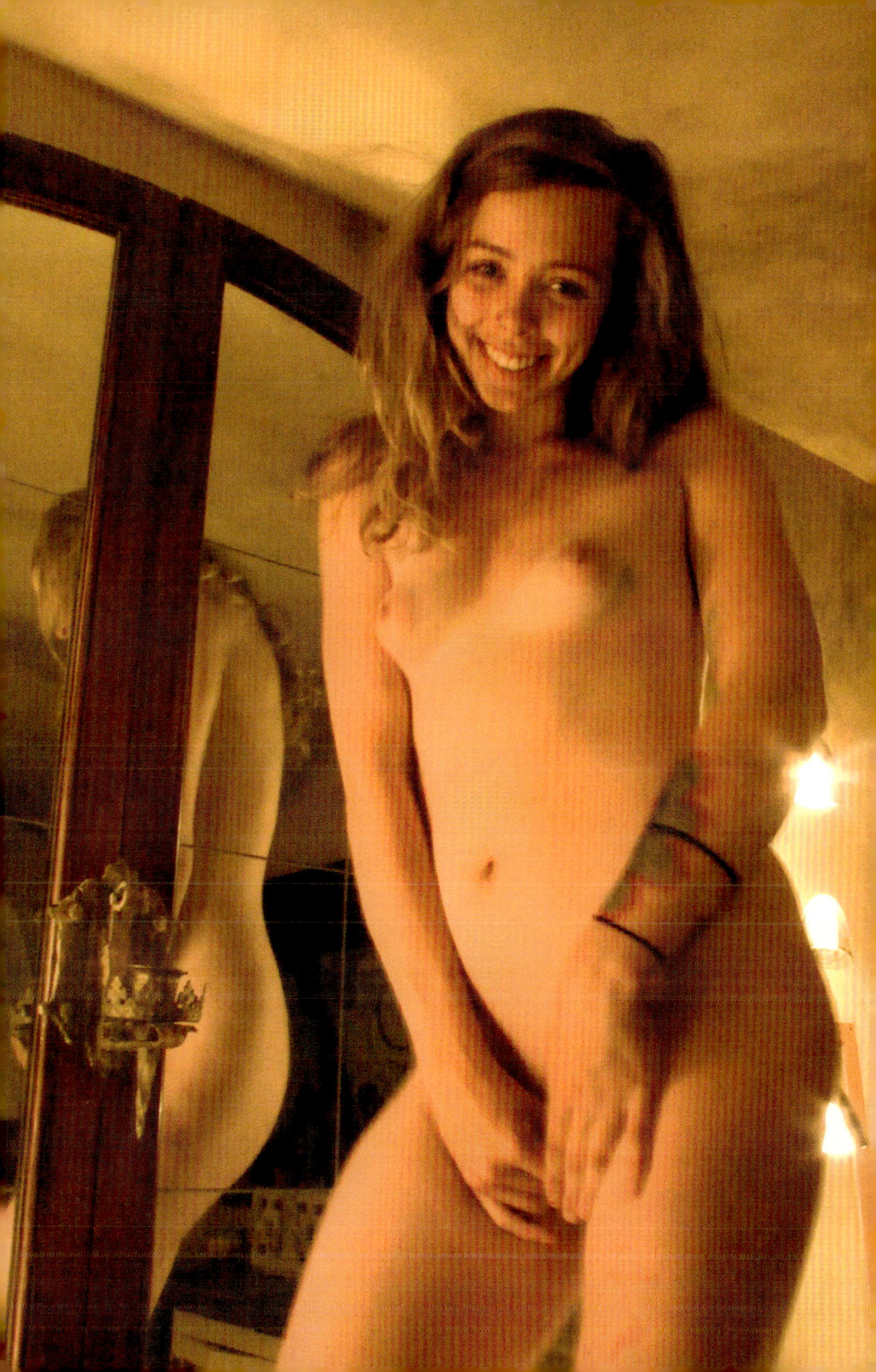

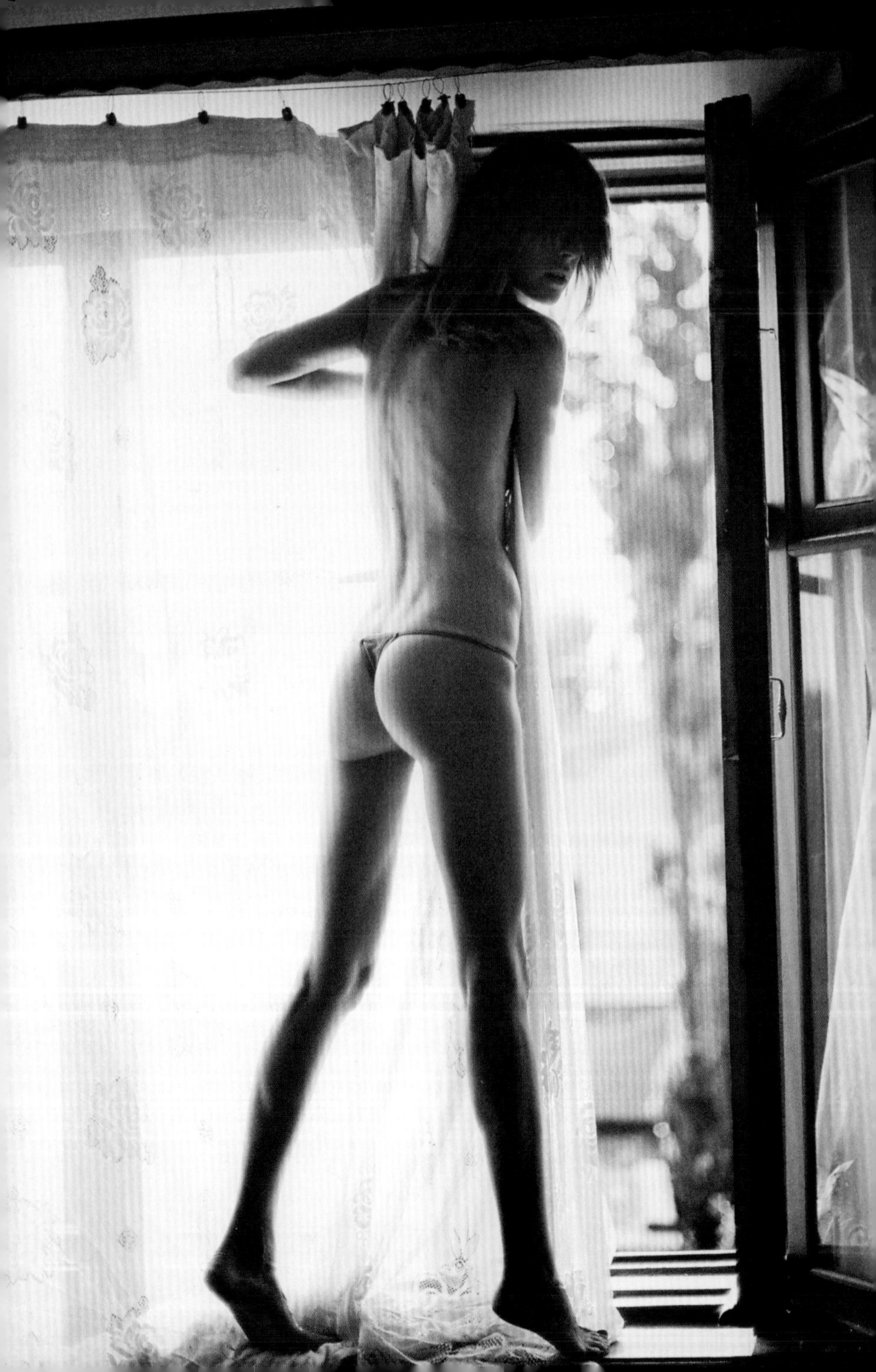

valeria lazareva

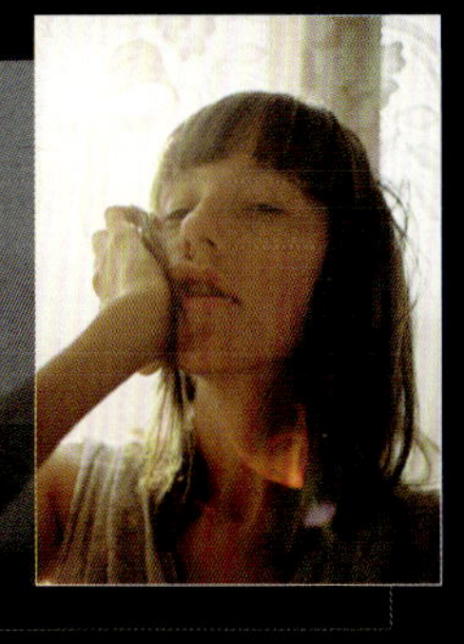

VALERIA WAS BORN IN KIEV, Ukraine in 1984. She is now based in Odessa, but also works in Kiev and Moscow, where she divides her time between architecture and photography. She is one of the most exciting new talents in the field, and contributes to several glossy magazines.

www.lazarevavaleria.com

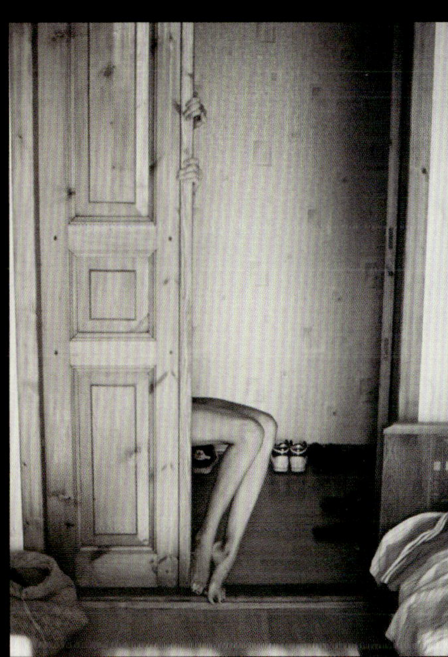

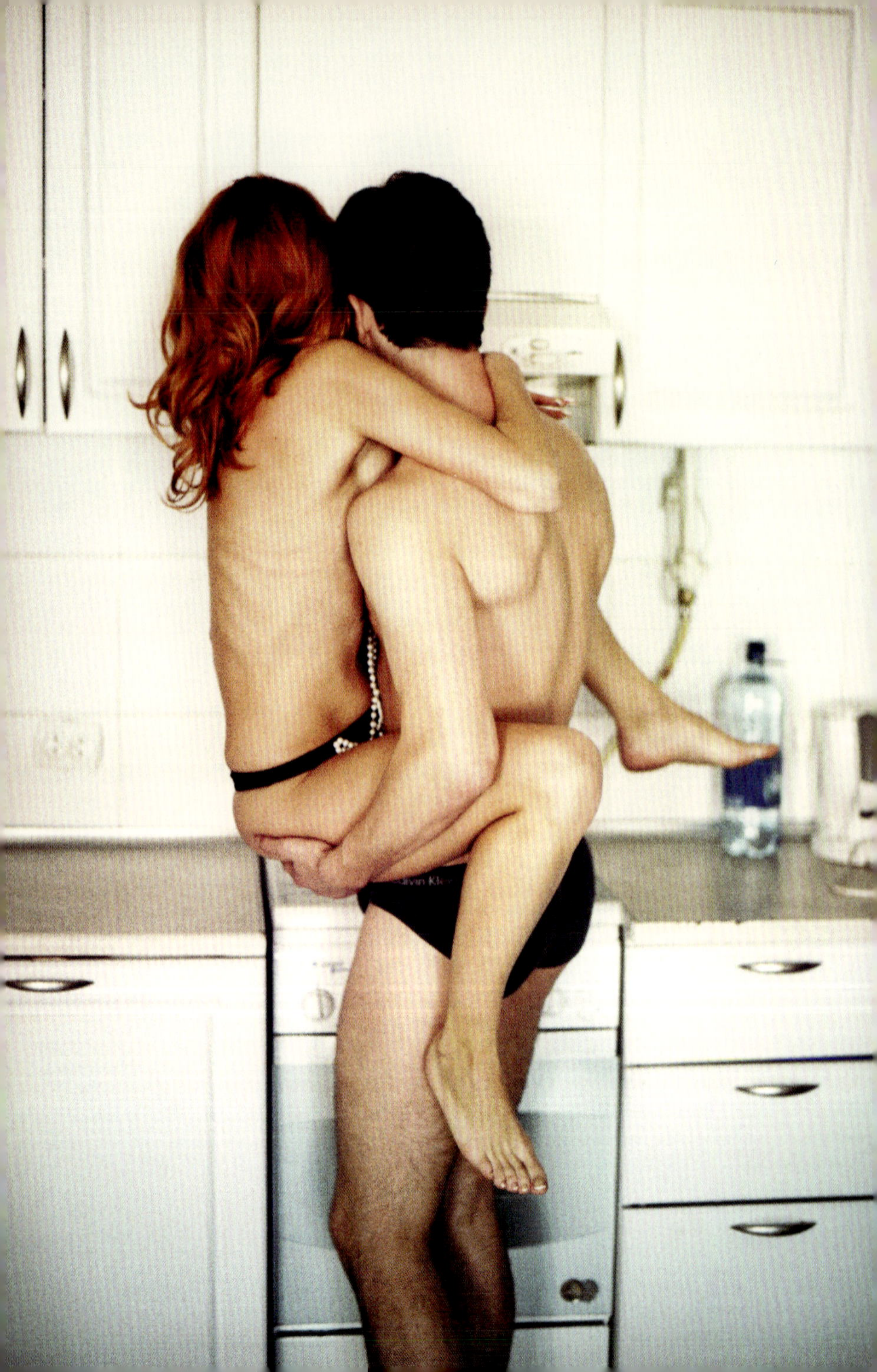

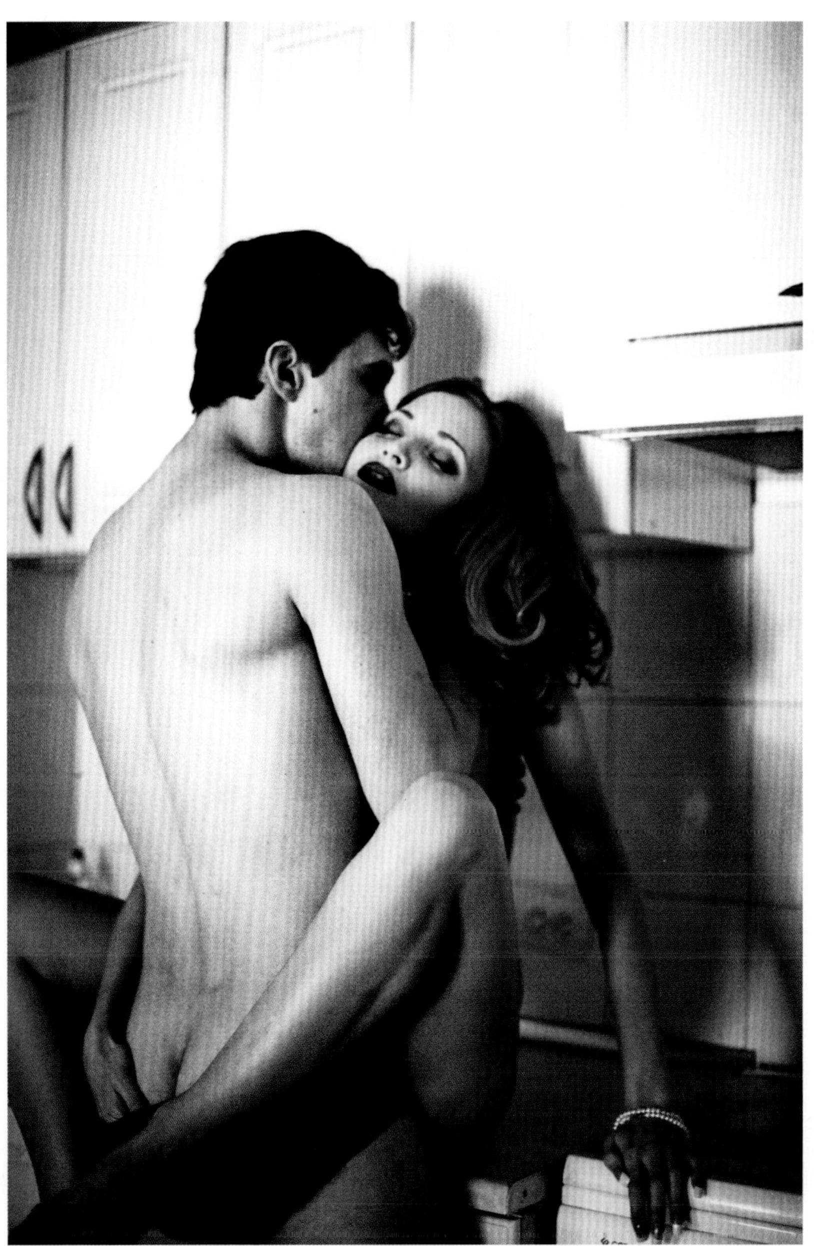

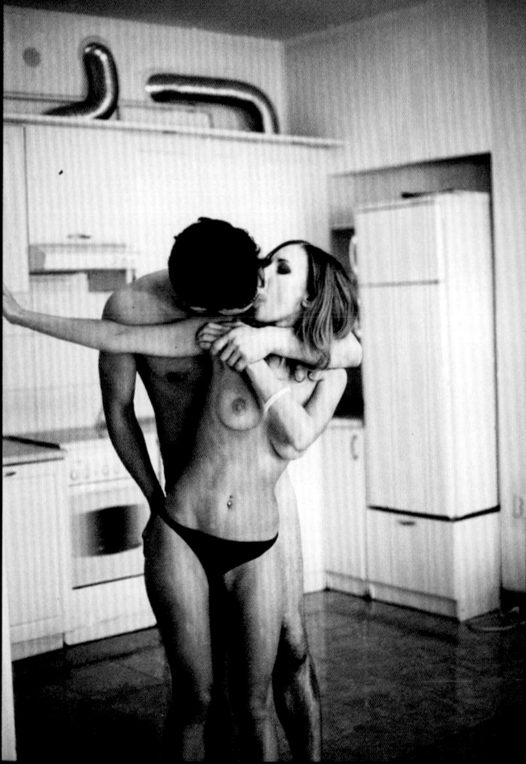

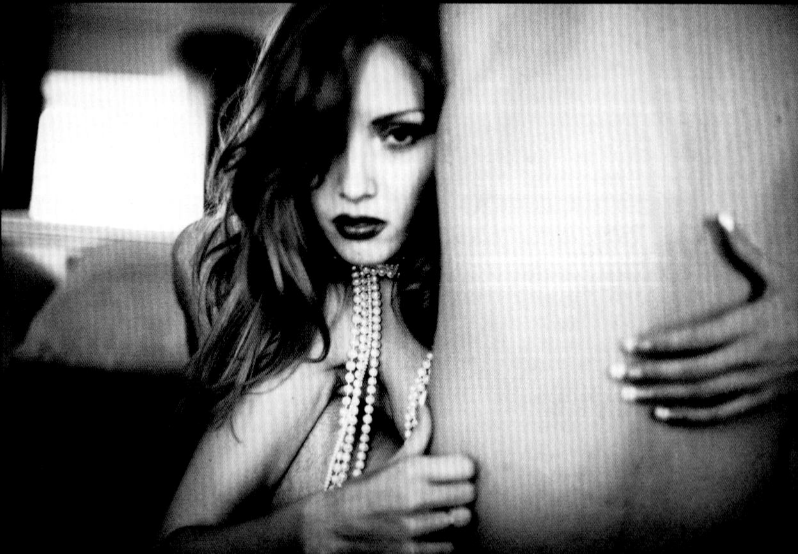

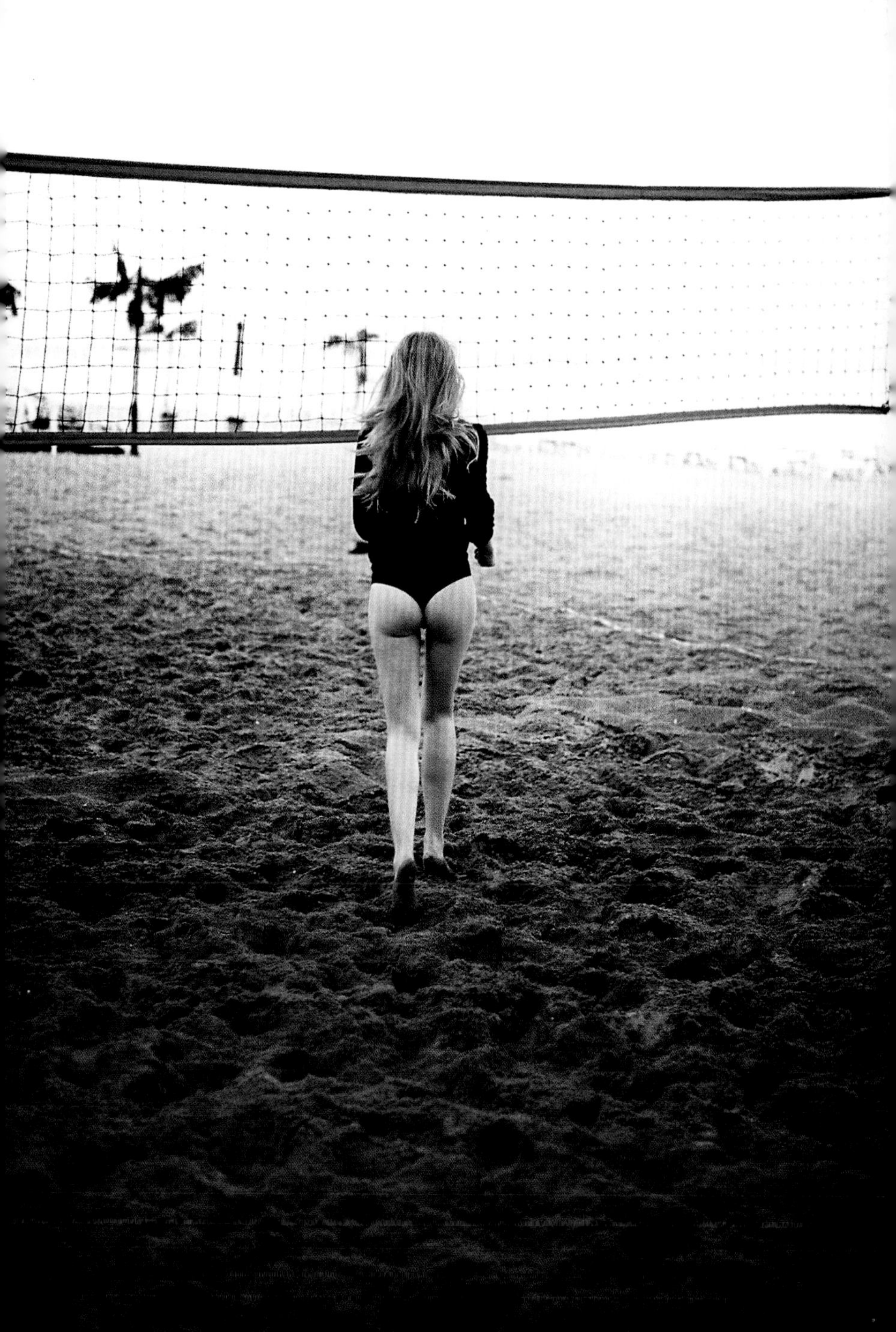

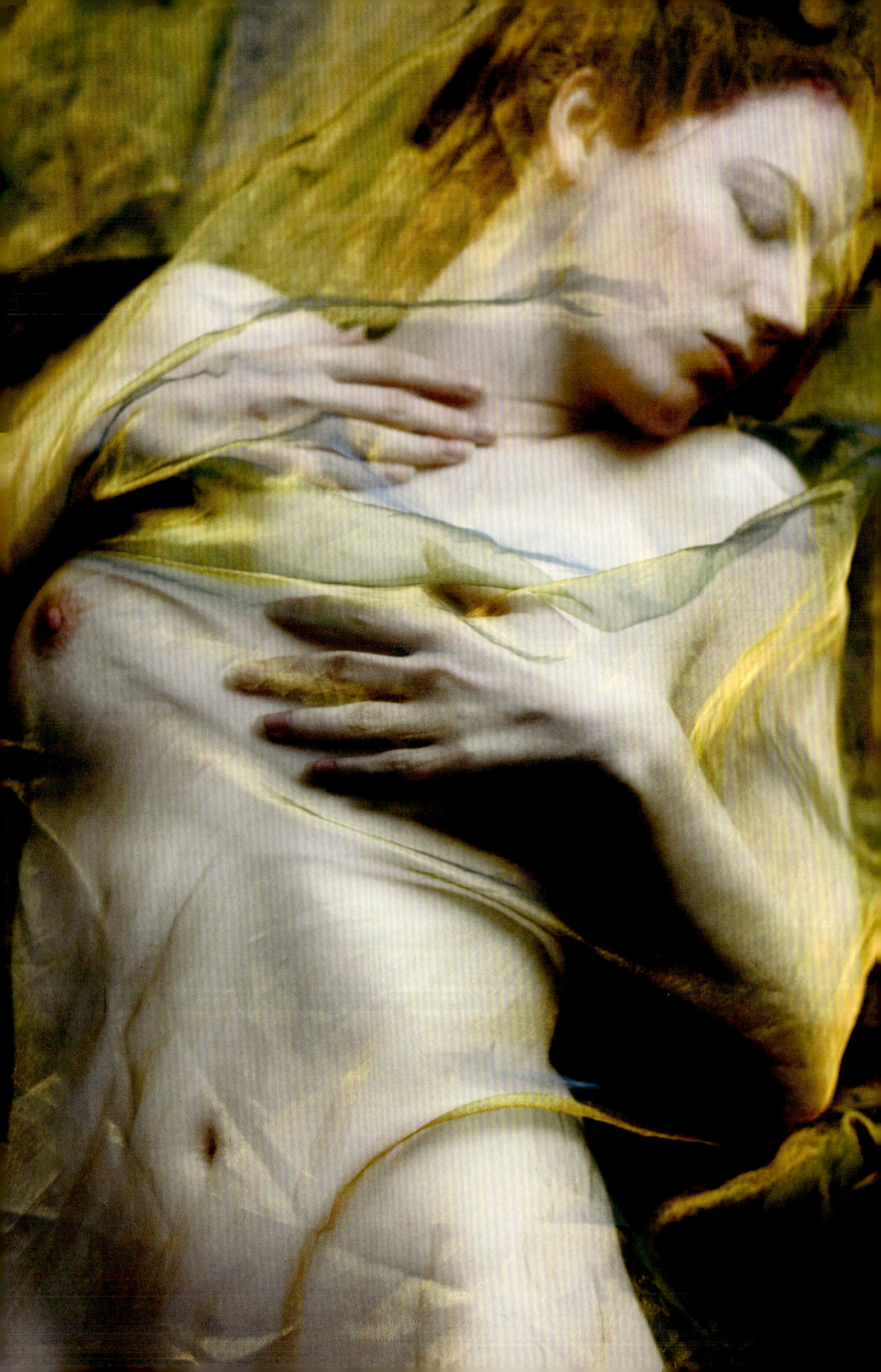

elisa lazo de valdez

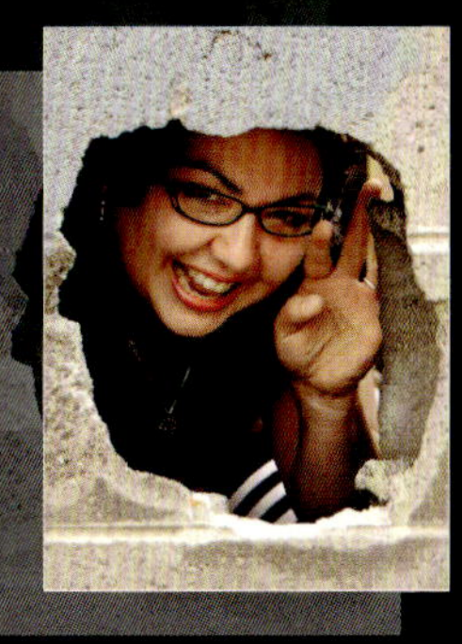

ELISA WAS BORN IN LIMA, Peru, in 1967 and has been an artist from the age of three. Her work expresses her fascination with dark sensuality, mythology and luxury of form. A traditional film photographer for a decade, she embraced digital photography after realizing the medium translated her artistic vision perfectly. Her work has appeared internationally on book covers, in magazines and advertising campaigns as well as being incldued in several photography anthologies. She currently lives in Portland, Oregon, USA and continues to explore the photographic themes of surreal sensuality and dark erotica.

www.visioluxus.com

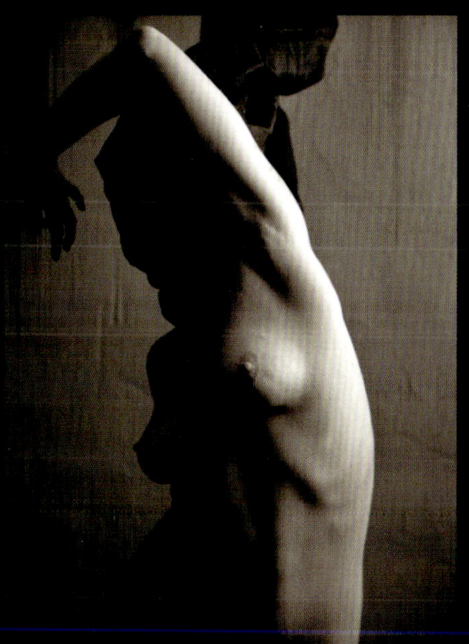

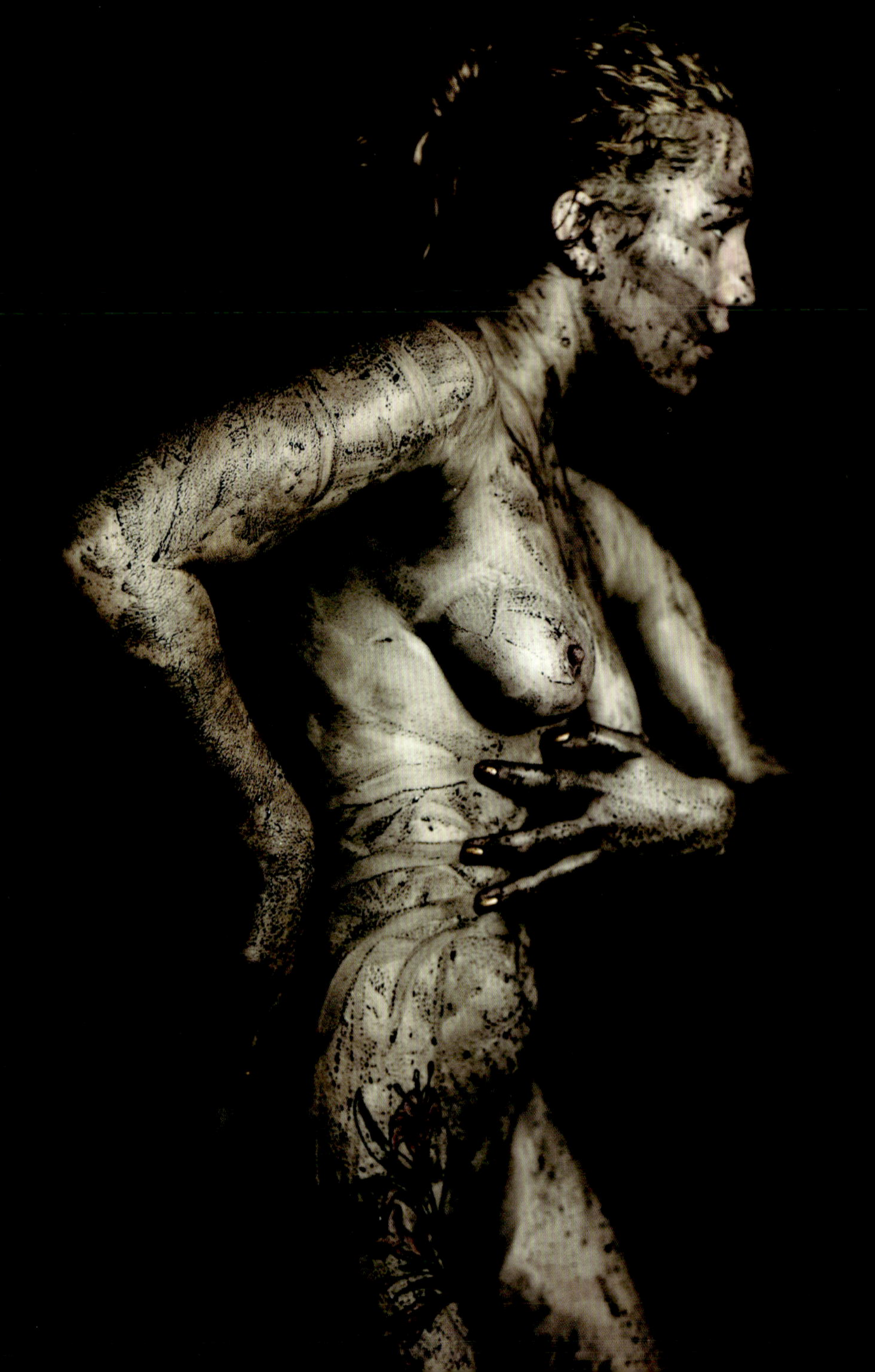

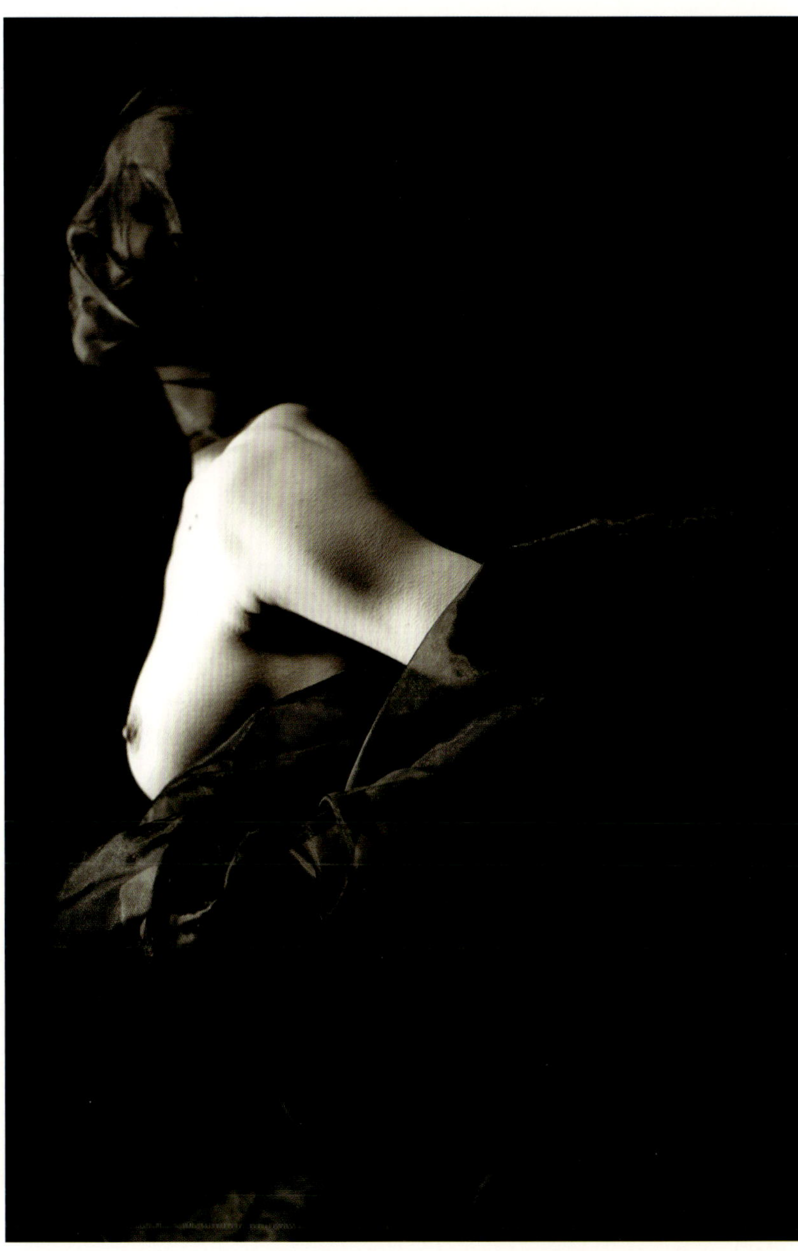

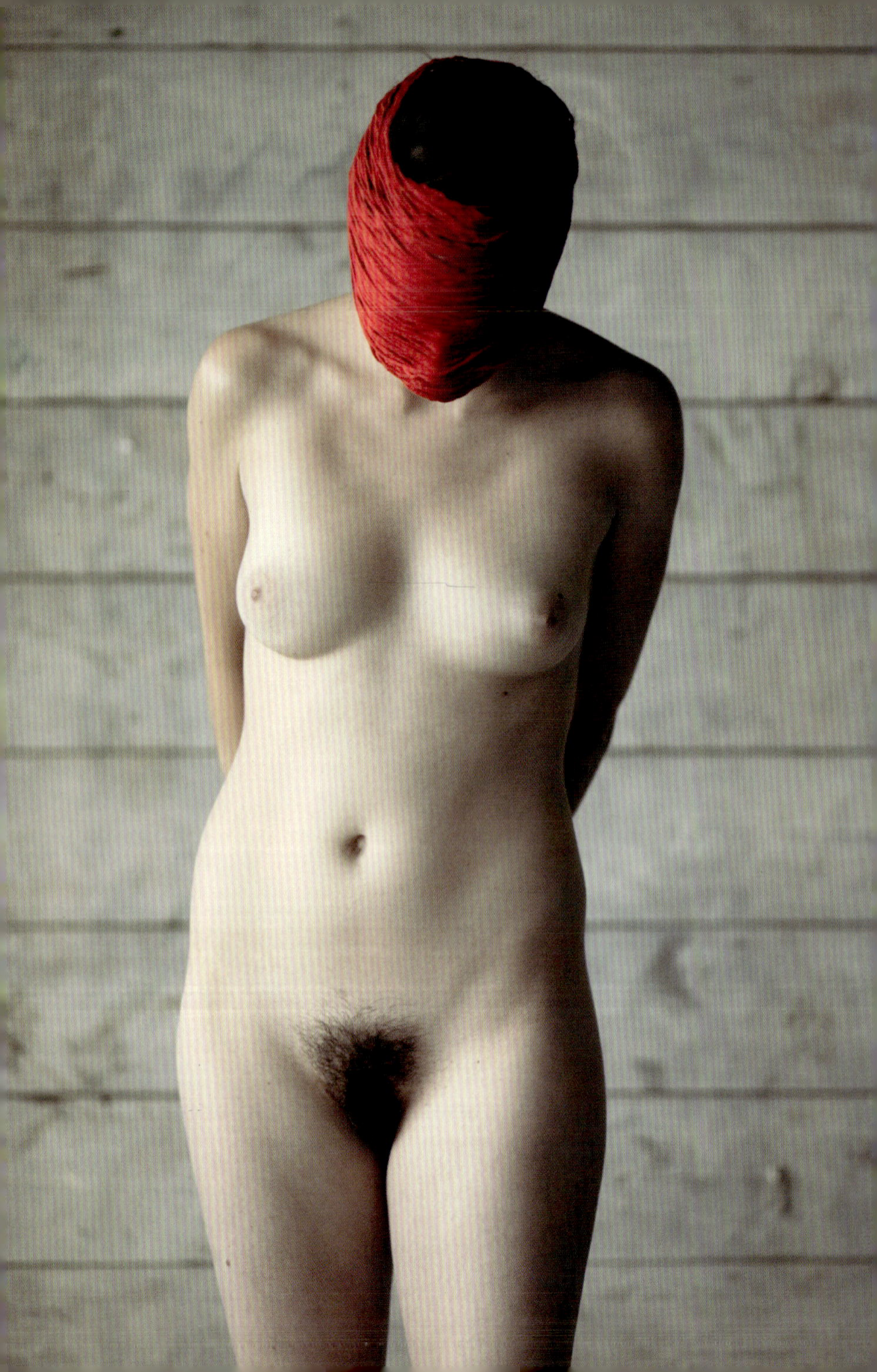

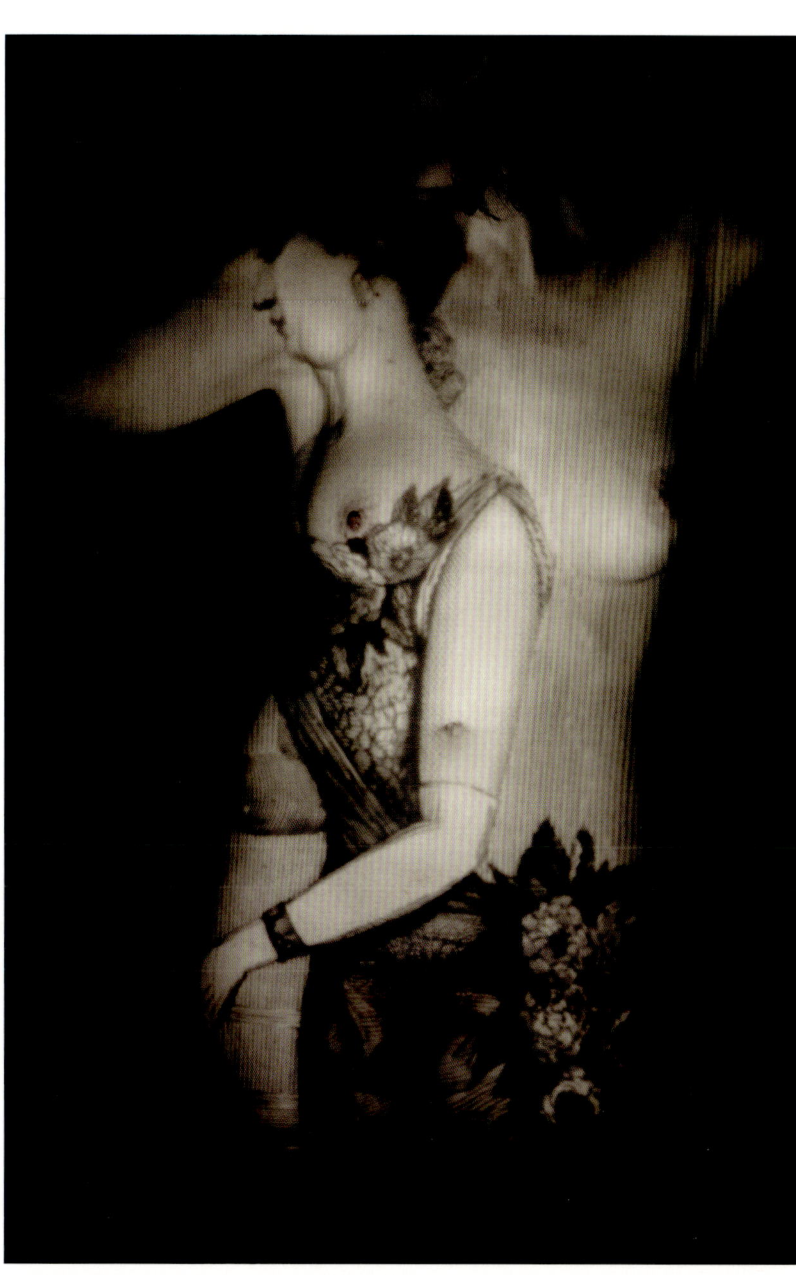

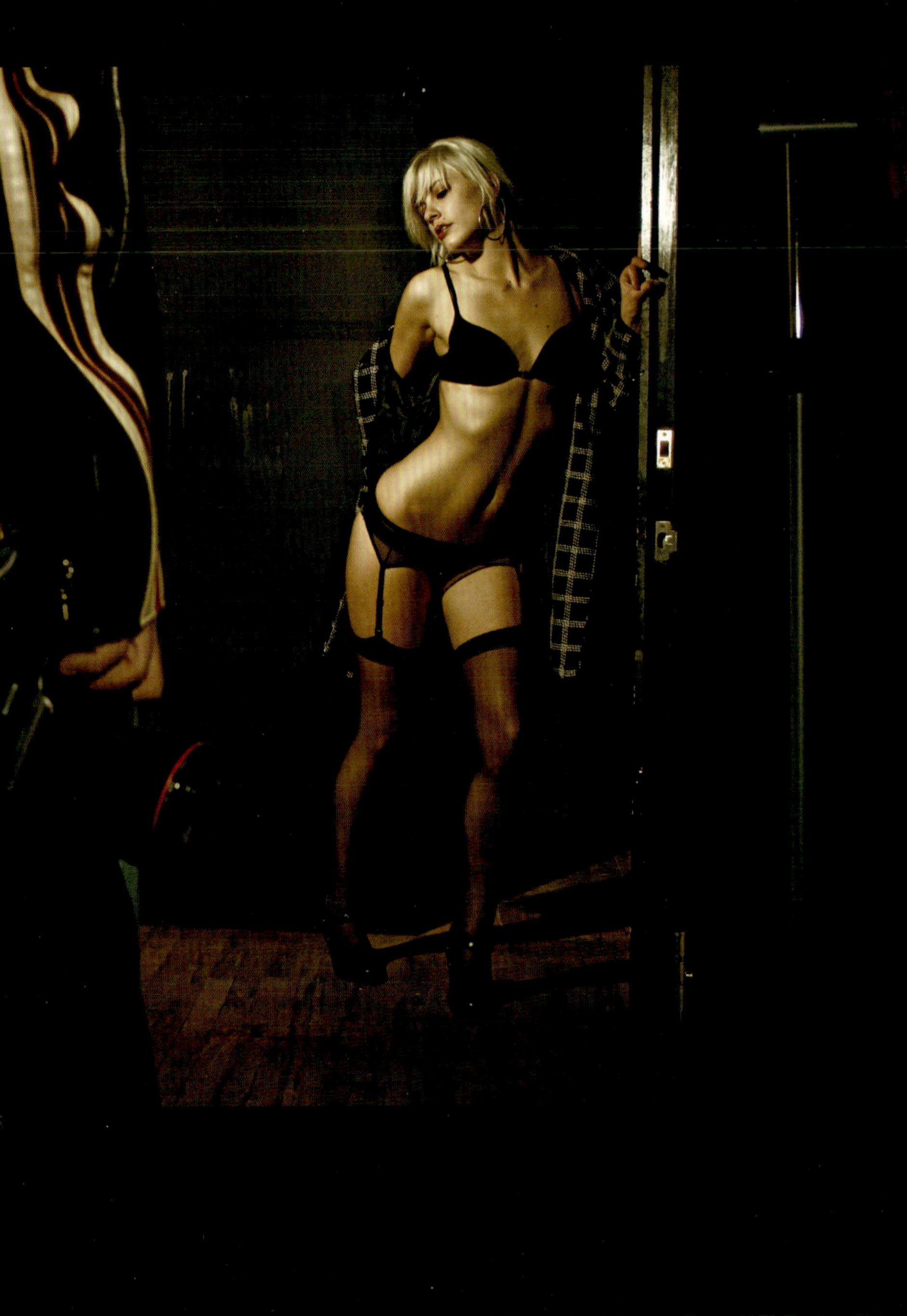

chris leblanc

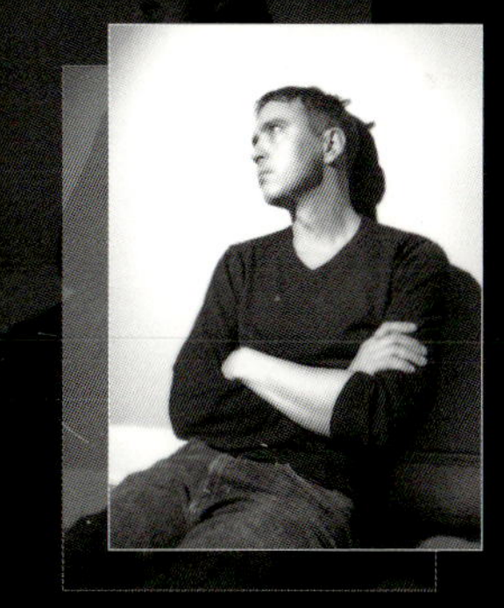

AFTER TOYING EVERY ONCE in a while with a camera at different periods of his life it wasn't until two and half years ago that Chris LeBlanc made a conscious decision to get more serious about it. Following a love of Helmut Newton and being drawn into his photographs definitely had an influence on his love for the more dark, moody, sexy and edgy side of women. He is self-taught, living in Calgary, Canada in an old 1918 house that he has shot models in almost every weekend for the past two years. The house perfectly blends atmosphere, character and mood with its dramatic lighting, a feature that he has come to love. After stumbling nervously for the first few shoots he could see a style start to develop and has rolled with it since. It was never his intention to show women as subservient or victims but on the contrary as strong and powerful, perhaps even dominant. The photographs themselves portray that fine line of sexy and edgy but still remain classy, and that's the way he wants to continue.

www.flickr.com/photos/chrisleblanc

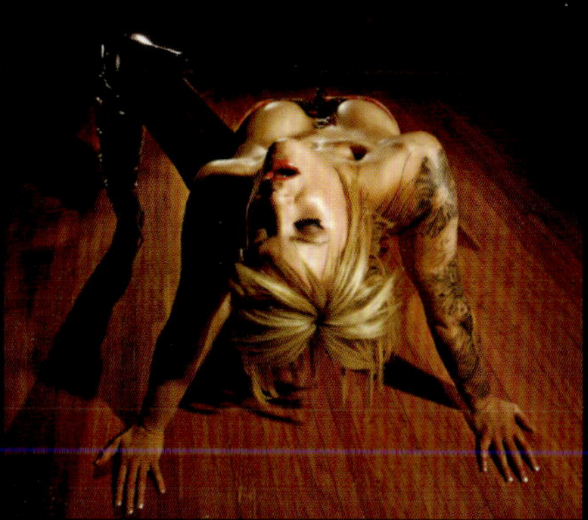

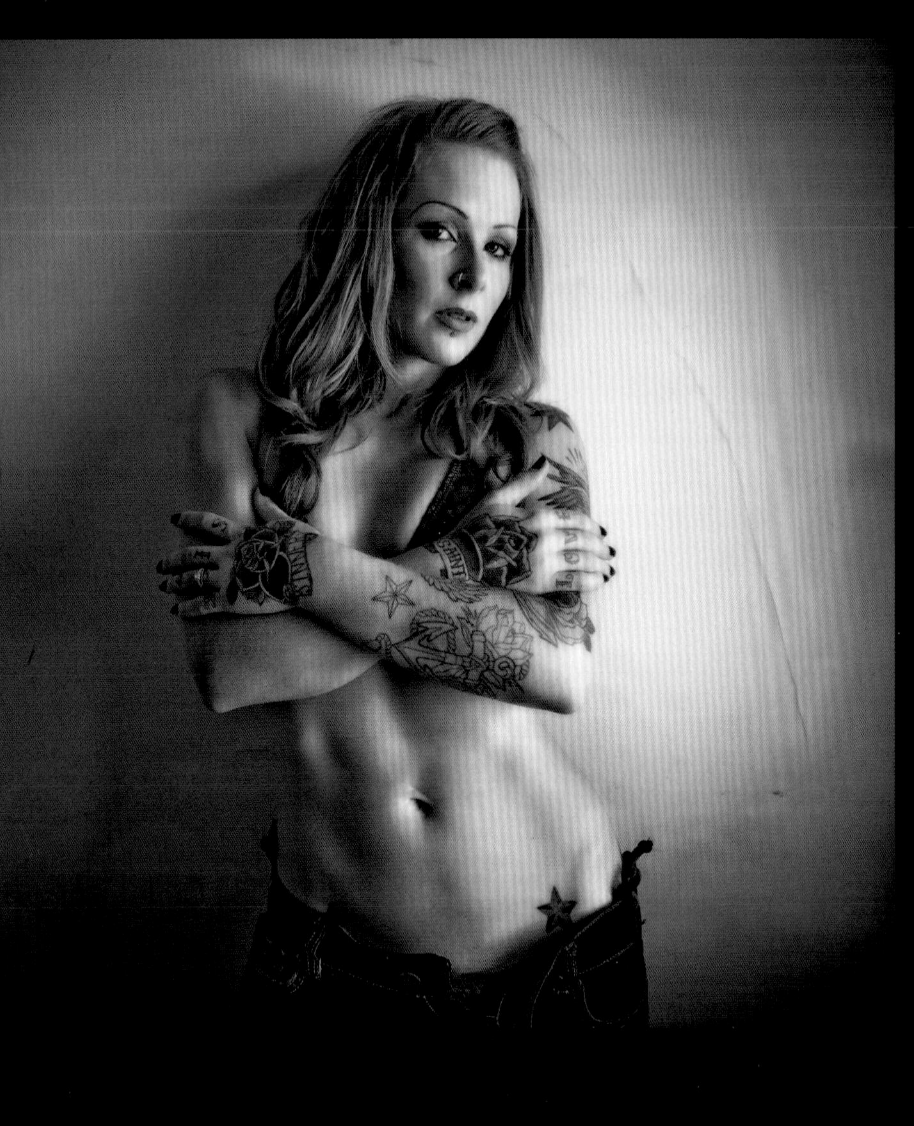

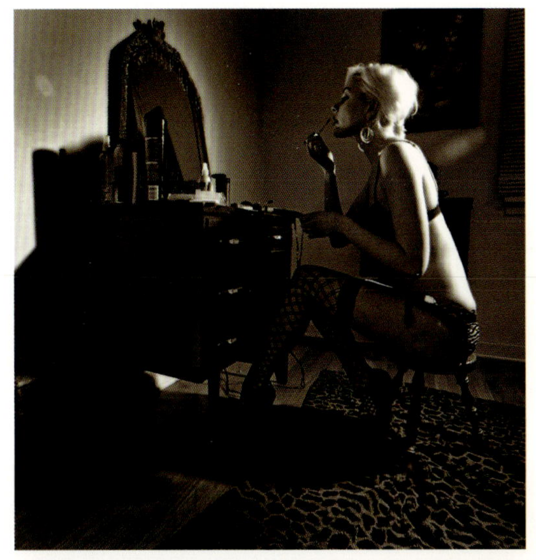

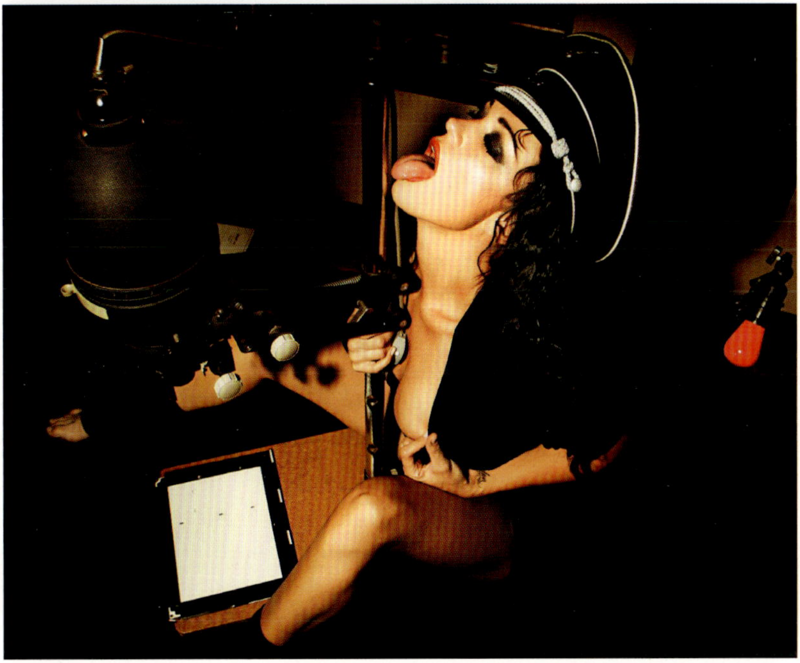

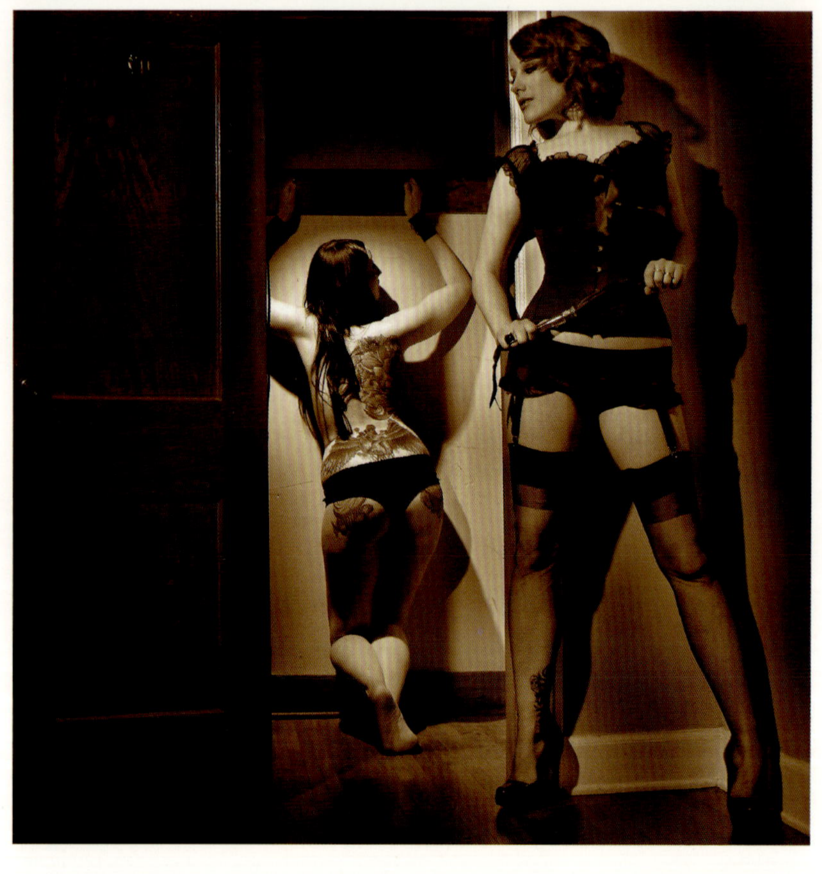

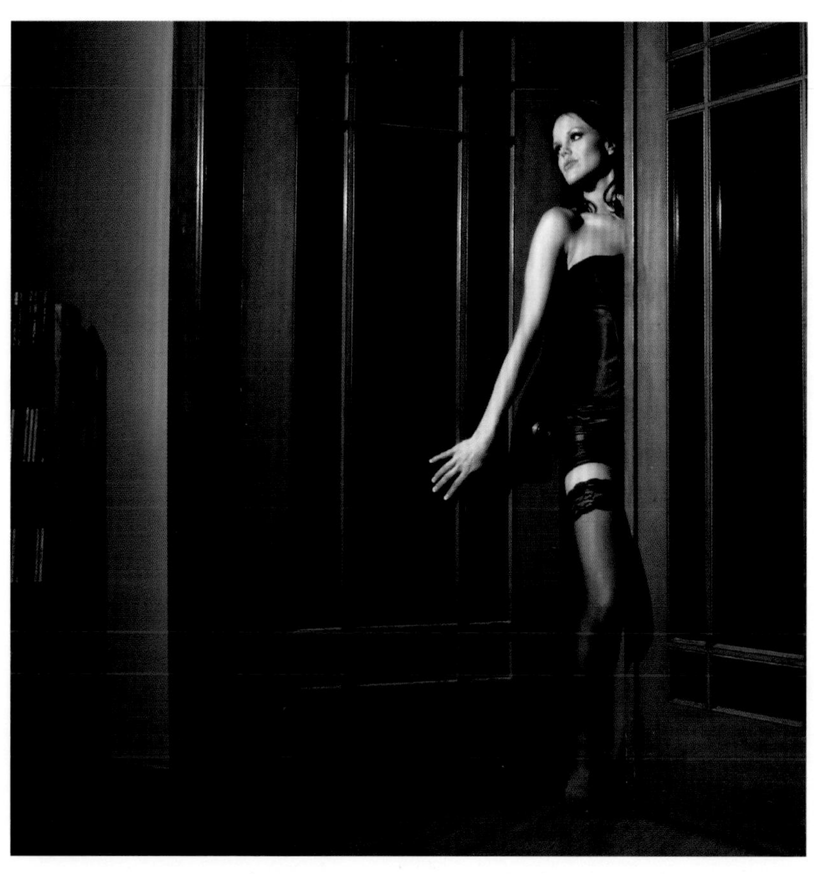

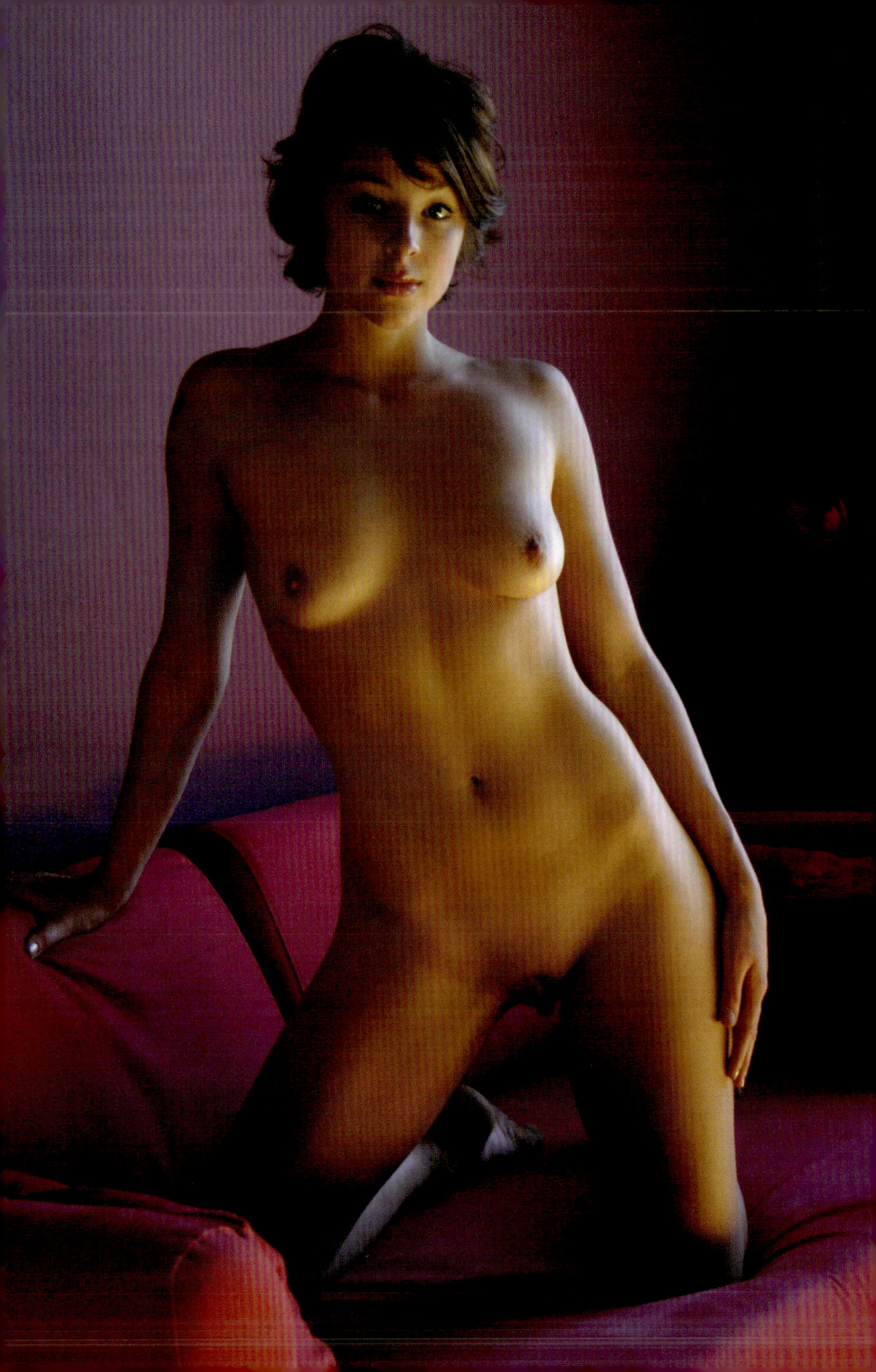

jp lefauche

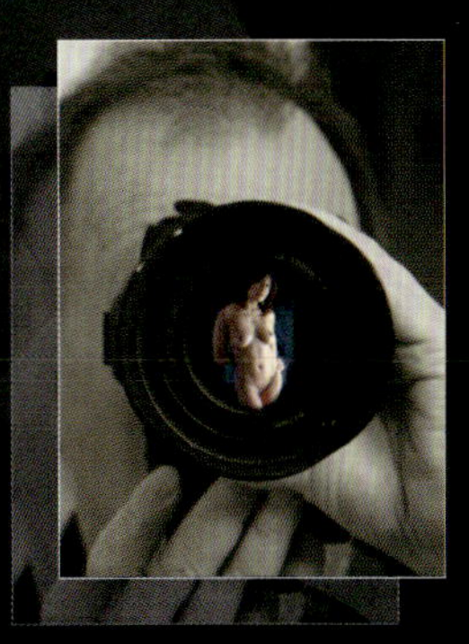

A LIFELONG PASSION FOR DRAWING, painting and illustration brought JP to the lens in 2004, with a colourful focus on artistic and carefree erotic nudes. Much of his work is created on location, often outdoors in the mountains, forests and beaches of Washington State, evoking a mix of influences from classical Renaissance painting, to Elvgren pinups, to modern edge.

www.free-form-studios.com

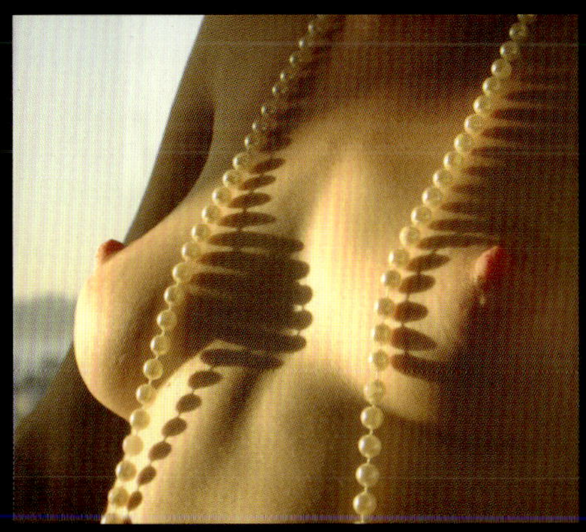

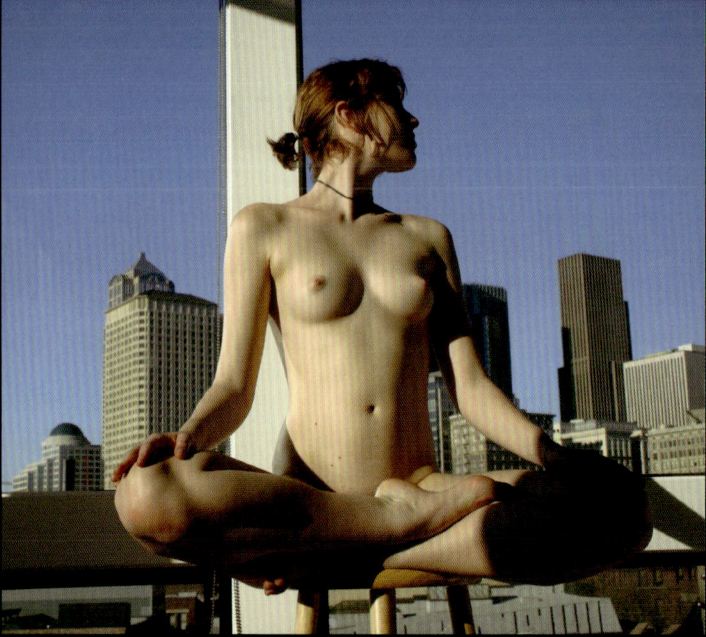

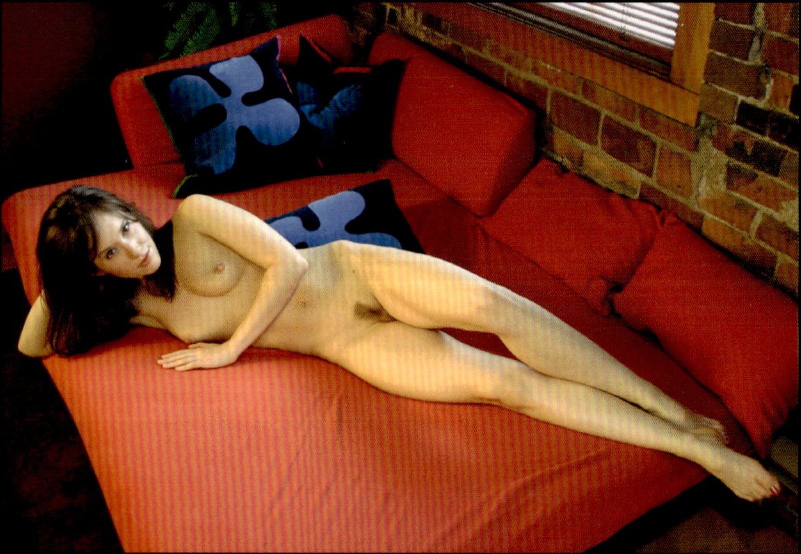

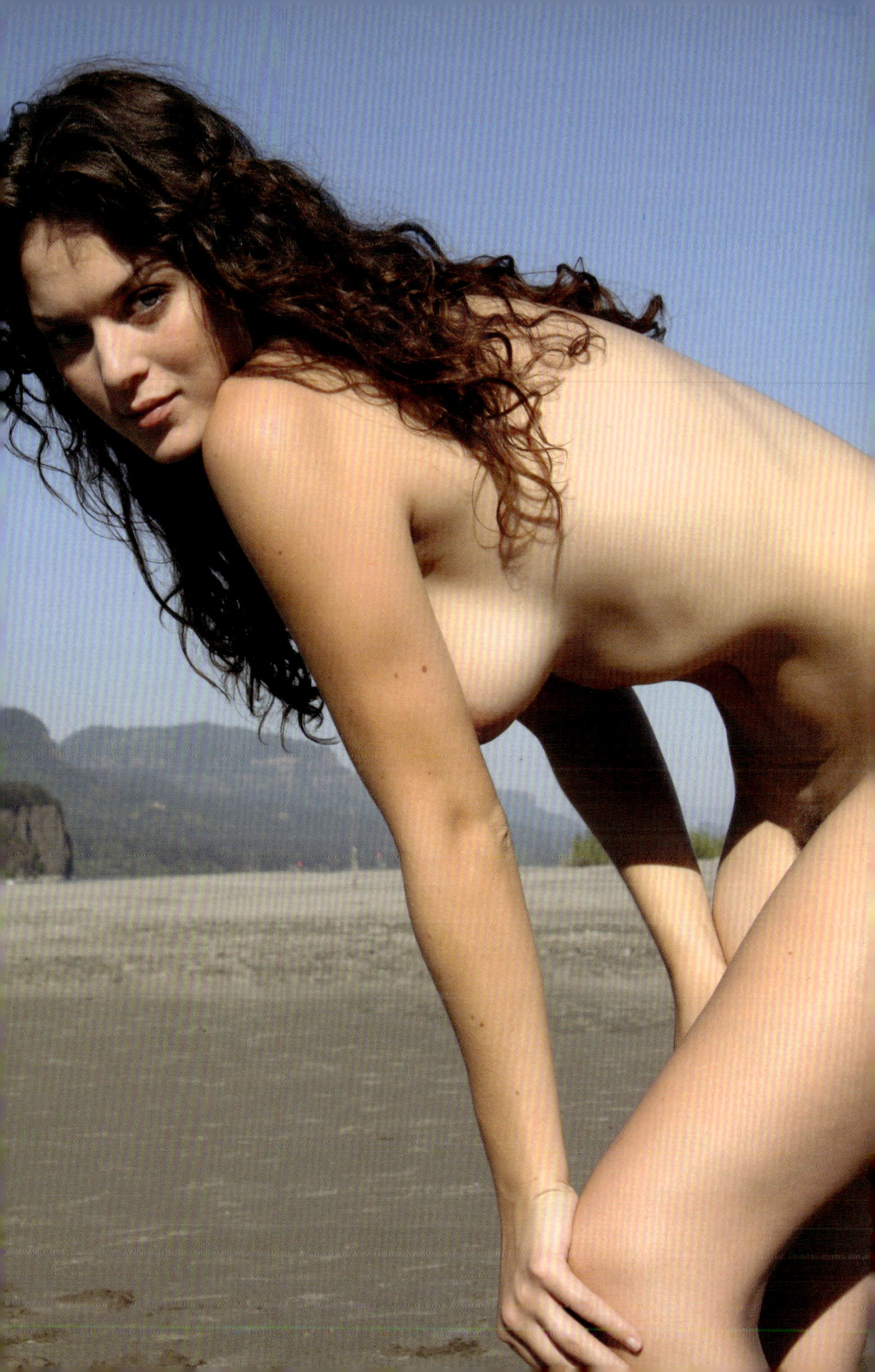

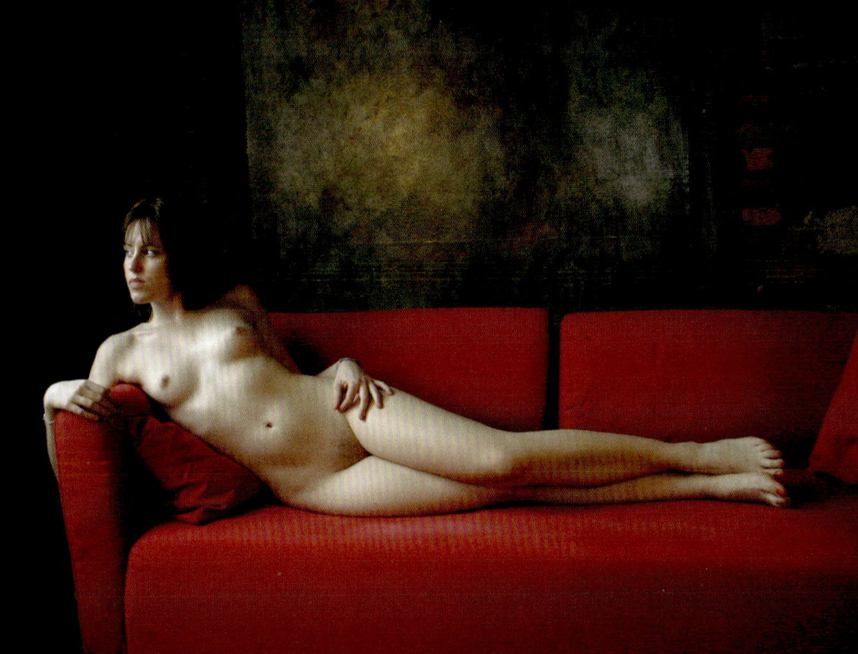

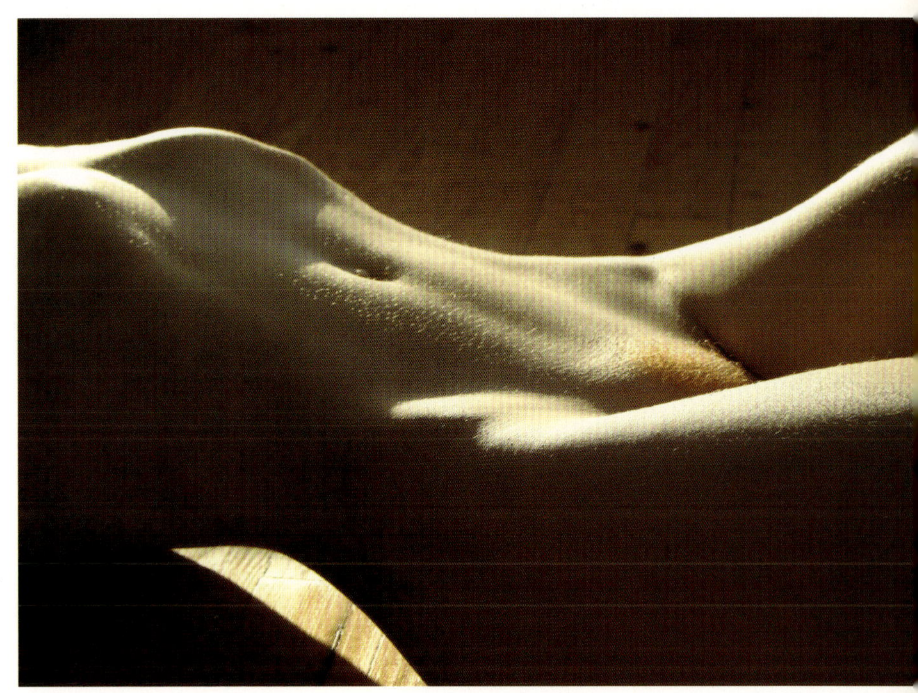

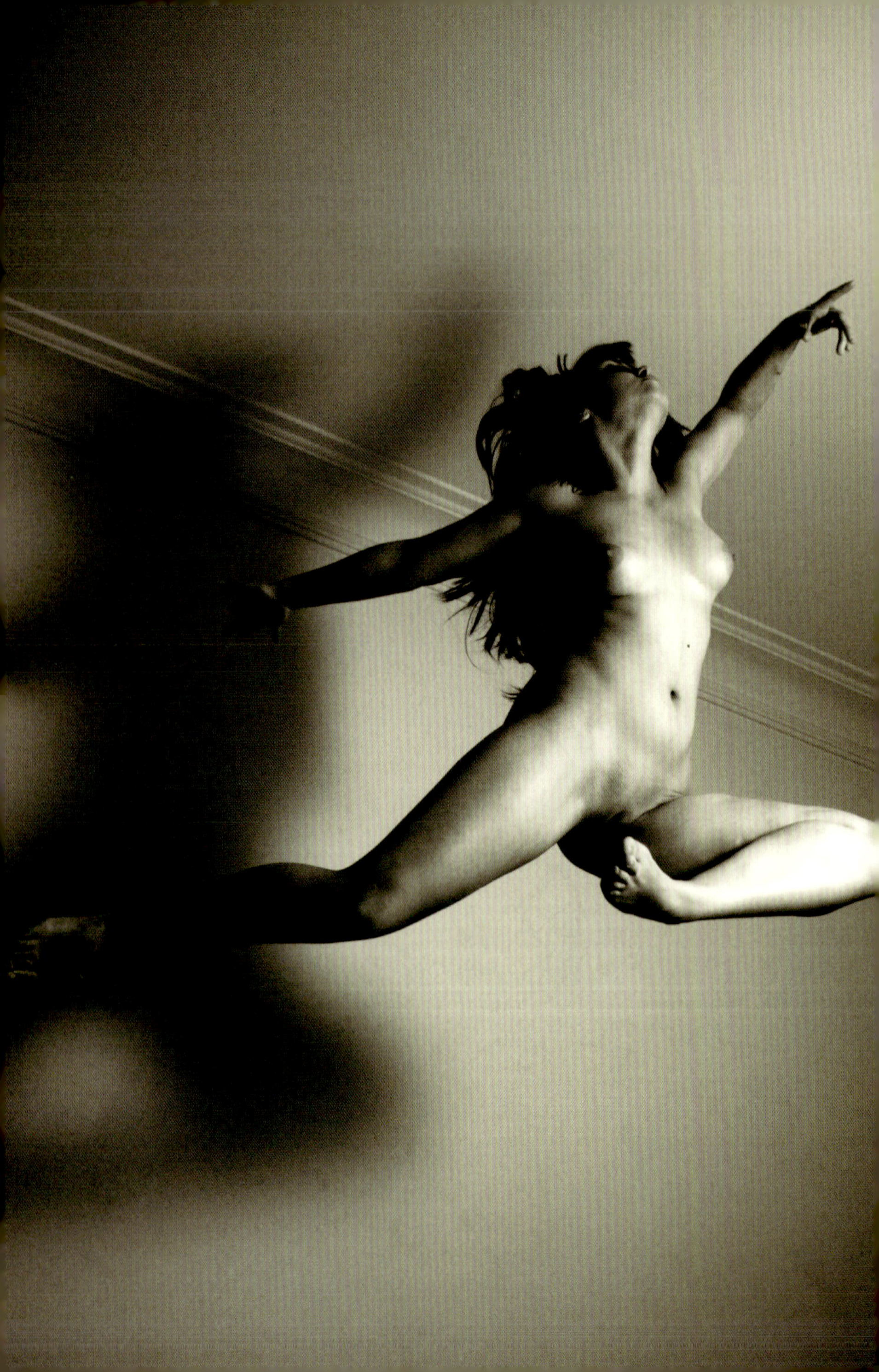

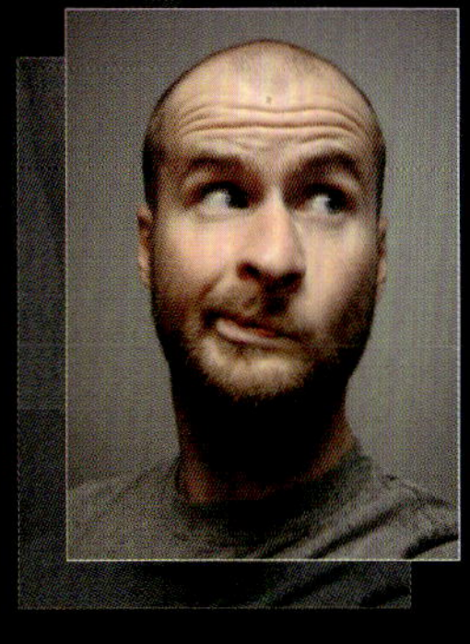

K LEO STATES: 'I believe in beauty. I trust Art. I seek implausible things. We live in a freakishly marvellous world. I am perpetually amazed at the places, faces and precarious situations that surround us all. Mirth and beauty throughout. Nothing is more impressive to me than people. It is my subject of choice. I believe that everyone has beauty.' Based in Chicago, K Leo is a fine art photographer whose work seeks to capture the beauty of his subjects. His photographs range form erotic artistic nudes to pensive emotive portraits.

www.mirthandbeauty.com

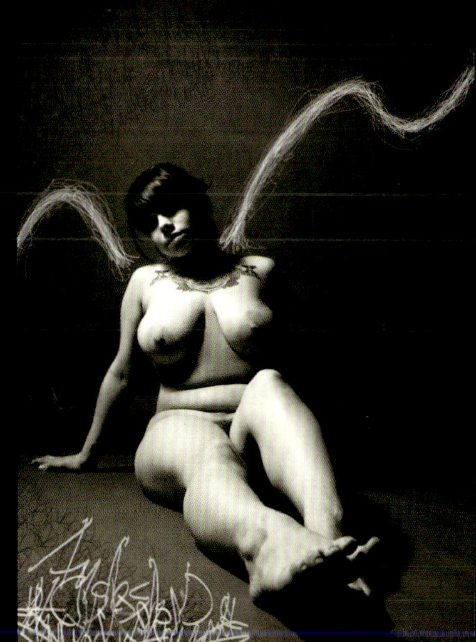

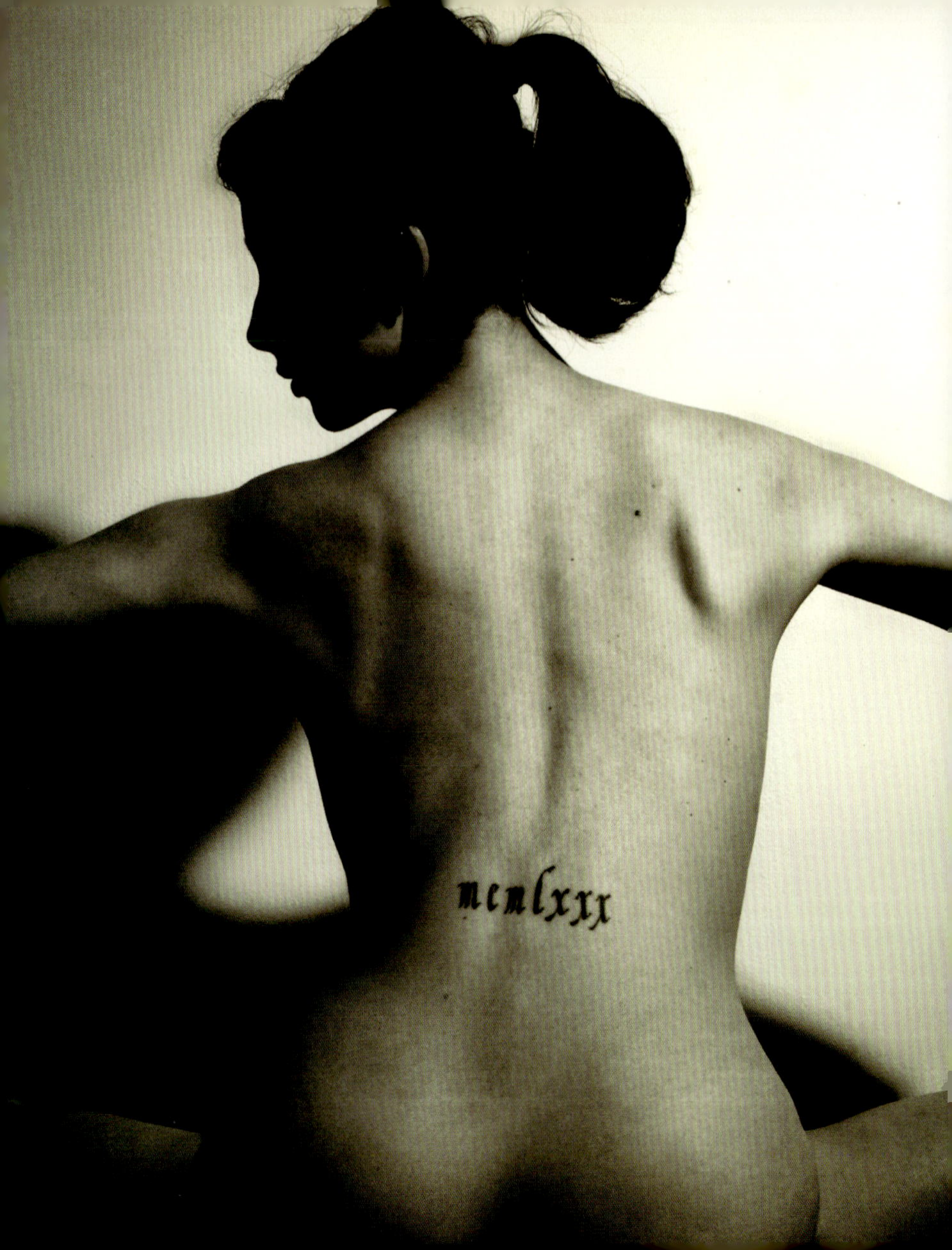
mcmlxx

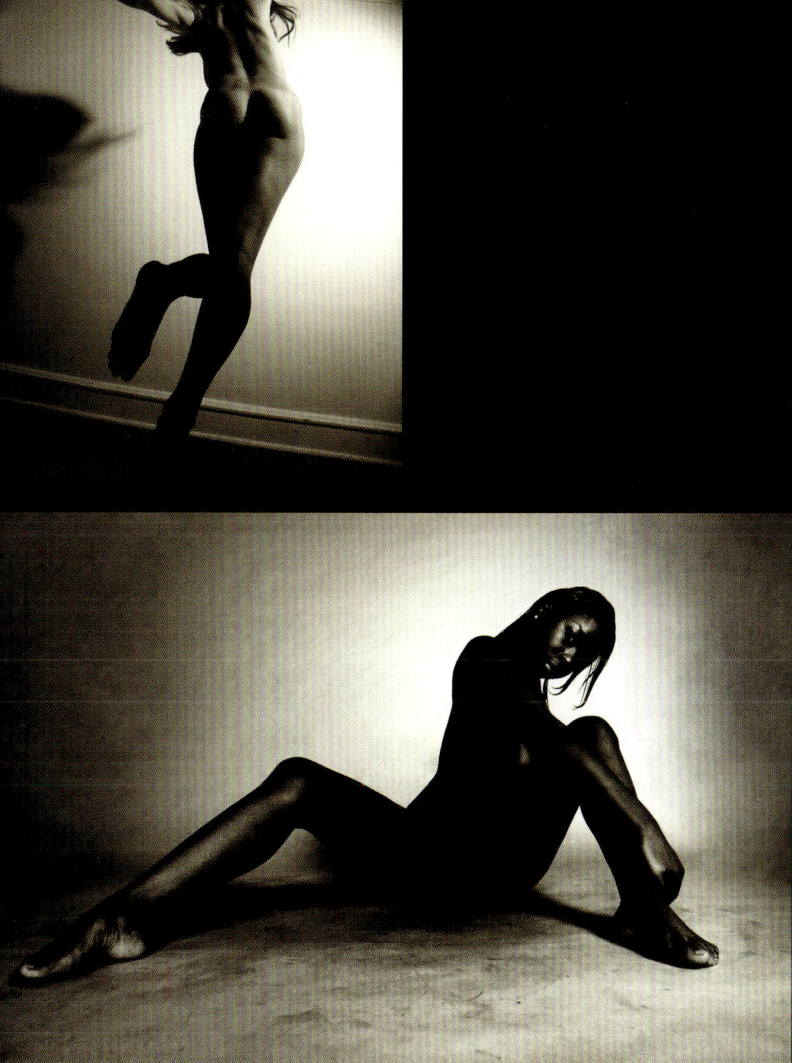

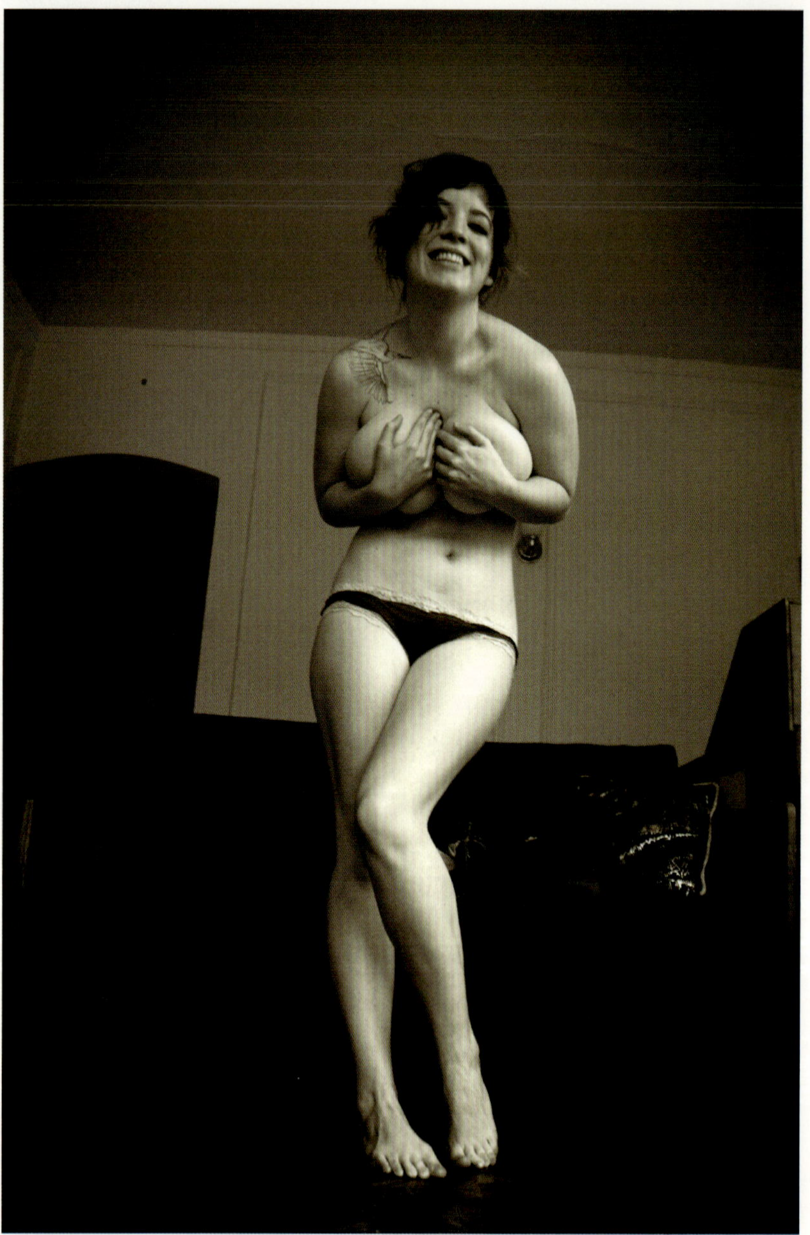

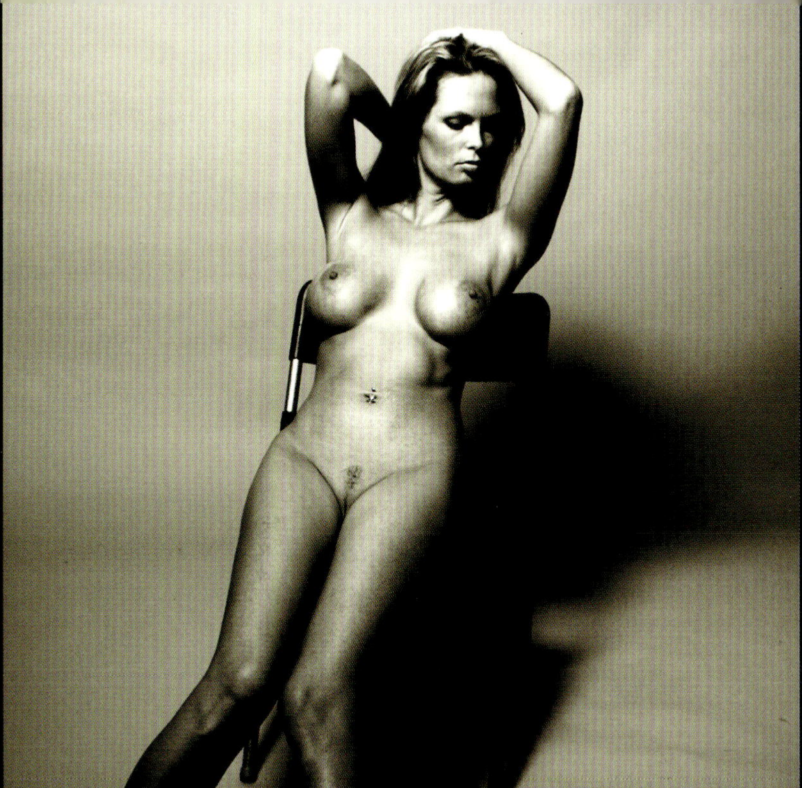

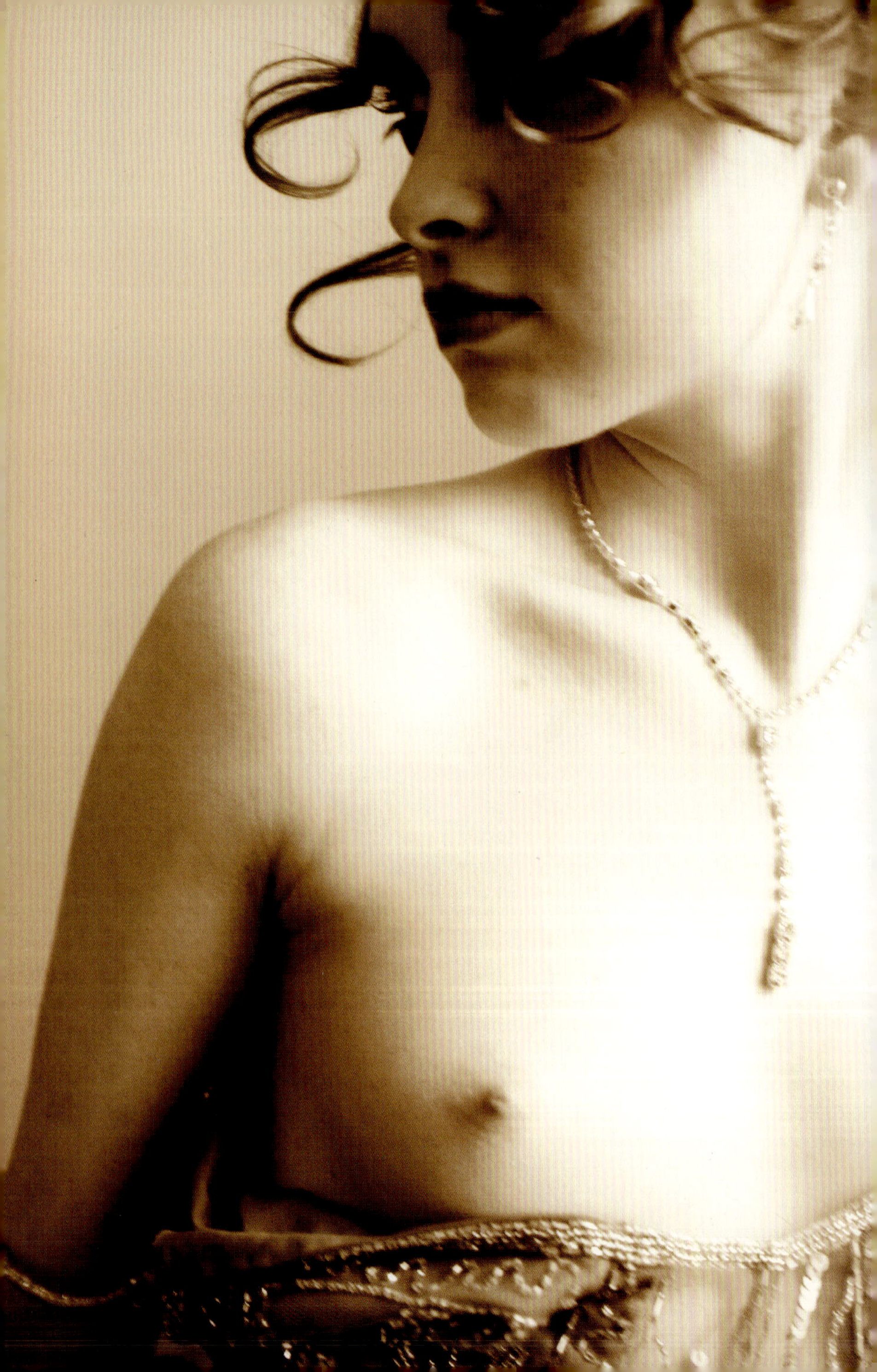

kitty maer

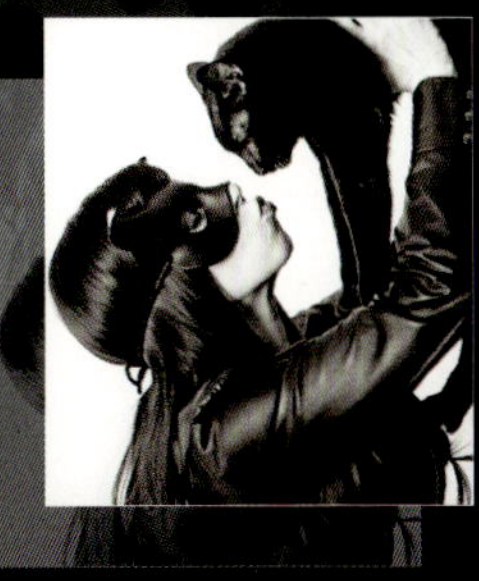

MANY YEARS AGO, fashion and portrait photographer Kitty Maer moved from New York City to Ohio in the American midwest, where she found herself indulging in new aspects of photography. Her commercial and erotic work has been published internationally.

www.kittymaer.com

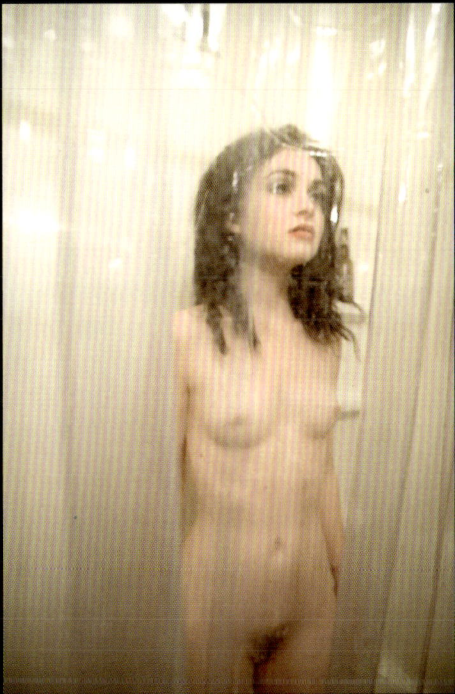

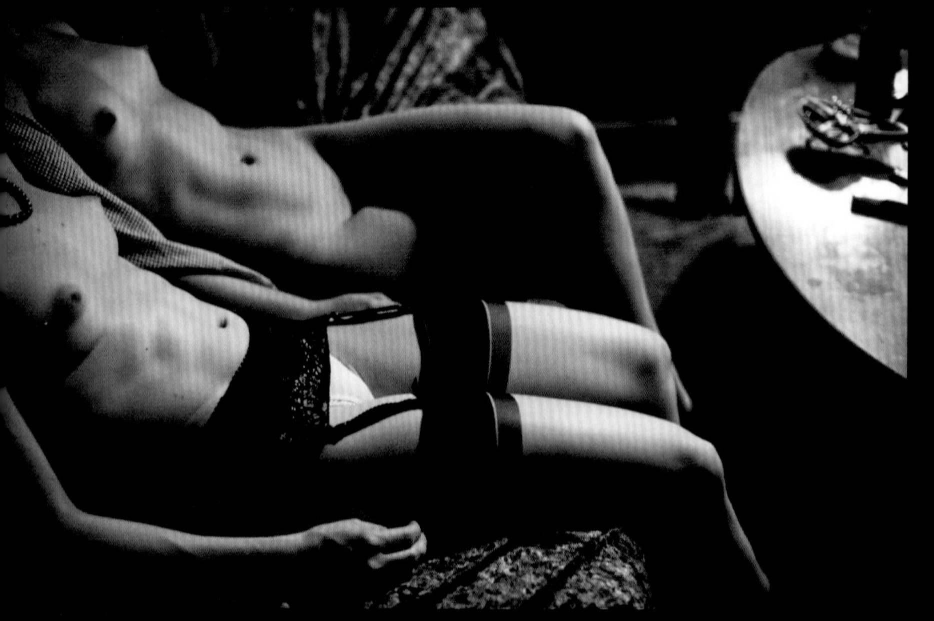

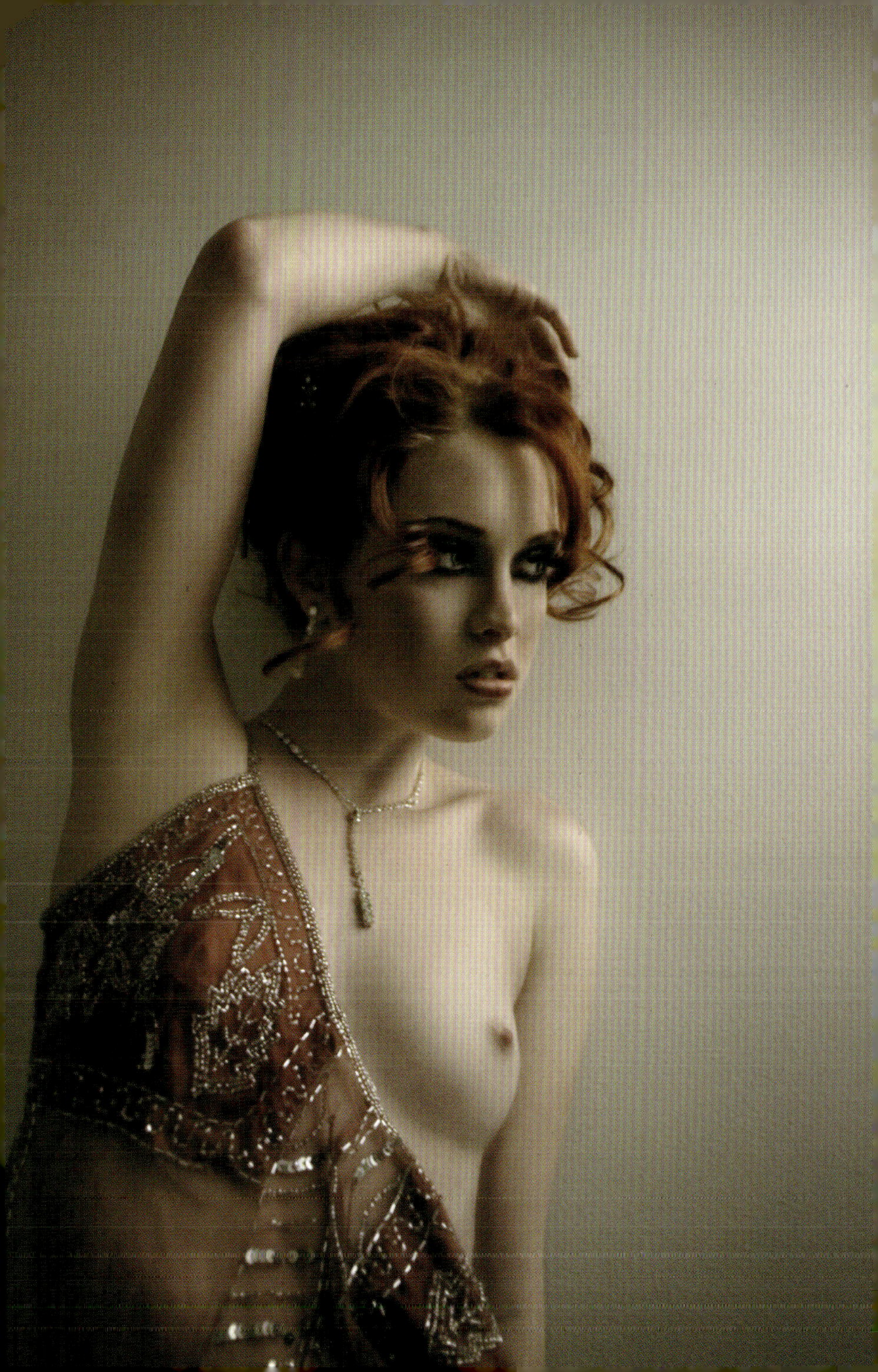

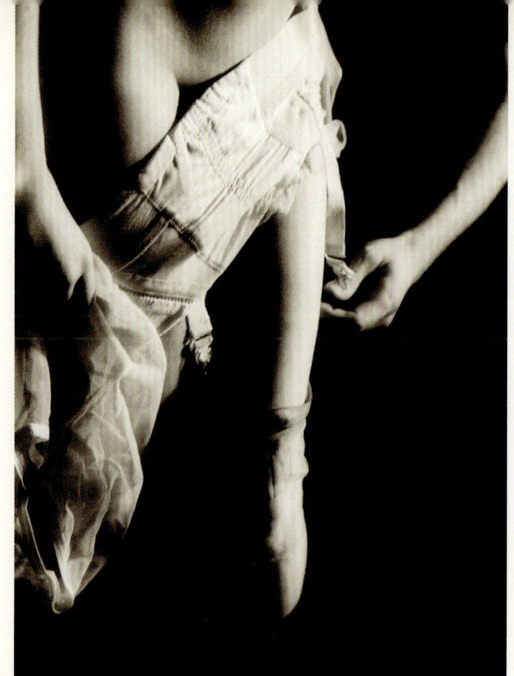

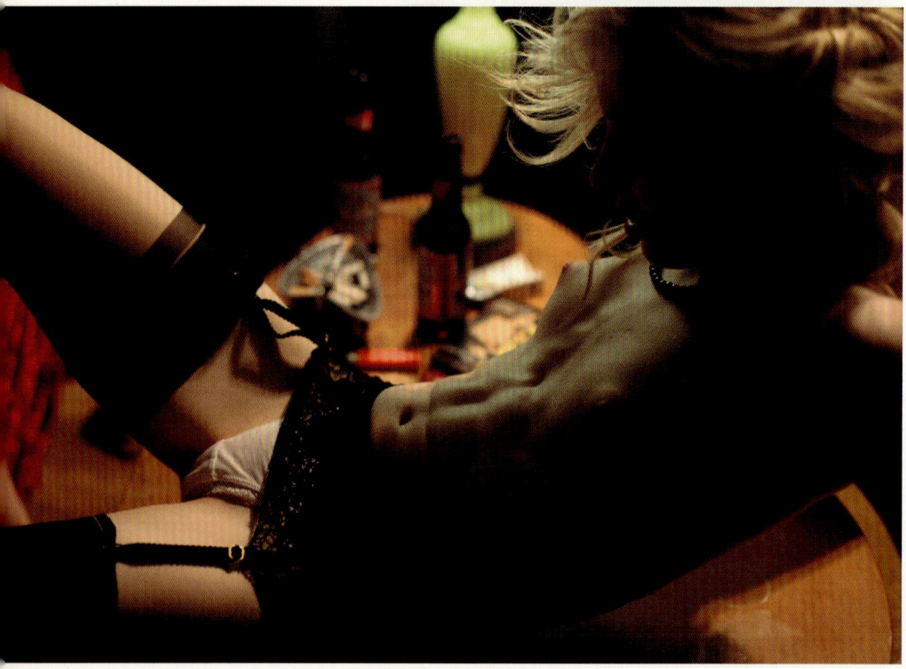

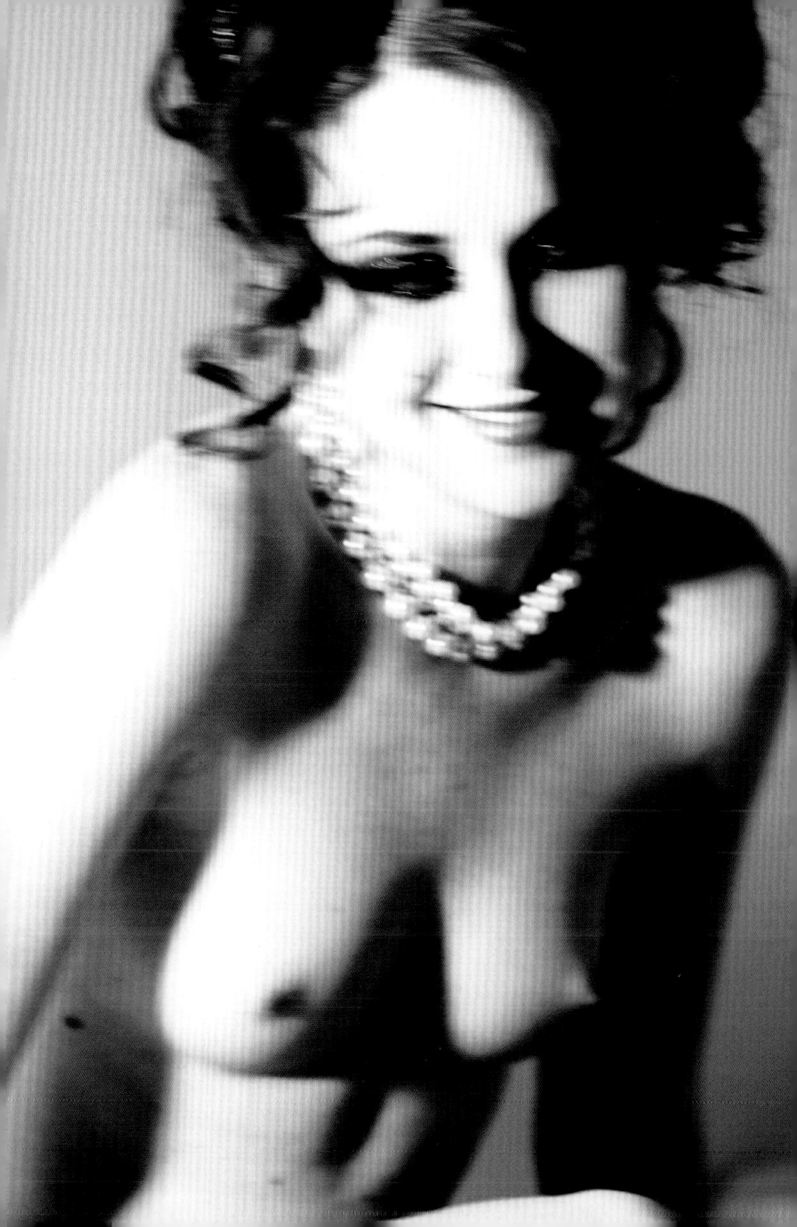

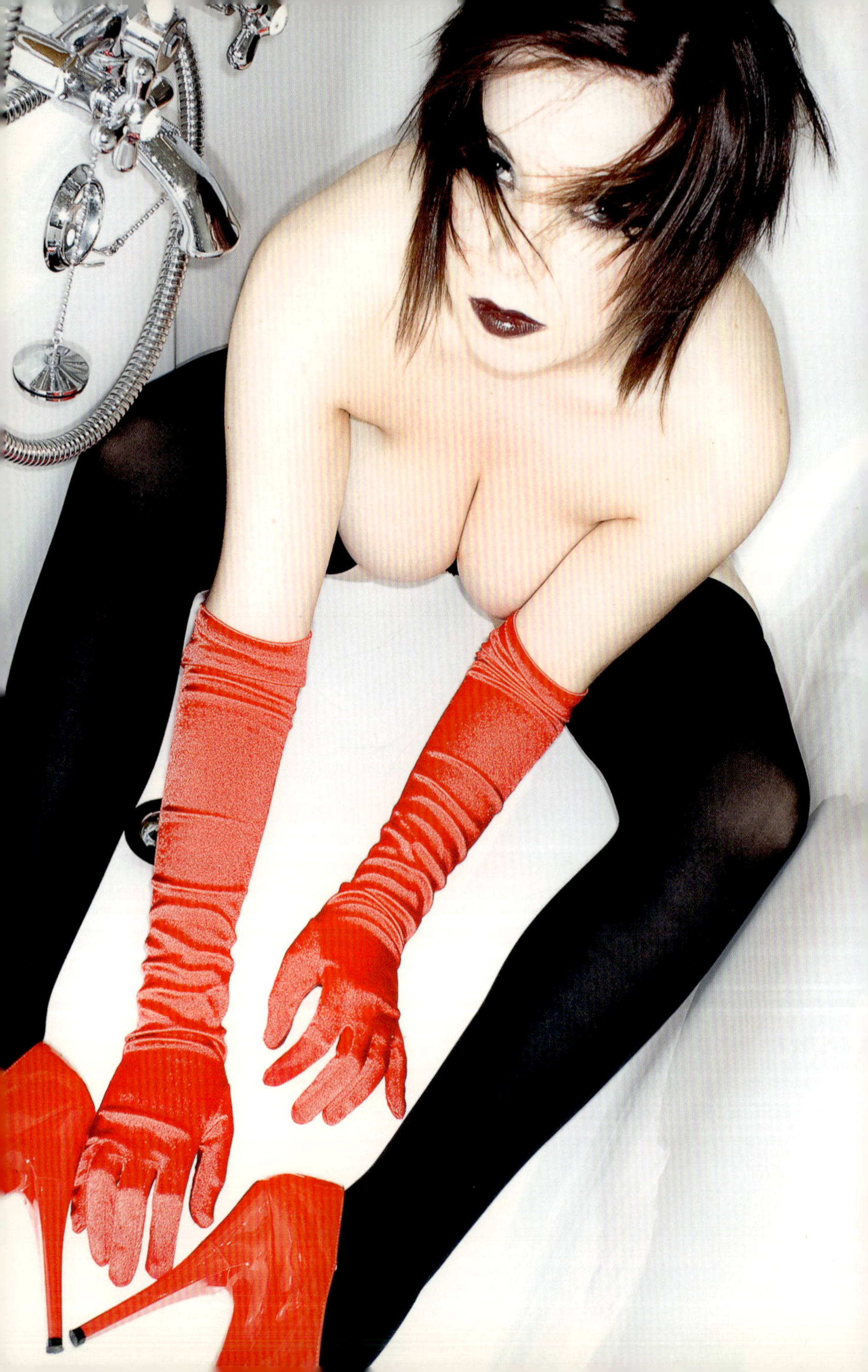

hudson manilla

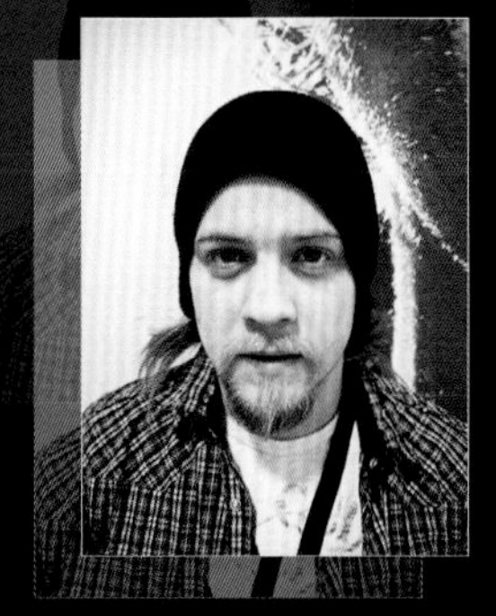

HUDSON MANILLA IS AN internationally acclaimed photographer who specializes in shooting the female art form. He is UK-based, but regularly shoots in the United States and Japan. From traditional cover style glamour photography to raw-edged fashion, to fine art eroticism, his imagery always has a unique signature. Appealing equally to both men and women, he excels at capturing emotional as well as physical beauty, but also knows how to improve upon it. In his imagery, a pretty girl is always transformed into a sensual and spectacular woman. Whilst his work has a strong aesthetic appeal, it also contains an underlying psychological connection and an intriguing narrative. Spontaneous moments of emotional intensity are perfectly captured, the models eyes intensely luring the viewer into her sensual world with such an aphrodisia of intimacy and seduction that the viewer can't help but wonder if the image captured a real or imagined passionate moment of rapture.

www.skyline-studios.co.uk

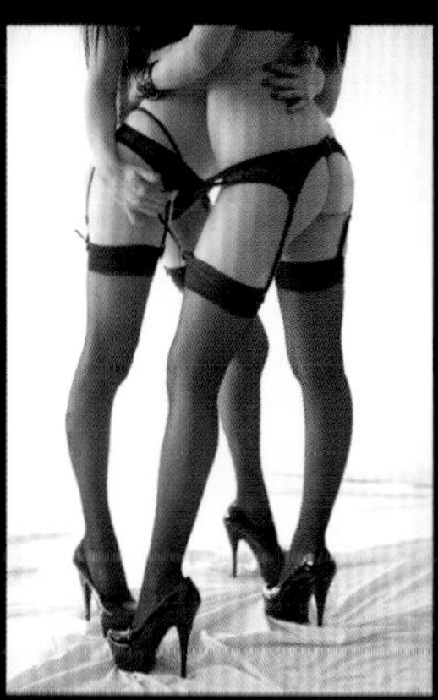

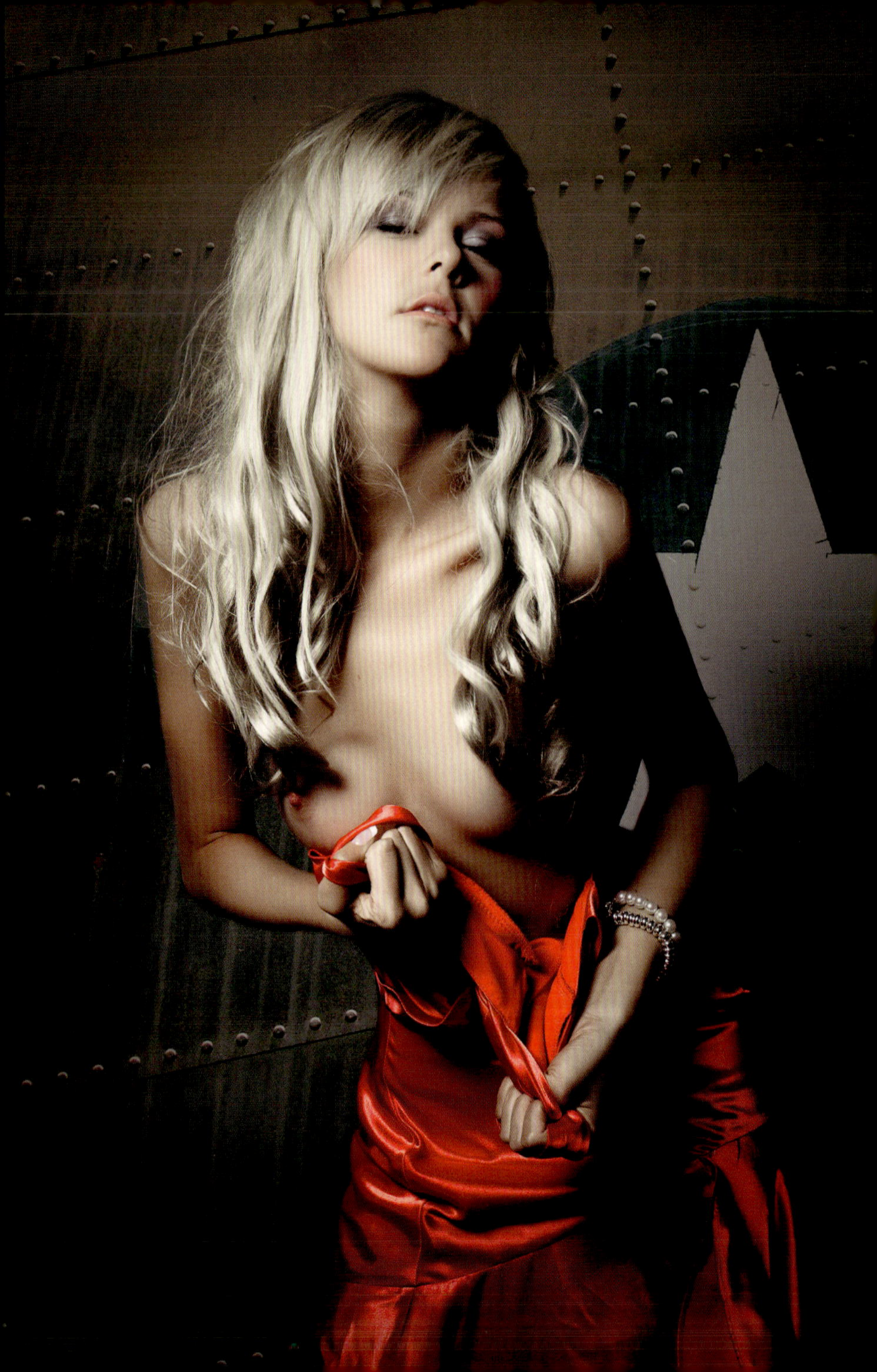

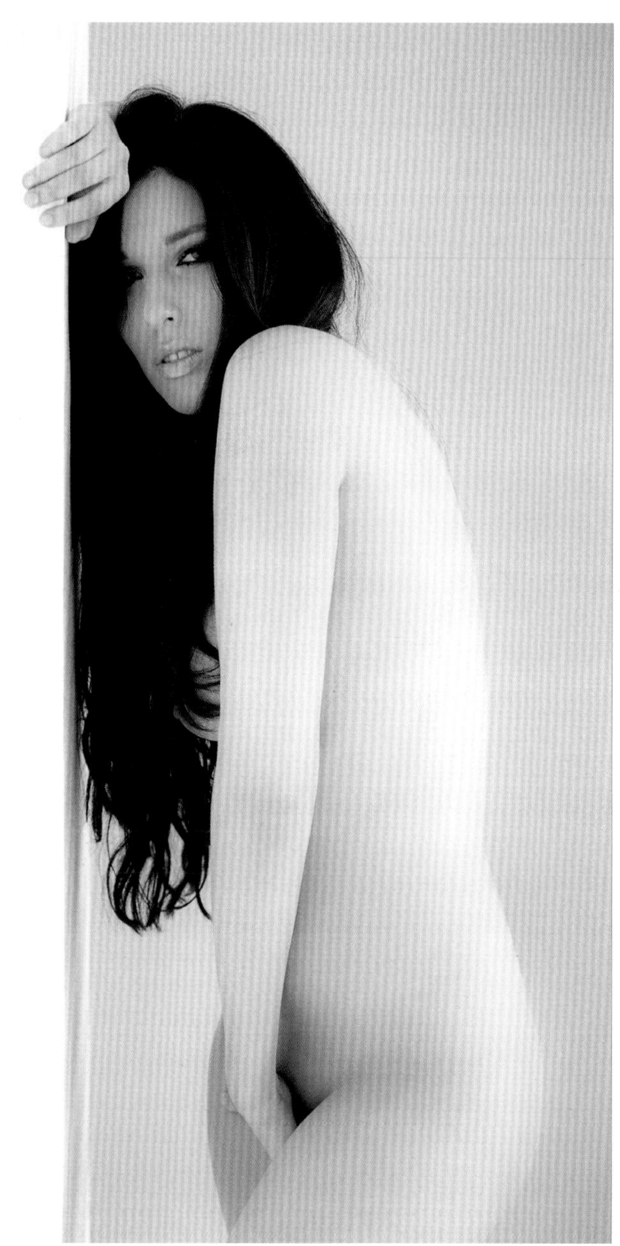

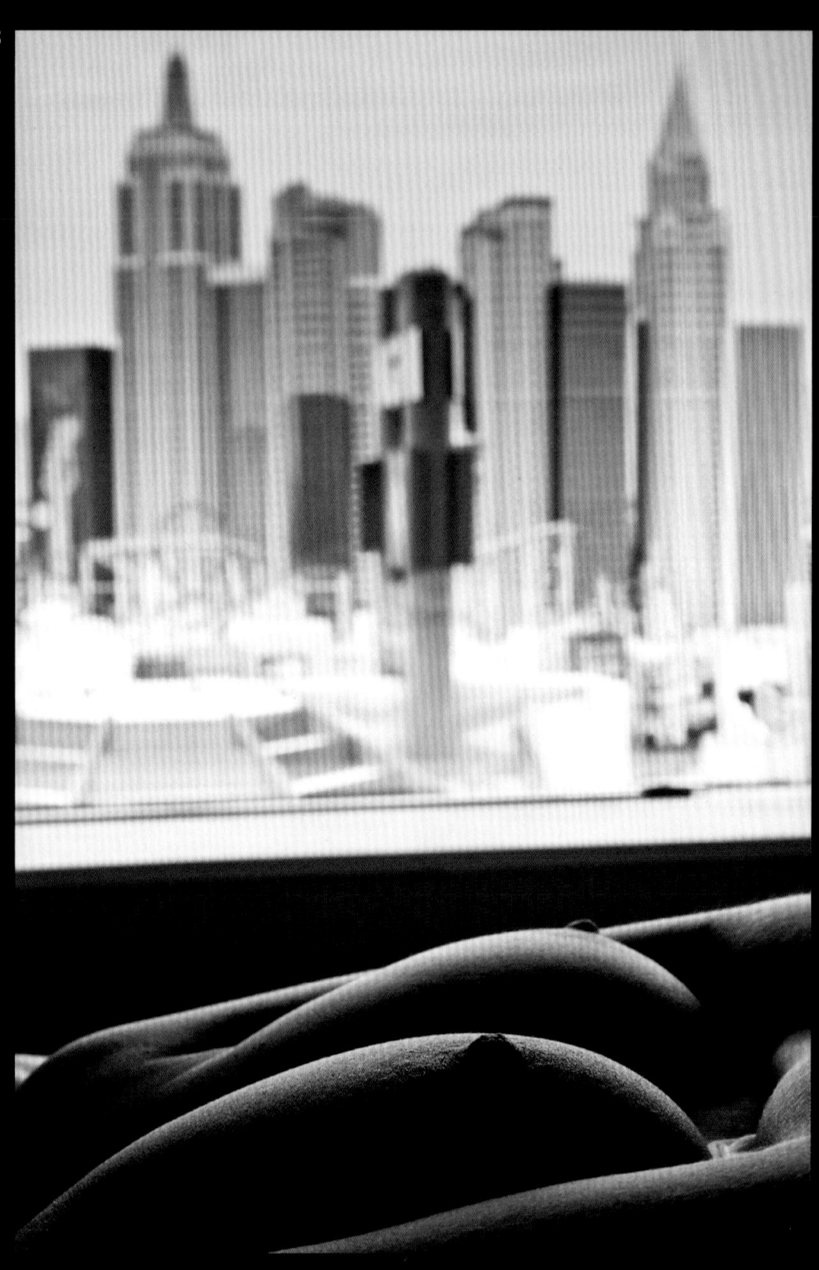

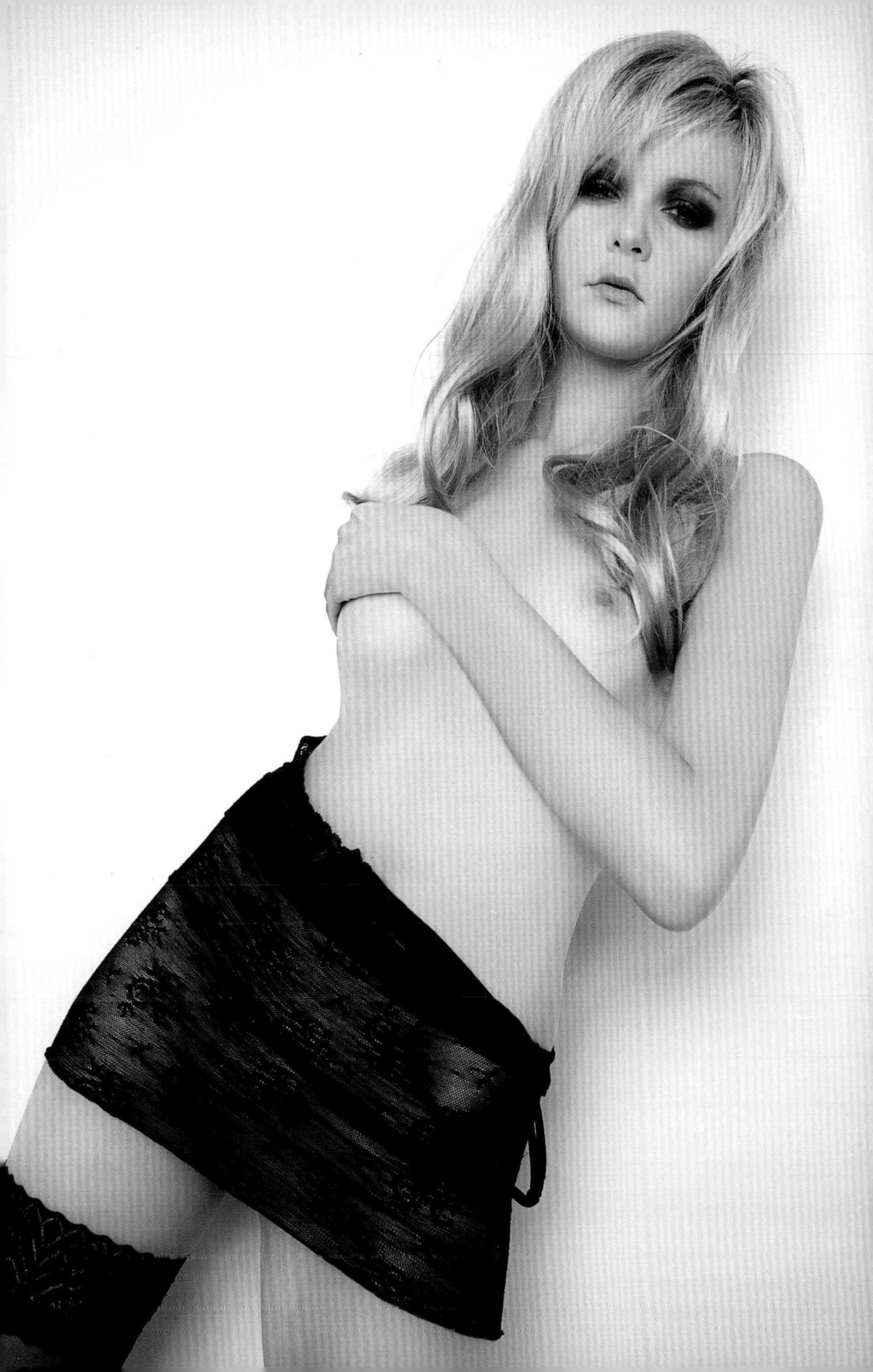

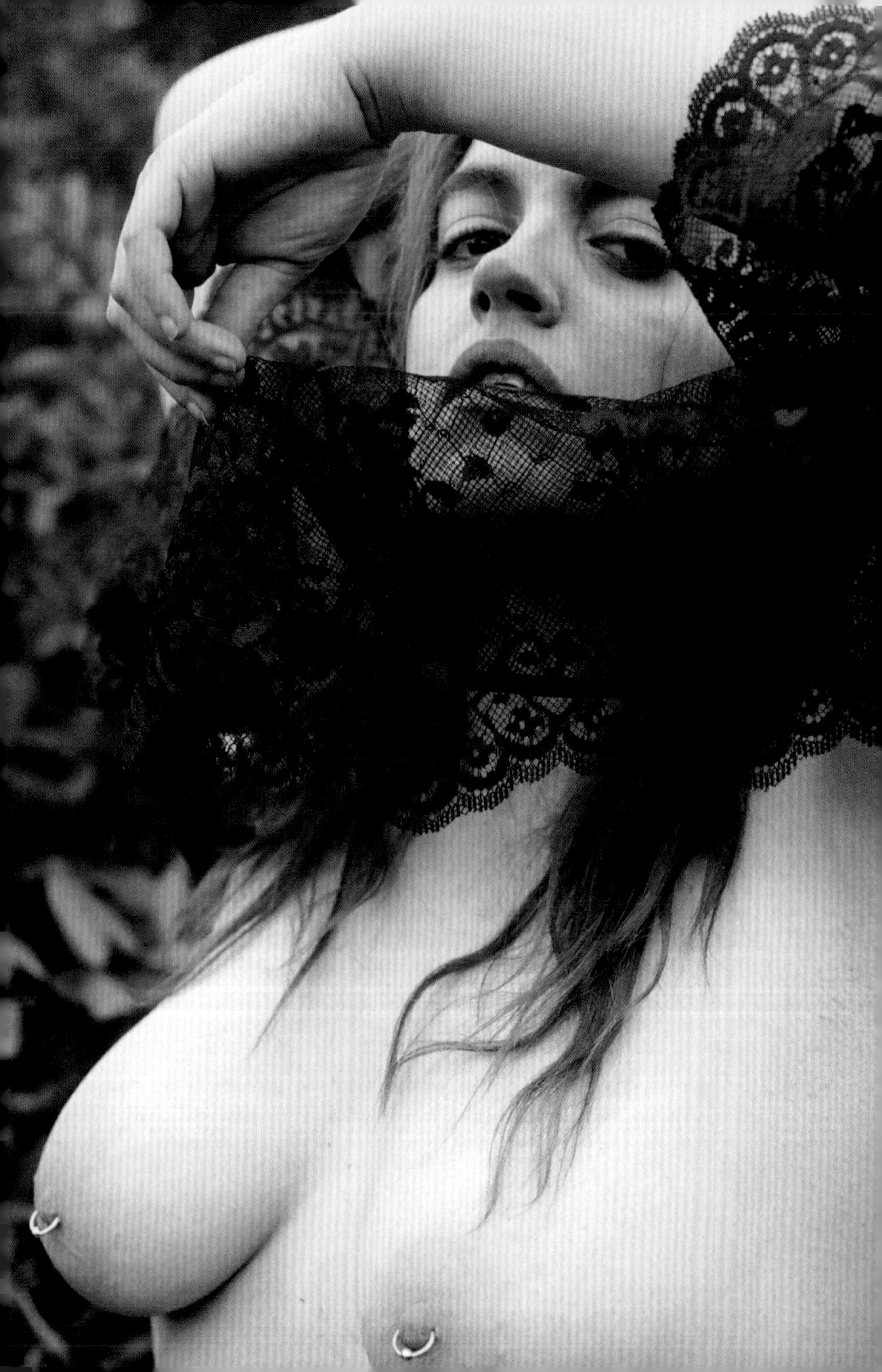

liz mares

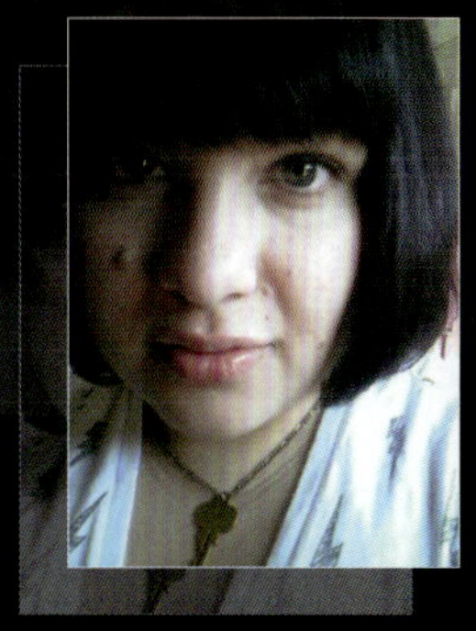

LIZ MARES IS A PHOTOGRAPHIC artist, living and working in the Chicago area. Her erotic works are a projection of her most intimate thoughts, fantasies and desires. As a newcomer to the erotic scene, she has often been referred to as abstract, vague and offbeat. She favours alternative methods over more traditional ones, using such devices as old Polaroid cameras and converted shoe boxes. Through a minimalist approach, Liz retains the mystique, charm and femininity of her subjects. Published both nationally and internationally, she hopes to continue her artistic career in the exhibiting circuit.

www.lizmares.com

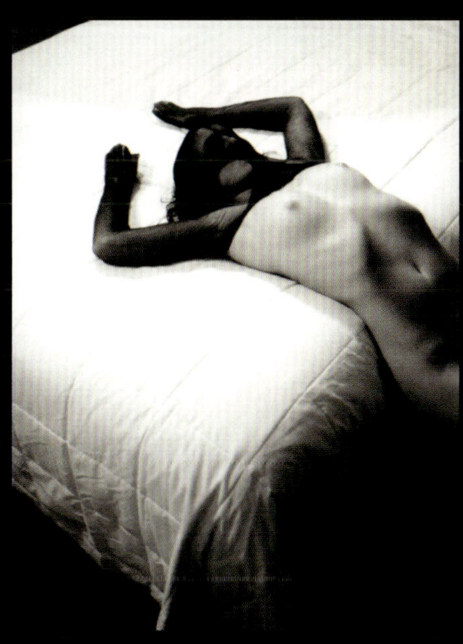

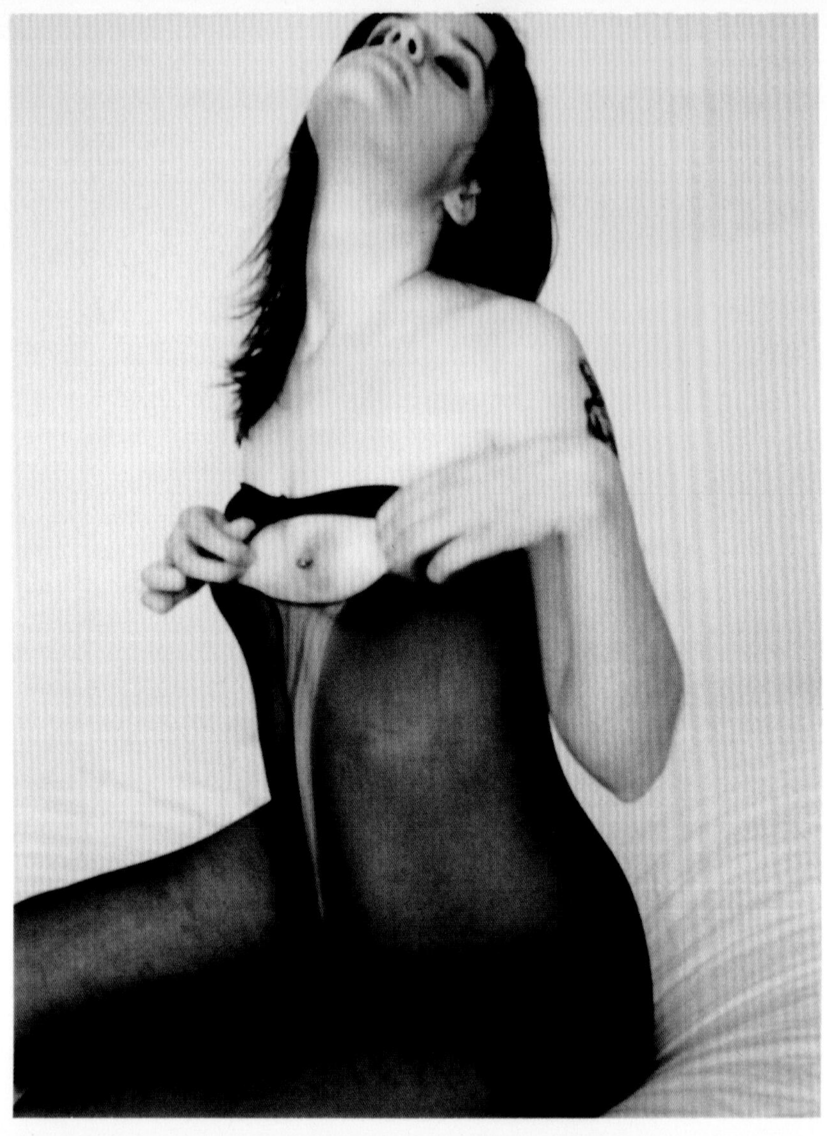

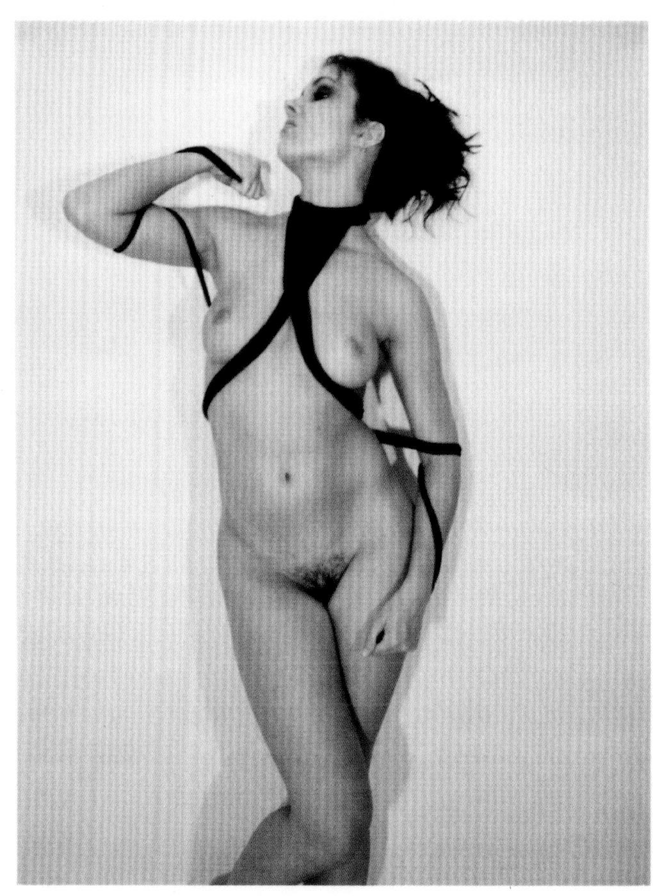

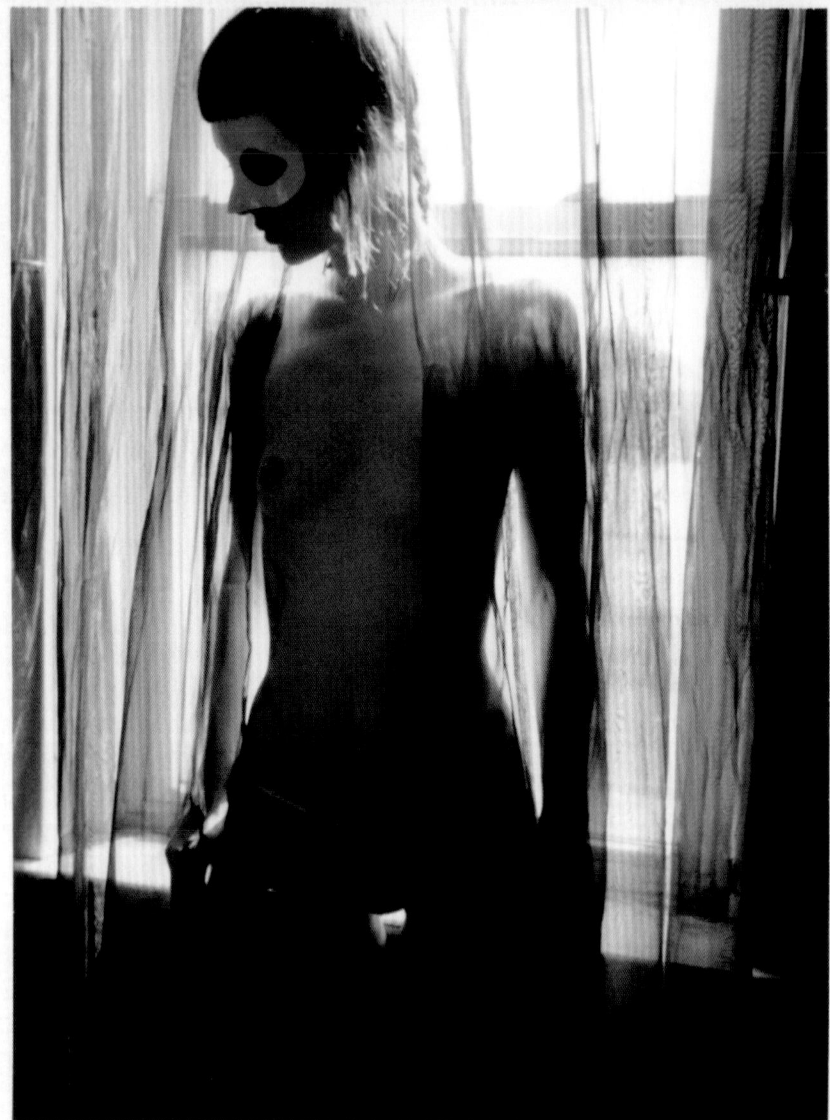

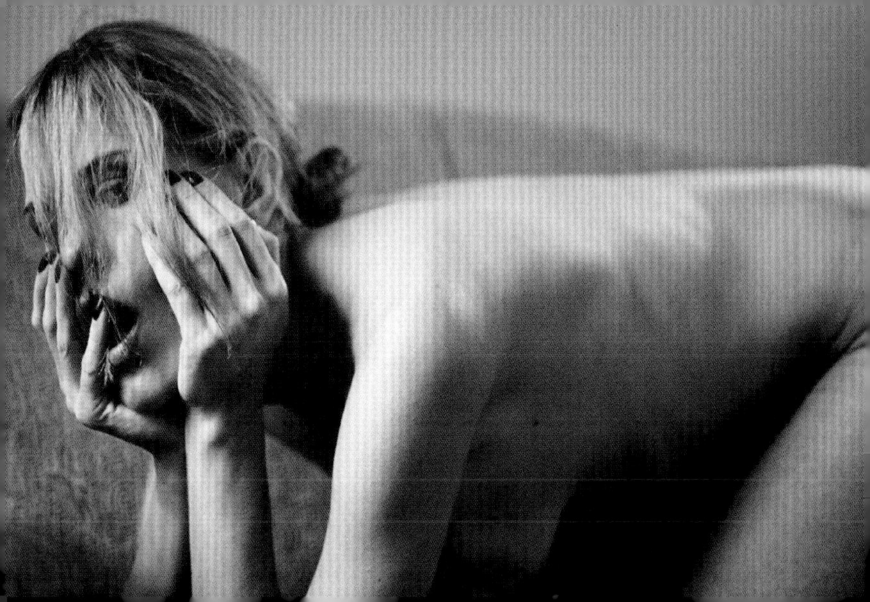

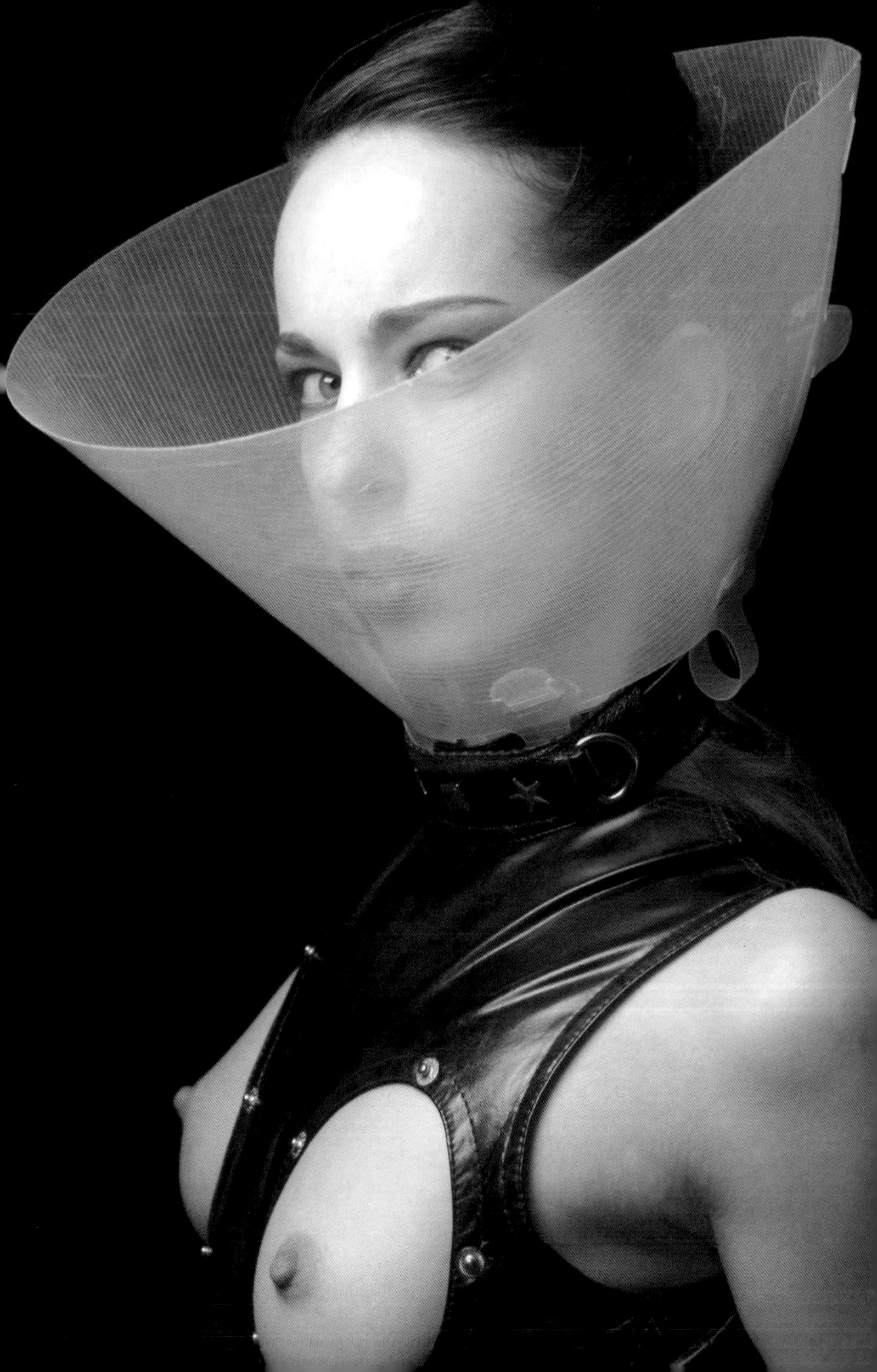

andy metal

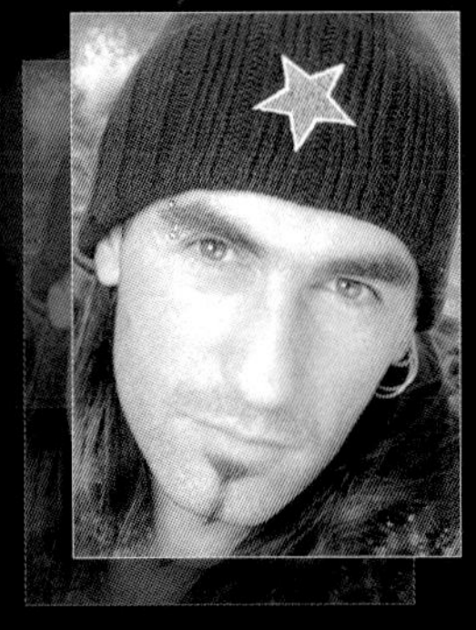

BORN IN 1969 IN TOULOUSE, Andy Metal now lives and works in Montpellier in the south of France. Since the age of fifteen he has processed all his own films, as taught by his father. He loves classic black-and-white photography, even though he now uses a computer to do the 'touching up' that was previously done in his photo lab. Andy Metal's main interest is in people. He likes to capture expressions, bodies, something special in a face or an attitude, and his strongest tributes go to women, who never stop seducing him. His work has been published in many photo magazines and books worldwide.

www.andymetal.com

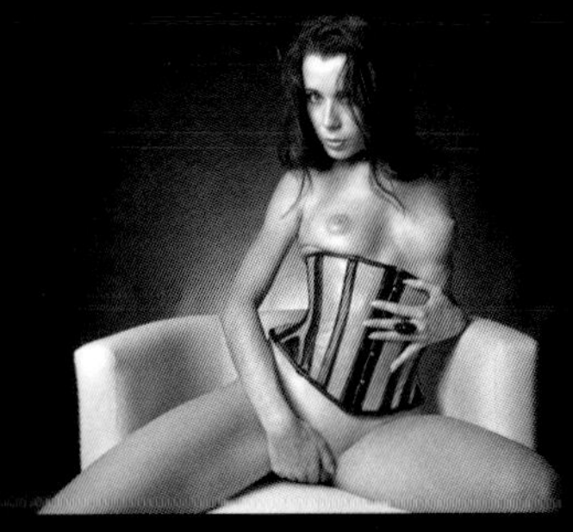

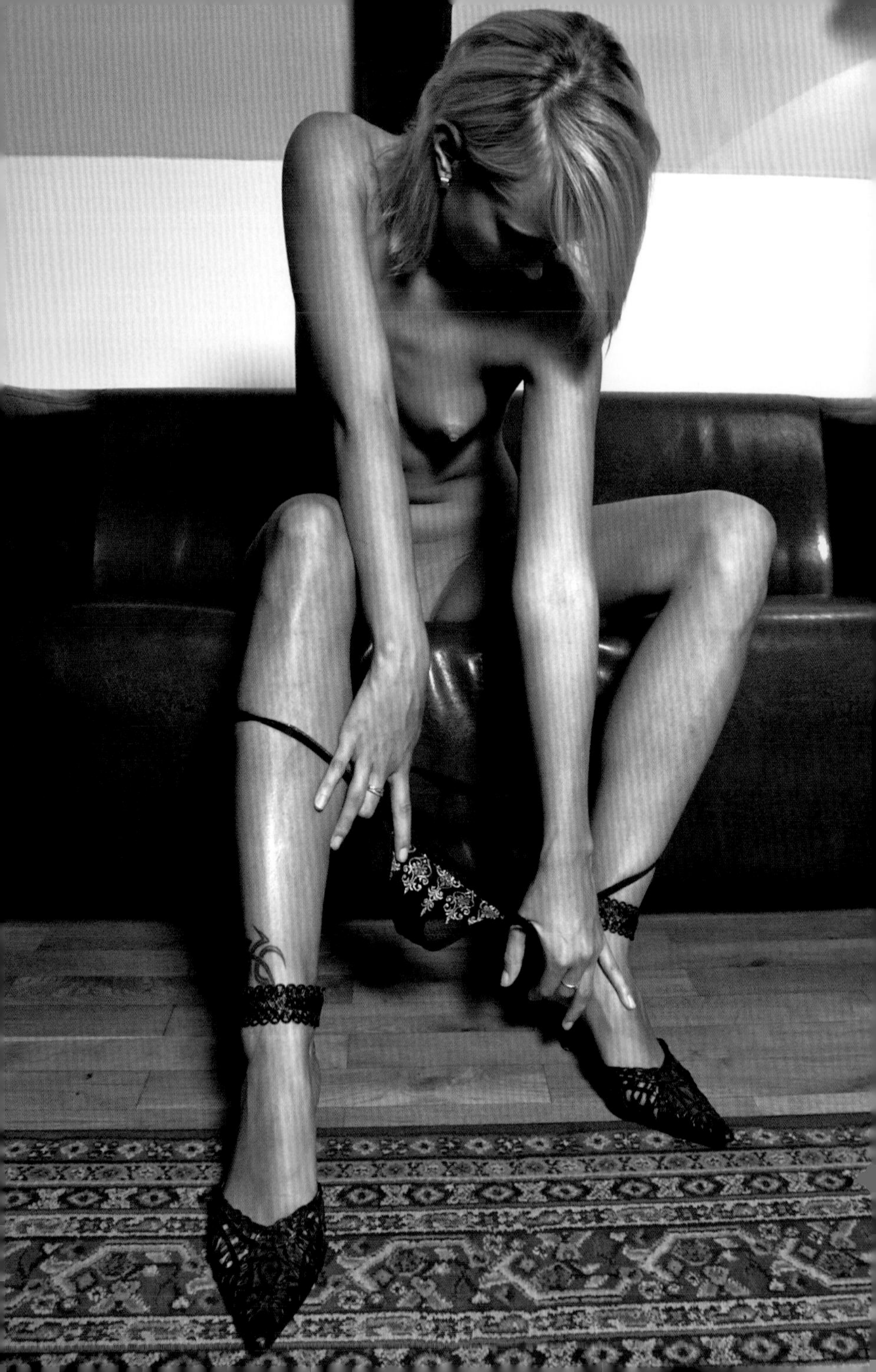

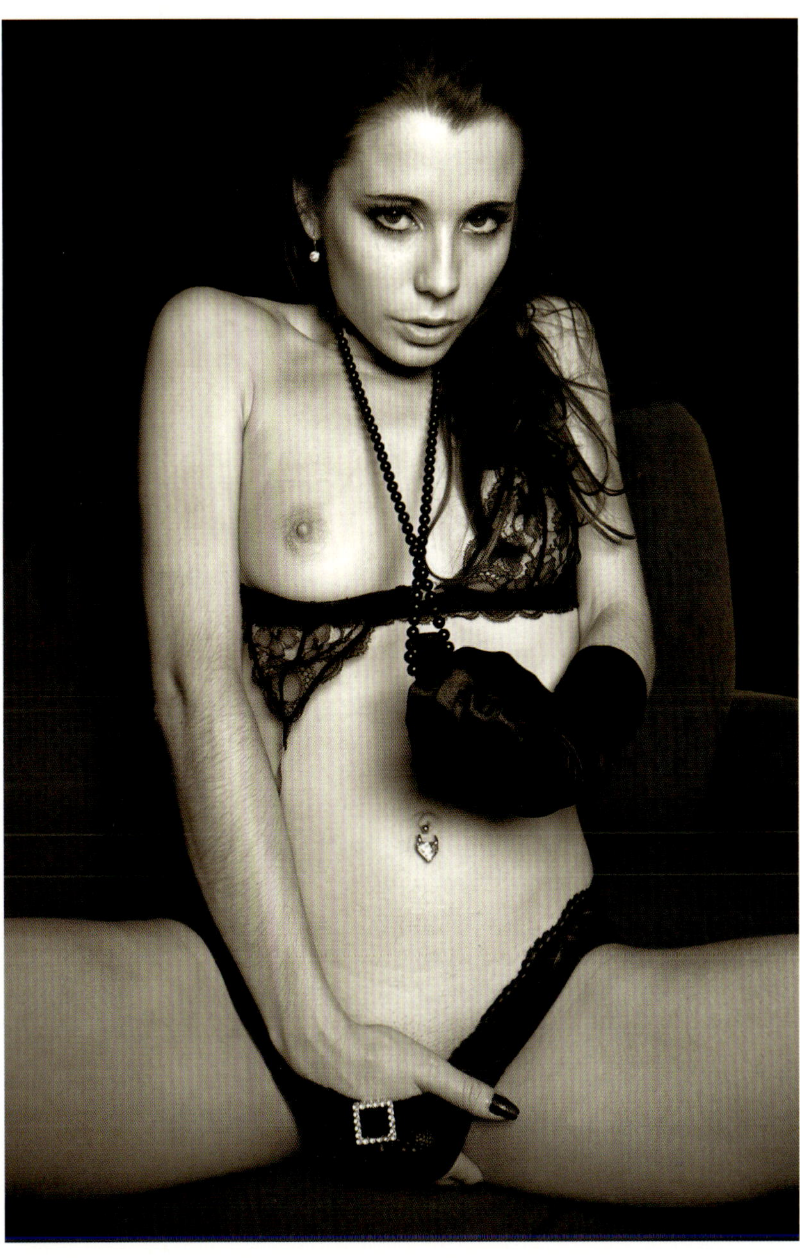

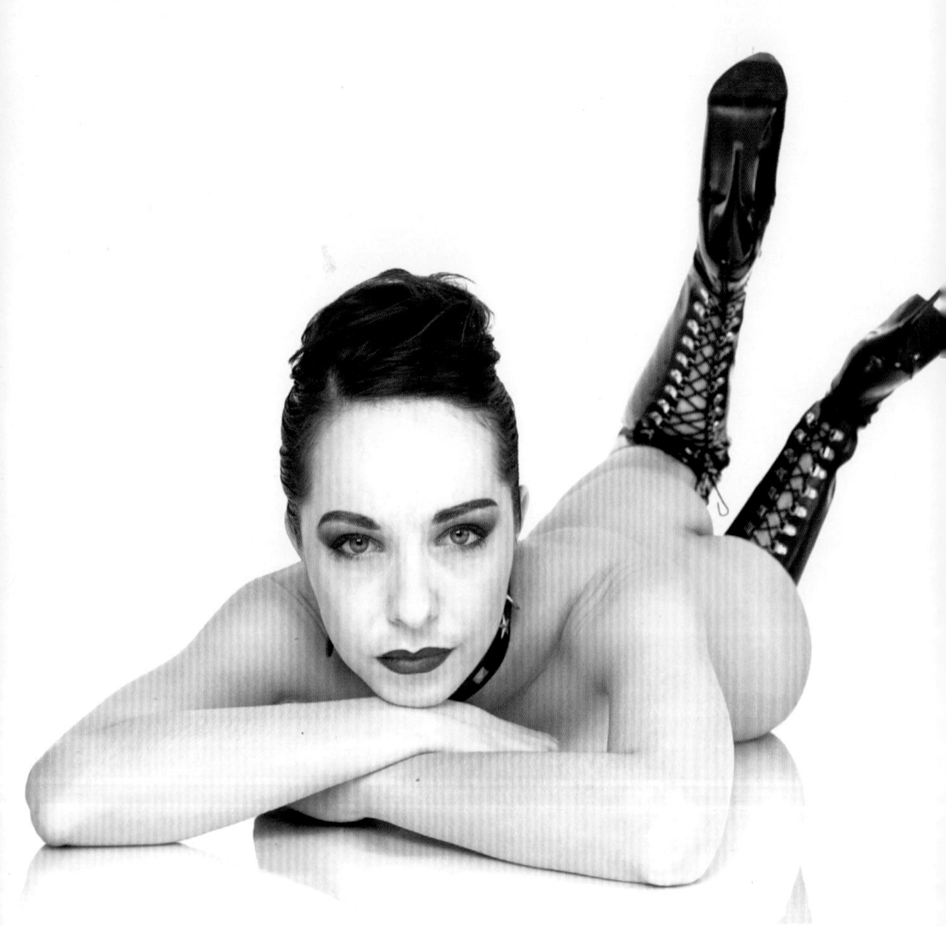

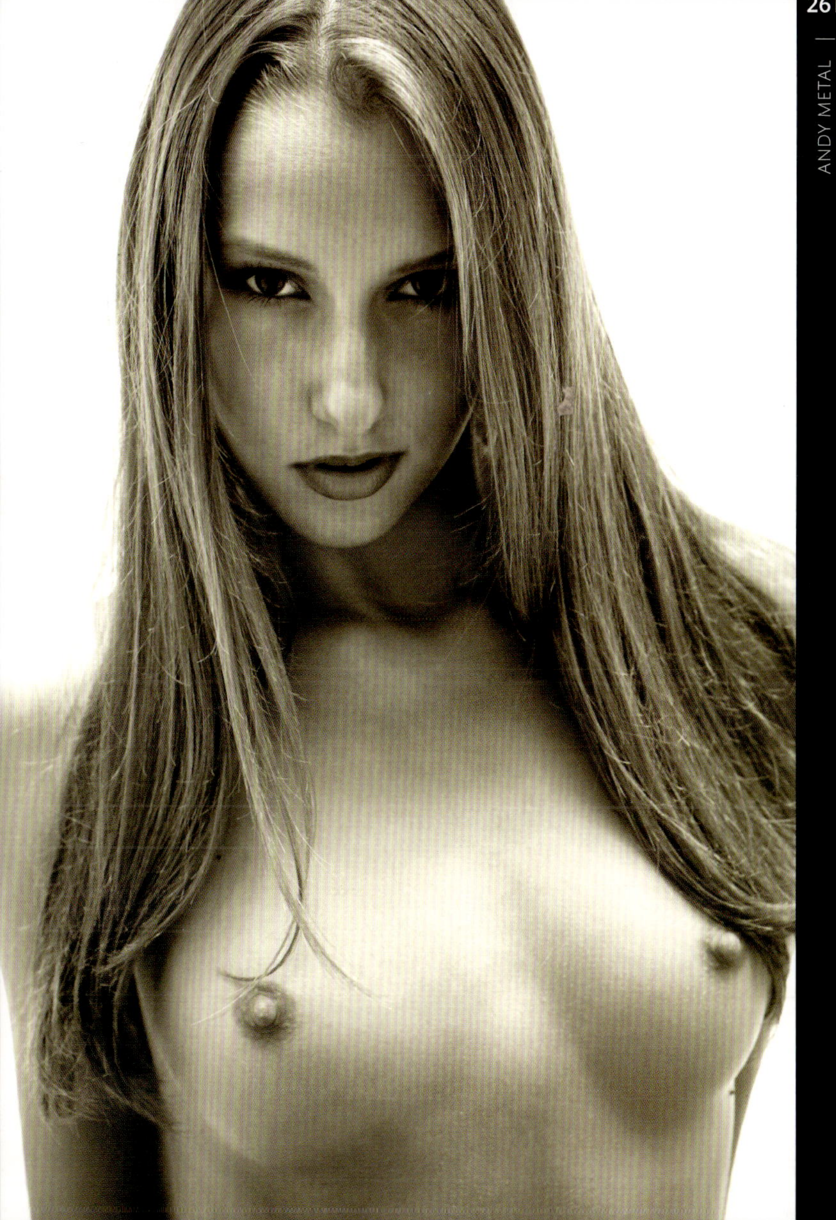

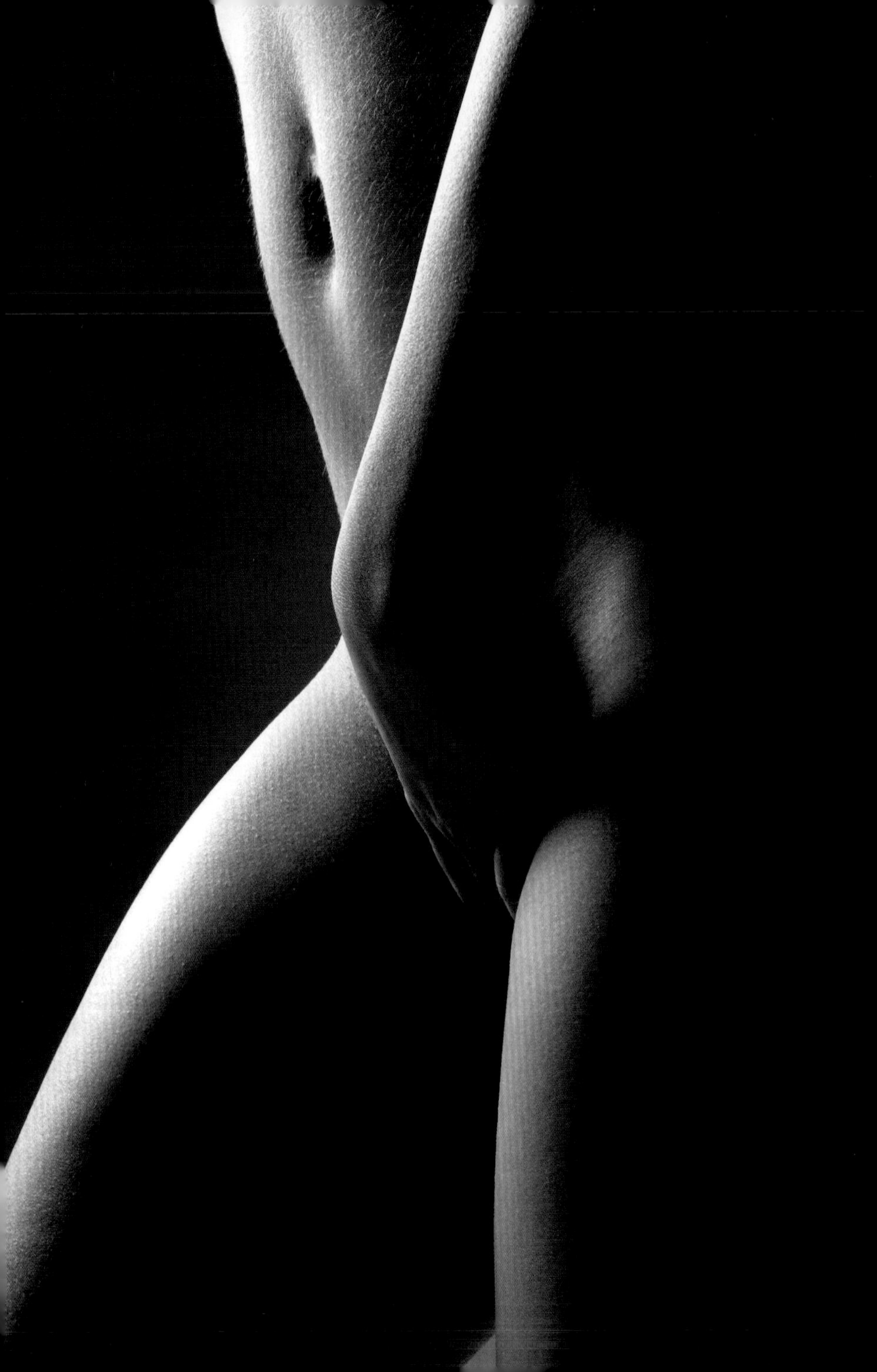

gary mitchell

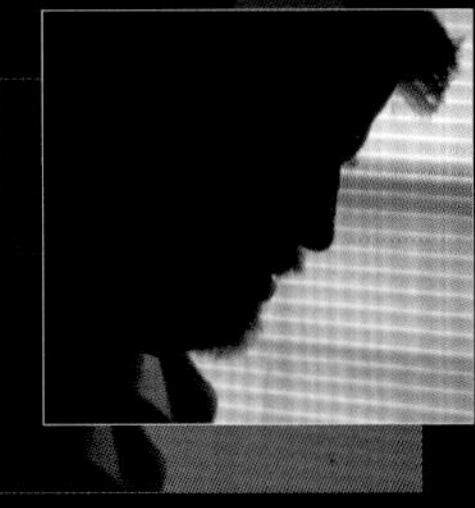

AMERICAN PHOTOGRAPHER Gary Mitchell strives to present the beauty of women and the eroticism of their nature. 'I generally avoid dramatic make-up, wardrobe, or extensive props, and concentrate on the nuances of the woman herself – although I do enjoy finding a dynamic location that complements the model. Often I feel that black and white adds the right emphasis to the light and the forms within an image. I don't rule out tones or colour, though I generally shoot with black and white in mind.' Since 2005, he has worked from studio space in Dayton, Ohio, and shot on location across America. His work has been published in the US and the UK and he was awarded the 2009 Readers' Prize by the *Erotic Review* magazine.

www.garymphoto.com

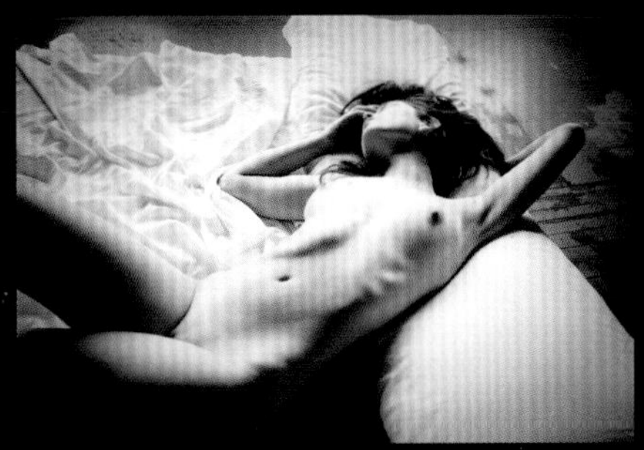

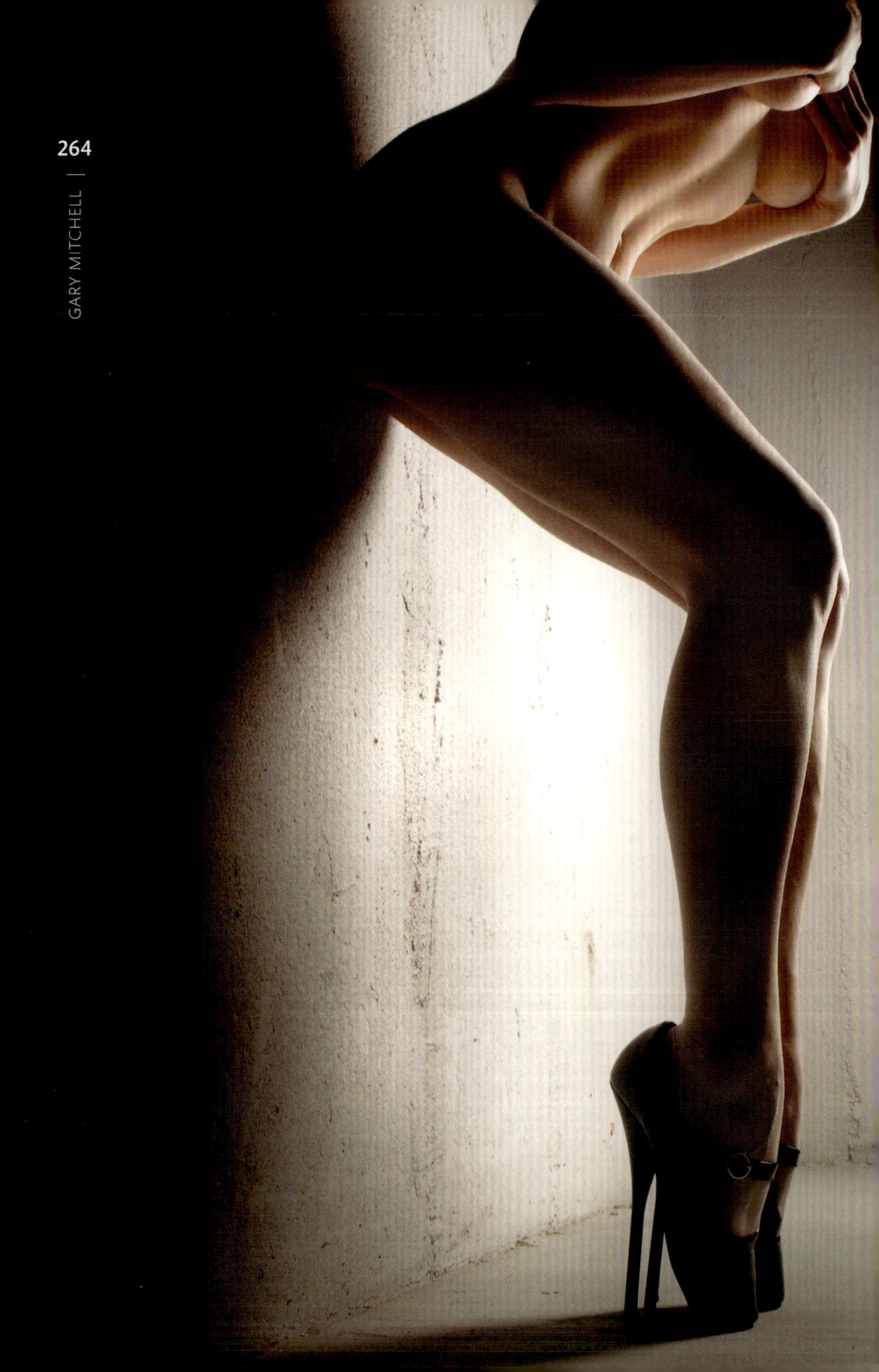

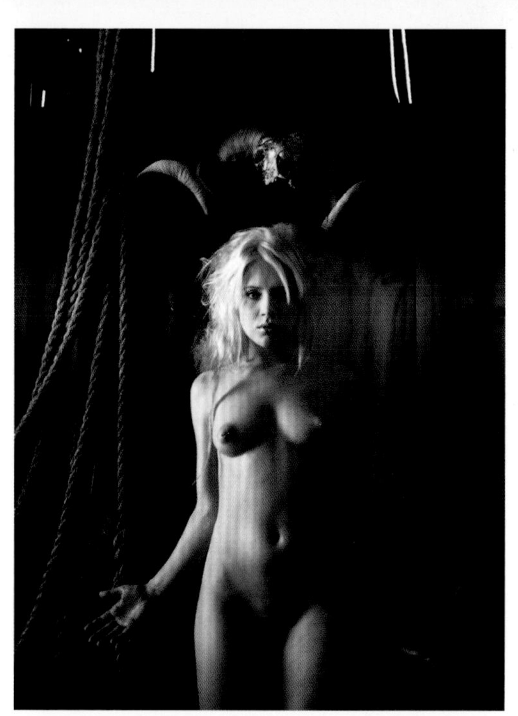

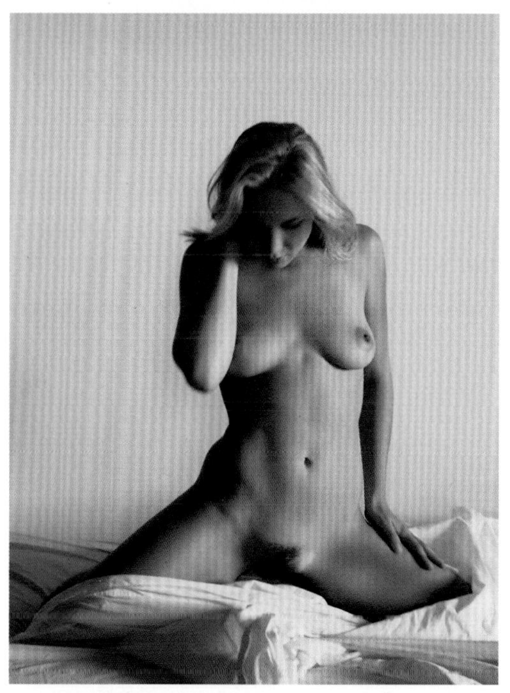

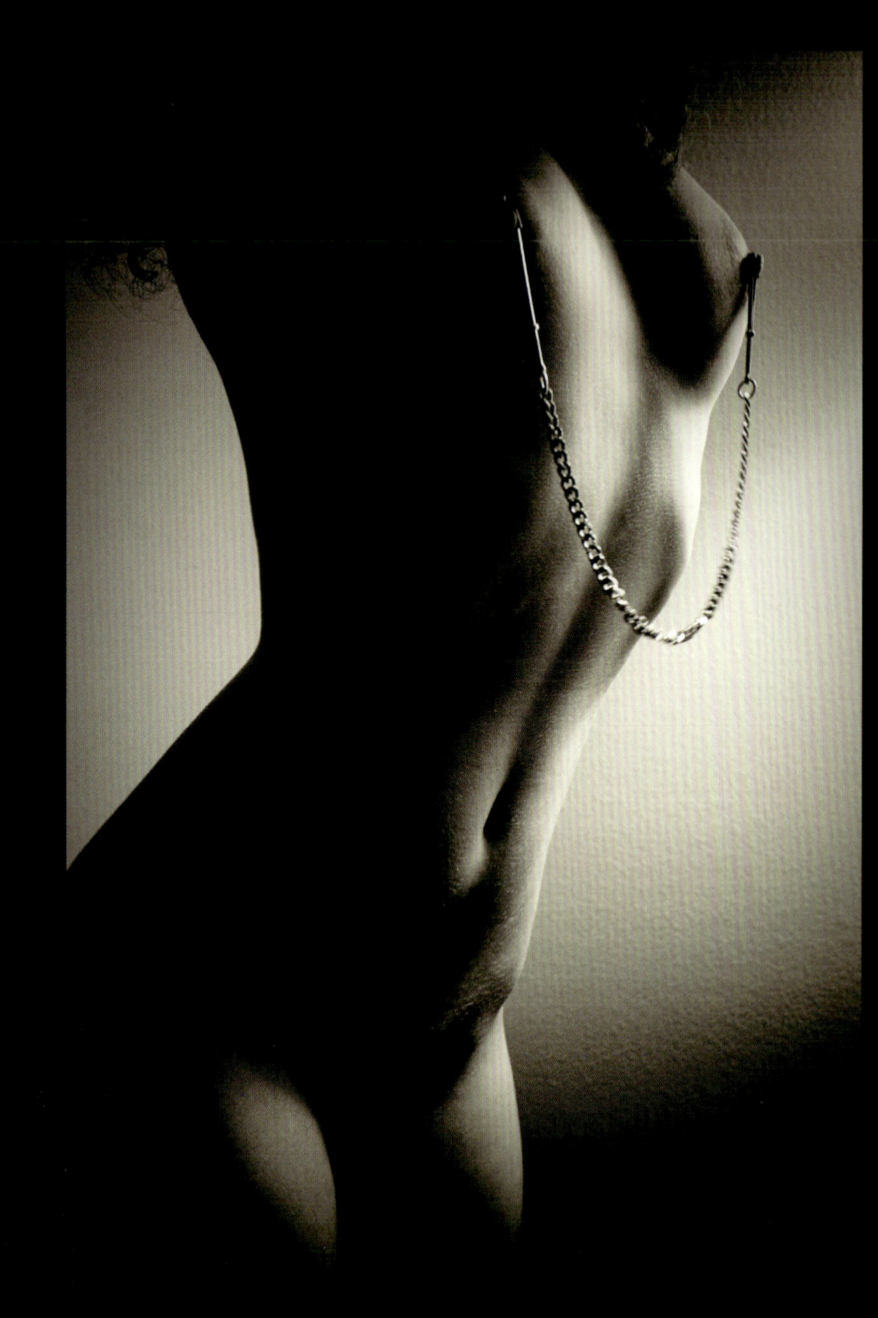

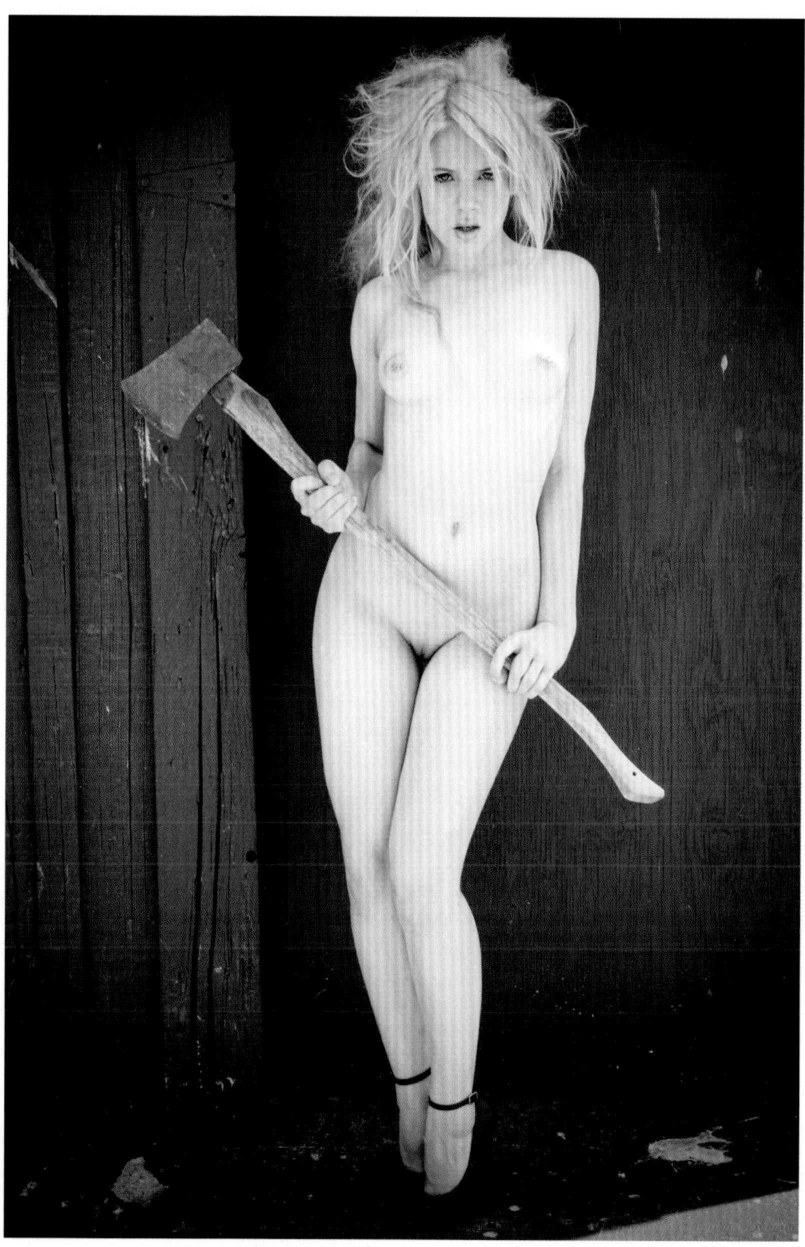

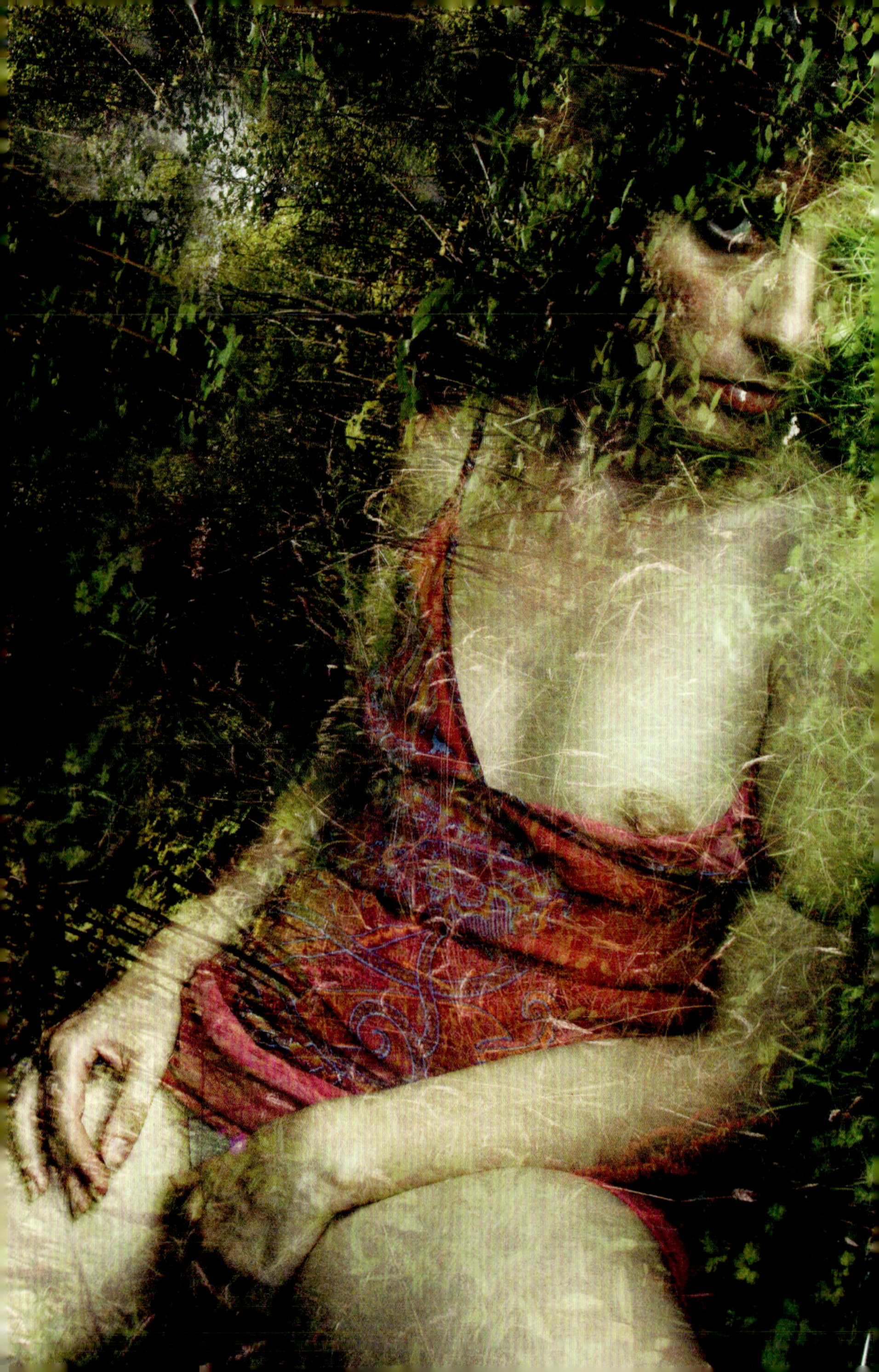

guy moberly

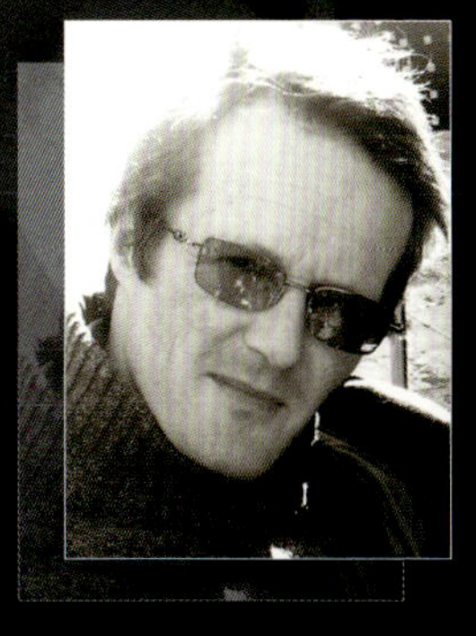

GUY STUDIED FINE ART and, later, documentary photography at Newport after extensive travel and two years working as a cruise ship photographer. Most of his published work has been travel, editorial and reportage. His erotic photography is relatively new, spontaneous, inspired and unhindered by deadlines, editorial restraints and nosey, prudish British processing labs. His work is still largely shot on film. It is a culmination of his love of light, the medium, the 'erotic' and a burning necessity to express himself, experiment and produce thought-provoking, stunning work as well as simply enjoying himself! He has been based in Barcelona for almost ten years, where attitudes towards eroticism are generally, in his experience, far more liberal. He wants to photograph all sorts of women, from all walks of life, though especially everyday girls that he might see on the bus or working in the supermarket.

Contact at GuyGuapo@yahoo.com

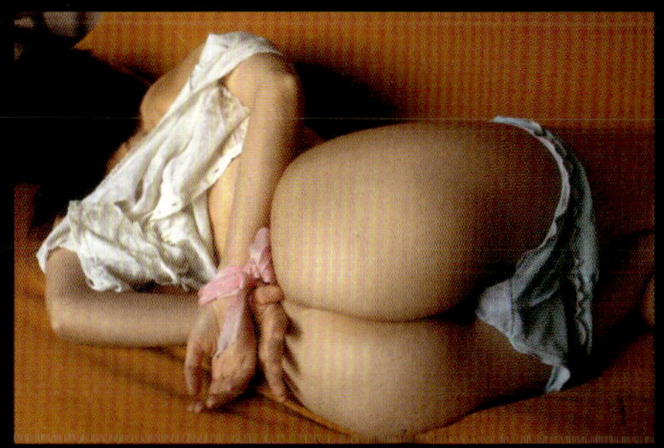

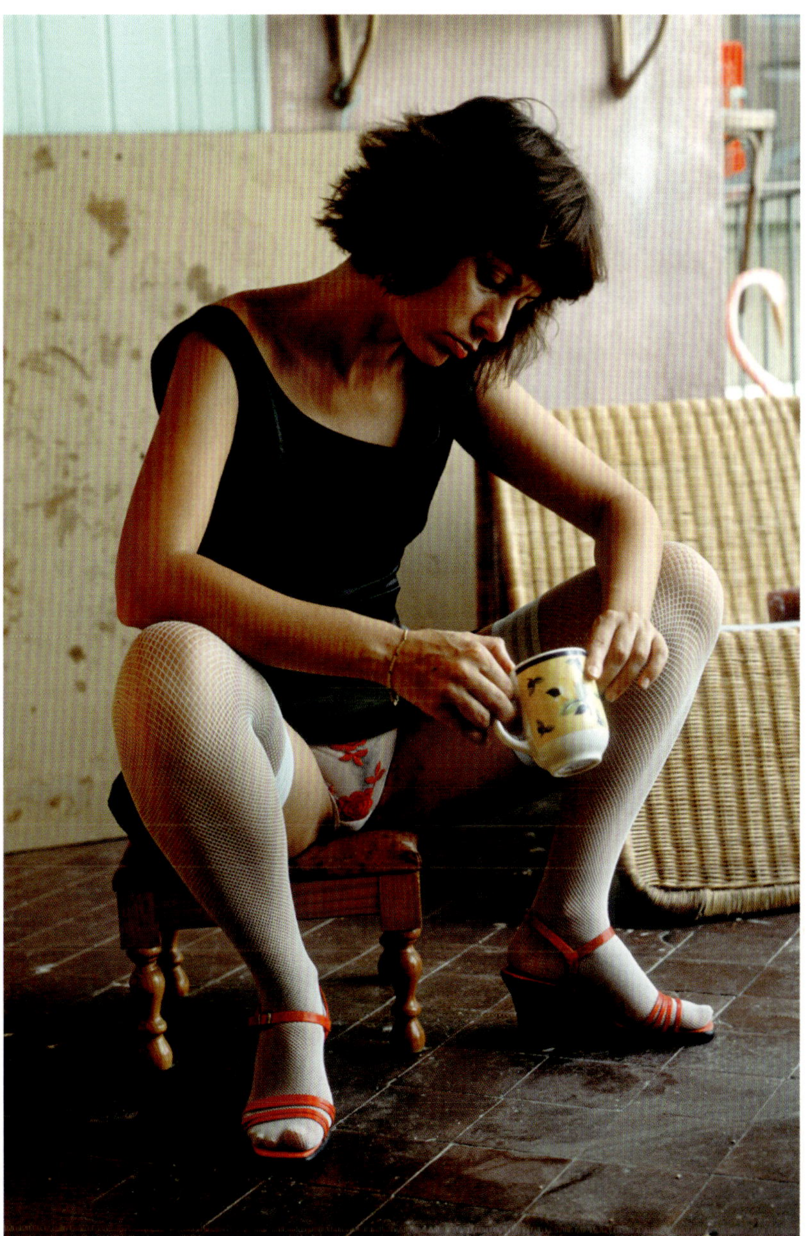

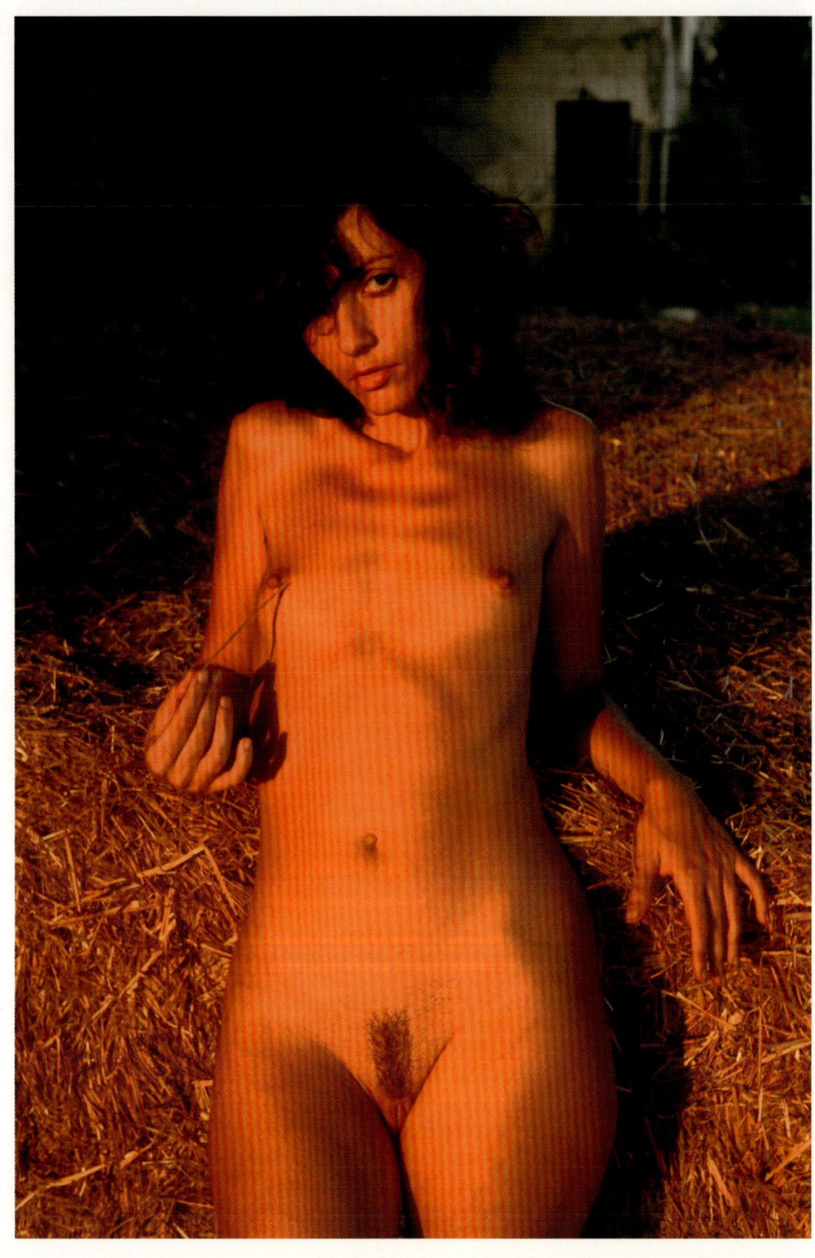

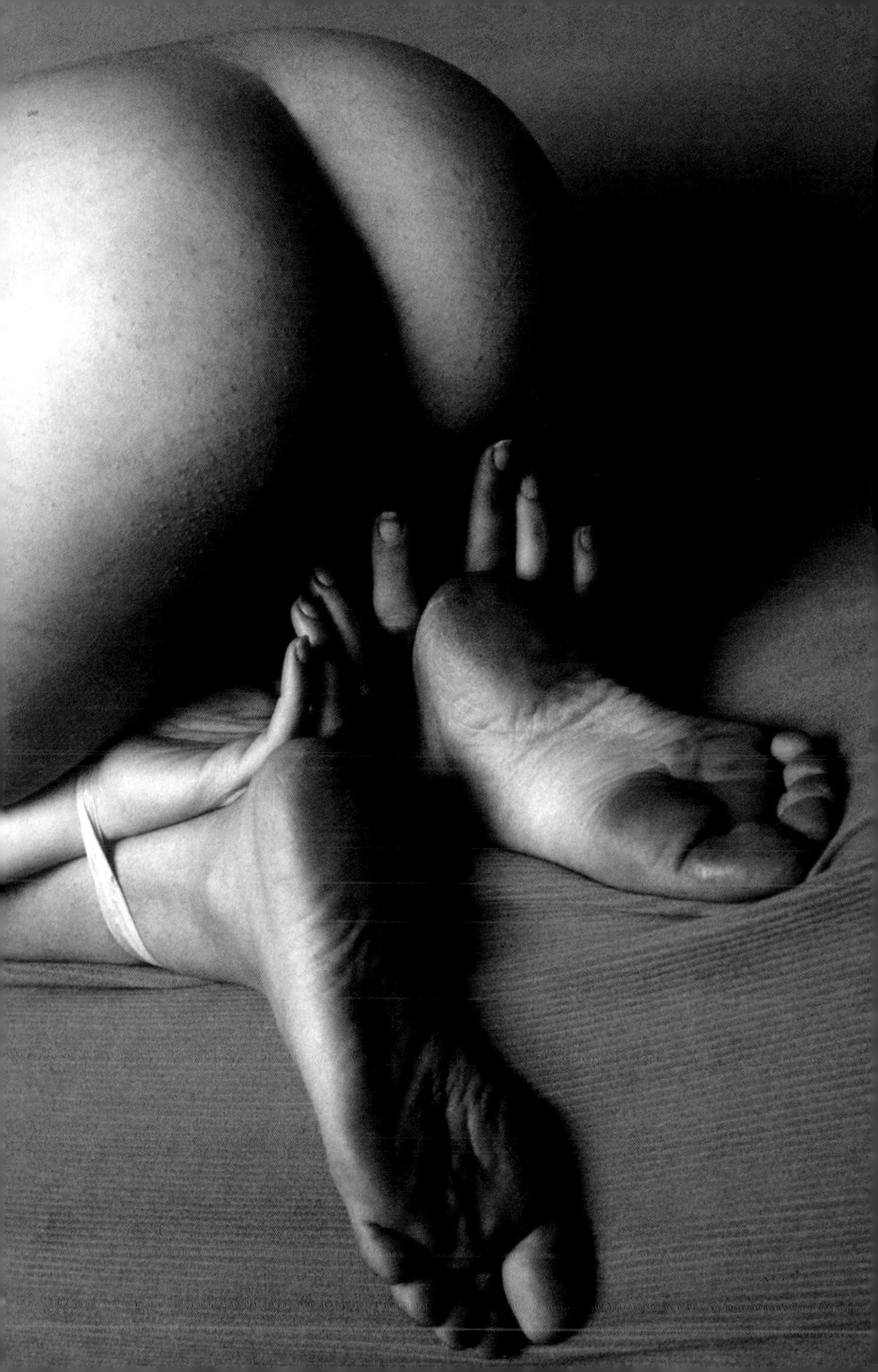

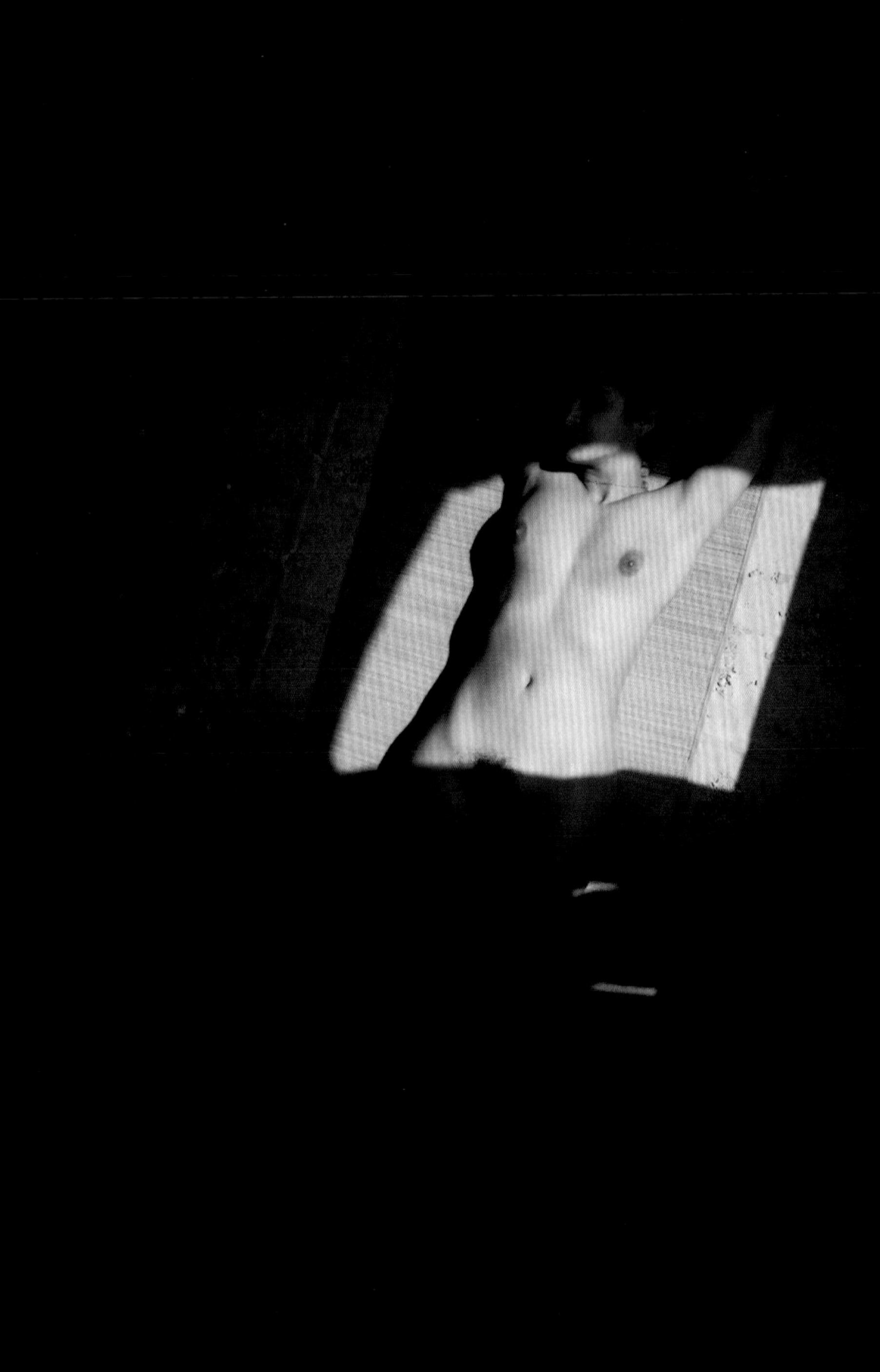

sabine modotti

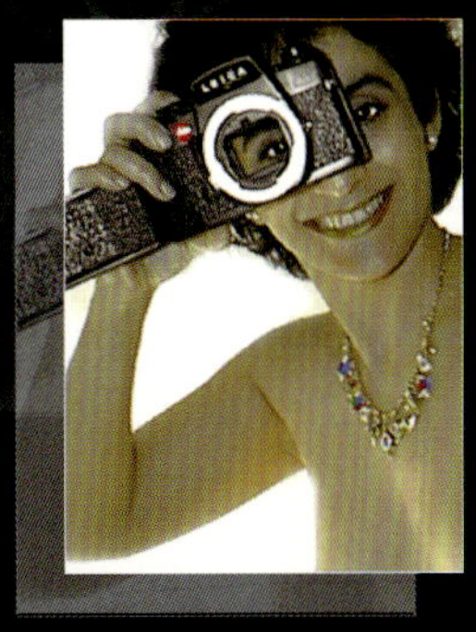

SABINE WAS BORN IN 1967 in Venice, but has lived and worked in Berlin since 1999. She has a degree in architecture but has always had a passion for female nude photography. For many years, she signed her work 'Aelia' and won many awards and had numerous exhibitions. Since her move to Germany, she now works principally in the studio, with German and Italian friends and models, attempting to connect with viewer's fantasies through light, vivid colours and arty elegance.

www.thenymphes.net
www.sabinemodotti.jalbum.net

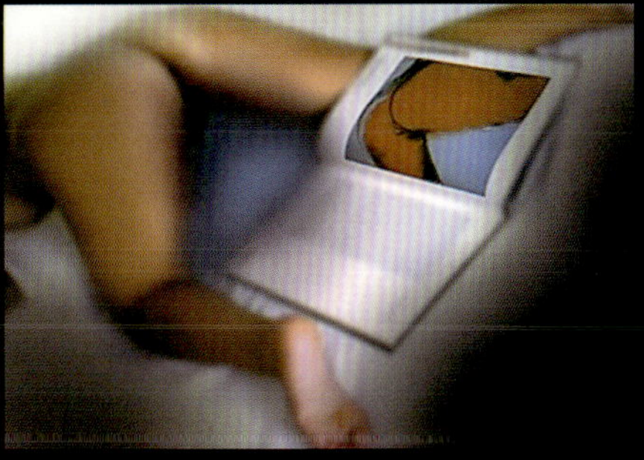

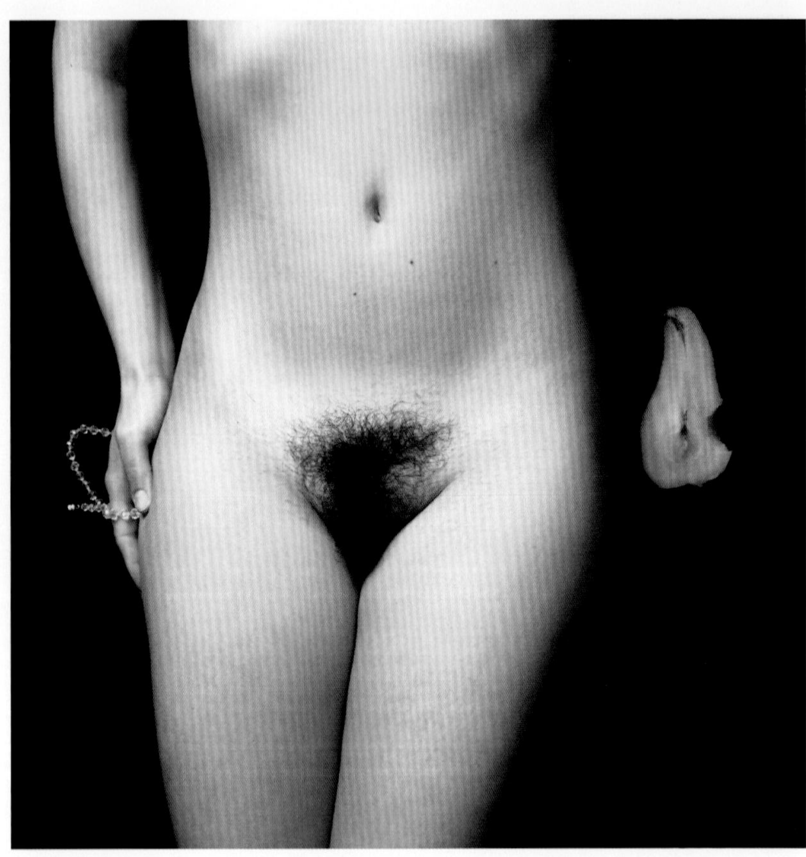

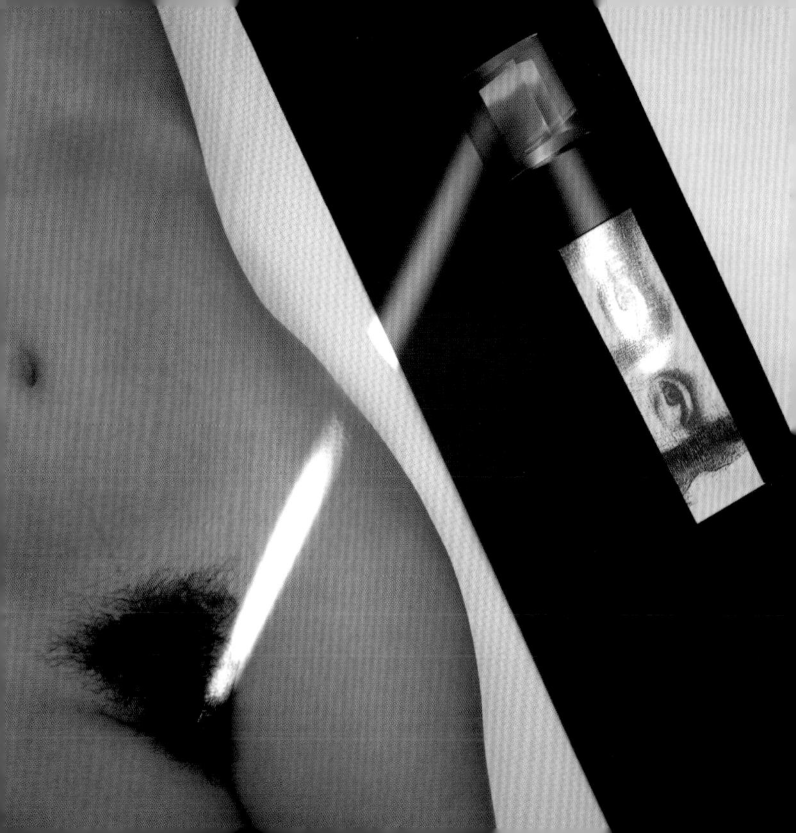

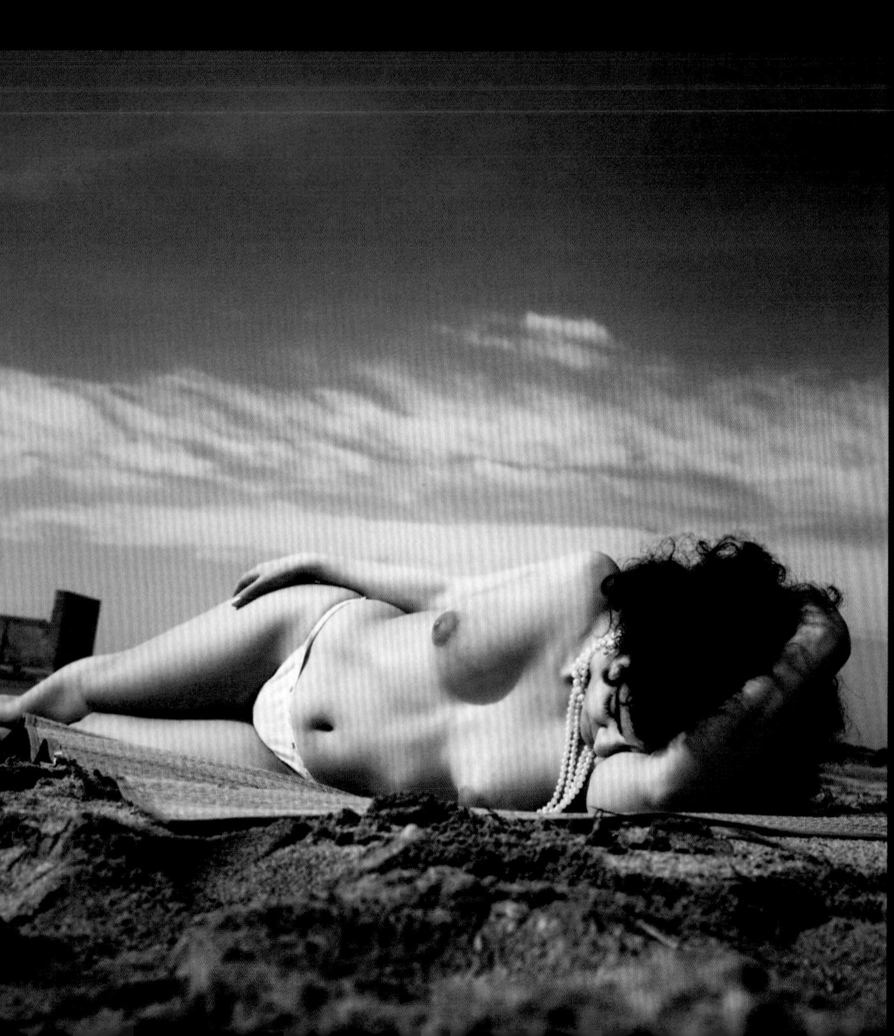

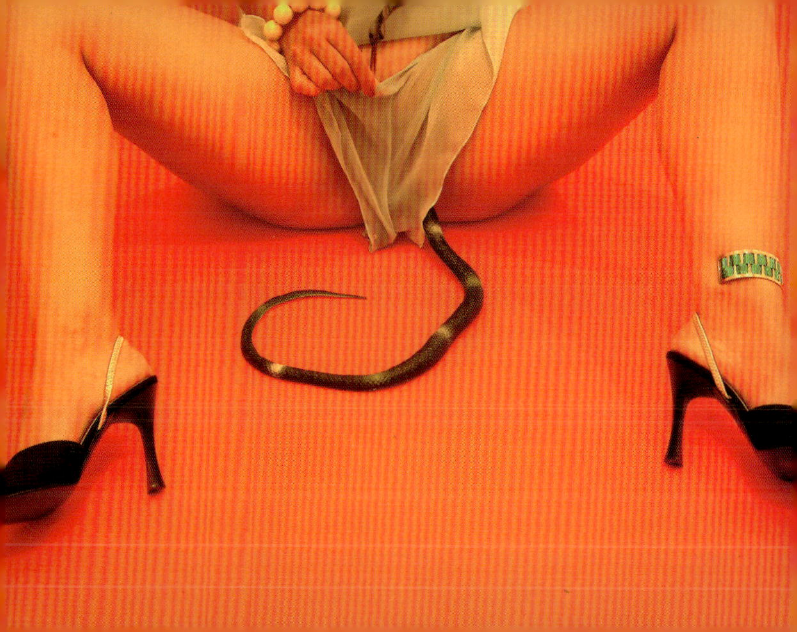

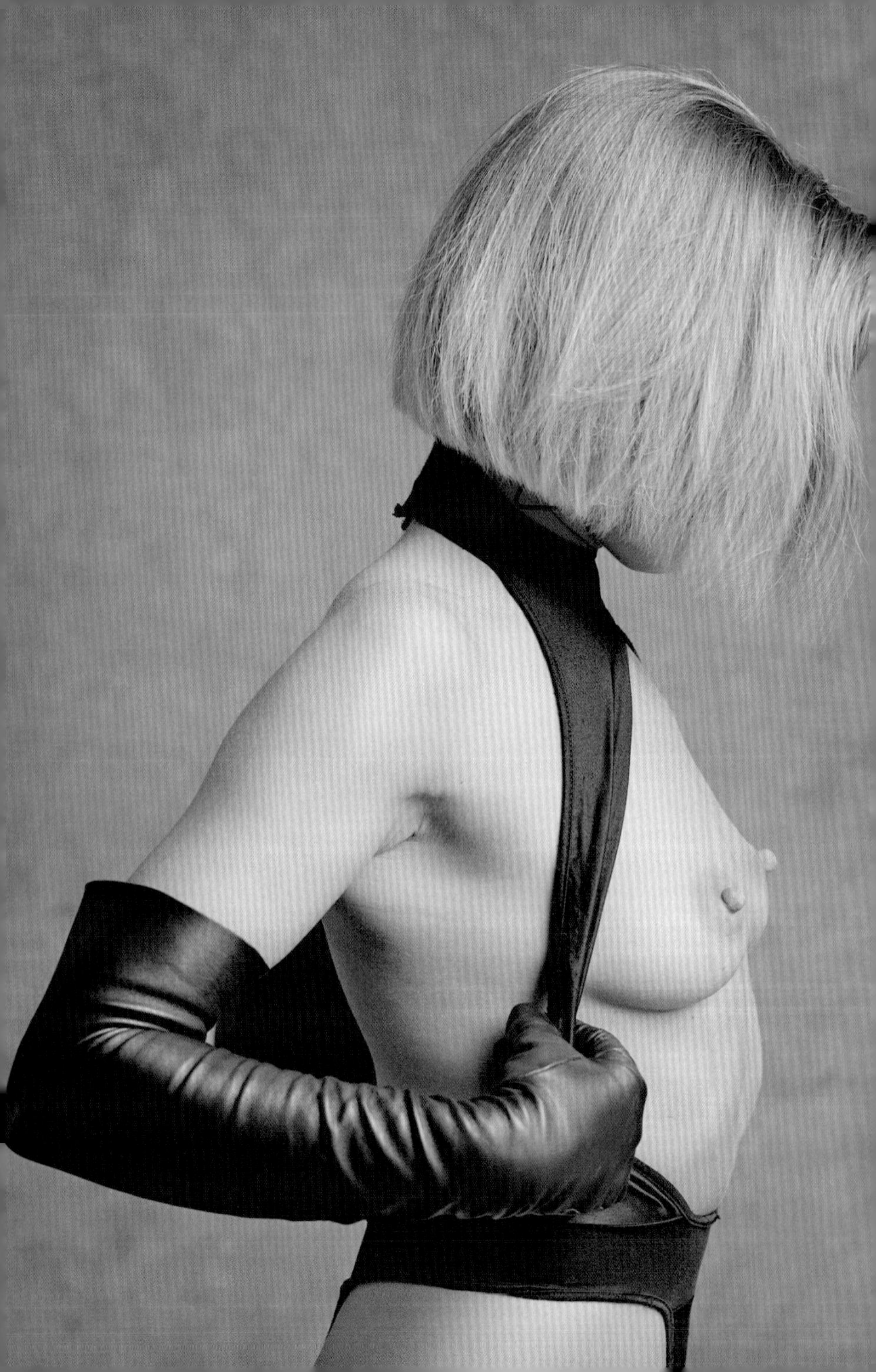

craig morey

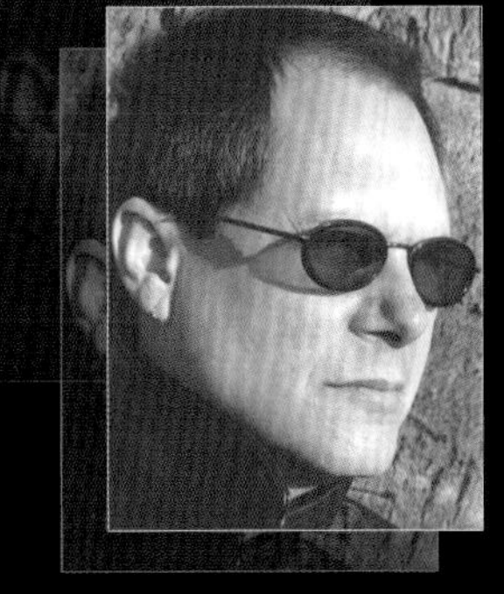

CRAIG MOREY IS AN AMERICAN photographer, known primarily for his black-and-white erotic nudes. He was a founding director of the well-known San Francisco Camerawork in the early 1980s, and has since won numerous awards with his work, including a Special Jury Prize at the International Triennial of Photography in Friebourg, Switzerland, First Prize at the California State Exposition, and inclusion as one of five worldwide 'Discoveries' by the editors of Time-Life Books. His photographs have been extensively published in the US, Europe and Japan, and he is the author of four books: *Studio Nudes* (Penthouse Intl, 1992), *Body/Expression/Silence* (Le Merche/Yashida, 1994), *Linea*, (Korinsha Press, 1996) and *Twentieth Century Studio Nudes* (Glaspalast ed. 2001).

www.moreystudio.com

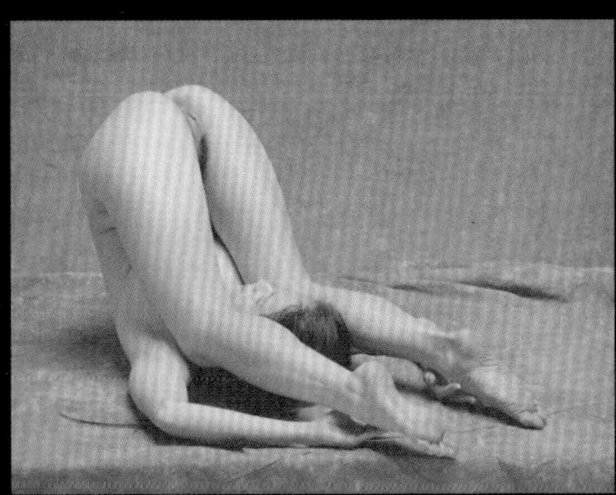

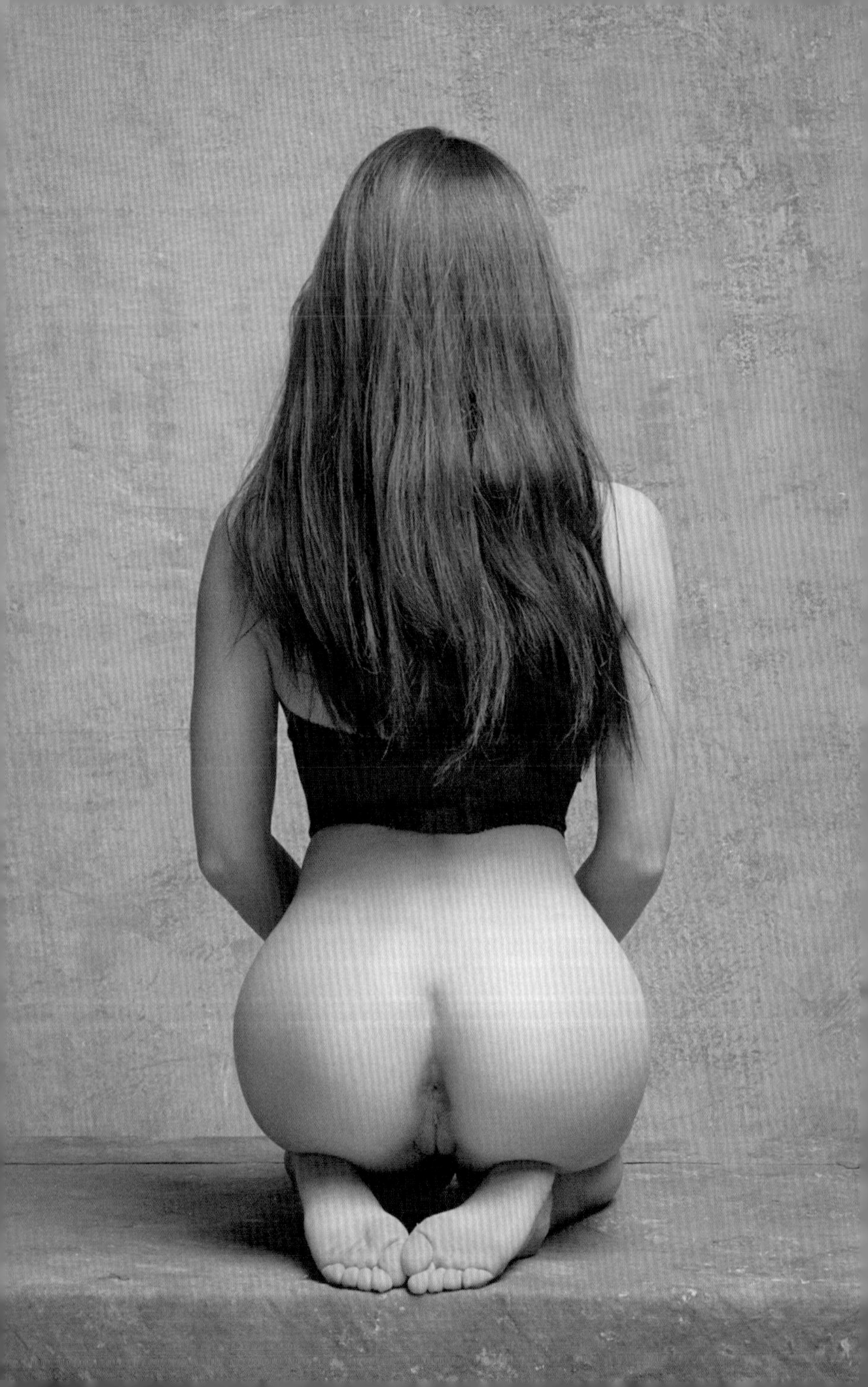

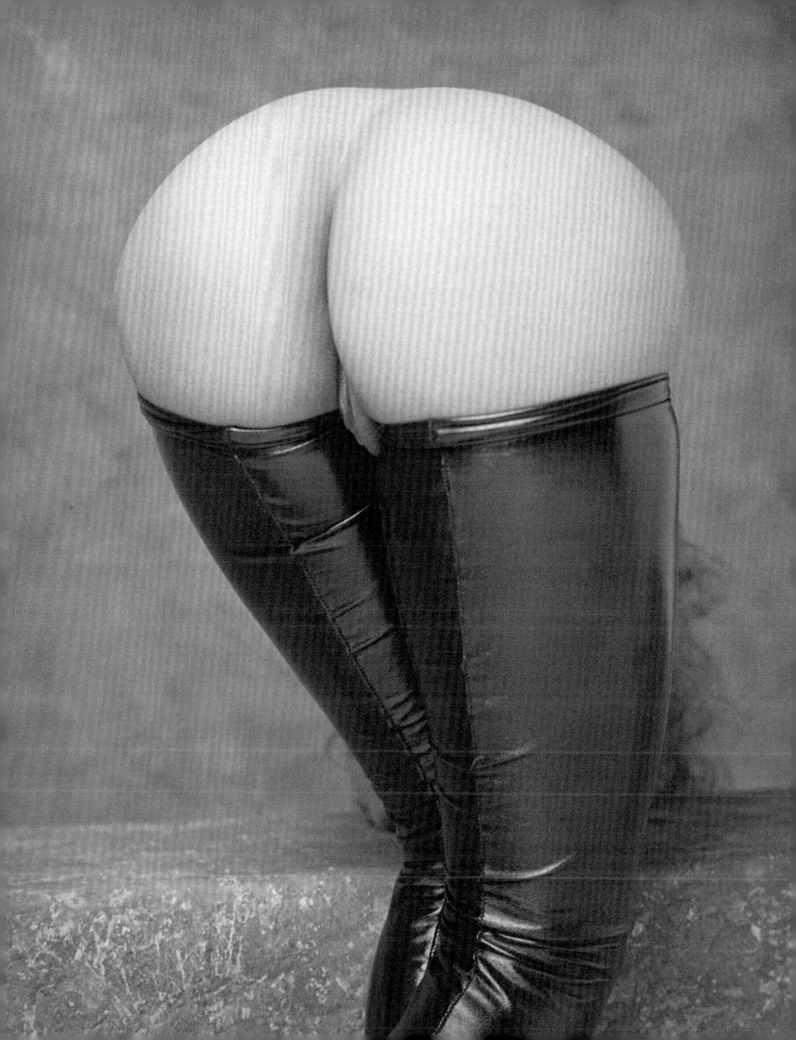

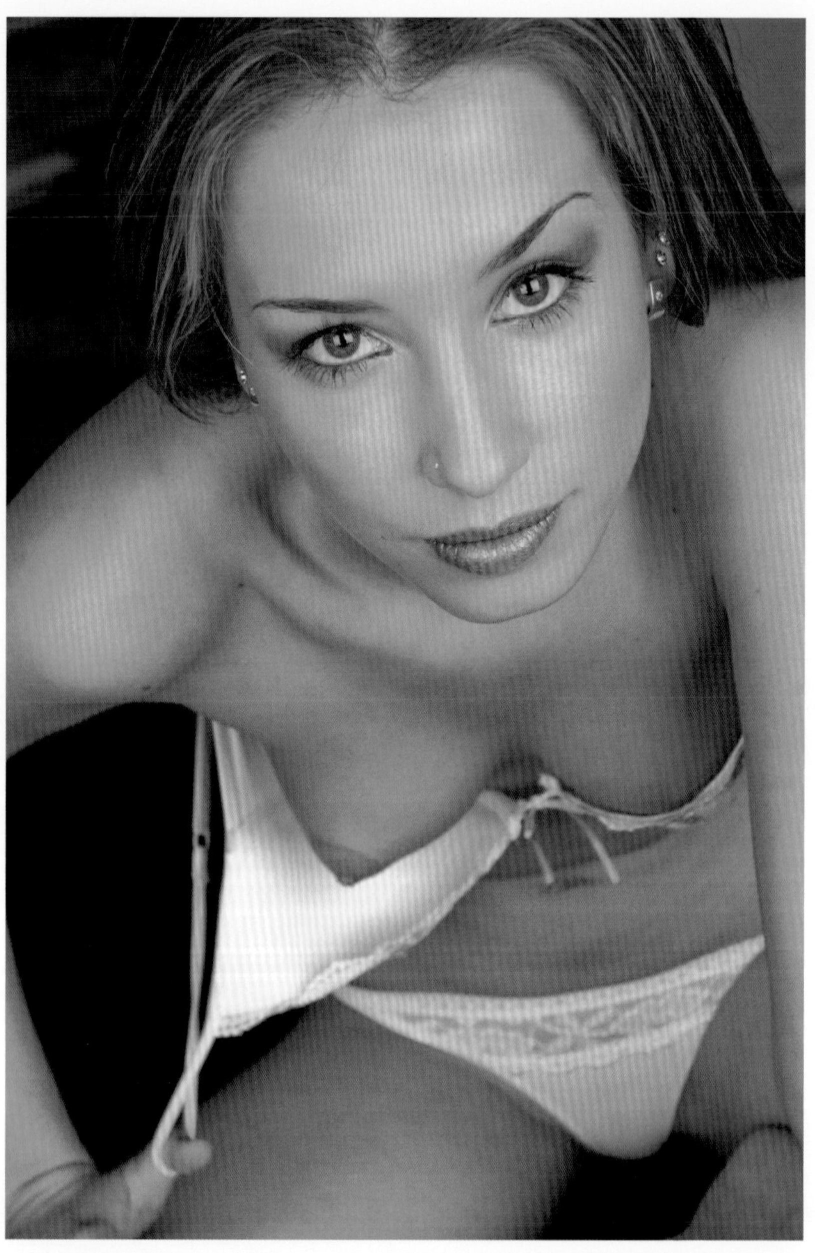

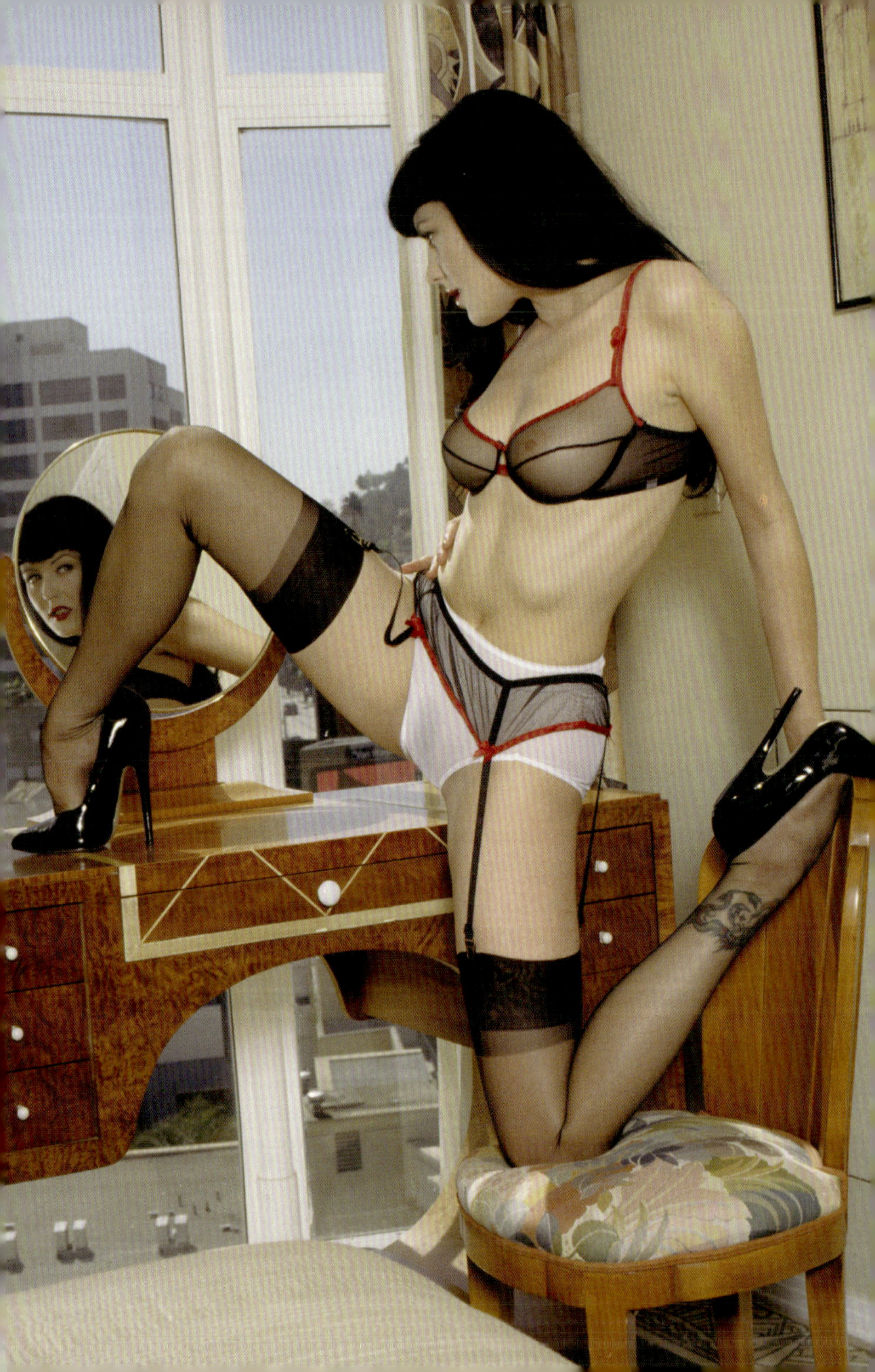

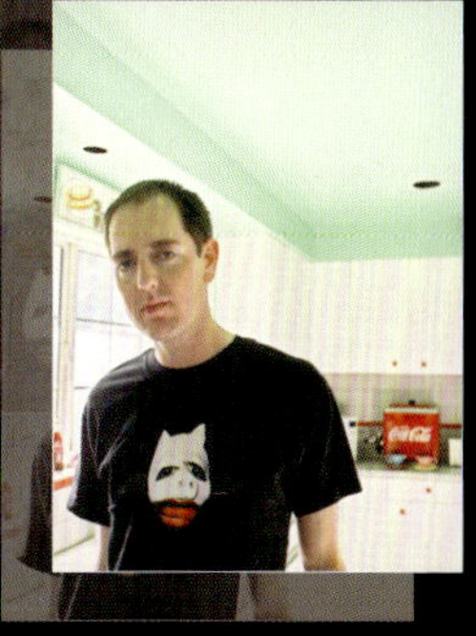

DAVE NAZ IS A PHOTOGRAPHER of sex and meaning, women and landscape. Innovative and self-taught, Naz has issued five books with Goliath Press: *Lust Circus* (2002), *Panties* (2003), *Legs* (2004), *Fresh: Girls of Seduction* (2006), and *L.A. Bondage* (2007), and his photographs have been shown all over the world. His work has appeared in *GQ*, *Maxim*, *Stern.de*, and *Salon*, and in many international collections, including *The New Erotic Photography* (Taschen, 2007) and *Self-Exposure: The Male Nude Self-Portrait* (Universe, 2005). He lives in the foothills above Southern California with his wife, Oriana.

www.davenaz.com

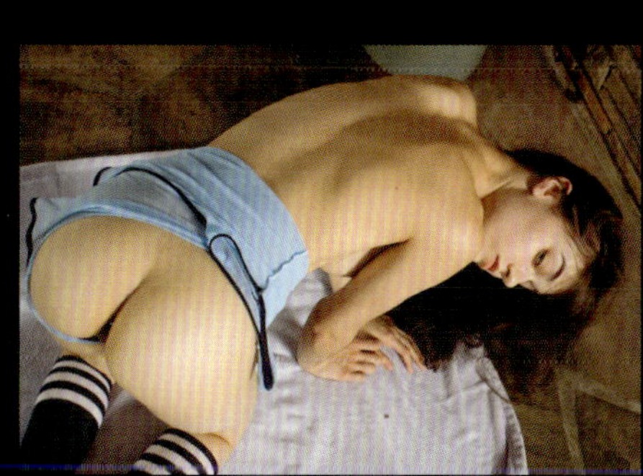

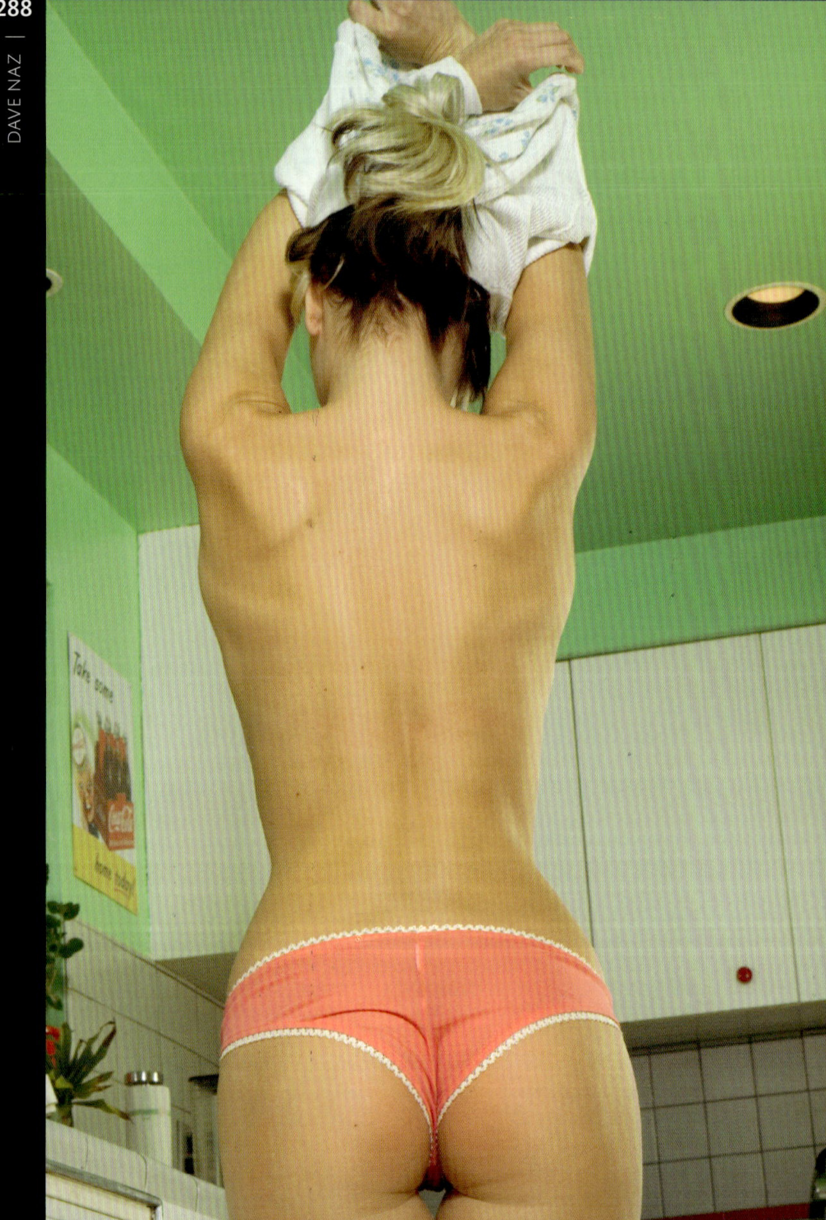
Take some
home today!

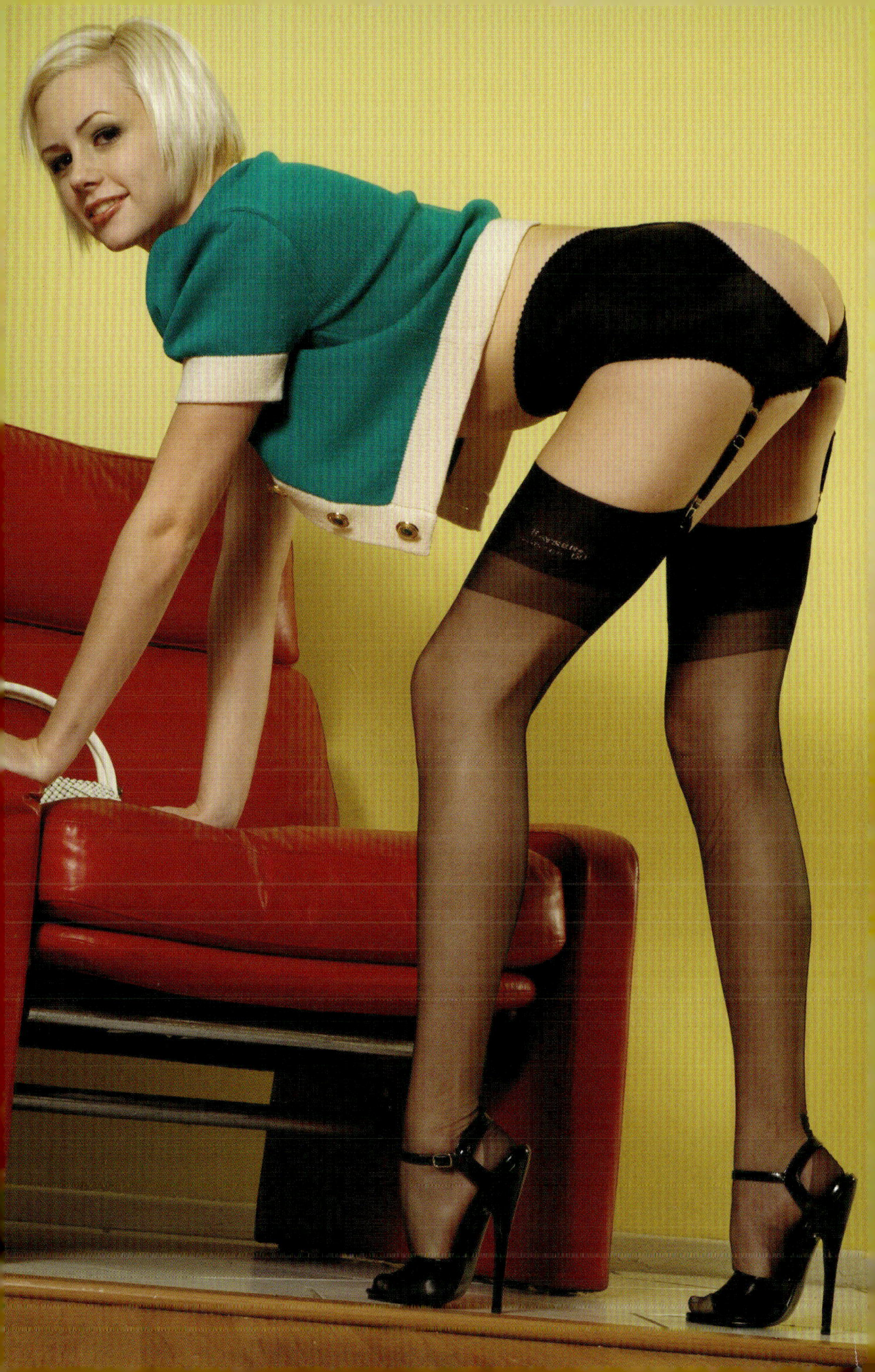

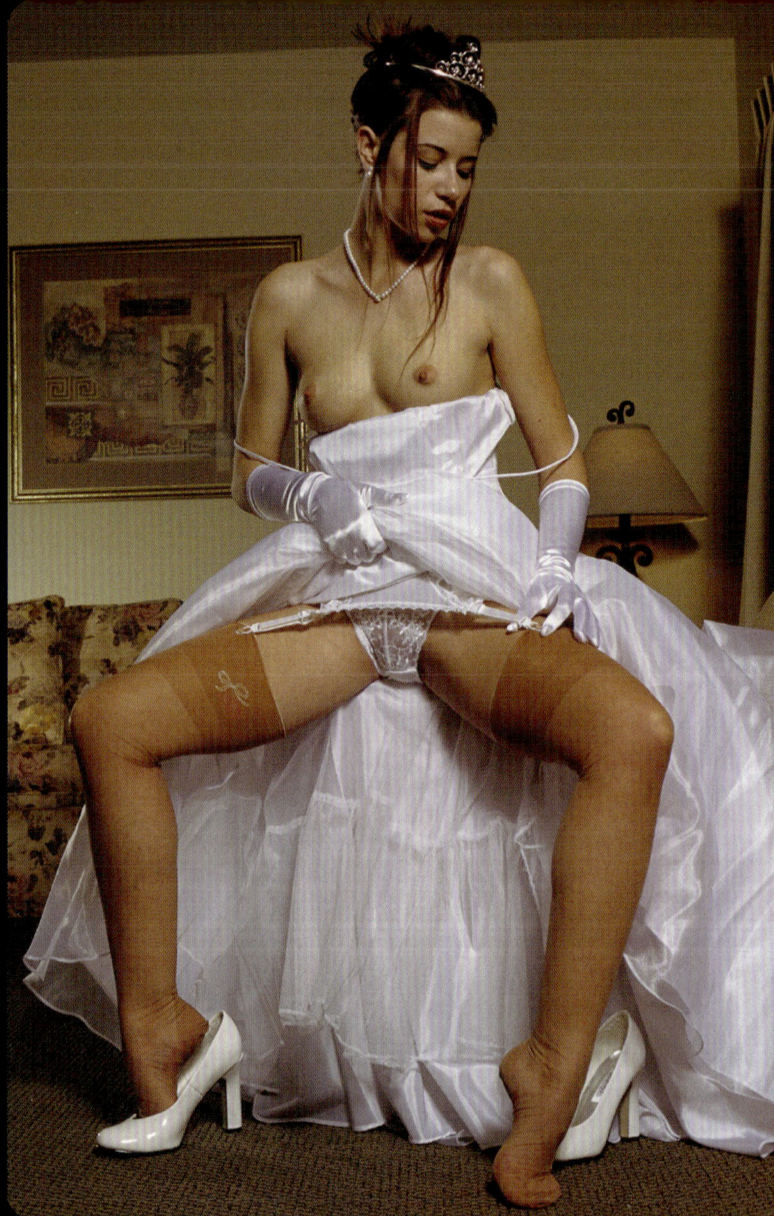

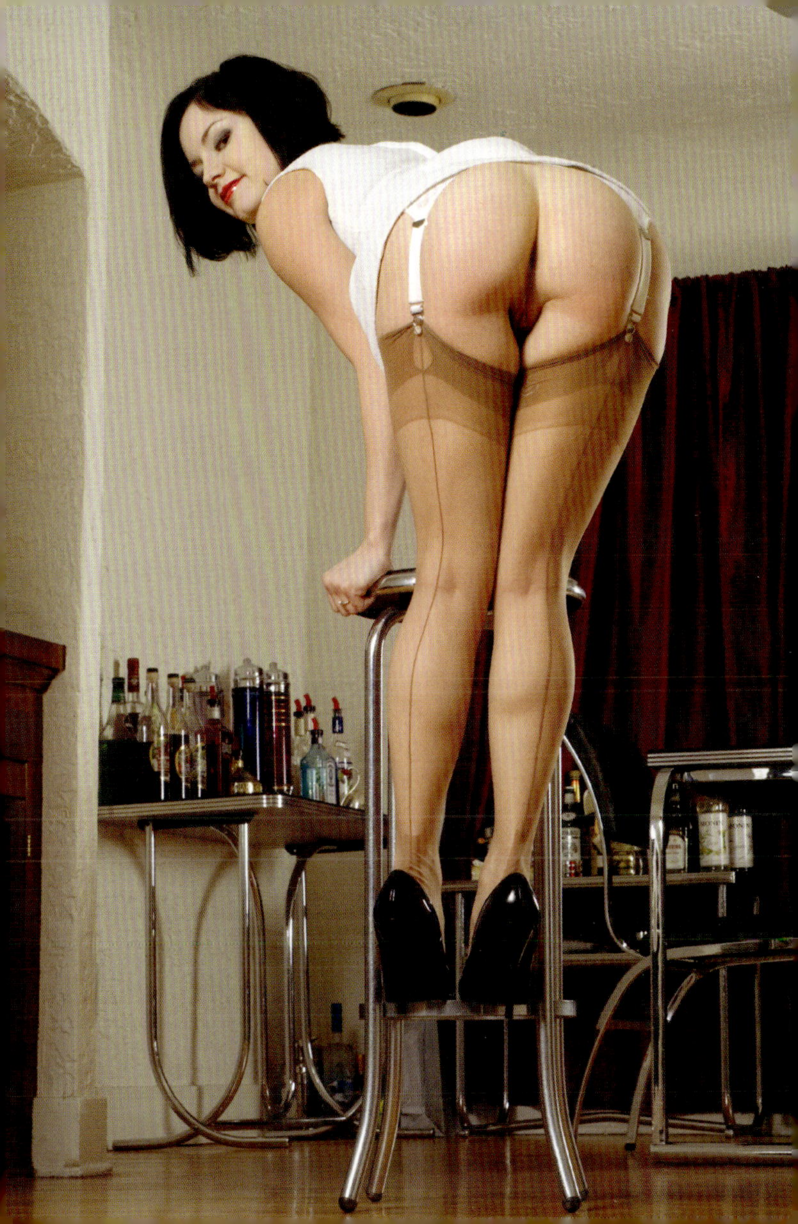

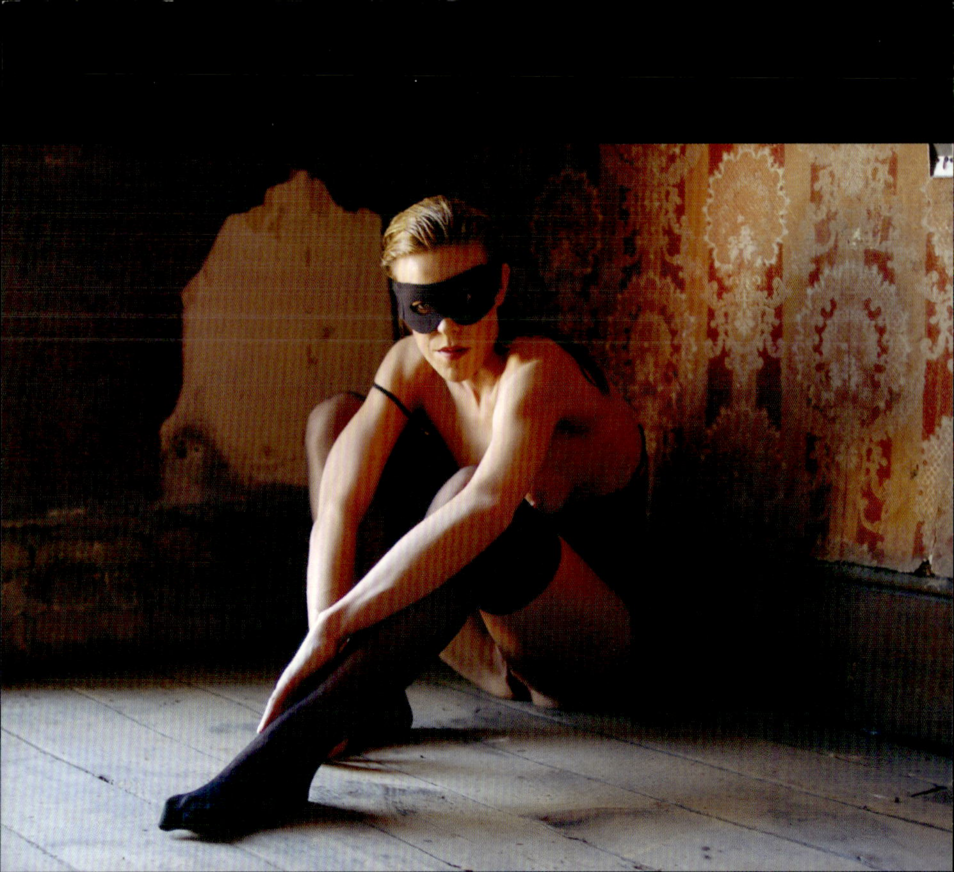

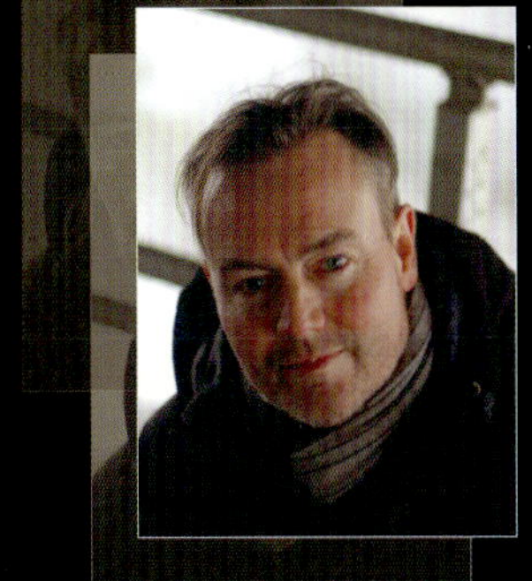

SECOND-GENERATION Canadian photographer Rob Nelson began his apprenticeship with his father as a teenager. He developed his craft doing aerial photography but his love for magazines led him to shooting fashion editorial assignments and exhibiting his work in galleries. Working internationally, Rob's portfolio includes credits in publications such as *Saturday Night*, *The Look* and *Interview*, documenting celebrities like Kirsten Dunst and Prince Andrew.

www.robnelsonphotography.com

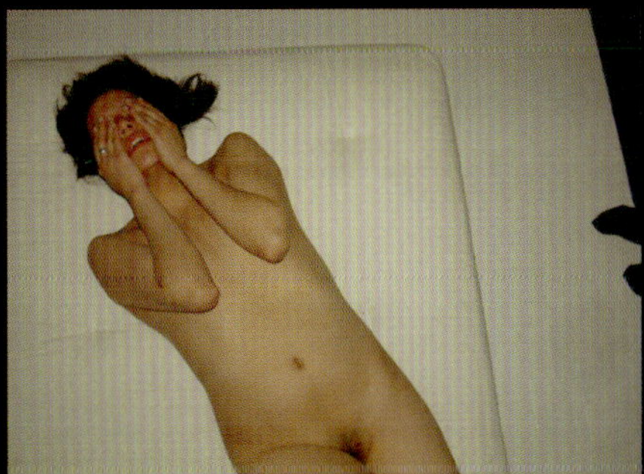

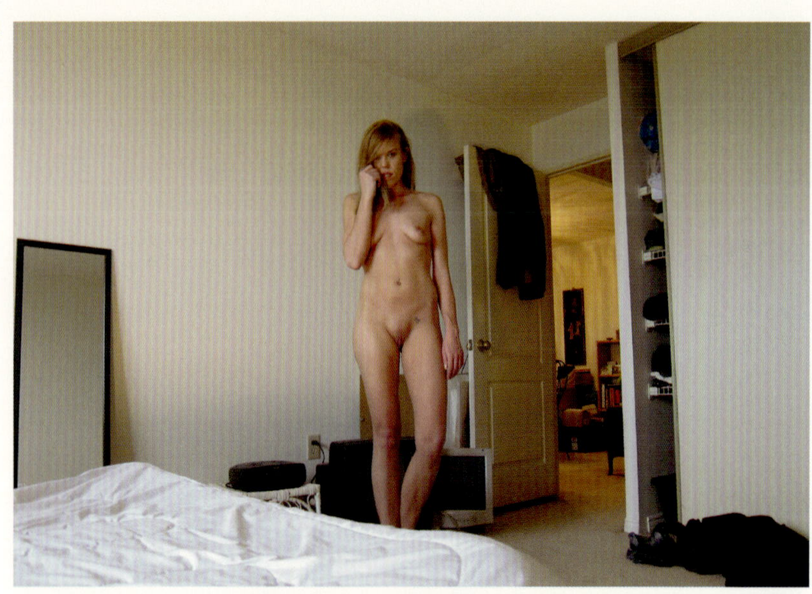

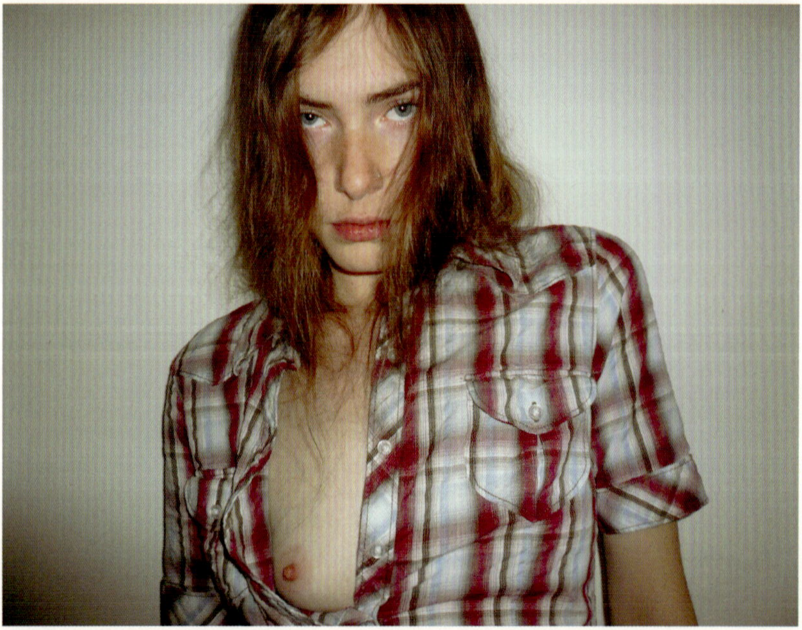

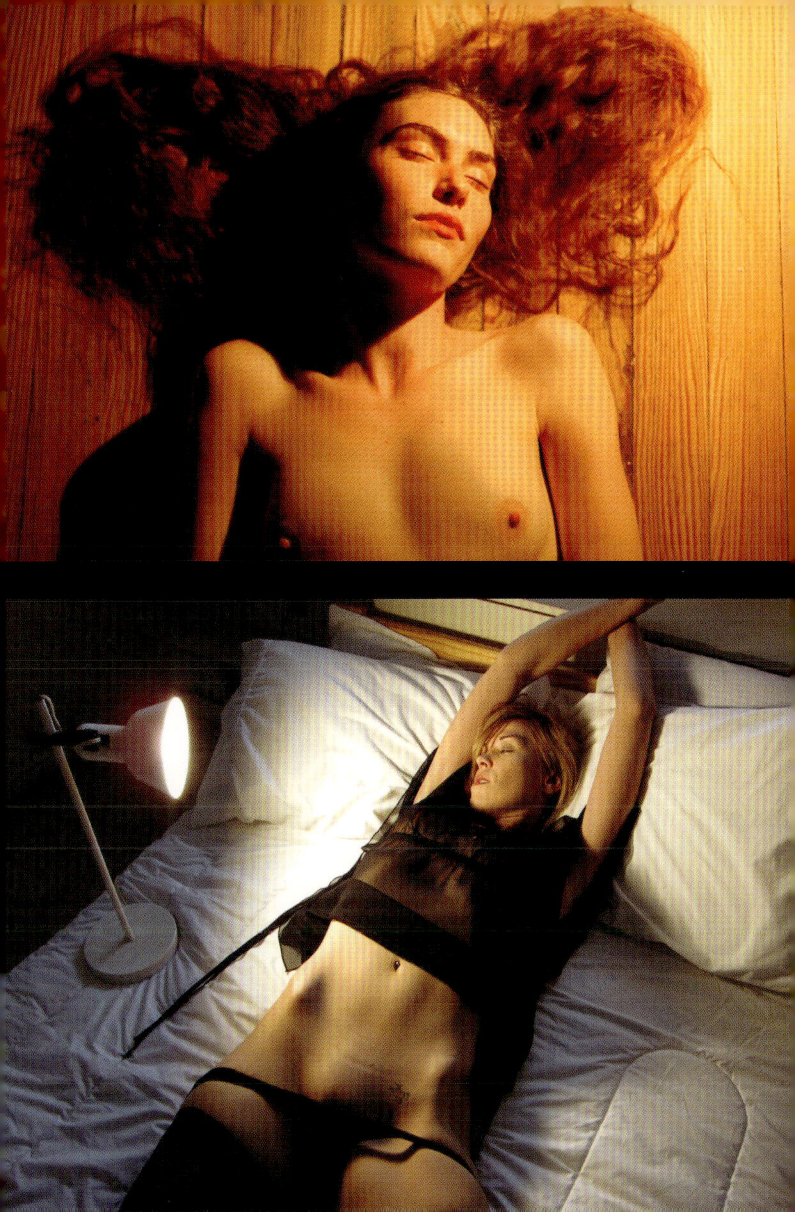

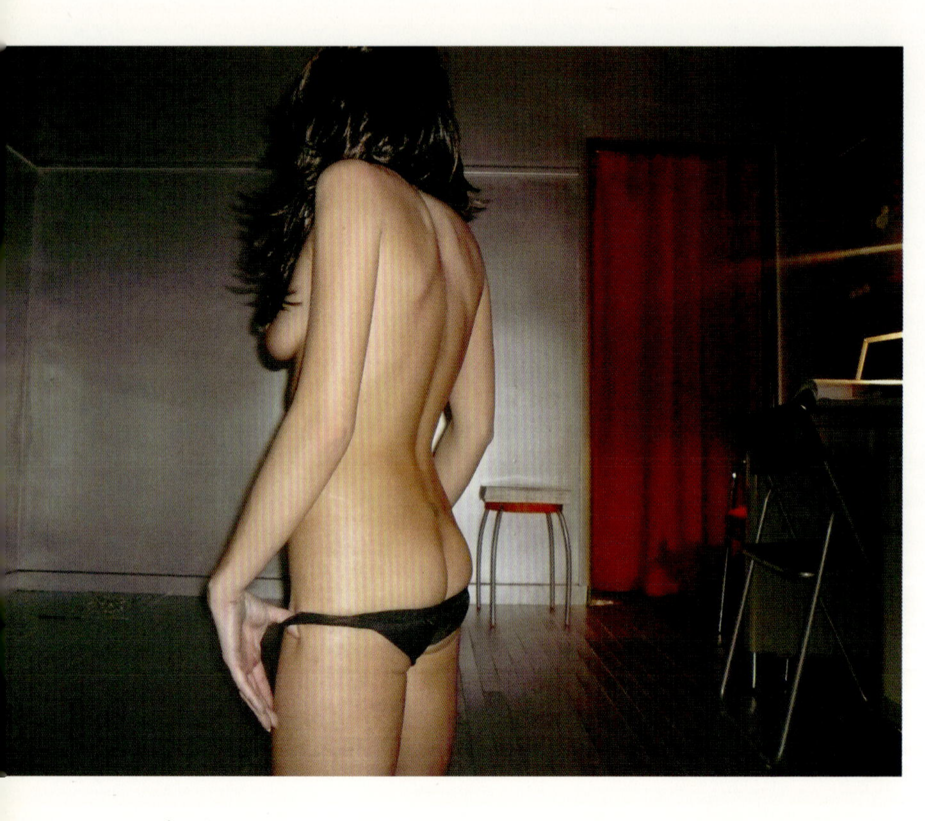

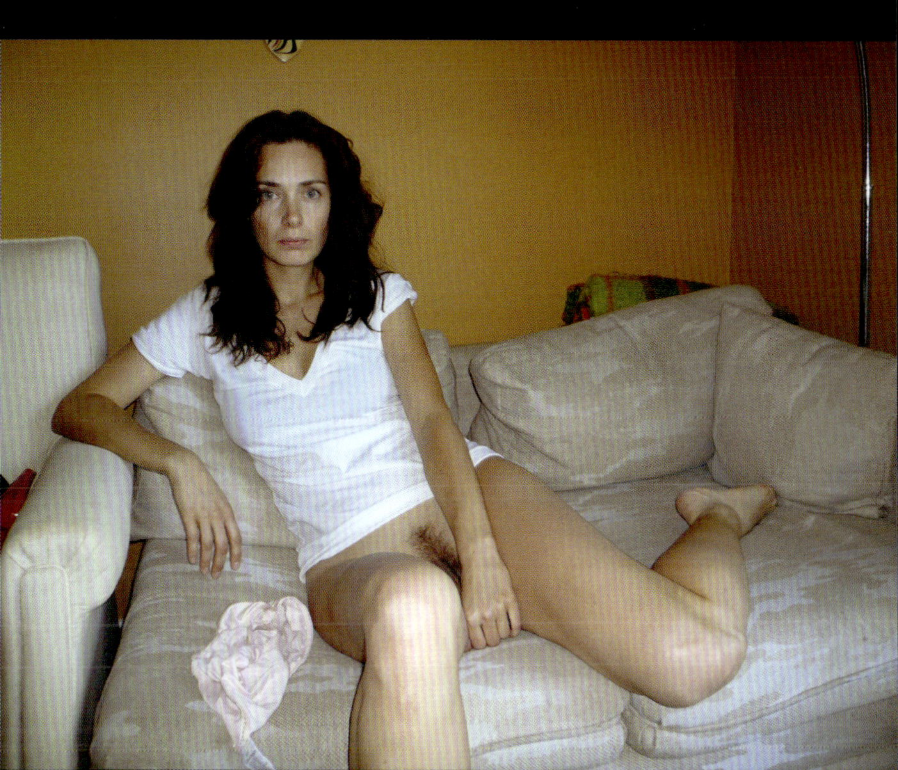

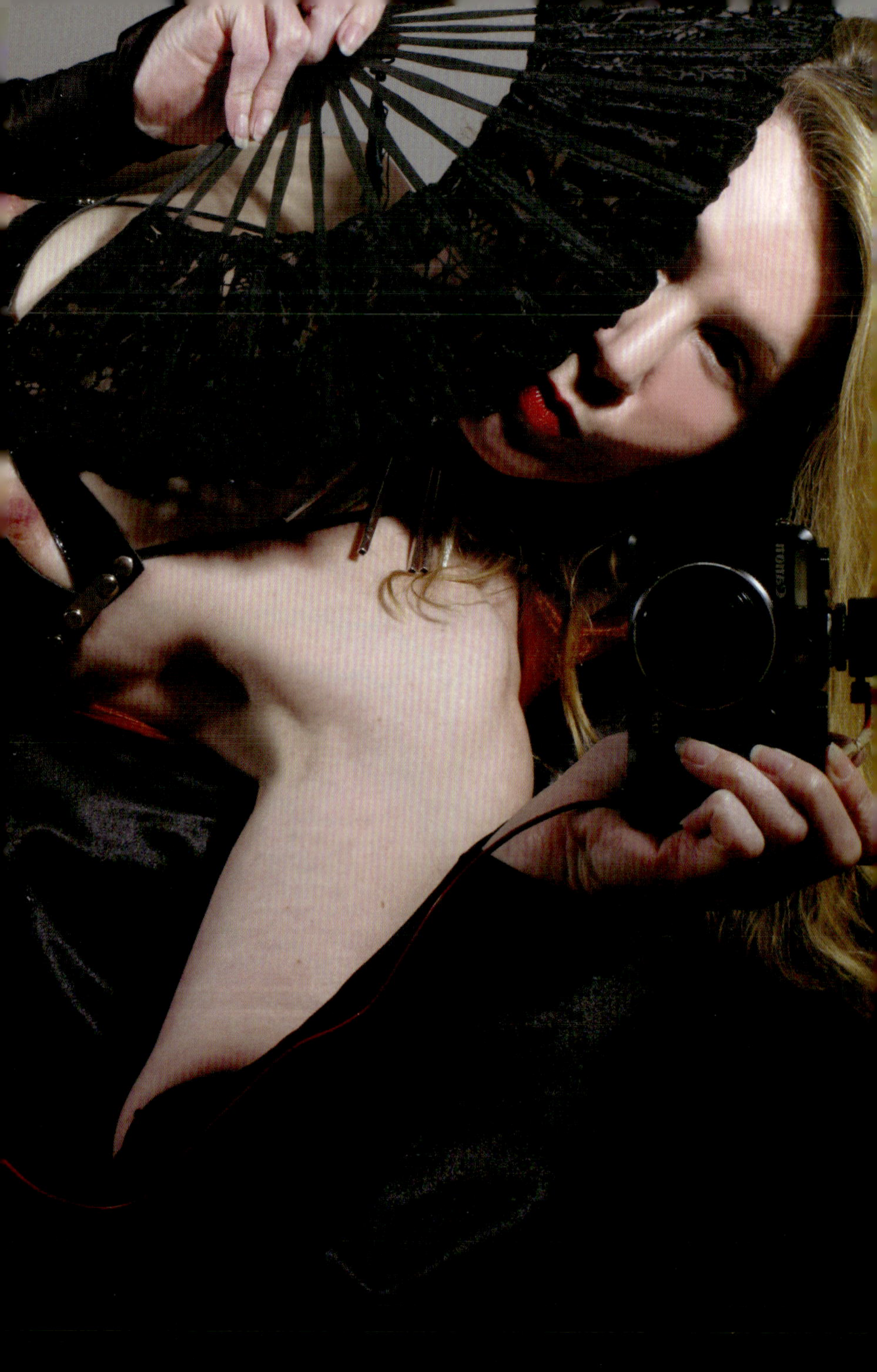

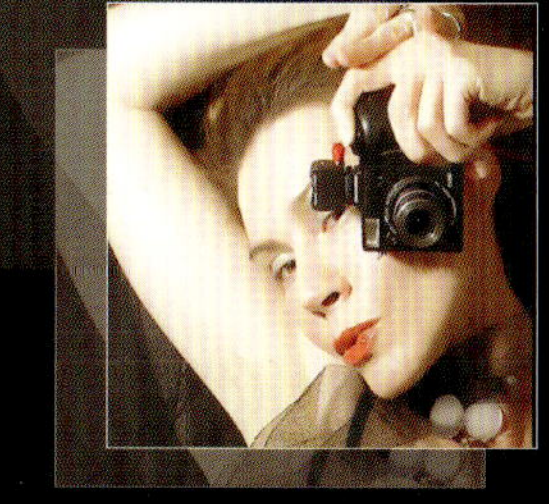

NORA NESS IS A SELF-TAUGHT German artist who specializes exclusively in self-portraits, created in front of a mirror, that seek to capture true erotic moments and passion. What differentiates her work from the mainstream of erotic photography is that she is not just the woman before and behind the camera but also the stylist and the arranger. Her work has been seen at a variety of Italian art fairs and at the Galleria Carini & Donatini.

www.eroticmirror.de

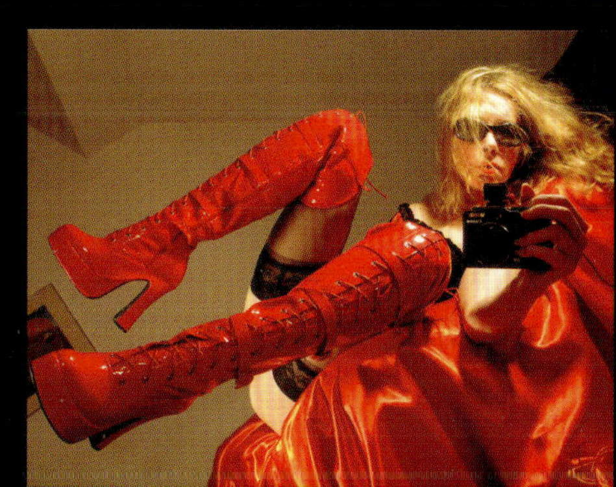

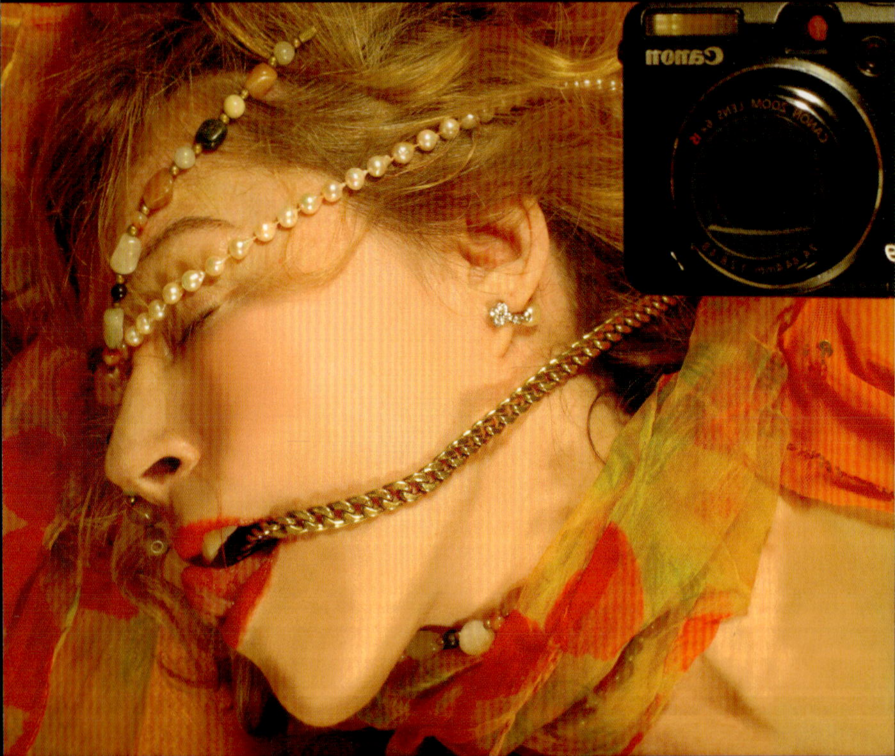

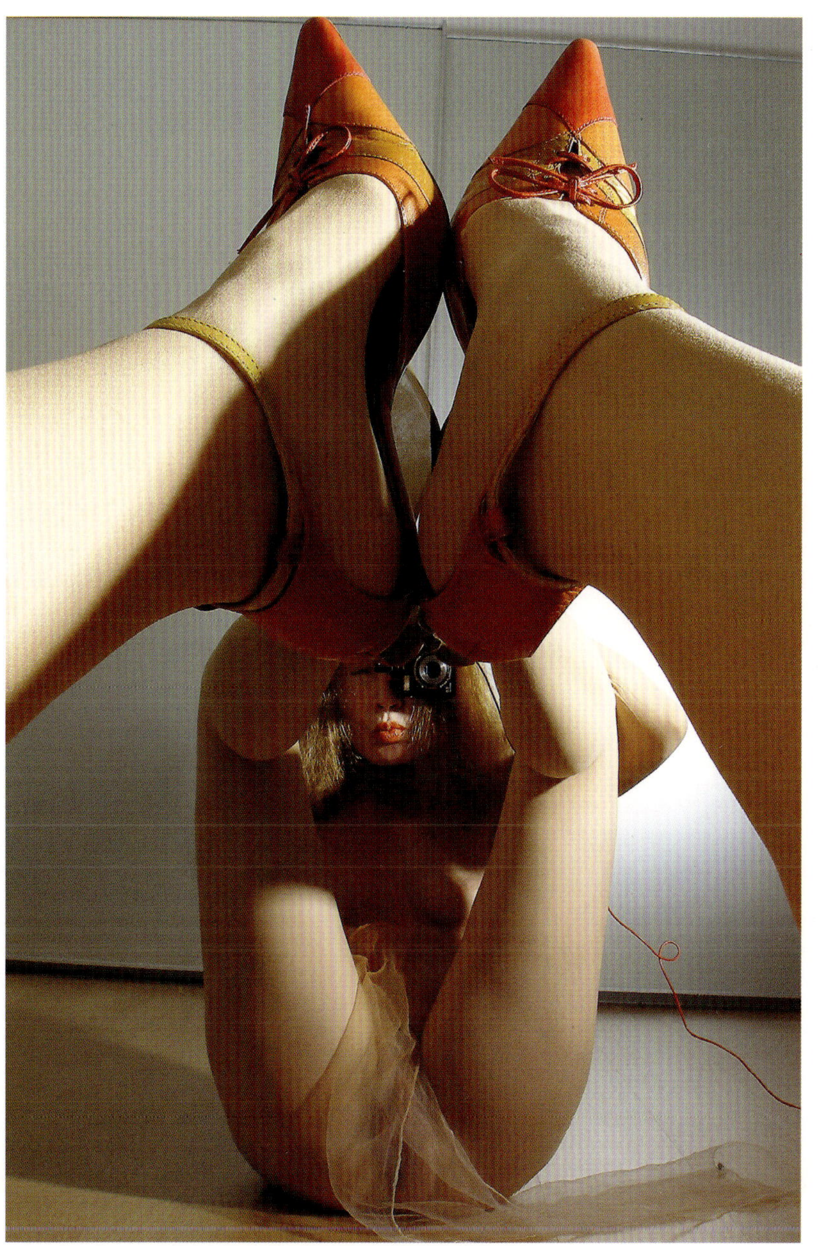

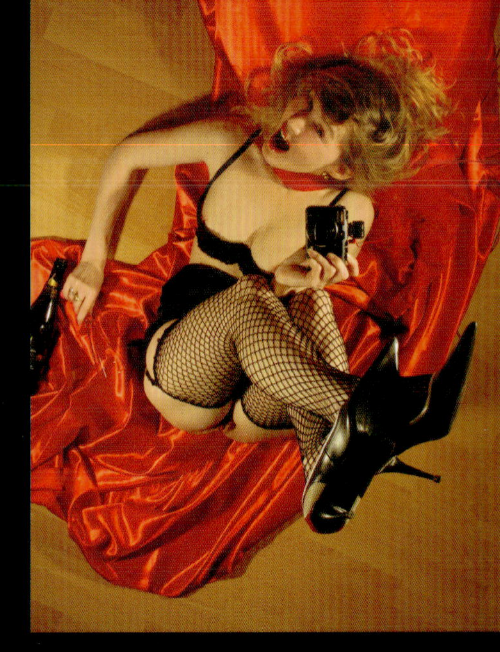

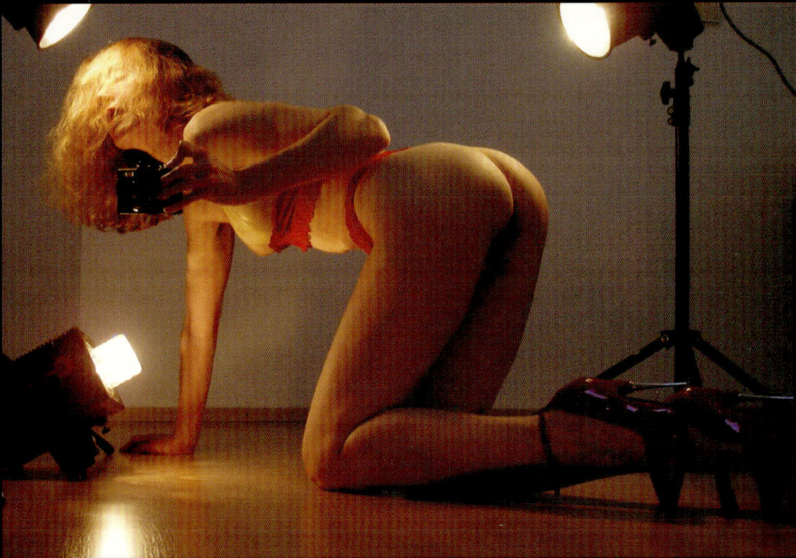

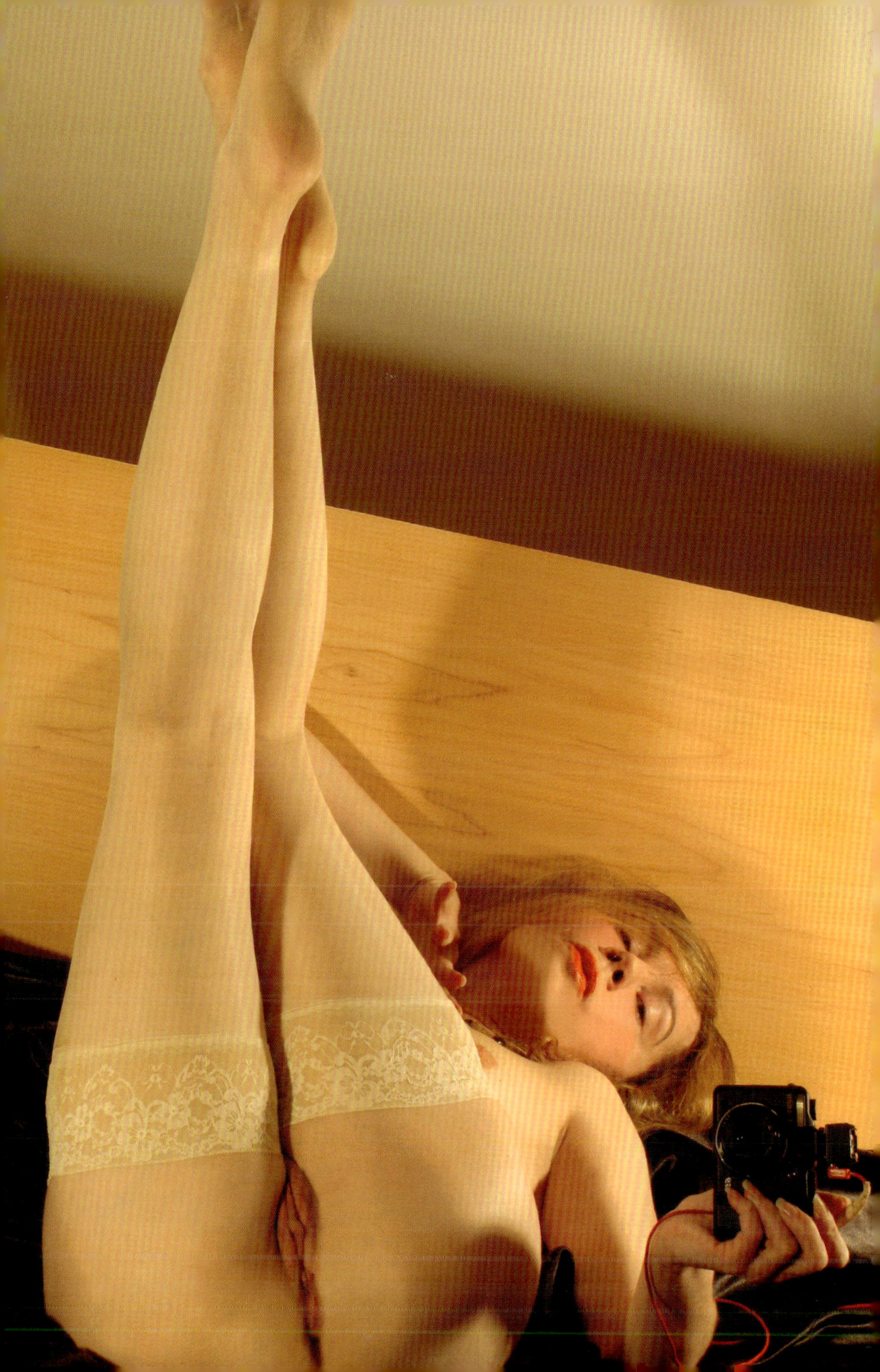

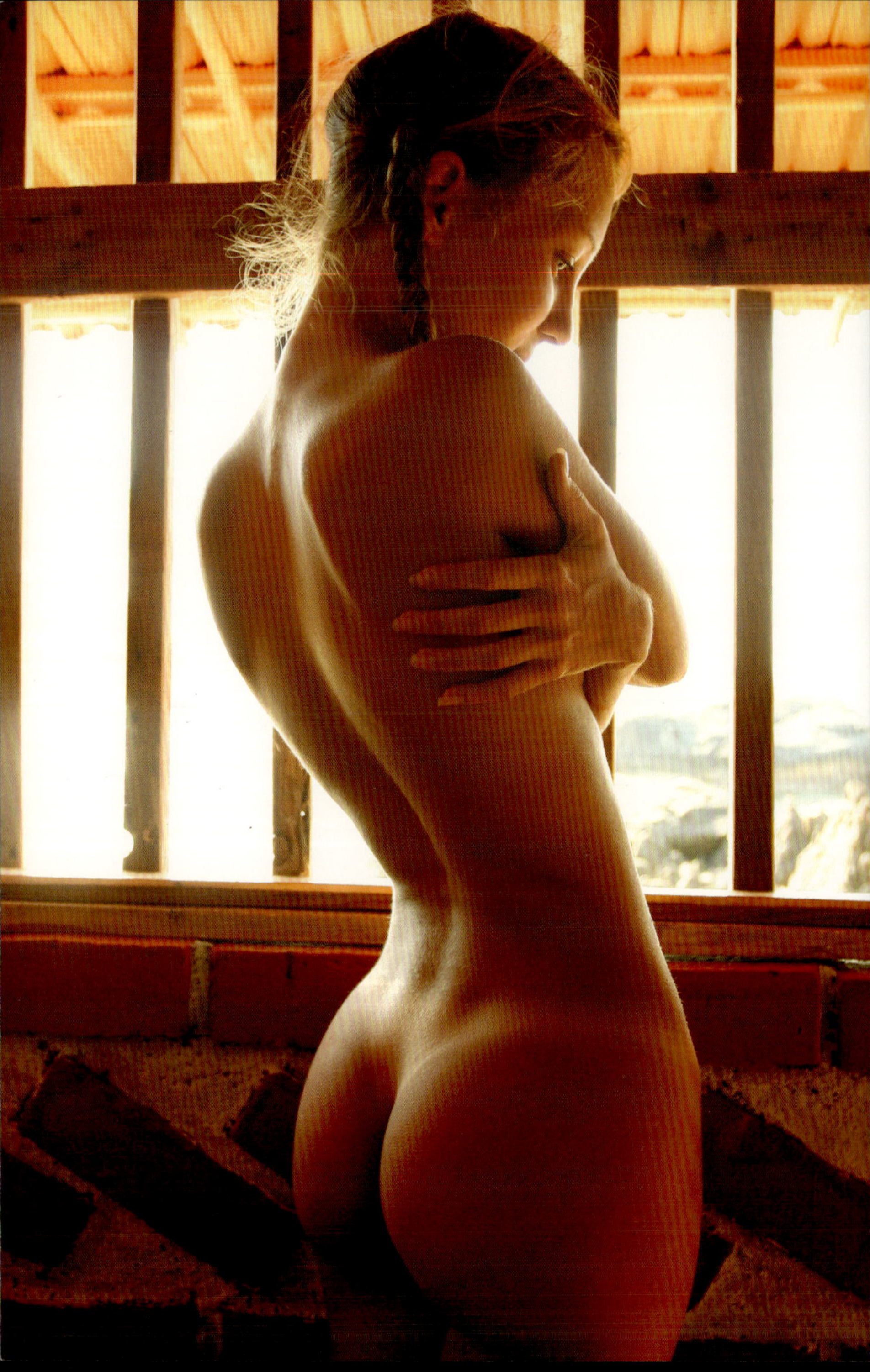

mikhail paramonov

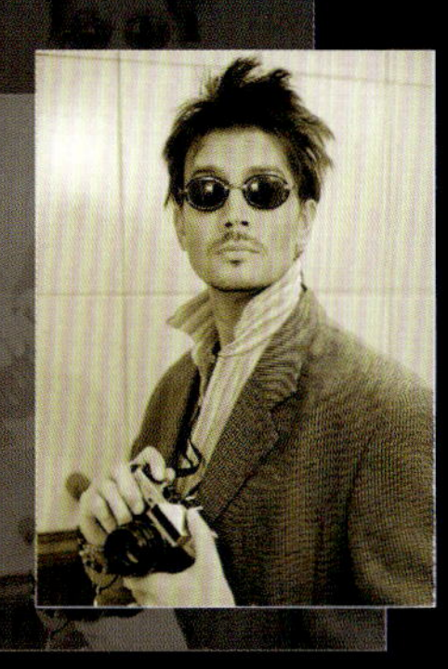

A RECOGNIZED MASTER of the erotic style, Mikhail Paramonov is a Russian photographer who was born in 1975 in St Petersburg. He first held a camera in his hands at the age of fourteen and has not let it go since. He studied at the faculty of arts of the St Petersburg State Theatre Arts Academy, and has concentrated on erotic work since 2002.

www.mikhailparamonov.com

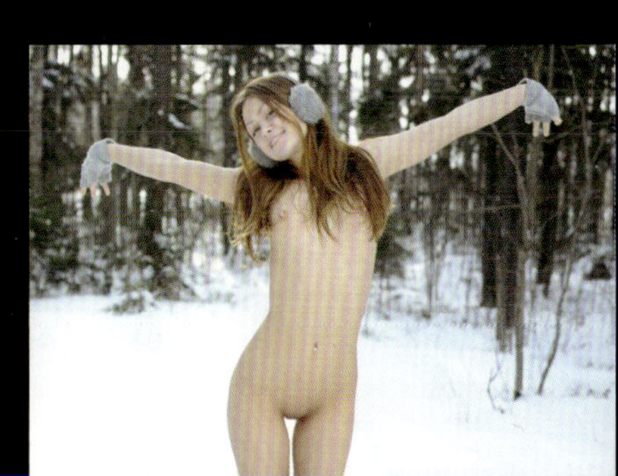

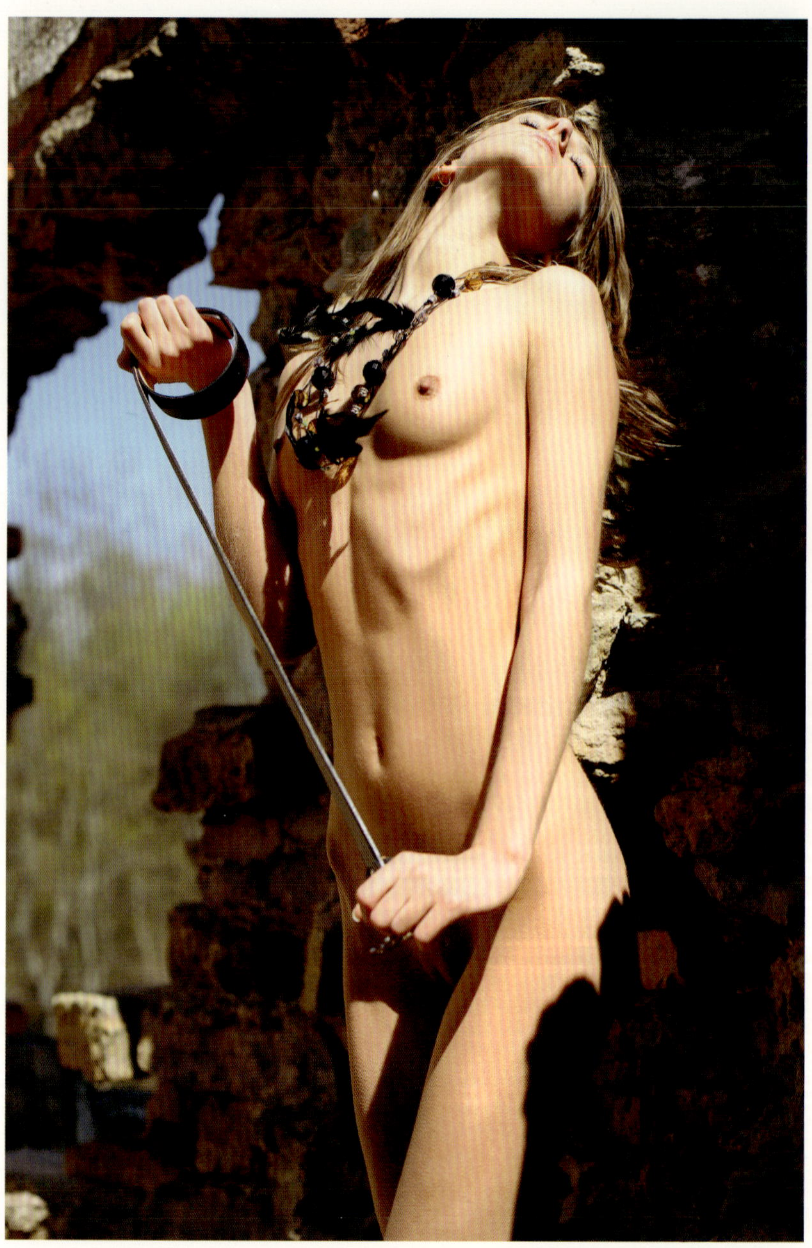

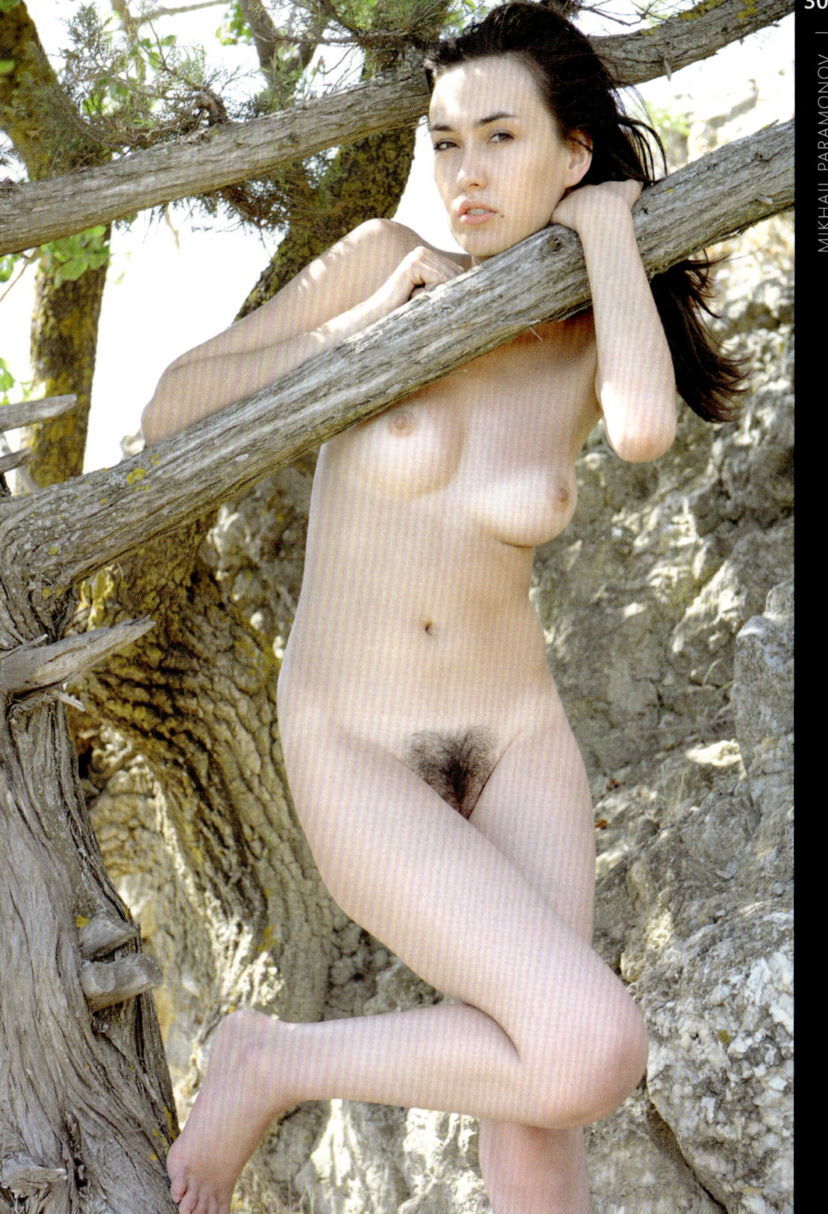

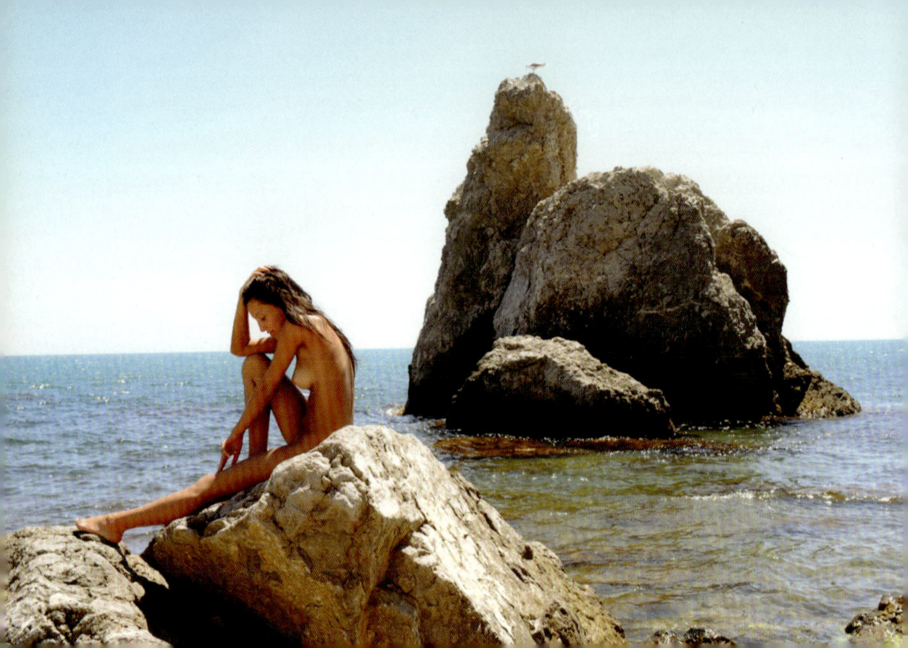

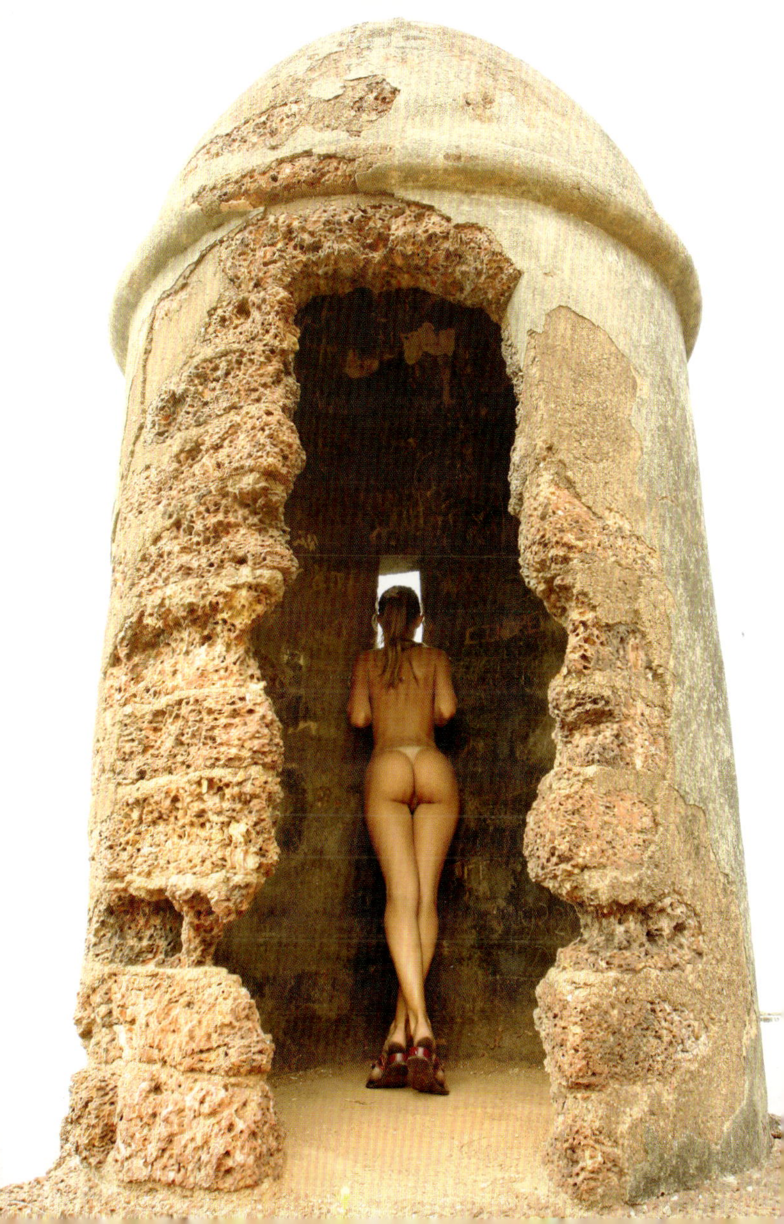

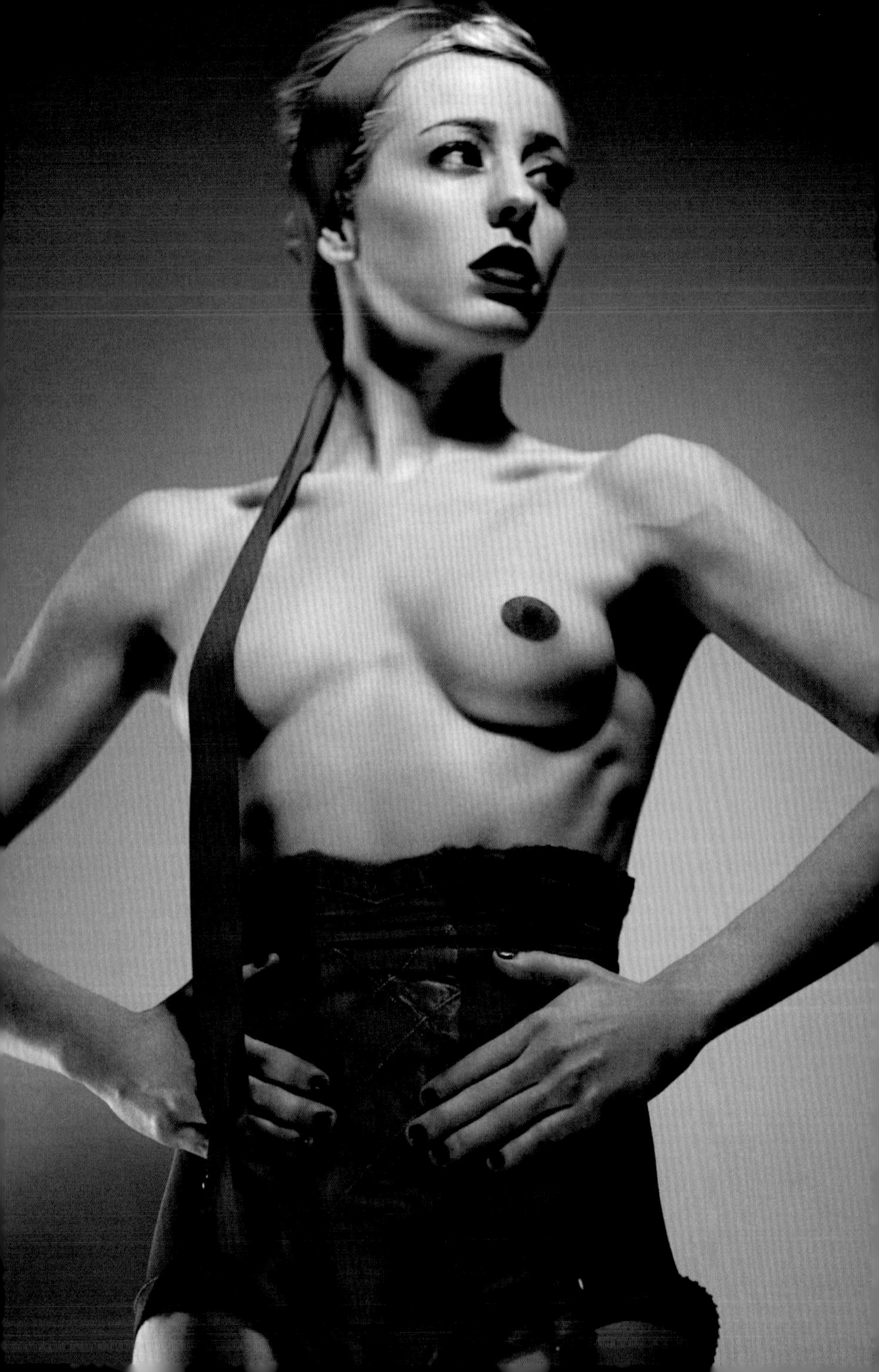

wolfgang parker

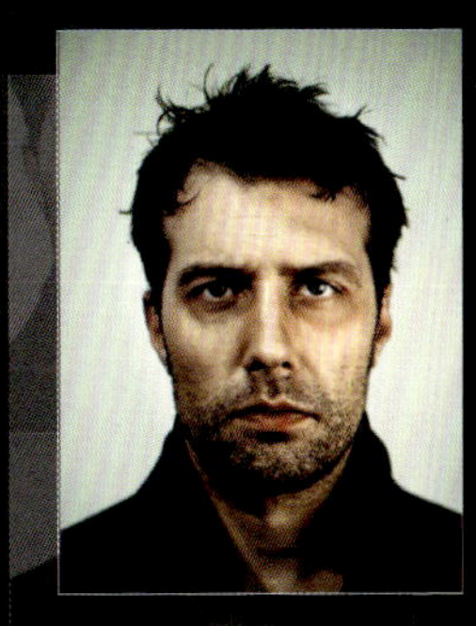

WOLFGANG PARKER IS AN American fashion and commercial photographer based in Columbus, Ohio. He is also a musician. His erotic work has been featured on Stern.de, filthygorgeousthings.com, and in *Secret Magazine*.

www.modelmayhem.com/wolfgangparker

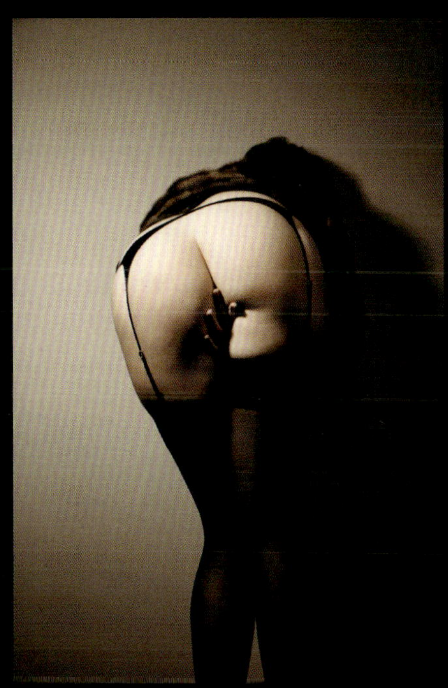

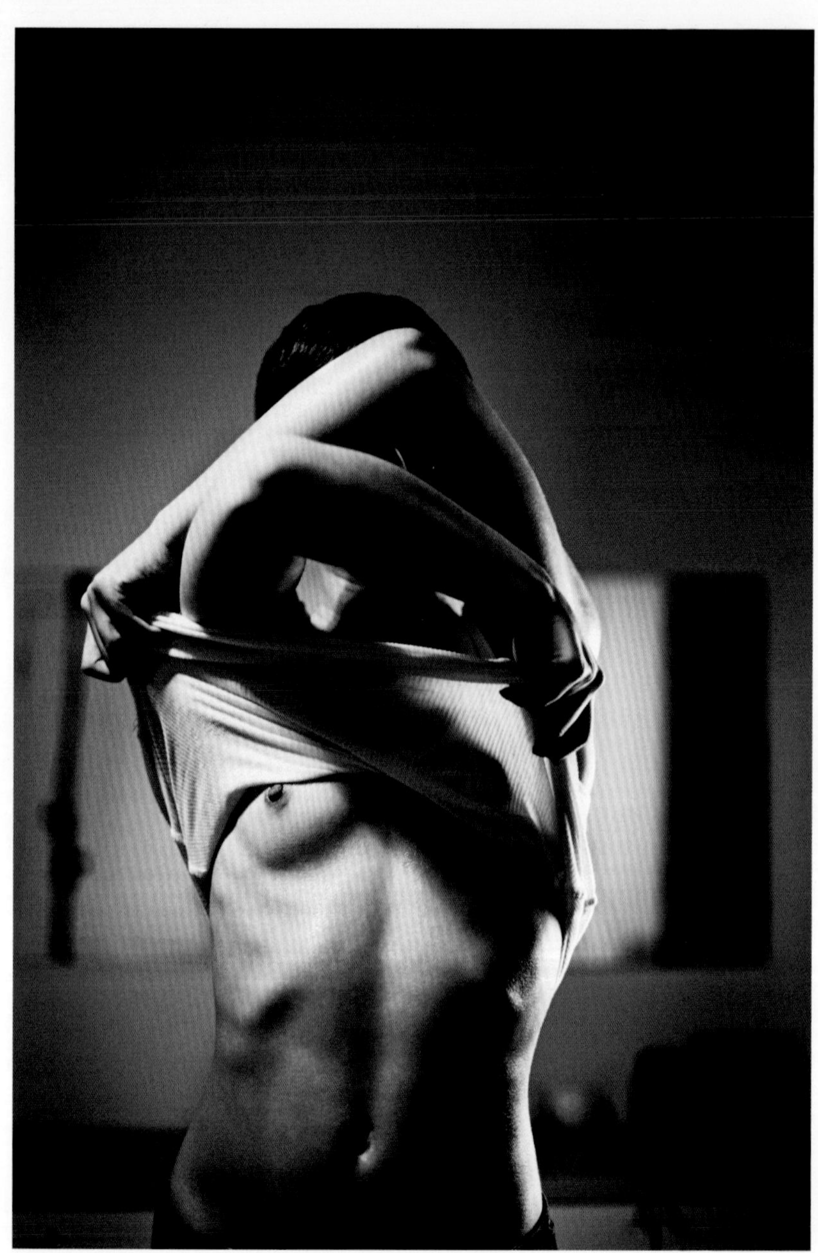

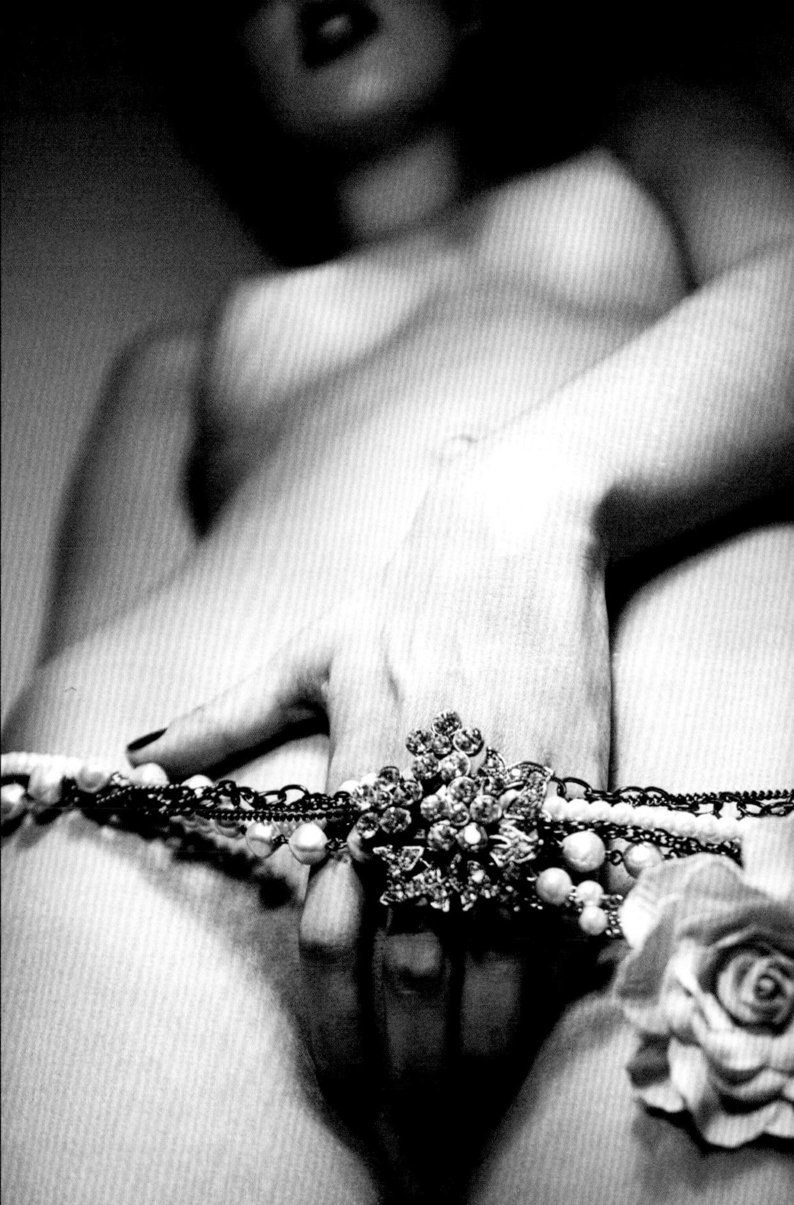

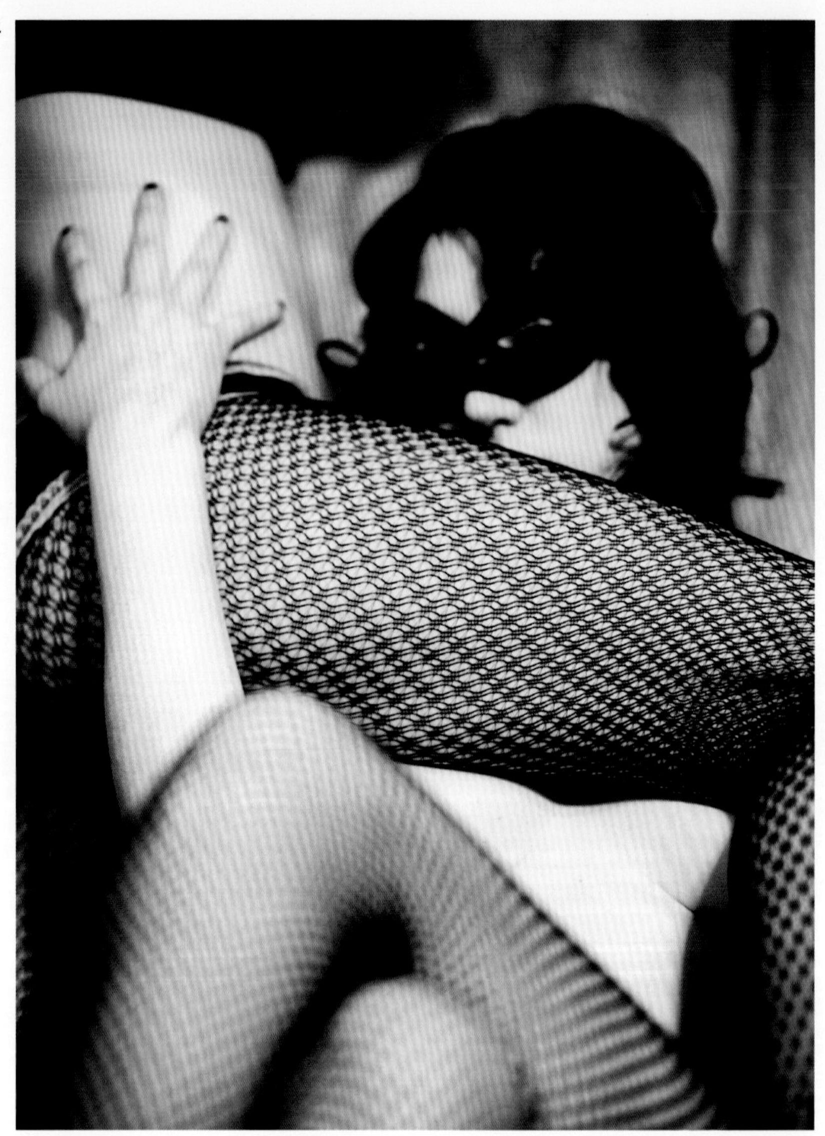

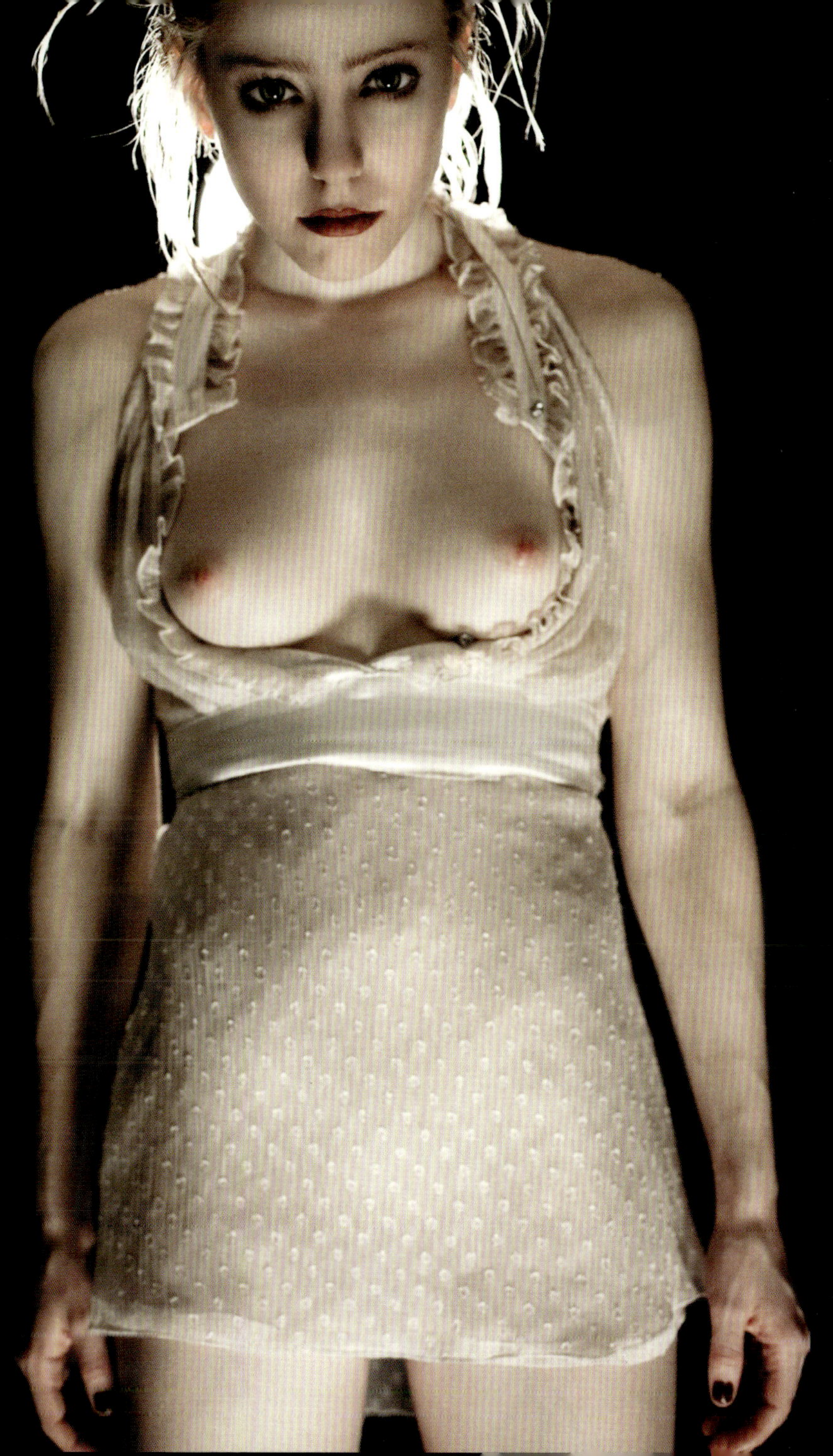

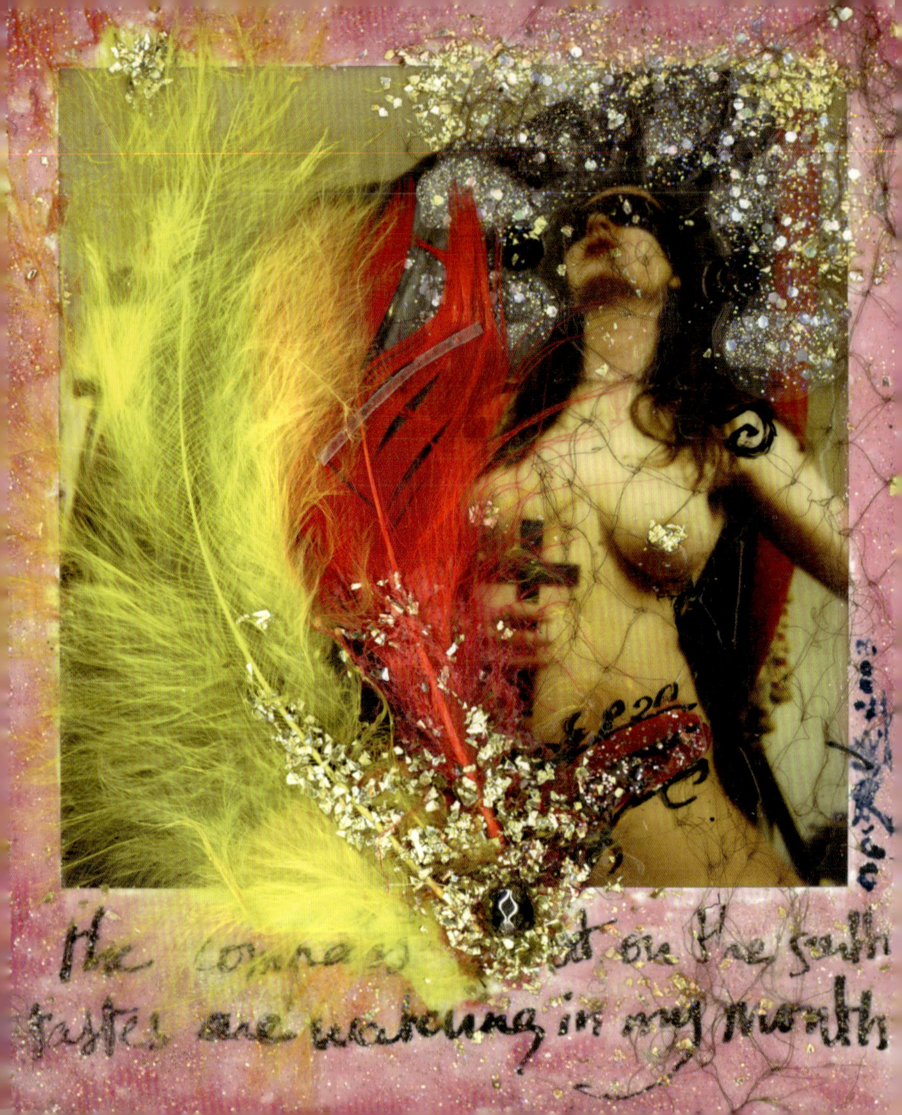
the compass
at on the south
tastes are waking in my mouth

anne pigalle

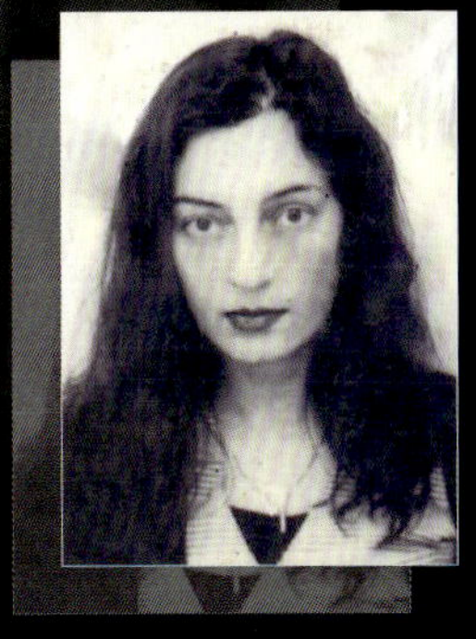

ANNE WAS BORN IN PARIS and lives in London. She is a singer, songwriter, painter and photographer and is currently working on an autobiographical film. Her performing and art have taken her across Europe, America, Mexico, Japan and Africa. Her Polaroids are part of her Amerotica body of work and often go hand in hand with poetry performances. She has been influenced by punk and surrealism and she is constantly redefining her own idea of eroticism.

www.annepigalle.com

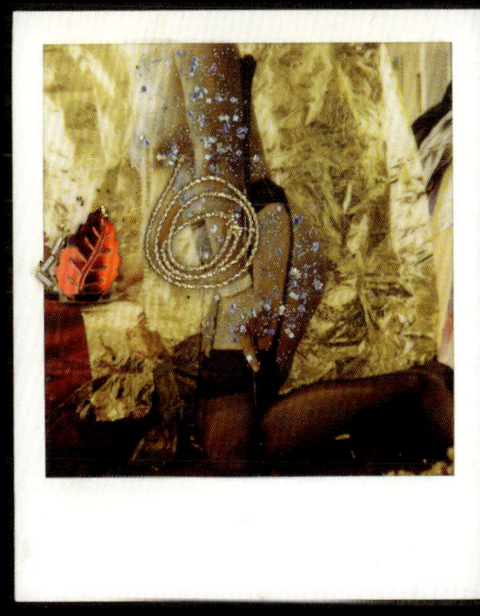

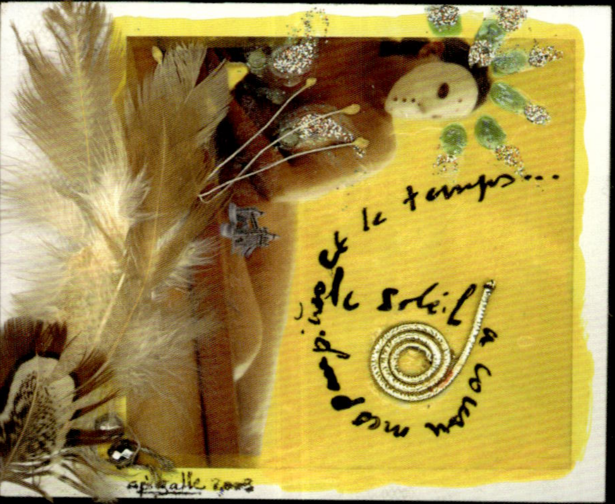

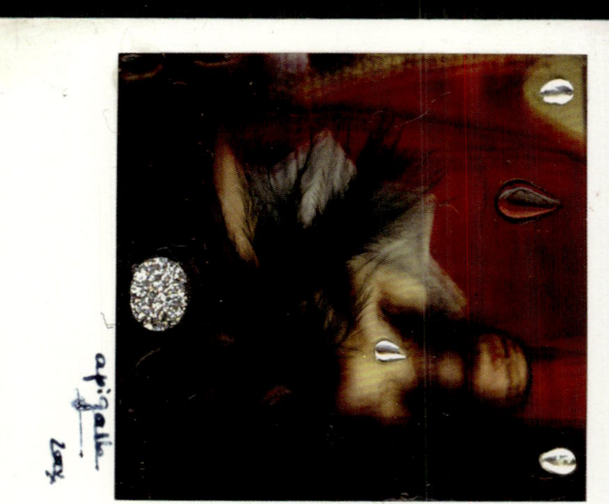
apigalle

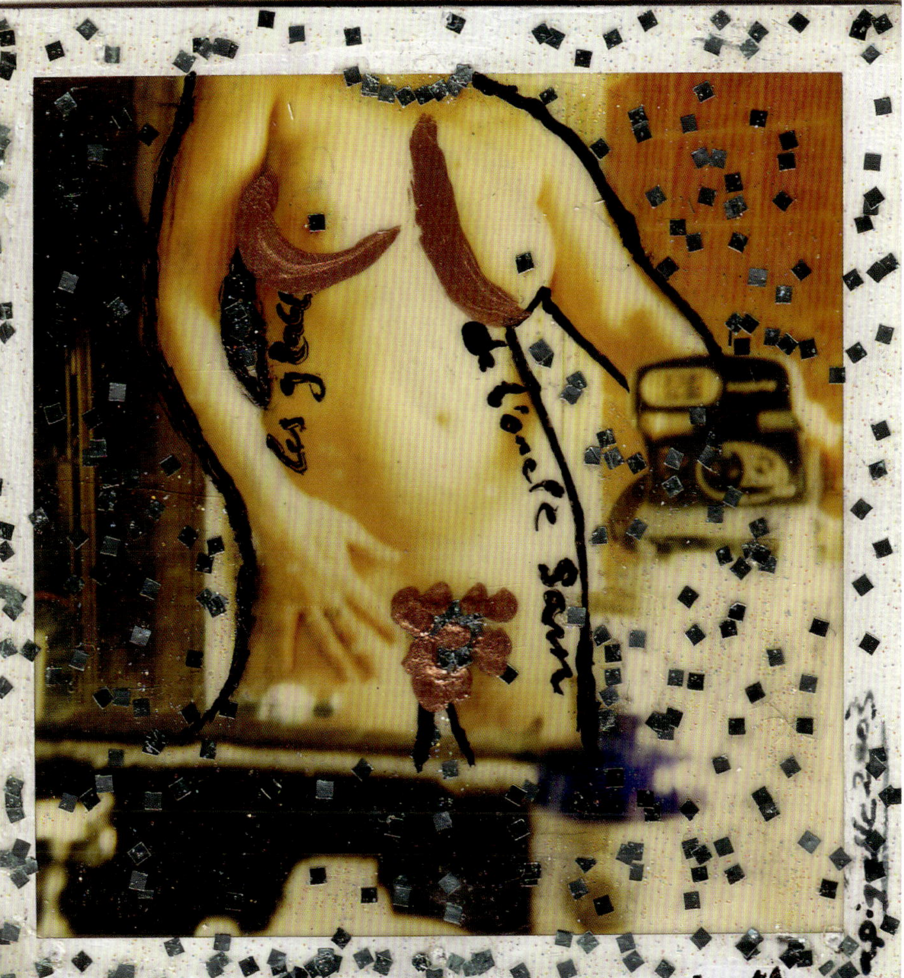
Un soleil de music hall

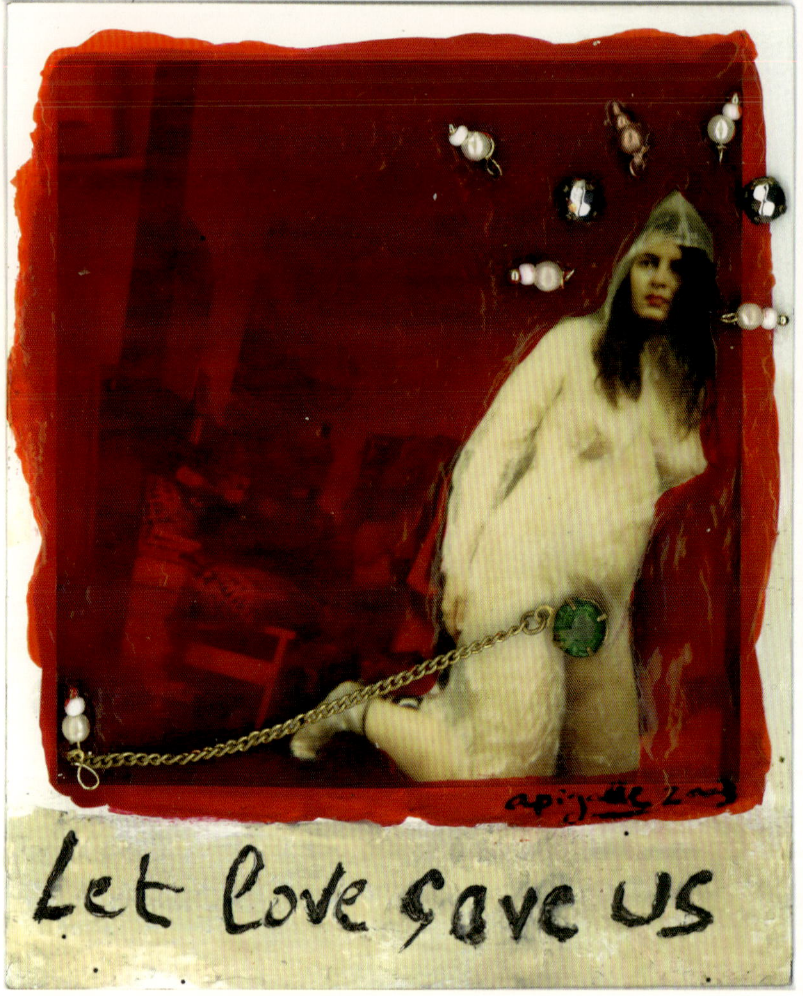
Let love save us

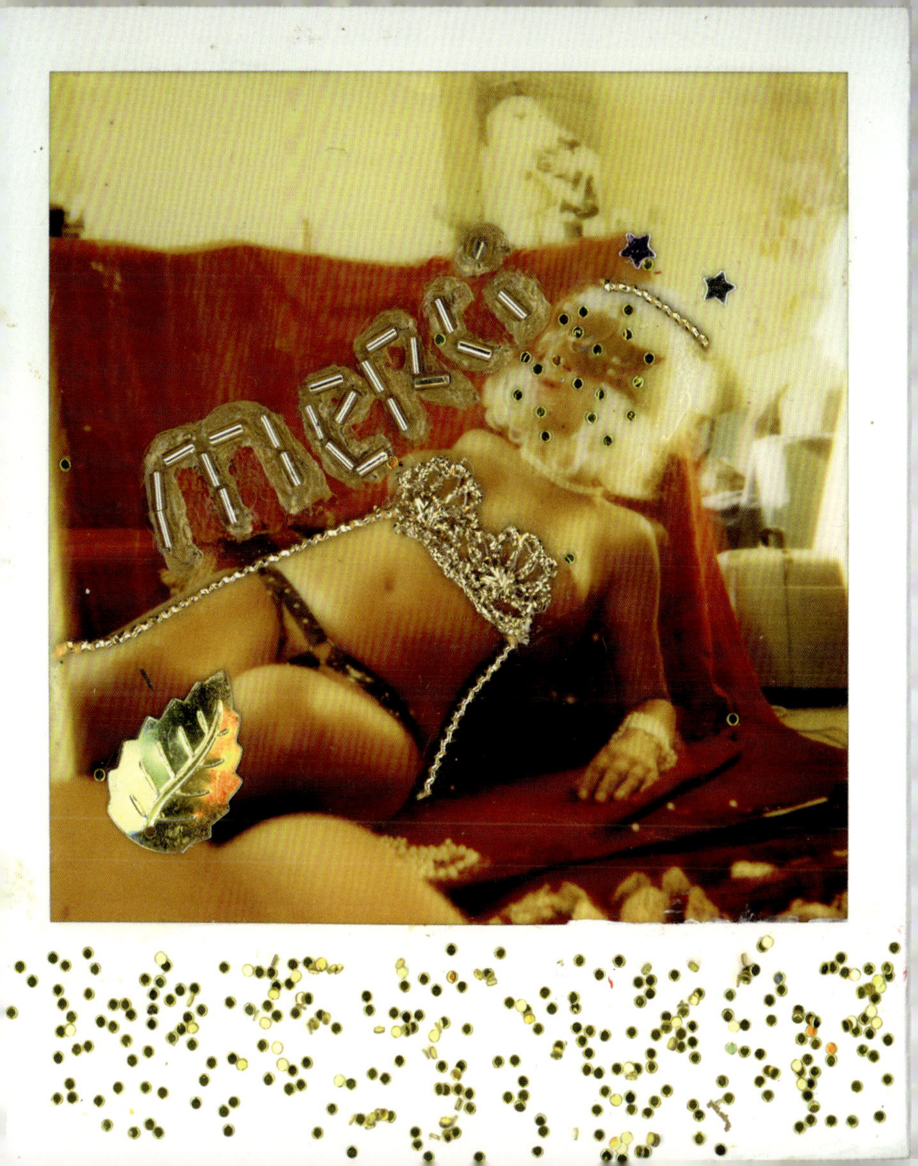

merci

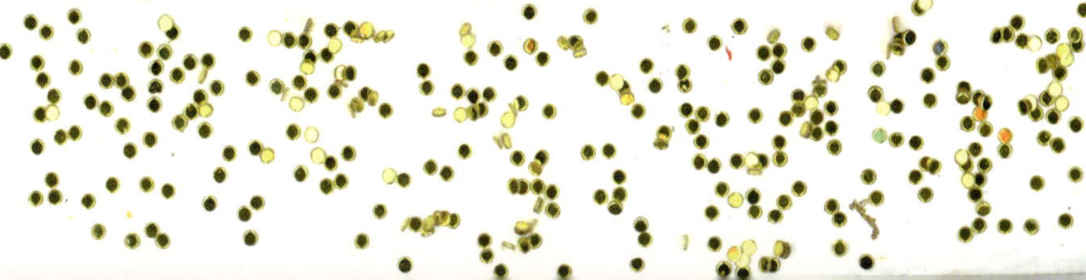

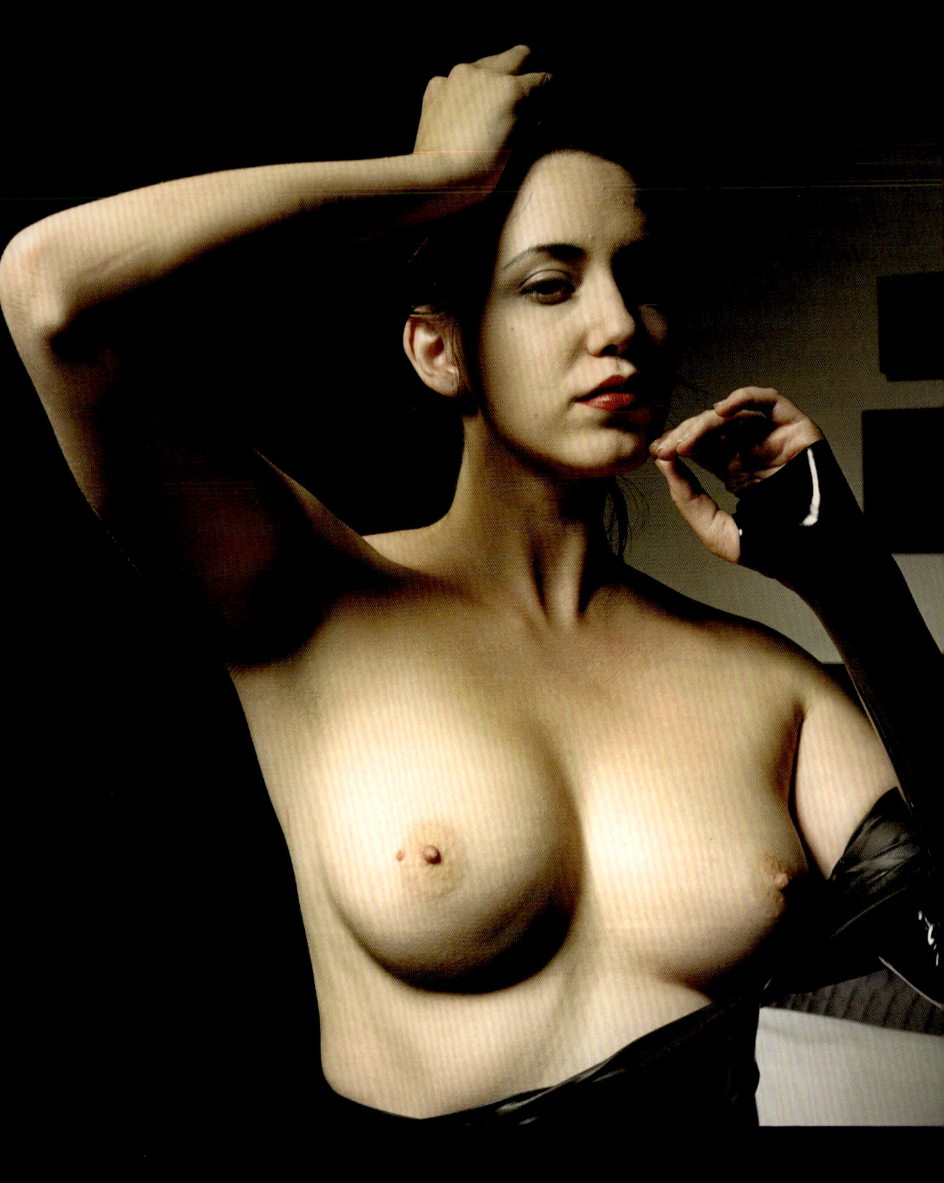

george pitts

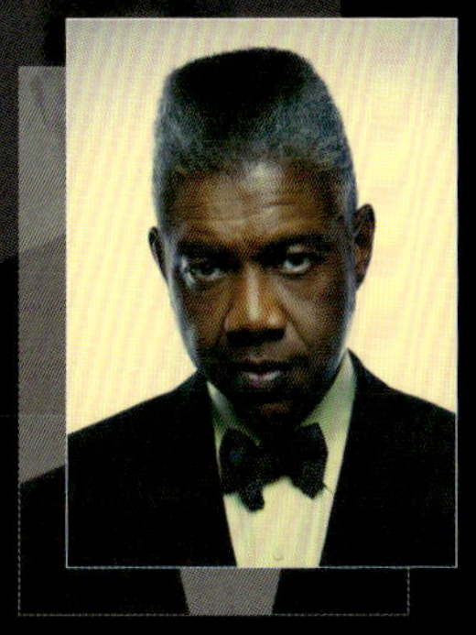

GEORGE IS A WIDELY PUBLISHED and exhibited US photographer. His work is an extensive meditation on women. Women as authentic autonomous figures, and as elusive, richly layered simulacra, are given dual significance, with the hope of capturing the daunting contradictions that bridge these cultural perceptions. He tries to capture the emotional complexity, the sheer physical presence, the innate or individual style, the degrees of sensuality or erotic candour, and the breadth of difference between women. Although rooted in portraiture, these photographs are not strictly portraits, because a fictive element inflects the work, and the images branch off into different tributaries of feeling. With women as the emotional navigators, intimate play is a constant in the photographs, enabling the photographer to look carefully yet quickly, making minute decisions that collect in the formal choice of images that memorialize the collaboration and gentle search for another world, where female identity is a hedonistic foxhole, a Pandora's Box, and an elaborately visual and physical conundrum, into which one freefalls through levels of bliss undercut with striations of melancholy. To photograph a woman is to reckon with the inevitability of shifting gears, seeing ideas through, or scrapping them at a moment's notice, buoyed by the gladness inherent in the promise of the sitting.

www.georgepitts.com

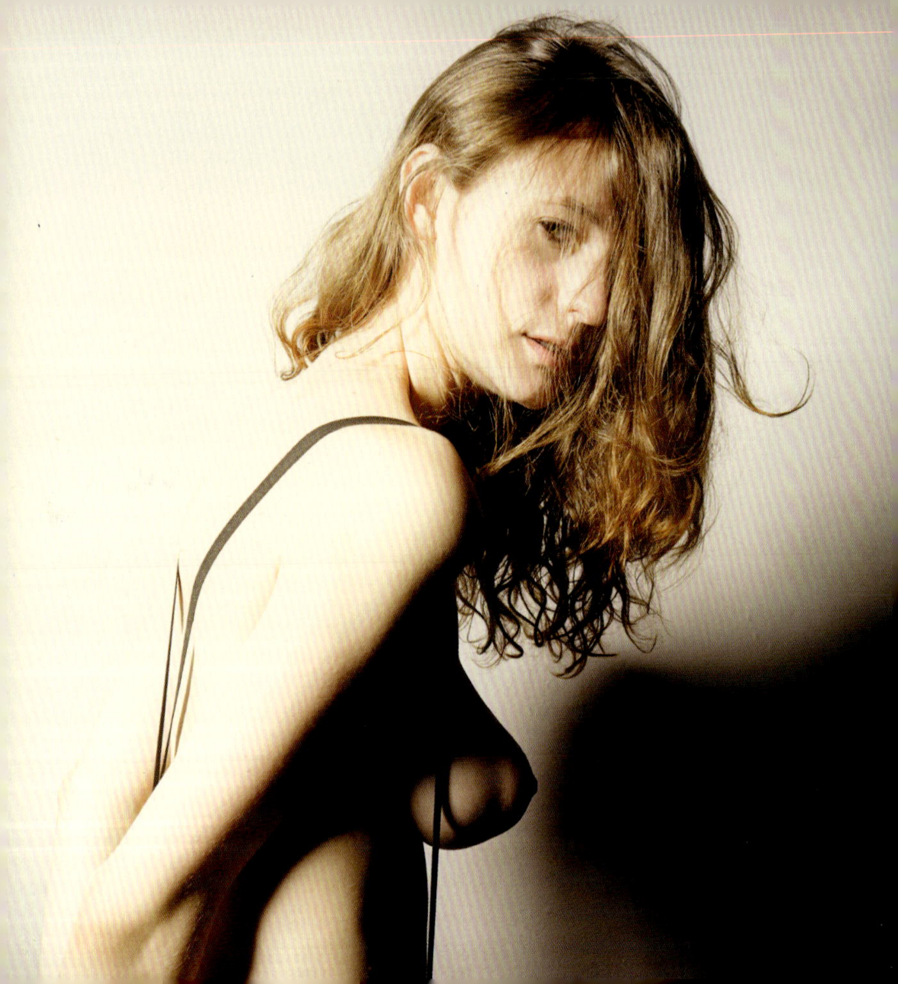

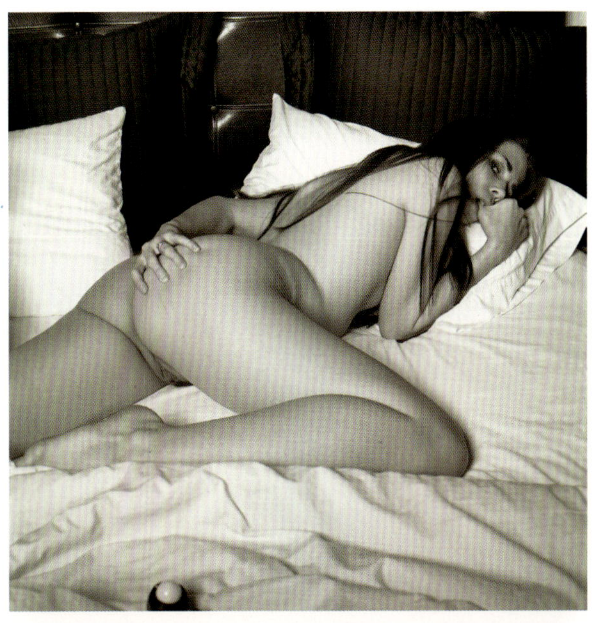

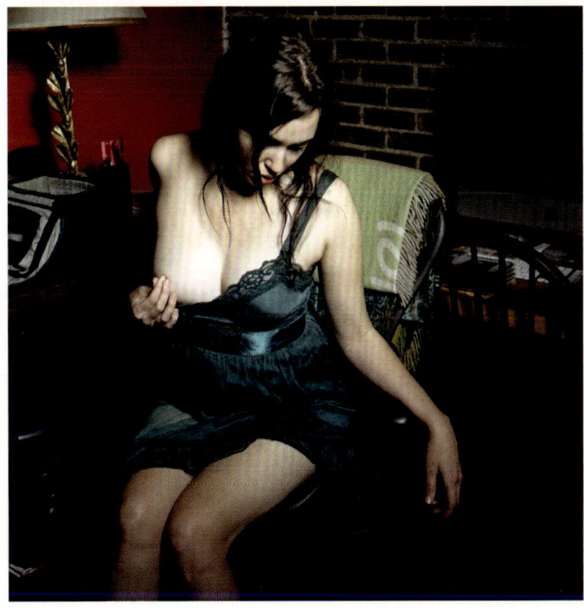

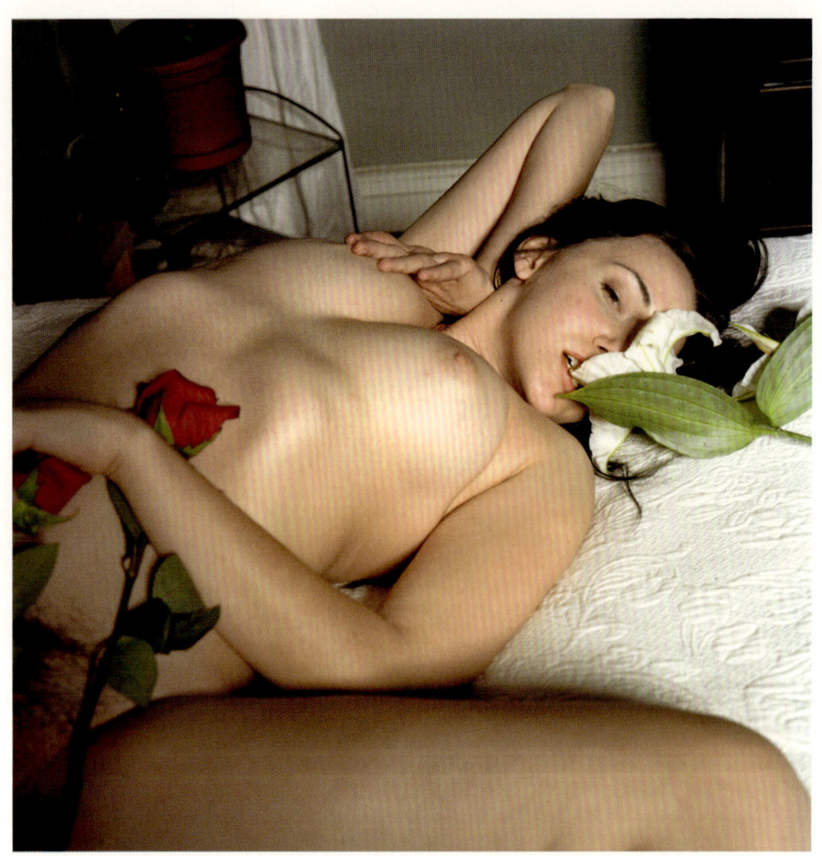

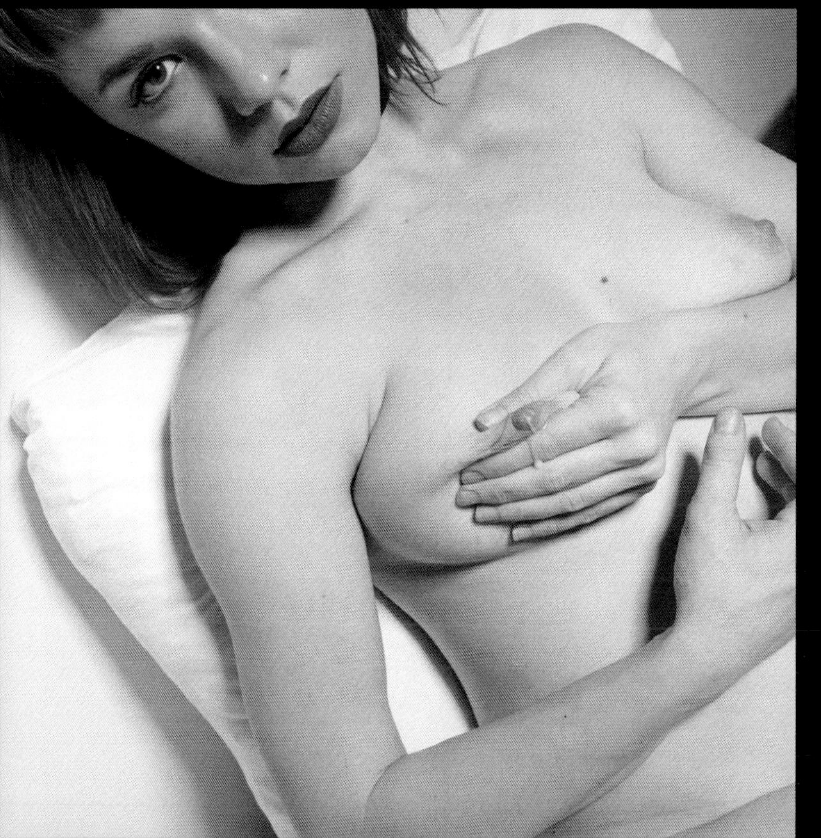

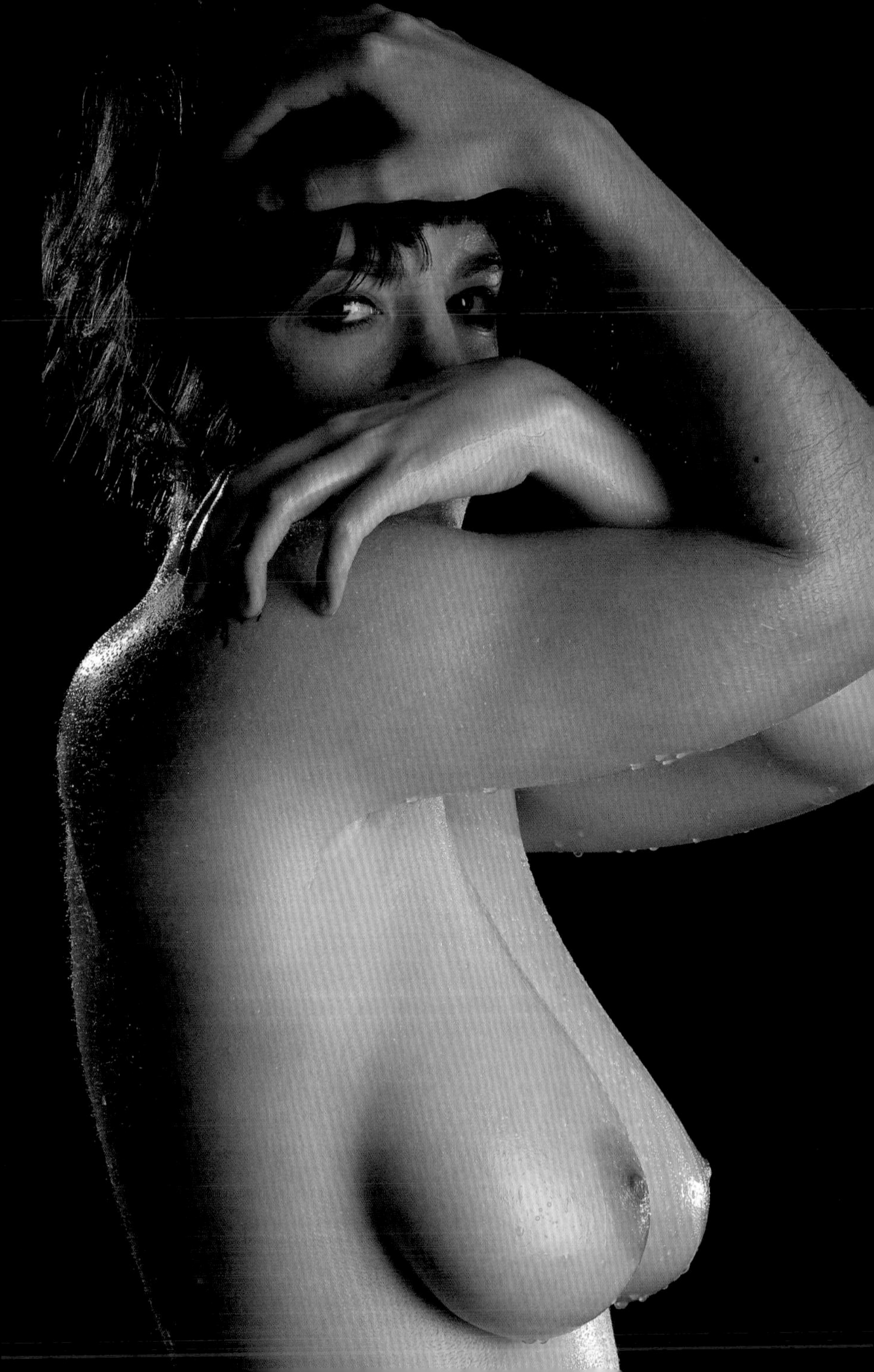

randem

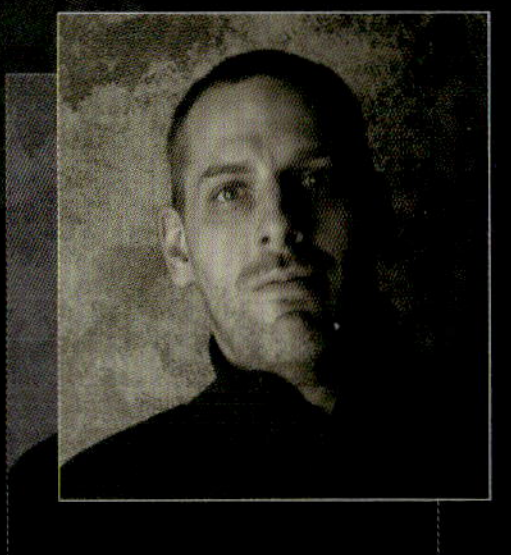

WITH HIS FRESH PERSPECTIVE and emotional imagery, Randem is quickly making a name in erotic photography. His photos are not creative expression; they are an exorcism of the distractions filling his mind. His first series, titled Just Bodies, explores the theme of anonymous vulnerability. Security disappears along with clothing, just as identity disappears when the face is covered. Like a car crash you can't look away from, what remains is a beautiful tragedy: awkward, perhaps even unpleasant, yet appealing in ways that are not always comfortable to admit.

www.randem.net

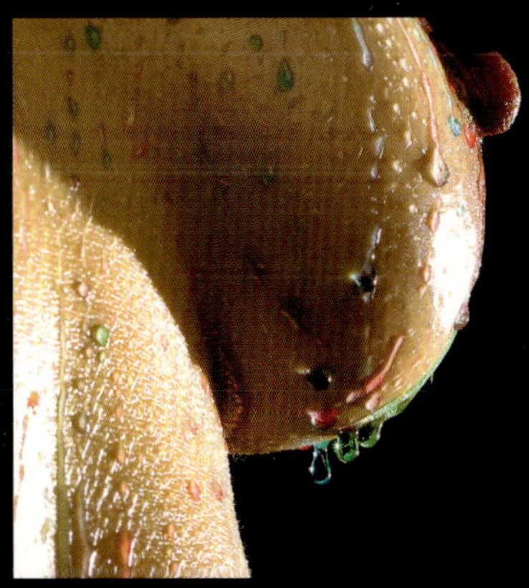

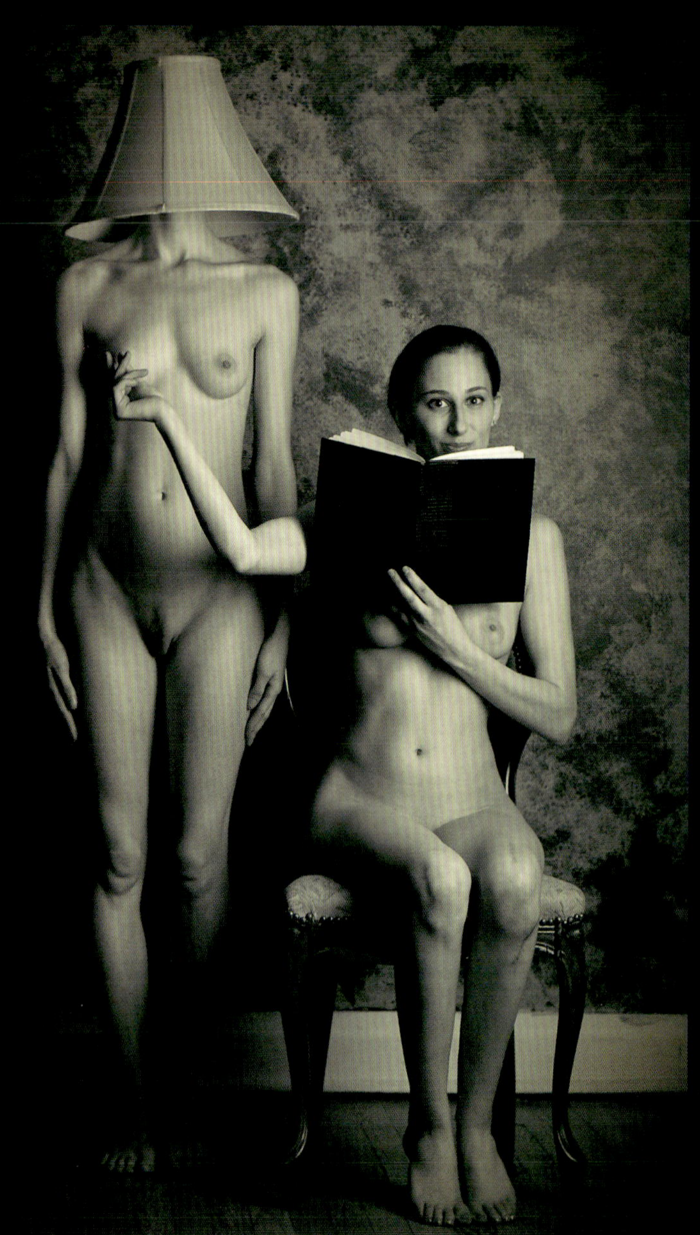

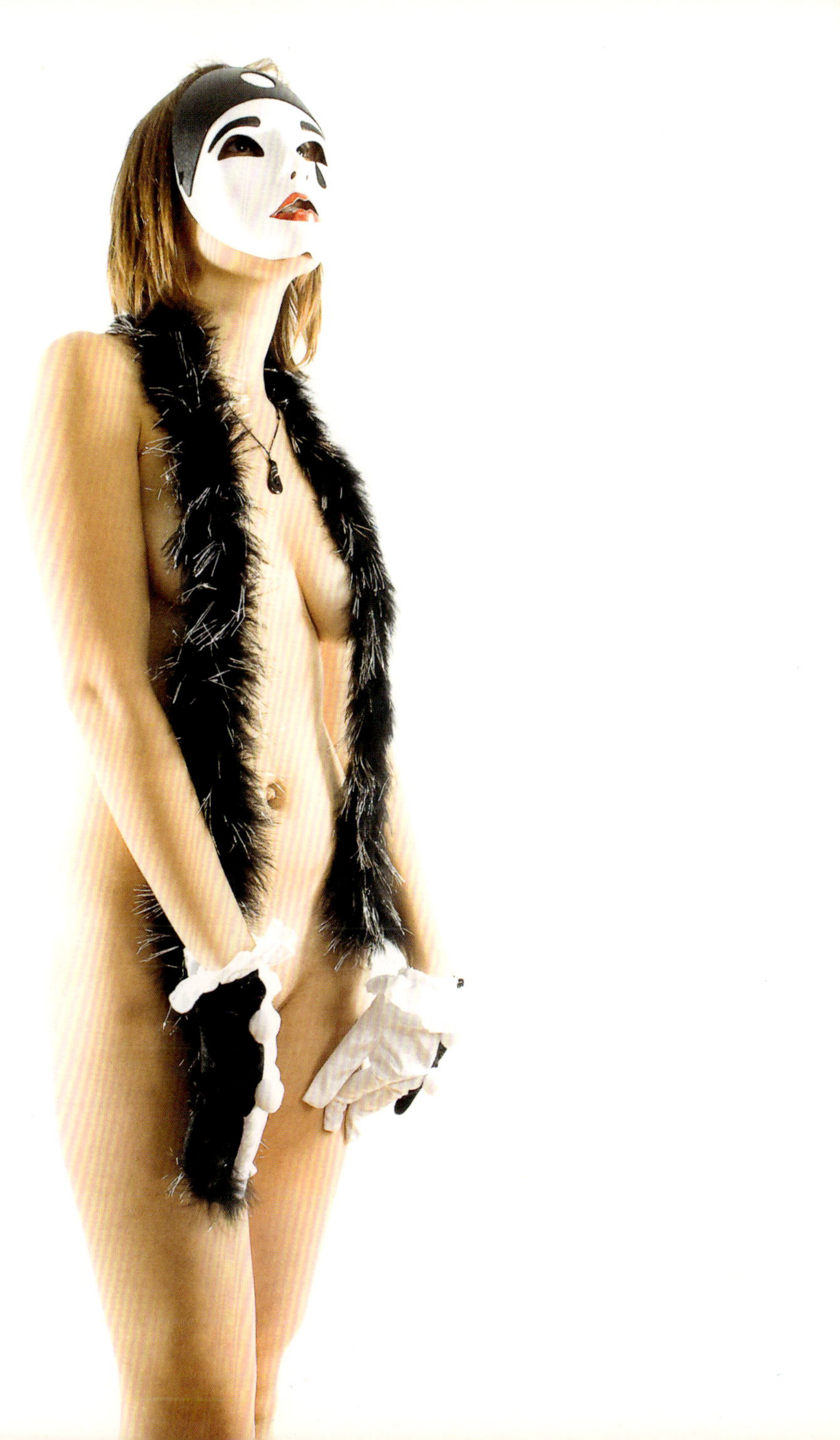

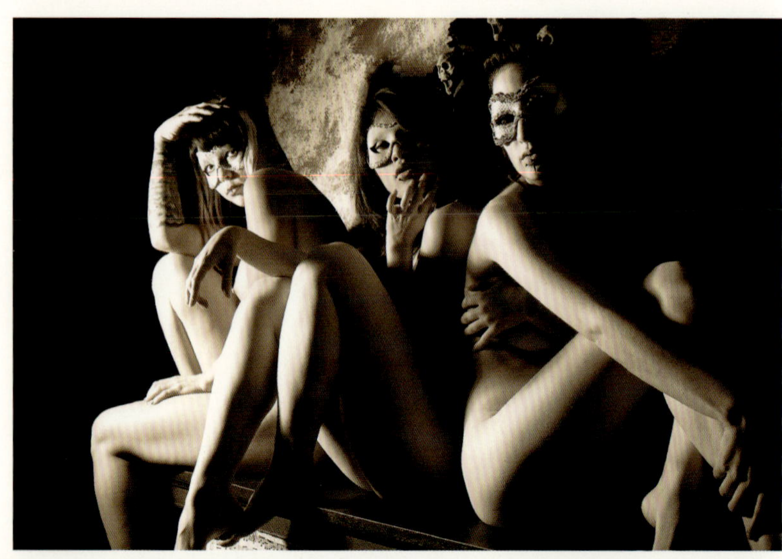

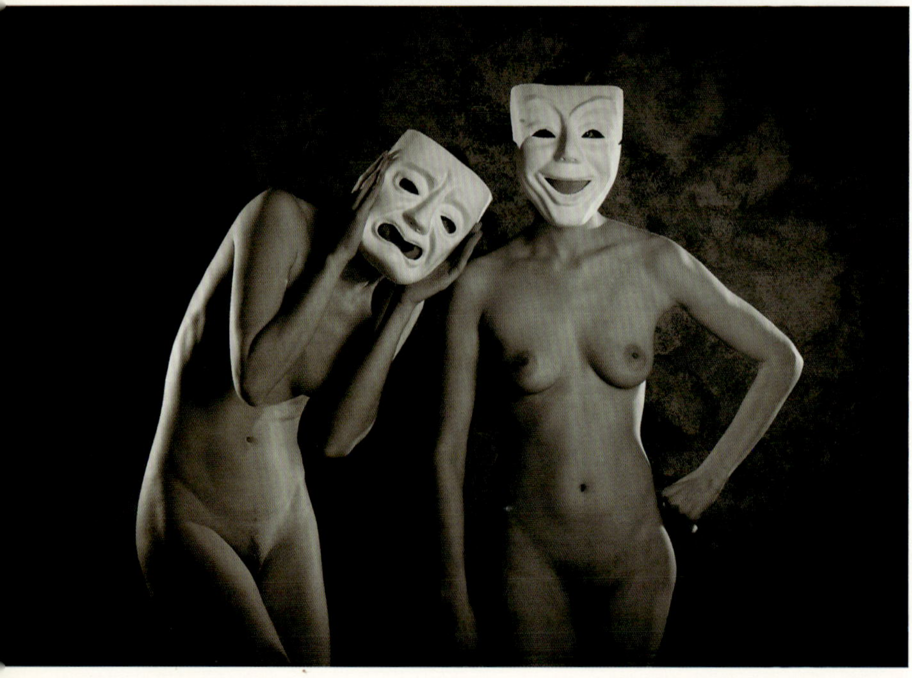

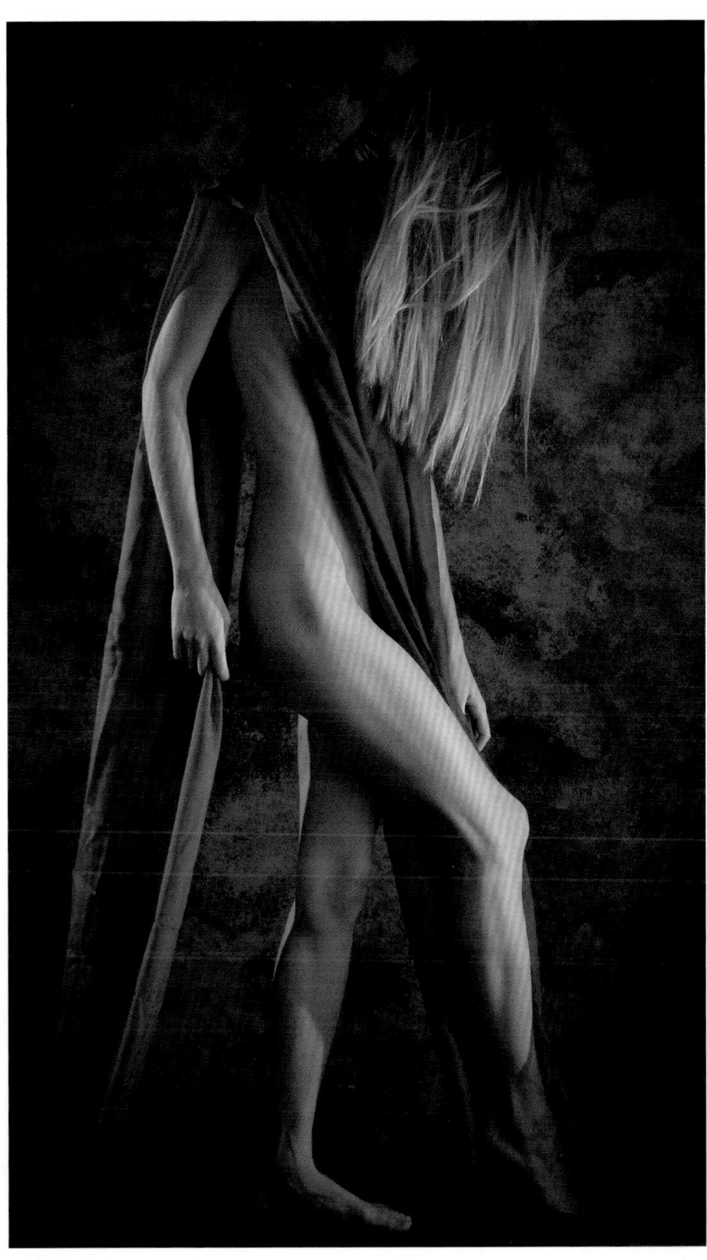

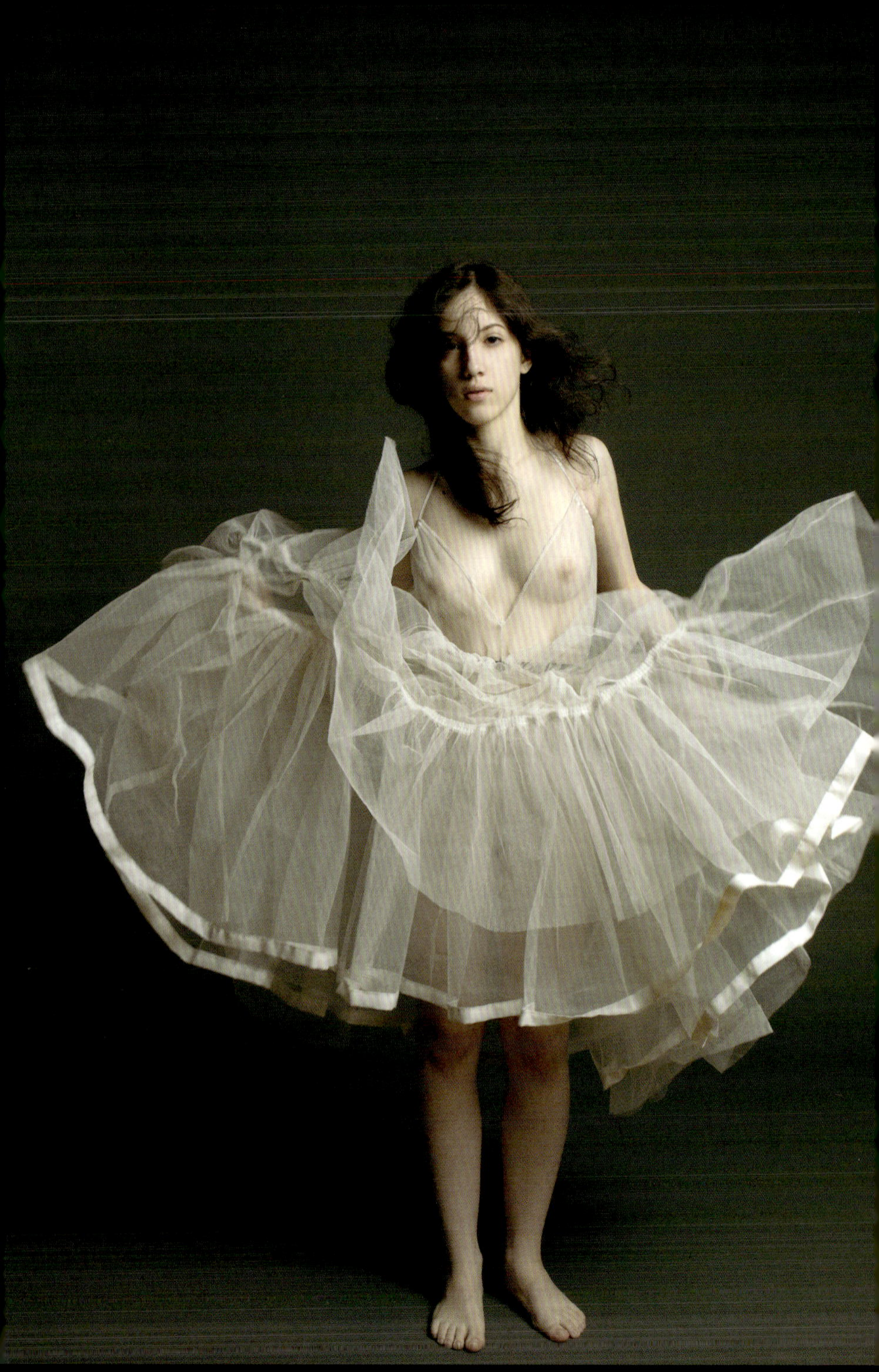

ned & aya rosen

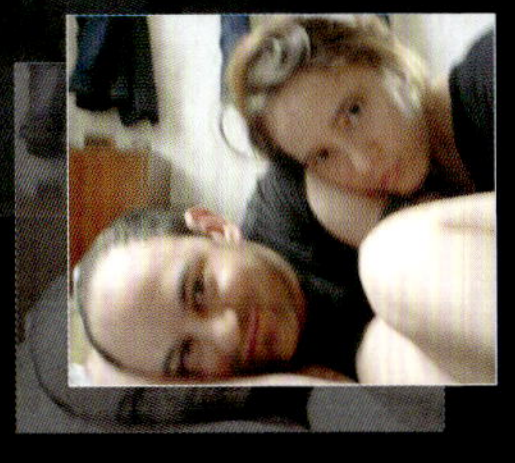

NED WAS LIVING IN BROOKLYN and Aya in Tel-Aviv. They spent a year in an online relationship complete with two web cams, and lots of masturbation. After that, and before going crazy, they decided that either he should go to her or she should come to him. To make a long story short(er), she came to the US, they got married, and they live, work, shoot and play side by side. They began making images for each other as a way to bridge their gap of the oceans, teasing, sharing and developing a visual language, a language that they've been working with and shooting from together.

www.nedandayaerotic.com
www.nedandaya.com

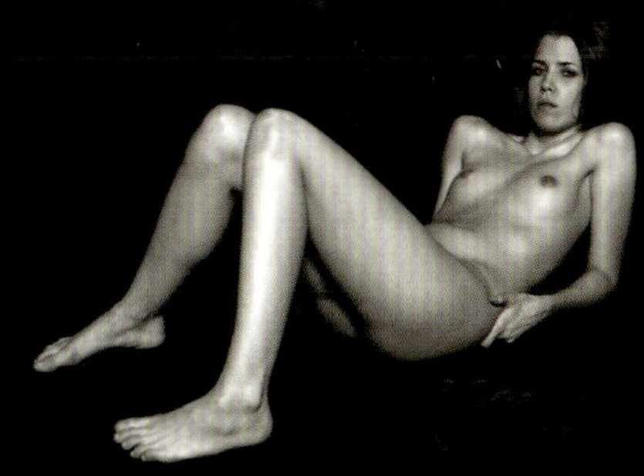

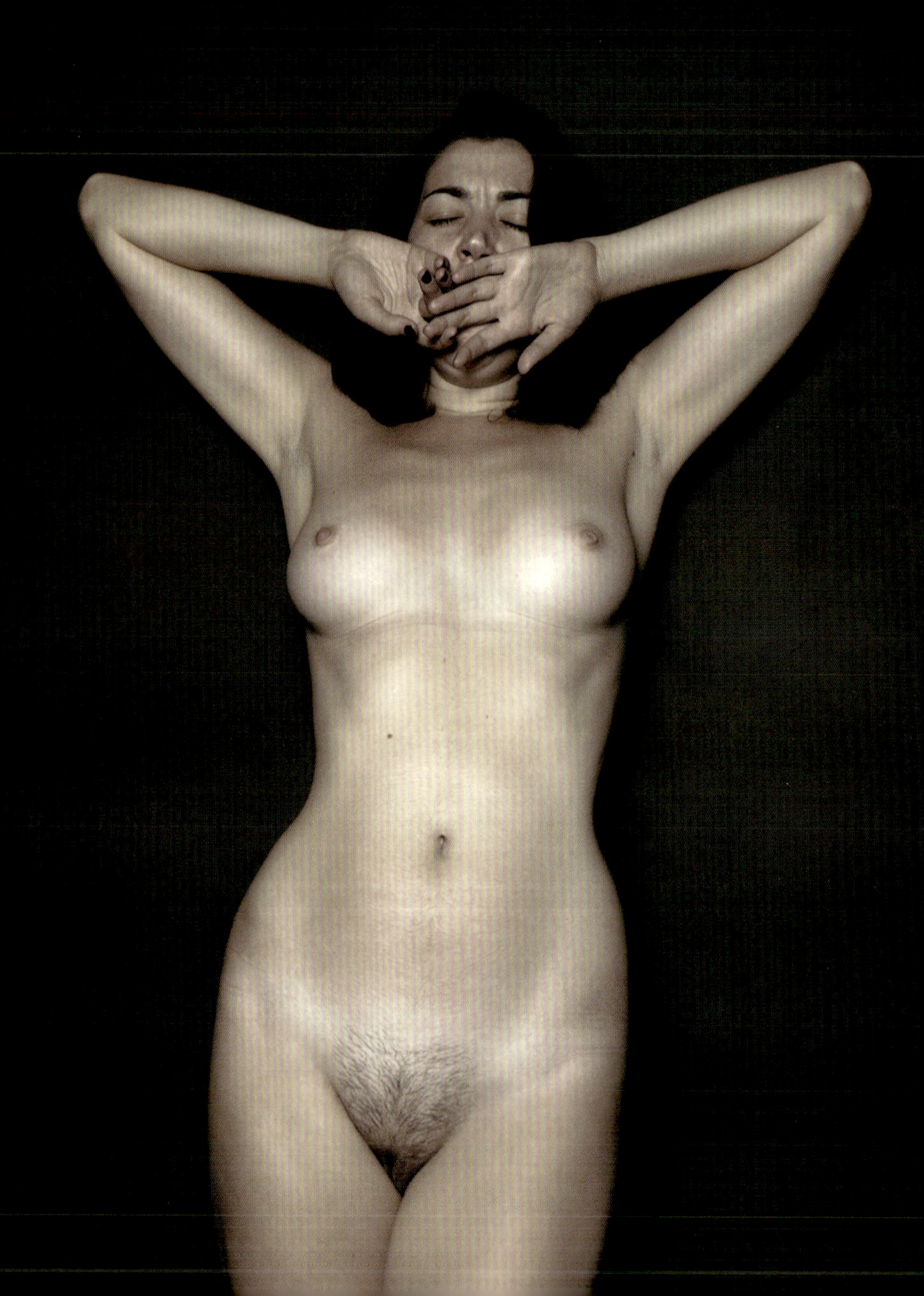

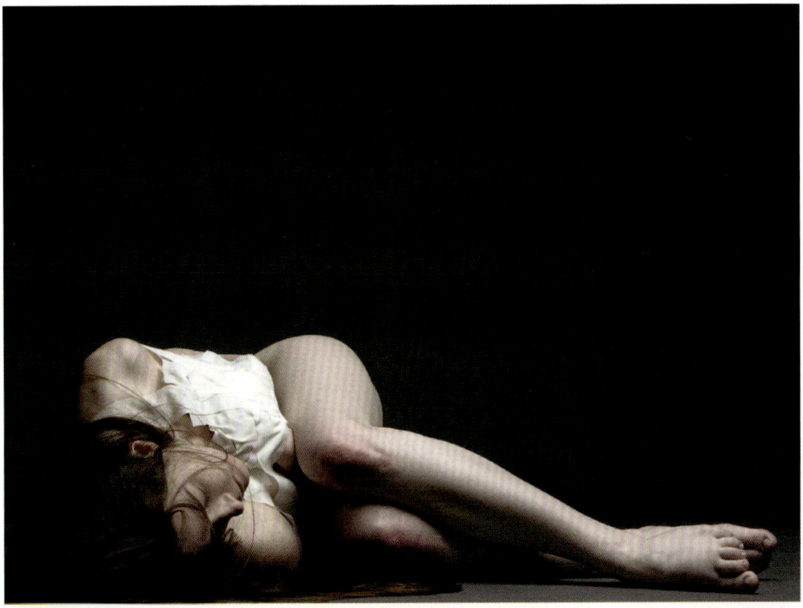

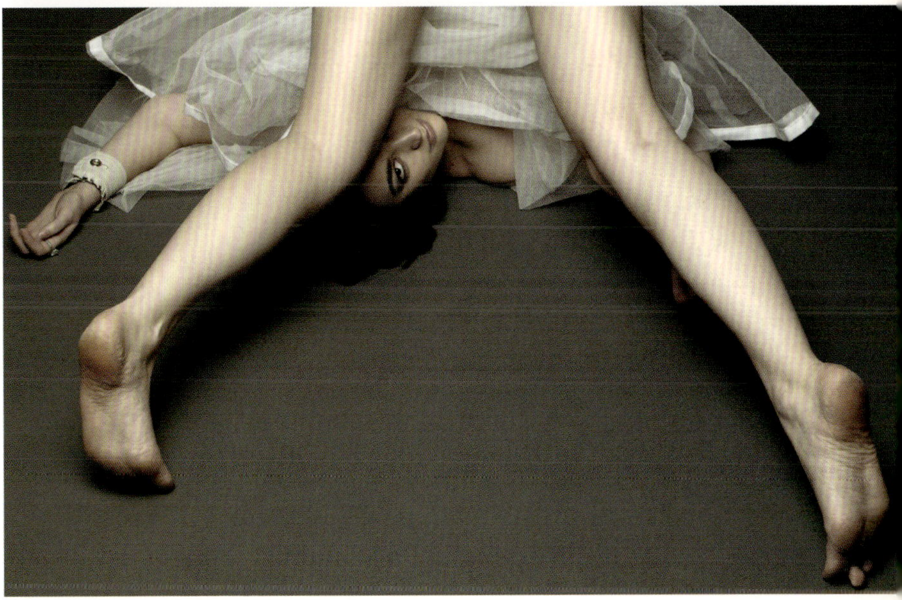

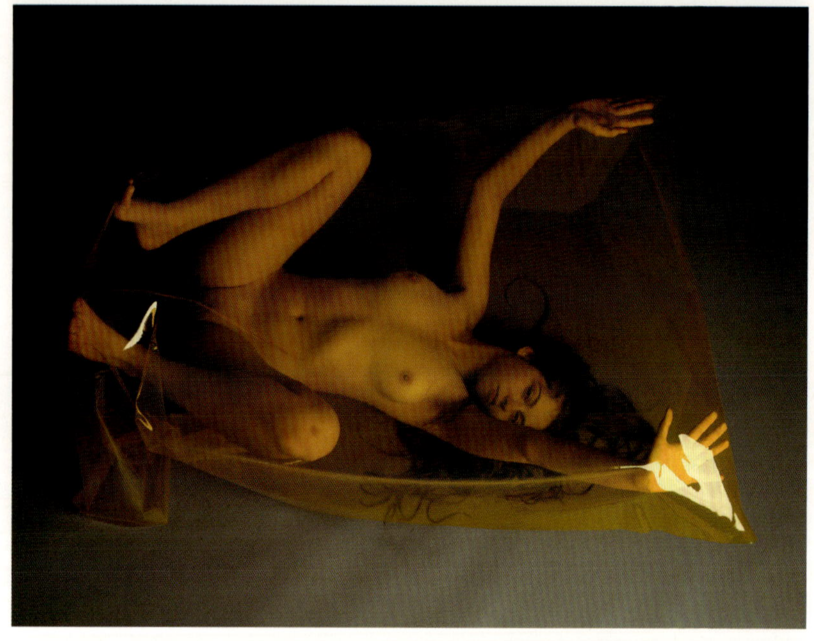

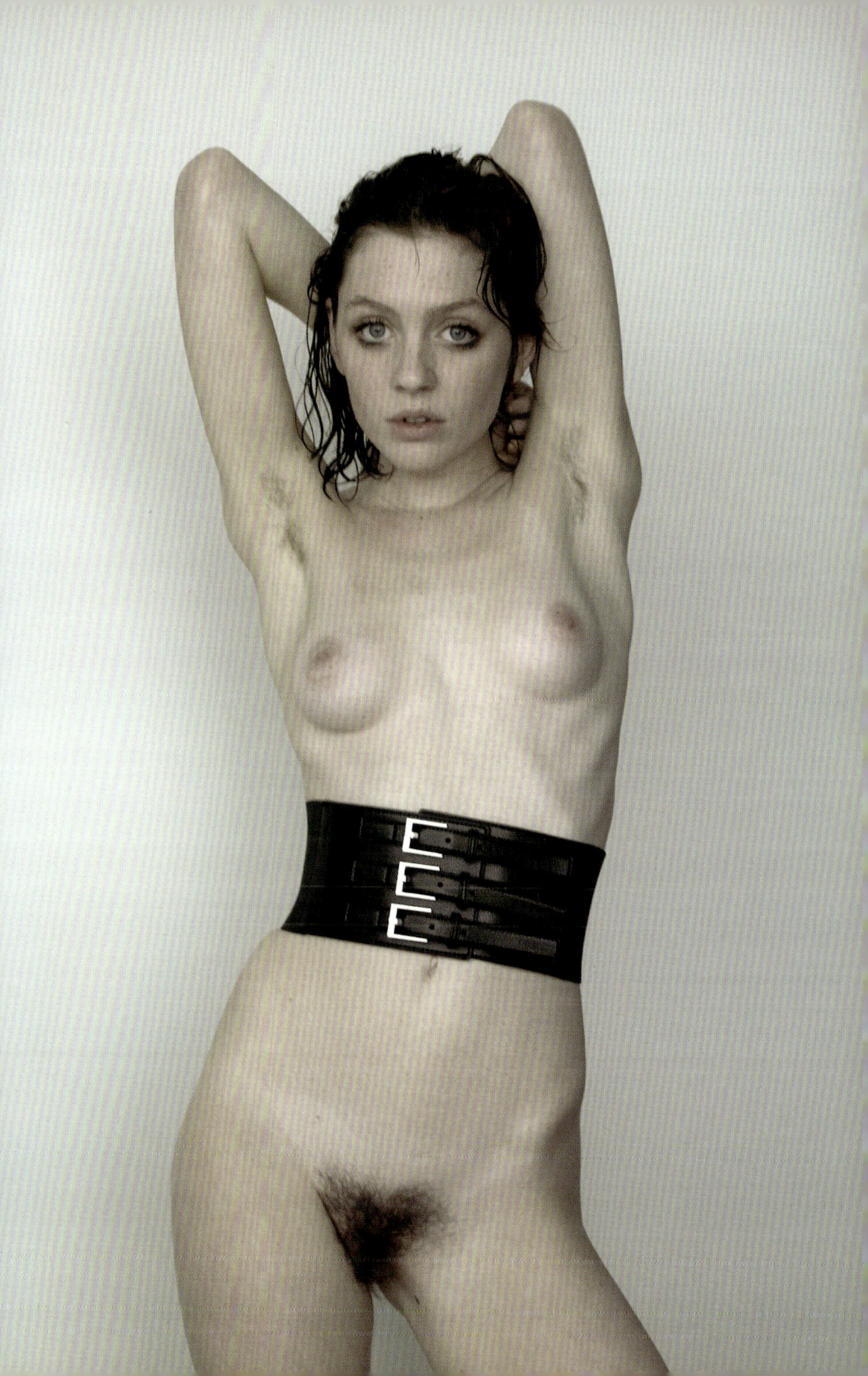

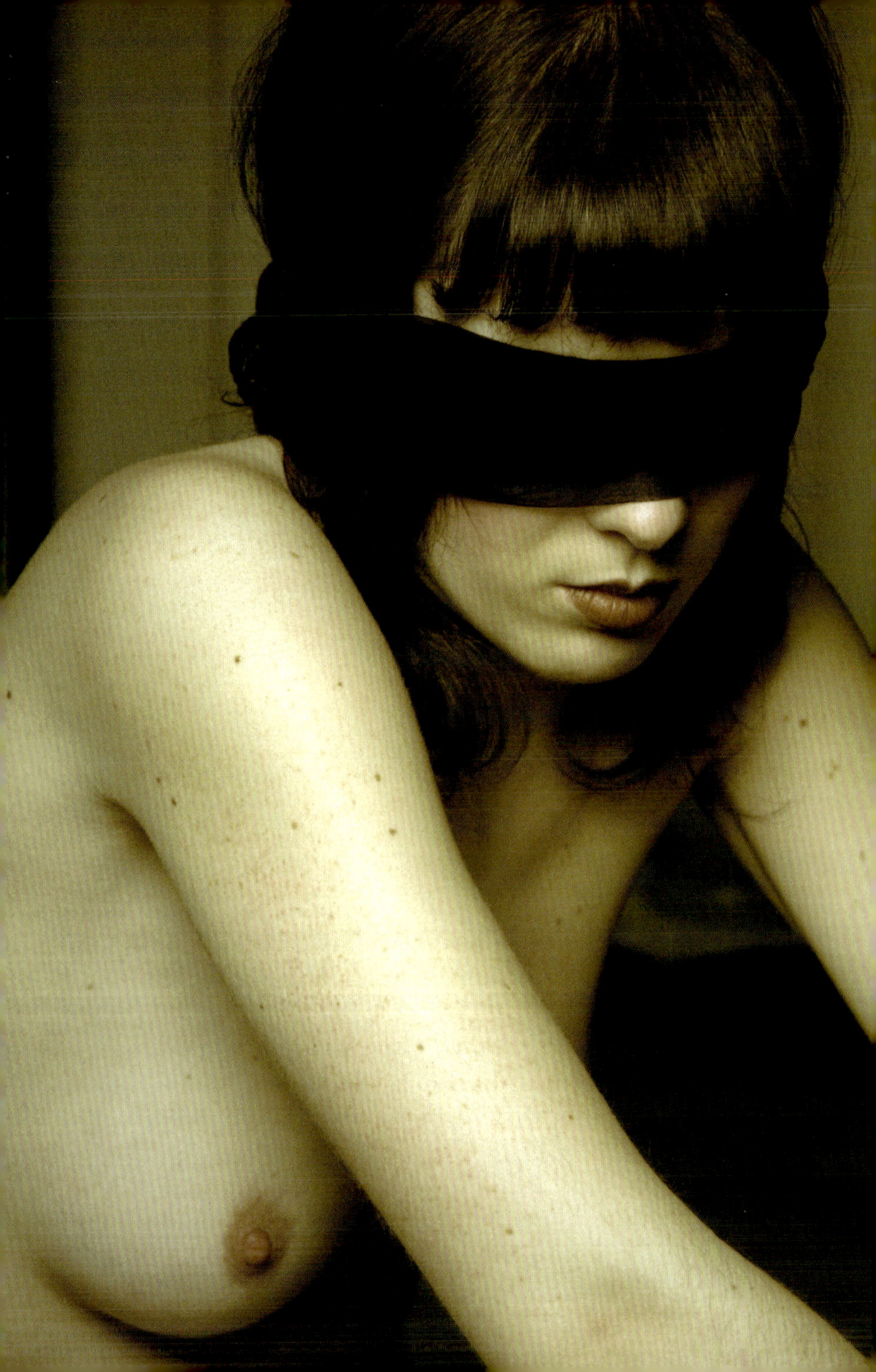

kati rudlova

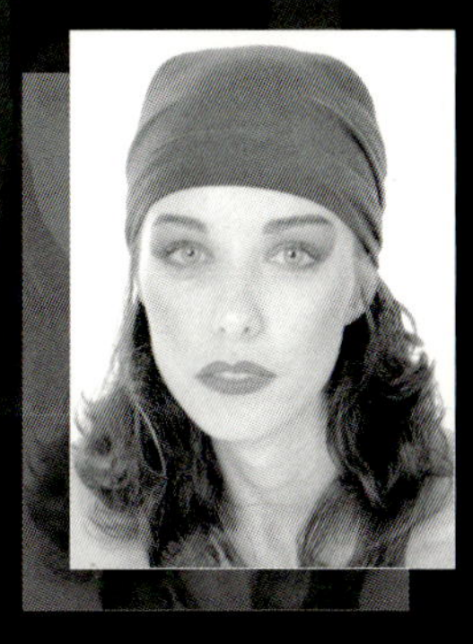

KATI WAS BORN IN 1974 in Ostrava, the industrial town in the Czech Republic where she grew up. She began to take photographs when she was twelve years old, after her parents gave her a first camera, and photography became her passion. She has now explored this world both as a model and as a photographer. Since first posing as a model in 1998, she has had the opportunity to work with many photographers. In 2002, she bought a Canon EOS 5, took up her position behind the camera, and began to take photographs of others and of herself. She focuses on self-portraits, portraits and outdoor fashion photography. Her work has been published in many photo magazines and books worldwide.

www.katirudlova.com

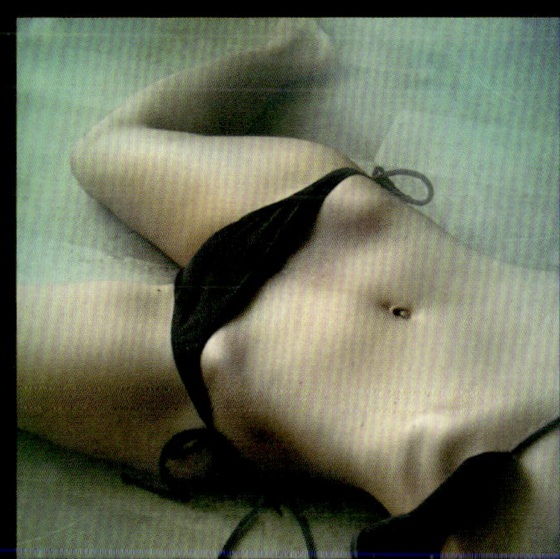

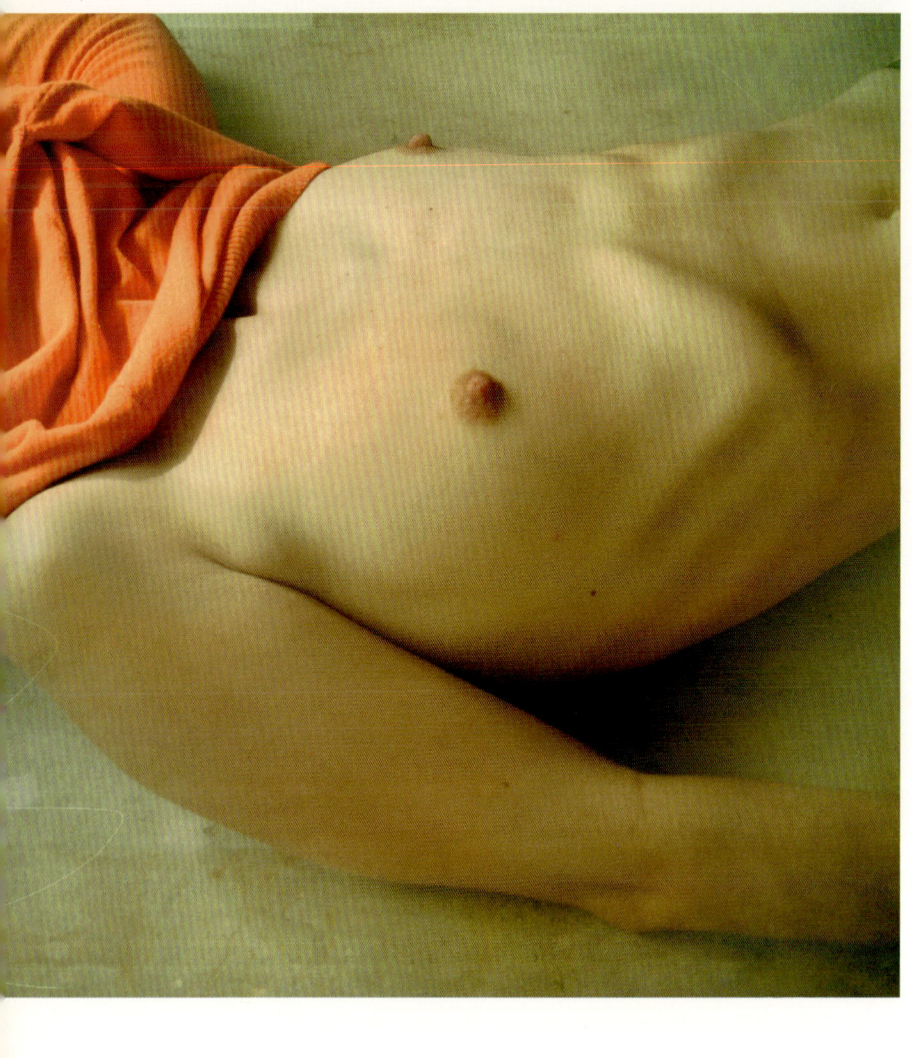

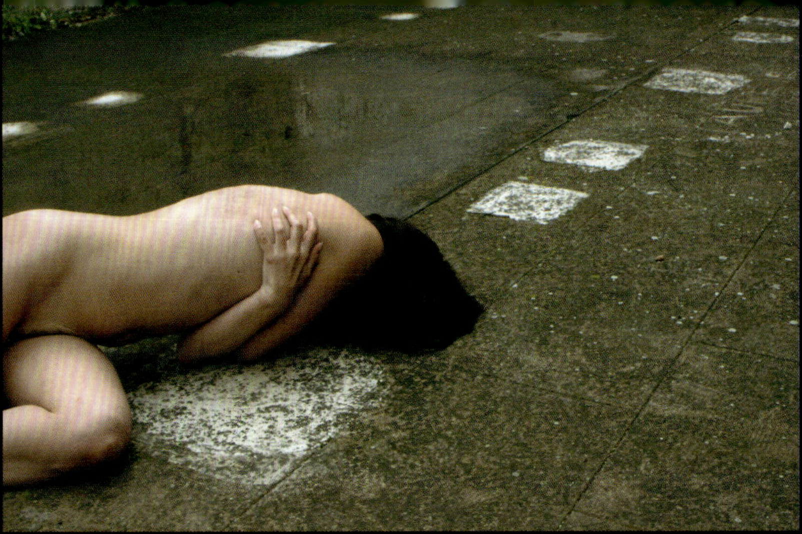

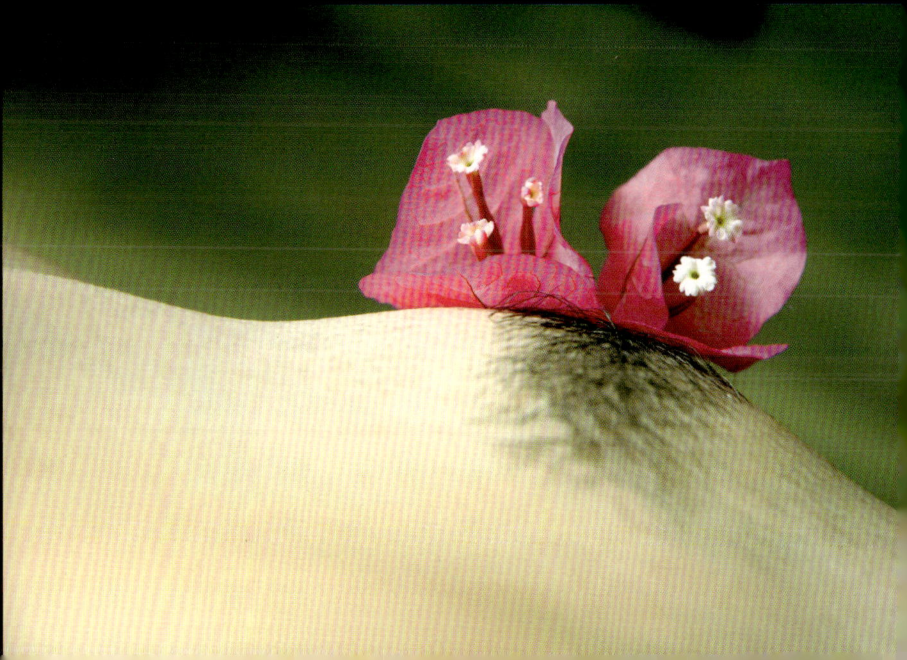

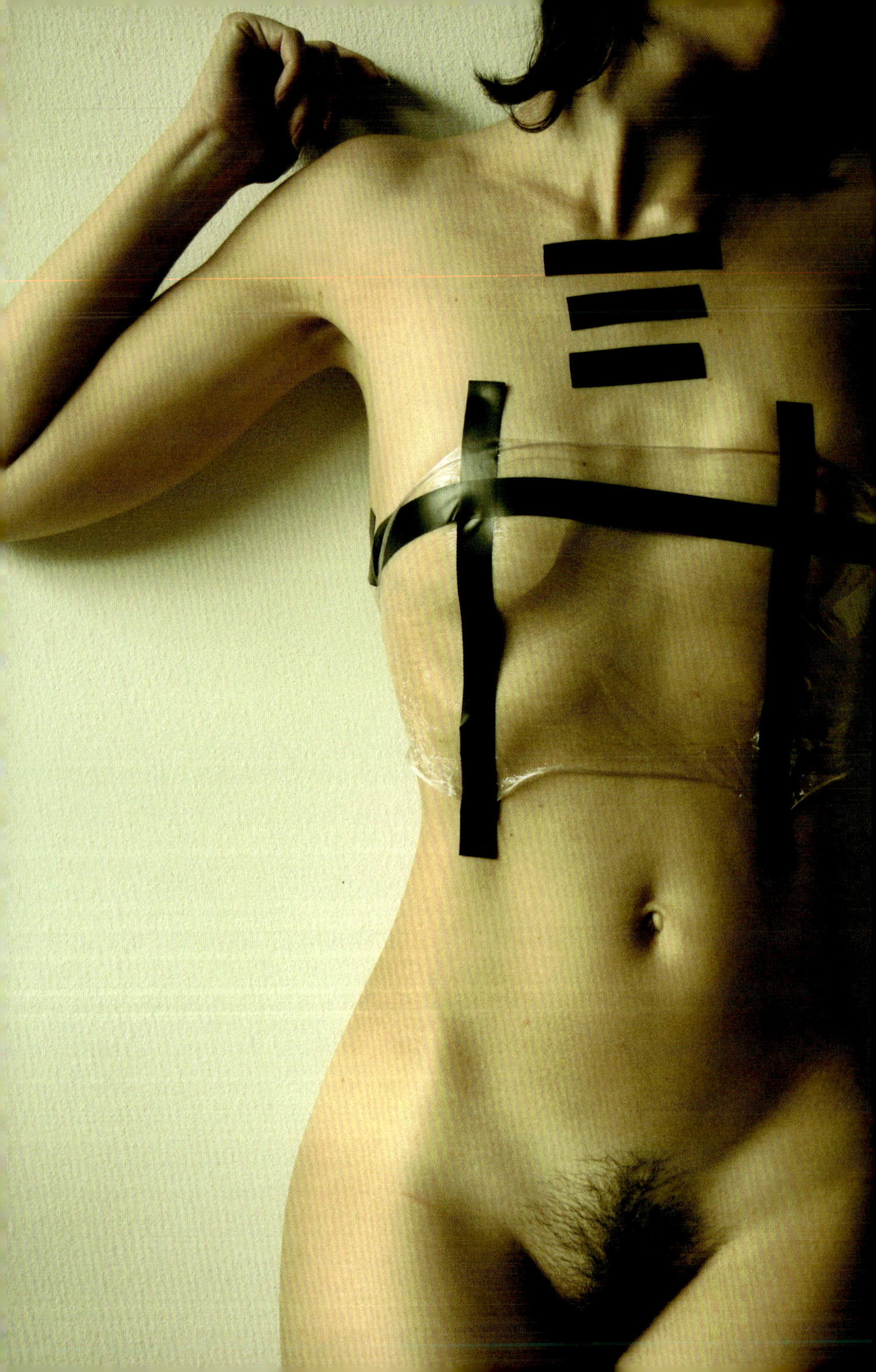

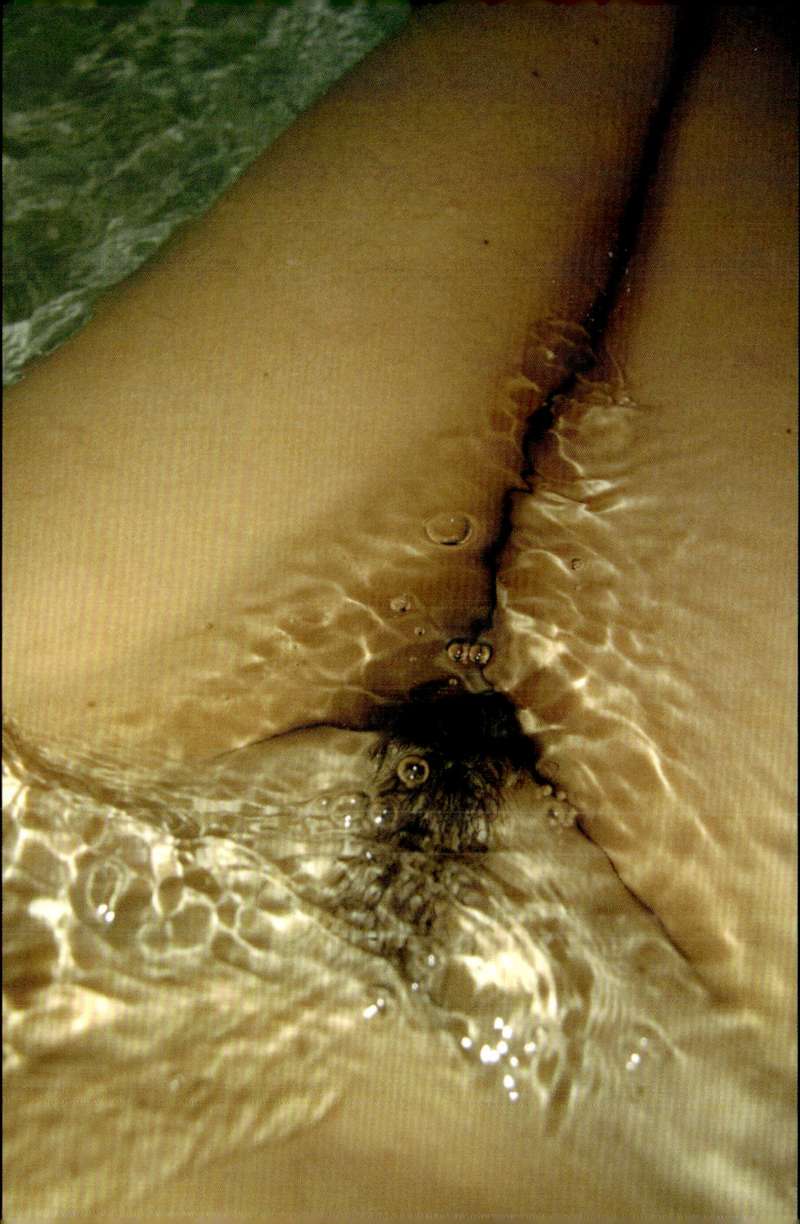

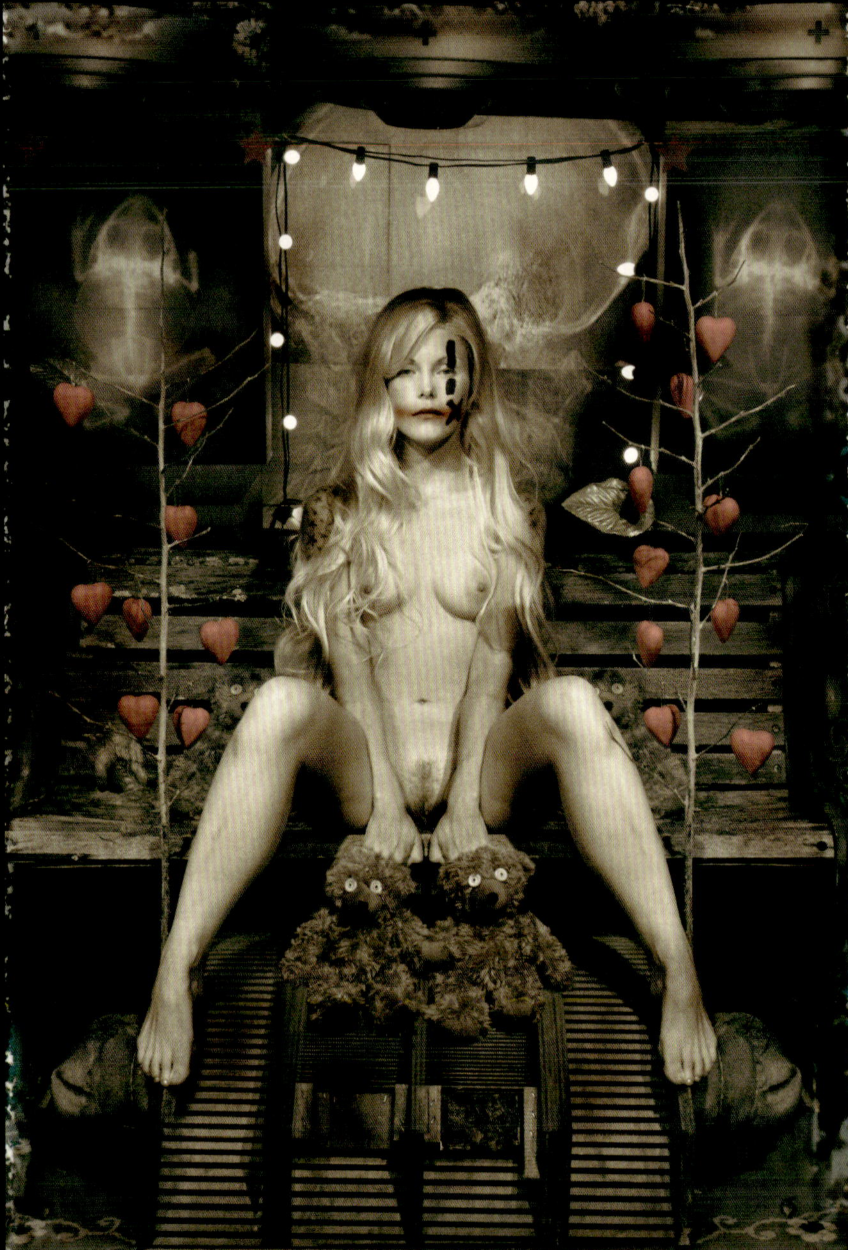

john santerineross

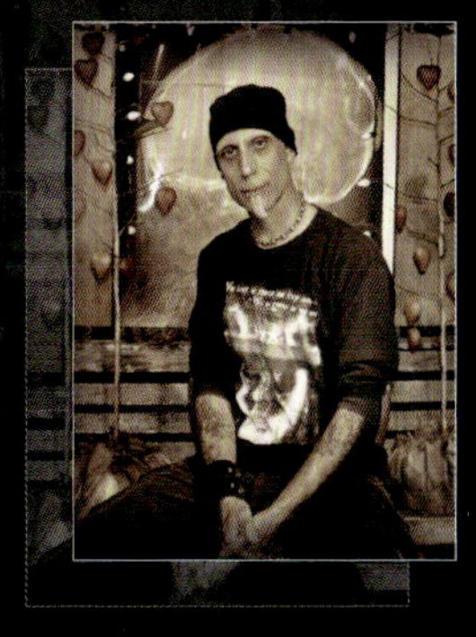

JOHN IS A US ARTIST who does not classify or categorize himself. He prefers to let viewers decide and define. He has been called everything from 'the world's leading neo-symbolist photographer' by *Profifoto*, Germany's leading photography magazine, to 'an artistic assassin who wants to artistically assassinate Christianity, especially Catholicism' by Bill Donohue, head of the American Catholic League. John never elucidates his imagery for fear of limiting viewers' personal interpretation. He is influenced by the early Symbolists' belief that 'the creation of a mood is as important as the transmission of information.'

www.santerineross.com

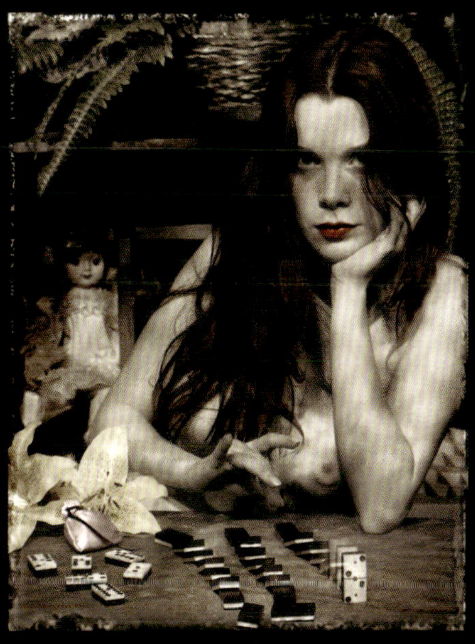

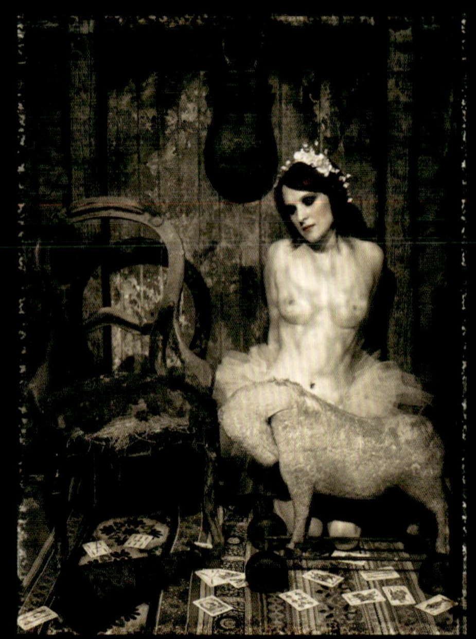

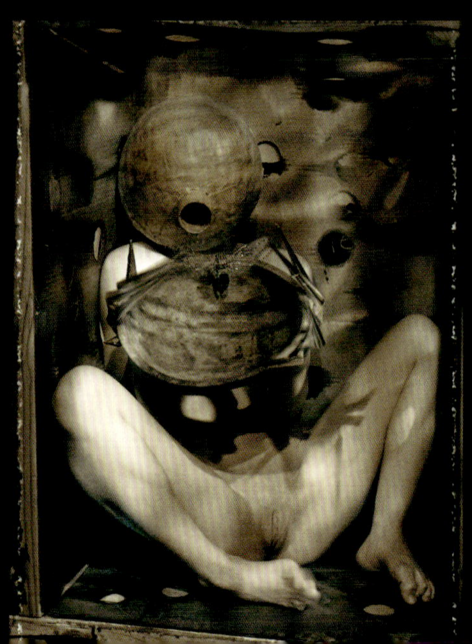

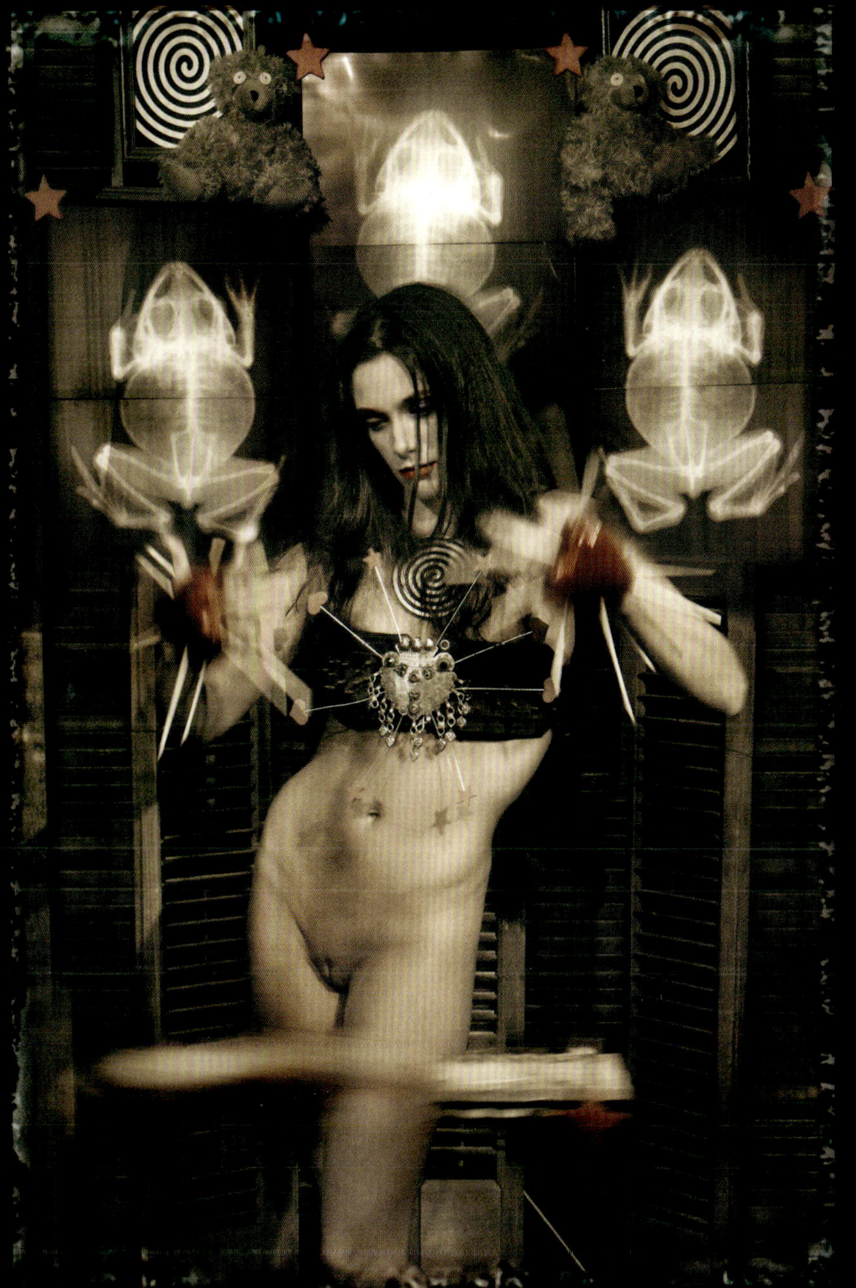

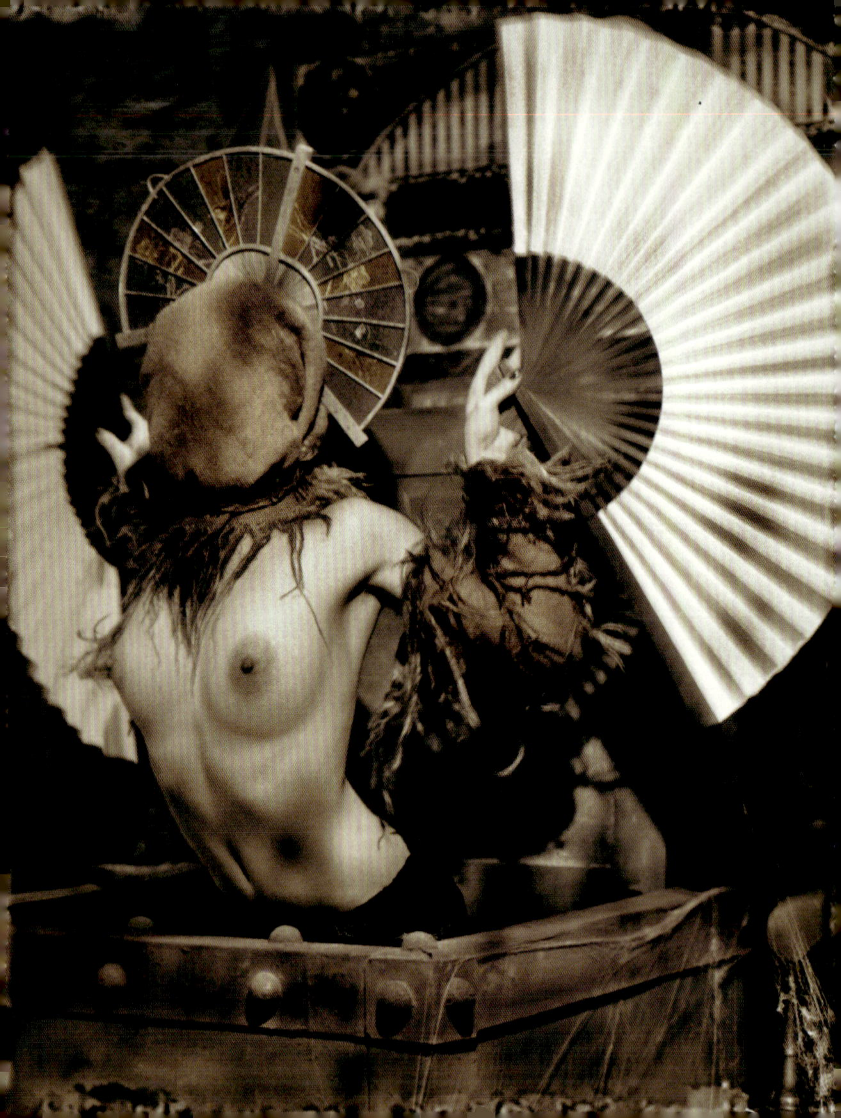

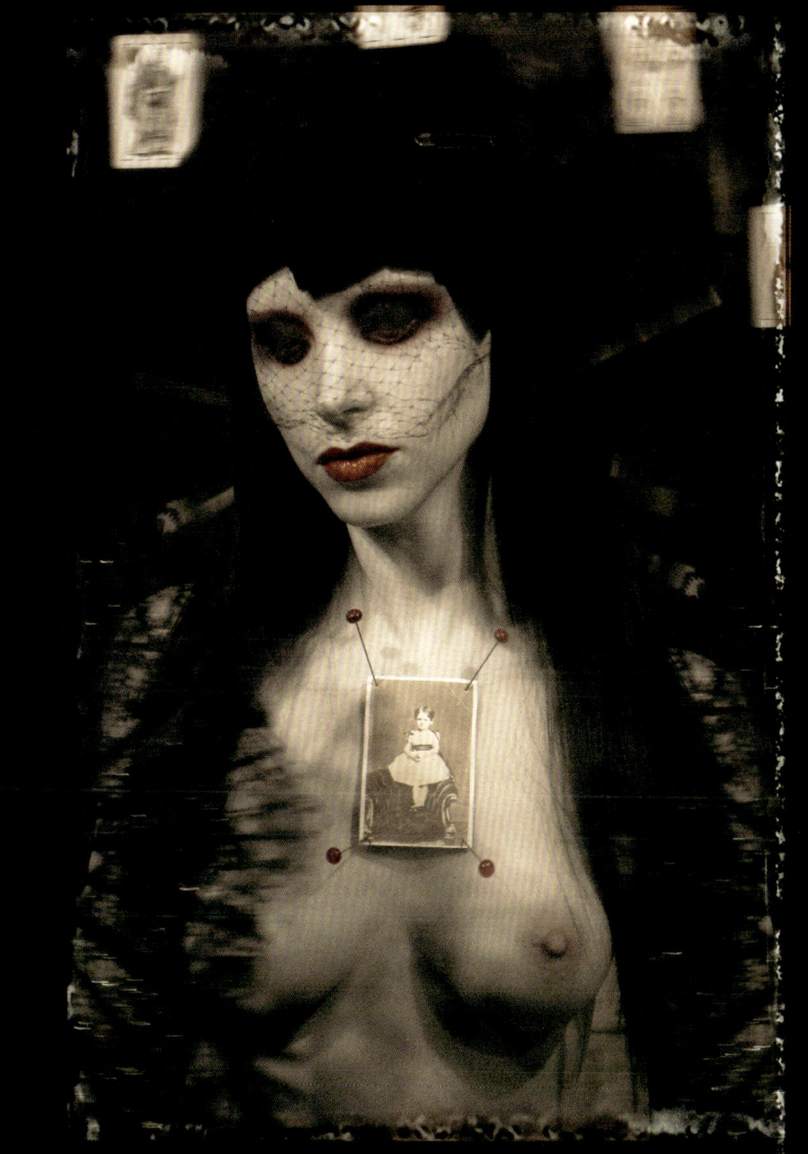

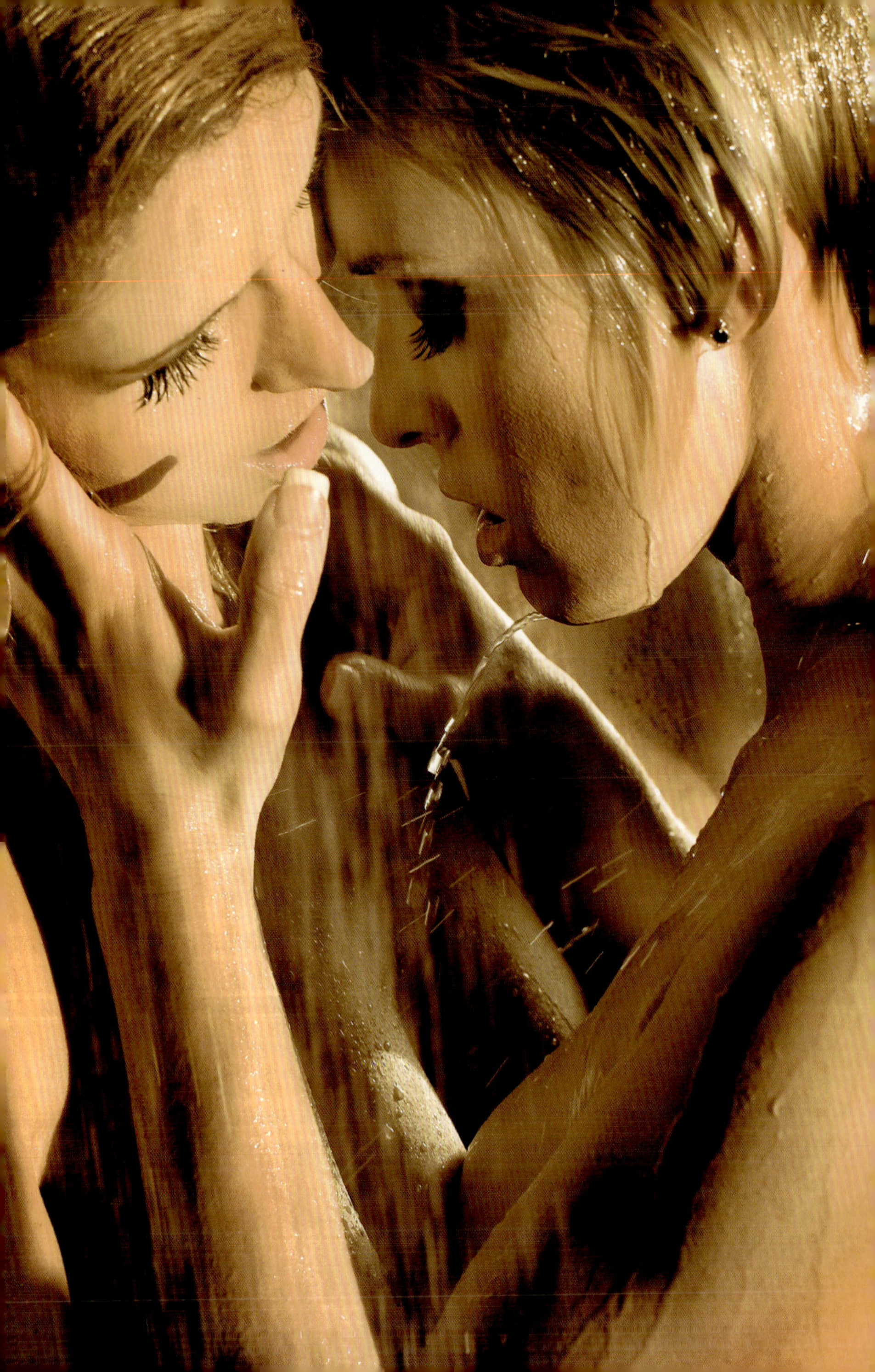

will santillo

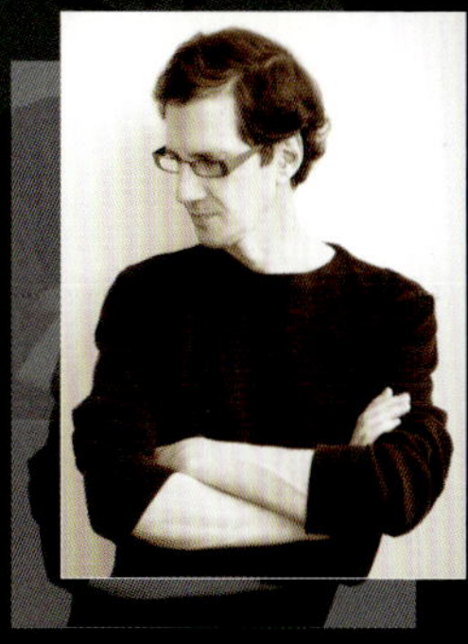

WILL WAS BORN OUTSIDE New York and, after completeing a degree in Art and Design at MIT, where he studied with renowned photographer Minor White, then moved to Canada where he still lives, to pursue architectural studies. After twenty-five years in commercial photography, architectural design and computer programming, he expanded his creative range to include erotic art. His ambition is to capture the Perfect Moment, the lingering, charged moods and memories that recall the often tender – but sometimes taboo – aspects of human desire. His work has been widely published and his first book, entitled F*lagrante Delicto (Caught in the Act)*, was published by Rosalbino Press in 2008.

www.santillophotography.com

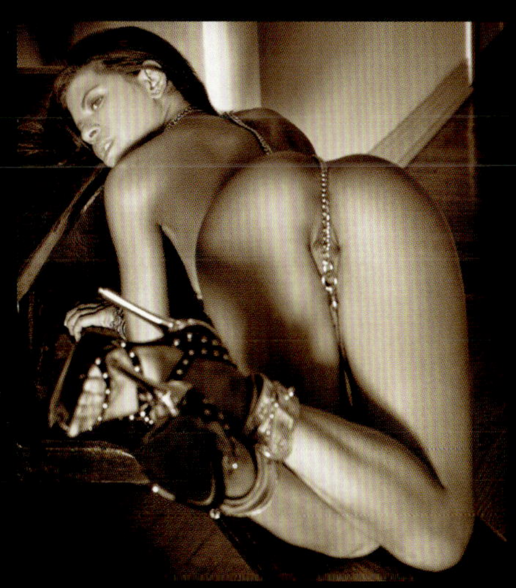

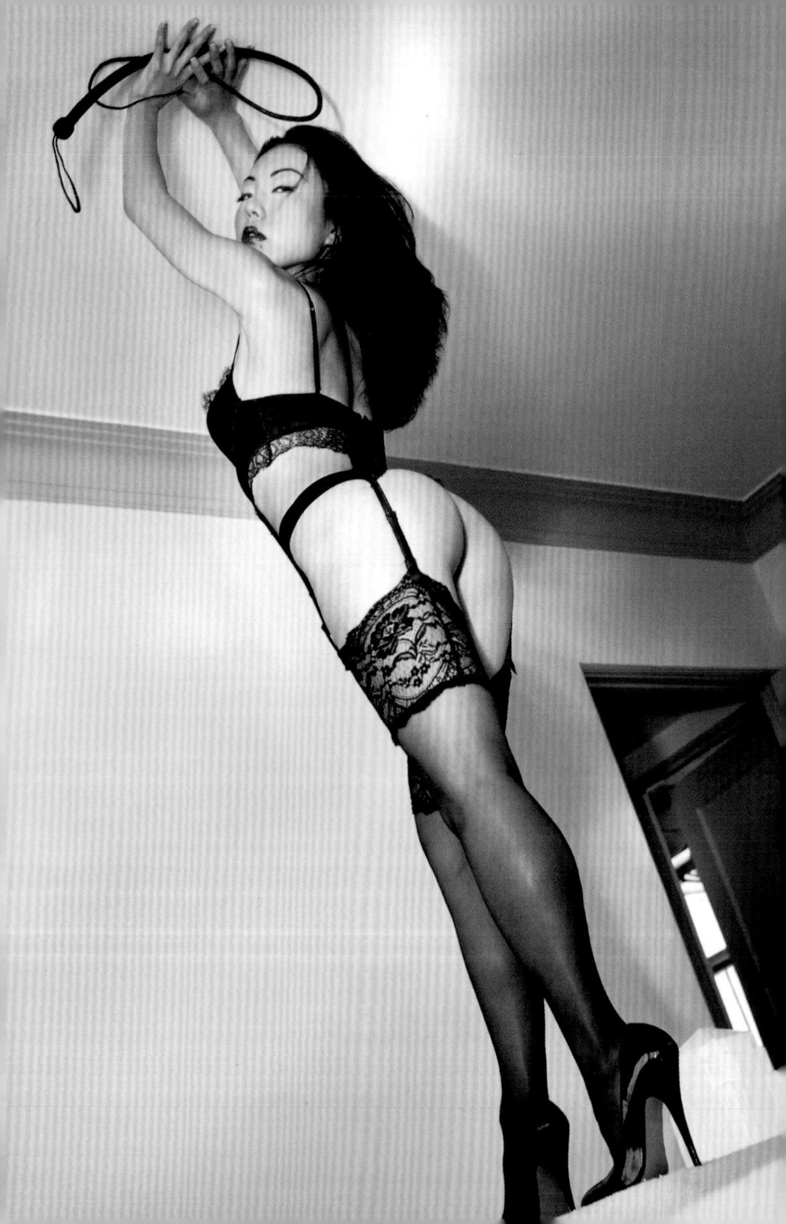

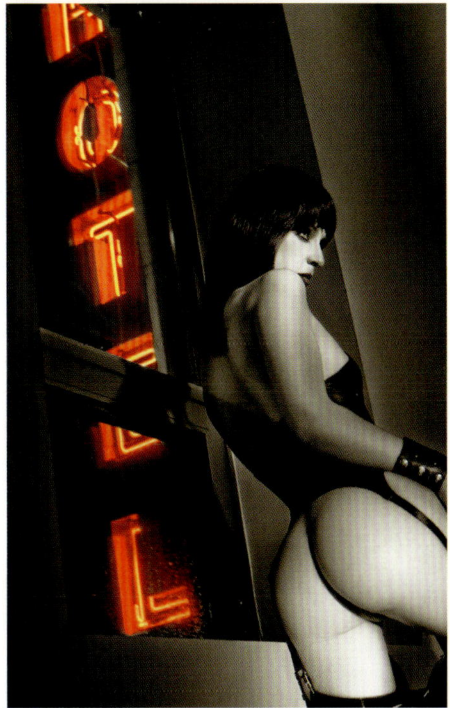

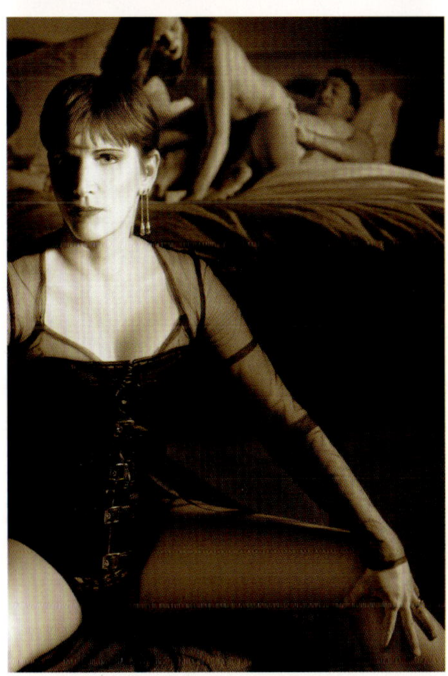

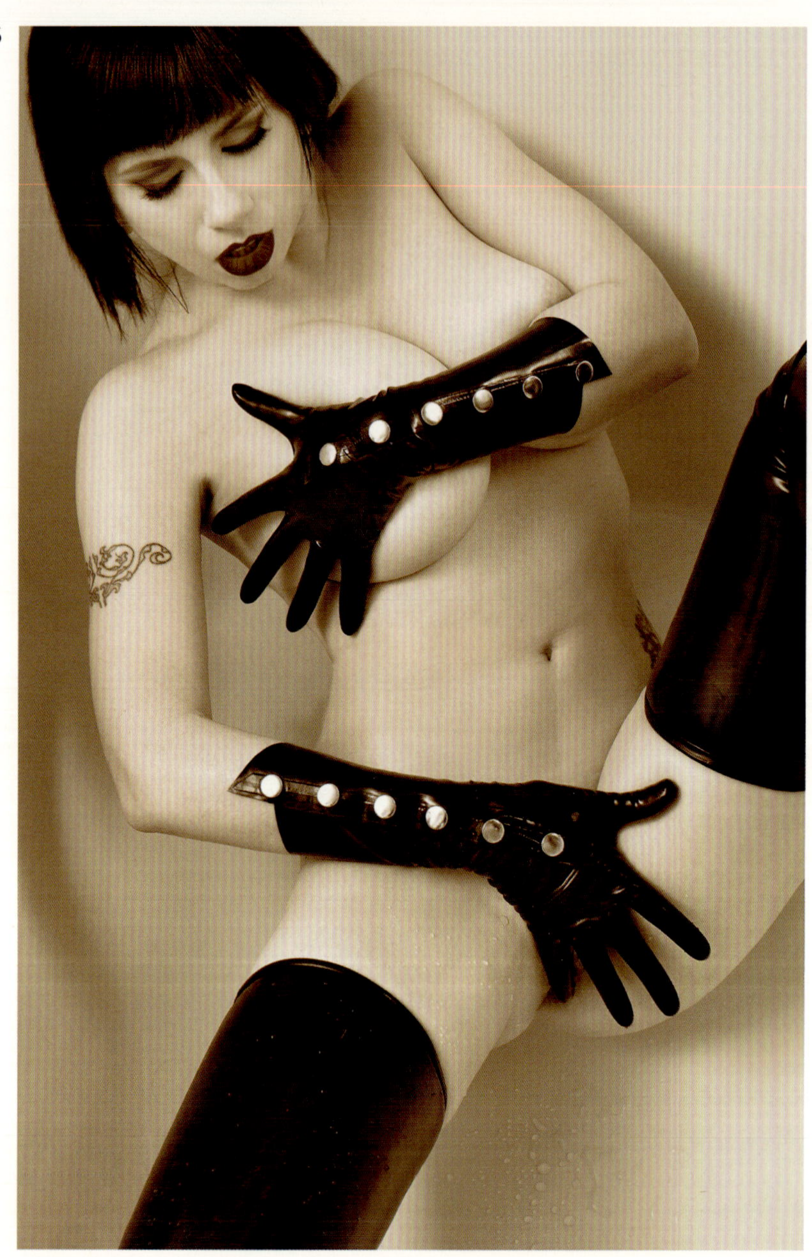

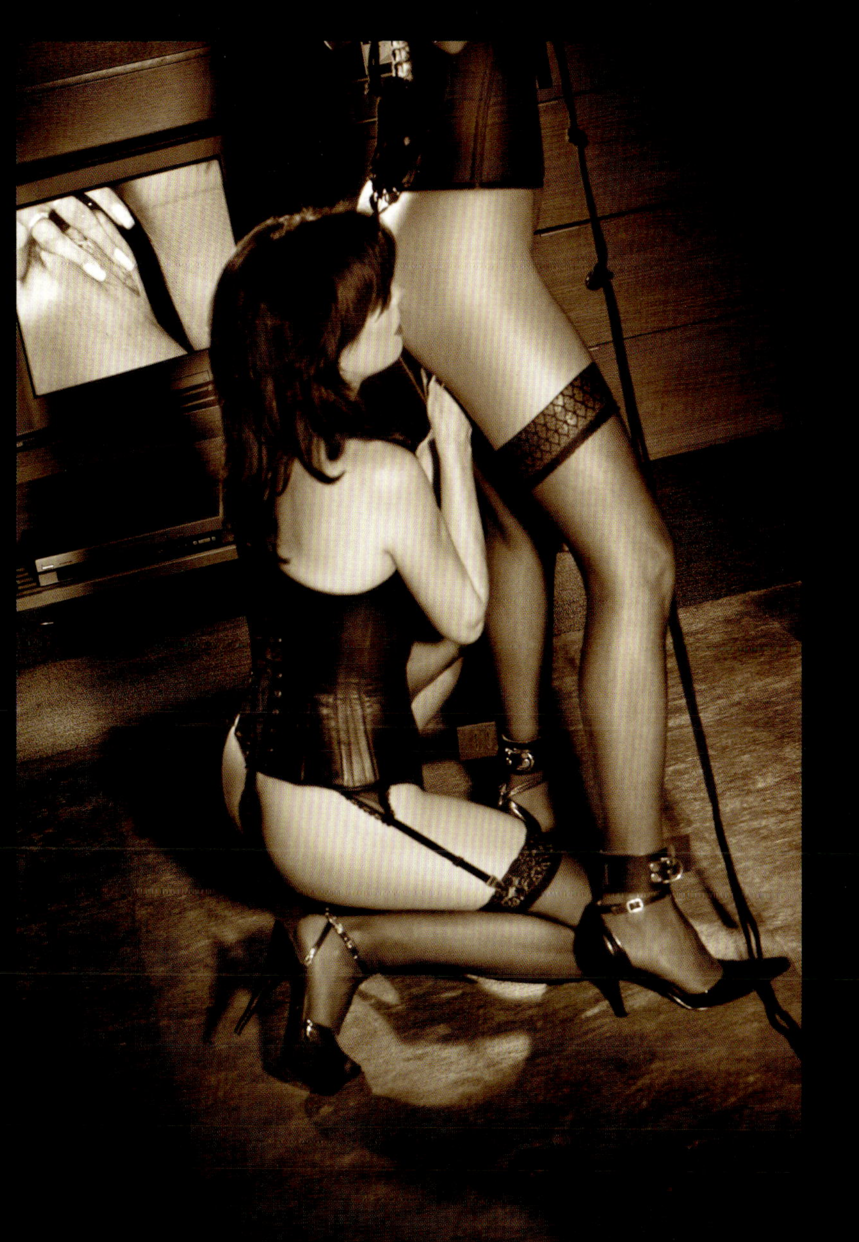

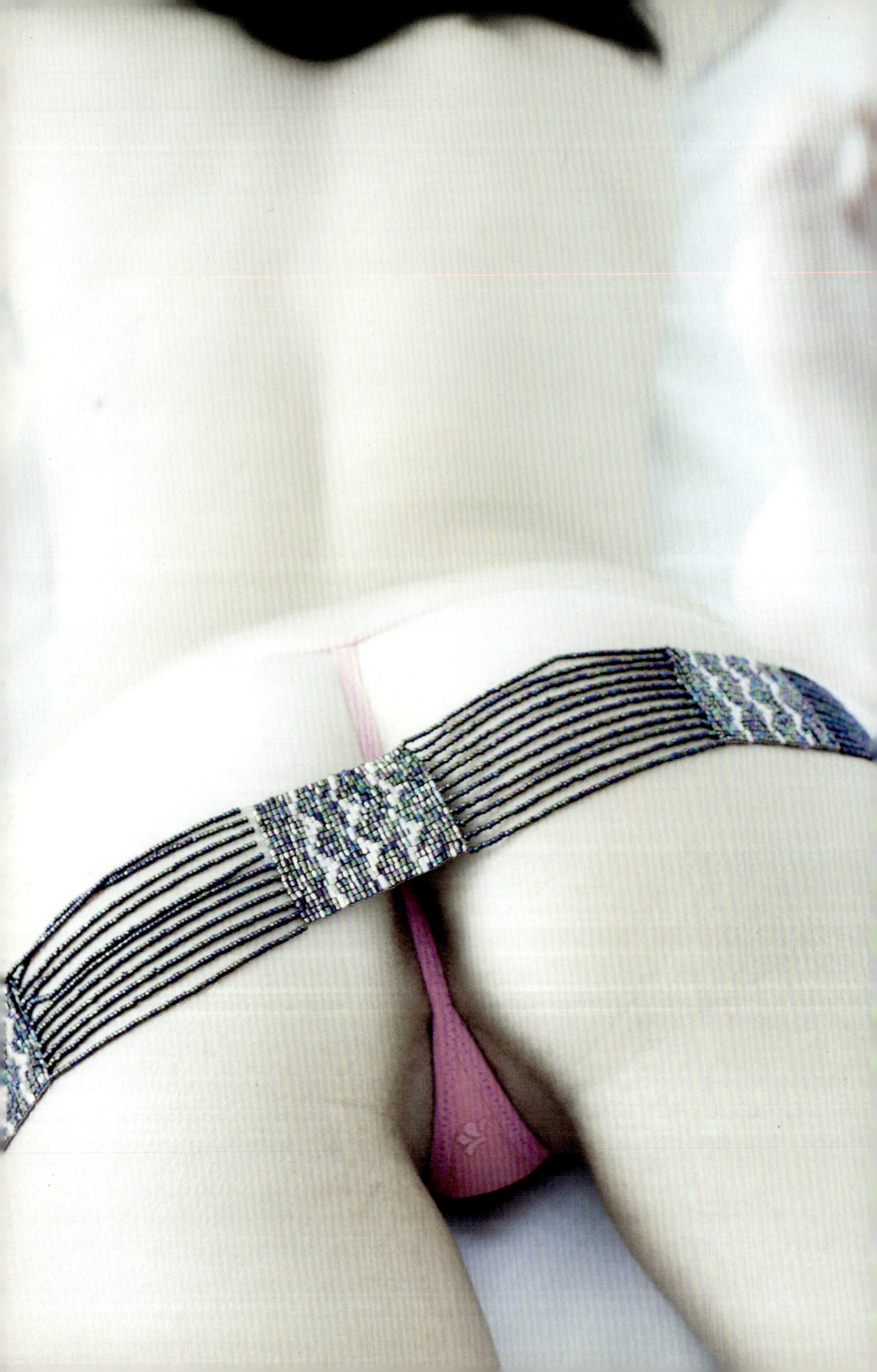

carlos santos

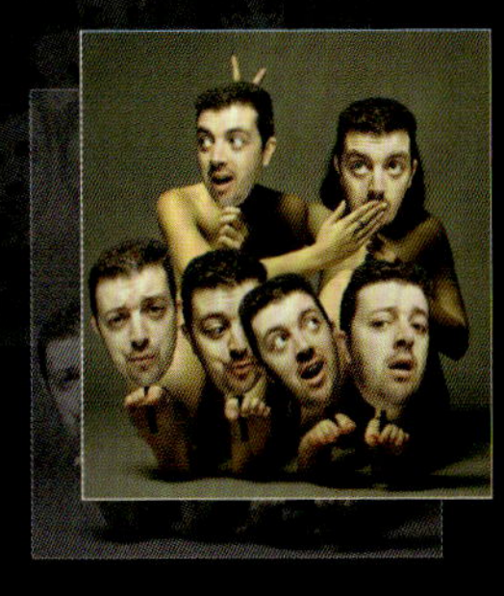

CARLOS BEGAN TO TAKE photographs about ten years ago. When he photographs, he concentrates his attention on the surrounding mood, emotions and personalities. His photos are mainly about the study of the feminine body, its features and feelings. In past years he has worked with several magazines and erotic sites including *FHM*, *Playboy* and *Suicide Girls*. His work can easily be found on the Internet, at individual exhibitions, and in photographic publications.

www.photograma.com

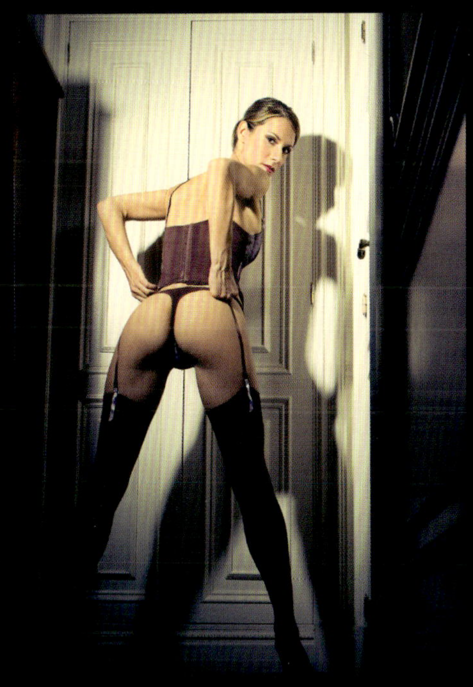

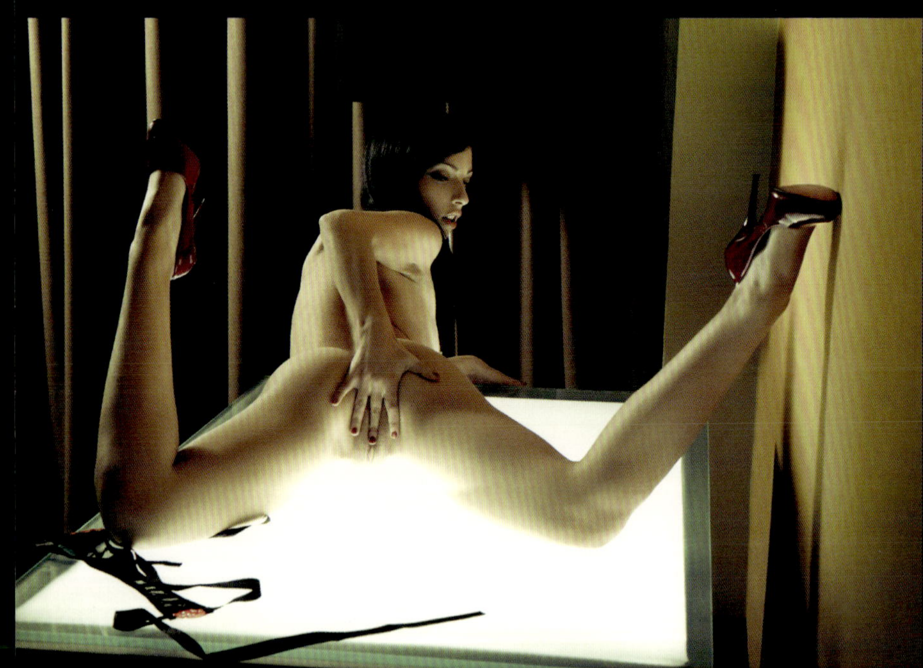

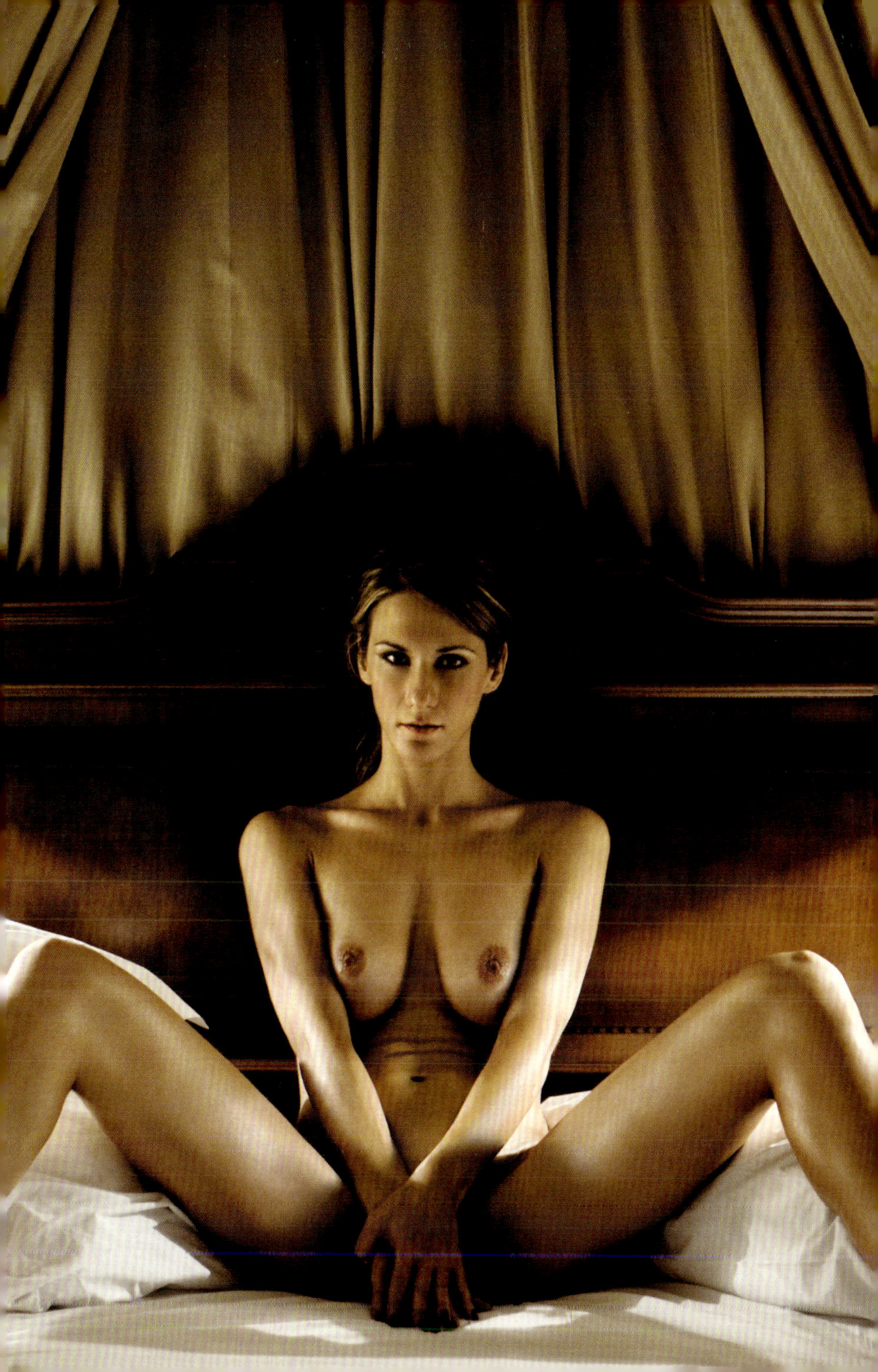

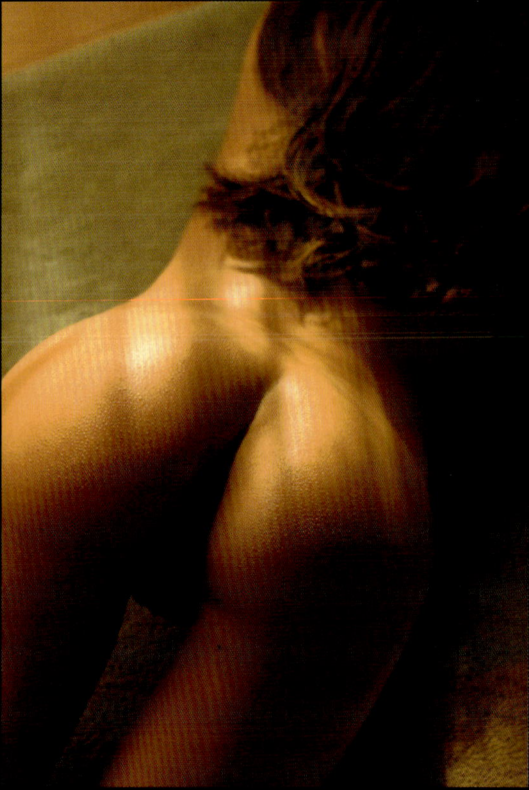

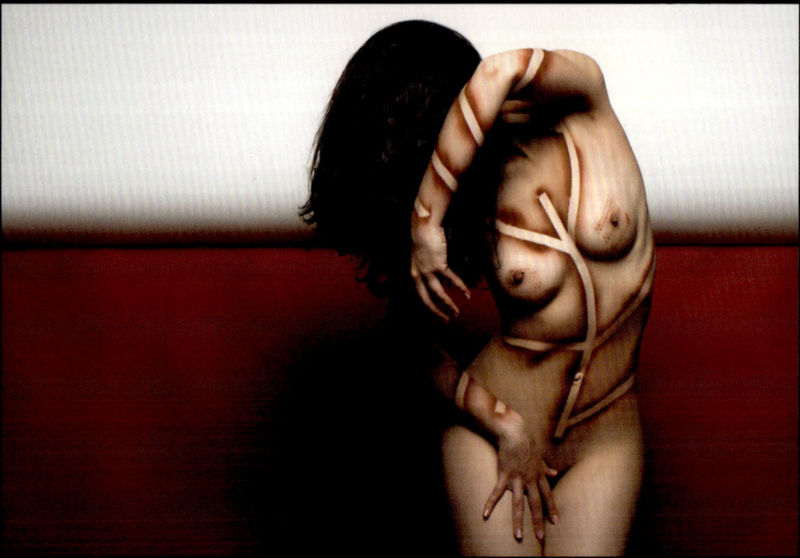

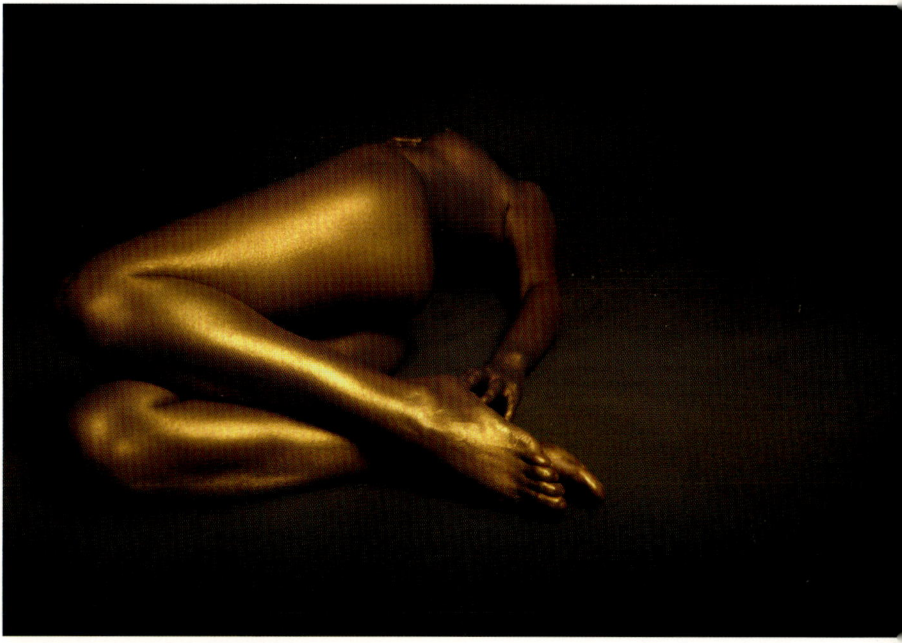

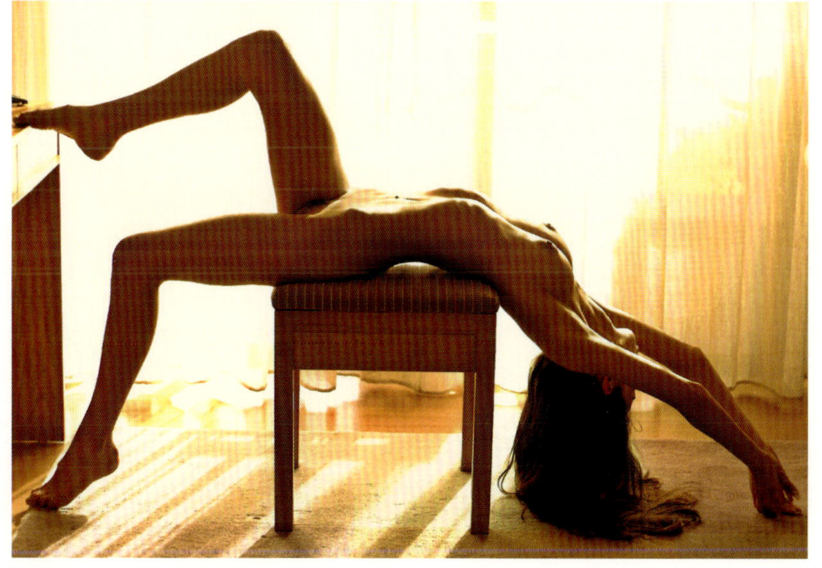

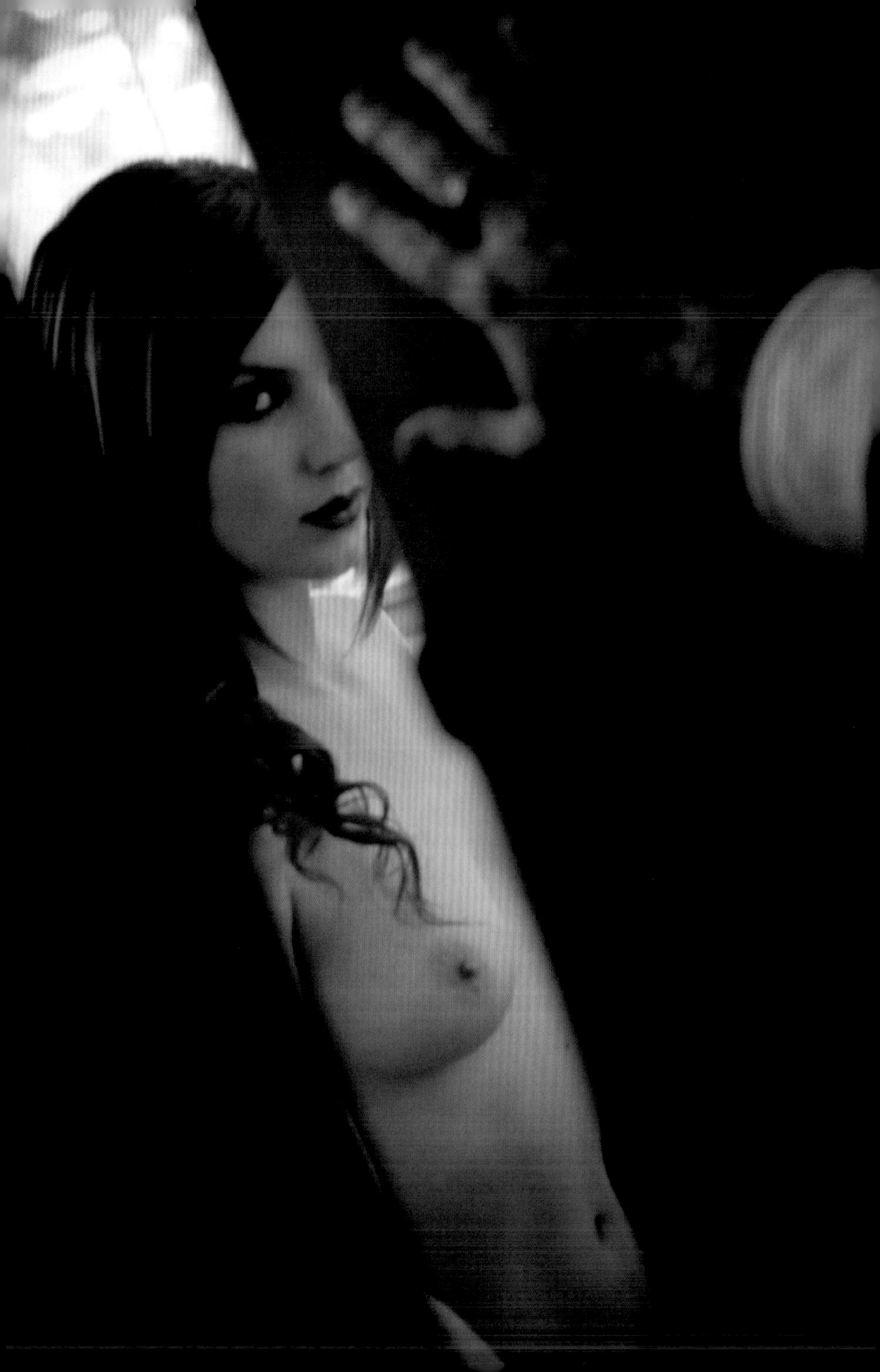

alessandro saponi

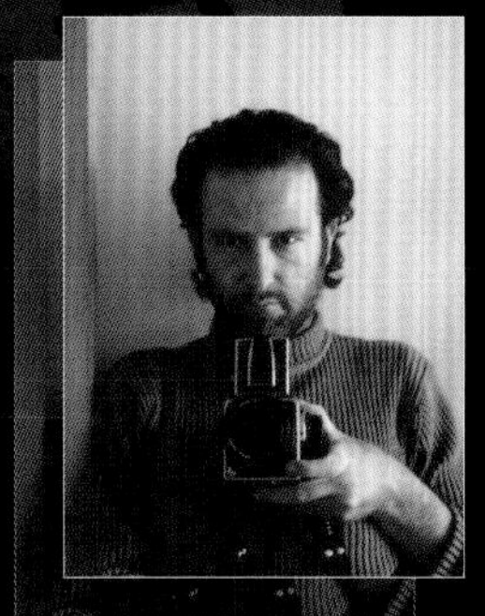

ALESSANDRO IS AN ITALIAN filmmaker with a passion for the arts. He mostly lives between Milan, Sydney and New Zealand, where he is currently based. After years of focusing on street and travel photography, he became interested in erotica as a way of discovering the more intimate side of strangers, and travelling the obscure zone between exhibitionism and the underworld of beauty.

www.flickr.com/photos/sapo74/

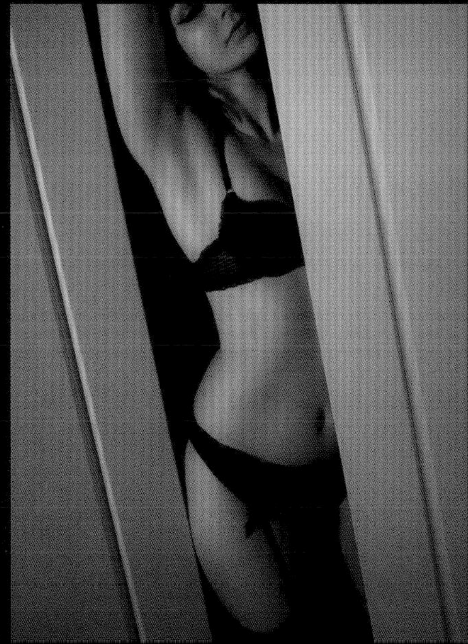

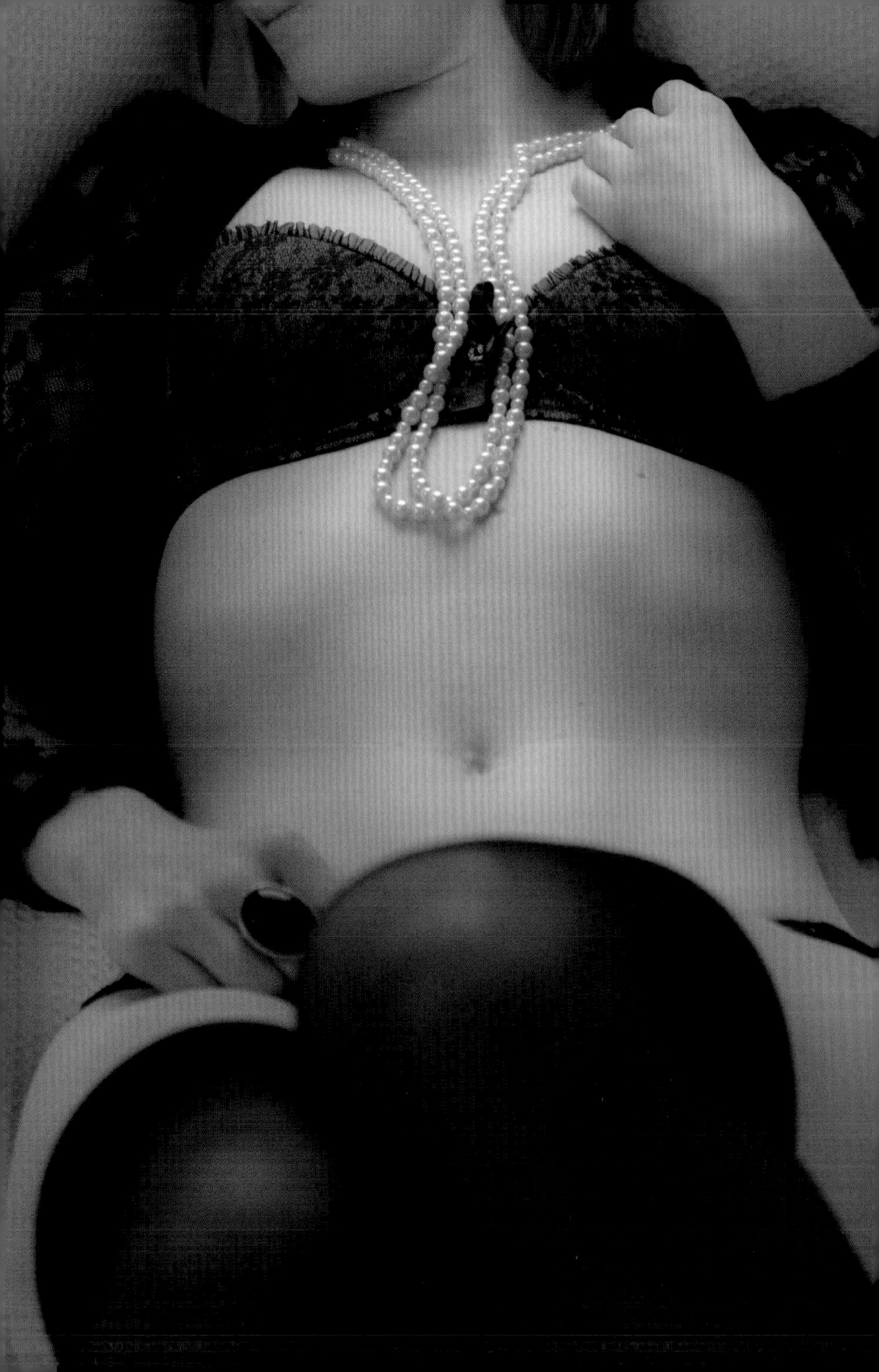

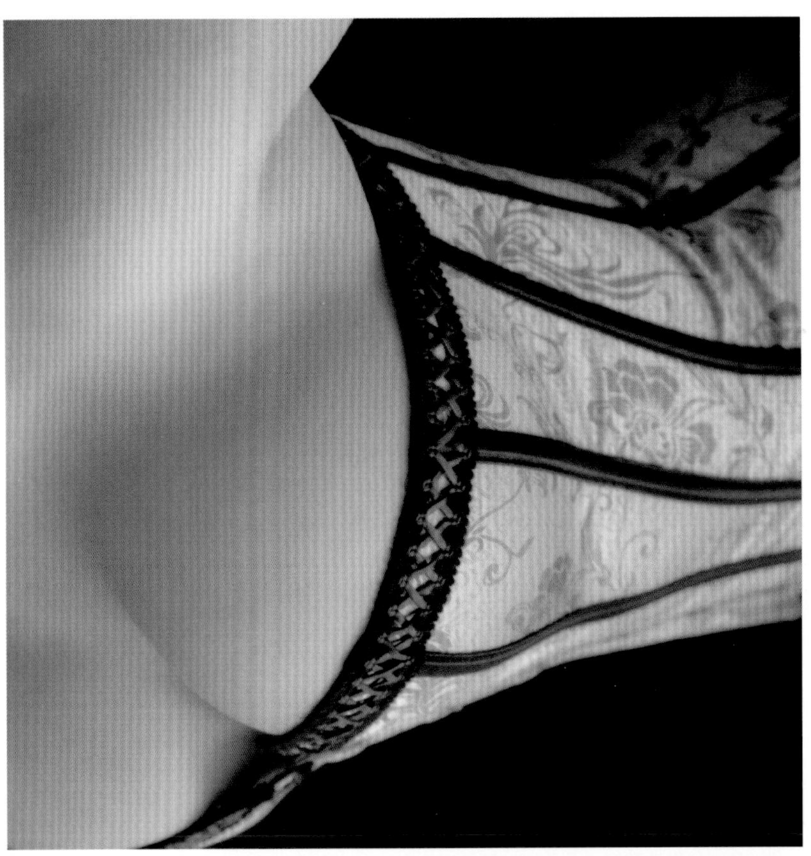

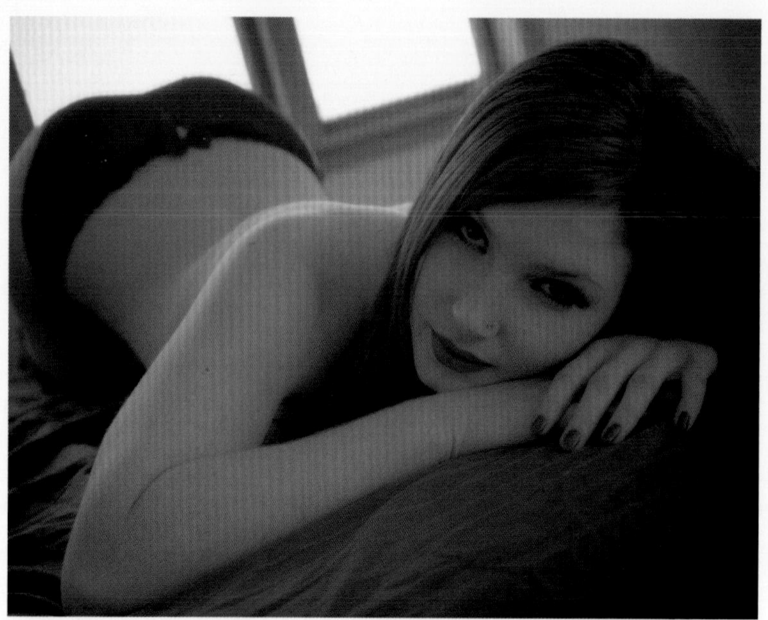

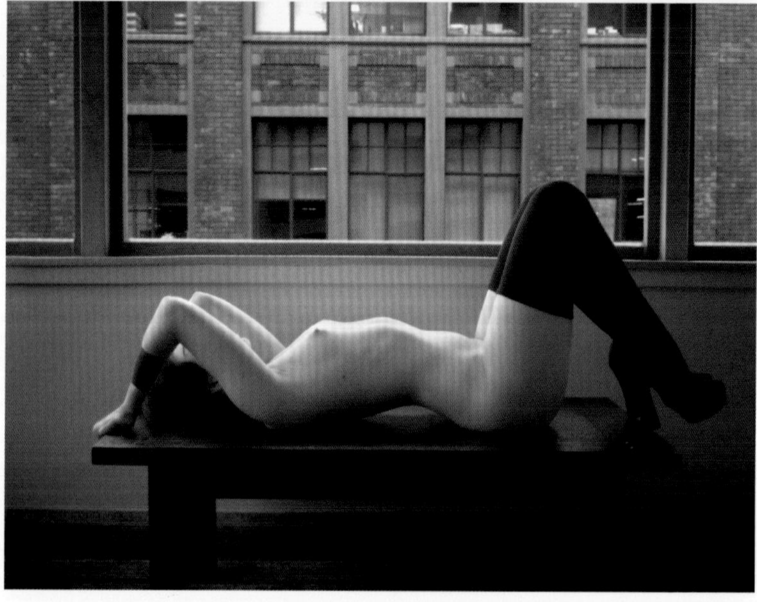

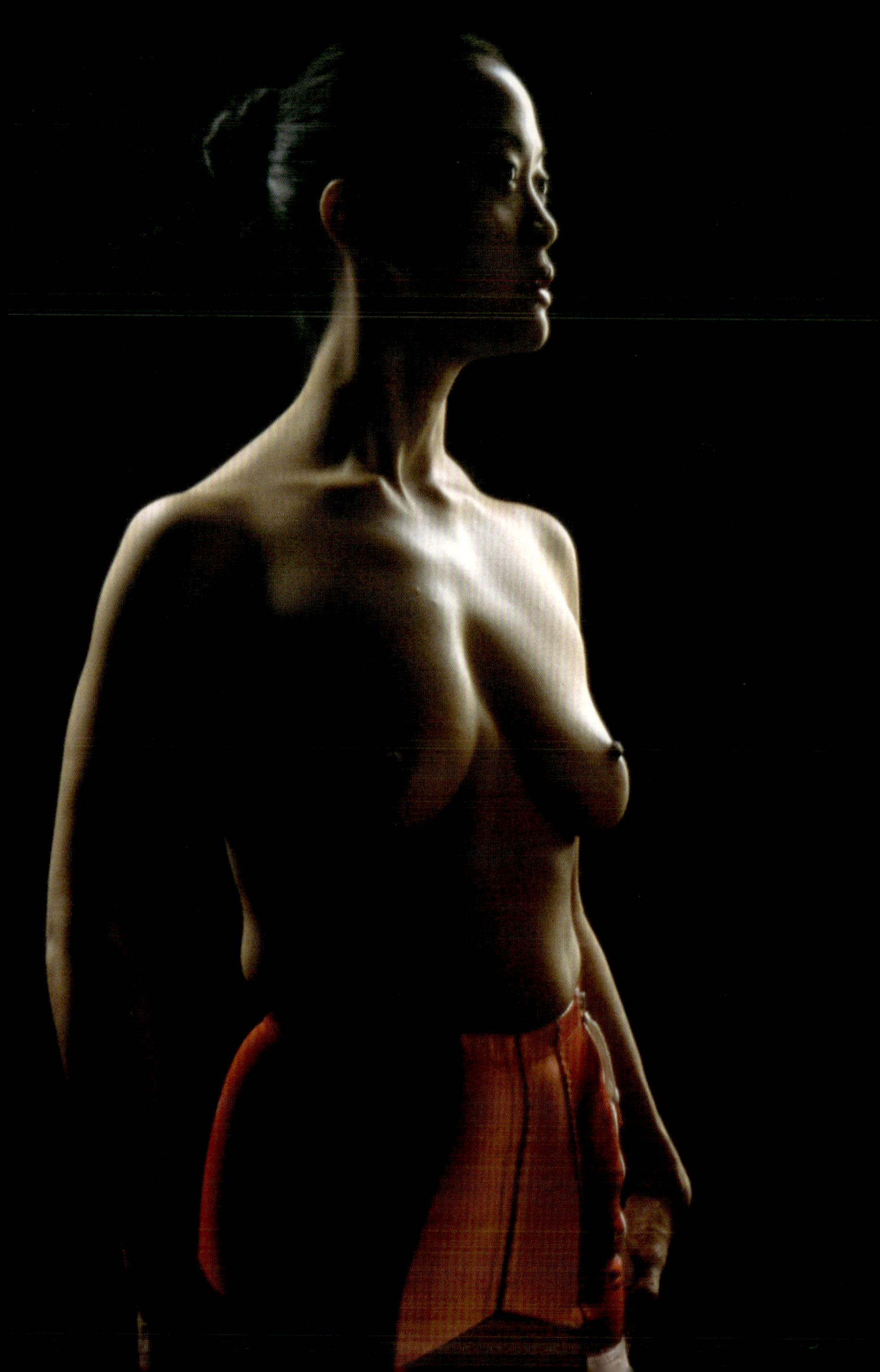

michele serchuk

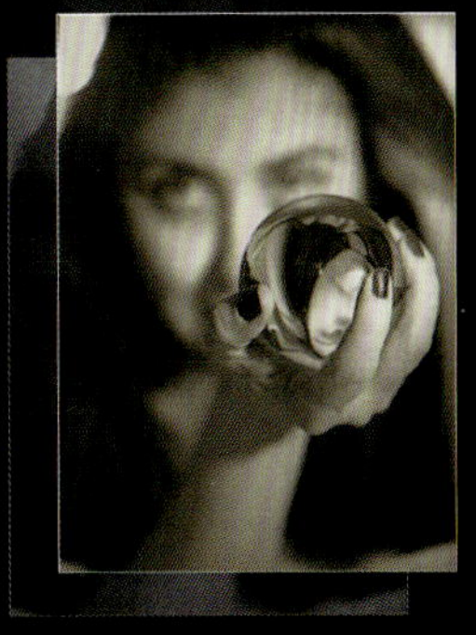

MICHELE HAS BEEN SHOOTING her evocative, intensely personal erotic portraiture in New York City for over a decade. She has lectured, presented workshops and events across the US and Canada and exhibited in several major cities, as well as being involved in TV, radio, webcasts, podcasts and magazines. She has published extensively in magazines and books and been the Photography Associate for OnOurBacks Magazine.

www.photodiva.com

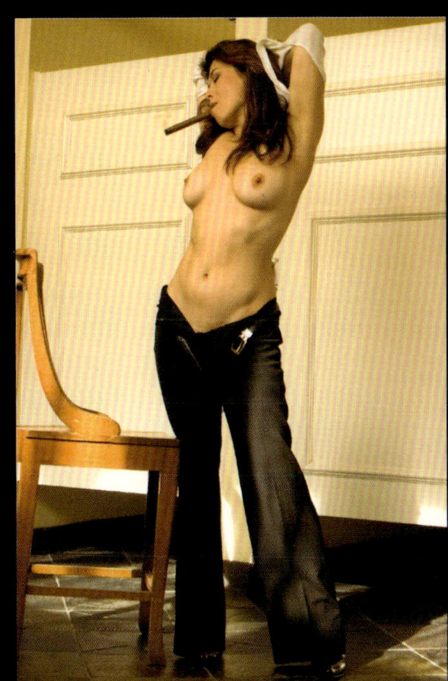

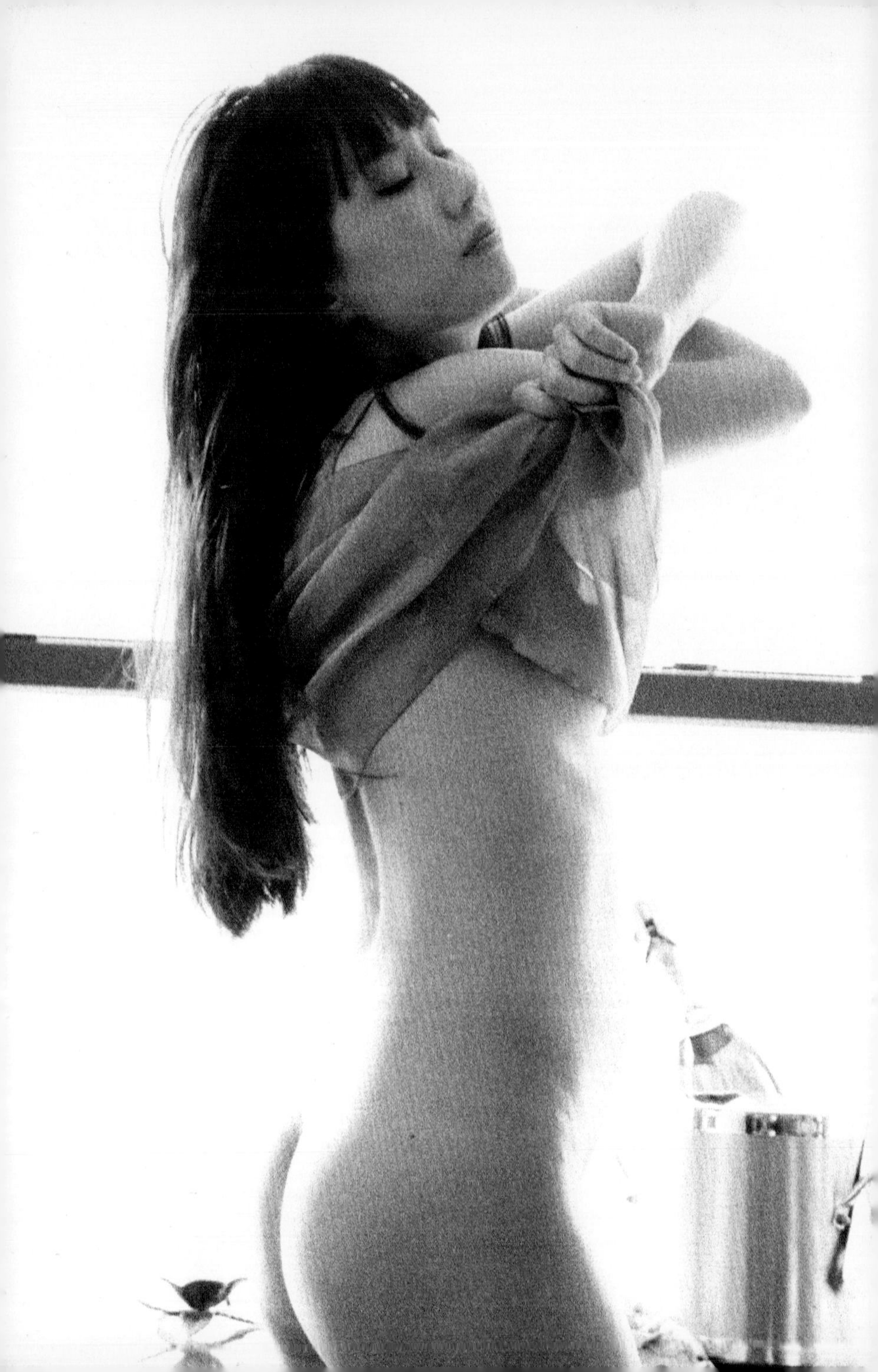

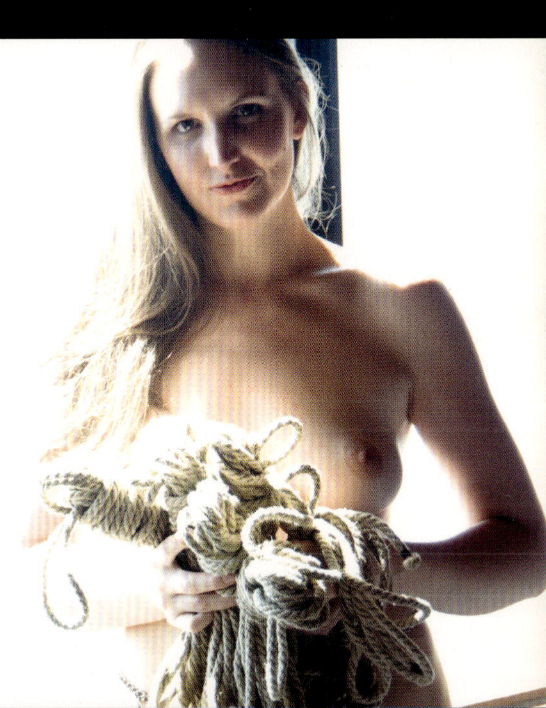

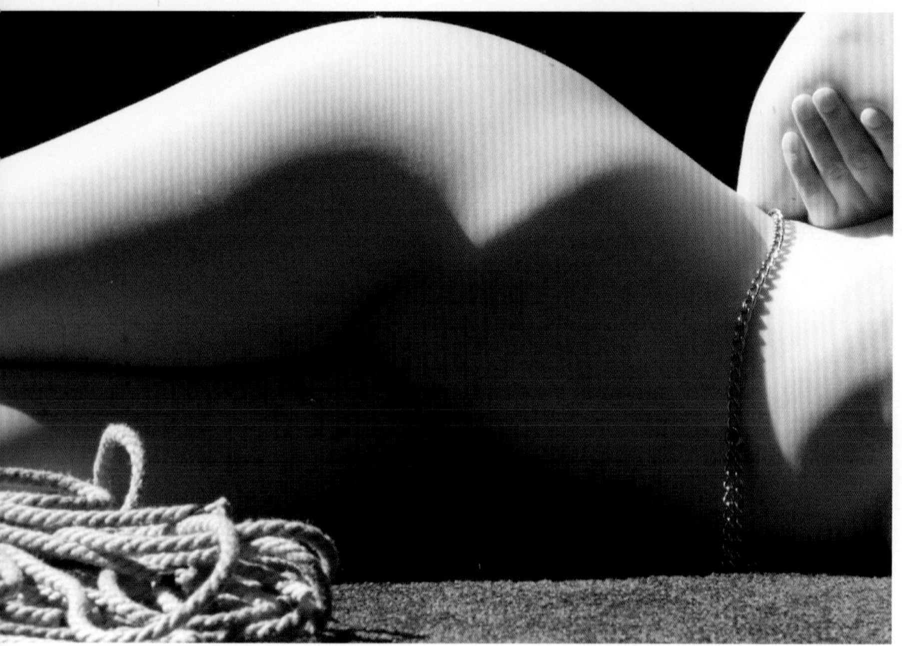

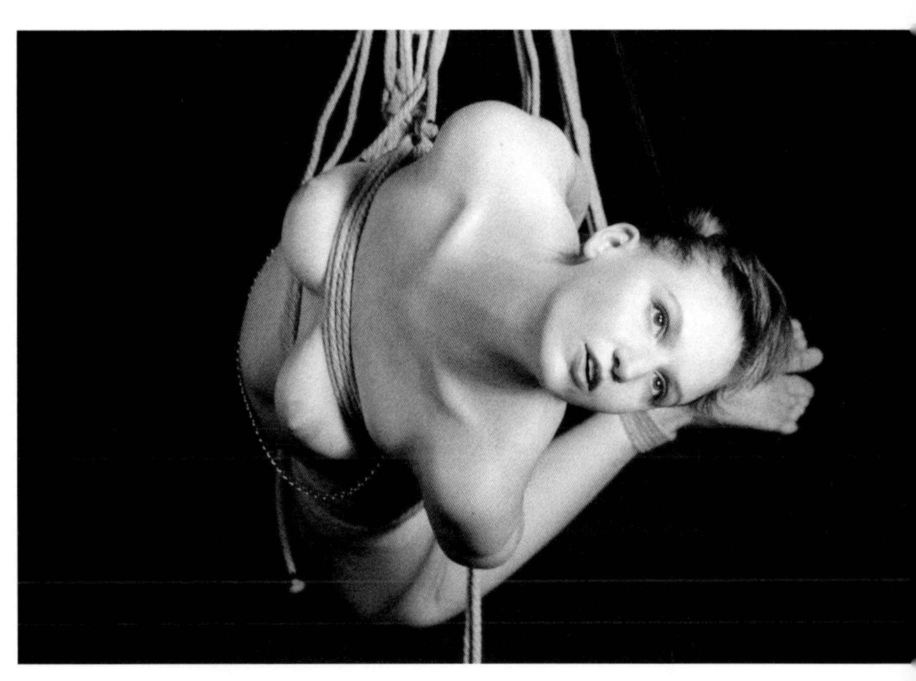

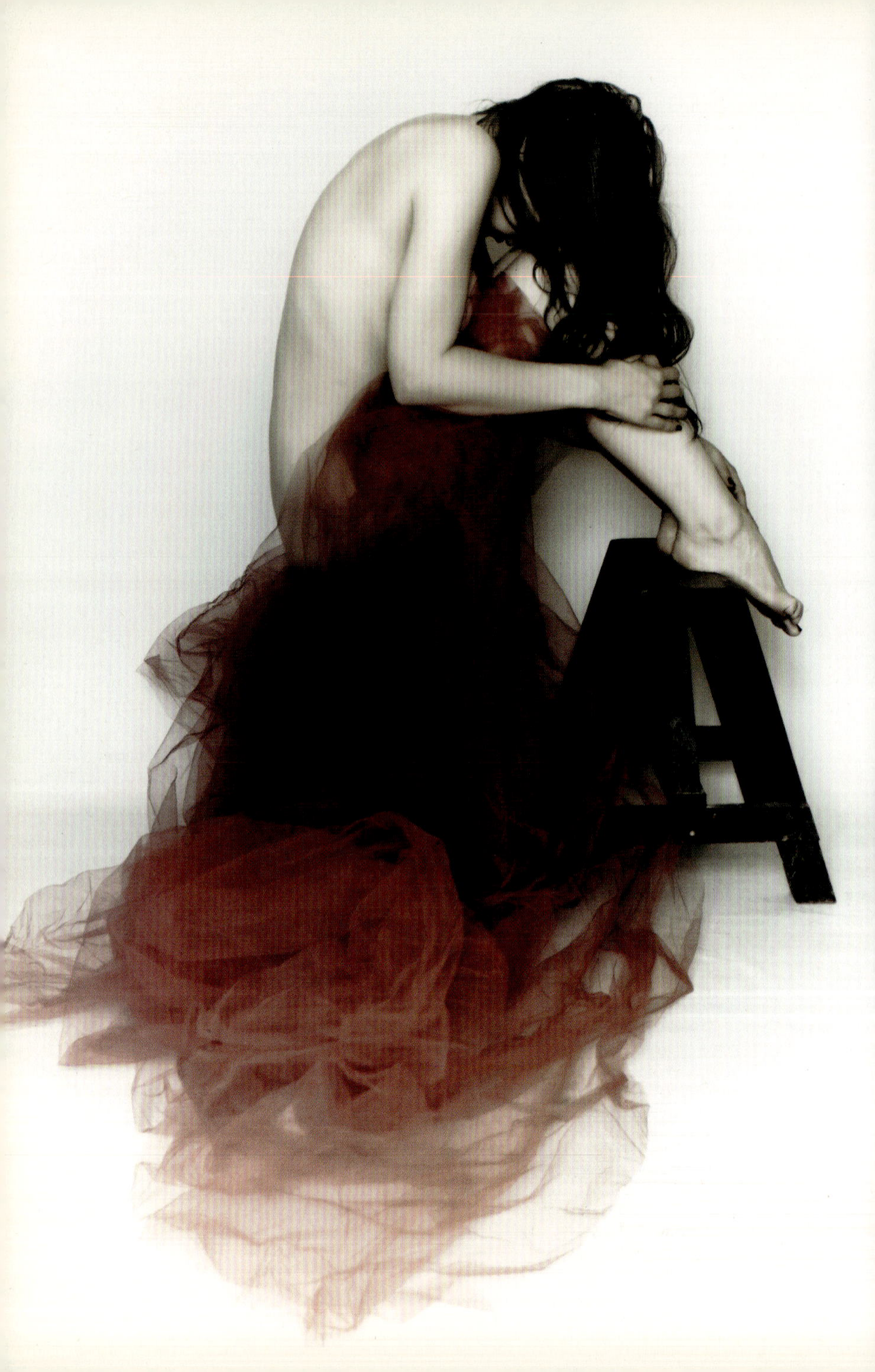

soukizy

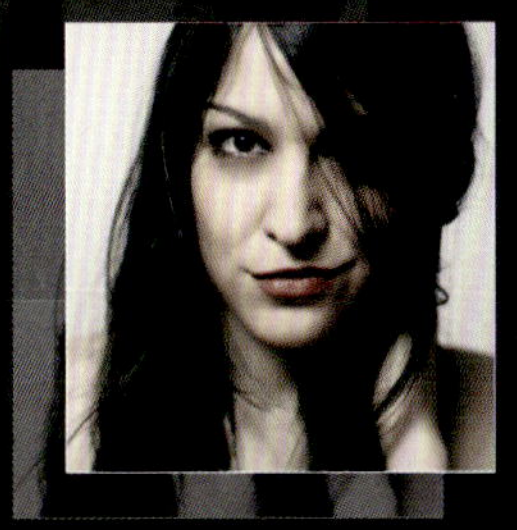

ANNARITA ACANFORA WAS BORN in 1983 in Naples, Italy, into a family of artists. Since childhood, music has been a major source of inspiration for her artistic endeavours, which include painting, writing, graphic design and multimedia experiments. Her photography, as Soukizy, forms part of a dream world from which she draws energy, and, in addition to her portraits of musicians and live music, she is involved in self-portrait sessions and nudes, which intensify the dominance of the erotic in her visual language.

www.soukizy.com

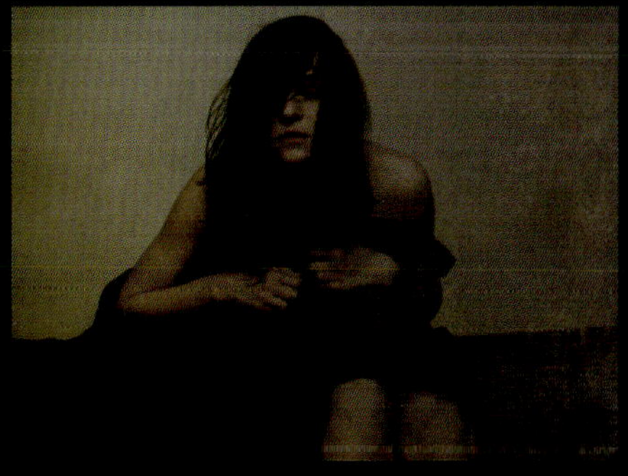

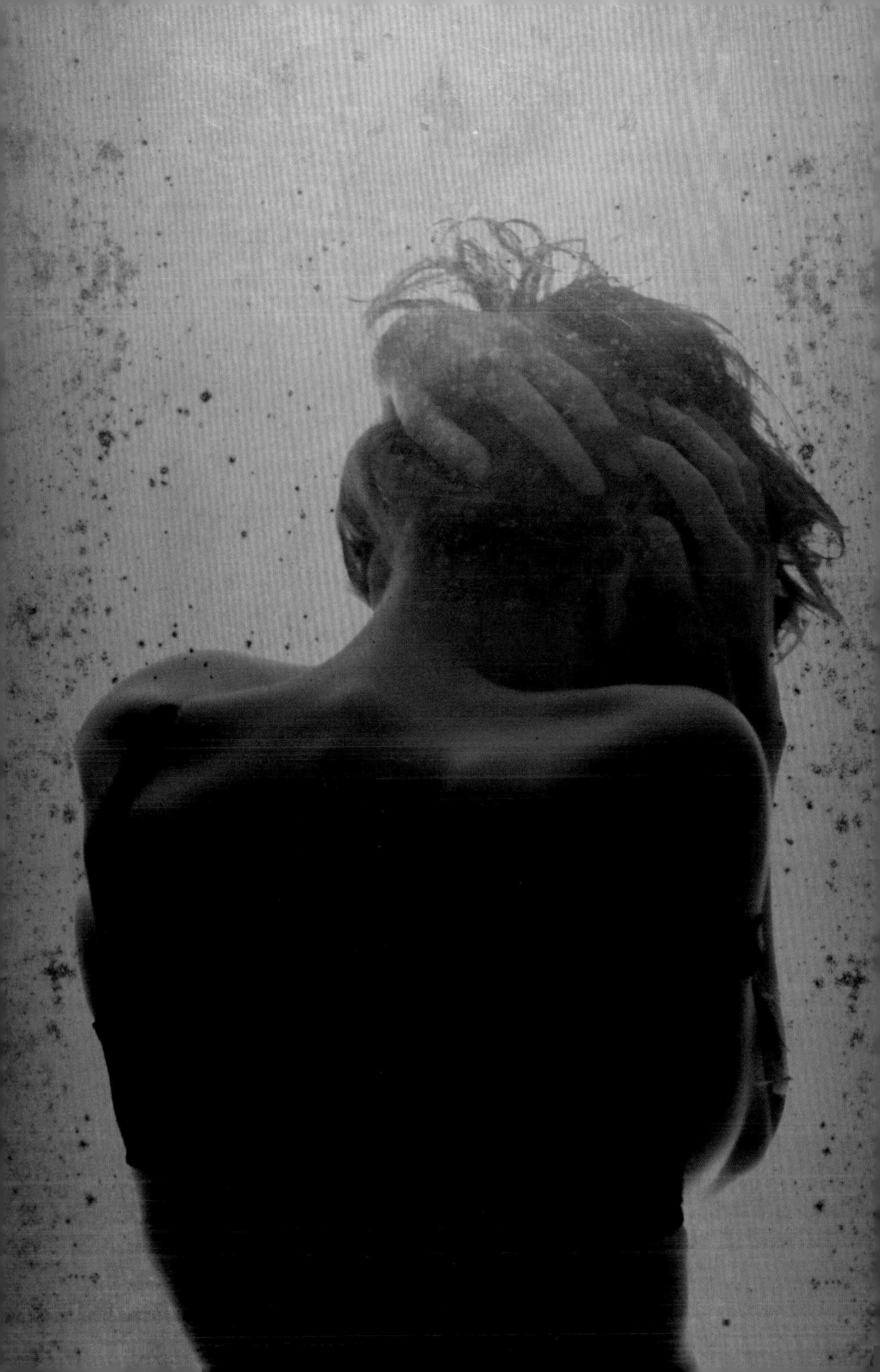

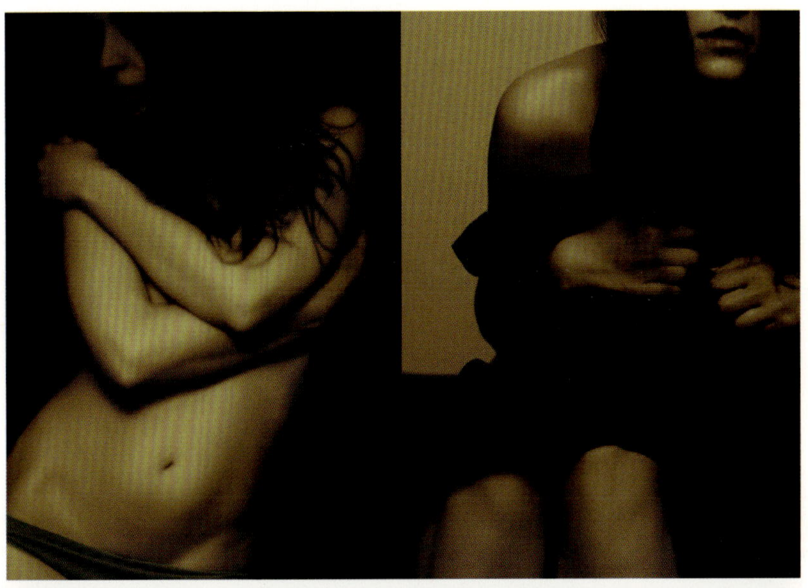

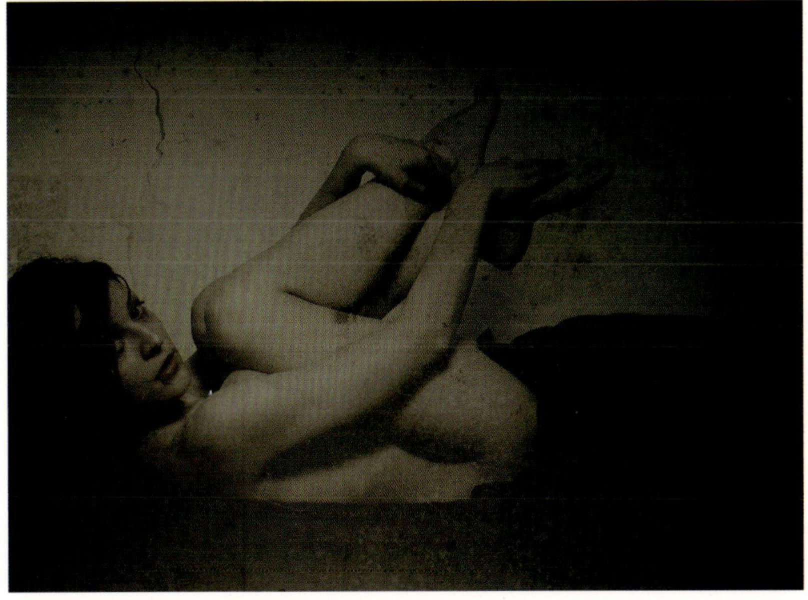

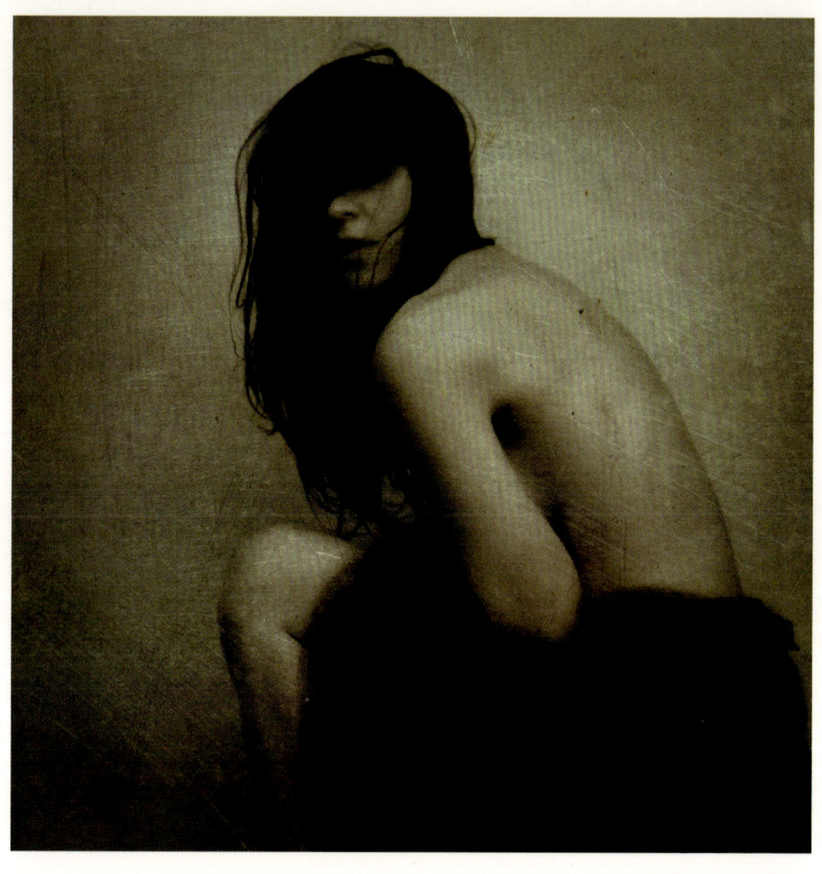

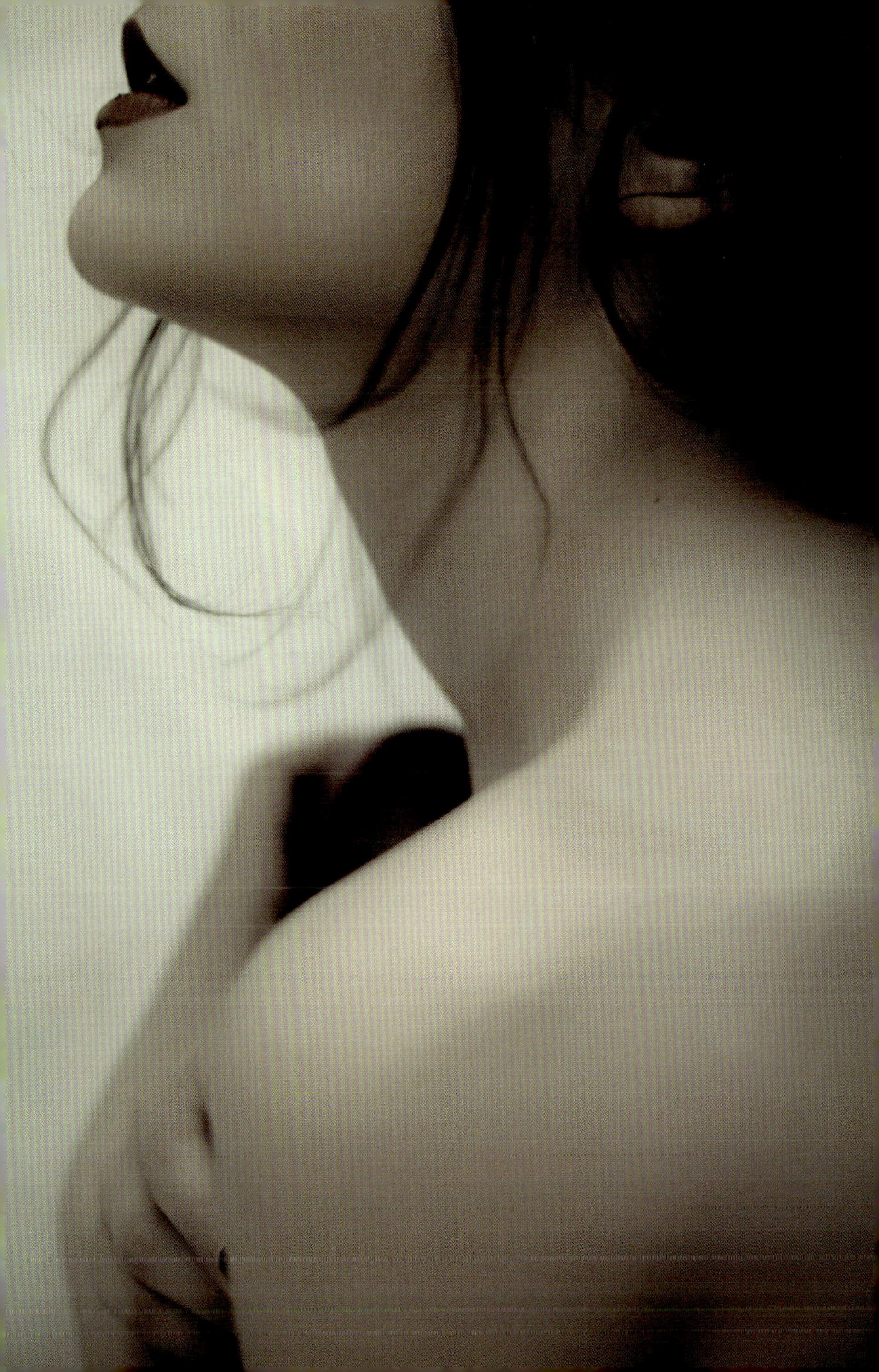

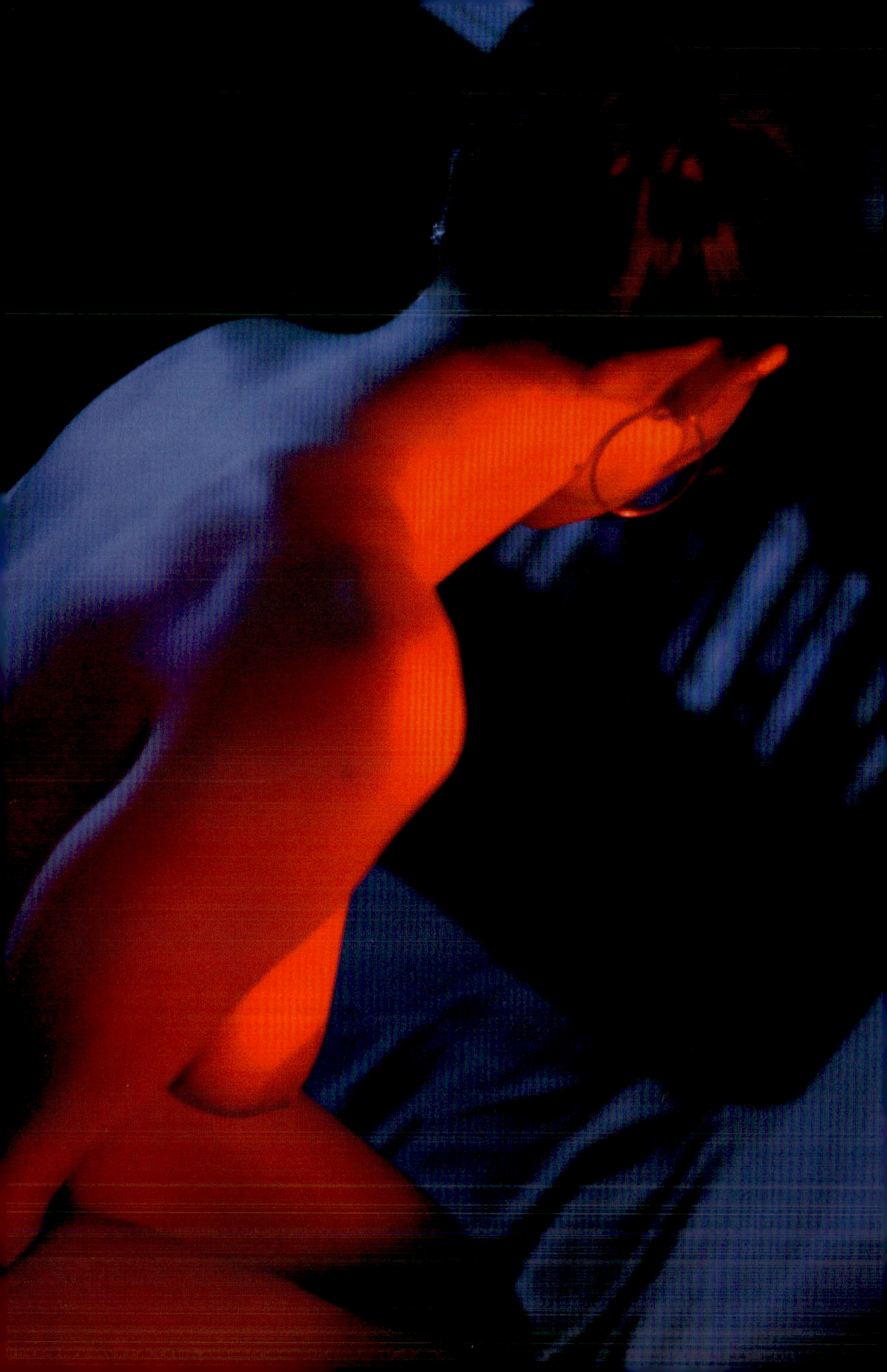

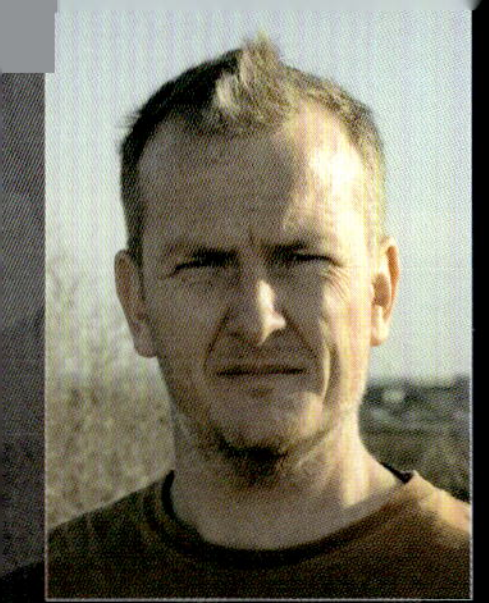

IAN CAUGHT THE PHOTOGRAPHY bug while stationed in Panama with the 82nd Airborne Division; there was a life in the jungle that was so much fun to try and catch on film. On returning to Los Angeles, he took composition and photography lessons while getting a music degree at UCLA. He loves darker pictures and wishes his photography to seem like a memory – not too posed and not too crisp – as we neve remember in sharp vivid pictures, our memorie being, rather, imperfect stylizations of reality.

www.iansouterphotography.com

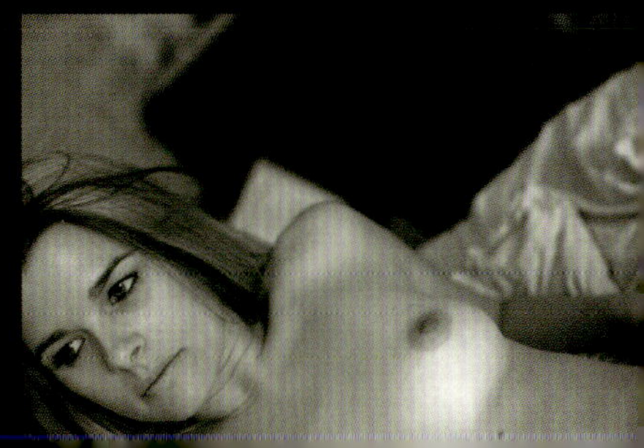

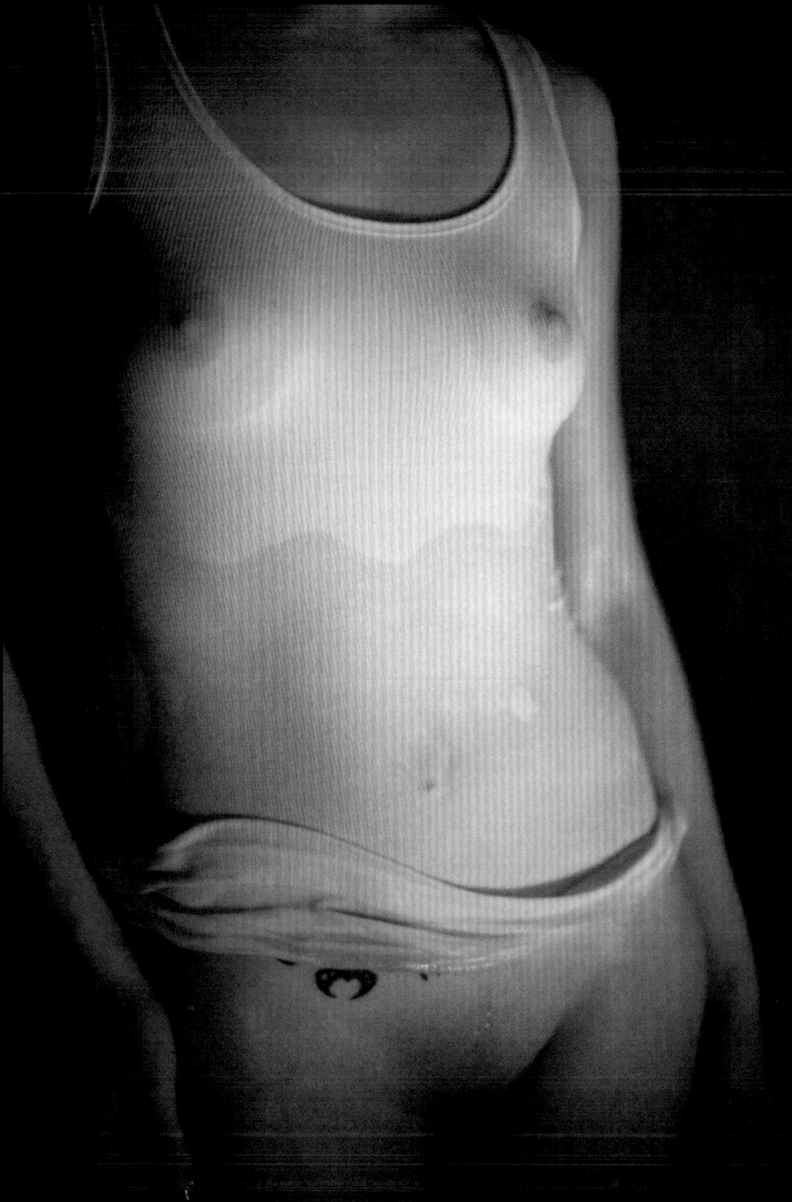

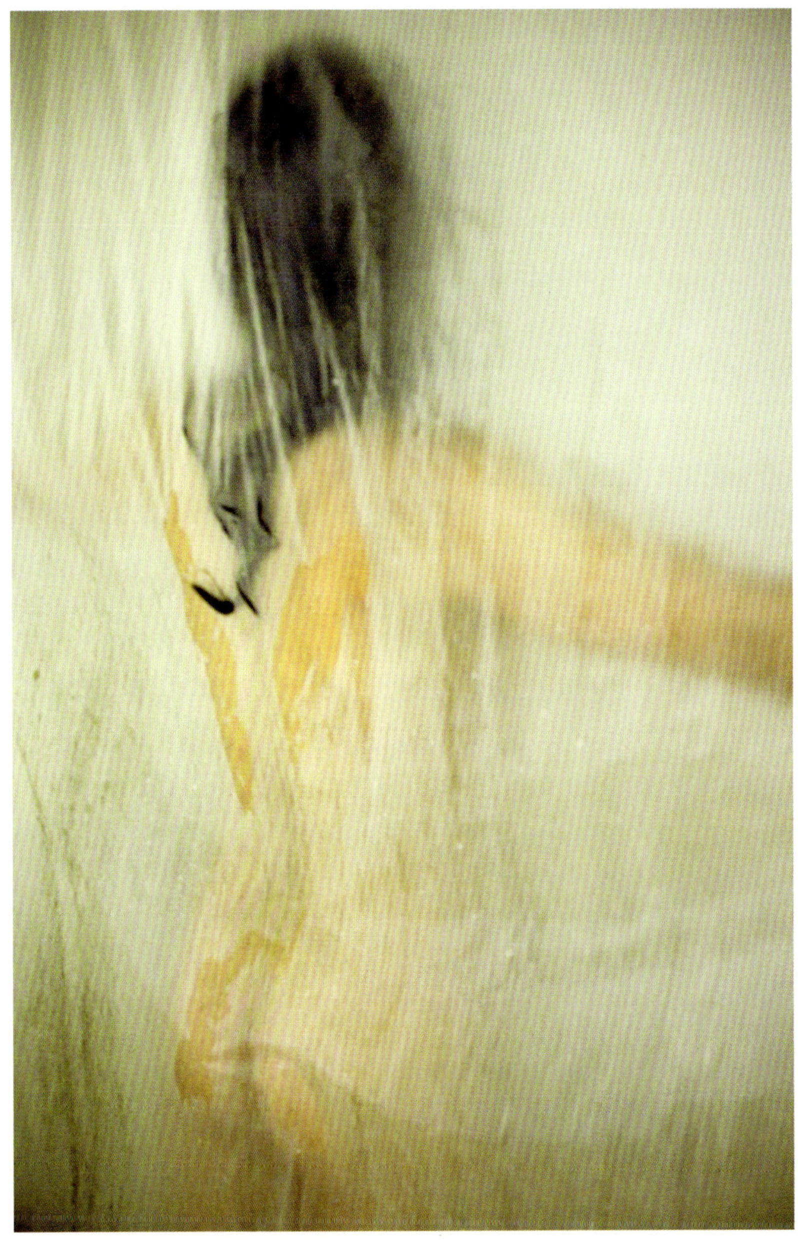

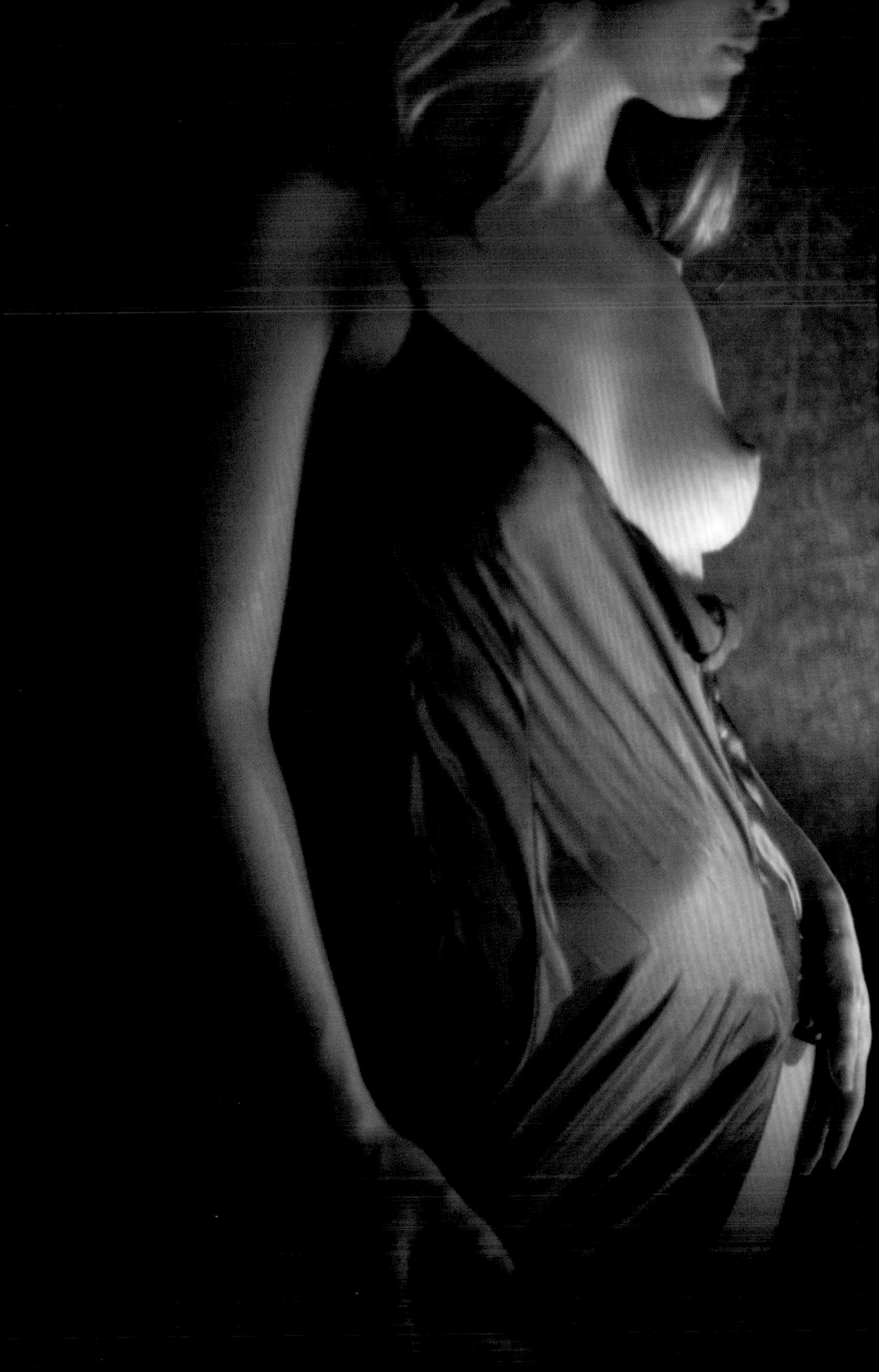

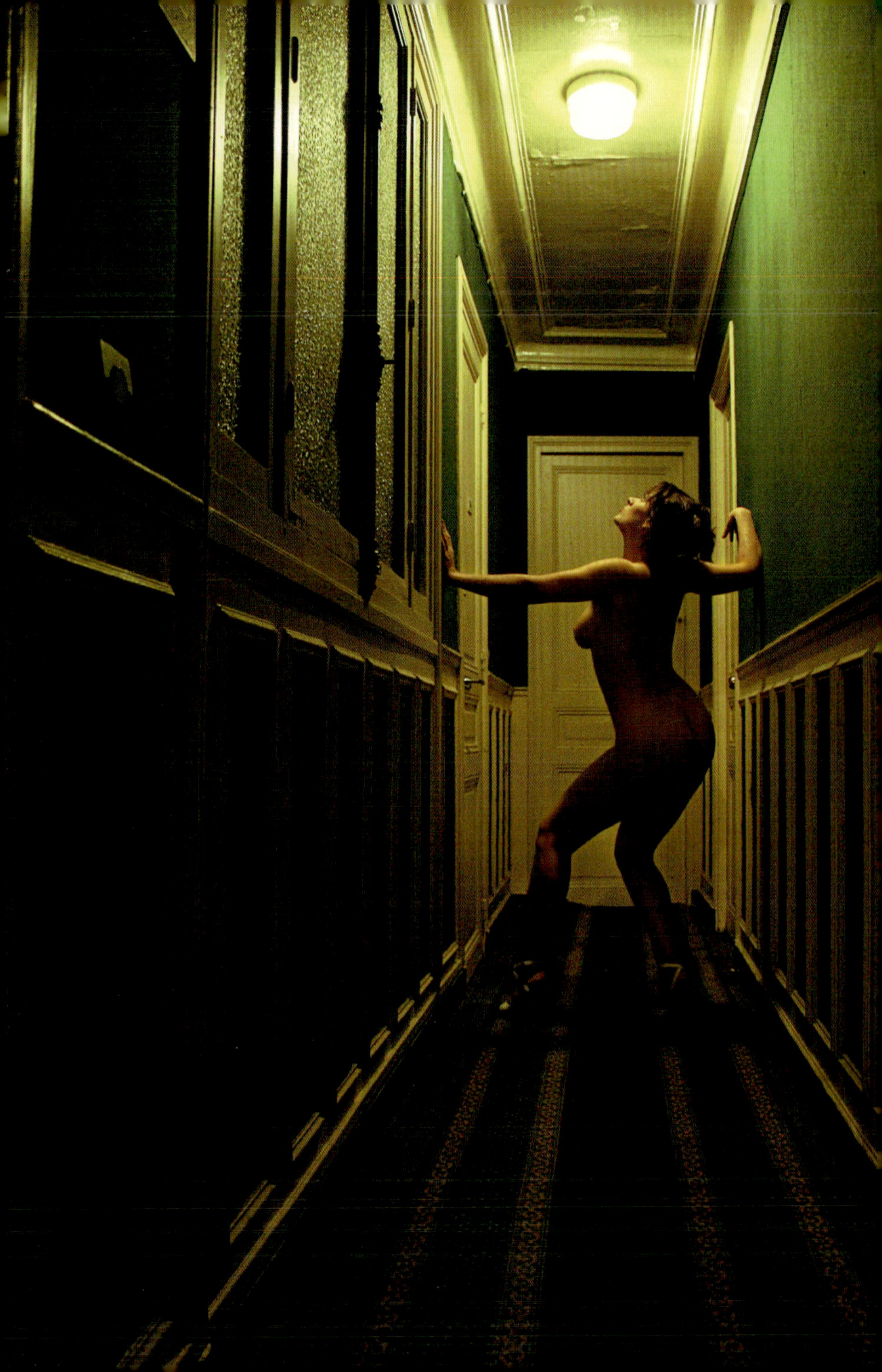

vanda spengler

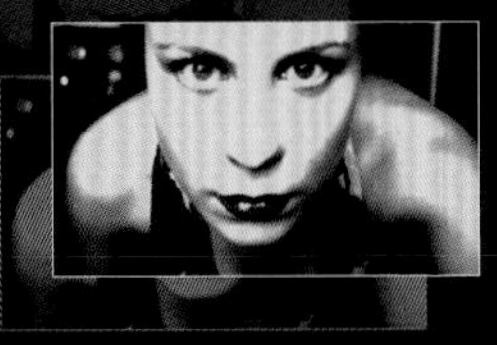

VANDA IS THE LATEST in a prestigious Franco-Swiss family of writers, artists and publishers. She is self-taught and began taking photographs in 2000 in an attempt to express her inner fears and thoughts through a number of nude self-portraits. Soon, friends and casual acquaintances came on board and she has never used professional models. Her photography reflects her state of mind, and her passion for science fiction and imaginary worlds. She is also a folk singer.

http://vanda.spengler.free.fr

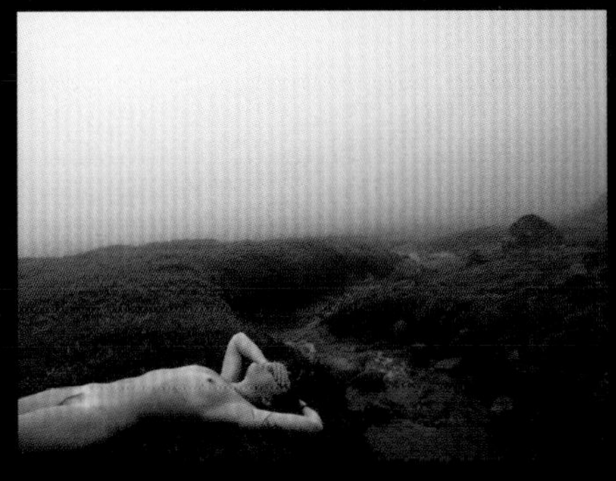

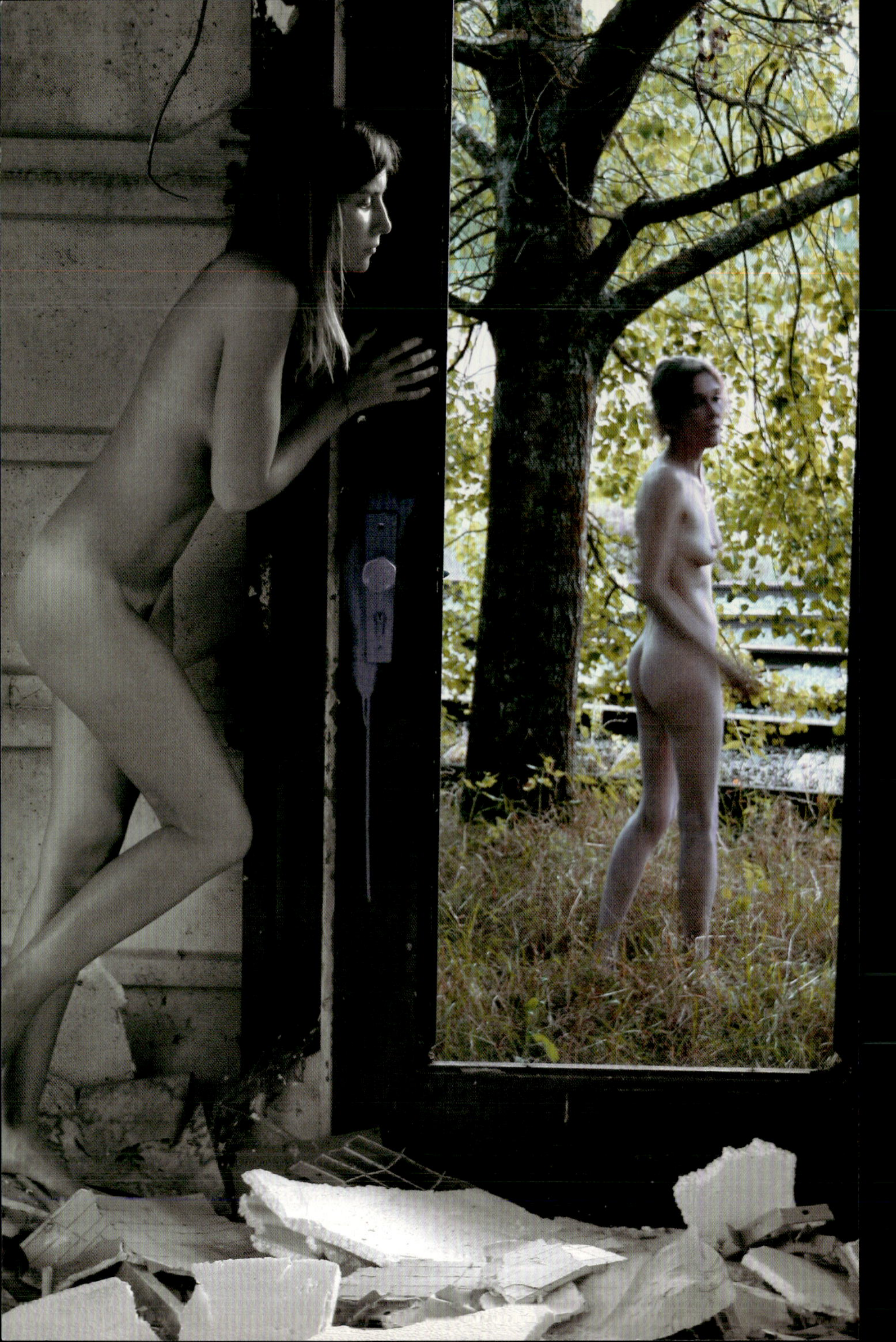

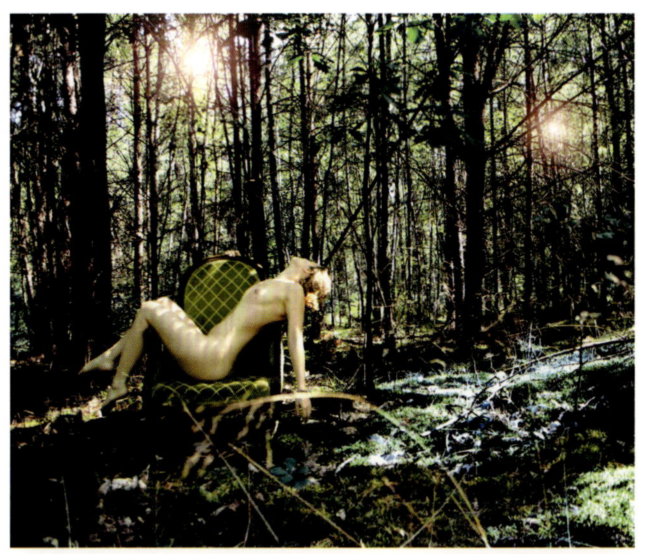

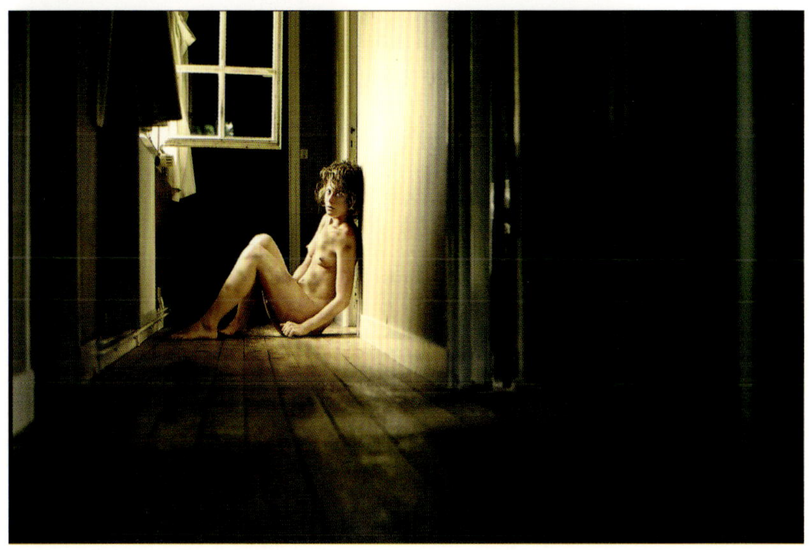

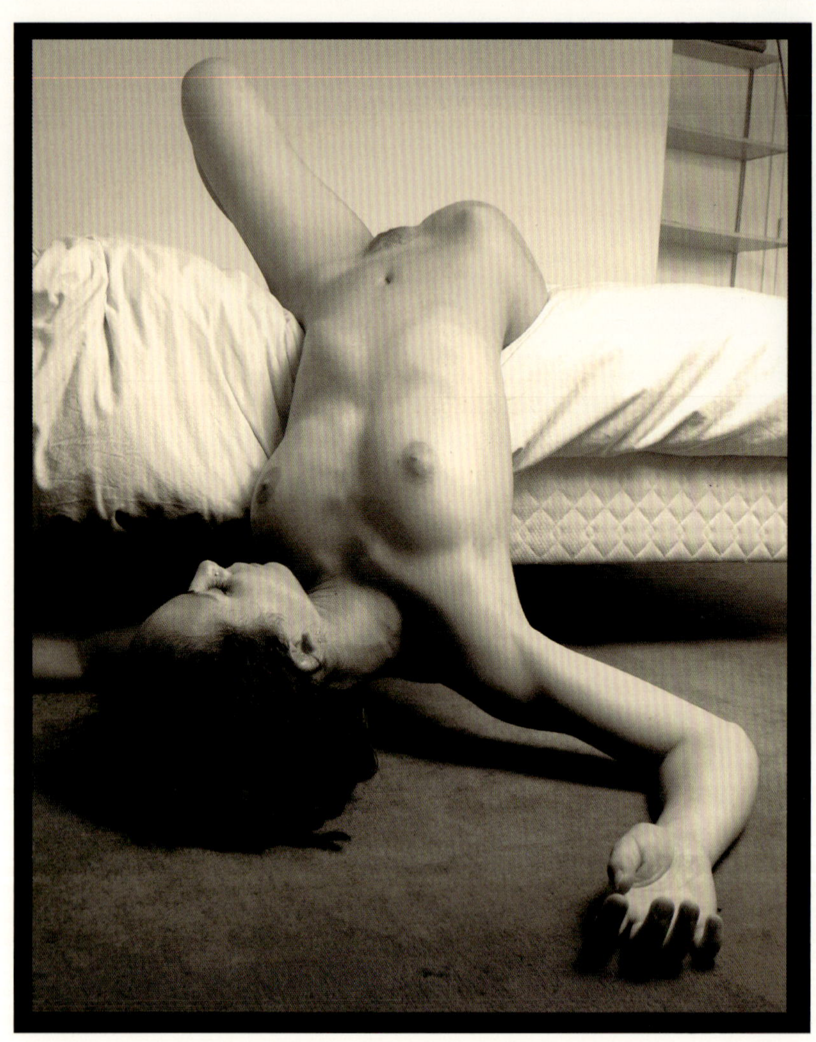

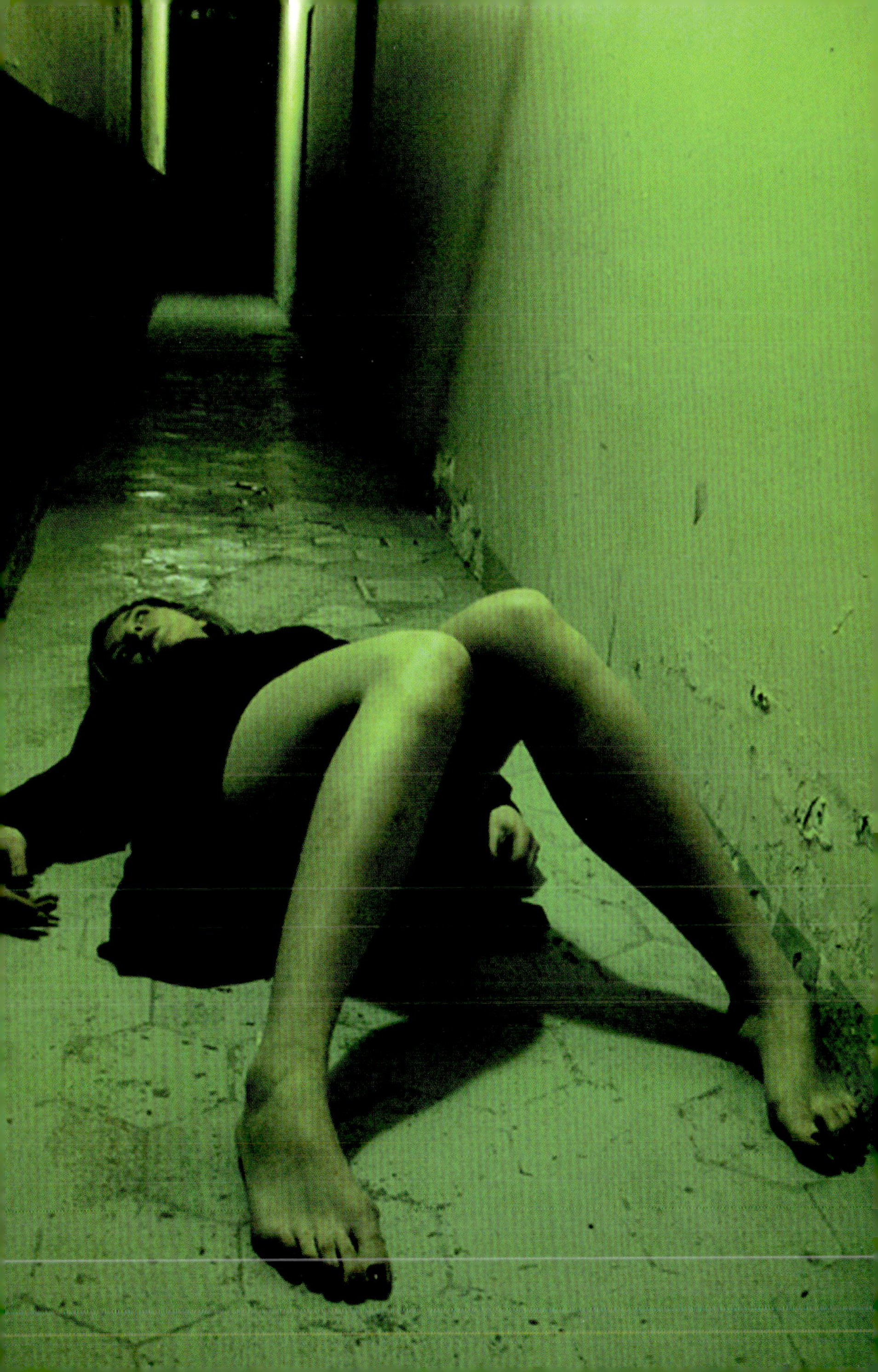

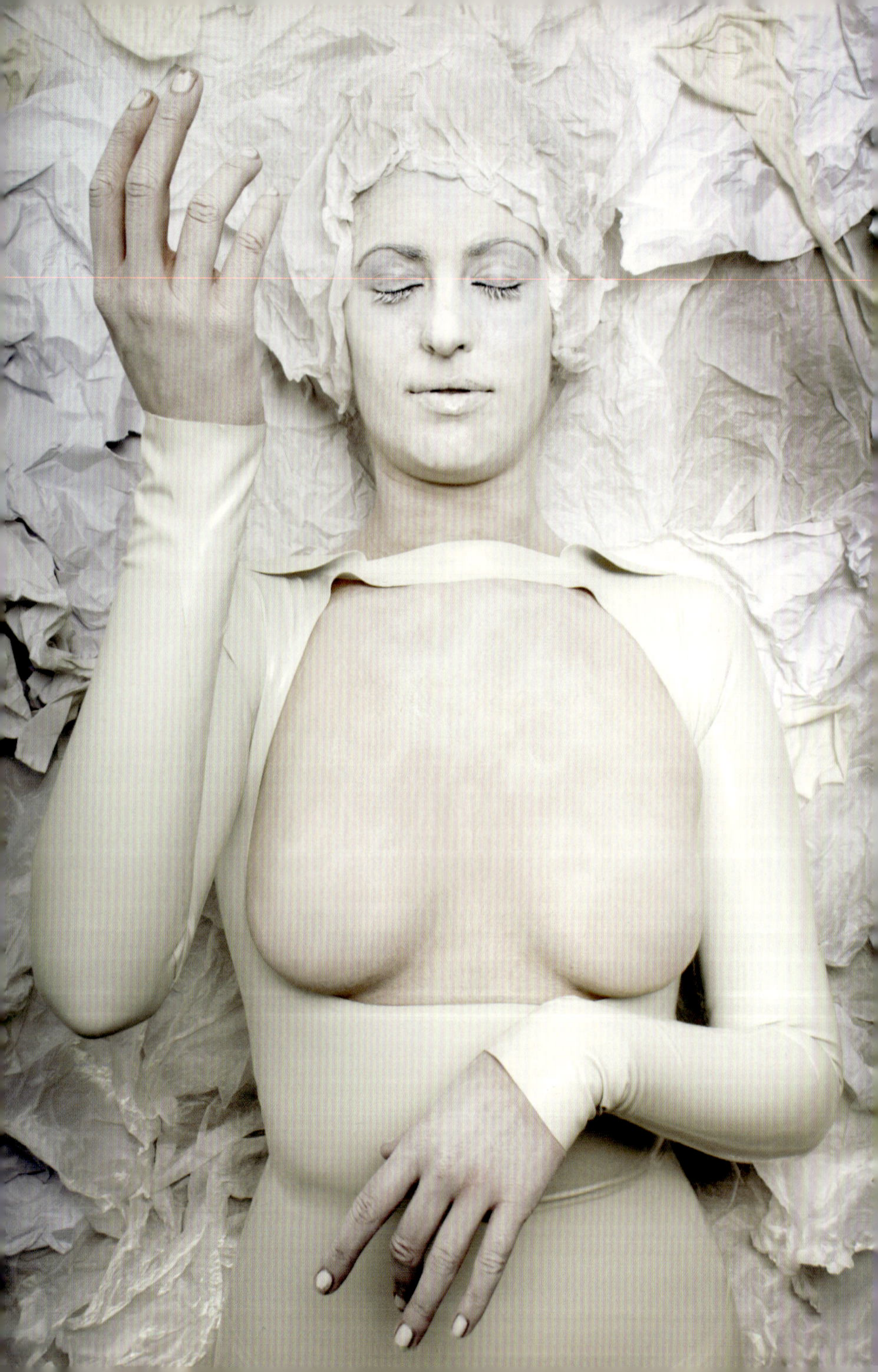

julischka stengele

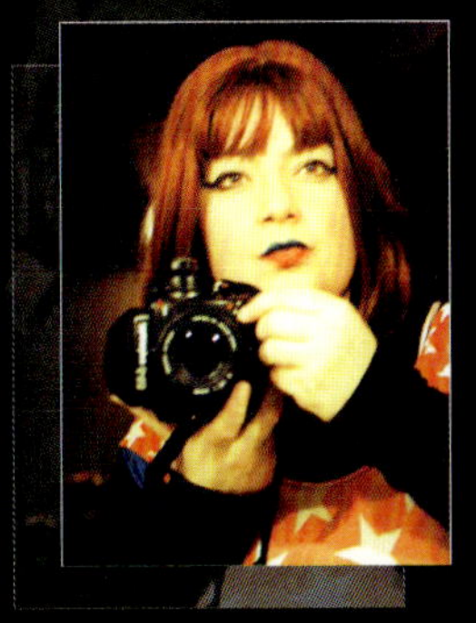

JULISCHKA IS A BERLIN-BASED photographer, performance artist and life model born in 1982. In her work, the body is clearly the centre of attention; she focuses on aspects of femininity, physicality, sexuality, interpersonal relations and social structures: 'A body is immediate and so is communicating through it. And communication is basically all I want.'

www.julischka.eu

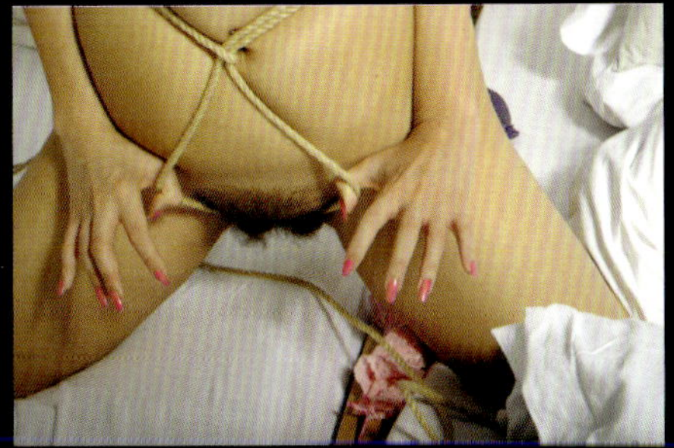

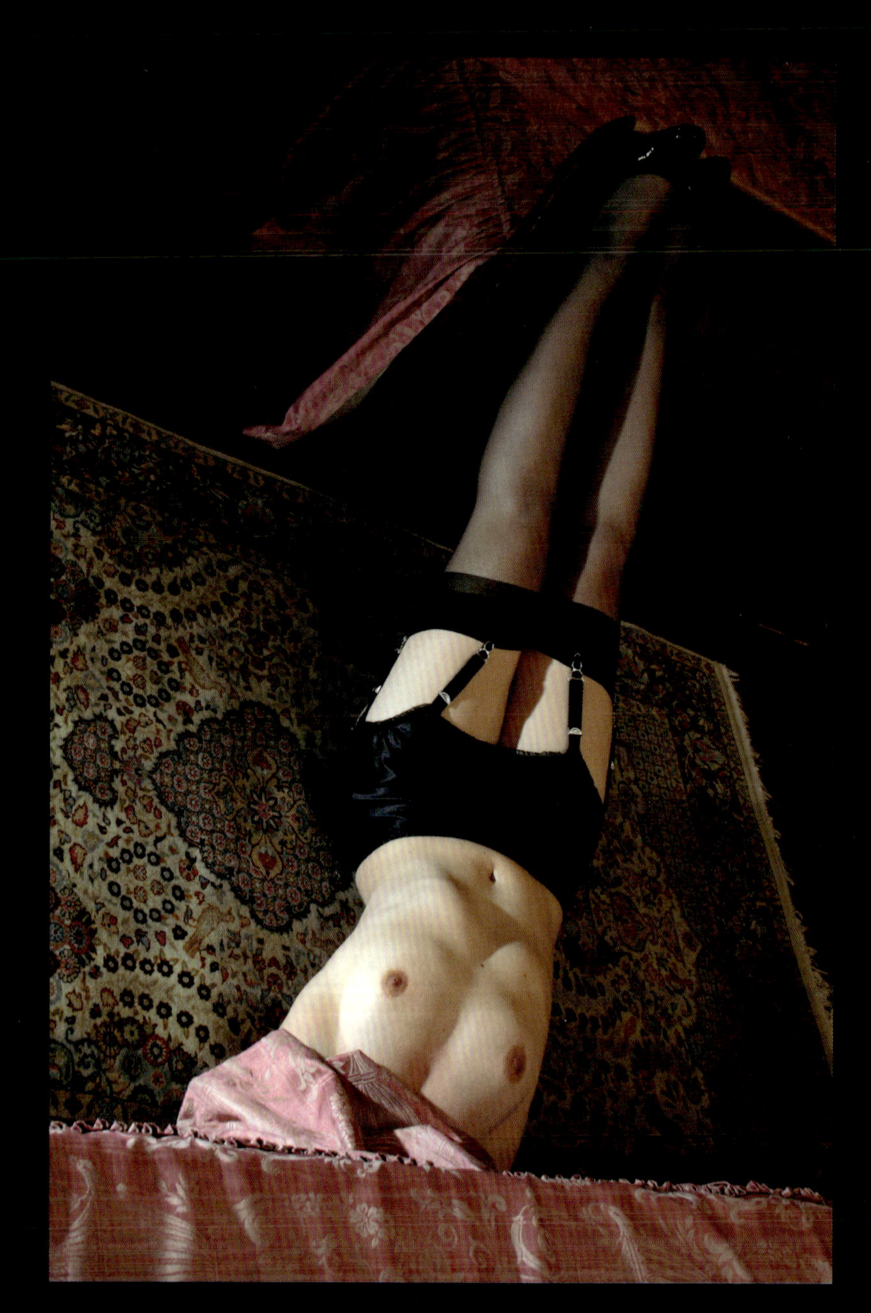

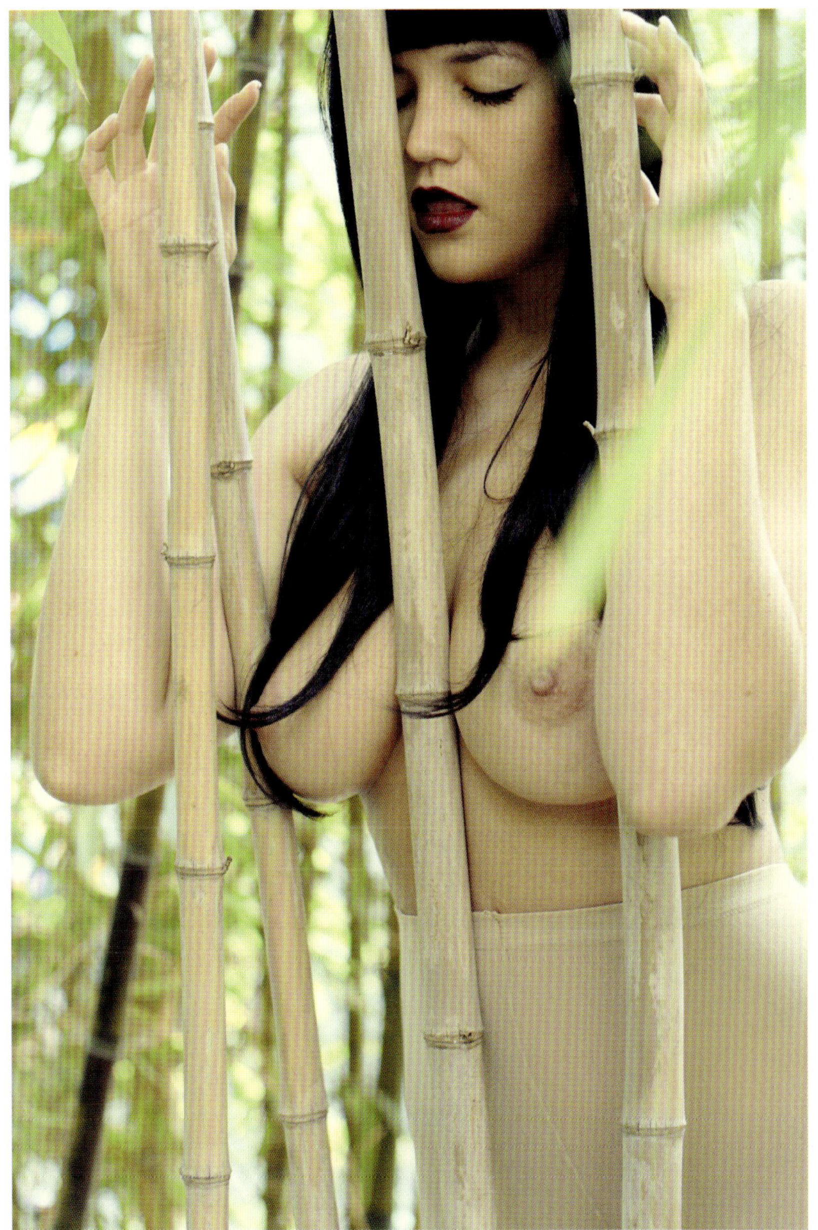

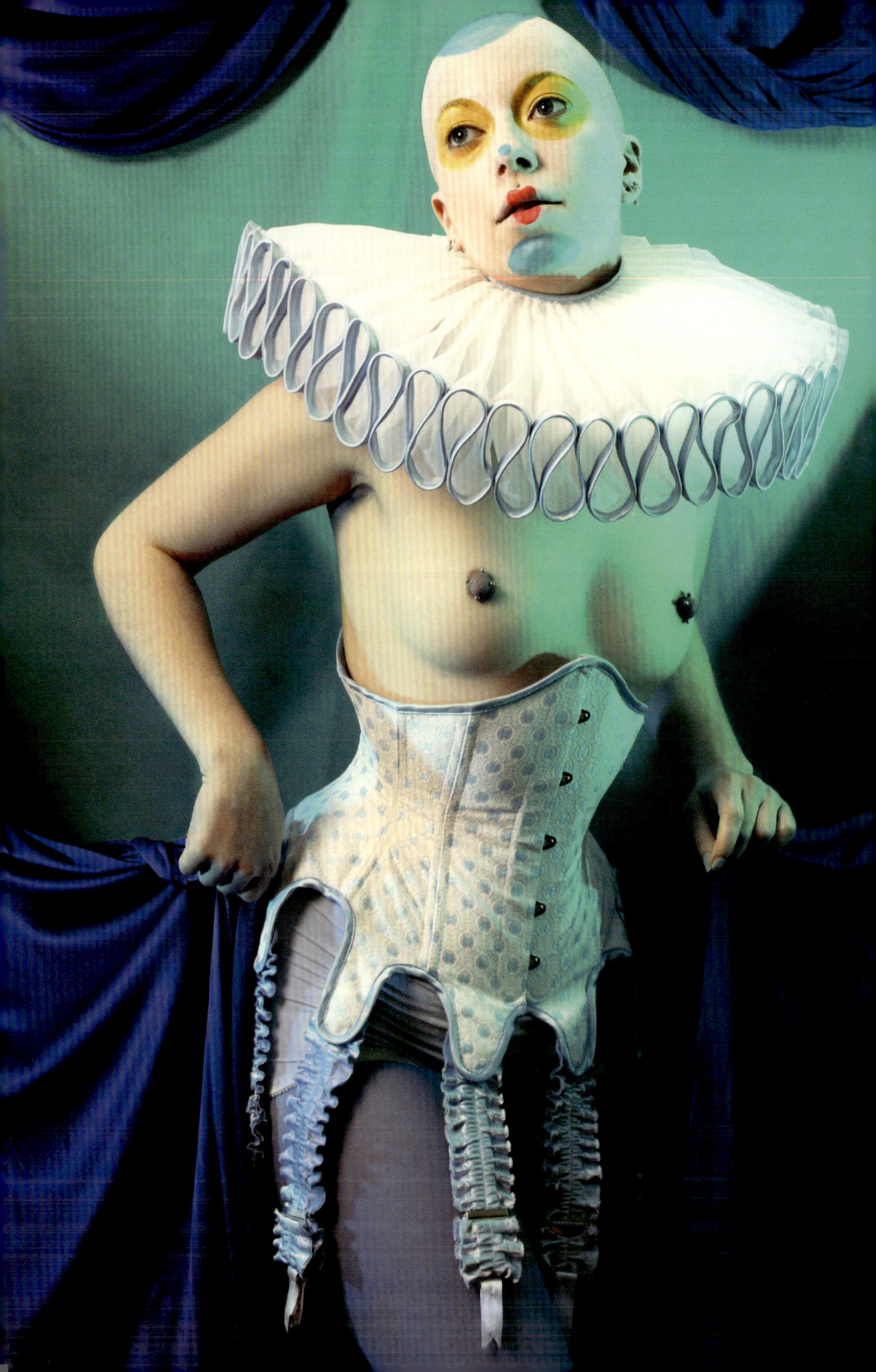

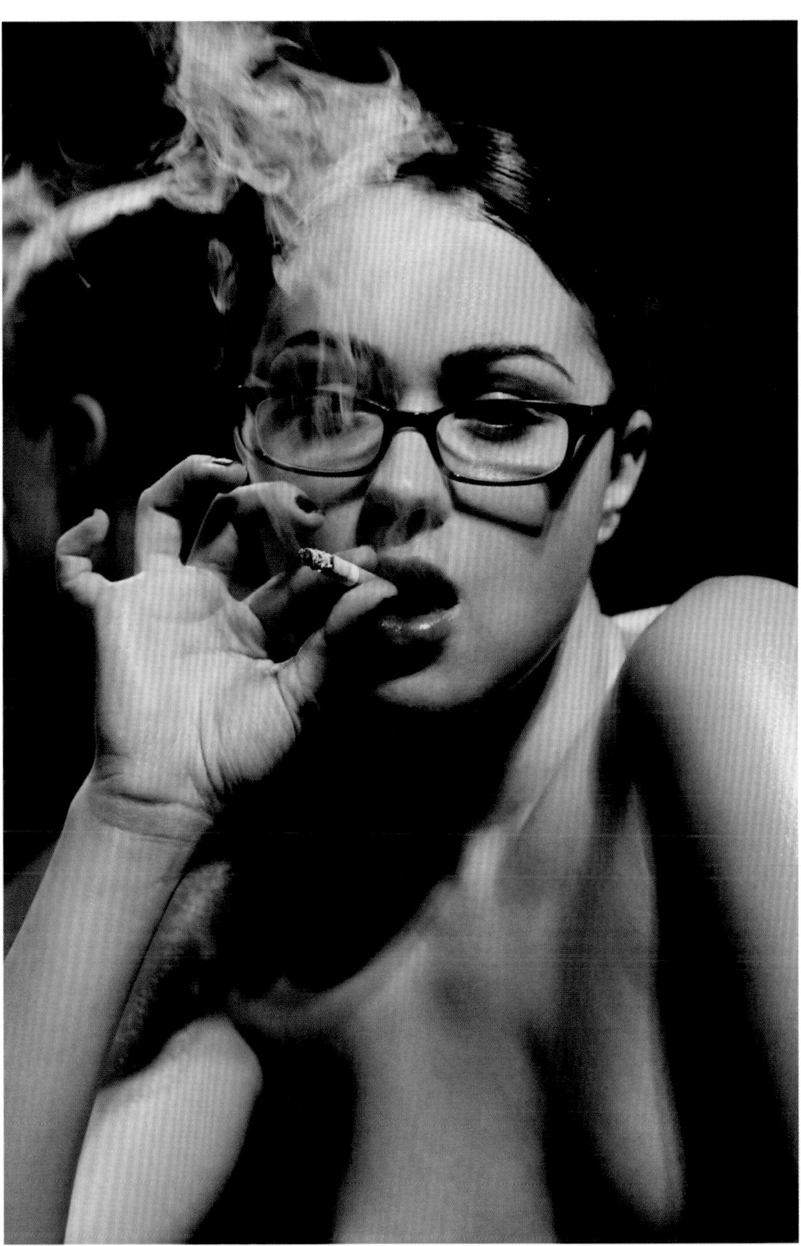

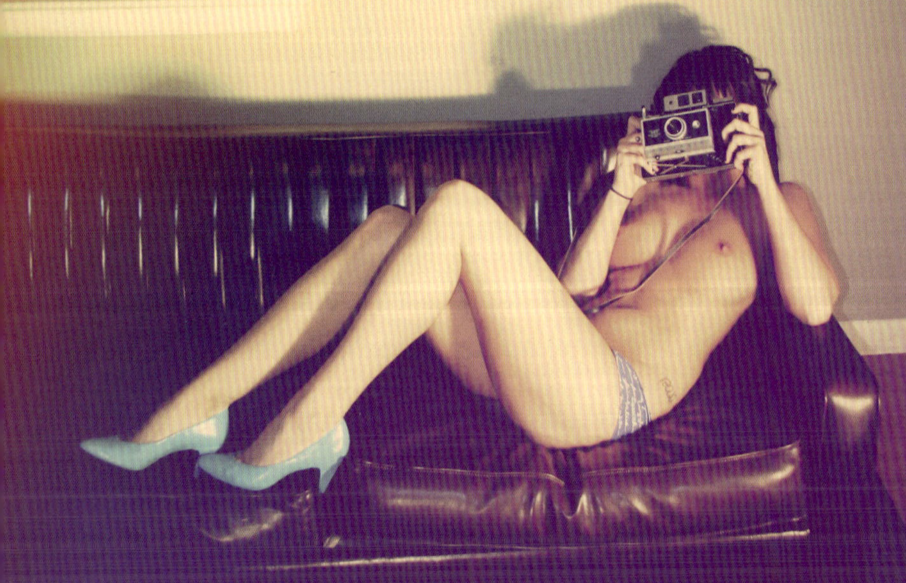
DO
NOT
ENTER

rebecca tillett

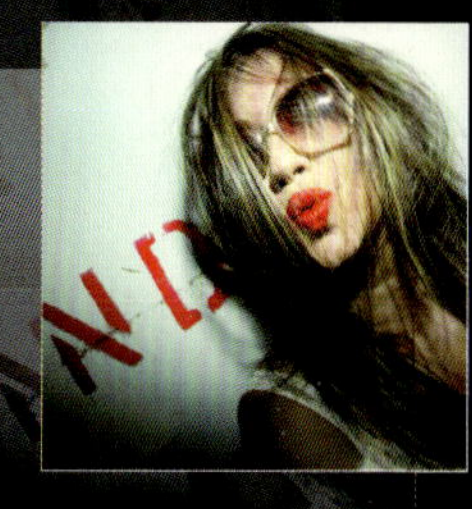

REBECCA IS A GRAPHIC DESIGNER currently residing in Colorado. She has considered photography a serious hobby for more than ten years and has been widely published and exhibited across the US, and been part of shows in Italy and the UK. Considered a highly accomplished, if quirky, photographer, she looks for subjects who are confident and experimental, in a bid to bring something new to the table.

www.rtillett.com

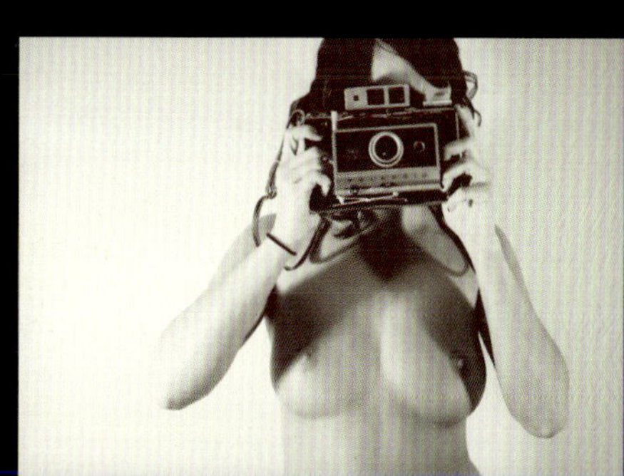

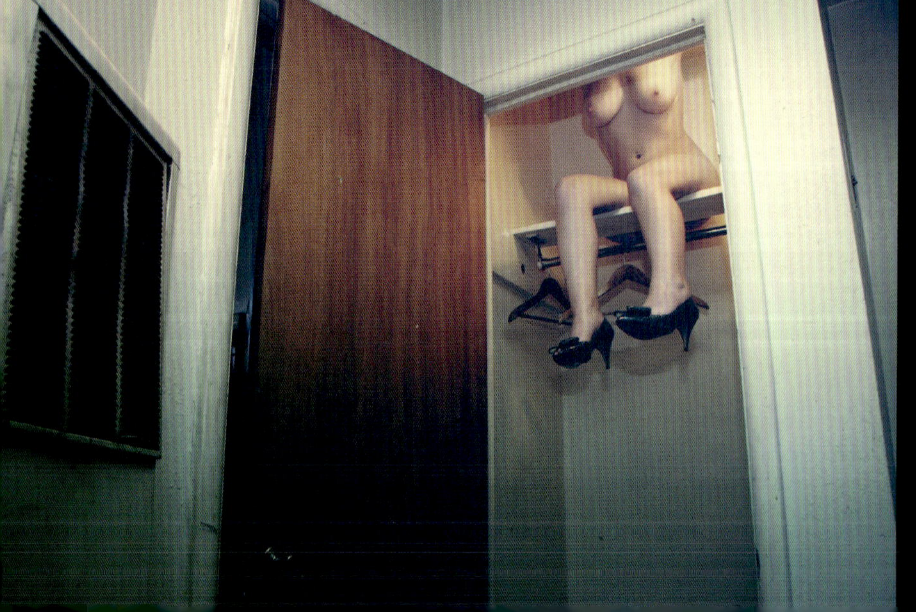

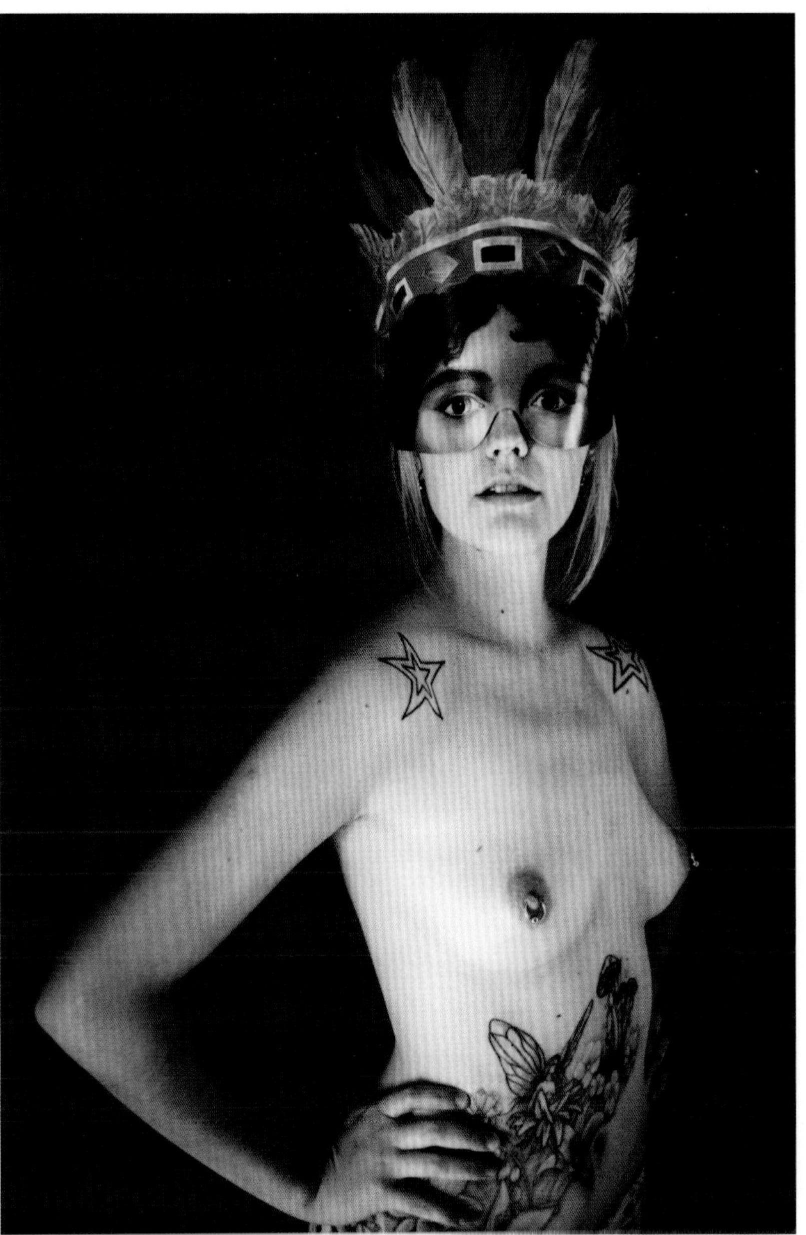

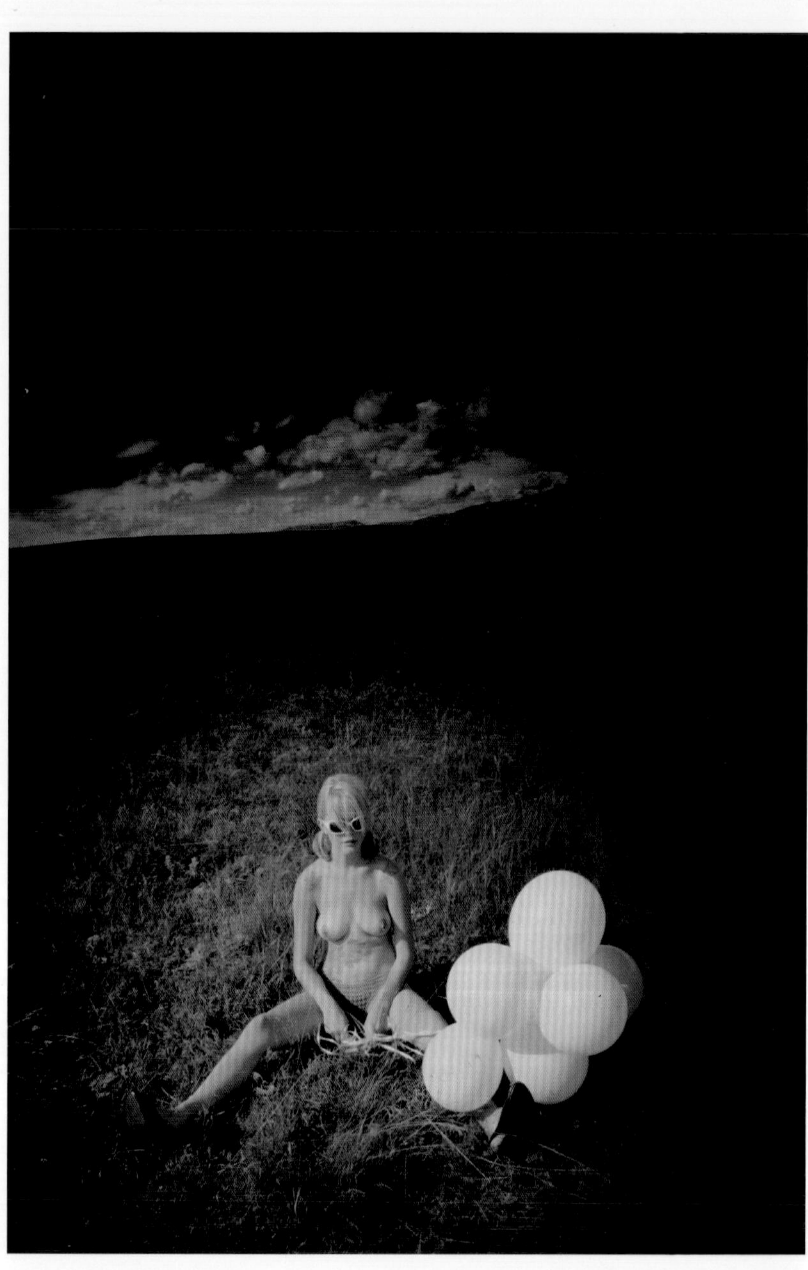

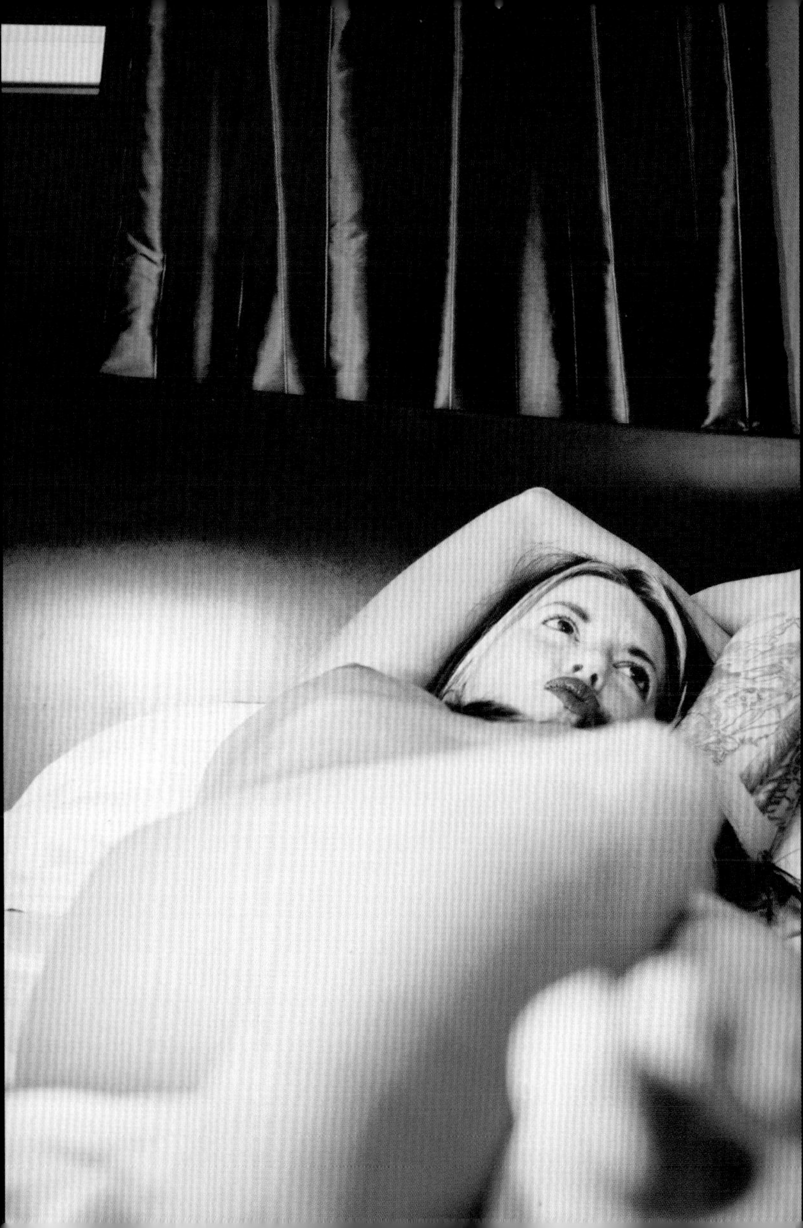

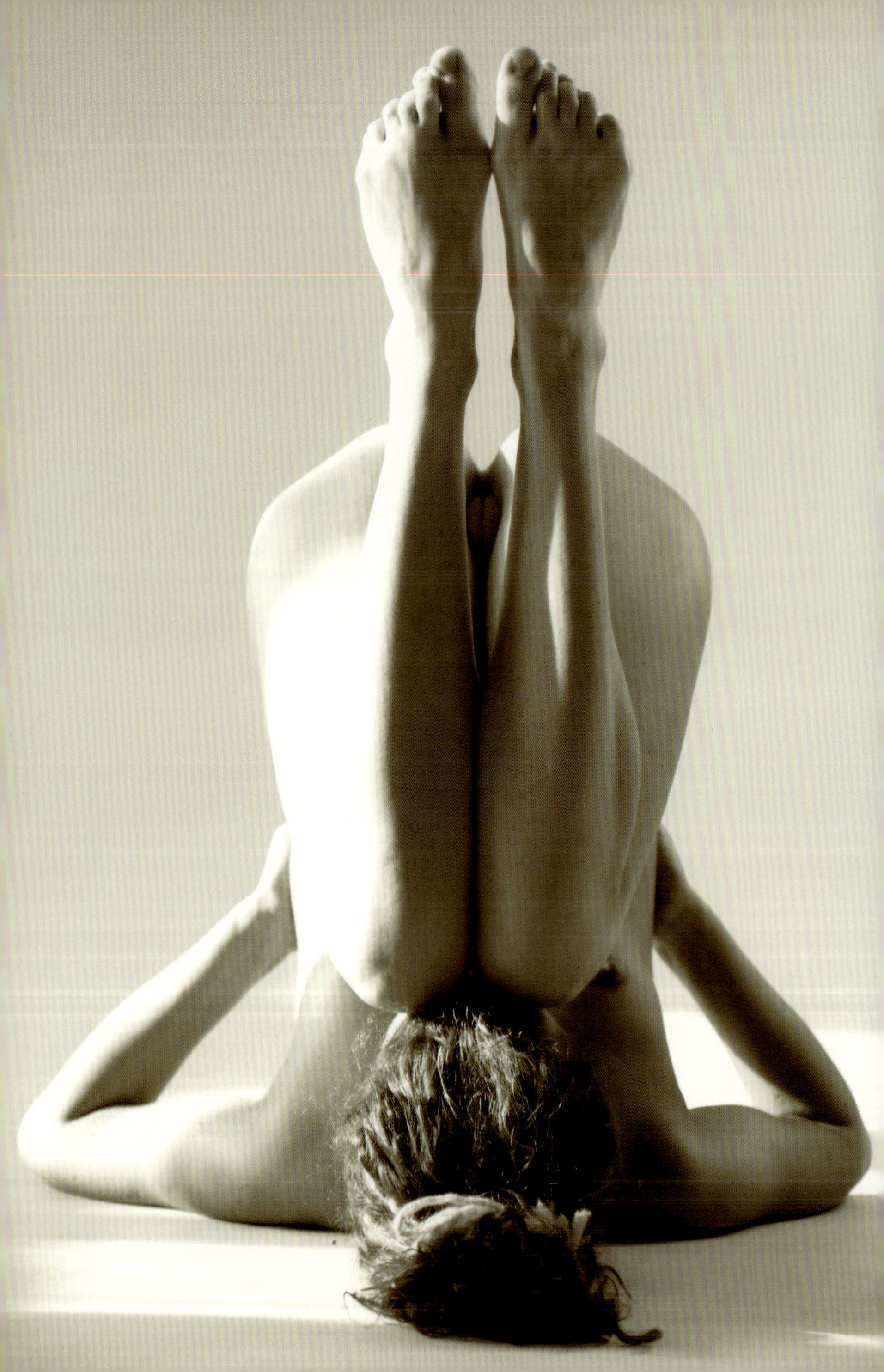

anton volkov

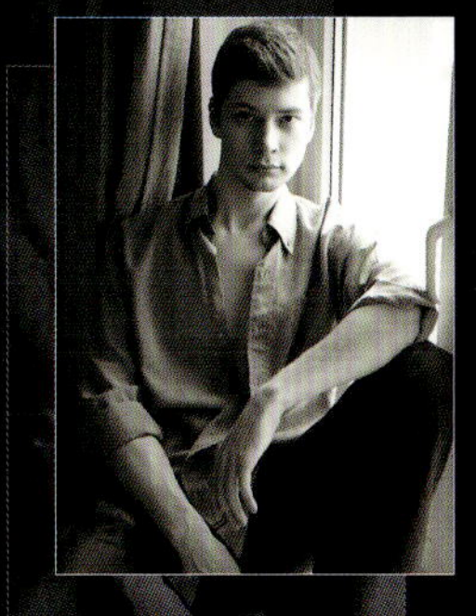

ANTON WAS BORN IN 1978 in Moscow, Russia. He graduated in 2000 and became a photographer the following year. He has always been fascinated in communicating true beauty to viewers. He has a preference for models who are also ordinary people who you could come across on the street.

www.antonvolkov.ru

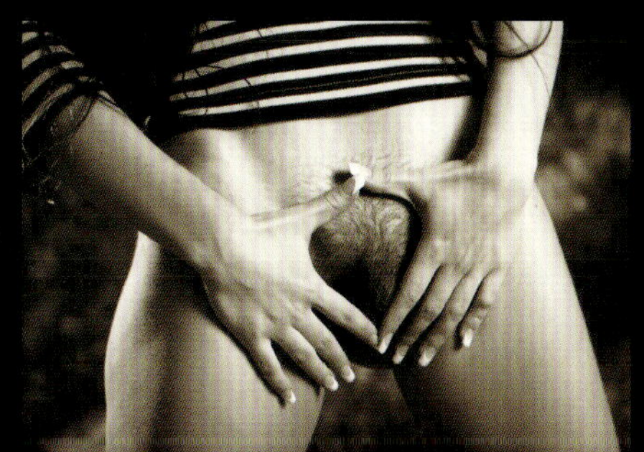

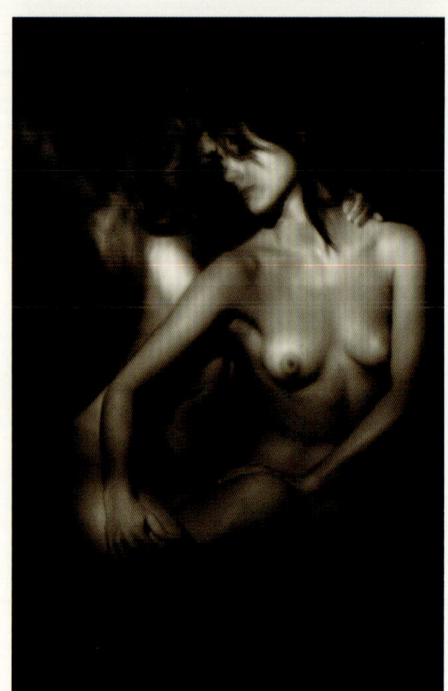

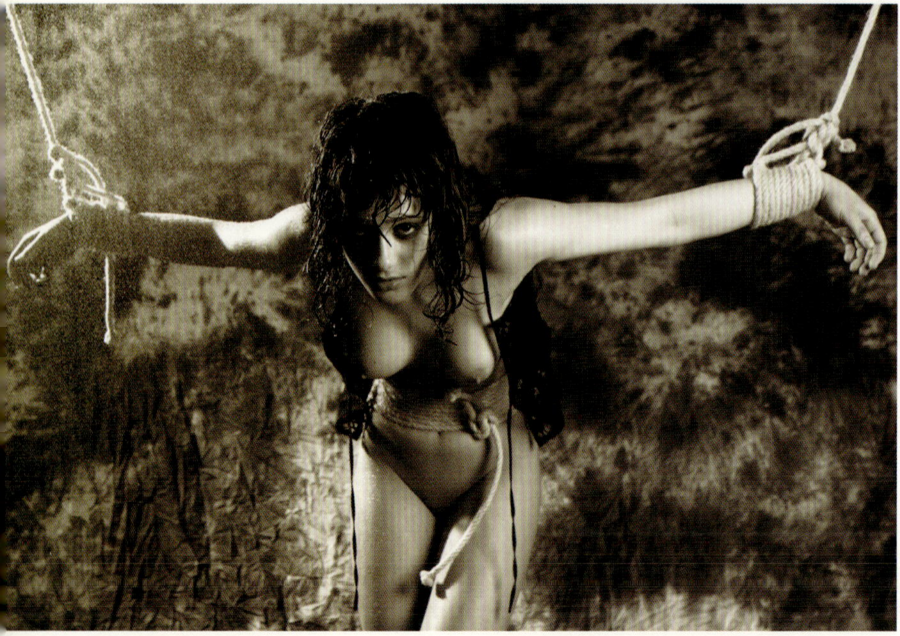

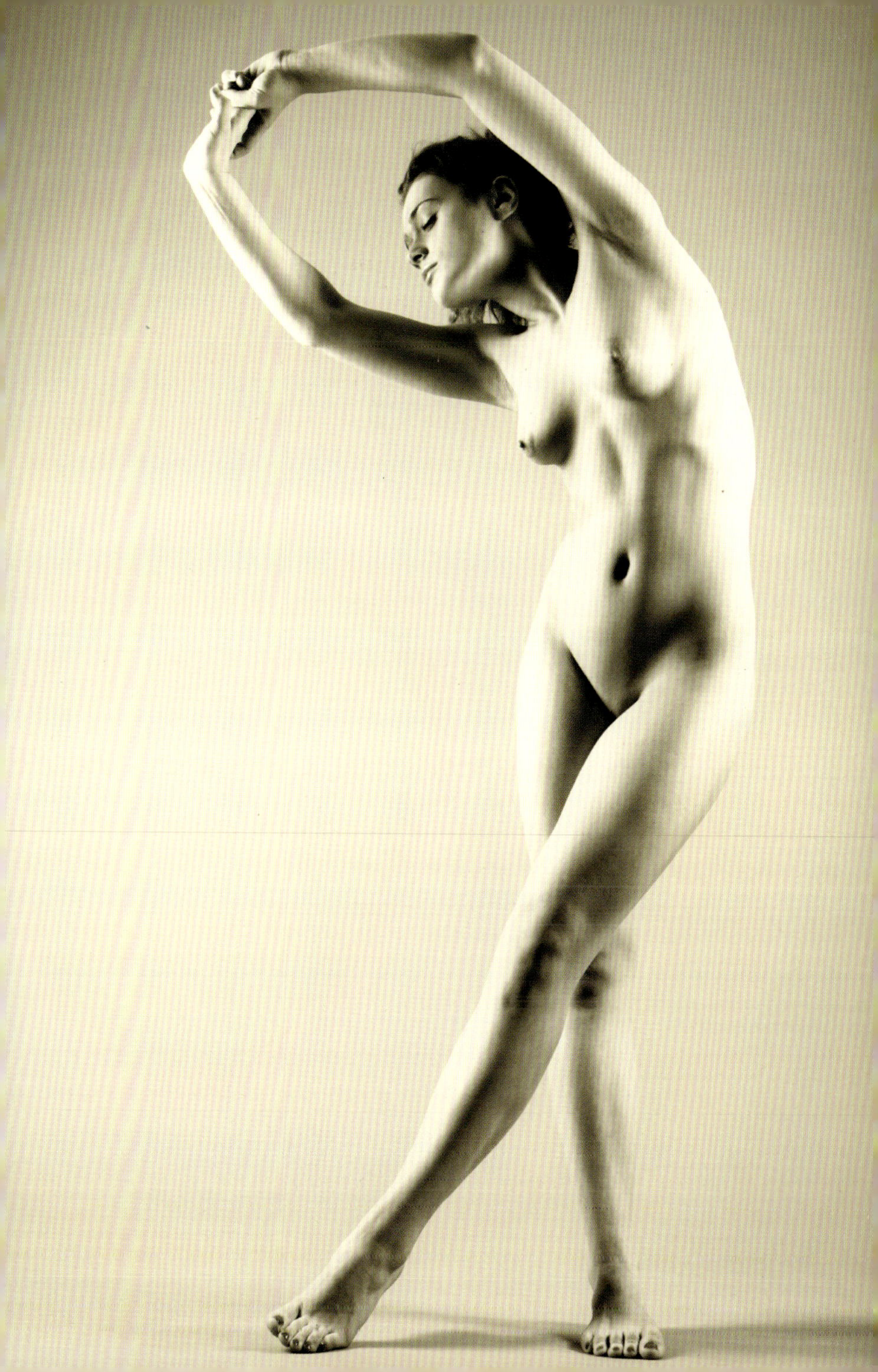

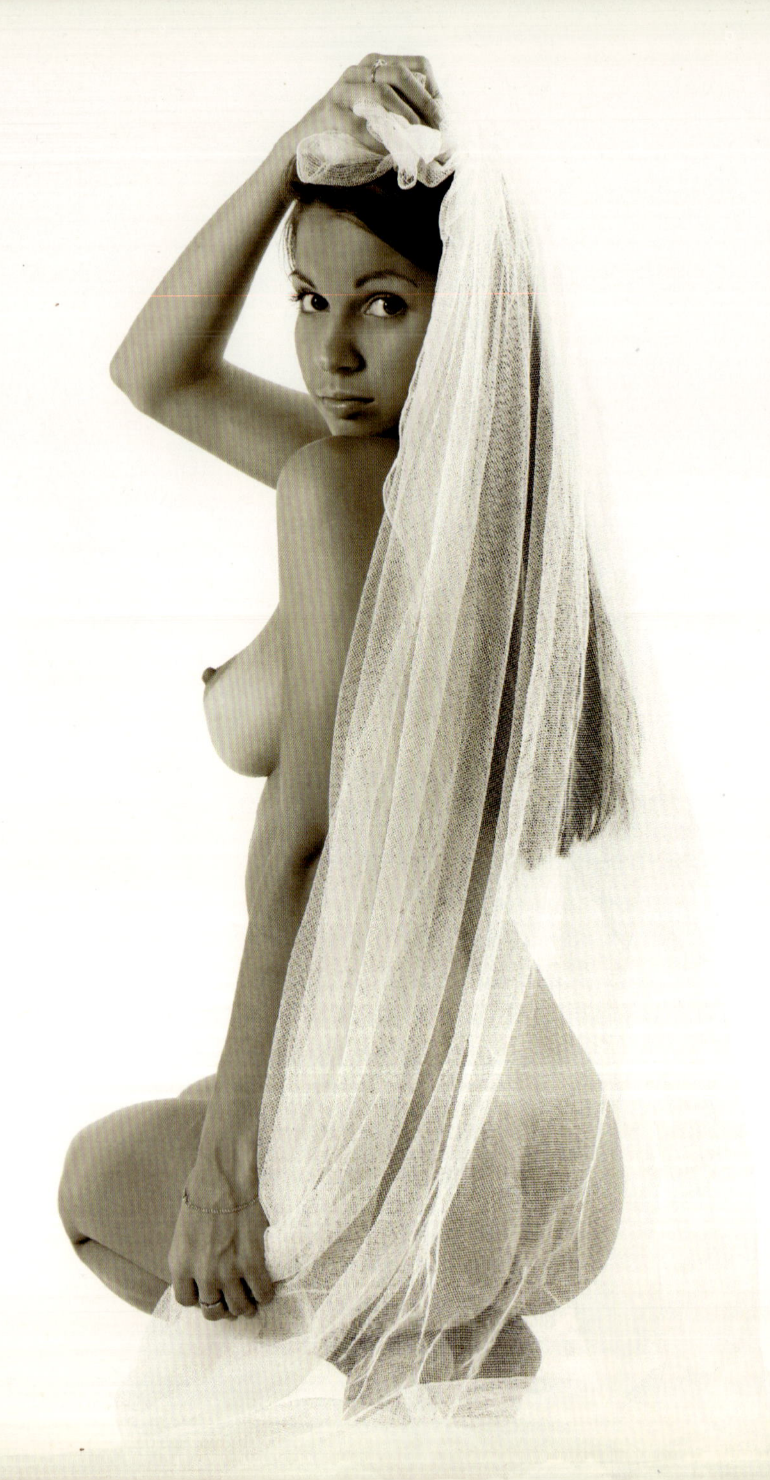

ANTON VOL

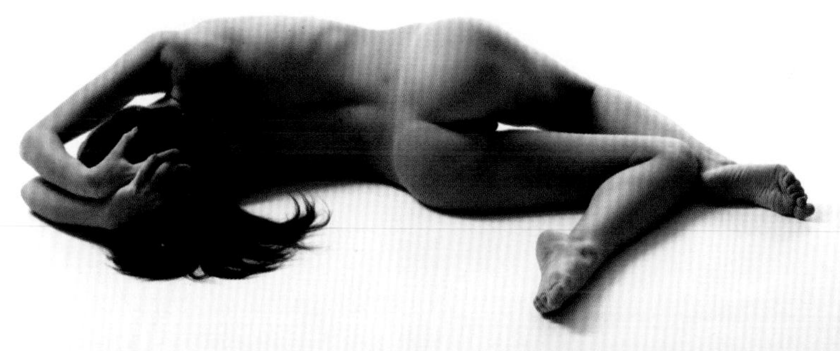

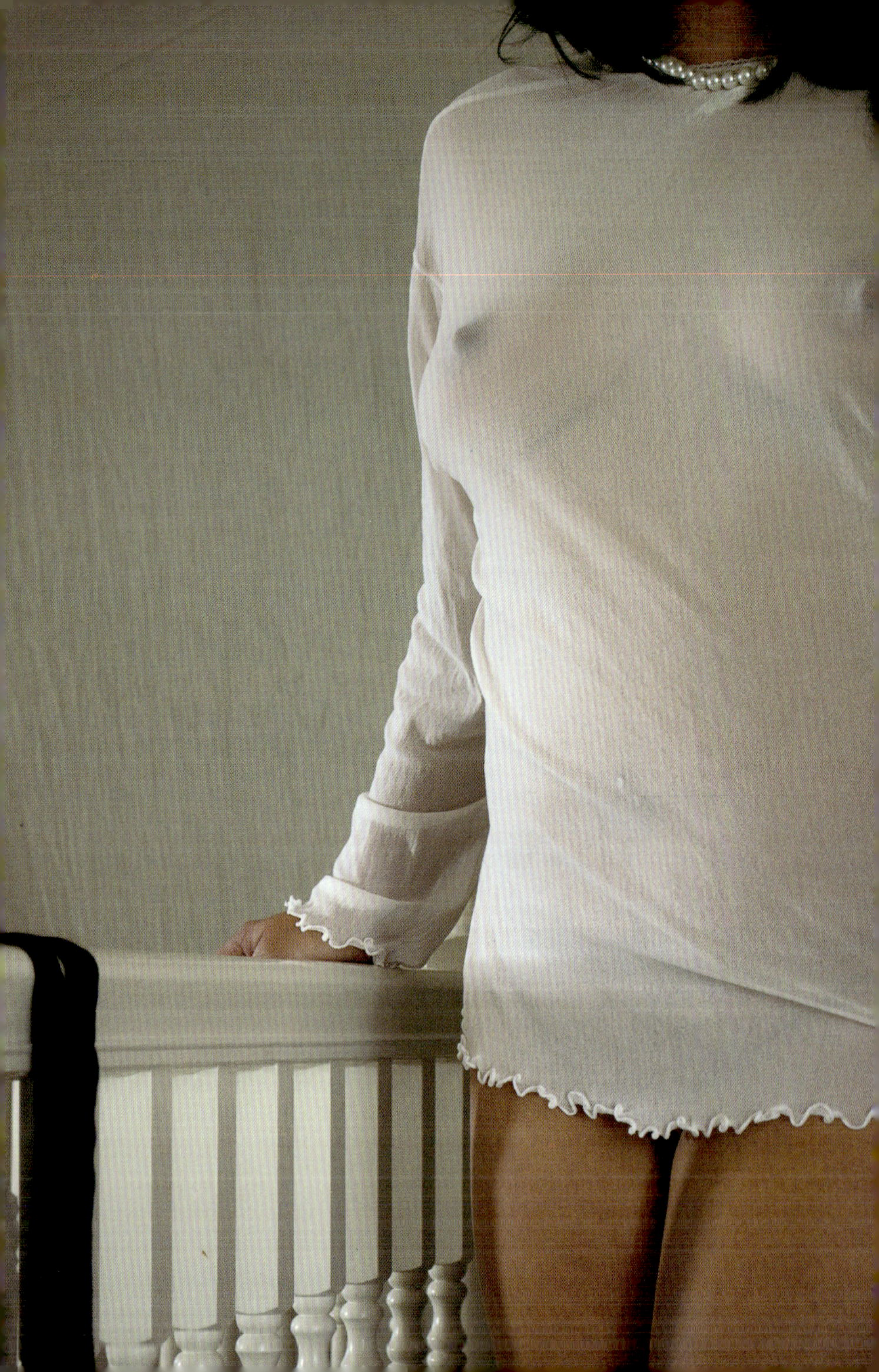

katerina vonwize

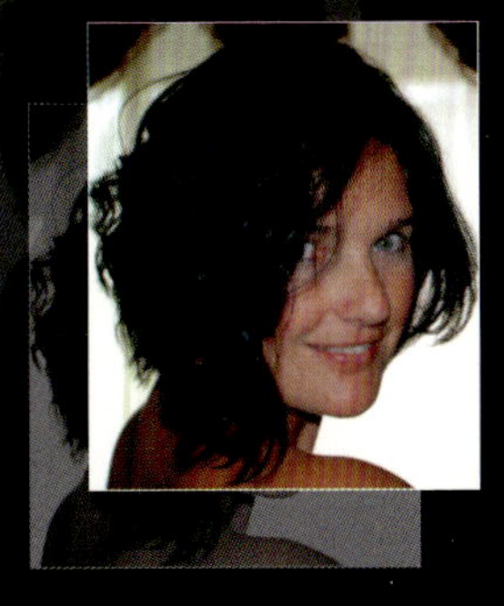

NAÏVE TO SAY THE LEAST, this suburban mother of three, and black sheep of the soccer moms, transformed at night into her alter ego, Katerina VonWize, which she created after the end of a bitter and abusive marriage and subsequently brutal divorce. Created solely under cover of darkness, these photos became her secret from the world. With her inhibitions checked at the bedroom door and the courage created by her fierce new persona, she transformed into a goddess creating erotic, stylish and imaginative images. After discovering the first edition of the *Mammoth Book of Erotic Photography* she learned others had an appreciation for this type of art and couldn't wait to share her photos with the world.

www.katerinavonwize.com

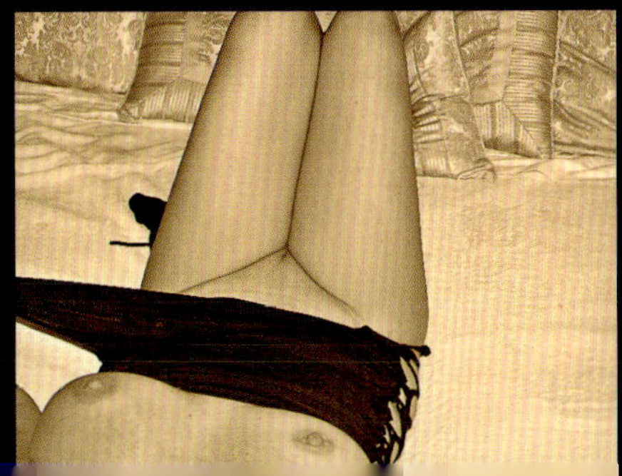

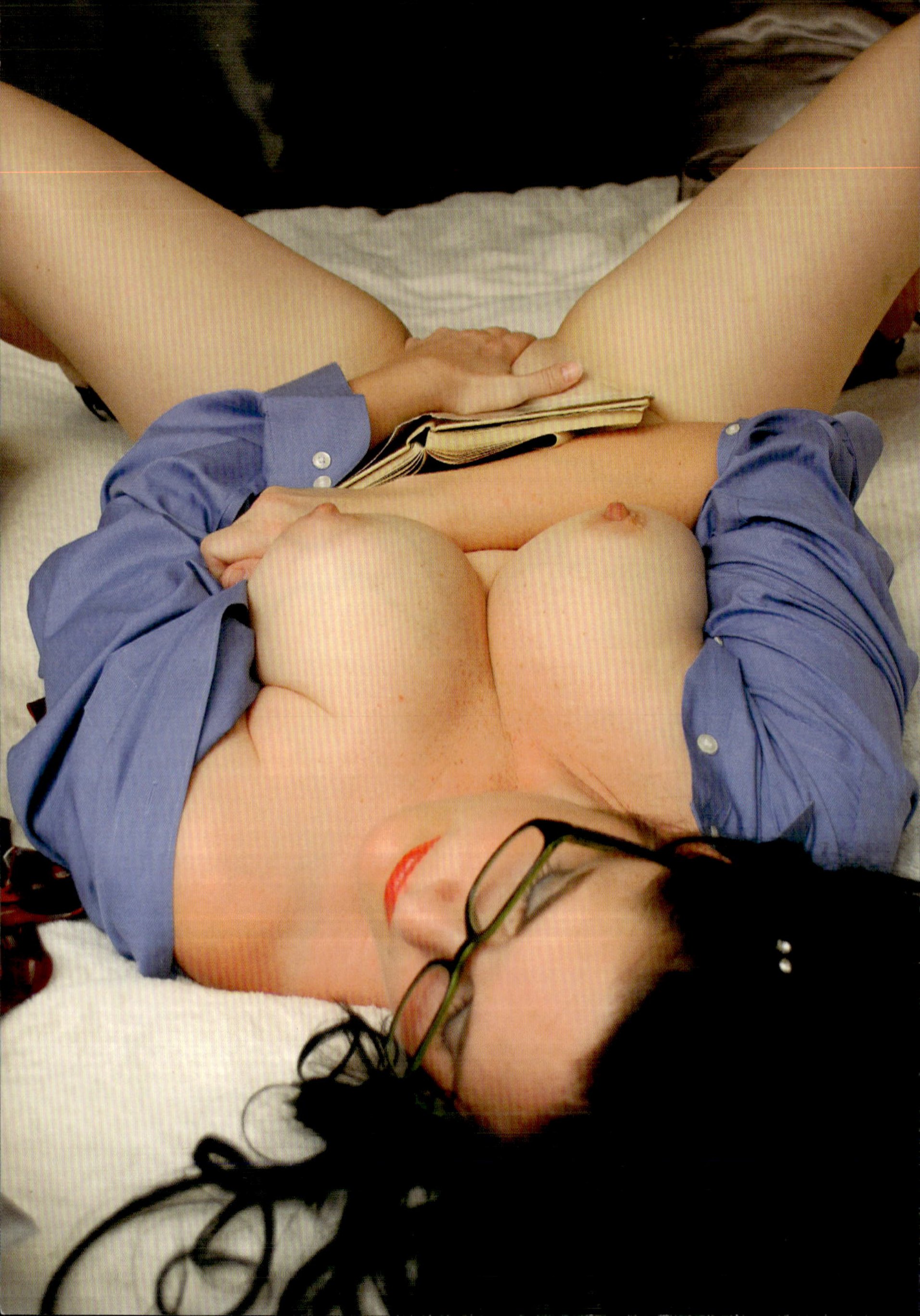

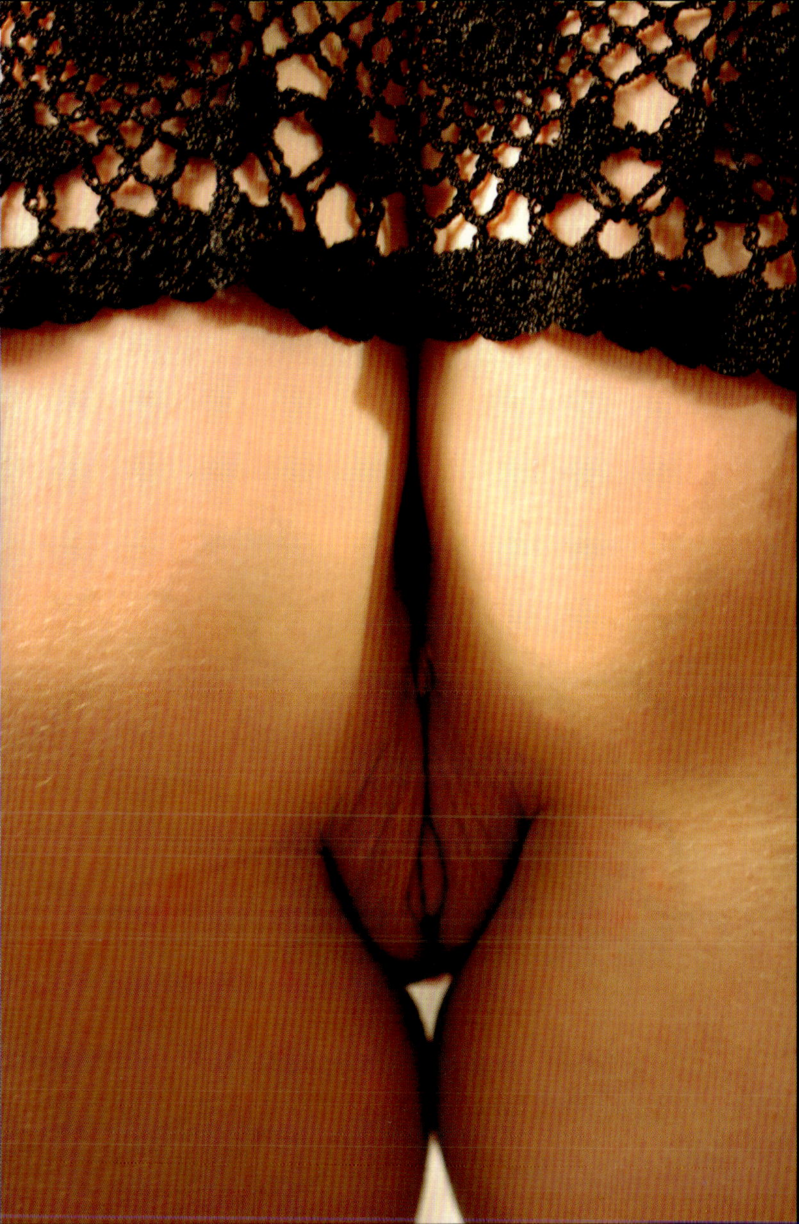

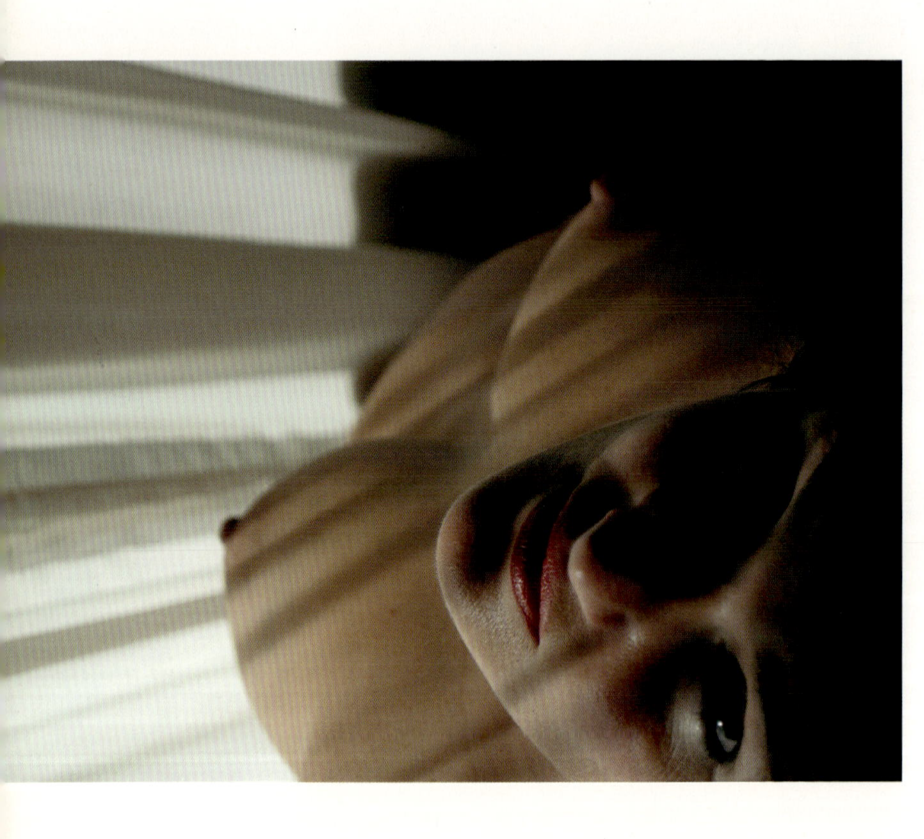

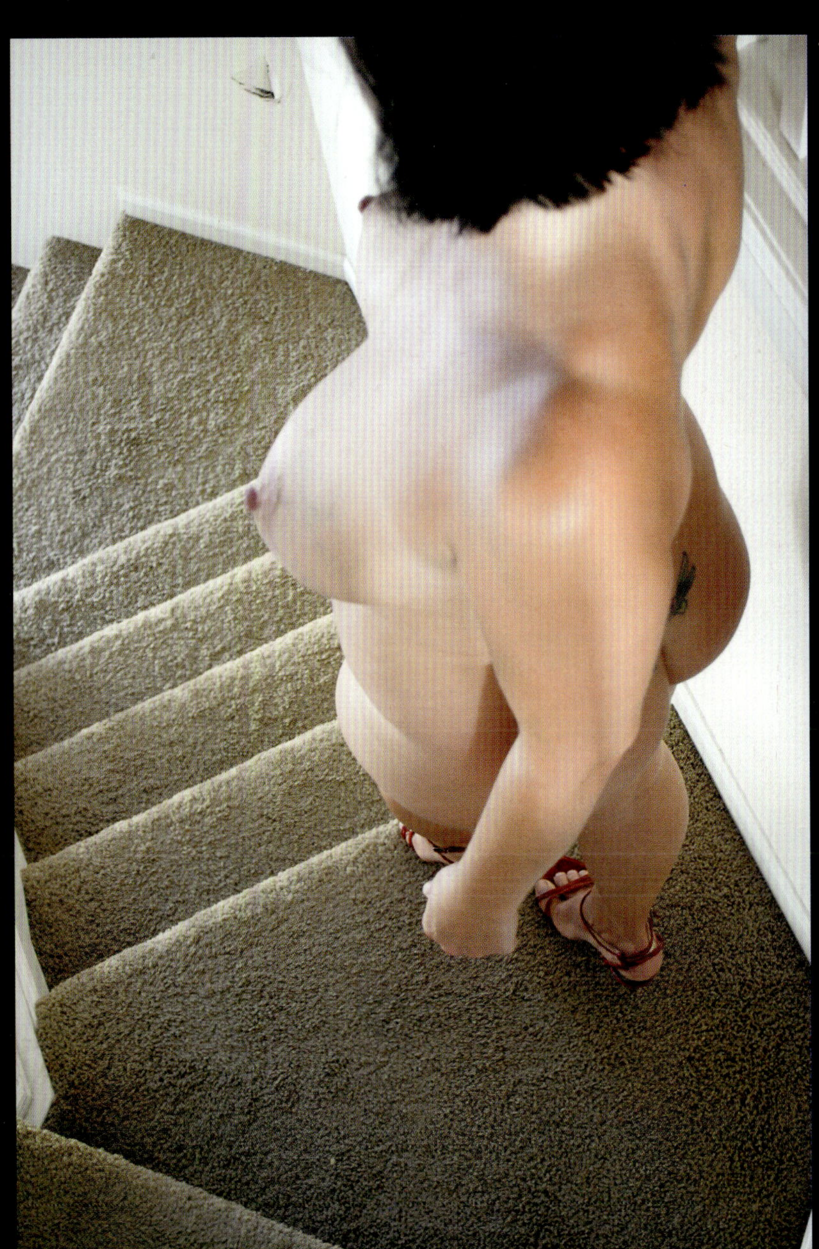

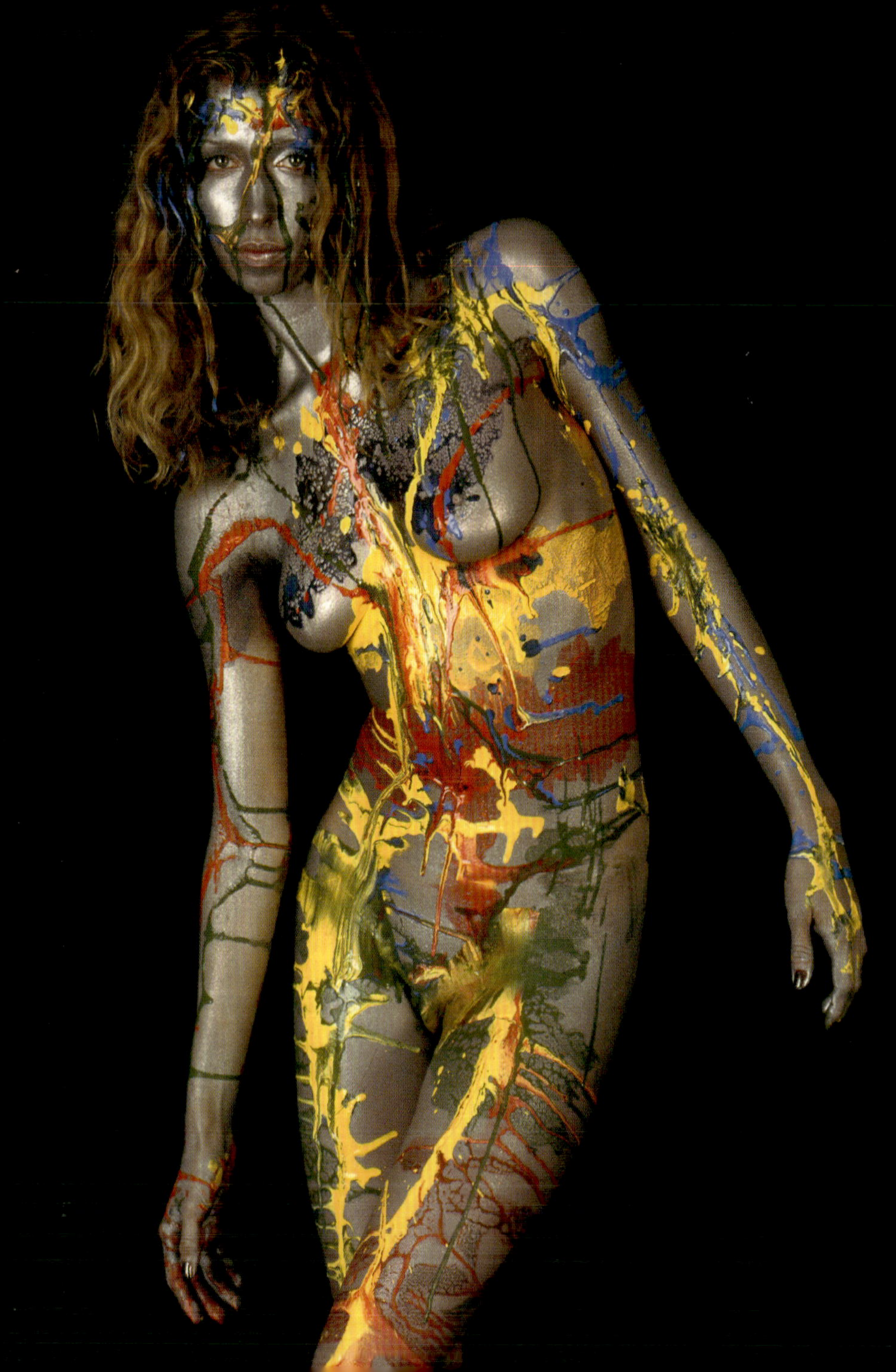

abraham wagner

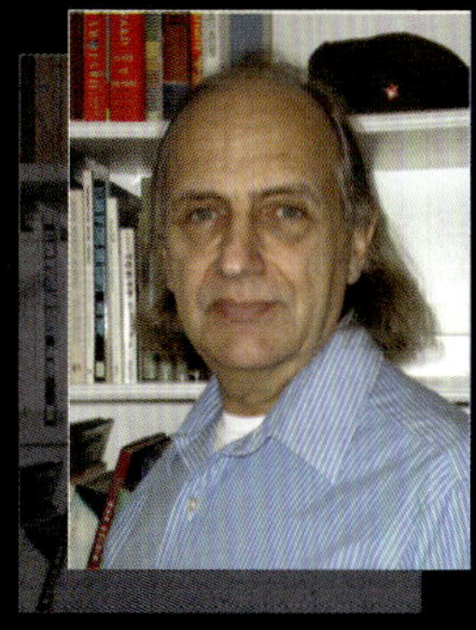

ABRAHAM IS AN AMERICAN photographer and teacher living in New York and Los Angeles. Born in 1947, he began photographing antiwar demonstrations and rock concerts as a student and has continued to do fine art and fashion photography for over 40 years for magazines in the US and Europe. He served for many years in the United States Government and, in 2005, joined the faculty of Columbia University in New York City where he teaches and works as a fine art photographer. He is inspired by Helmut Newton and Greg Gorman and is working on a book, *Shooting Naked*.

www.wagnerpix.com

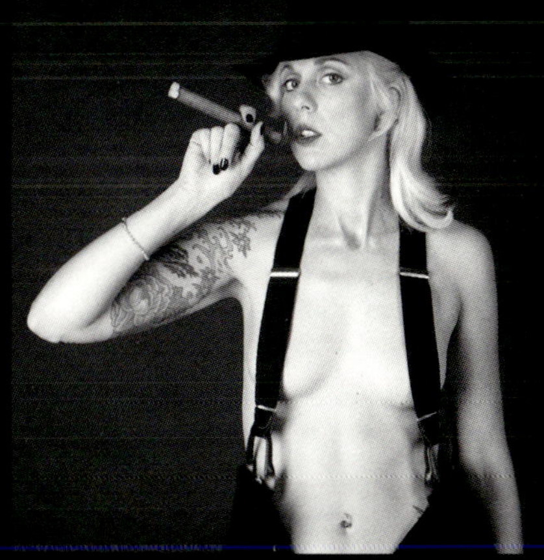

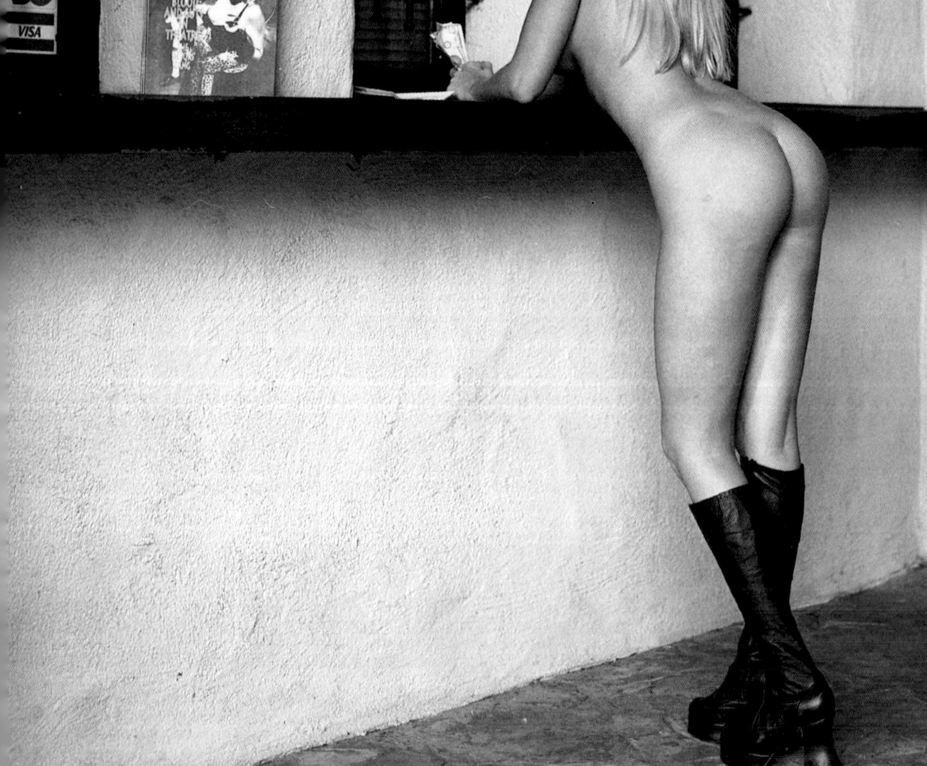
PURCHASE
BOX OFFICE
MasterCard
VISA

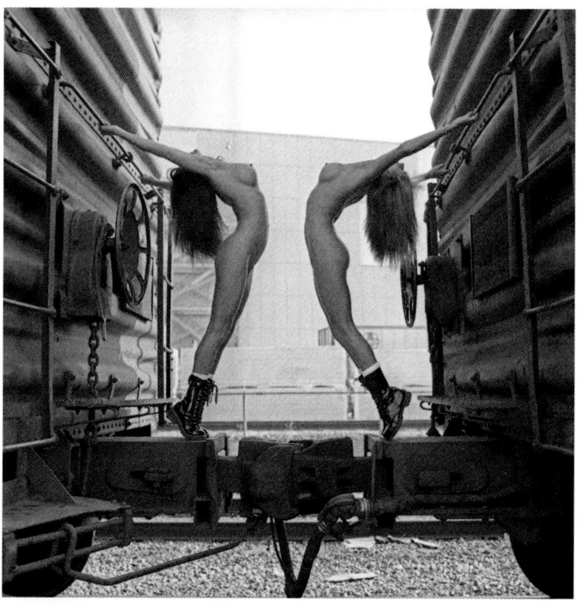

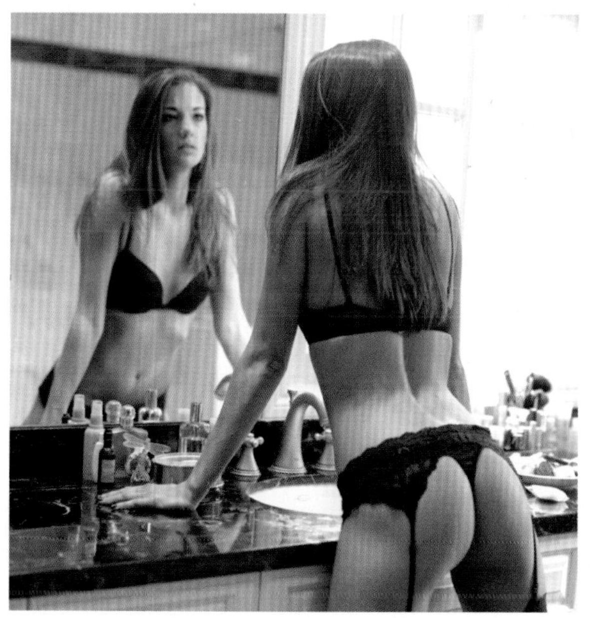

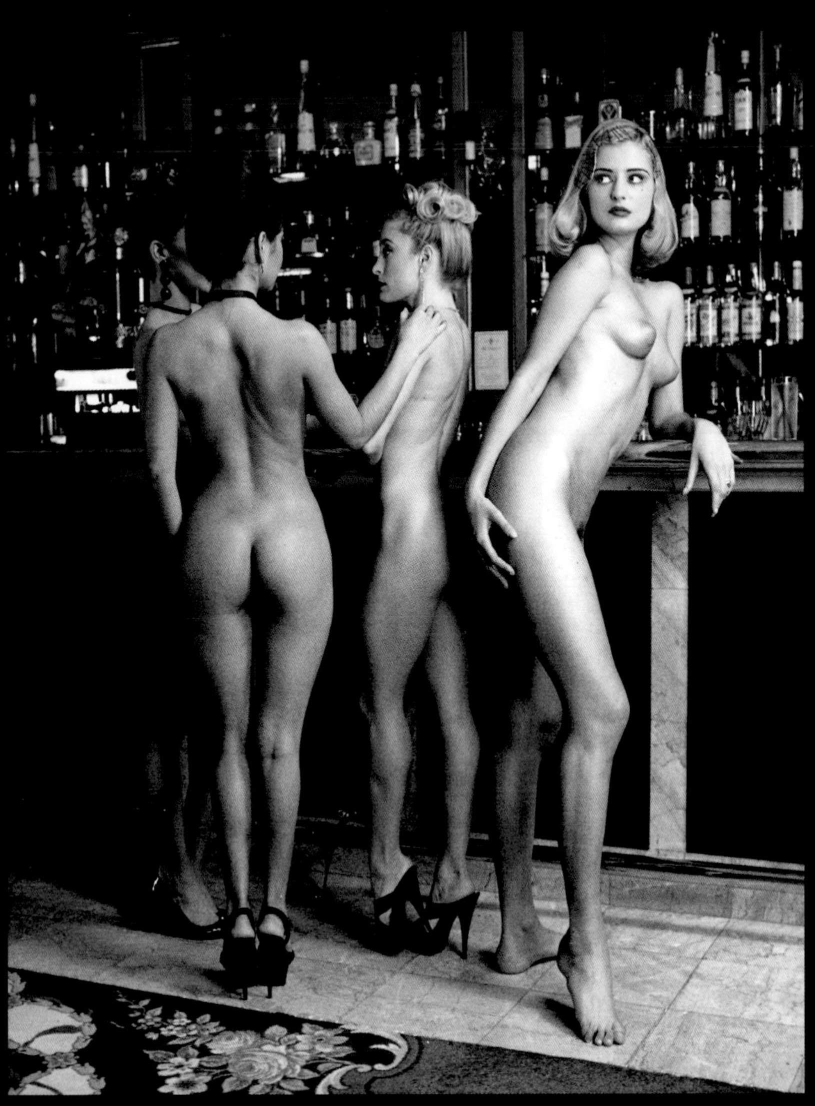

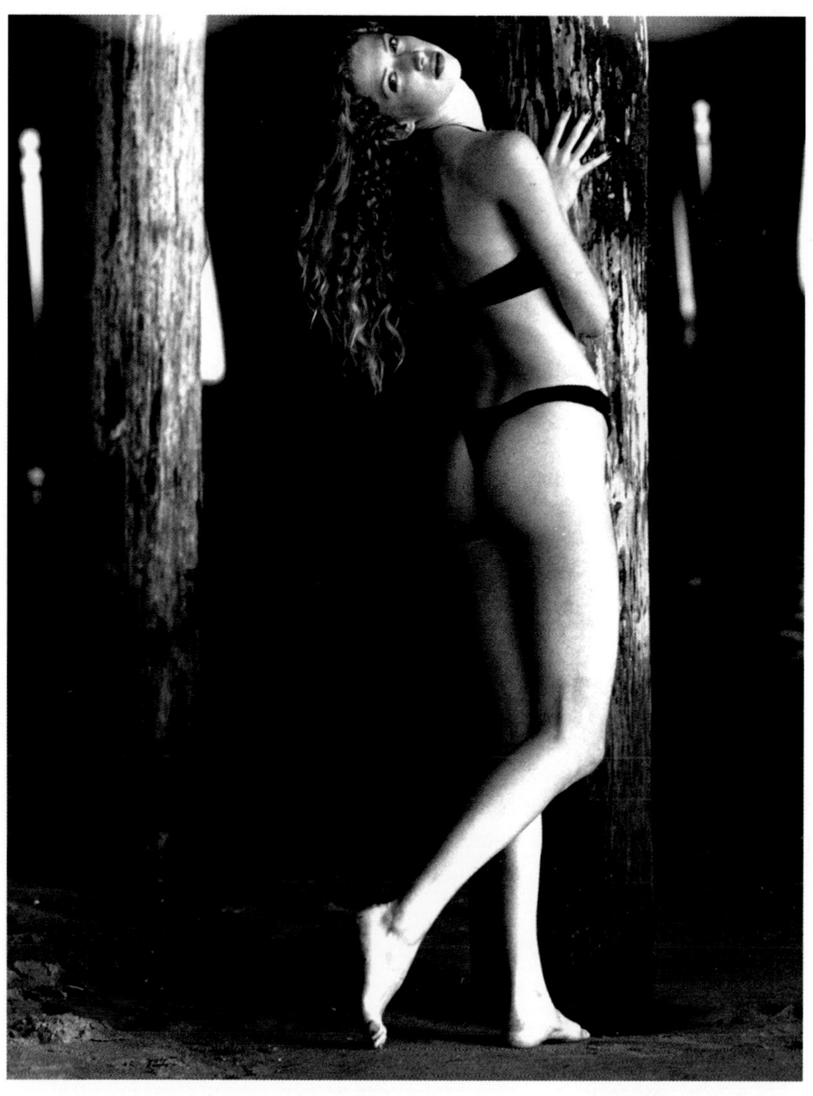

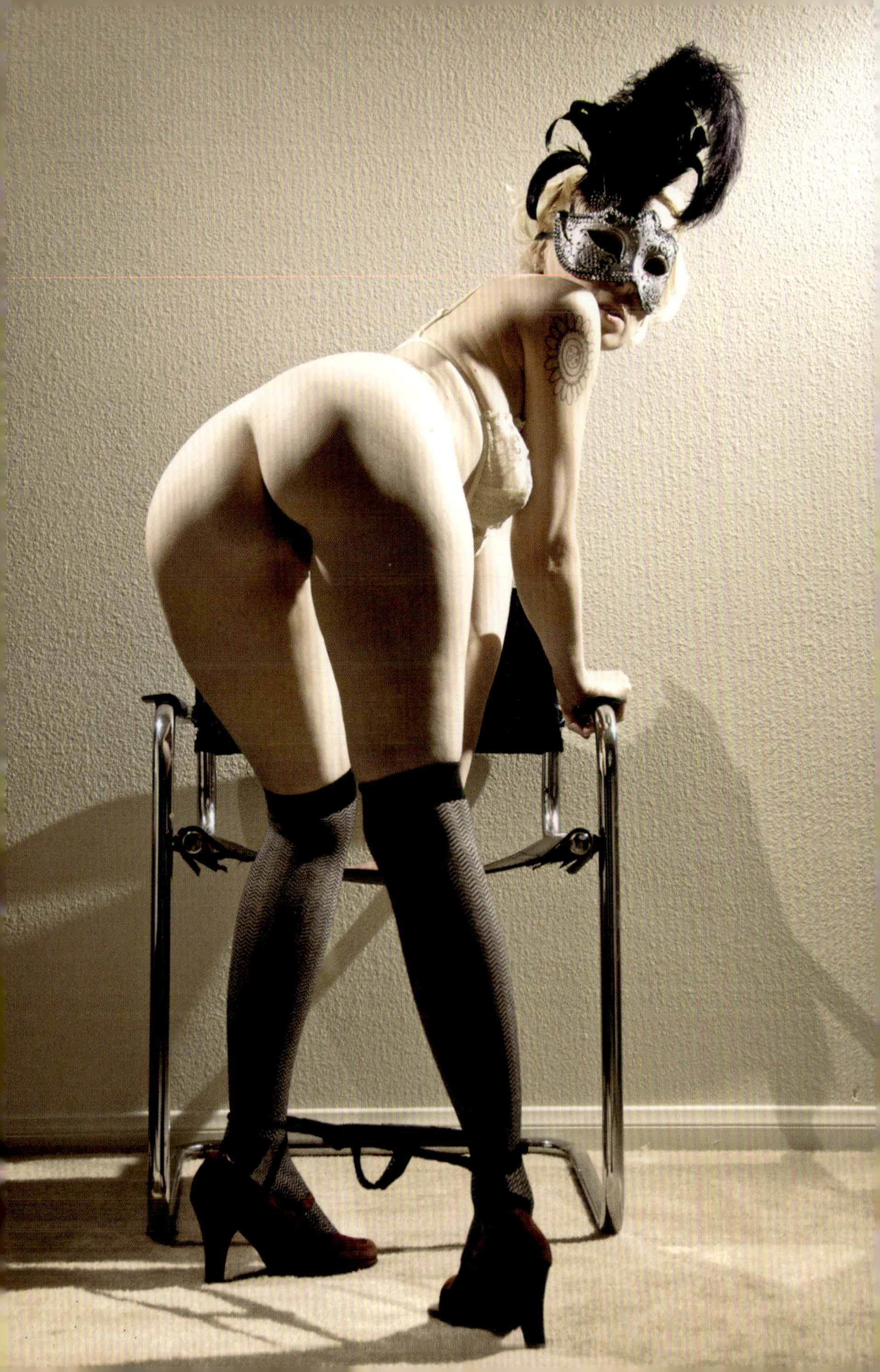

curtis joe walker

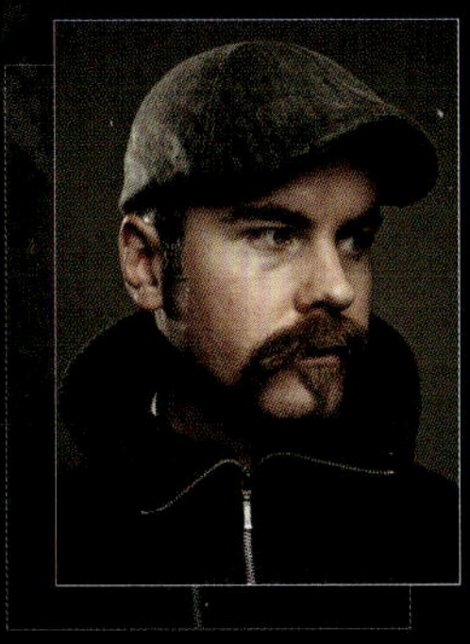

CURTIS IS A LAS VEGAS NATIVE and modern Renaissance man, working as an actor, musician, photographer and writer. He shoots both digitally and on analog film. His erotic work has been celebrated simultaneously as both disturbing and beautiful. His current projects include Analog Bondage and Truth, both long-term works in progress. His work has appeared extensively online and on the *Alt Pinup* site deviantnation.com, where he works as a staff photographer. His influences include Richard Kern, Frédéric Fontenoy and Annie Leibovitz.

www.curtisjoewalker.com

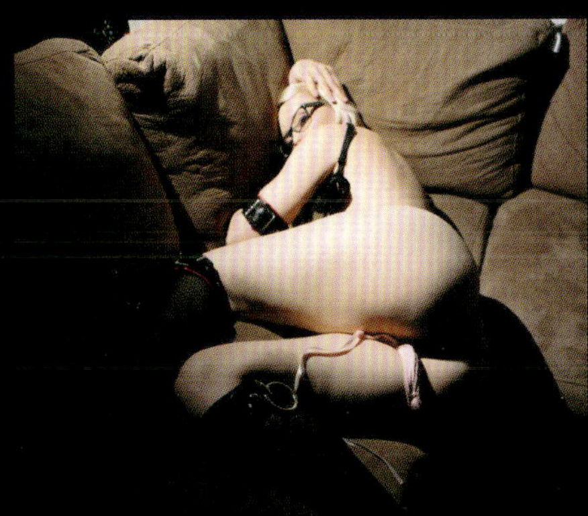

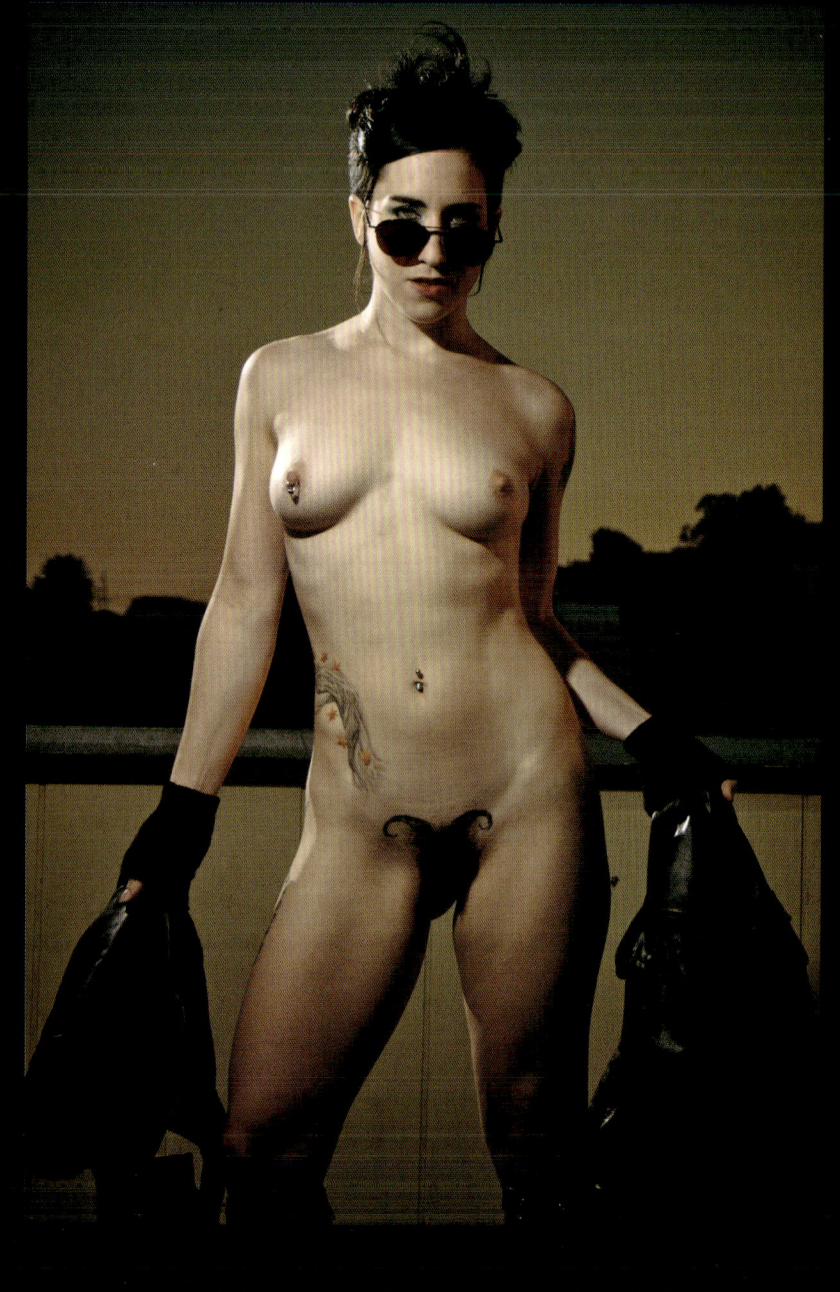

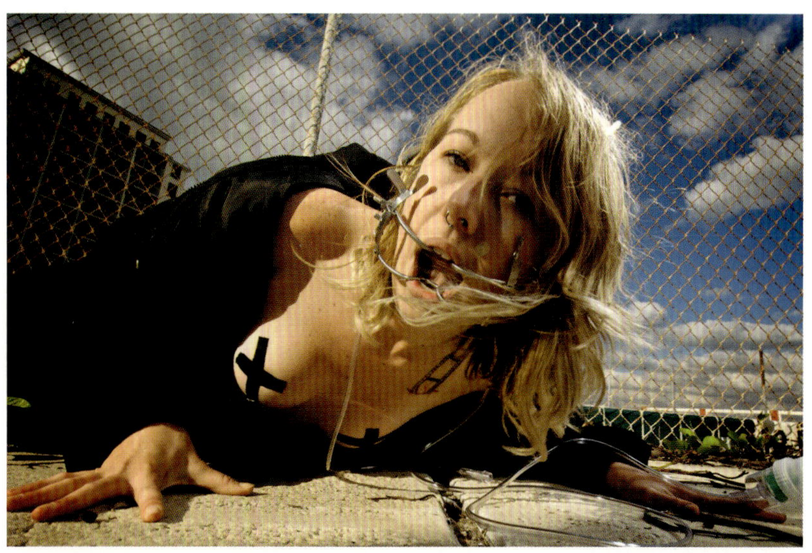

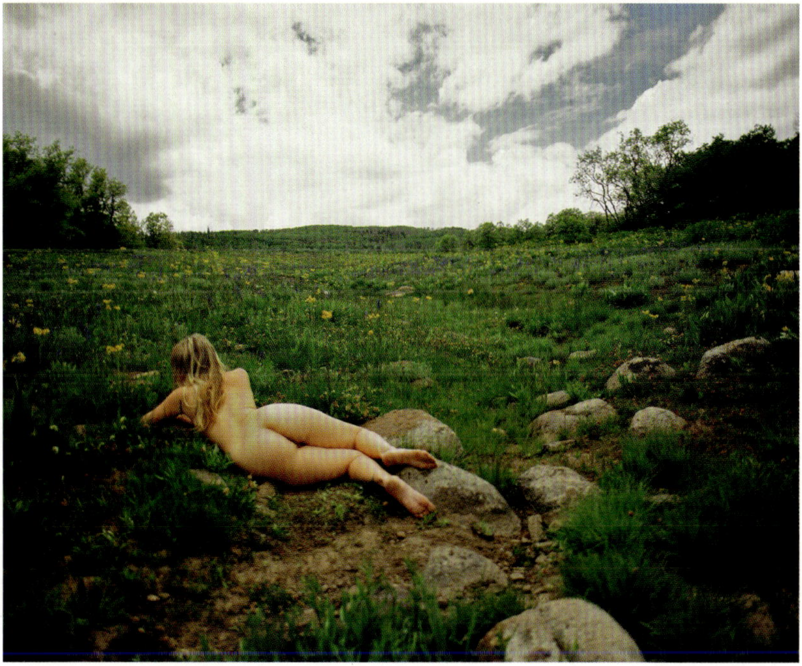

CURTIS JOE WALK

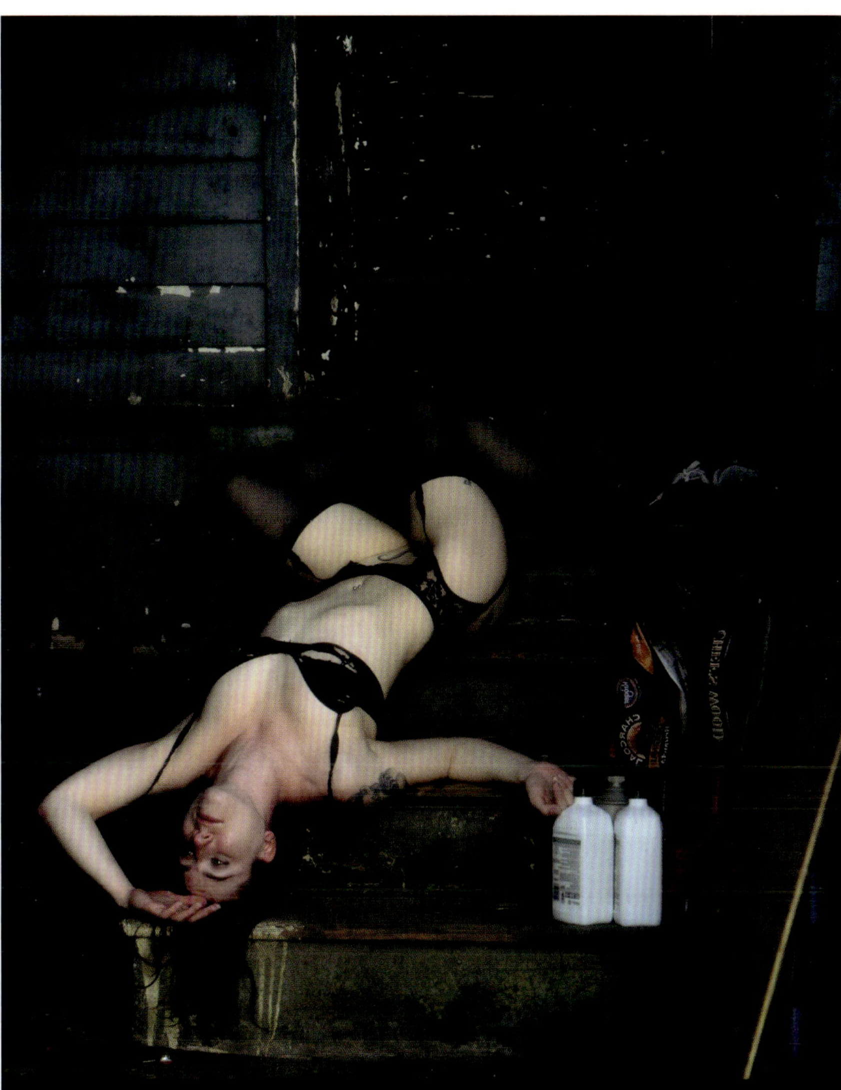

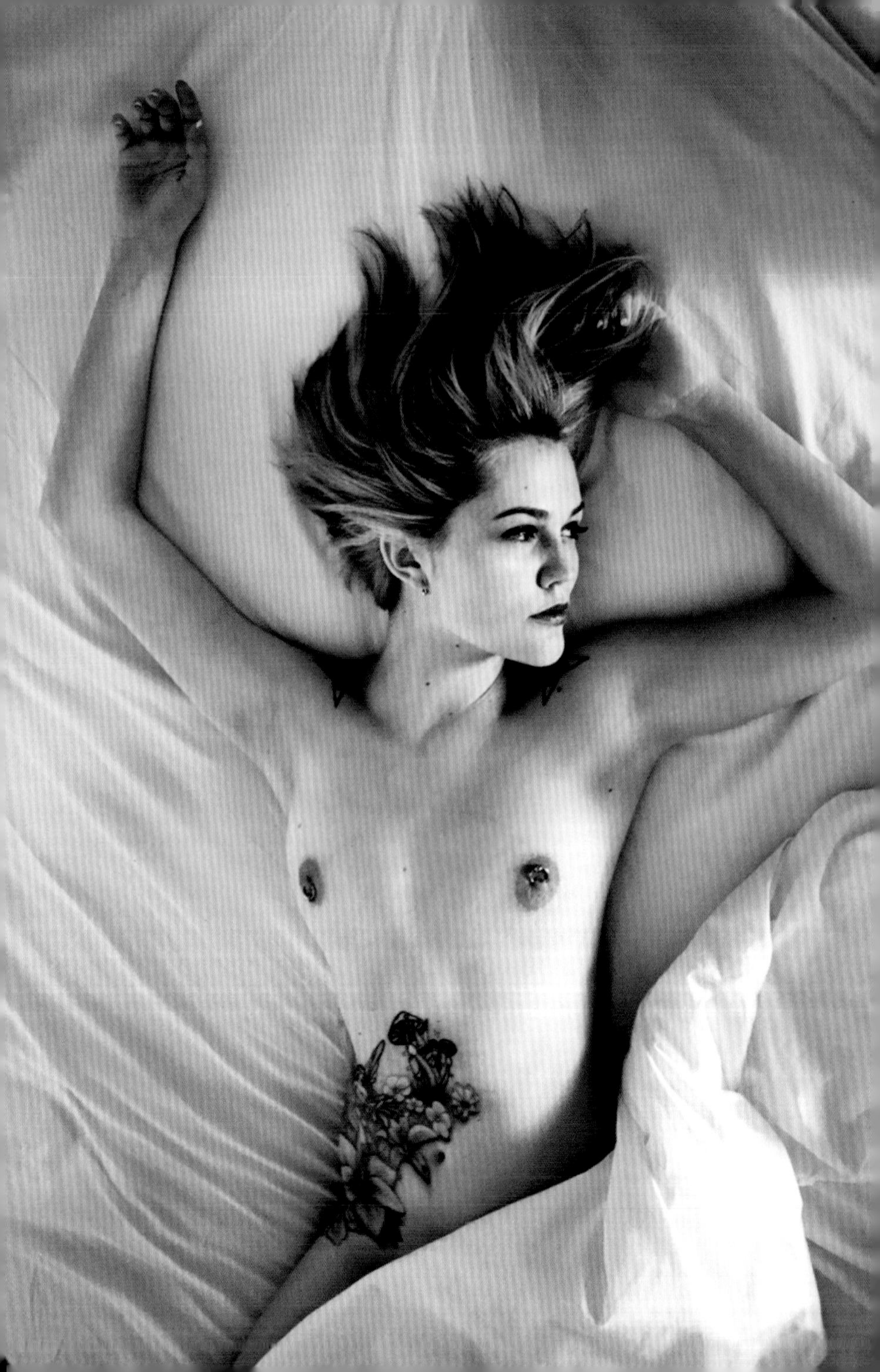

wolf189

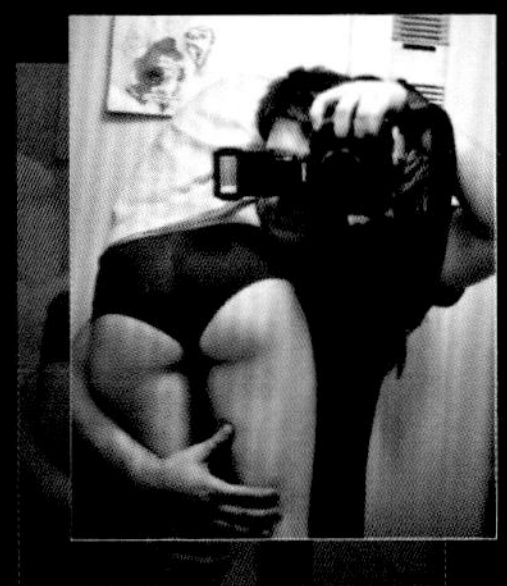

WOLF189 IS AN INTERNATIONALLY published and exhibited American photographer, artist, editor and film-maker. He is active in various fields including editorial fashion, erotica, documentary and portrait photography.
It has been said of him: 'A photographer always offers a secret, voyeuristic thrill to the viewers of his or her artistic product, but aliased artist Wolf189 elevates the private, sensual moments of his models to extreme voyeuristic levels. The viewer often gets the feeling that not even the photographer was in the room. His skilful composition, framing and lighting capture naturally intimate images that reveal the sadness and desires we all hold inside' (Sez Go).

www.wolf189.com

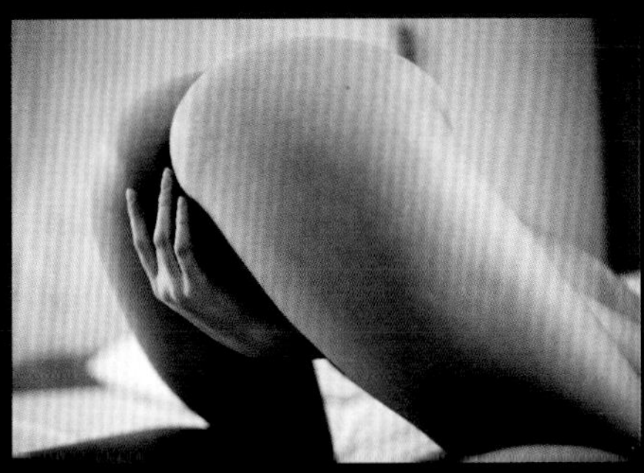

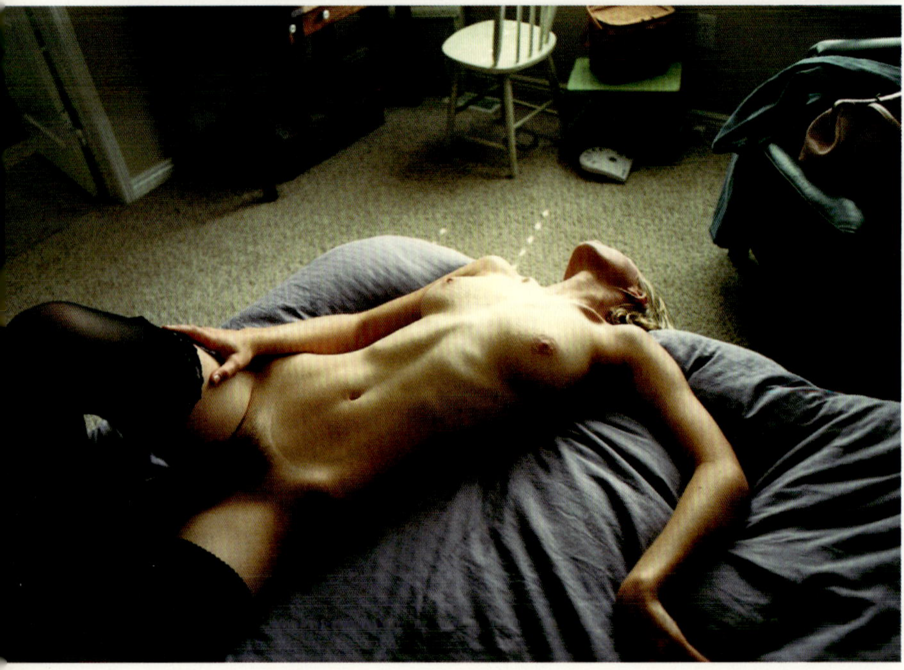

WOLF189

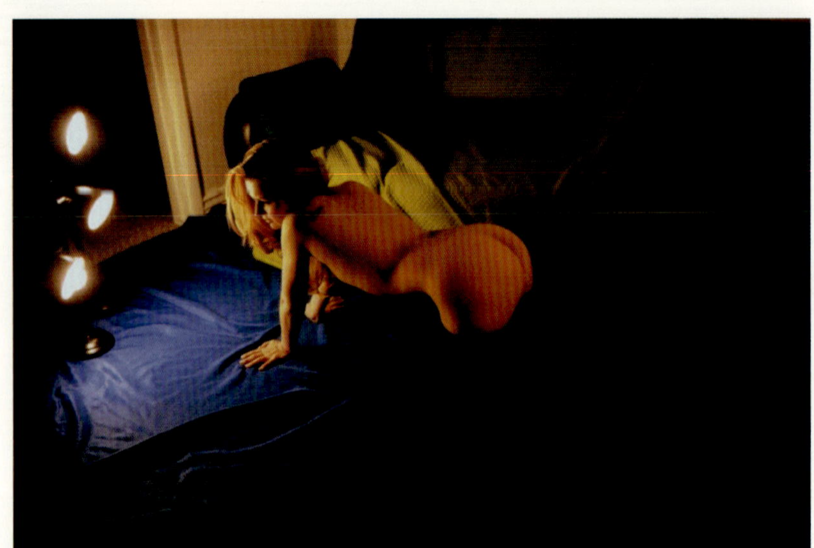

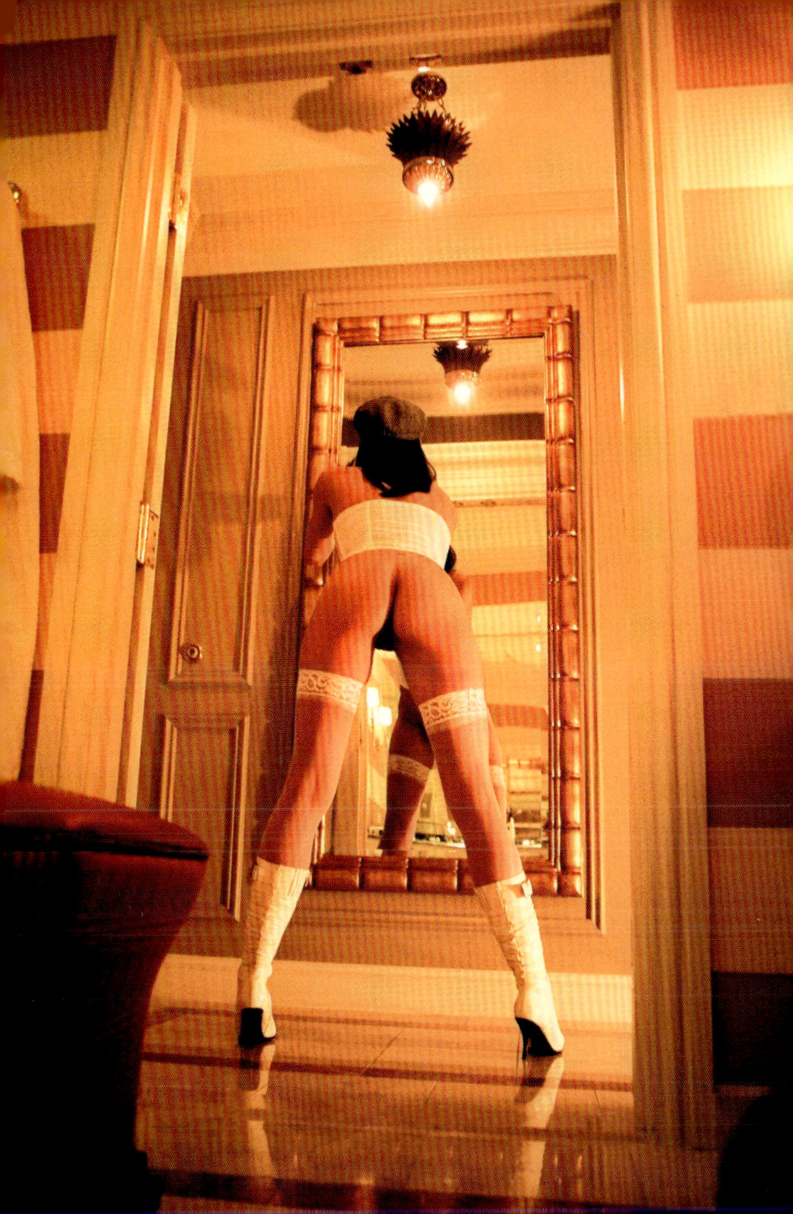

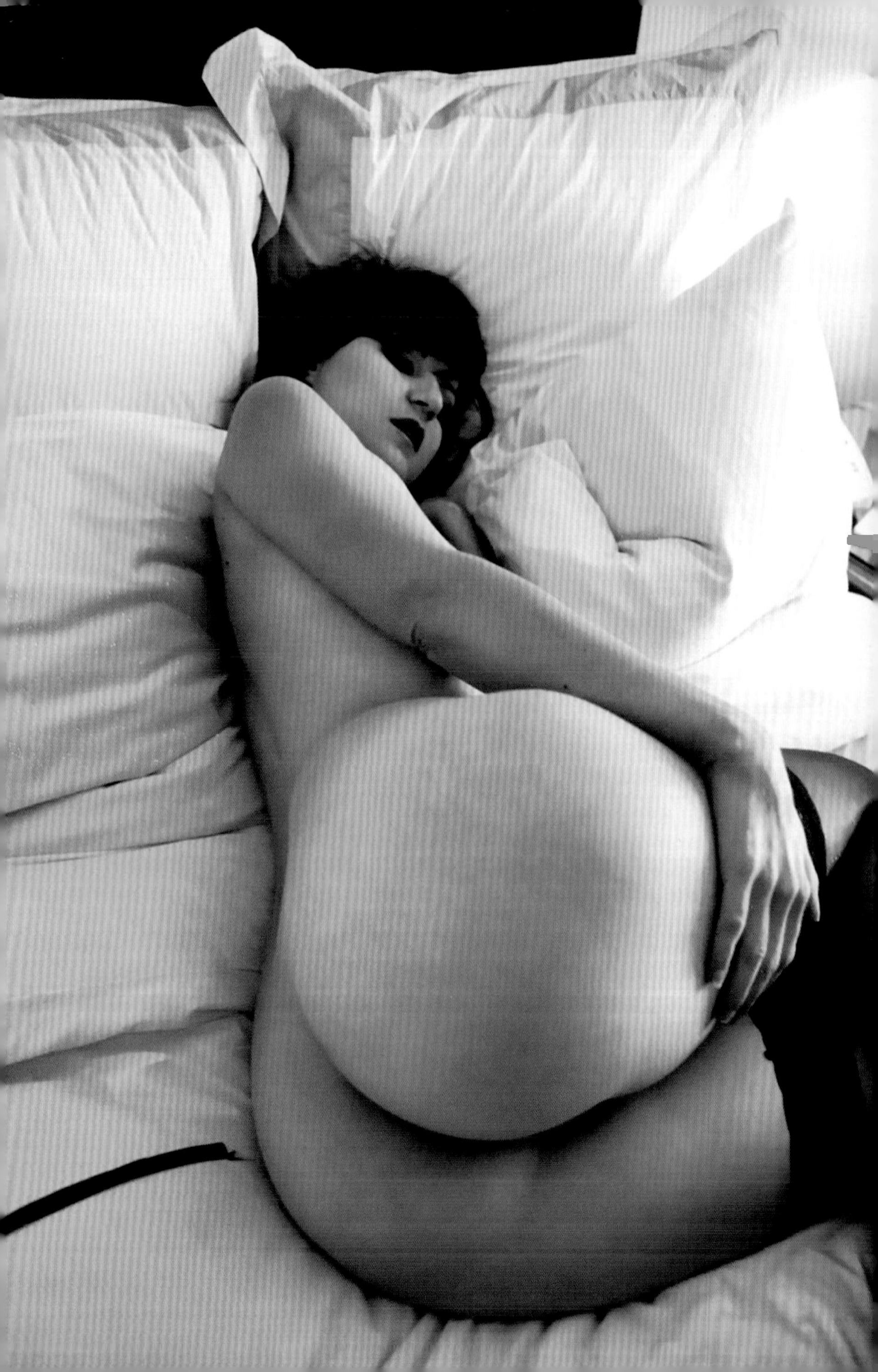

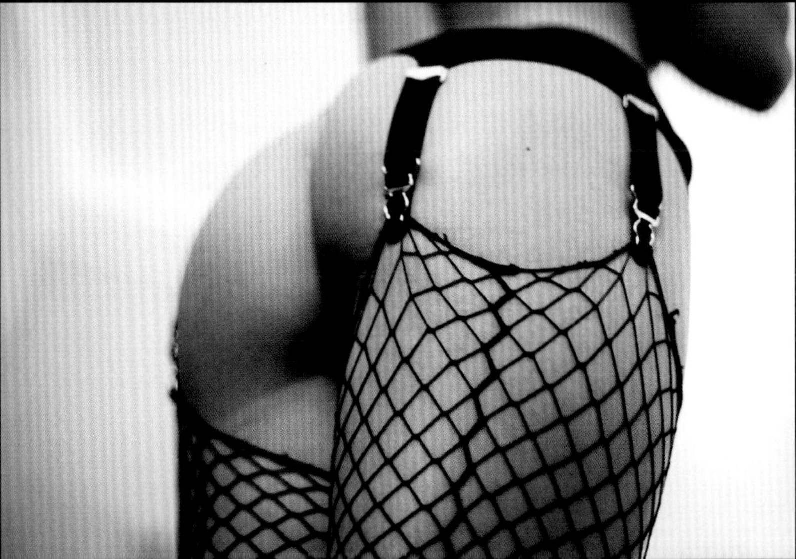

WOLF189

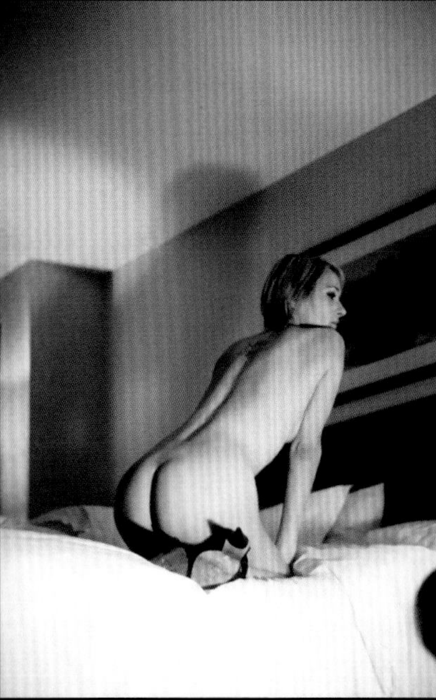

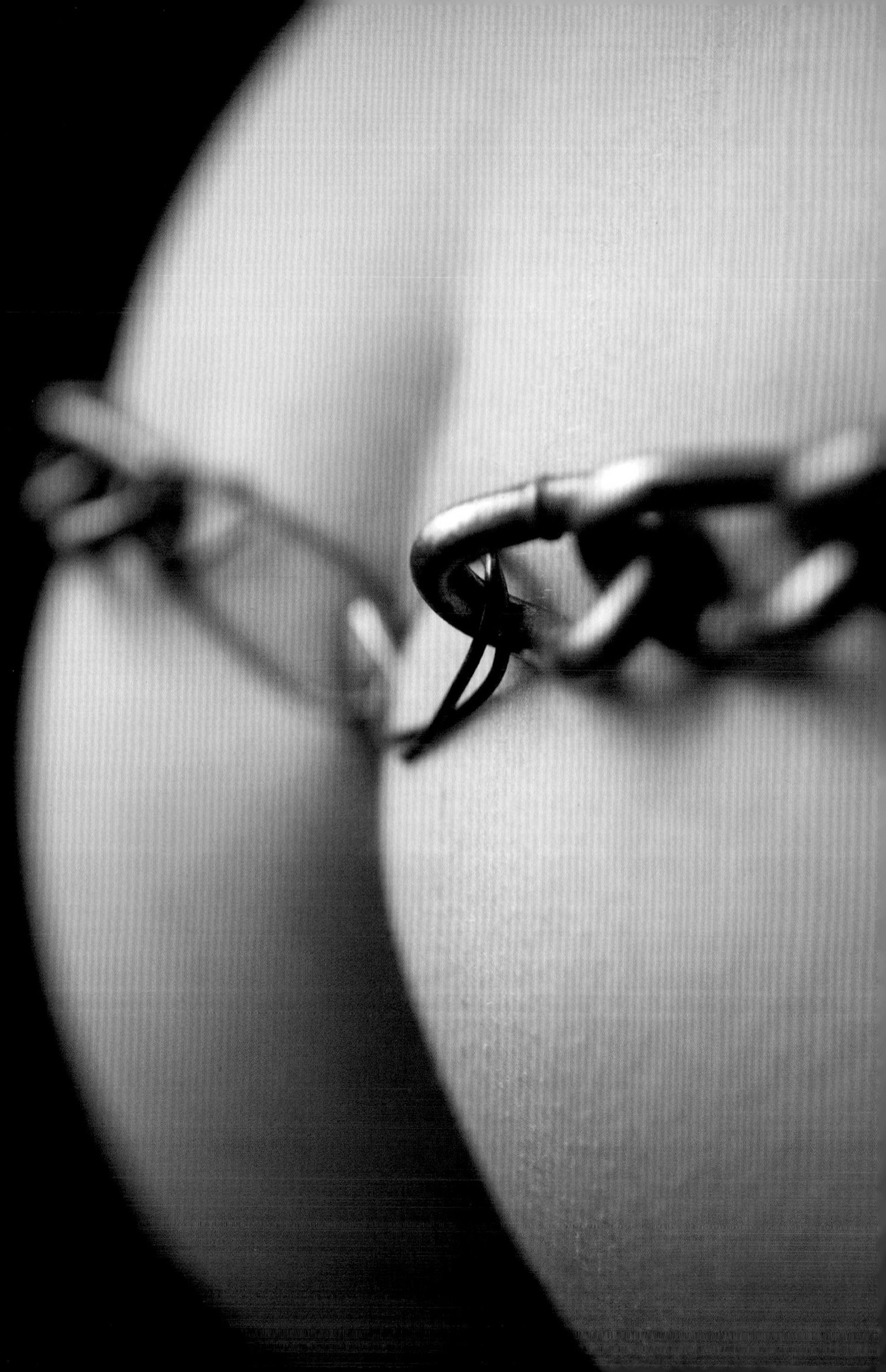

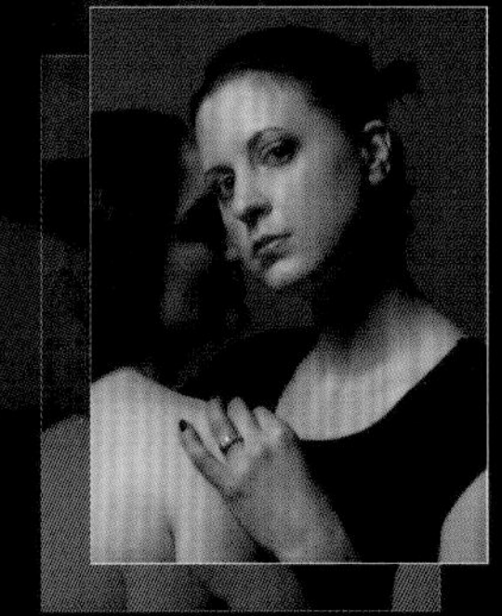

RENEE AZCRA WOODWARD has been practising her photography for seven years and shoots a variety of styles and subjects, although her passions are erotica and fashion. She has won awards and been exhibited internationally. She has recently completed two art book projects: *Hidden Ink*, about the conflict faced by people with tattoos and *She*, about bisexual and lesbian women, which pairs erotic images with anecdotes about her past lovers.

www.woodwardstudios.com

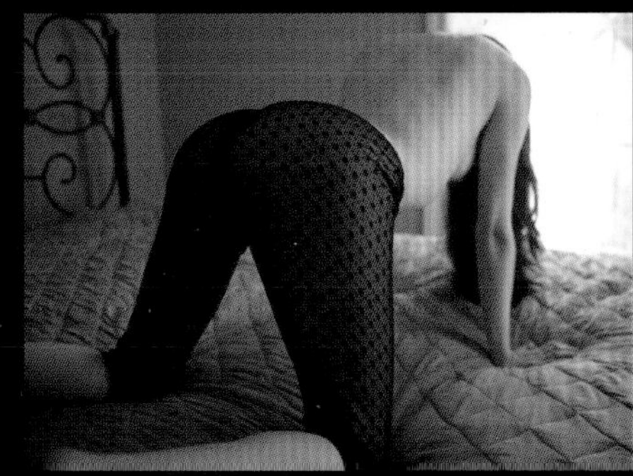

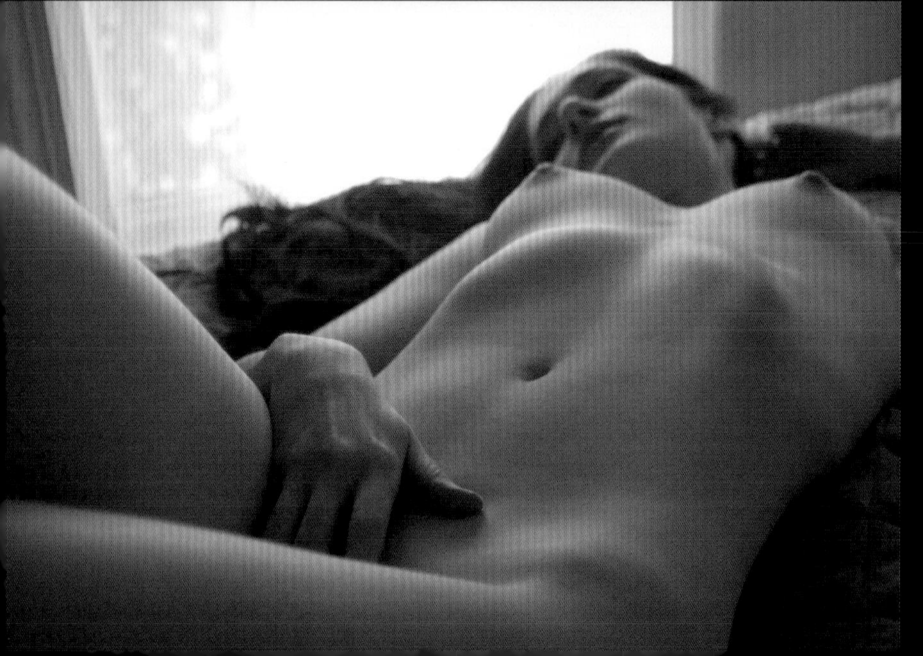

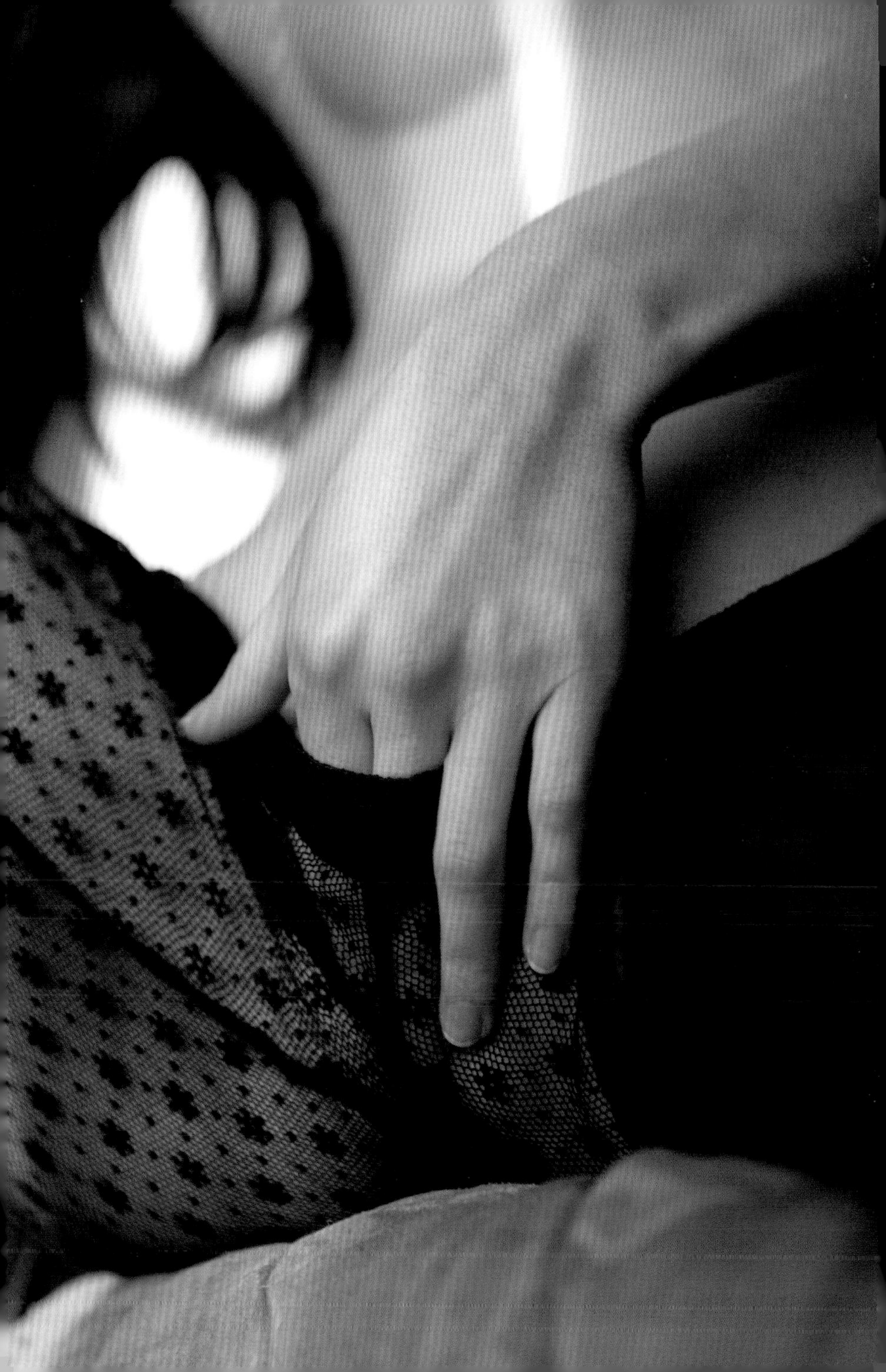

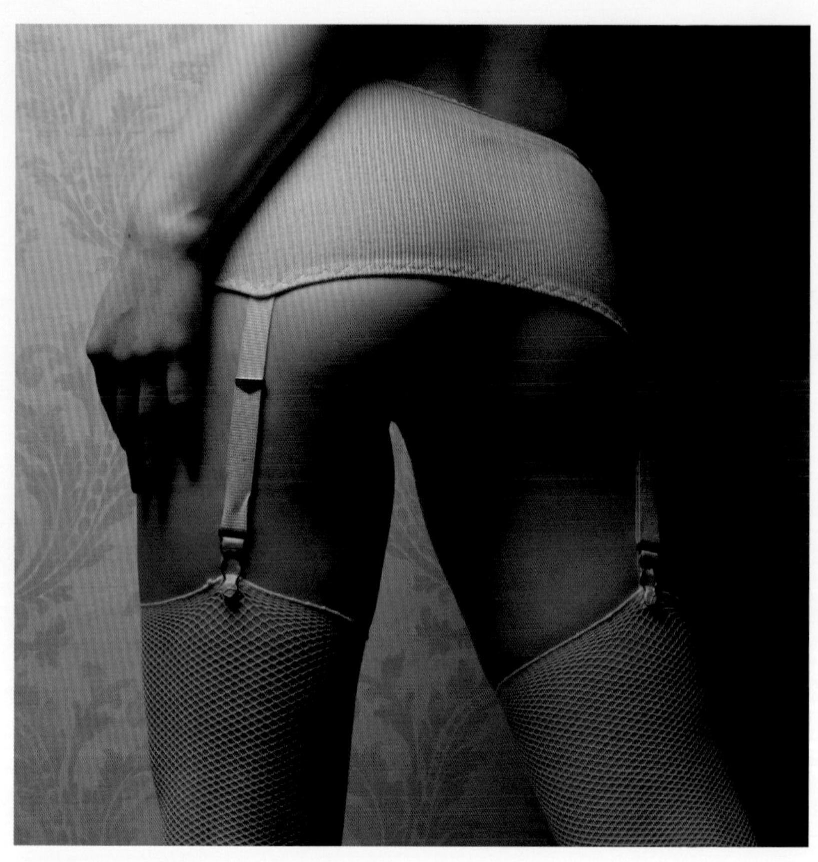

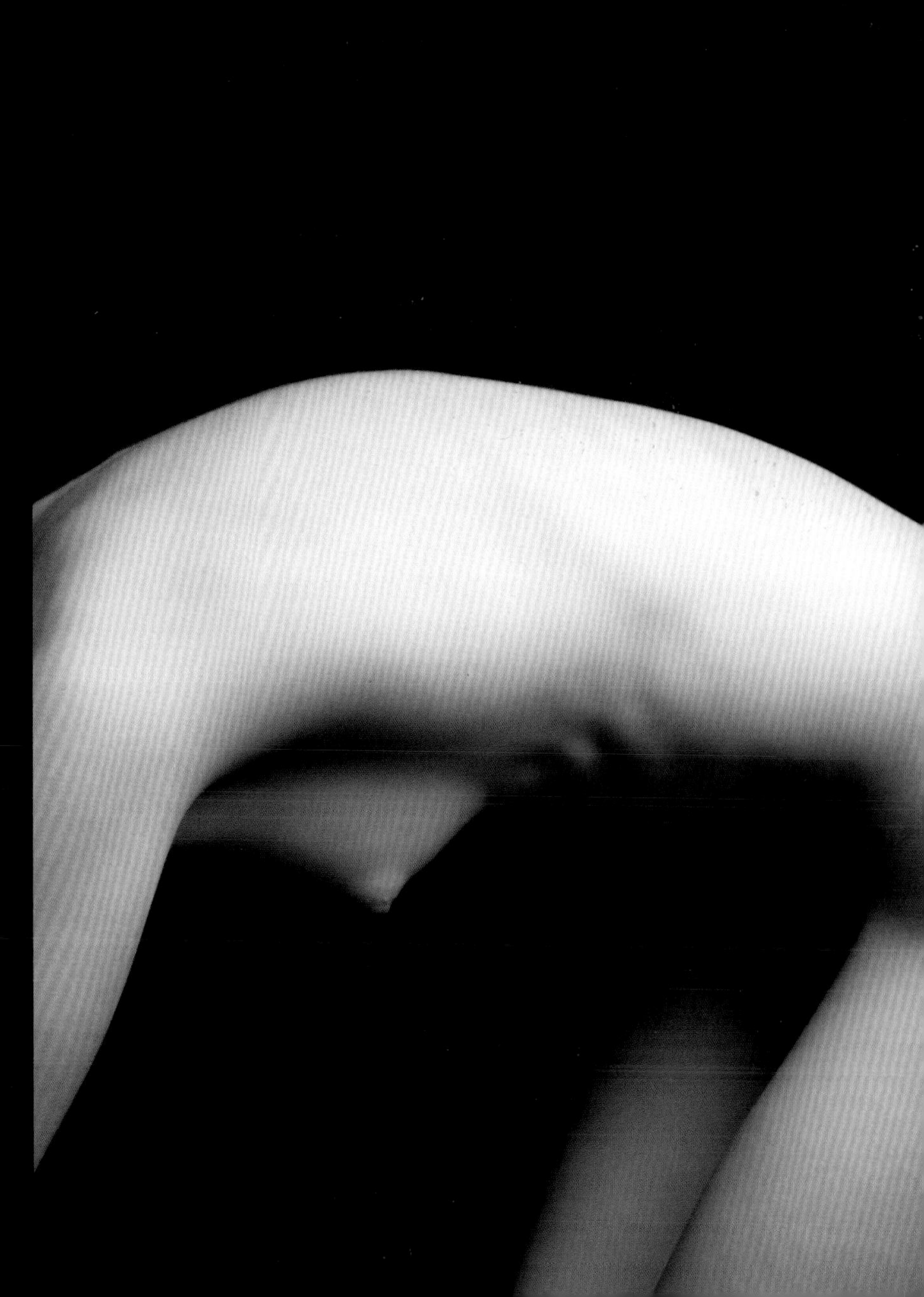

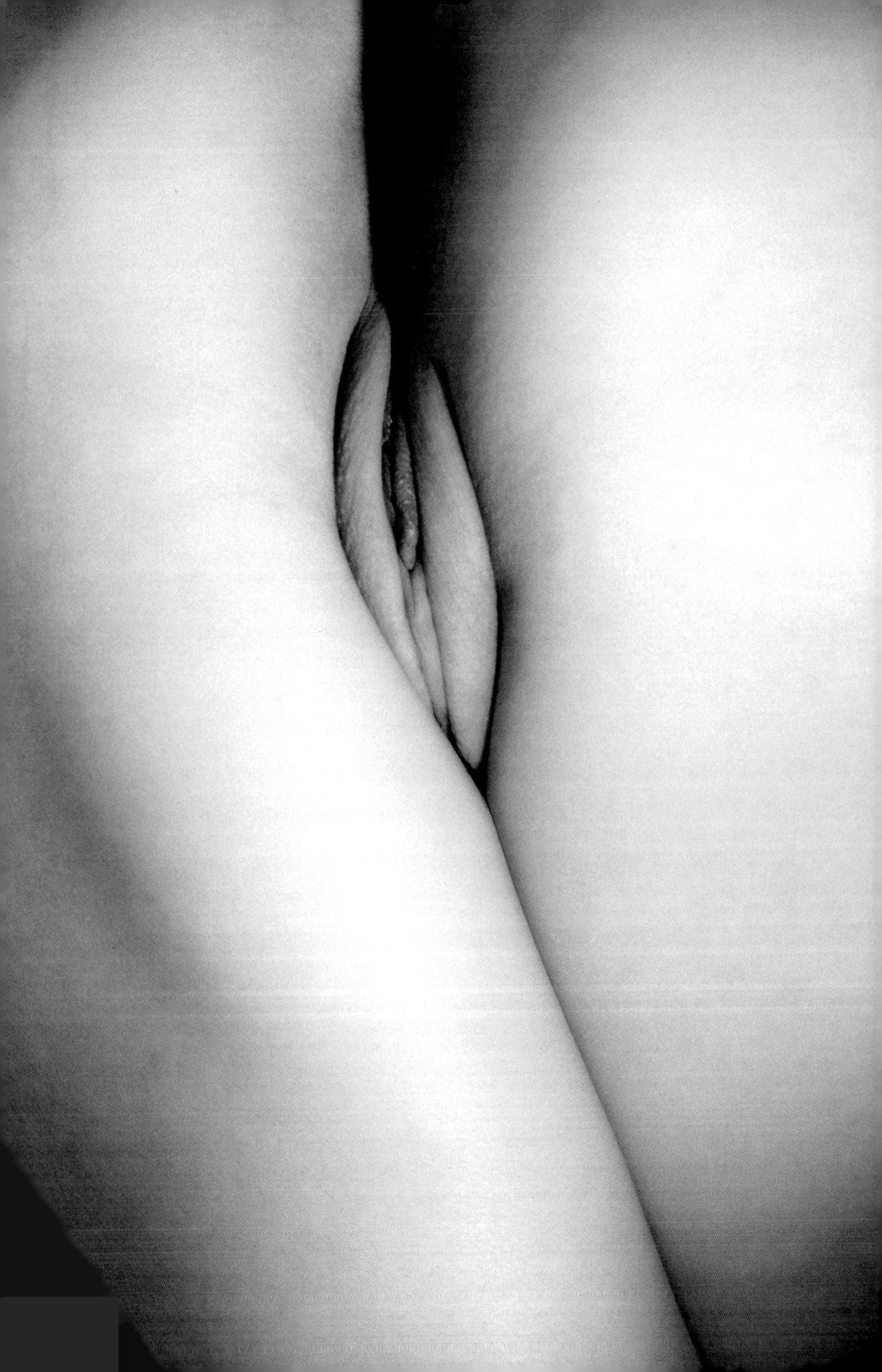

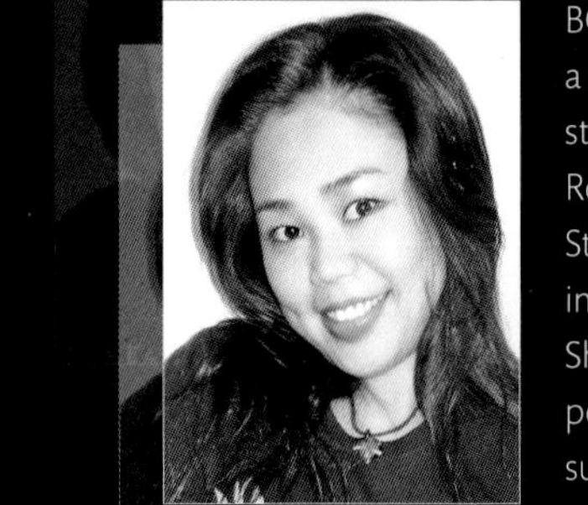

BORN AND RAISED IN JAPAN, she has been a resident of New York since 1995. She studied photography under the legendary Roy DeCarava, and earned a BA degree in Studio Art and Psychology. Nudity is central in her photography and takes many direction She uses nudity to reflect her personal perception of sexuality and to expose her subject's emotion. She creates BDSM/fetish

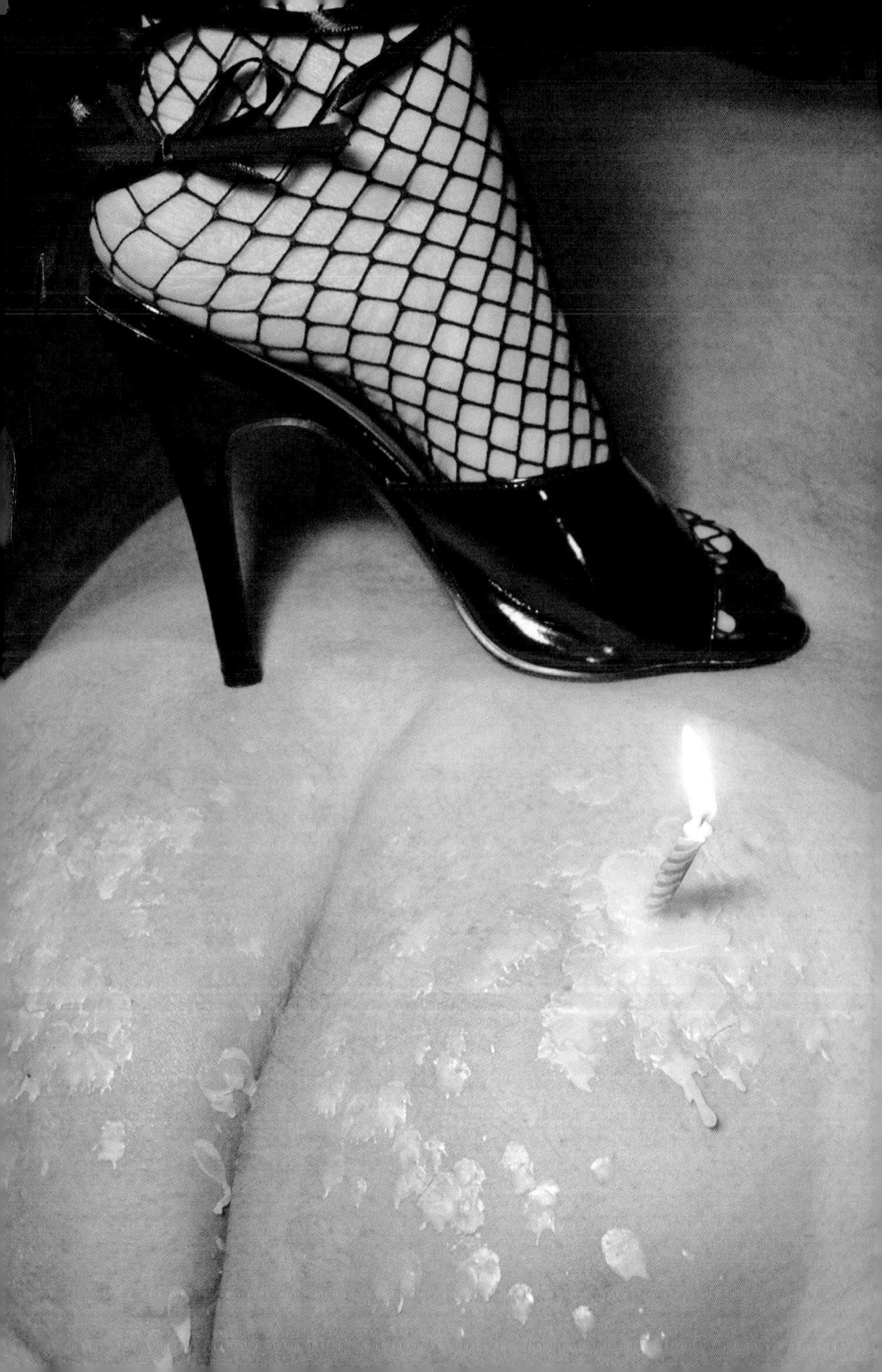

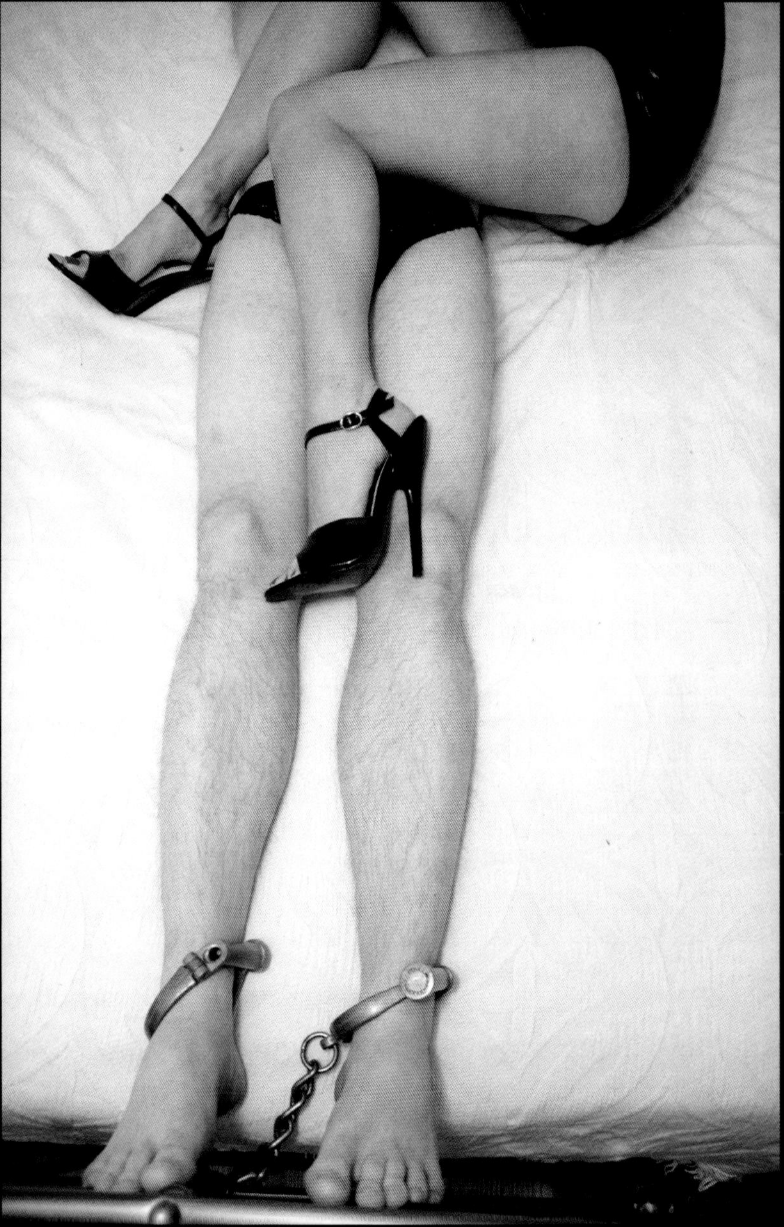

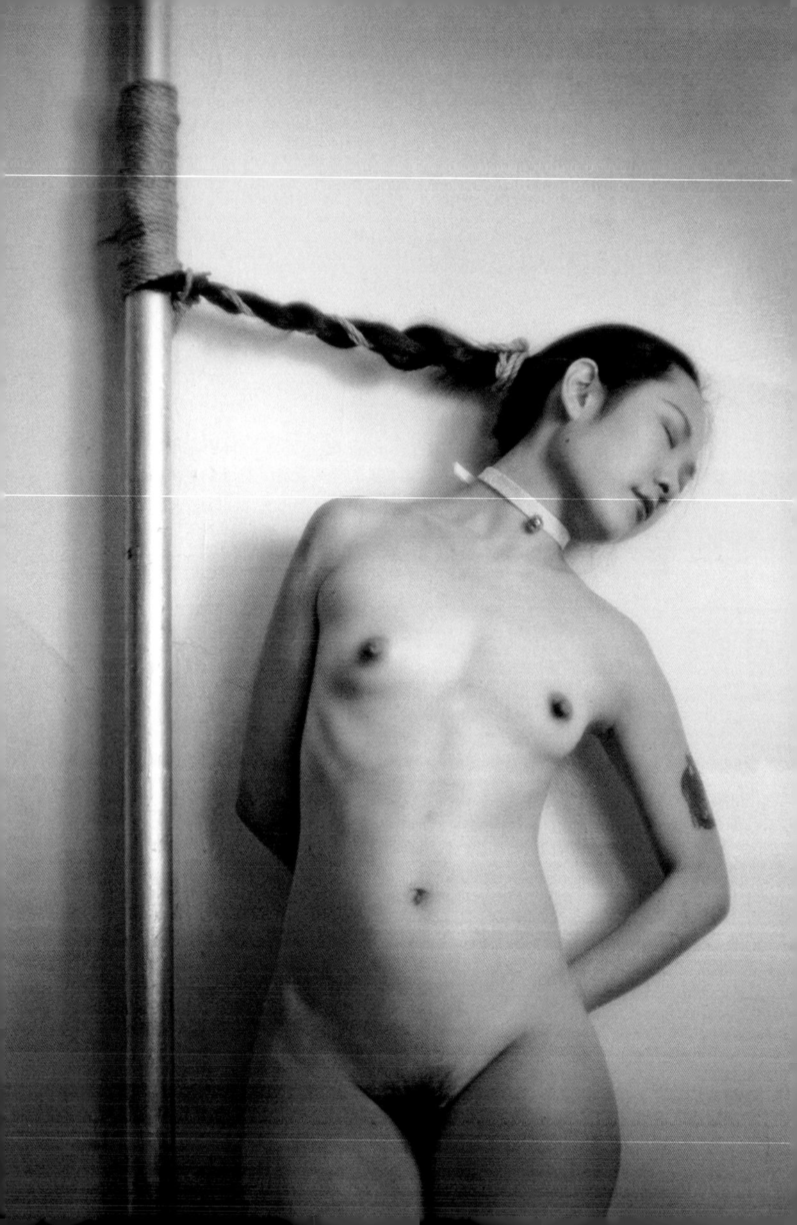

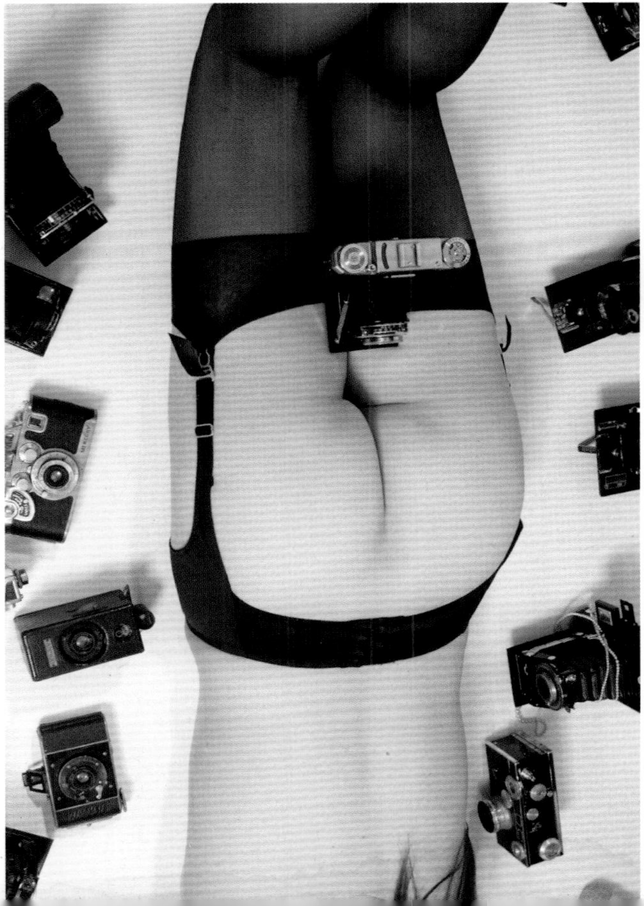

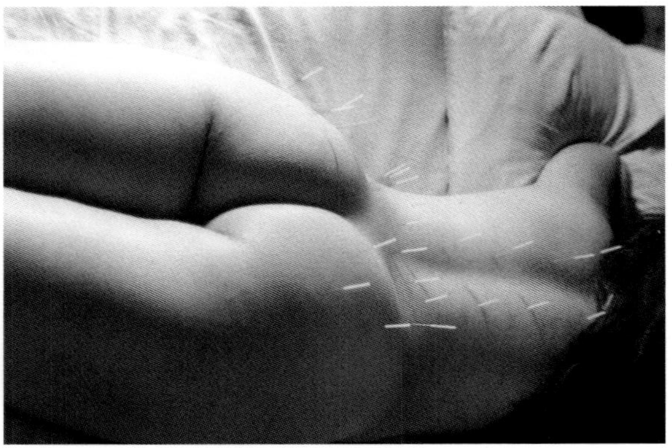

about the editor

MAXIM JAKUBOWSKI IS the editor of the best-selling *Mammoth Book of Erotica* series, now into fifteen volumes, and two previous volumes of *Erotic Photography*. A columnist for *Time Out* and the *Guardian*, novelist and broadcaster, he lives in London, where he used to own the world-famous Murder One bookstore. His latest novel is *I Was Waiting For You*.